URBAN POLITICS

Power in Metropolitan America

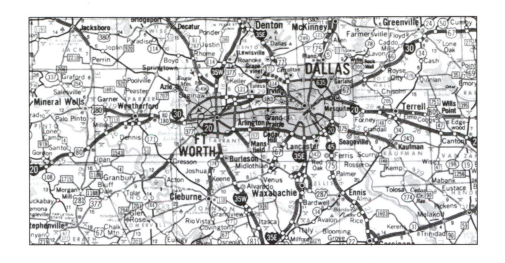

URBAN POLITICS

FIFTH EDITION

 F.E. Peacock Publishers, Inc. ITASCA, ILLINOIS

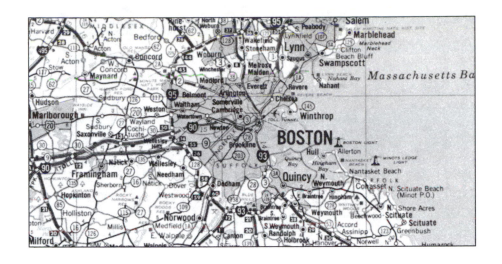

Power in Metropolitan America

BERNARD H. ROSS   AMERICAN UNIVERSITY

MYRON A. LEVINE   ALBION COLLEGE

To Nettie and
the memory of Len,
both of whom taught me
to love the city.
B.H.R.

To my mother and father.
M.A.L.

Bernard H. Ross and Myron A. Levine
would like to dedicate this edition
to the late Charles H. Levine,
our friend and colleague
who taught us both so much
about urban politics and administration.

Cover photo:
© Daniel Furon/Photonica

Contents

4. FORMAL STRUCTURE AND LEADERSHIP STYLE   101

5. MACHINE POLITICS   143

9. SUBURBAN POLITICS AND METROPOLITAN AMERICA   283

10. THE POLITICS OF METROPOLITAN GOVERNMENT   321

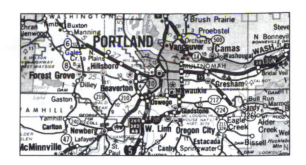

Figures

Tables

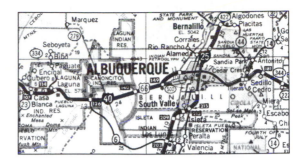

Preface

Since the appearance of the fourth edition of *Urban Politics* in 1991, much has changed. Tensions in Los Angeles exploded in the wake of the jury verdict in the Rodney King trial in 1992. By the mid-1990s, new fiscal troubles emerged in New York City, Philadelphia, Detroit, the District of Columbia, Los Angeles County, and even affluent Orange County! After an era of Republican presidents, Bill Clinton's election seemed to embody the promise of new aid and assistance to cities. But the promise proved short-lived. The Republican victory in the 1994 mid-term congressional elections only reinforced the sense of limits that had already been imposed by national budgetary pressures.

The study of urban politics has been reinvigorated by the new theoretical insights offered by regime theory. Political scientists have begun to ask "Who benefits?" from city politics, especially when so much of a city's attention is devoted to the pursuit of economic development. Just when, and under what conditions, does a city respond to the needs of elite corporate interests? What are the prospects that a more progressive coalition can emerge to challenge the power of corporate interests? Questions of political power and democracy once again occupy the center of the study of city politics.

As a result of these changes, the fifth edition of *Urban Politics* represents a substantial revision over previous ones. Every chapter has been thoroughly rewritten. The new insights of regime theory are incorporated into the text. Special attention is paid to discerning the exact "limits" that intercity economic competition imposes on city decision making. New material also focuses on the immigration of new racial minorities to the United States, the place of women in the postindustrial city, and the prominence of such trends as gentrification and homelessness in the emerging "dual city." The fifth edition also presents much new material on the potential growth of African-American and Hispanic power.

The book's opening chapter on the Los Angeles riots (or, maybe, the Los Angeles *rebellion*?) introduces the overall themes of the book: the importance of private power; the continuing importance of the formal rules and structures of local government; the similarities and differences between Frostbelt and Sunbelt urban patterns; the critical importance of intergovernmental influences on city politics; and the continuing ambivalence of people in the United States on questions of race.

Chapter 2 has been revised to present a more comprehensive overview of the historical evolution of cities, suburbs, and metropolitan areas in the United States. Special care is taken to point out where private sector power and governmental policy have helped to determine metropolitan and regional settlement patterns. Central cities have lost population, economic activity, and political power to the suburbs. Frostbelt cities have yielded power to the Sunbelt.

The book's material on decision making, city governing structures, machine politics, and the reform movement has all been greatly revised to include the extensive insights offered by the regime theory literature. We present case studies of New York, Atlanta, Detroit, and San Francisco in order to examine the tendency toward corporate regimes and the potential for progressive regimes. The picture of the urban political machine presented here is one of great complexity: Was the machine "functional" in the services it provided immigrants and the urban poor? Or did the machine attempt to construct a "minimal winning coalition," and, in doing so, did it deny a fair share of benefits to ethnic and racial groups who were not the dominant ethnic group in the ruling coalition? This edition of *Urban Politics* also pays much greater attention to the leadership roles played by city managers in council-manager cities and suburbs.

We continue to describe the institutionalization of citizen participation and decentralization. New material from Jeffrey Berry et al., *The Rebirth of Urban Democracy*, is used in an effort to identify the keys to successful participation. Just why is it that citizen participation efforts succeed in some cities but not in others?

Our discussion of urban service delivery devotes considerable attention to the new trend toward privatizing city services. We discuss the pros and cons of "contracting out." We also present detailed discussion of various school "choice" programs—including the private management of public schools, the School District 4 experiment in East Harlem, and Milwaukee's nascent use of school vouchers for the city's poor—in order to illustrate the controversy that surrounds privatization efforts.

We continue to examine the critical policy area of education—tracing the history of school finance reform and integration efforts—in our chapters on suburban and metropolitan politics. We also note the heterogeneity of suburbs and the changing face of suburbia, including the generally different social composition of inner-ring and outer-ring suburbs. The New Jersey *Mount Laurel* decisions allow us to assess the prospects of "opening" more exclusive suburbs to greater racial and social diversity. Cleveland-area case studies are presented as all-too-rare efforts by suburbs that have taken active steps to maintain stable integration in order to avoid the prospects of racial transition and resegregation. The difficulties of metropolitan reform are detailed, and the prospects of more informal and cooperative regional arrangements are reviewed.

Much of the fourth edition's detailed discussion of the Nixon, Carter, and Reagan policies has been greatly condensed or eliminated. In the fifth edition we pay greater attention to the continuing impact of the New Federalism and how cities fared during the Reagan-Bush era. We show the significance of the relatively new budgetary rules in Washington. Greater emphasis is also placed on such contemporary initiatives as Clinton's reinventing government ideals, his empowerment zone legislation, and HUD Secretary Henry Cisneros' plans for the dramatic overhaul of both his department and assisted housing programs.

What role should the federal government play in responding to urban problems? There are three general options: Should the United States develop a more comprehensive national urban policy? Should the federal role in urban affairs be greatly reduced? Or is there a pragmatic path by which the federal government can help cities in an anti-city age? In the concluding chapter of this book, students are presented with the arguments for and against each of these three dramatically different approaches to the future of urban policy.

Several friends and colleagues helped to improve the quality of the manuscript in more ways than they will ever know. Al Hyde at The American University provided us with current information on urban budgeting and finance issues. Bev Cigler at Penn State–Harrisburg was extremely gracious in sharing her work on management, counties, and intergovernmental relations. David Walker at the University of Connecticut was always supportive and available when we had questions about intergovernmental relations. Bill Peterman provided "hands on" insights as he introduced us to the intricacies of citizen participation and neighborhood politics in Chicago. Bob Waste, too, was an excellent source of ideas. At Albion College, Len Berkey helped to show that there are no great walls that separate urban sociology from urban politics. Rowan Miranda of the University of Pittsburgh and John Pelissero of Loyola University, Chicago, provided numerous helpful comments in their review of the fourth edition.

Throughout the writing of the manuscript, the authors had an opportunity to share ideas and opinions with numerous practitioners who helped us to focus on the day-to-day issues confronting urban officials. Among the most helpful were Larry Jones, the National Association of Counties; Jim Martin, the National Governors' Association; Steve Borko, the Metropolitan Washington Council of Governments; Revan Tranter, the Association of Bay Area Governments; and Enid Beaumont, formerly with the Academy of State and Local Government.

Myron Levine wishes to acknowledge the generous support he received from a number of Albion College faculty development grants. An

Occasional Fellowship provided by the Midwest Faculty Seminar made possible his visits to the Regenstein Library at the University of Chicago. At home, Nancy, Alex, and Evie were supportive and, more importantly, understanding.

A special debt of gratitude also goes to Bridget Brocken, a graduate research assistant at The American University who worked tirelessly for a year helping the authors collect and update information, check facts, and badger agency and city officials for current data. Mike Van Houten also helped with fact-checking at Albion.

P. J. Dillon and Ruth Ann Boyd typed several drafts of the manuscript. Ted Peacock, Dick Welna, and Jura Avizienis provided us with fine support (and encouragement!) at F. E. Peacock Publishers. John Beasley and Kim Vander Steen were most helpful, respectively, with gentle editing and with "proofing" under pressure. Leo Wiegman, too, deserves our thanks for his help with earlier editions of this book.

Professors who have used this volume in past years will immediately notice one significant difference. This is the first edition of *Urban Politics* that does not carry the name of Murray Stedman on its cover. The book was originally Murray Stedman's creation and we are indebted to him for allowing us to become a part of the authorship. We are also indebted to him intellectually and hope that this edition continues his approach of trying to identify the changing style of urban politics. In the 1970s and 1980s, it was enough to note that machine politics yielded way to reform and postreform politics. In the 1990s, clearly the politics of race and economic development dominate.

1

The L.A. Riots and the Urban Situation

The violent explosions that flared in Los Angeles in the wake of the 1992 Rodney King trial verdict stand as dramatic testimony to the condition of urban America. During the second half of the twentieth century, the United States enjoyed immense prosperity. People bought houses in the suburbs. The shift to a high-technology economy created many new growth industries. A growing black middle class shared in the nation's wealth. Yet, as the civil disorder that started in the impoverished South Central section of Los Angeles vividly reminded us, all was not well. Not all communities and people fully shared the nation's abundance. Some communities were left behind by the economic transformation that had taken place.

[handwritten margin note: Sounds like a great excuse to have a riot!]

The South Central riots were not the first major civil disorder to hit Los Angeles in the second half of the twentieth century. In 1965, riots in another poor inner–Los Angeles neighborhood, Watts, were the first in a chain of major violent outbursts that would sweep across cities in the United States in the years that immediately followed.

The 1960s riots led to the enactment of numerous governmental programs in an attempt to alleviate the conditions that led to the violence. While these programs had their successes, over the years the conditions of many inner cities deteriorated further. In many ways—in terms of drugs, crime, gang violence, out-of-wedlock pregnancies, welfare dependence, lost job opportunities, and inadequate schools—the problems that plagued the inner city in the 1990s were worse than they were in the 1960s.

For a brief moment, the South Central riots focused the attention of policy makers on the conditions of America's cities. Urban advocates proposed numerous solutions to correct the ills that led to the riots (or, as some preferred to term it, the urban "uprisings" or "rebellion"). But, as we shall see, few of the proposed solutions were ever enacted or effectively implemented.

1

In this book we shall examine the politics of governing metropolitan America. We shall see how populations are distributed throughout the metropolis and the problems that result. We shall observe how cities, suburbs, and their governing arrangements have changed over time. We shall also explore why certain solutions are attempted while others are ignored.

A review of the 1992 Los Angeles riots, the events that led up to them, and the limited nature of government's response in their aftermath will reveal much of importance about the state of contemporary urban America. We believe that Los Angeles is not unique, that Los Angeles suffers from the same problems that plague many American communities. A review of the events in Los Angeles will help to illustrate the five themes that guide this book's study of the politics of American cities and suburbs:

1. **The importance of private power.** Urban conditions are more the result of private sector action than of government programs. Any attempt to solve those problems will require the joint efforts of both the government and the private sector.

2. **The continuing importance of the formal rules and structure of American cities and suburbs.** Despite the importance of private power, the formal rules and organizations of municipal government continue to be of importance. As we shall see, the formal rules in Los Angeles allowed the hierarchy in the city's police department to shape that city's style of policing while remaining relatively free from outside accountability.

3. **The importance of intergovernmental relations and the rise of the dependent city.** Troubled cities like Los Angeles simply lack the means to solve urban problems on their own. They are dependent for their continued good health on the assistance provided by state and national governments.

4. **The continued existence of urban problems in Sunbelt cities despite the general distinction that can be made between Frostbelt and Sunbelt communities.** In recent years, a regional shift in jobs and population has given a peculiar shape to the urban crisis. The nation's most distressed cities are generally found in the declining Northeast and North Central regions of the country. Yet, as the events in Los Angeles remind us, it would be a mistake to stereotype Sunbelt communities as enjoying universal growth and prosperity. Sunbelt cities, too, suffer major problems.

5. **The reluctance of Americans to confront fully the issue of race.** Although Americans profess a belief in integration, they have not come to grips with the issue of race. Metropolitan areas in the United States are not integrated. Segregated schools and communities continue to exist. As a more extensive examination of the 1992 Los Angeles riots reveals, the issue of race in American life

has become even more complex over the years. Racial issues in American communities are no longer simply black versus white. The arrival of new immigrant groups has raised new dividing lines in U.S. cities.

In order to illustrate these themes, we turn to a brief review of both the 1960s riots and the events that took place in Los Angeles in 1992.

THE URBAN RIOTS OF THE 1960s

On August 11, 1965, in the Watts section of Los Angeles, a police officer named Lee Minikus pursued and stopped a young black man named Marquette Frye for speeding, driving without a license, and driving while intoxicated. By the time the police arrested Frye, an angry crowd had gathered. The crowd included Frye's mother and brother, who, too, were arrested during the altercation. The officers waded into the crowd in an attempt to find an assailant who spat on them. After the officers grabbed a woman wearing a smock, the rumor spread through the neighborhood that the police had brutalized a pregnant black woman. So began the Watts riot in which thirty-four persons (thirty-one African-Americans and two white law enforcement officers and one white firefighter) died.[1]

In 1966 and 1967, riots flared in large and small urban areas alike, including Chicago, Cleveland, Detroit, Newark, Milwaukee, Atlanta, Phoenix, Houston, Cincinnati, New Haven, Tampa, Grand Rapids (Michigan), Plainfield and Paterson (New Jersey), and Cambridge (Maryland). During the first nine months of 1967, 164 disorders were recorded by the National Advisory Commission on Civil Disorders.[2] Another wave of riots rocked cities across the nation in the wake of the April 1968 assassination of Martin Luther King, Jr.

President Lyndon Johnson established the National Advisory Commission on Civil Disorders to examine why the disturbances had occurred and what could be done about preventing further violence. The commission did not limit itself to identifying the immediate incidents that precipitated each riot. Instead, the commission also sought to identify the more fundamental, long-term causes of the violence. The commission was popularly referred to as the **Kerner Commission**, after Otto Kerner, the governor of Illinois, who headed the group.

According to the commission, the fundamental cause of the violence was inherent in the fact that the United States had become "two societies, one black, one white—separate and unequal."[3] Population migration patterns—the influx of poor blacks into the central city and the exodus of middle-class whites to the suburbs—exacerbated the **two societies** separation. The commission found **white racism** to be responsible "for the explosive mixture which has been accumulating in our cities since the end of World War II."[4] Among the ingredients of this explosive mixture were pervasive discrimination and segregation, the black in-migration to and white exodus from major cities, and the continued maintenance of black ghettos. The black community's sense of frustrated hopes only added to the incendiary situation, especially as the promises of both the civil rights movement and civil rights legislation were unfulfilled. The commission further identified **powerlessness** as a major cause of the riots. Inner-city blacks were unable to gain access to the power centers of government to bring about change.[5]

Were the commission's conclusions regarding the causes of riots in the 1960s equally applicable to Los Angeles in the 1990s? Were the roots of the Los Angeles disturbances in 1992 to be found predominantly in the fundamental inequalities of urban society? Or were the riots of the 1990s fundamentally different, with different causes and different patterns of violence?

THE RIOTS IN SOUTH CENTRAL, 1992

On March 3, 1992, Los Angeles police officers pursued and finally stopped a black motorist named Rodney King for driving at excessive speeds. A resident of a nearby apartment videotaped a circle of police officers as they arrested and repeatedly clubbed King as he resisted and attempted to get up from the ground. The dramatic footage of the beating, repeatedly aired on national television, shocked the nation. Young black males had often been the victims of brutality as law enforcement officials in Los Angeles adopted an aggressive approach to policing a city where drugs, gangs, and guns posed obvious dangers. The only exceptional aspect of the Rodney King beating, according to the police department's critics, was that the brutality had been captured on tape.

Four white police officers were charged for their involvement in the Rodney King beating. Out of concern that they could not get a fair trial in the heated L.A. environment, the trial was moved to nearby Simi Valley, a predominantly white suburban community in Ventura County.[6]

There had been no violent disturbances in Los Angeles at the time of King's arrest or the initial airing of the videotape. But the situation would be much different when the Simi County jury delivered its verdict.

On April 29, 1992, a predominantly white Simi Valley jury found the four officers "not guilty."[7] The jury seemingly accepted the defense attorneys' arguments that the officers had acted acceptably, that they used no undue force in subduing King, and that stop-action of the videotape replay showed that they had softened the blows they delivered to King. The verdict seemed incredible to a great many viewers who had themselves seen actual footage of the beating on television.

As news of the verdict spread, the impoverished, inner-city community of South Central Los Angeles exploded. The three-day riot was not confined to Los Angeles' poorest neighborhoods, but extended into neighboring communities, covering selected parts of an area of almost sixty square miles.[8] News cameras recorded the scene from helicopters as fires burned in different areas of the city. One particularly dramatic piece of tape showed a gang of violent thugs pulling a white driver, Reginald Denny, from his truck, kicking him, and dropping a large block on his head. Denny survived the attack as several black men and women in the community came to his assistance.

Ultimately, fifty-eight persons died in the conflagration. Smaller disturbances broke out in Las Vegas, Atlanta, and other cities. By the time the Los Angeles riot ended, it had become the most costly civil disorder in United States history, measured in both civilian deaths and property burned, looted, and destroyed. Amazingly, though, while a number of other cities experienced lesser disorders, the streets in many big-city, African-American communities remained calm.

Even before the Rodney King beating, the Simi Valley verdict, and the subsequent violence, African-Americans and other reformers had objected to the militaristic approach to law enforcement taken by L.A. Police Chief Daryl Gates. They had placed on the ballot a measure to reform the police department. After the King beating, they escalated their demands for both Gates' removal and greater citizen control over what had become a highly independent and unaccountable police department.[9] Soon after the beating, city council member Michael Woo, the city's most prominent Asian-American elected official, and Congressman Howard Berman, a Jewish liberal, joined the call for Gates' resignation. Mayor Tom Bradley, a political moderate and the city's first elected black mayor, proceeded more cautiously, first working behind the scenes in an attempt to arrange Gates' ouster before finally calling publicly for the chief's removal. The city council, however, fearing a lawsuit threatened by the chief, reversed a decision by the police commission to place Gates on indefinite suspension while an investigation of the department proceeded.

Racial attitudes in Los Angeles were polarized. At first, more conservative citizens in the predominantly white parts of Los Angeles, seeing the police as a "thin blue line" that separated good citizens from the forces of disorder, came to Gates' defense. In the early stages of the affair, Gates enjoyed greater support among Latinos than among blacks, as Latinos had greater confidence in the ability of the police to fight crime in their neighborhood.[10]

But in the wake of further revelations of the chief's mishandling of a potential riot situation, support for Gates eroded among whites and Latinos as well as among blacks.[11] Further investigations had shown that the police chief had failed to initiate adequate preparations in anticipation of a riot that might occur coincident with the announcement of the trial's verdict. The chief had even refused to meet with Mayor Bradley, his long-time political rival, to discuss preparations as a tense city awaited the Simi Valley verdict. In a number of riot-torn neighborhoods, the police were obviously slow to respond to the violence and the looting.

The dramatic footage of the rampaging mob that pulled Reginald Denny from his truck and brutally beat him showed no police officers in sight. Citizens were particularly aggrieved by what seemed to be Gates' negligence when he decided to attend a political dinner to raise funds to fight a police reform referendum rather than take more direct charge of the police response to the riot situation. In July, a blue-ribbon commission headed by Warren Christopher (later to be Secretary of State) further attacked Gates for his failure to root out the racism and brutality that plagued the police department.

Despite the diminished public faith in Gates' performance, neither the mayor nor the city council possessed the authority to dismiss the chief, as will be explained. Gates stayed on, postponing the date of his retirement. Eventually, though, Gates did decide to leave and was replaced by Willie Williams, an African-American, who, as police chief in Philadelphia, had adopted a community-relations-oriented approach to law enforcement that stood in marked contrast to Gates' more militaristic approach.

In the wake of the riots, the Bush administration provided Los Angeles with $1.3 billion in emergency relief, with an emphasis primarily on loans to aid small businesses. President Bush promised a "weed and seed" program, under which increased law enforcement efforts would weed crime out of urban neighborhoods and the seeds of new educational and job opportunities would be planted. The program that Bush promised was heavy on weed (law enforcement) and short on seed (job training and other opportunity programs). Congress broadened the purposes of the urban aid bill by loading it up with all sorts of provisions unrelated to the urban condition—including provisions for tax deductible IRA's, the repeal of the luxury tax on expensive boats and cars, and new incentives to aid the real estate industry. The program, which had started out as a mere $2.5 million urban aid bill, had ballooned to a five-year cost of $27 billion, of which only $7 billion would go to cities. The day after the 1992 presidential election, Bush vetoed the program as excessive.[12]

Civic leaders understood that, given the fiscally conservative mood of the early 1990s, only the most minimal infusion of federal aid could be expected. Rather than rely on government assistance, the city would attempt to rebuild itself by relying on private corporations to invest in, and provide jobs in, the city's poor neighborhoods. Mayor Bradley recruited Peter Ueberroth, the former Baseball Commissioner and successful organizer of the 1984 Los Angeles Olympic Games, to head a private-sector initiative called **Rebuild L.A.** (later, more simply, **RLA**) to secure new investment in the riot-damaged area, aid minority entrepreneurship, and provide new skills training and opportunity for the people of the riot area.[13] Immediately upon its creation, the city's different racial constituencies fought over what was to be the exact goal of RLA and over who would get the jobs on each rebuilding project. A spokeswoman for

Korean-American business owners also complained that, as RLA focused on new supermarkets and job training centers, small-business owners did not receive sufficient assistance to reopen their shops.[14]

URBAN RIOTS AND THE URBAN SITUATION

The violence and outrage that engulfed Los Angeles can be seen in the context of the urban situation. Studies of the urban riots of the 1960s generated a great volume of work that adds to our understanding of the causes of civil disorder. In many ways the riots in Los Angeles parallelled the disturbances of the 1960s; in other ways, they represented something new.

As we have already noted, the Kerner Commission emphasized the social and political causes of the 1960s riots—that the roots of the urban violence could be found in the substantial inequality of urban society and the powerlessness of the inner-city poor. To a great extent, this characterization applies to the 1992 riots as well. Racial isolation, "white flight" to the suburbs, continued ghettoization, and the hard-line enforcement practices of the Los Angeles Police Department all added to the frustrations of inner-city residents.[15] Housing segregation for blacks in big cities was only slightly less severe than it had been in the 1960s.[16] Despite the gains of a black middle class, there was little governmental effort to promote scatter-site public housing or curb the exclusionary land use powers exercised by suburban jurisdictions. In the area of education, desegregation efforts had slowed and a new pattern of resegregation began to emerge. Studies of school systems in metropolitan areas reported "a tendency toward declining contact between black and white students."[17] The perceived injustice of a jury verdict that acquitted the four officers, despite the videotape evidence that seemed to have established their clear guilt, touched off a powder keg of accumulated frustrations.

Lynn A. Curtis, President of the Milton S. Eisenhower Foundation, testifying before Congress in the wake of the Los Angeles disturbances, spoke of the long-term causes of the potentially explosive situation in America's cities:

> Overall, in spite of some gains since the 1960s but especially because of the Federal disinvestments of the 1980s, we conclude that the famous prophesy of the Kerner Commission, of two societies, one black, one white—separate and unequal—is more relevant today than in 1968, and more complex, with the emergence of multiracial disparities and growing income segregation.[18]

The title of a best-selling book by Andrew Hacker summarized the urban situation even more succinctly: *Two Nations: Black and White, Separate, Hostile, Unequal.*[19]

Writing before the South Central outburst, the nongovernmental Commission on the Cities, too, concluded that, twenty years after the Kerner Commission completed its work, "The Kerner Report is coming true: America *is* again becoming two societies, one black (and, today, we can add to that, Hispanic), one white—separate and unequal."[20] America's cities suffered from violence. Even where there were no manifest outbreaks of civil disorder, central cities in the United States were marred by the **quiet riots** of "unemployment, poverty, social disorganization, segregation, family disintegration, housing and school deterioration, and crime."[21] Political scientist Robert Waste phrased the point only somewhat differently, noting that the absence of civil disorder meant that Los Angeles, Miami, and other large cities were only "between riots."[22]

Still, a number of differences separate the Los Angeles riots of 1992 from the Watts riots and other uprisings of the 1960s. Violence during the latter-day disorders was not confined to poor, minority neighborhoods as had been the case in the 1960s. In 1992, substantial looting of stores also occurred in Hollywood and areas of the city that were not obviously poor and oppressed.[23] Acts of violence in the 1992 riot were more sadistic. This sadism, sadly, was also evident in the 1980s riots that occurred in the predominantly black Overtown and Liberty City areas of Miami, Florida.

Further, the 1992 Los Angeles outburst was clearly multiracial. Persons arrested in the 1965 Watts riots were almost exclusively black, but such was not the case in 1992. News reports in 1992 initially framed the event from the stereotype of a black riot; the dramatic footage of the Reginald Denny beating at the hands of a violent group of black assailants also reinforced images of an African-American rebellion. But arrest report data strikingly reveal that over half of those arrested during the disturbance were Latino, not black, underscoring the multiracial character of the outburst.[24] As one review of arrest data from the riots concluded, "The heavy involvement of Latinos suggested that they too used the opportunity to vent their frustrations."[25]

The Kerner Commission's "two societies" prophesy is deficient only in its failure to predict the population diversity and resulting tensions that would characterize urban America in the 1990s. The population of U.S. cities and suburbs is no longer comprised largely of ethnic groups of European descent and African-Americans. In recent years, a **new immigration** has brought new population groups from Asia, Mexico, and Central America—including, to name only a few, Salvadorians, Caribbean blacks, Chinese, Japanese, Iranians, Indians, Filipinos, Vietnamese, and Koreans—to U.S. cities and suburbs.[26]

The complex, new social cleavages that resulted from this new migration were apparent in Los Angeles and other cities. Blacks, Latinos, and Asians were all struggling for a piece of the shrinking economic pie that was South Central Los Angeles.[27] Unlike the 1960s, when looting and arson were often directed against stores owned by whites and Jews, in 1992 much of the property violence was directed against Koreans, other Asian-Americans, and Hispanics—a new generation of inner-city, small-store proprietors. In the 1992 disturbance, Hispanic store owners suffered greater property damage than did black owners.

Even before the South Central violence, African-Americans often complained that they received little respect in the Asian-owned shops that populated their neighborhoods.[28] They were especially angered when a Korean grocer received no jail time after having shot a thirteen-year-old African-American girl named Latasha Harlins in the back of the head after a store altercation. In 1990, in New York's Flatbush section of Brooklyn, African-Americans organized a boycott of Korean shopkeepers, whom they accused of showing disrespect for Haitian customers.

In Miami as well as in Los Angeles, blacks and Hispanics have often seen themselves as competitors.[29] Antagonism between the two groups even surfaced during the 1990 visit to Miami by South African leader Nelson Mandela, then deputy president of the African National Congress (ANC). The visit was part of Mandela's triumphal tour across America. But the city's Cuban-Americans were outraged by Mandela's refusal to condemn Fidel Castro for human rights violations in Cuba. Castro had provided the ANC with much needed help in its liberation struggle in South Africa, and, as Mandela observed, the ANC lacked the luxury of being able to comment on the internal affairs of other nations. Miami Mayor Xavier Suárez and four other Cuban-American mayors publicly criticized Mandela's stance and refused to extend Mandela an official welcome. Local black activists, outraged by the slight, urged blacks to register and vote Suárez and other Cuban-Americans out of office.

POLITICAL POWER AND URBAN AMERICA

The story of the Los Angeles uprisings and their aftermath illustrates a number of essential urban themes. In particular, it points to the importance of *power* in determining whose needs are met and whose needs are ignored, in determining what gets done and what does not get done in urban America.

The particular focus of this book is on power—how it is distributed and how it is exercised in the urban political arena. **Power,** as the word is commonly used, implies threat or the ability to use sanctions to achieve compliance. In this simple definition, power can be understood as **social control;** a political actor exercises power when he or she can force others to comply with his or her wishes.[30]

Power is oftentimes confused with influence. **Influence** is the ability of a person or a party to persuade or cajole others to act in a desired manner. But influence does not always entail coercion or threats. Influence can be seen to run along a continuum, with the far end characterized by coercion (the imposition of severe penalties for noncompliance). It is this far end of the continuum, coercive influence, that is often referred to as power.

But it is too simple to look at power only as social control. According to Clarence Stone, power also denotes **social production** or the ability to get significant things done: *"power to,* not *power over."* [31] Power denotes a capacity to act and is exercised when an actor has the ability to ensure the achievement of important objectives or, alternatively, to frustrate goal achievement by others. Power does not always denote situations of conflict. Defined as the ability to act or get things done, power can entail cooperation in the pursuit of goals. Power is evident when people from different sectors of the community cooperate in the making of important governing decisions. [32]

In the urban arena, there are numerous important policy changes that need be made. We need to find out who has the ability to get these things done and who has the ability to stop or veto proposed changes. Who has the power? Whose cooperation is essential to the realization of important urban outcomes? Whose interests are served?

An examination of power requires that we go "behind the scenes" of urban government. We must look at the formal procedures and institutions of government. A study of the formal rules will afford us great insight as to who has the right to make important decisions. But a formal structural analysis, by itself, is an insufficient method for the study of political power. Governmental officials make decisions, but they may be severely constrained by the power of private sector actors. Business groups, labor unions, religious groups, civic associations, charitable foundations, non-profit social service organizations, and community and neighborhood groups are all frequent participants in the urban political arena. We need to find out which of these, under what conditions, can be seen as truly powerful.

As we noted at the beginning of this chapter, five dominant themes emerge throughout our study of urban political power:

1. Private sector institutions and their actions have played an important role in shaping metropolitan America.
2. The structure of municipal government, its formal institutions, and its procedures continue to be important as they influence who gets what from city politics.
3. Intergovernmental actors, especially the federal government, but more recently state governments as well, have gained a new prominence in influencing city affairs.
4. There are important regional variations in patterns of urban development and the structure and exercise of urban power. We need to compare Sunbelt communities with Frostbelt communities in order to discern just where urban problems, problem solving, and the exercise of power are similar and where important regional differences exist.

5. Race constitutes an important dividing line in American politics. We need to discern just how the exercise of power has affected patterns of racial succession and prospects for racial equality. We also need to assess just what leadership strategies are capable of crossing the chasm too often posed by race in urban affairs.

THE IMPORTANCE OF PRIVATE POWER

Many of the most important decisions that affect local communities are made not by governmental institutions but by private sector actors. Suburbs have grown as Americans show a preference for suburban living and businesses have pursued suburban locations. The result has been an exodus to the suburbs that has produced racially imbalanced communities, development sprawl, and fiscally hard-pressed central cities with only a limited ability to provide services to a population in need.

Prominent members of a metropolitan area's business community, including the executives of national and international corporations, play a key role in determining the economic health of local jurisdictions. It is private business that decides just where its facilities will be located and, ultimately, just which localities will gain and which will lose jobs and taxes. The cooperation of business elites is often essential to the completion of local projects; their refusal to cooperate can frustrate municipal hopes. Consequently, private sector elites often occupy a privileged position in civic affairs, and municipal officials generally come to terms with business interests.[33]

In many European countries, private sector power is counterbalanced by a tradition of strong governmental planning and action. In these countries, government officials seek to ensure that private development decisions bring public benefits as well as private profits. In Europe, for instance, city and regional planning officials often insist on aesthetic standards in new construction. They also insist on more balanced development, often requiring developers of new commercial projects to have a housing component in their plans, including subsidized units for the poor.[34]

The American political culture, in contrast, grants no similar role to government officials in guiding private sector development. Just the opposite. Americans, on the whole, are an antigovernment people who tend to see strong urban planning requirements and land use restrictions as violations of their individual rights. Under the American attitude of **privatism**, private sector freedom is equated with liberty; government intrusions and regulations are kept to a minimum as private sector actors are allowed maximum leeway in a free market system to pursue their interests and to develop and dispose of their property as they see fit.[35]

The Los Angeles riots can be understood within the framework provided by a free-market, privatist culture and private sector power. The roots of the South Central disturbances can be found in migration patterns and the changed structure of the nation's economy. Citizens who could afford to do so moved out of inner-city neighborhoods, in effect making these areas **reservations** for the urban poor.[36] Businesses, too, fled the inner city for suburban sites more convenient to their customers and middle-class work force. Multinational corporations, too, shifted production facilities to low-wage nations overseas, depriving cities of the good-paying, entry-level manufacturing jobs that characterized urban economies in a previous era.[37]

WHY DID THEY LEAVE?

The flight of both better-off residents and businesses beyond the city's borders acted to deprive Los Angeles of both jobs and a source of funds to cope with social problems. The loss of white students, to private schools as well as to the suburbs, meant the resegregation of the city's schools. Free-market profitability determined the availability of local services. As a result, residents in South Central lacked the facilities that other Americans tend to take for granted. Banks did not even open branch offices in poor neighborhoods such as South Central, leaving inner-city residents with no alternative but to rely on "Checks Cashed Here" stores as a substitute. Supermarkets, too, ignored South Central, leaving residents to shop in smaller stores that charged high markups. At the time of the riots, South Central had only 11 grocery stores but 728 liquor stores.[38]

In the aftermath of the riots, America's privatist culture explains why plans for recovery focused not so much on government programs but on a Rebuild L.A. (RLA) effort to increase private sector investment. Ultimately, RLA produced very little—certainly not enough to bring new opportunity to and transform inner-city Los Angeles. Although Rebuild L.A. was able to negotiate a few notable reinvestment projects, including a decision by Vons Supermarkets to open ten to twelve new stores in Los Angeles' inner city, overall the efforts of RLA proved insufficient to the task at hand. RLA claimed to have invested $500 million in the riot area and to be responsible for the creation of several thousand jobs. Yet a *Los Angeles Times* editorial reported that "the fruits of those efforts have been barely visible amid burned buildings and abandoned businesses."[39] Two years after the riot, *The New York Times* provided an even more discouraging assessment of the private enterprise effort, observing that "Today, Rebuild L.A. has virtually disappeared from the Los Angeles landscape, and Mr. Ueberroth and his cochairmen have all stepped aside."[40]

RLA attempted only limited action consistent with its private power structure. There was little public authority to order more. Nor was it directly answerable to community residents: "RLA was never more than a private sector driven organization with minimal participation of public sector representatives and even more limited contact with community organizations and individuals."[41] RLA had a top-down, decision-making style devoted to secrecy. A corporate-led organization, RLA showed no great willingness to open the process and bring community residents into the making of decisions.[42]

In the privatist system in the United States, the private sector, not government, holds the resources necessary for urban prosperity. Yet there was not enough profit in the rebuilding of Los Angeles for most private sector actors to reverse the past decisions that had led them away from the inner city. Government has only limited power to mobilize the commitment of private sector resources necessary to solve critical urban problems.

THE CONTINUED IMPORTANCE OF GOVERNMENTAL INSTITUTIONS AND FORMAL RULES

Despite the great influence exerted by private sector actors, the institutions and formal rules of government remain important. As we shall see, a city's voting rules—whether a city has a system of ward-based elections or at-large elections or whether a city has a partisan or a nonpartisan voting system—help to determine the extent of representation gained by minorities in a city. Similarly, federal government rules requiring citizen participation can also give citizens a new opportunity to raise their voices and challenge the decisions made by a city's elected officials. In city after city, the landmark federal Voting Rights Act of 1965 proved essential for helping minorities achieve elective office and a share of the power. Simply put, the rules and formal procedures of government count. They help determine who gets what from politics.

The formal structure of the municipal government in Los Angeles explains why Police Chief Daryl Gates was able to exercise power so independently and hold on to his position long after he had lost the confidence of the city's mayor and large portions of the public as well. In many other big cities, mayors have the power to dismiss a disappointing police chief. But Los Angeles operates under a form of government known as a weak mayor system. In Los Angeles, the mayor and the city council lacked the formal authority to force cooperation from the chief or remove him from office.

As Chapters 4 through 6 of this book will detail, many of the rules and institutions for governing cities have their genesis in the long battle between political machines and reformers. The reformers have, for the most part, won the war. Many cities today have elements of reformed rules, including nonpartisan and at-large elections, the council-manager form of government, independent city planning commissions and professionalized service agencies, and local bureaucracies protected by merit system hiring and firing rules. In Los Angeles, municipal government is structured to minimize the influence of "politics" on government. As much as possible, power is placed in the hands of professional administrators who are, by the rules of the municipality, assured of their independence.

In Los Angeles, the reformed rules insulated the police chief from direct accountability to the city's elected officials.[43] Chief Gates had the power to dictate the department's militaristic approach to policing with little regard for the opinions of elected officials or the representatives of minority communities. As Gates reported in his book *Chief: My Life in the LAPD*, he felt no need to work with Mayor Tom Bradley; the two "were scarcely on speaking terms," and, over time, they had learned "to tolerate each other, barely—speaking only when we had to, mainly by telephone."[44] After the outbreak of the riots, Mayor Bradley recalled that he had not spoken to Gates, the city police chief, in thirteen months![45]

Even Willie Williams, the community-oriented police chief who succeeded Gates, confessed, "I don't have one operating superior" to whom to report. The new chief did not have to meet with the mayor or other department heads to coordinate actions: "The first six months I thought I was mayor!"[46] Only after Gates mishandled the South Central disturbances did the public vote to change the city charter—the city's formal rules—to limit the police chief's tenure and give public officials greater authority in his tenure and removal from office.

Los Angeles' reformed rules also help to explain the city's lack of responsiveness to the concerns of impoverished, minority neighborhoods. Earlier in L.A.'s history, the reformers had sought to structure a government that would reflect a citywide, public interest. The reformers wanted to avoid the parochialism that results when city council members represent small geographic districts.

Given the immense size of Los Angeles, each member of the fifteen-member city council winds up representing thirty-one square miles and 250,000 people. At the county level, there are only five supervisors, each of whom has the virtually impossible task of representing millions of people with all their diversity. The representative of such a large and diverse district cannot act as the advocate of a particular minority community. With such large districts, there are no strong council voices to represent the needs of impoverished minority communities.

THE RISE OF THE INTERGOVERNMENTAL CITY

As already noted, cities like Los Angeles lack the resources to solve the extensive economic, social, and educational problems their communities confront. The nature of public finance places them in a bind. They have the problems, but much of the metropolis's tax base lies beyond their borders. They can raise taxes in an effort to fund needed programs only at the risk of driving residential and commercial activity outside the city. As a result, each city is limited in its ability to undertake redistributional social programs.[47] More distressed cities are **dependent** on state and federal assistance to provide an adequate level of basic services.[48]

Since the Reagan years, however, intergovernmental assistance to cities has fallen. The Reagan administration terminated Urban Development Actions Grants and general revenue sharing with local governments.

TABLE 1.1
Federal Grants-in-Aid to State and Local Governments
(in Billions)*

Fiscal Year	Amount (Current Dollars)	Percent Increase or Decrease Over Previous Year	Amount in Constant Dollars (1987 dollars)	Percent Real Increase or Decrease Over Previous Year
1955	$ 3.2	—	$ 15.3	—
1960	7.0	—	29.1	—
1965	10.9	—	41.8	—
1970	24.0	—	73.6	—
1975	49.8	—	105.4	—
1980	91.5	10.4%	127.6	-0.4%
1981	94.8	3.6	121.5	-4.8
1982	88.2	-7.0	106.5	-12.3
1983	92.5	4.9	107	0.5
1984	97.6	5.5	108.4	1.3
1985	105.9	8.5	113	4.2
1986	112.4	6.1	115.9	2.6
1987	108.4	-3.6	108.4	-6.5
1988	115.3	6.4	110.8	2.2
1989	122.0	5.7	112.2	1.3
1990	135.4	11.0	119.7	6.7
1991	152.0	12.3	129.0	7.8
1992[e]	182.2	19.9	149.8	16.1
1993[e]	199.1	9.3	158.4	5.7
1994[e]	220.1	10.5	169.4	6.9
1995[e]	235.5	7.0	175.3	3.5
1996[e]	255.1	8.3	183.7	4.8
1997[e]	275.2	7.9	191.8	4.4

*Office of Management and Budget estimate.
Source: Compiled from Advisory Commission on Intergovernmental Relations, *Significant Features of Fiscal Federalism, 1992 Edition:* vol. 2 (Washington, DC: ACIR, 1992), p. 60.

It virtually stopped assistance for the construction of new subsidized housing units; it sharply reduced funds for public housing modernization and other urban programs. Overall, federal aid to local governments, which stood at $22 billion when Reagan came to office in 1980–81, was reduced to $17 billion in 1987–88 as Reagan was about to leave office.[49] Reagan succeeded in reducing, but not eliminating, federal aid to states and cities (see Table 1.1). Better-off cities survived the Reagan onslaught in fairly good shape,[50] but distressed cities and impoverished communities like South Central, which were most dependent on federal aid, were hurt greatly by the cutbacks.

The federal government's response to the 1992 Los Angeles riots was quite different than its response to the urban rebellion of the 1960s. The public had tired of "big government" domestic problem-solving approaches. They saw the programs of the Democratic Great Society era as ineffectual and wasteful.[51] The huge size of the Reagan and Bush budget deficits also imposed a new sense of fiscal constraint on policy makers, a sense that there were no new federal funds available for major, new urban programs.

President George Bush visited Los Angeles and offered some immediate relief, mainly in the form of loans to small businesses. But when Congress proved unable to produce a targeted urban aid program, Bush vetoed the resulting "porked up" bill. The Clinton administration expanded certain urban aid programs. But even the new Democratic administration limited its urban efforts as a consequence of budgetary constraints and a recognition that the federal government possessed only a limited ability to solve complex urban problems. Rather than launch major, new urban aid programs, Clinton emphasized **reinventing government**—to allow states and localities greater flexibility to do more with the funds that were already available.

The relative paucity of new federal spending after the South Central riots may also have been the result of the general calm that prevailed in cities nationwide in the wake of the Rodney King verdict. While a number of cities did experience limited disorder, there was no nationwide wave of urban riots as there had been after the 1968 assassination of Martin Luther King. In the wake of the Rodney King verdict, streets in cities such as Detroit and Cleveland remained calm, perhaps because these cities had black mayors and were no longer seen by minority groups as the enemy of their communities. Even in Atlanta, there was only a miniriot rooted in the student community, which turned mildly violent when it went downtown and the police attempted to intervene. Students in Atlanta for the most part accepted as legitimate the actions that a black mayor, a black-controlled city council, and a black police chief took to suppress the disorder.[52]

In *Regulating the Poor*, Frances Fox Piven and Richard Cloward argue that the 1960s urban riots constituted a threat of unrest that led to an expansion of federal aid programs. But once civil order was restored, the government could again cut social programs. In 1992, the government could more safely ignore the more limited, isolated nature of the outbursts that had occurred.[53]

The California state government, too, was constrained in responding to the situation in Los Angeles. A taxpayer's rebellion in the state had led to a new sense of fiscal conservatism. The post–Cold War reductions in military-related spending also took their toll on the state's economy. The problems of the inner cities competed for attention as California sought to find the funds for economic conversion, education, earthquake relief, and other statewide needs.

Our analysis of Los Angeles points to the rise of the **intergovernmental city**, where the health of troubled communities is greatly dependent on the action of the state and federal governments. Cities, especially more troubled cities, are precariously dependent on the actions of governments outside their borders. Any contemporary description of local affairs must take into account the expanded role played by intergovernmental actors and the problems posed by the vicissitudes of intergovernmental assistance.

FROSTBELT-SUNBELT: REGIONAL VARIATIONS IN THE URBAN CRISIS

In recent decades the United States has witnessed a shift in population from the Northeast and the Midwest to the South (particularly Florida), the Southwest, and the West. A restructuring of the nation's economy has been accompanied by the decline of both jobs and population in the older, "smokestack" cities of the **Frostbelt**—the Northeast and Midwest. Entire metropolitan areas centered around declining industries have shrunk in size as they lost population to other parts of the country. In contrast, Los Angeles, Houston, San Diego, Dallas, San Antonio, Phoenix, San Jose, and a great many other cities in the Sunbelt have gained substantially in population and economic activity over the past three decades.

There is a general recognition that the term **Sunbelt** denotes those areas of the American South, Southwest, and West that have experienced a general growth of population and economic activity the past few decades. Yet there is no clear consensus as to the precise boundaries of this region.[54] There is a substantial consensus that the Sunbelt includes, at the very least, the states south of a line from North Carolina running west through Oklahoma and southern California. Yet different authors have used different definitions: A number include Virginia within the region; others look at the growth of population and economic activity as the defining characteristics of the region and hence include Colorado, northern California, and the Pacific Northwest as parts of the Sunbelt—forming a "Sunbelt" that in some places is rather cool, cloudy, rainy, and even snowy.[55] (See Figure 1.1.) Ann Markusen uses a similarly expansive definition of the **gunbelt** to underscore the importance of defense-related expenditures to communities in the states of Washington and California, as well as the Southwest and Florida. The gunbelt clearly extends beyond the more traditional borders of the Sunbelt to include Seattle, Colorado Springs, Washington, DC, high-tech suburbs in the greater Boston area, and other centers of defense-related prosperity.[56]

Of course, there is an analytical danger entailed in dividing the country into two such large and loosely defined regions as Frostbelt and Sunbelt. Such regional division may hide and distort as much as it may reveal. Cities in the Frostbelt do not all suffer advanced decay. In fact, beginning in the 1980s, a number of Frostbelt cities began to reverse over two decades of population losses and fiscal problems. By the early 1990s, numerous states in the Northeast and Midwest showed substantial economic recovery. While cities like Philadelphia, Detroit, Bridgeport (Connecticut), Jersey City, and Newark (New Jersey) continued to suffer serious fiscal distress, other cities—notably Baltimore, Boston, Cleveland, and Pittsburgh—exhibited evidence of resurgence and renaissance. New York went from a fiscal crisis in the 1970s to a new economic dynamism in the 1980s and 1990s. The downtowns and trendy residential districts in these Frostbelt cities prospered, even while severe economic and social problems continued to plague other neighborhoods.

FIGURE 1.1
Three Views of the Sunbelt

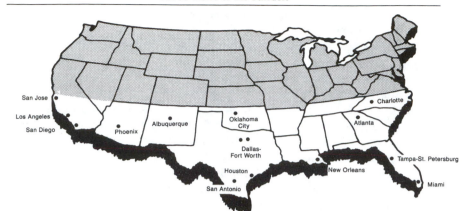

Map 1.1
A Common View of the Sunbelt

Map 1.2
A Broader View of the Sunbelt,
Including Virginia and Sacramento, California

Map 1.3
A Very Expansive View Based on Growth,
Including Colorado, Northern California, and the Pacific Northwest

Similarly, it is a mistake to speak in stereotypical terms of Sunbelt growth. The time bomb that erupted in South Central underscores the fact that growing Sunbelt cities suffer many of the same social problems experienced in cities of the Northeast and the Midwest. A great many urban problems are the same no matter the region in which a city is located.

Further, not all Sunbelt states and cities shared equally in the region's prosperity. States in the Southeast—Alabama, Louisiana, Mississippi, and Arkansas—generally did not share in the Sunbelt's dynamic population growth of the 1980s. In a number of southern states, rapid growth and prosperity were confined to resort and retirement communities. Louisiana actually lost population! In many ways, New Orleans more closely resembles an aged and troubled city of the Frost-belt than it does the more dynamically growing cities of the American Southwest. In a developing trend, New Orleans, Galveston (Texas), and Biloxi (Mississippi) are among the Sunbelt cities that have turned to, or are considering, casino gambling in an effort to uncover new sources of revenue to fight urban problems.

Periods of regional economic downturn have also hurt Sunbelt cities. The 1980s decline in oil prices, followed by the collapse of the savings and loan industry, brought new economic problems to Houston and other once-dynamic cities of the "oil patch" and the American Southwest. The downturn of southern California's economy in the early 1990s also provided part of the setting for Los Angeles' civil unrest. Jobs had increased by 27 percent in southern California during the economic boom of the 1980s. But the end of Cold War defense-related spending helped bring an end to that prosperity. In the eighteen months preceding the riots, southern California lost 600,000 jobs.[57]

Still, whatever the diversity within the regions and whatever the economic problems that plague the Sunbelt, important Frostbelt-Sunbelt regional differences remain. In fact, the gap between the regions may increase still further as the Southwest shows signs of an economic recovery and the economic boom in the Northeast begins to fade. Patterns of job growth may only serve to broaden, not narrow, the economic gap between the regions. In surveying the fifty states for job growth for 1988 and 1989, the Bureau of Labor Statistics found that seven of the nine states from Pennsylvania northeast to Maine finished in the bottom ten in terms of job growth. In contrast, seven western states and Florida finished in the top ten. As the regional commissioner commented after reviewing the situation of the Northeast, "The economic renaissance of the 1980s is now history."[58]

Has the renaissance of U.S. cities, particularly in the Frostbelt, led to an improvement in the lives of neighborhood residents and the poor? Evidence presented by Harold Wolman and his associates has forced a reassessment of the "urban success stories" of the 1980s. Only in Atlanta,

Baltimore, and Boston has urban revitalization been associated with the improved economic well-being of city residents. In contrast, the downtown and commercial comebacks of Cleveland, Pittsburgh, Louisville, Cincinnati, and other generally recognized revitalized cities did not lead to improved economic conditions for city residents. In these North Central cities, indicators of economic distress in 1990 were little different than they had been in 1980; in some cases, conditions had become even worse.[59]

In Philadelphia the renaissance was clearly over. As the city entered the 1990s, it faced an escalating crime rate, an austerity budget, the curtailment of many municipal services, and the imposition of new taxes—in a city where residents were already among the highest taxed in the nation. A reduction in the city's bond rating also meant a possible increase in municipal borrowing costs by $10 million a year.[60] Newly elected Mayor Ed Rendell faced a formidable task in his high-profile efforts to revivify the city.

Patterns of power in many Sunbelt communities appear quite distinct from those of their northern counterparts. Sunbelt cities tend to lack strong labor unions and political party organizations. Sunbelt cities also have traditionally been more likely to be ruled by local business elites. Only recently has this traditional pattern undergone change and transformation. In studying cities and suburbs, we must take special care to observe the ways in which patterns in Sunbelt communities are similar to, and diverge from, patterns in their Frostbelt counterparts.

AMERICA'S AMBIVALENCE TOWARD RACE

Americans as a whole are ambivalent on matters of race. Americans condemn blatant acts of racism and discrimination and overwhelmingly disapprove of *de jure* **segregation** (that is, segregation mandated by law, as existed in the South in the 1950s and preceding decades). Yet, there is no similar willingness by white Americans to take action against *de facto* **segregation** (segregation that exists in fact but is not mandated by law), the sort of separation that characterizes school and housing patterns in the North as well as in the South.

The Supreme Court's famous 1954 *Brown v. Board of Education* decision began the prolonged process of bringing to an end the *de jure* segregation of school systems in the South. But in succeeding decades, the most significant desegregation battles, as often as not, were fought in the North. In the late 1960s, South Boston became the national symbol of community resistance to school busing. Metropolitan school desegregation efforts effectively came to an end in a great many cities nationwide as a result of the Supreme Court's 1974 *Millikin v. Bradley*[61] ruling against an interdistrict plan for desegregating Detroit's schools. In the late 1980s, Yonkers (New York) stubbornly refused to comply with court-ordered housing integration despite the imposition of heavy fines by a federal judge.

According to urban analyst Anthony Downs, American society since 1968 has essentially abandoned the goal of racial integration. Instead, the nation has pursued a strategy of "mild ghetto enrichment"—giving governmental aid to both individuals and city governments while maintaining continued racial segregation.[62] The Reagan administration's social service and urban program cuts represented a retreat from even this limited goal of ghetto enrichment, offering instead only "segregation and serious poverty for minorities."[63] Downs underscored the tolerance for ghettoization in the United States:

> The white-dominated U.S. society has clearly chosen to create and maintain two racially separate and unequal societies, as the Kerner Commission feared it might. In spite of all the pious statements to the contrary, the leaders and citizens of nearly all parts of U.S. society have no intention whatever of changing that deliberate policy.[64]

In Los Angeles and other cities, the costs that result from maintaining separate societies are becoming increasingly evident. The different societies had quite different views of the disturbances that had occurred. Where white residents spoke of the "civil disturbances," African-Americans often chose more political terms, such as **uprising** or **rebellion**. The rebellions were a response to political causes. While there were extensive incidents of looting and some dramatic incidents of senseless violence during the Los Angeles disturbances, it is too simplistic to characterize all participants only as opportunists rioting "for fun and profit," as Edward Banfield had viewed an earlier generation of urban civil disorders.[65]

Studies of the 1960s riots refuted the "riff-raff" theory that rioters represented only a small criminal element in the community. Quite the contrary, a broad cross section of the community residents participated, and even nonparticipants expressed sympathy for the riots as a strike against inequality and oppression.[66]

Today the picture is a bit more complex. The urban situation has changed as the economic and social conditions of central cities have worsened. No single interpretation can capture the complexity of the 1992 events and the motivations of participants in different neighborhoods. Instead, it is more appropriate to view the events as several different riots that occurred more or less simultaneously.[67]

Racial tensions, too, have become more complex as a result of the new immigration to America's shores. In Los Angeles and other U.S. cities, racial conflict has gone beyond black versus white. When Los Angeles attempted to rebuild, black activists protested at reconstruction sites where Latino laborers—and no blacks—had been hired. Latinos, in turn, vowed to resist efforts to shut down the sites; they protested efforts to keep them from working as a result of their race.[68] Ueberroth's Rebuild L.A. was similarly paralyzed by racial polarizations and the resulting lack of consensus over its mission. Korean-American merchants demanded that RLA help rebuild and restock their stores. Leaders in the black community, in turn, demanded that capital assistance be given to African-American entrepreneurs to start up businesses to serve their own people.

At times, cities have been able to transcend racial polarizations. In Los Angeles, long-time Mayor Tom Bradley maintained office by fusing together a coalition of blacks, Latinos, and liberal whites, especially Jews. While this coalition exhibited severe strains over time, outrage over the Rodney King beating helped, at least momentarily, to remobilize the coalition on issues of police reform and accountability.[69] In the nation's two other largest cities, the mobilization of multiracial coalitions similarly led to the elections of two progressive black mayors—Harold Washington in Chicago and David Dinkins in New York. But in all three cities—New York, Los Angeles, and Chicago—the multiracial coalition fractured and could not be sustained over time. In each case, these mayors were succeeded in office by more moderate and conservative leaders.

The study of contemporary urban politics cannot ignore the issue of race. It is always there, and the future of American cities and suburbs to a great extent depends on how the nation's citizens deal with it.

CONCLUSIONS

The 1992 riots in Los Angeles and other cities point to the persistence of unresolved urban problems. While economic restructuring and the transition to a post-industrial society have brought a general economic prosperity to a great many communities, others have only suffered accelerated decline and distress. Even in growing Sunbelt areas such as Los Angeles, the benefits of growth have been spread unevenly; they have not filtered down to all communities. The verdict that freed the four officers in the first Rodney King beating trial was seen to embody all the inequalities and injustices suffered by members of inner-city, impoverished communities.

In retrospect, it is not so surprising that South Central and other parts of Los Angeles burned after the announcement of the jury's verdict. What is more surprising is that few cities suffered major disturbances in the wake of the acquittals. The number of cities that "burned" in 1992 was much smaller than the number that suffered from the wave of urban rebellion in the 1960s. The election of black mayors and the consequent reform of urban police departments were factors that helped to increase the legitimacy that city governments enjoyed among the residents of poor, minority, inner-city communities. But as the violent outbreak in Los Angeles and the experience of Mayor Tom Bradley attest, even black political leaders cannot maintain their credibility as community representatives if they choose to preside over growth coalitions and ignore the social and economic destruction of inner-city communities.[70]

An important difference between the South Central riot as compared to the riots of the 1960s was the failure of the federal government to respond to the latter-day situation with a great expansion of urban and social programs. Budgetary restrictions have imposed a new sense of limitations on government. Even the Clinton administration, despite releasing certain new funds for housing and other urban programs, for the most part urged cities to "reinvent" government in order to deliver services better without the infusion of new program money.

This book will focus on power. It will seek to determine whose demands are being met in the local arena and whose are being ignored. Who has the power to get things done in local politics? Whose cooperation is essential for effective governance?

Five major themes—the importance of private power, the continuing significance of formal governmental structure and formal rules, the importance of the state and federal governments as players in urban affairs, continuing Sunbelt-Frostbelt regional variations, and the continuing significance of race—will guide our exploration of the changes that have taken place in American communities. In Chapter 2 we will begin to see the importance of these influences on the evolution of U.S. cities, suburbs, and metropolitan areas.

NOTES

1. For a detailed account of the Watts riot, see Robert Conot, *Rivers of Blood, Years of Darkness* (New York: Bantam Books, 1967).
2. *Report of the National Advisory Commission on Civil Disorders* (New York: Bantam Books, 1967).
3. Ibid., p. 1.
4. Ibid., p. 10.
5. Ibid., pp. 9–11 and 203–06. For similar analysis of the causes of the 1980 riot in the Liberty City section of Miami, Florida, see United States Commission on Civil Rights, *Confronting Racial Isolation in Miami* (Washington, DC, June 1992).
6. For a discussion of the issues involved in the change of venue and the jury selection, see Hiroshi Fukurai, Richard Krooth, and Edgar W. Butler, "The Rodney King Beating Verdicts," in *The Los Angeles Riots: Lessons for the Urban Future*, ed. Mark Baldassare (Boulder, CO: Westview, 1994), pp. 73–102.
7. As a response to the public outrage that followed the verdict, federal authorities later retried the police officers on federal charges for having violated Rodney King's civil rights.
8. Peter A. Morrison and Ira S. Lowry, "A Riot of Color: The Demographic Setting," in *The Los Angeles Riots*, p. 19.
9. Raphael J. Sonenshein, *Politics in Black and White: Race and Power in Los Angeles* (Princeton, NJ: Princeton University Press, 1993), pp. 210–26.
10. Ibid., pp. 213–14.

11. Raphael J. Sonenshein, "Los Angeles Coalition Politics," in *The Los Angeles Riots*, pp. 54–56.
12. Testimony by Lynn A. Curtis, President, The Milton S. Eisenhower Foundation, before the U.S. Senate, Committee on Banking, Housing, and Urban Affairs, *The State of Urban America*, 103rd Congress, 1st session, April 28, 1993, pp. 94–95.
13. J. Eugene Grigsby, "Rebuilding Los Angeles: One Year Later," *National Civic Review* (Fall 1993): 348–53.
14. John E. Yang, "Help for L.A. Business Has Begun, But to Some It Seems Too Late," *Washington Post*, November 18, 1992.
15. David O. Sears, "Urban Rioting in Los Angeles: A Comparison of 1965 with 1992," in *The Los Angeles Riots*, pp. 244–45.
16. Gary Orfield, "Separate Societies: Have the Kerner Warnings Come True?" in *Quiet Riots: Race and Poverty in the United States*, ed. Fred R. Harris and Roger W. Wilkins (New York: Pantheon Books, 1988), p. 106.
17. Ibid., pp. 117–18.
18. Curtis, testimony before the U.S. Senate Committee on Banking, Housing, and Urban Affairs.
19. Andrew Hacker, *Two Nations: Black and White, Separate, Hostile, Unequal* (New York: Ballantine, 1992).
20. 1988 Commission of the Cities, "Race and Poverty in the United States—and What Should Be Done," in *Quiet Riots: Race and Poverty in the United States*, p. 177.
21. Ibid., p. 181.
22. Robert J. Waste, "Between Riots: Urban Reservations and Urban Poverty" (Paper presented at the annual meeting of the Urban Affairs Association, Indianapolis, April 21–24, 1993).
23. Sears, "Urban Rioting in Los Angeles: A Comparison of 1965 with 1992," p. 249.
24. Joan Petersilia and Allan Abrahamse, "A Profile of Those Arrested," in *The Los Angeles Riots*, pp. 135–47; Sonenshein, *Politics in Black and White*, pp. 222–23; and Testimony of Jesse L. Jackson, National Rainbow Coalition, Inc., in Hearings Before the U.S. Senate, Committee on Banking, Housing, and Urban Affairs, *Fiscal, Economic, and Social Crises Confronting American Cities*, 102nd Congress, Second Session (May 14, 1992), p. 368.
25. Petersilia and Abrahamse, "A Profile of Those Arrested," p. 145.
26. For a description of the diversity of Los Angeles' population, see David Rieff, *Los Angeles: Capital of the Third World* (New York: Simon and Schuster/ Touchstone, 1991). Also see Sears, "Urban Rioting in Los Angeles: A Comparison of 1965 with 1992," pp. 242–44.
27. Ibid., p. 243.
28. See Regina Freer, "Black-Korean Conflict," in *The Los Angeles Riots*, pp. 175–203.
29. Raphael J. Sonenshein, "Biracial Coalition Politics in Los Angeles," pp. 33–48; and Christopher L. Warren, John G. Corbett, and John F. Stack, Jr., "Hispanic Ascendancy and Tripartite Politics in Miami," pp. 155–78, both in *Racial Politics in American Cities*, ed. Rufus P. Browning, Dale Rogers Marshall, and David H. Tabb (White Plains, NY: Longman, 1990).
30. Clarence N. Stone, *Regime Politics: Governing Atlanta, 1946–1988* (Lawrence, KS: University Press of Kansas, 1989), pp. 222–26.

31. Ibid., p. 229.

32. Ibid., pp. 8–9.

33. Ibid., pp. ix and 242.

34. For an overview of the ability of European states to insist on balanced growth and other public values in land use, see Ashok K. Dutt and Frank J. Costa, eds., *Planning in the Netherlands* (London: Oxford University Press, 1985); Michael Keating, "Local Economic Development Politics in France," *Journal of Urban Affairs* 13, 4 (1991): 443–59; Myron A. Levine, "The Transformation of Urban Politics in France: The Roots of Growth Politics and Urban Regimes," *Urban Affairs Quarterly* 29 (March 1994): 383–410; Myron A. Levine and Jan Van Weesep, "The Changing Nature of Dutch Urban Planning," *Journal of the American Planning Association* 54 (Summer 1988): 315–23; and Elizabeth Strom, "In Search of the Growth Coalition: American Urban Theories and the Redevelopment of Berlin," *Urban Affairs Review* (forthcoming).

35. Sam Bass Warner, Jr., *The Private City* (Philadelphia: University of Pennsylvania Press, 1968).

36. Norton E. Long, "The City as Reservation," *The Public Interest* 25 (Fall 1971): 22–32; and Waste, "Between Riots: Urban Reservations and Urban Poverty."

37. William Julius Wilson, *The Truly Disadvantaged: The Inner City, The Underclass, and Urban Policy* (Chicago: University of Chicago Press, 1987).

38. Fahizah Alim and Robert D. Davila, "South Central's Woes Still Burn," *Sacramento Bee*, April 18, 1993, cited in Waste, "Between Riots: Urban Reservations and Urban Poverty."

39. *Los Angeles Times* (editorial), April 30, 1993, cited in Grigsby, "Rebuilding Los Angeles: One Year Later," p. 350. Also see Eric Mann, "The Poverty of Corporatism: Los Angeles—One Year After," *The Nation* (March 29, 1993): 406–11.

40. Calvin Sims, "Who Said Los Angeles Could Be Rebuilt in a Day?" *The New York Times*, May 22, 1994.

41. James A. Regalado, "Community Coalition-Building," in *The Los Angeles Riots*, p. 206.

42. Ibid., pp. 207 and 220–21.

43. James Q. Wilson, panel discussion on the Los Angeles riots, at the annual meeting of the Midwest Political Science Association, March 4, 1992.

44. Daryl F. Gates, *Chief: My Life in the LAPD* (New York: Bantam Books, 1992), as reported by Jane Fritsch, "Los Angeles Mayor Comes Under More Attacks in Police Chief's New Book," *The New York Times*, May 6, 1992.

45. Jane Fritsch, "Los Angeles Mayor Criticizes Chief for Slow Action on Riot," *The New York Times* (May 4, 1992).

46. Los Angeles Police Chief Willie Williams, comments to the annual meeting of the National Civic League, Los Angeles, November 13, 1992.

47. Paul E. Peterson, *City Limits* (Chicago: Univ. of Chicago Press, 1981).

48. Roy Bahl, *Financing State and Local Government in the 1980s* (New York: Oxford Univ. Press, 1984), pp. 14–15; and Paul Kantor with Stephen David, *The Dependent City* (Glenview, IL: Scott, Foresman, 1988), pp. 207–18.

49. Figures provided by the National Governors' Association, January 1990.

50. George E. Peterson, "Urban Policy and the Cyclical Behavior of Cities," in *Reagan and the Cities*, ed. George E. Peterson and Carol W. Lewis (Washington, DC: Urban Institute Press, 1986), pp. 11–35.

51. John E. Schwarz, *America's Hidden Success: A Reassessment of Twenty Years of Public Policy* (New York: W. W. Norton, 1983), argues the opposite point of view: that despite widespread public perceptions to the contrary, a great many of the Great Society programs did work!

52. Georgia A. Persons, panel discussion on the Los Angeles riots, at the annual meeting of the Midwest Political Science Association, March 4, 1992.

53. Frances Fox Piven and Richard A. Cloward, *Regulating the Poor: The Functions of Public Welfare*, updated ed. (New York: Random House, 1971, 1993), especially p. 348.

54. For a review of the different boundaries given by different authors to the "Sunbelt" as well as a discussion as to the lack of homogeneity of the region, see Richard M. Bernard and Bradley R. Rice, eds., *Sunbelt Cities* (Austin, TX: University of Texas Press, 1983), p. 207; and Robert Kerstein, "Sunbelt Regimes Past, Present and Future: A Review of Some of the Literature" (Paper presented at the annual meeting of the Urban Affairs Association, New Orleans, March 1994).

55. See, for instance, the very expansive definition of the Sunbelt used by Carl Abbott, *The New Urban America*, rev. ed. (Chapel Hill, NC: University of North Carolina Press, 1987). Robyne S. Turner and Judith A. Garber have a similarly expansive view of the Sunbelt as they observe the commonalities of the boom-and-bust politics of the "oil cities" of Houston (Texas) and Edmonton (Canada). See their "Responding to Boom and Bust: Urban Political Economy in Houston and Edmonton" (Paper presented at the annual meeting of the American Political Science Association, New York, September 4, 1994).

56. Ann Markusen, Peter Hall, Scott Campbell, and Sabina Deitrick, *The Rise of the Gunbelt: The Military Remapping of Industrial America* (New York: Oxford University Press, 1991). Also see David L. Carlton, "The Sunbelt Debate Revisited," *Urban Affairs Quarterly* 20 (November 1993): 114–22.

57. Jane G. Pisano, "After the Riots: Multiculturalism in Los Angeles," *National Civic Review* 81 (Summer-Fall 1992): 313.

58. Richard Levine, "Northeast Lags on Jobs; Northwest Enjoys Gains," *The New York Times*, April 25, 1990.

59. Harold L. Wolman, Coit Cook Ford III, and Edward Hill, "Evaluating the Success of Urban Success Stories," *Urban Studies* 31 (June 1994): 835–50.

60. Michael deCourcy Hinds, "After Renaissance of the 70s and 80s, Philadelphia Is Struggling to Survive," *The New York Times*, June 21, 1990.

61. *Millikin v. Bradley*, 418 U.S. 717 (1974).

62. Anthony Downs, "The Future of Industrial Cities," in *The New Urban Reality*, ed. Paul E. Peterson (Washington, DC: Brookings Institution, 1985), p. 288.

63. Ibid., p. 289.

64. Ibid., pp. 289, 293.

65. Edward C. Banfield, *The Unheavenly City Revisited* (Boston: Little, Brown, 1974), pp. 211–33; Sears, "The Los Angeles Riots: A Comparison of 1965 with 1992," pp. 247–49.

66. Richard M. Fogelson and Robert B. Hill, "Who Riots? A Study of Participation in the 1967 Riots," in *Supplemental Studies for the National Advisory Commission on Civil Disorders* (Washington, DC: USGPO, 1968).

67. Sears, "Urban Rioting in Los Angeles: A 1965 and 1992 Comparison," p. 251.

68. Henry Weinstein, "Tensions Escalate Between Leaders of Blacks, Latinos," *Los Angeles Times*, July 11, 1992; Stephanie Chavez, "Racial Tensions Over South L.A. Jobs Grow," *Los Angeles Times*, July 22, 1992.

69. Sonenshein, *Politics in Black and White*, pp. 67–84, 101–14, and 224–25.

70. Richard E. Rubenstein, "The Los Angeles Riots: Causes and Cures," *National Civic Review* 81 (Summer-Fall 1992): 320–21.

2

The Evolution of Cities and Suburbs

3 VIEWS:
1) NATURAL FACTORS
2) GOVT. INFLUENCE
3) CORPORATE & PRIVATE POWER

The present-day problems of cities and suburbs can be seen as the end product of metropolitan evolution. In this chapter we will describe three different views as to why cities and suburbs have evolved as they have. As we shall see, the distribution of jobs and residences within a single metropolitan area and among regions is not the result purely of natural forces, as is commonly believed. Government policies and private sector power have been extremely important factors in determining the shape of the metropolitan landscape.

THE GROWTH OF METROPOLITAN AMERICA: NATURAL FACTORS — *The conservative view*

Urbanist Edward C. Banfield takes the view that metropolitan growth is primarily the result of natural forces. According to Banfield, the extent of metropolitan development is the consequence of three "imperatives."[1] The first is **demographic;** as a city's population increases it must expand. The second is **technological;** the available transportation and communications technology determines just how far outward the expansion of metropolitan areas will go. The third factor is **economic;** persons who can afford the costs of new housing and the commute to the city will seek to escape the older sections of the city, with their noise, traffic congestion, and decayed and cramped housing, for a "better life" in more desirable areas on the periphery.

The importance of transportation to cities can even be seen in their location. The original settlement of most American cities occurred near a major locus of transportation—a harbor, river, canal, or important railroad or trail junction. American cities developed in areas that were easily accessible, where commerce would be made easy. Only a few cities in the United States developed from a fort or army settlement that provided protection in a hostile environment.

North American cities in the 1700s and early 1800s were relatively small in size. People had to live close to their work, and, as a result, there was a clear distinction between the city and the countryside. These relatively small cities had to contain within their borders the full mixture of functions and a cross-section of the population. Merchants, shippers, laborers, and the rich and poor all lived inside the city. As a person could easily transverse the entire distance of the city, historian Kenneth Jackson has labeled the preindustrial communities in North America **walking cities.**[2] Indeed, walking was a major form of urban transportation in the early American city.

Most rural hamlets and farm villages existing at that time could not be considered suburban. Transportation difficulties imposed strict limitations as to how far a person could reasonably travel; residents of the rural countryside consequently had little interaction with the larger city.

Because cities have historically been centers of opportunity, poorer migrants came from the countryside to the early American cities in search of jobs and wealth. The result was congestion and overcrowding in the city centers. Those who could afford it sought "the good life" in residences on the edge of urbanized areas, far from the congestion and deteriorated housing stock of the central city. But there was a limit as to how far out the more affluent could move. It would take innovations in transportation technology to redefine the urban landscape.

Each transportation innovation—the horse-pulled streetcar, the electric trolley, the steam railroad—extended the urban population farther and farther outward from the city center. Even though suburbanization in the United States dates from about 1815, suburbs did not gain significant populations until the latter half of the nineteenth century.[3] In the early American city people either had to remain within walking distance to their jobs or they could move only as far out as a horse-pulled car could take them. Even with the introduction of later transit systems, urban areas in the United States remained very compact as compared to the sprawling megalopolis of today. By the 1880s and 1890s advances in architectural technology saw the construction of the first skyscrapers (or, at least, the predecessors of modern skyscrapers), allowing the city to expand upward before it greatly expanded outward.

For a long while the city simply extended its boundaries with each new outward movement of the population. Cities often used their **annexation** powers to adjoin neighboring areas to the city. Residents in these rapidly growing areas, where streets were often barely paved, gave their approval to annexations in order to receive public water, drainage, gas and light, road paving, and other municipal services that the more established cities could provide.

However, resistance to annexation began in 1873 when the growing suburb of Brookline, Massachusetts, surrounded on three sides by the city of Boston, refused to be incorporated into Boston. Residents of Brookline had come to see themselves as apart from Boston and, despite the promise of service improvement, were happy with the way things were.[4] By the latter part of the 1800s, "Boston was something to be feared and controlled,"[5] and opponents of annexation portrayed Brookline as a "refuge" from an industrial Boston and its corrupting influences. They charged that "the high levels of city services maintained by Boston meant higher taxes, and, further, they frankly stated that independent suburban towns could maintain native American life free from Boston's waves of incoming poor immigrants."[6] The **streetcar suburbs** of the era would now continue their growth beyond the reach of the central city.

Brookline was the first of what would be a wave. More and more suburbs would assert their independence and refuse incorporation with the central city. In spurning annexation, as historian Sam Bass Warner, Jr., has observed, "[T]he metropolitan middle-class abandoned their central city."[7]

The rural poor continued to pour into industrial cities in search of jobs. In need of labor, some factories in the early 1900s even sent recruiters to the South to bring poor black tenant farmers to work in the mills and the foundries of the North. The mechanization of agriculture and the phasing out of the sharecropper system in the South soon displaced many more rural poor and accelerated the migration to cities. The pace of this migration was accelerated by the labor needs of factories in these cities during and after World War II. Millions of poor blacks from the South made their way to the cities of the North in search of civil rights as well as jobs and prosperity.[8]

The automobile revolutionized the shape of metropolitan areas. With the automobile, suburban residents no longer needed to live in close proximity to the streetcar and railroad tracks; suburban homes could now fill in the spaces between the "fingers" of the rail and streetcar systems. Residents also could live farther and farther away from the old center of the city.

Business followed the move of its better-quality work force to the suburbs. Business also sought suburban locations where land was cheaper and sites were more suitable to assembly-line production. New transportation technology, in the form of the trucking industry, enabled the move of warehousing and distribution activities to the suburbs. By the 1970s, advances in containerization would put a further premium on suburban sites; city streets proved too congested, and older warehouse loading docks too antiquated, to handle the new shipping techniques.

The retail and entertainment industries also eventually began the shift to the suburbs. The middle class, with its buying power, lived on the city's rim and did not want to be bothered with long commutes, traffic jams, and the search for parking downtown. Plaza-type shopping centers and, later, enclosed shopping malls developed at the intersections of major highways with the urban rim highway or beltway. Retail activity in the older downtown shopping districts dropped off markedly. By the mid-1980s Hudson's department store, long associated with Detroit, closed the doors of its downtown store. The company, however, retained its stores located at various suburban shopping malls throughout the metropolitan area. Detroit gained the dubious distinction of being the largest city in the nation not to have a major department store within its borders. Baltimore and Toledo, too, saw their major downtown department stores close their doors.

New technological advances in the field of telecommunications freed white-collar offices from sites in the old downtown. Suburban office parks competed with central city downtowns as potential sites for new office development. Outside Chicago, a virtual second downtown was created by the office towers of the city's northwest suburbs. Orange County, California, witnessed an office boom south of Los Angeles. Similar growth occurred on the rim of a great many metropolitan areas, including the Route 128 area outside Boston; White Plains, New York; Rosslyn and Crystal City, Virginia (just across the Potomac River from Washington, DC); Troy and Southfield, Michigan; the corridor between Dallas and Fort Worth, Texas; and the Silicon Valley region between San Francisco and San Jose, California—to name only a few. According to historian Robert Fishman, these new developments redefined suburbia by creating **technoburbs** which essentially duplicate the job, retailing, and entertainment resources traditionally associated with central cities.[9]

The metropolitan area had begun to lose its older central-city focus. Vast new **edge cities** developed in places where, in the 1950s, there had been relatively little suburban development. These full-fledged outer cities were giantized, modernized, dynamic, and seemingly vastly improved versions of suburbia, as compared to the relatively tranquil bedroom communities of the 1950s. Functions and services once found only in central cities now were commonly found in new spread-out urban centers. For a great many people, daily life evolved around the corporate office parks, shopping malls, entertainment complexes, and cultural centers of these new suburban villages, not the old central city. Suburbs were at the cutting edge of technology, and life on the city's rim no longer seemed to be "sub" to central cities in any way.[10] The new perimeter cities, though, did not contain a fair share of the region's poor and minority populations.

The shift from a manufacturing-based economy to a service economy reinforced these anticity trends. In the eyes of one city observer, "The industrial city has become an institutional anachronism."[11] As a result of the transition to a post-industrial era, cities such as Philadelphia were hard-hit by the erosion of their economic base. Declining economic opportunity, racial conflict, severe budgetary cutbacks, a desperate search for economic development, and a hovering threat of insolvency were all ever-present aspects of Philadelphia politics in the 1980s and early 1990s.[12]

Of course, not all cities suffered such extensive decline. A number of Sunbelt cities continued to grow. In the Frostbelt, some cities were able to attract new office development to help compensate for the loss of manufacturing jobs. Vital downtowns—capable of attracting international corporate headquarters and sustaining convention activity—remained in "world class" cities.[13]

New York, Los Angeles, Chicago, and other major cities have lost their older industrial character and have been transformed into **post-industrial cities.** By the 1980s, less than 15 percent of the work force in Los Angeles was employed as manufacturing production workers; in New York, the figure had fallen to 10 percent. Production jobs had been lost to automation and recession; corporations moved manufacturing to the suburbs and overseas. New York rebounded from its financial crisis of the 1970s by becoming a center of global finance and corporate services. Los Angeles and Chicago became headquarters cities for national corporations. Low-paid, predominantly female, clerical work replaced the older jobs on the docks and in the factories. Both the ghettoized poor and the new immigrants from Latin America and Southeast Asia had a difficult time finding good-paying, entry-level jobs in a high-tech, corporate economy.[14] As John Hull Mollenkopf sums up, New York is clearly no longer an industrial city:

> While always important as a headquarters city, New York's single largest social stratum in the mid-1950s was blue-collar white ethnics. Turn-of-the-century immigrants and the children they bore before World War II constituted an industrial working class of considerable proportions. Today, few white blue-collar workers remain; many once categorized this way are now elderly. New groups have replaced them, ranging from white professionals and managers to minority and female clerical workers, to immigrant service workers. Office workers in corporate, social service, and government settings vastly outnumber production workers.[15]

In the Sunbelt, Miami used the advantages afforded by geography and its Cuban enclave to emerge as a center of Caribbean banking and finance.[16]

In labeling as "imperatives" the three factors shaping metropolitan growth—population pressures, transportation technology, and distribution of income—Banfield is stating that government can do relatively little to ameliorate urban problems by attempting to reshape an urban landscape that was naturally formed: "The argument is not that nothing can be done to improve matters. Rather, it is that only those things can be done which lie within the boundaries—rather narrow ones, to be sure—fixed by the logic of the growth process."[17] City-suburban (and increasingly intersuburban) inequalities will continue to exist, as no government in a free society can easily reverse the choices of its people.

But do Banfield's three factors constitute "imperatives" that dictate the shape of metropolitan areas? While Banfield's three factors explain much of the pressure for outward urban growth, they do not dictate the exact pattern of metropolitan growth that will occur. The present-day shape of metropolitan areas in the United States was not inevitable. Nor was it purely the result of unhindered, free market choice. As Clarence Stone observes in his criticism of Banfield's work, "[T]he market does not operate in isolation from government policy."[18] Governmental action and private sector power, too, have throughout history been important influences in accelerating suburbanization and in promoting central city decline and transformation. Banfield understates the importance of government and private power in shaping the metropolis.

GOVERNMENTAL INFLUENCES ON METROPOLITAN DEVELOPMENT

Natural growth tendencies provide only a partial explanation of how American cities and suburbs wound up in their present condition. Governmental policies, especially those of the federal government, have also played a crucially important role in determining the shape of metropolitan America and the health of America's urban communities.

The federal programs that shaped metropolitan America were often not even explicitly urban in their orientation. They existed for other quite laudable objectives. They sought to help Americans buy homes of their own; they sought to improve the interstate highway system; and they sought to help finance the construction of much-needed facilities such as hospitals and sewage plants. At the time these policies were being implemented, few people perceived the negative effects they would have on urban America. Still, these programs produced adverse effects on cities that were so large and substantial that they can be said to constitute a **hidden urban policy**. In this section we will identify some of the more significant components of that hidden urban policy.

FEDERAL HOUSING POLICY: THE FHA AND VA

Many middle-class families would not have been able to buy homes of their own if it were not for federal assistance. The key to financing many of these new homes was Section 203 of the 1934 Housing Act, which enabled the creation of the **Federal Housing Administration (FHA)**. The purpose of Section 203 was to help families acquire new or existing one- to four-unit homes. FHA would provide insurance up to 80 percent of the value of the property. In the event that an FHA-insured homeowner proved unable to repay a loan, FHA would repay 80 percent to the creditor. The risk of making home loans was thereby reduced. As a result, financial institutions were willing to finance homes for millions of Americans who otherwise would never have received credit. With less risk, lenders could also lower down payment requirements and interest rates.

It seems the author is stating that the inner city was already in decline, so VA & FHA did not want to insure homes in these areas but previously the author wants us to

The federal government also sought to provide further assistance to the millions of veterans returning home after World War II. Under the GI Bill of Rights of 1944 the **Veterans Administration (VA)** was authorized to insure home mortgages to veterans. No down payment was required from the buyer under this act. As "the VA very largely followed FHA procedures and attitudes…the two programs can be considered as a single effort."[19] Together, the VA and FHA programs offered prospective home buyers a very attractive package of low or no down payment, easy credit, and a twenty-five- to thirty-year period of relatively small monthly payments. The programs also put the federal government heavily into the mortgage market, where it has remained to this day.

While these programs insured the purchase of new homes, they gave little attention to the purchase of apartments or the renovation of older housing stock. As a result, the programs subsidized growth in suburban areas; the revitalization of central cities was ignored. This anticity bias was even explicit in the agency's 1939 *Underwriting Manual*; FHA underwriters were instructed to minimize credit risks by looking for "economic stability" when making neighborhood evaluations; they were told that "crowded neighborhoods lessen desirability."[20] FHA's administrators did not wish to guarantee loans for houses in neighborhoods where declining market conditions might lead homeowners to default on their obligations.

The FHA and VA programs helped young marrieds obtain a home of their own. As more and more middle- and upper-income people fled the city, the less desirable and more run-down housing in the central city became available for lower-income residents, particularly for blacks and Hispanics, to inhabit. The federal housing finance programs thereby helped exacerbate the racial and financial imbalance between central cities and suburbs.

But FHA policy was more pernicious than even the above description indicates. Until the 1950s and 1960s, the FHA pursued a policy of explicit racial segregation in the award of home loans. As the agency's *Underwriting Manual* warned, "If a neighborhood is to retain stability, it is necessary that properties shall continue to be occupied by the same social and racial classes."[21] The manual instructed federal underwriters to give a low rating to mortgages that would lead to the "infiltration of inharmonious racial or nationality groups" into a neighborhood.[22] The FHA had even endorsed the use of **restrictive covenants** or deed restrictions that prohibited a buyer from reselling a home to someone of a different race! As a consequence, very few FHA-insured loans were given to black families; only 2 percent of the housing built in the postwar period under FHA mortgage insurance was sold to minorities. And half of that total was for housing built in all-minority subdivisions![23] The FHA would not approve loans to minorities who sought to move into all-white suburbs.

believe that VA & FHA caused the decline — which is it? I suspect that middle class people do not want to live near the dirt bags that cause decline!

So if not for the FHA — whites and blacks would have moved into & occupied the same subdivisions and lived harmoniously!!

How could the federal government so explicitly endorse segregation? As political scientist Dennis Judd explains, FHA administrators "were drawn from the ranks of the housing and banking industries." Consequently, "FHA administrators shared the real estate industry's view that segregation was preferable to integration."[24] Selling a home to a family whose background or skin color differed from those already in the neighborhood was seen to jeopardize the property values in that community. The National Association of Real Estate Boards endorsed this philosophy in its code of ethics; the FHA subscribed to a similar set of principles.

By 1949, the FHA had dropped its references to "racial groups" and "infiltration." But it was too late; the harm was already done, as thousands of racially segregated neighborhoods had been established. In the early 1970s, under pressure from Congress to respond to the situation that had created the urban riots, the FHA began to reverse its pro-suburban bias. In 1973 the clear majority of FHA loan guarantees were made inside central cities. But even here, the FHA often continued to ignore the poor, as it had strict income guidelines to ensure that families had the means to support home ownership.[25] Where loans were extended to the poor, FHA guarantees at times even acted to hasten neighborhood decline by advancing loans that eventually led to boarded-up, abandoned property. Unscrupulous lenders and realtors would help marginally qualified people obtain FHA-insured loans, knowing that the FHA would repay when the borrower defaulted on the loan.

THE FEDERAL TAX CODE'S PROVISIONS FOR HOMEOWNERS

The FHA and VA programs helped promote both suburban growth and a racially segregated metropolis. But the impact of these two programs pales by comparison to that exerted by still another element of the "hidden" federal urban policy: the federal tax code's provisions for home owners.

Homeowners are allowed to deduct mortgage interest and property taxes from their gross income. The billions of dollars deducted by homeowners each year dwarfs the amount the federal government allocates to subsidized housing for the poor. For instance, in 1989 alone, tax expenditures for homeowners totalled $63 billion—nearly four times the amount ($17.3 billion) spent on all low-income subsidized housing. Two-thirds of these tax benefits went to households with incomes of greater than $50,000.[26]

As a result of these tax write-offs, millions of Americans who could not otherwise afford to do so can now meet the purchase price of buying a home in the suburbs. In the flight to the suburbs, the central cities lost much of the next generation of their middle class as well as civic, business, and political leaders. The flight of the middle class also represented a loss of disposable income, as consumer dollars were now being spent in suburban shopping malls, movie theaters, and automobile showrooms rather than in downtown retail shops.[27]

In more recent years these same tax provisions have stimulated condominium and cooperative apartment conversions in many cities. Simply put, you get a generous tax break if you own a home, condominium, or cooperative; you get no such subsidy if you continue to rent an apartment. Given this set of federal tax advantages, the economics of the situation is clear; it "pays" to convert to a condominium or cooperative. Those tenants who lack the funds to buy into the new arrangement are forced to move elsewhere; they often must accept units that offer less space at higher prices than did their previous dwellings. The victims of the conversion process too often are the elderly and the poor, tenants on limited incomes who suddenly find themselves ousted from their long-time dwellings.

The federal tax code further hurts central cities by allowing home sellers to defer the tax liability on the capital gain realized in selling a home if they purchase a home of equal or greater value. This provision of the tax code was intended to encourage mobility; people who move from one place to another should not be penalized by being made to pay a tax on the increase in value over time represented in the sale price of their old home. But if homes of greater value in a metropolitan area are generally located in suburbs, as they often are, then this provision in the IRS code effectively steers higher income residents to suburbs; a buyer of a lower-priced home in the central city will have to pay a capital gains tax that the buyer of a home in a higher-priced suburb does not. In effect, the tax code encourages the decline of many central cities and poorer small towns as homeowners are given an incentive to move to higher-priced communities.[28]

The higher priced homes are located, inside the perimeter!

FEDERAL HIGHWAY PROGRAMS

The Highway Act of 1944 committed 25 percent of federal highway monies to the construction of roads in cities. The federal role in highway construction increased over the years as advocates for a strong national defense argued that a national highway network was needed in order to move military personnel and matériel quickly and efficiently. The 1956 National Defense Highway Act increased the federal share of funding highway construction projects from 50 percent to 90 percent, giving a major new impetus to road construction and suburban development.

While the federal highway program had once sought only to link major cities via an interstate highway network, now the program was helping to build major commuting roads from suburbs to cities. The construction of new urban freeways allowed people to live in the suburbs without losing access to the jobs and cultural opportunities offered by the central city. The new urban freeways also opened up vast new areas for residential and commercial development.

The greatly expanded urban highway and beltway system not only expedited commuting trips from the suburbs to the central city but also expedited traffic flow from one suburb to another. As a result, huge shopping malls opened in the highly developed suburban communities, wherever the highway system made property easily accessible. The decentralization of manufacturing, warehousing, distribution, and retailing activities soon followed. The urban freeways even enabled "reverse commuting" whereby residents of the central city could commute to jobs in the suburbs. The freeways, built with extensive federal subsidies, have in effect become the new "main streets" of a growing suburban America.[29]

Federal highway programs also had the effect of destroying viable neighborhoods in city areas. Highways divided neighborhoods, cutting off residents from local stores and their friends. The Cross Bronx Expressway in New York uprooted a solid working-class, Jewish neighborhood. Once displaced by the new highway, many of the residents left the city, never to return. Highway building was also used as a tool to destroy ghetto housing, displacing African-Americans and other minorities to other neighborhoods. In Miami, the building of I-95 "ripped through the center of Overtown," a large black community of at least 40,000 people, pushing residents to settle in more distant black neighborhoods in Miami, most notably Liberty City. With the completion of the expressway, there was little left to Overtown, once known as the "Harlem of the South."[30]

OTHER FEDERAL PROGRAMS

Other federal programs also encouraged suburbanization. Generous federal grant programs subsidized the cost of new hospitals and sewage plants, thereby underwriting the infrastructure costs of new suburban development. Government tax incentives to businesses helped pay for the costs of new physical plant and equipment investment in the suburbs; equivalent tax write-offs were not offered to rehabilitate aging plants in the central city.

Even the **urban renewal** program of the 1950s contributed to the "push" to suburbanization. Urban renewal cleared large parcels of land that were allowed to lie vacant for long periods of time. In a number of cities, homes were torn down to make way for new upper-income apartments, modernized university and hospital campuses, and an expanded central business district. Many people displaced by renewal chose to leave the city altogether for homes in the suburbs, far away from the city and its problems.

THE ACTIONS OF LOCAL GOVERNMENT

The extent of racial and class imbalances in the metropolis has not been the result of governmental action at the federal level alone. Local governments have played a major role in contributing to patterns of metropolitan segregation. Each local community can use its control over **zoning** to determine just which forms of development may or may not take place within its borders (see "Zoning and Its Impact: The New York Metropolitan Area" on pages 40–41). Suburbs can, and quite often do, choose to limit or ban the construction of townhouses, apartment buildings, and subsidized housing for the poor within their borders. A suburb can also sharply drive up the price of buying a house within its borders by requiring that new houses be built only on excessively large lots and that they meet expensive construction requirements exceeding any concern for health and safety.

The poor and even working-class families are effectively locked out by many such suburbs. Racial minorities, too, have a problem gaining access to more exclusionary suburban communities, as only very wealthy minority families have the ability to buy houses in these communities. As a result, central cities and certain inner-ring aging suburbs wind up with populations that are disproportionately poor, minority, and in need of government services. Suburban exclusion can even be seen as helping to produce central city ghettoization.

But in a great many cases, suburbs are not the only local actors that have proven responsible for central city ghettoization. In many cases, the cities themselves undertook policies that helped to promote the formation and expansion of racial ghettoes. For instance, from the 1940s through the 1960s, governmental policy in the city of Chicago actively pursued racial segregation. The Chicago Housing Authority did not simply give an available public housing unit to the next family on a waiting list; instead assignments were done on the basis of race, in order to keep public housing segregated. Each city council member was also allowed a virtual veto over the placement of new public housing in his or her ward, thereby guaranteeing that no public housing for minorities would be built in white neighborhoods; new public housing would reinforce the ghetto. The city also used its powers to move blacks out of areas in order to facilitate urban revitalization projects.[31]

New York City, too, in settling a lawsuit in 1992, admitted that it had violated the federal Fair Housing Act by setting racial quotas on certain public housing projects and steering black and Hispanic applicants away from largely white projects. The city gave preferential treatment to applicants who lived in a neighborhood surrounding a project; in effect, white families in a neighborhood had priority in gaining entrance to predominantly white housing projects.[32]

Zoning and Its Impact: The New York Metropolitan Area

In 1916 New York became the first city to adopt a zoning ordinance. The idea soon spread like wildfire and is now the primary land use control tool employed by cities and suburbs throughout the nation. The idea behind zoning is simple: to prevent incompatible land uses. No homeowner today, for instance, wants to see a factory or an automobile service station built next to his or her home. Zoning prevents that by setting out an orderly pattern of land development. Certain land parcels are designated for industrial and commercial uses; other parcels are reserved for residential development. Greater distinctions in parcel designation can be made. Light industry can be kept separate from heavy industry. Homeowners can be permitted to take in lodgers in certain neighborhoods, but not in others. Likewise, zoning can be used to keep apartment dwellings in a city separate from single-family homes.

Suburbs have used zoning to keep nuisance industrial and commercial activities and lower-income people outside their borders. Communities in Westchester County, north of New York City, have used zoning and other land use restrictions in an attempt to prevent the "Bronxification" of their area: "their goal was to attract 'class' not 'mass' to Westchester."* Zoning restrictions typically prevent or sharply limit the construction of apartment buildings and other forms of high-density development; poorer people are thereby excluded. Tax burdens on suburban residents are further kept low, as only better-off families can afford the purchase price of homes built on required large lots or with the requisite large-size rooms and other expensive construction features.

Not all communities in the greater New York region have used exclusionary zoning as effectively as did Westchester. In Nassau County on Long Island, pressures from large-scale developers were more intense, and local political leaders generally took less interest in developing effective land use controls. Communities like Oyster Bay, though, did adopt land use barriers every bit as strict as those utilized in Westchester.

Within a community, zoning can be used to maintain income and racial segregation. In 1985 Federal District Court Judge Leonard B. Sand linked residential segregation to school segregation in ordering the city of Yonkers, on the border of the Bronx, to desegregate both its housing and its schools. According to the judge, the city had engaged in a patterned practice of racial discrimination by concentrating its subsidized housing in the minority-dominated southwestern part of the city, not in the white eastern part.

In the face of escalating fines that were bankrupting the city, Yonkers in 1988 agreed to a court-ordered desegregation plan under which the city agreed to change its zoning laws to allow the construction of 1,000 low- and moderate-income housing units in the predominantly white, middle-class areas of the city. The city agreed to rezone certain potential building sites and to increase the density of development allowed on others. Angry citizens in Yonkers feared for the destruction of their neighborhoods and vociferously protested against the court's order. As a result, implementation of many parts of the desegregation plan lagged.

One section of the New York region shows what would happen if development could take place in the absence of stringent zoning laws. In 1964 the Verrazano-Narrows Bridge was opened, connecting Staten Island to the New York mainland. Until that time Staten Island had remained relatively undeveloped. The bridge opening touched off a building boom on the island. As part of New York City, Staten Island lacked the power to enact zoning restrictions of its own; zoning was controlled by a seemingly distant and insensitive city. As a result, development proceeded relatively unabated: "Compared with the region's typical suburb, Staten Island has been a paradise for the home building industry."[+] The city permitted high-density development on small plots of land. As Michael N. Danielson and Jameson W. Doig observe in their book on New York: "Freed from the constraints imposed by local government's typical strategy for maximizing internal benefits, the private sector has produced housing on Staten Island that is smaller, less expensive, more crowded, and less attractive than that built during the same period in the suburbs of the New York region."[++] Planning and environmental values were also ignored in the quick pace of development.

Zoning, then, has its virtues. But as we have also seen, zoning is employed by suburbs as a potent weapon of exclusion that prices less advantaged people out of their communities. We will discuss the debate over zoning in greater detail in Chapter 9.

[*] Michael N. Danielson and Jameson Doig, *New York: The Politics of Urban Regional Development* (Berkeley, CA: University of California Press, 1982), p. 79.
[+] Ibid., p. 106.
[++] Ibid., p. 107.

In reviewing the various programs that have influenced American metropolitan development, historian Kenneth Jackson asks, "Has the American government been as benevolent—or at least as neutral—as its defenders claim?"[33] The answer must be a resounding No! The development of metropolitan America and its resulting problems were not purely the consequences of natural ecological evolution; rather, they were also the product of government action. A bold proponent of this perspective might also proclaim that the government has an obligation to remedy the problems it helped create.

THE IMPORTANCE OF CORPORATE AND PRIVATE POWER

Even a recognition of the role played by government does not fully explain why spatial patterns in the metropolis took the shape they did. Indeed, new transportation technology and government programs only "*facilitated, but did not create*"[34] the flow of population and industry to the suburbs. We must try to identify the driving forces that produced the contemporary patterns of city and suburban development. As Joe R. Feagin and Robert Parker observe in their book *Building American Cities: The Urban Real Estate Game*:

> Cities are not chance creations; rather, they are human developments. They reflect human choices and decisions. But exactly who decides that our cities should be developed the way they are?[35]

According to Feagin and Parker, more traditional explanations of urban growth neglect the role played by "the most powerful players on the urban scene—the array of visible real estate decision makers in industry, finance, development, and construction."[36] Cities are shaped by powerful private and corporate actors who seek spatial patterns of development that enhance profit maximization.[37]

Economist David Gordon observes that the more orthodox explanations of metropolitan development fail to account adequately for the motivations that lay behind the dispersion of industry to suburban sites. As Gordon points out, the movement of industry to sparsely populated sites at the edge of the urban area began around the turn of the century, before trucks had become an effective substitute for rail transport and before any major suburbanization of the industrial work force had occurred:

> Between 1899 and around 1915, corporations began to establish factory districts just beyond the city limits. New suburban manufacturing towns were being built in open space like movie sets. Gary, Indiana,

constructed from 1905 to 1908, is the best-known example. Other new industrial satellite suburbs included Chicago Heights, Hammond, East Chicago, and Argo outside Chicago; Lackawanna outside of Buffalo; East St. Louis and Wellston across the river from St. Louis; Norwood and Oakley beyond the Cincinnati limits; and Chester and Norristown near Philadelphia.[38]

No way, according to Gordon, can the suburbanization of industry be explained simply as a consequence of new transportation technology and the desire of industry to locate its facilities near an already suburbanized work force. Likewise, this decentralization of industry preceded the major government programs that catalyzed suburbanization.

How does Gordon account for the sudden and massive investment in new suburban plants around the turn of the century? Gordon sees only one possible answer: the need of factory owners to isolate workers and control labor unrest. The late 1880s and 1890s were a period of labor conflict in downtown central-city districts: "Employers quickly perceived an obvious solution. Move!"[39] The testimony of the president of a contracting firm in Chicago during this time period only reinforces the point. According to this business executive,

> [A]ll these controversies and strikes that we have had here for some years have…prevented outsiders from coming in here and investing their capital.…It has discouraged capital at home.…It has drawn the manufacturers away from the city, because they are afraid their men will get into trouble and get into strikes.…The result is, all around Chicago for forty or fifty miles, the smaller towns are getting these manufacturing plants.…[40]

The actions, manipulations, and self-interest of private enterprise can also be seen to be at work in residential dispersion. Suburban residential development was not simply the result of citizens' natural desires for the "good life." Instead, in what Dennis Judd has labeled "Selling the American Dream," landowners and other real estate interests actively marketed suburban living as the epitome of the American way of life.[41] Their advertisements portrayed suburbs as idealized, segregated living environments. They then built for, and profited from, the desires they helped to create.

The role played by private enterprise in the shaping of metropolitan areas is even apparent in the development of Los Angeles. Urban sprawl in greater Los Angeles is often viewed as the result of the automobile; Los Angeles never took on the central-city focus of those older East Coast and Midwest cities that grew and prospered in the preautomobile age. But what is often overlooked is that the dispersion of population in Los Angeles, America's present-day automobile city, actually began well before the appearance of the automobile as a dependable means of transit. Amazing as it may seem, Los Angeles' dispersed nature was to a great degree prompted by mass transit!

Henry Huntington's Pacific Electric Railway in the early 1900s made possible the growth of Los Angeles' suburbs. Perhaps the finest mass transit system of its day, the Red Cars (featured in the movie *Who Framed Roger Rabbit*) traveled along at speeds of forty-five to fifty-five miles per hour. Los Angeles became the fastest growing area in the country. The system was overbuilt and operated at a loss. But the losses did not matter:

> The Pacific Electric lost millions of dollars extending lines far ahead of demands for service, but the loss was compensated many times over by the profits from land sales by the Huntington Land and Improvement Company. In fact, the system was built not to provide transportation but to sell real estate.[42]

Huntington and other subdividers built railways for horse-drawn cars, cable cars, and electric streetcars all in order to sell their lots.[43] Los Angeles' dispersed settlement pattern was established well before the arrival of the automobile; it had been ingrained by the needs of real estate speculation.

PRIVATE POWER AND CENTRAL CITY DECLINE

Private sector and corporate power can also be seen at work in the decline of central-city neighborhoods. The practices of private credit institutions go a long way to determining which neighborhoods receive an injection of cash for new housing construction and upkeep and which, receiving no such investment, suffer accelerated deterioration.

Redlining refers to the practice whereby credit institutions make few if any loans to areas of a city or county considered as less desirable financial risks. The red line denotes an area within which home loans are seen to be too risky an investment; at one time banks and other credit institutions actually drew a line on a map to indicate those parts of the city in which they would make no investments. The result of such **disinvestment** was to take away the potential for rehabilitation or growth in economically depressed areas of the city.

As a result of public outrage over redlining, banks and other financial institutions are now prohibited by federal law from writing off entire sections of a city when dispensing loans. Yet redlining still continues in a more modified form; mortgage finance institutions can extend loans for condominium and cooperative conversions while denying financing in the neighborhood to owners of low-income apartment buildings and owners of older single-family homes who wish to make structural repairs in their dwellings.

The **Community Reinvestment Act (CRA)** of 1977 required mortgage finance institutions to disclose where they make their loans; community groups could then use this information to pressure these credit institutions to make loans in inner-city neighborhoods.[44] However, it is debatable how effective such public disclosure is except in those few neighborhoods with active community organizations organized around the disinvestment issue. Some mortgage banking institutions have begun to reorient their credit practices toward inner-city needs. The Mortgage Bankers Association of America is insistent that "lenders are often unjustly accused of redlining when they apply sound underwriting criteria" in refusing to make loans to properties and applicants that are not considered to be "creditworthy."[45] Yet evidence of continued redlining persists. One study of successful and unsuccessful loan applications has found that determinations of creditworthiness are still influenced by race and not just by economic factors.[46]

Some banks have looked upon the requirements of the CRA as an opportunity to make new loans, strengthen the community, and, in the process, strengthen the bank. They advertise the availability of residential and commercial loans. They work with community organizations to identify potential home buyers and counsel low-income prospects as to how to budget their funds. Other credit institutions, however, have dragged their feet from fear of the financial risks involved.

It often takes an activist, grassroots organization to motivate credit institutions to extend loans to areas and people they otherwise would not serve. Banks are rated according to how well they are meeting the goals of the CRA and actively promoting credit to the area served. In the late 1980s and early 1990s, a wave of bank mergers gave housing advocacy groups an opportunity to leverage credit institutions to make new loans to the community. As the merger of banks must be approved by federal regulators, a community's objection that a bank has not met its obligations under the CRA could pose a serious financial threat to a bank considering a merger. In Philadelphia, ACORN, an activist group, used the threat of opposing specific bank mergers as a means of getting the financial institutions concerned to commit millions of dollars in new loans for inner-city businesses and low-income mortgages. Yet, despite the CRA's successes, mortgage institutions complain of the costs of compliance. In 1995, the Republican majorities in the House and the Senate began consideration of bills that would relax the CRA's requirements, exempting nearly 88 percent of the nation's banks from CRA coverage.[47]

PRIVATE POWER AND CENTRAL CITY REVIVAL AND TRANSFORMATION

Even where there has been a revival of an inner-city neighborhood, such a comeback may be the result of corporate manipulation and not just the result of natural demographic trends or market factors. **Urban renewal** was a program in the 1950s and 1960s that professed the laudatory goal of rebuilding slum neighborhoods. Yet in a number of ways urban renewal made the living conditions of the urban poor even worse. Urban renewal tore down more housing than it built; housing conditions worsened as displaced residents were crowded into other impoverished neighborhoods. Also, segregation was increased, as in numerous cities urban renewal became synonymous with "Negro removal" and the "federal bulldozer" was used to remove minorities from sections of the city near more exclusive white neighborhoods.[48]

How could all these negative effects come from a program that seemed to have such good intentions? Private sector and governmental actors shaped the program to achieve their own ends, which had little to do with improving the living conditions of the poor. Downtown businesses sought an expanded and more modernized central business district; local hospitals and universities sought room for expansion. Urban renewal was often used to clear out the poor and minorities who lived on the periphery of the old downtown and stood in the way of much commercial and institutional expansion. When new houses were built in renewal areas, these houses were often too expensive to be afforded by the former residents of the neighborhood. Commercial elites used urban renewal as an attempt to bring new customers with good buying power to their fading downtown businesses; improving the housing conditions of the poor was a secondary concern.

All these outcomes were apparent in urban redevelopment in Chicago.[49] Downtown business officials designed a redevelopment plan to reattract potential customers to the city. But the city's poor first had to be cleared from the targeted renewal areas. The city exercised its power of **eminent domain** to take (or, more appropriately, to buy) the land from private owners for public purposes. The renewal sites were then turned over to developers at a fraction of their real costs. Displaced minority residents were rehoused in a long row of massive public housing projects (known in Chicago as "The Wall") that effectively enlarged the city's South Side black belt.

Michael Reese Hospital and the Illinois Institute of Technology used urban renewal as the keystone to claiming South Side land for expansion. The University of Chicago used the program to establish a buffer zone that would prevent the university's annexation by the growing black belt; the university opposed construction of public housing in the immediate renewal area and actually demolished sound buildings and displaced residents in order to establish a buffer zone between itself and the burgeoning black community.

Even today's **back-to-the-city** or **gentrification** movement (a movement we will discuss in more detail toward the end of this chapter) can be seen to be shaped by the decisions of private business elites. Gentrification does not occur simply because singles and young marrieds have placed new value on urban life. In at least one case, the turnaround of an inner-city neighborhood, Philadelphia's Society Hill area, was the result of the orchestration of that city's downtown real estate community working in league with governmental planners. Roman Cybriwsky and his research associates concluded that "the shift toward smaller households or the tightening of housing markets…might be portrayed as but a passive backdrop to a stage upon which powerful actors, a civic elite, *will* the new city into being."[50] The strategy to reclaim Society Hill was "'top-down' in conception and execution."[51] All but a few of the residents already living there were expelled to make way for a new socially homogeneous neighborhood that could be marketed to a higher class of tenant. These efforts succeeded in doing what was once thought to be impossible—reversing deterioration on the edge of Philadelphia's downtown. The results serve as evidence of "the undeniable impact that a small number of individuals can have in guiding—or even partly reversing—established urban trends."[52]

PRIVATE POWER AS A CAUSE OF HOMELESSNESS

Finally, even the problem of the homeless can be seen to be rooted to a great extent in the actions of private enterprise. Of course, there are numerous reasons why people go homeless. Some are drug users and alcoholics. Others are former mental patients who have been left to wander the streets as a result of deinstitutionalization. Still others are left homeless as a result of being unable to pay the rent because of low pay, loss of a job, marital breakup, or a family crisis.

Yet it is too simplistic to view homelessness as resulting solely from the internal characteristics of the poor. Homelessness also has its roots in the shrinkage of the supply of cheap housing offered by both the private sector and the government. In many cities the stock of low-rent housing has shrunk dramatically as cheap housing units were removed by the private sector to make way for more profitable activities. These units, while often in a state of disrepair, could be afforded by the poor. Now these units have been torn down to make way for new office and retail complexes, high-rise luxury apartment buildings, and parking lots. The cheap **single room occupancy (SRO) hotel**, while never very desirable to begin with, at least offered the poorest of the poor a place to sleep. Now, under the pressures of redevelopment, these hotels and the other flophouses of skid row have all but disappeared from many cities, leaving the city's poorest residents no place to sleep.[53]

According to Joel Blau, homelessness has increased as corporations have sought to maintain their competitiveness by moving production facilities overseas.[54] The high-paying industrial jobs once found in cities in the United States have given way to new service jobs. Central city residents often lack the skill and educational requirements to secure the better jobs available in a high-tech, information economy. The low-wage service jobs that they can secure do not guaranty long-term security; dismissed from a job, a worker and his or her family may be unable to meet their monthly rent.

[handwritten margin note: I DON'T THINK IT IS TOO SIMPLISTIC !!!]

[handwritten note at bottom: It's always someone elses fault !!!]

Economic restructuring has acted to make families headed by women especially vulnerable to homelessness. "Women's jobs" often pay low wages and lack economic security. Homelessness among women and children also results because young men facing economic uncertainty do not make good partners.[55]

Government policy, too, has contributed to the rise of homelessness. Local governments have often worked hand-in-hand with developers in central city revitalization plans that resulted in the destruction of SROs. Cutbacks in social welfare and public housing during the Reagan-Bush era, too, resulted in increased homelessness.[56]

THE SHIFT TO THE SUNBELT

The in-migration of the poor to the cities and the out-migration of the middle class to the suburbs constitute two of the major demographic trends that have shaped American cities. A third and more recent demographic trend has been the shift of population and jobs from the Frostbelt to the Sunbelt. By 1980 this regional shift had become quite pronounced. Almost all those cities that gained population in the 1970s were located in the South and the West; those that lost population were for the most part in the Northeast and North Central parts of the country (see Table 2.1).

Explaining Sunbelt Growth

As we have seen in Chapter 1, there is no exact consensus as to just what states and parts of states constitute the Sunbelt. Still there is general agreement that the term **Sunbelt** denotes those areas of the South and West that have enjoyed a general increase of population and economic activity over the past few decades. We must exert a bit of caution in making generalizations that characterize such a broad and diverse region; not all parts of the South and the West have shared in the region's newfound growth and prosperity.

What are the reasons that underlie the long-term growth of the Sunbelt? The three general factors that explain suburban growth also explain Sunbelt growth. Sunbelt growth is not simply the result of natural factors; it is also the product of governmental policies and of corporate and private sector power.

Natural Features

Sunbelt growth can be seen as a natural demographic trend resulting from affluence, innovations in technology, and citizens' preference for the good life. Citizens came to the Sunbelt in search of warm weather, sunny skies, and good beaches. Florida and Arizona proved especially hospitable to those seeking retirement homes. Other newcomers sought to flee the congestion, overcrowded conditions, crime, and social problems of the

TABLE 2.1
Growing and Declining Cities by Region:
Cities over 100,000 Population, 1980

U.S. Region	Number of Cities with 100,000 Plus Population	Number of Cities Gaining Population	Number of Cities Losing Population
Northeast	23	—	23
North Central	39	8	31
South	60	46	14
West	47	39	8
Total	169	93	76

Source: Bureau of the Census, *U.S. Department of Commerce News* (Washington: June 3, 1981), p. x.

cities of the Northeast and Midwest. The arrival of immigrants from Mexico, the Caribbean, and Central America only further fueled the growth of Sunbelt cities, especially those in Florida, southern California, and the American Southwest. Business came too when technology permitted, as a result of the availability of cheap land.

Technological advances made possible the regional shift in jobs and population. The development of the interstate highway system and jet plane travel as well as breakthroughs in telecopying and telecommunications made it possible for businesses and people to locate in new regions of the country. Branch firms could be sited there; corporate executives could fly to meetings as required; face-to-face meetings could be dispensed with altogether as executives could "meet" by teleconference and "fax" documents around the country as needed.

One often overlooked technological innovation that made possible the growth of the Sunbelt is air conditioning. With the marvel of machine-cooled air, no longer was much of the South a "hot belt," inhospitable to office work and comfortable living.

Government Policy

Government programs also helped assist the growth of Sunbelt communities. Most important among these programs was spending by the defense department and defense industry. It is generally recognized that World War II provided the major stimulus to Sunbelt growth. Historians Richard M. Bernard and Bradley R. Rice observe that "the armed forces made deliberate efforts to relocate their personnel and training facilities around the country and to spread out defense contracts in order to make bombing and even invasion more difficult for the enemy."[57] Warm weather cities provided ideal sites for port activities, troop training, and airplane testing. New Orleans, Atlanta, Fort Worth, Oklahoma City, San Antonio, Albuquerque, Phoenix, Los Angeles, and San Diego all witnessed great expansion as a result of the location of aircraft production facilities and military bases.[58] Production in many of these facilities continued after the end of the war, through the Cold War period.

It is not just the siting of military bases and production facilities that has worked to the benefit of Sunbelt cities. Military procurement, too, has aided Sunbelt growth. From 1951 to 1981 the amount spent by the Defense Department on prime contracts increased by 810 percent in the South and 402 percent in the West; during the same period the amount allocated to the Midwest decreased by 1.5 percent.[59] The military simply sought to buy supplies from contractors conveniently located near its installations; often southern suppliers also proved to be cheaper in providing services as a result of the low levels of unionization and the wage structure of the region. Aircraft carriers were retrofitted in the naval yards of Norfolk, Virginia, and not in those of Philadelphia or New York City. Spending by military personnel, the Defense Department's suppliers, and spin-off industries all fueled Sunbelt prosperity. Defenders of the Frostbelt blasted "the Pentagon tilt"[60] and labeled the Pentagon "a five-sided building that faces South."[61]

But Defense Department spending and contracting are not the only big ticket spending programs that spurred Sunbelt growth. The massive expenditures on the space program, too, fueled the economies of Florida and Texas (with NASA's Manned Spacecraft Center located close to Houston).

The activity of the Federal Housing Administration has helped promote new home construction in the region. The FHA sees its job as assisting people in obtaining mortgages wherever they wish to buy a home. If people wish to buy homes in the Sunbelt, the FHA is only too willing to guarantee loans made to qualified buyers. As a result, in 1975 California, Florida, and Texas were the three states that led the nation in the number of FHA-insured mortgages; Arizona, too, received a disproportionately large share of FHA guarantees.[62] In the absence of the FHA, a much smaller number of families would have been able to undertake the move to the Sunbelt.

The federal tax code, too, played an important role in spurring Sunbelt growth. The tax code's provisions for homeowners helped facilitate home purchases in the region. Such tax write-offs as the investment tax credit and accelerated depreciation on the purchase of new facilities and equipment subsidized new commercial activity in the region. Tax incentives were also given to the oil, gas, and energy industries in the South and West. Houston's growth, for instance, has been to a great extent the product of favorable tax treatment given to the petrochemical industry and investments in real estate. The federal government further assisted Houston's development with grants for highway construction and port development and the infusion of spending related to the space program.[63]

The 1993 **North American Free Trade Agreement (NAFTA)** may prove to be the most recent addition to the series of federal policies that have served to promote Sunbelt growth. While it is too early to determine the exact regional effects of NAFTA, it appears that the agreement may boost the economies of such border cities as San Antonio. Representatives from states in the Northeast and the Midwest also voiced their concern that the legislation gave the Southwest an unfair advantage by steering job-creating pollution clean-up and developmental funds to Southwest border states to the exclusion of other regions of the country. According to the legislation's critics, NAFTA focused assistance on the United States–Mexico border while ignoring similar environmental and developmental problems in the Great Lakes and along the country's border with Canada.[64]

But the federal government was not the only public institution supporting Sunbelt growth. Sunbelt growth has not been purely the result of either free-market natural forces or federal policy, as is commonly claimed. Instead, active local governmental intervention has often been an essential element in the emergence of cities such as Houston, San Antonio, and San Jose. In each of these cities, the municipal government incurred vast debts in order to undertake the sewer, street, highway, and other infrastructure improvements necessary for Sunbelt expansionism. In the post–World War II period, Houston boosted its debt almost eight times in order to finance the city's public construction boom. As Heywood Sanders observes, "Contrary to the notion that Houston's development was built on a *limited local state*, or a form of urban development fully dominated by free enterprise, the city's public sector actively fueled and sustained the urban development process with public dollars."[65] Development in San Antonio lagged until city officials copied the Houston model of undertaking a large public debt to finance new capital investment. Similarly, in California, "San Jose's boom in the 1960s was supported and sustained by public capital investment on a scale unprecedented in the city's twentieth century history."[66]

Private Power

The profit-maximization drive of the profit sector provides much of the motivation behind the shift of commerce and industry to the South and West. Factory owners and the directors of corporations sought Sunbelt locations for their facilities in order to undercut work force unionization, minimize tax burdens, and lessen the degree of intrusion posed by state and local environmental and social regulations. The textile industry, for instance, moved from New England to the South in the face of increased militancy of northern work forces. Right-to-work laws, a general anti-union climate among state and local governments in the South, and the prospect of paying lower wages soon led other industries to make the shift.[67]

In other industries, corporations took advantage of times of economic recession to close plants with relatively high costs of production, energy, wages, taxation, and regulation—costs often associated with more aging plants in the industrialized Northeast and Midwest. When good times came, these plants were not always reopened. Instead, it only made good economic sense to expand output at the more productive, newer facilities located in the less costly, less unionized areas of the country.[68]

The economic boosterism of local governments in the region further explains why business entrepreneurs and corporate managers found the Sunbelt a desirable location for business. In northern cities, according to political scientist John Mollenkopf, powerful coalitions of Democratic party politicians and their ethnic constituencies, vocal minority groups, and labor unions all challenged the business community for control over city affairs. In southwestern municipalities, in contrast, the political terrain was much less contested; the business community could rule essentially without challenge. As a consequence, the business climate created by municipal governments in the Southwest reflected the desires of the business community. In cities in the Southwest, the size of the public sector was kept smaller, tax burdens were lower, and spending was less oriented toward social problems as contrasted to cities in the Northeast and the Midwest.[69] Only recently have minority and neighborhood groups begun to challenge the business community's hold on public affairs in Sunbelt cities.

THE EMERGENCE OF PROBLEMS IN THE SUNBELT

It would be quite misleading to paint a picture of unqualified Sunbelt prosperity and uniform Frostbelt decline. Growth brings with it problems as well as advantages. Cities such as Dallas, Houston, and Los Angeles suffer monumental automobile congestion problems. Numerous cities in California and the Southwest suffer from water shortages. Houston faces the problem of subsidence, as parts of the city are actually sinking as a result of water having been pumped out of the ground to make way for development.[70] The growing cities of the Sunbelt must also find the means to pay for new highways, schools, and other improvements in infrastructure.

Coping with overcrowded schools in fast-growing cities is a particularly difficult problem. Constitutional and statutory limitations on taxing and borrowing often make impossible the construction of new school facilities. In numerous communities referenda to authorize the issuance of new school construction bonds repeatedly fail to win public approval. In overcrowded districts students are often shunted off to makeshift classrooms in annexes and trailers. In Los Angeles the school board has considered year-round schooling, having students attend schools on different overlapping schedules throughout the entire twelve months of the calendar year, thereby relieving classroom overcrowding without having to incur the huge expense of building new schools.

Growth also compounds environmental problems. Florida's rapidly growing urban areas have led to the disturbance of wildlife habitats and a reduction in the acreage devoted to agriculture. In the Los Angeles basin, the problem of air pollution has become so severe that very drastic solutions may have to be imposed. Under one plan to reduce emissions advanced by the South Coast Air Quality Management District and the Southern California Association of Governments, residents "may be forced to buy methanol and electric cars, ride to work in van pools, mow their lawns by hand and spray their underarms with manually pumped deodorant."[71] Much of the pollution is generated by heavy industries concentrated on the coast in Los Angeles and Orange counties; the pollution then drifts east over Riverside and San Bernardino counties. Under a plan that seeks to improve the jobs-housing balance in the region, commercial development near the coast would be discouraged and businesses would be induced to locate inland; daily commuting from the more affordable outlying areas to Orange County and Los Angeles would thereby be reduced.

The general portrait of Sunbelt prosperity also overlooks the fact that growth has been unevenly distributed in the Sunbelt. The new prosperity does not reach every small and mid-sized city. Even such larger cities as Fresno, California, and New Orleans, Louisiana, have suffered fiscal and social problems so severe that in a number of ways they appear to have more in common with Frostbelt cities than with their Sunbelt neighbors. As two New Orleans officials observed, "Like older northern cities, New Orleans suffers a declining tax base, a large population of unemployed and untrained persons, and a very small middle class population."[72]

Even the more economically dynamic large cities of the region contain substantially large pockets of poverty. In 1970, during the heyday of its economic growth, Houston contained a distressed area of over 350,000 population; Dallas had one of 215,000; and Memphis had a pocket of poverty of 270,000.[73]

In Miami the unevenness of Sunbelt development has led to tensions that peaked in a series of riots in the 1980s. The poverty-stricken black communities in Overtown and Liberty City did not share in the area's new wealth. The January 1989 Miami riot occurred in the midst of the glitter and flamboyance surrounding the city's hosting of the Super Bowl.[74]

The Sunbelt's economic bubble also burst in the 1980s. The region lost many of its textile mills to low-wage competition in Taiwan and Singapore. By the mid-1980s eleven of the nineteen Sunbelt states had unemployment rates greater than the national average.[75] A tumble in oil prices greatly hurt the economies of Texas, Louisiana, and the rest of the "oil patch." By 1989 nine of the ten metropolitan areas with the highest rates of unemployment were in the Sunbelt: McAllen, Laredo, Brownsville, and El Paso in Texas; Shreveport, Houma-Thibodaux, and Alexandria in Louisiana; Modesto, California; and Mobile, Alabama. Flint, Michigan, was the only Frostbelt representative among the ten cities on the list.[76] Cutbacks in defense spending undermined California's economy in the 1990s.

SUNBELT-FROSTBELT: HOW GREAT A DIFFERENCE?

Urban journalist Neal Peirce has surveyed both the Sunbelt, with its emergent problems, and the Frostbelt, with its comeback cities such as Boston. In both regions he found urban success stories and permanent poverty. Peirce concludes that the distinction between Frostbelt and Sunbelt has been overplayed: "All regions, in a real sense, are a very 'mixed bag.'"[77]

As the bloom has come off the Sunbelt rose, Sunbelt cities may have to undertake new strategies to attract investment. The rebound of a number of Frostbelt cities was to a great degree the result of the infrastructure spending and quality-of-life services provided by the region's city and state governments. High-amenity states such as Michigan, Wisconsin, Minnesota, and Massachusetts were able to attract businesses despite their reputation for high taxes. As Peirce observes, faced with such competition, Sunbelt states and cities can no longer afford to rely solely on their low-wage, antiunion reputations to attract business. Instead, they may have to find the resources to make the investments in education, human resource development, and community amenities that many business leaders expect.

A new division may also be emerging among Sunbelt communities. Continuing local prosperity in the Sunbelt may depend on the position a city occupies in a globalized economy. While Los Angeles, Dallas, Miami, Atlanta, and other internationally connected communities have emerged as centers of global information and corporate headquarters, other Sunbelt cities have begun to see their economies slow or stagnate.[78]

As we have seen, Sunbelt communities have begun to confront quite serious problems, and certain Frostbelt cities have experienced a renaissance. Yet the rebound of Frostbelt cities is far from complete. While Boston, Baltimore, and Pittsburgh have begun comebacks, other cities such as Detroit continue their long-term decline.[79] In 1995, Washington, DC, faced a major fiscal crisis that necessitated drastic cutbacks in municipal personnel and city services. Still other cities such as Cleveland enjoyed a revival only after first losing a substantial part of their population and industrial base. Cleveland may be seeing a rebirth, but there are fewer Clevelanders today to share in its benefits.

Finally, even where Frostbelt cities have come back, their gains have been made predominantly in the information-processing industries. They continue to lose jobs in the manufacturing and traditional blue-collar industries. The result is both a displacement of workers from the older industries as well as a loss of relatively unskilled entry-level jobs that could be taken by disadvantaged first-time entrants to the work force. In contrast, large cities in the South and West, including Atlanta, Houston, Denver, and San Francisco, experienced gains not only in the information-processing sector but in other industries as well.[80]

Sunbelt cities are not quite as well off as the stereotype once made them out to be. Yet regional differences still remain. Whatever rebound there has been in Frostbelt cities does not match the long-term gains represented by Sunbelt growth. The Frostbelt continues to lose population to the Sunbelt.

For all of its recent problems, the Sunbelt continues to be a region of long-term population growth. And growth brings with it both resources and new opportunities. The distinction between the Frostbelt and the Sunbelt, while not as great as it once was, still retains its validity.

IS THE URBAN CRISIS OVER?

In a number of obvious ways, the crisis of America's cities clearly continues. The "crack" and drug problems of inner cities appear to be more severe today than they were in the past. Urban poverty persists; the problems posed by an urban underclass appear to be more difficult than ever to deal with.[81] Many major cities and metropolitan areas remain segregated on a de facto basis. Coping with the needs of the homeless and AIDS victims are relatively new items that have emerged on the urban agenda.

Yet a number of commentators have argued that the urban crisis is over. Cities like New York City and Cleveland are no longer teetering on the edge of bankruptcy. Impressive new building construction is apparent in the downtown of city after city. Apparent comebacks have been made by a whole broad range of Frostbelt cities, including Boston, New York, Pittsburgh, Baltimore, Cleveland, Cincinnati, Worcester (Massachusetts), and Stamford (Connecticut).

Journalist T. D. Allman in his article "The Urban Crisis Leaves Town and Moves to the Suburbs" has argued that the urban crisis argument is overemphasized and out of date.[82] He maintained that proper reading of the data showed that America's largest cities, particularly those in the Northeast and Midwest, were nowhere near the crisis levels articulated by some politicians, academics, and journalists. Allman further argued that while capital investment was increasing in the downtown areas of the nation's largest cities, crime and other problems associated with America's cities were now spreading to the suburbs. The gap between cities and suburbs appeared to have narrowed.

Yet Allman's analysis clearly overstates the degree of good health of cities as a whole. City downtowns have been revitalized. Certain trendy "candleshop" districts have shown a new vitality as a result of urban resettlement. New York City, for instance, has experienced a building boom in its downtown; neighborhoods like Columbus Avenue in upper Manhattan have become suddenly attractive residential and nightlife areas. Yet these developments do not necessarily bring any positive improvement to the lives of residents of the South Bronx,

Bedford-Stuyvesant in Brooklyn, or any of the other outer-borough dis-tressed neighborhoods. The continued development of downtown Washington, DC, does not translate into anything meaningful for the residents of the poverty-stricken Anacostia neighborhood in the south-eastern part of the city. Philadelphia's downtown transformation and the development of its hospitals and medical research institutions do not produce much in the way of new job opportunities, services, or a desegregated society for the permanent poor of the city's ghettos. For these people, the urban crisis continues. The problem of urban dualism is even more severely pronounced.

A more complete reading of the statistical evidence points to contin-uing urban distress. Unemployment rates remain higher in central cities than in suburbs. Private sector employment growth in central cities still lags behind such growth in the suburbs. Also, despite the impressionistic evidence that wealthier people are moving back to the city, dual migration persists to the disadvantage of central cities; on the whole, poorer people move to cities in search of opportunity, and better-off citizens continue to move to the suburbs.[83] Major cities in the United States continue to face severe economic and social problems that cannot be minimized by anec-dotal evidence to the contrary.

GENTRIFICATION

Much of the debate as to the continuing existence of the urban crisis has to do with the extent of gentrification and its impact on cities. **Gentrifi-cation** refers to the restoration of deteriorated urban neighborhoods that occurs when middle-class families, particularly singles and young marrieds, place new value on city living and declining property values make certain inner-city neighborhoods ripe for development. *Urban regeneration, inner-city revitalization, neighborhood renewal, rehabilita-tion, neighborhood reinvestment,* and *urban reinvasion* have all been used as synonyms for gentrification.[84]

Gentrification was assumed to bring new vitality and tax sources to cities. Yet gentrification has not been as widespread or universal as the journalistic accounts originally assumed. Not all cities have experienced substantial amounts. Extensive gentrification can be found most fre-quently in those cities that maintain an attractive downtown core, espe-cially corporate headquarters cities and cities that maintain an active administrative central business district.[85] Substantial neighborhood rein-vestment also is likely to occur only if a city has a stock of housing of good architectural character and historic interest; that housing must be located near a downtown that offers a good postindustrial white-collar job base as well as numerous cultural opportunities and an active nightlife. As a result, neighborhood reinvestment has occurred in New York, Boston, Philadelphia, Washington, DC, Atlanta, Chicago, Los Angeles, and San

Francisco; it is much more limited in extent in Detroit, Cleveland, Newark, and many of the cities of the Sunbelt.[86]

But gentrification even in a world class city does not necessarily produce any upgrading of its more troubled neighborhoods. One study of New York City in the 1970s concludes that, despite widespread perceptions of neighborhood reinvestment, there has been little overall improvement in these neighborhoods: "In sum, if there are neighborhoods that are revitalizing, they are improving in the midst of a continuing decline for the inner city as a whole."[87]

Nor has gentrification drawn a wealth of new taxpayers or taxable resources to the cities. Study after study has refuted the popular perception that gentrification is a back-to-the-city movement. Most of what was assumed to be a back-to-the-city movement is really the result of two separate processes that do not bring much in the way of new revenues to the city's coffers. A substantial amount of inner-city renovation is simply the result of "incumbent upgrading" by people who already reside in the neighborhood. A majority of the gentrifiers were also found to be people who moved from other parts of the city, not from the suburbs. The back-to-the-city viewpoint retains its validity only to the extent that a large number of these new inner-city investors were found to be persons who had spent their childhoods in the suburbs.[88]

Even where neighborhood reinvasion does occur, new residents are often unwilling to support the sharing of resources with other parts of the city. Gentrifiers demand service improvements for their neighborhoods; they want to protect their investments. A large number of these new residents have no children or have children who attend private schools; as a result, the new urban gentry is not always very willing to support increased taxation for the improvement of public education.[89]

Finally, gentrification results in a substantial problem of **displacement** as existing residents are moved out to make way for the newcomers. Those who are displaced must bear the burden of moving; often they can find housing elsewhere only at a price higher than that which they were already paying.[90] The burden is especially troublesome for the poor, the elderly, and those on fixed incomes. Some observers find particularly troubling the fact that displacement related to gentrification often entails a change in the social composition of the neighborhood; poorer people and minorities are forced to vacate their housing in order to make way for more attractive units made available to a new class of buyers. Reinvestment may improve neighborhoods, but it is improvement for the upwardly mobile middle class, not for the poor who were already residents in these transition areas. As one critic of the gentrification/displacement process asked, what is the ultimate goal of neighborhood reinvestment, "Saving the buildings or saving the people?"[91] Due to the higher rates of poverty among female householders, gentrification might also lead to a disproportionate displacement of women and female-headed families.[92]

Gentrification is a complex phenomenon. Is it saving cities or destroying poor neighborhoods? Does it enhance the city's tax base or displace the poor and minorities? There are no easy answers when it comes to assessing the effects of gentrification.[93]

In the privatist, free-market American system, gentrification can be expected to continue. Urban reinvestment in newly attractive neighborhoods will occur even while disinvestment in more distressed communities proceeds unabated.

What can be done? Organized community action can at times mitigate some of the ill effects that accompany gentrification, as a comparison of two gentrifying neighborhoods in New York City underscores. In Washington Heights, in upper Manhattan, a multiethnic coalition of community groups fought to ensure that the housing opportunities for the poor would be included in plans for the upgrading of the area. The coalition fought for increased public and private rehabilitation programs that improved the neighborhood's housing stock and stabilized the area while maintaining community diversity. In the Park Slope neighborhood of Brooklyn, in contrast, there was no equivalent level of community action to push for similar government programs. As a result, market forces alone determined the pace and scope of gentrification. SROs were converted into duplexes; extensive cooperative conversions took place; and a greater displacement of the poor occurred in Park Slope than in Washington Heights.[94]

While neighborhood-based groups can provide the focus of resistance to gentrification, though, such groups can also weaken over time. They lose members as displacement proceeds, and new community activists will often come from the ranks of new neighborhood residents who often have a vision of the community far different from that of the poor.[95]

CONCLUSIONS

Natural growth, governmental policies, and private sector power have all acted to produce a contemporary urban situation marked by extensive suburbanization and the shift of population and jobs to the Sunbelt. In recent years production has shifted to Latin American and Pacific Rim nations as well. The downtown revival, the renaissance of Frostbelt cities, the downturn of Sunbelt (especially oil patch) cities, and the gentrification of residential neighborhoods all do little to alter the long-term trends. While prospects for municipal bankruptcy have diminished (with the fiscal problems of Washington, DC, and Orange County, California, as notable exceptions in the mid-1990s), the urban crisis continues in a good many other ways.

What are the implications of the ecological trends and power patterns discussed in this chapter? In summary, the evolution of metropolitan areas has produced the following patterns:

1. **The fragmentation of metropolitan areas.** Each metropolitan area comprises an integrated economic entity.[96] Cities and suburbs cannot survive without each other. Such interdependence is clearly evident in commuting patterns. Many suburbanites commute to central-city workplaces. The continued dispersion of work sites in the metropolitan area has brought with it a rise in both reverse commuting from city to suburb and commuting from one suburb to another.

   Yet when it comes time for governance, there is no need to respect such economic interdependence. Instead, for purposes of governance, the metropolitan area is *fragmented* or divided into numerous smaller, independent units—cities, counties, townships, suburbs, and special districts—all of which owe no legal responsibility to the other. Each can afford to pursue those actions in such areas as land use and taxing that most benefit its own residents. The negative effects of such actions on surrounding communities need not be considered.

2. **The separation of resources from need.** The selective migration patterns discussed in this chapter have resulted in an unbalanced metropolis. As a result of **dual migration**—where the poor and racial minorities continue to move into cities while the well-to-do middle class moves out to the suburbs—central cities have become centers of populations in need. Yet at the same time, residential and corporate tax bases have seen an exodus to the suburbs. Central cities have to provide for a population increasingly in need of expensive services in such areas as education, language instruction, mental health, and social welfare. Taxable resources, however, increasingly lie in suburban jurisdictions beyond the reach of central-city governments.

   Of course, not all suburbs are characterized by wealth and prosperity. Not all fit the stereotype of the well-to-do bedroom community. Instead, many suburbs are the sites of antiquated industrial plants, aging infrastructure, and populations in need. The situation for such troubled suburbs is the same as it is for troubled central cities; both lack the ability to tap the taxable resources of the metropolis in order to provide for their populations in need.

3. **Racial imbalance in the metropolis.** As a result of both dual migration and the ability of suburbs to enact exclusionary zoning ordinances, the distribution of population in the metropolis is marred by severe racial imbalance. The mechanization of agriculture in the South, job opportunities created by World War II production, and prospects for increased civil rights protection all led large elements of the black population to abandon the southern countryside and search for a better life in cities, particularly

in cities of the North. In more recent years the arrival of new population groups from Latin America (and to a lesser extent from Asia as well) has only served to reinforce the minority character of central-city populations.

Not all suburbs are white, or predominantly white, enclaves. Some suburbs have experienced substantial integration. Others, such as Baldwin Park in suburban Los Angeles, are minority-dominated. The small increase of minority incorporation into suburbia in recent years, however, does not change the overall picture. The white middle class continues to leave the central city in search of the suburban good life. Minority families do not find all suburbs in a metropolitan area equally open to their settlement. The result is the severe problem of racial isolation, not just in residential neighborhoods but in the public schools as well.

4. **Prospects for minority power in the central city.** As a result of the fragmented metropolis, central-city minority populations have suffered from both segregation and underservice. Yet in one respect the increased minority composition of central cities offers minorities a certain advantage—a heightened chance of political power. Over the years large black populations in central cities have helped elect black mayors in a number of cities, including New York, Chicago, Cleveland, Detroit, Gary, Philadelphia, Newark, Oakland (California), New Orleans, Charlotte, Atlanta, and Birmingham (Alabama). Among the cities that have seen the election of Hispanic mayors are Miami, San Antonio, and Denver.

5. **The changing position of cities in the postindustrial economy.** The American economy has changed. No longer is heavy industry the dominant element in the American economy it once was. The United States has moved to a postindustrial economy marked by increased levels of education, a shift to a service economy, and technological breakthroughs in such areas as communications and information processing.

The effect of this economic transformation on cities has been immense. The emergence of new industries and new means of communications and transportation has increased the viability of suburban and Sunbelt commercial sites. These areas have been marked by growth and in some cases by the problems associated with rapid growth.

In contrast, cities dependent on the older manufacturing sector of the economy have suffered a long-term decline. Some have undergone a difficult but successful transition; others have been unable to diversify their economic base or find a new role for themselves in a changed national economy.

Urban sociologist John Kasarda argues that cities must adapt to their new roles in a service economy if they are to prosper.

According to Kasarda, headquarters offices, finance, marketing, research, and communications are the new growth industries for cities. To be competitive, cities must invest in rewiring and other infrastructure improvements in order to meet the needs of modern information-processing offices. They must also spend funds on quality-of-life amenities that will make a city attractive to higher-income residents and corporation personnel.[97]

Yet even long-term economic adaptation is no guarantee of local fiscal health in a rapidly changing economy marked by strong international competition. Even American cities with relatively healthy economies are facing increased competition from low-wage nations in Latin America and the Pacific Rim. The health of cities is dependent on larger economic cycles and forces over which they have no control. The sudden downturn in economic vitality of certain Sunbelt communities in the 1980s and 1990s, especially those in the oil patch, reminds us as to just how tenuous local economic health may be.

The poor occupy a precarious position in the postindustrial city. Cities may economically adapt or transform, but the jobs available in a technology-based age may be beyond the skills of the poor. And the subsidies given new businesses may only drain resources away from community development programs designed to aid neighborhoods and persons in need.

The viability of suburban and Sunbelt commercial sites has also served to make interlocal and interstate competition for business more intense. Cities need businesses for the job opportunities and the tax resources they provide. Yet business capital is mobile; each business can choose in which suburb or city it will locate its facilities. As a result, business has been put in the driver's seat.

Private sector influentials have always been important actors in city affairs. The new regional and global competitiveness for business has only enhanced that power. The exact degree to which private sector power shapes the actions of cities is the subject of much debate. We will discuss this topic at some length in our next chapter.

NOTES

1. Edward C. Banfield, *The Unheavenly City Revisited* (Boston: Little, Brown, 1974), pp. 25–51.
2. Kenneth T. Jackson, *Crabgrass Frontier: The Suburbanization of the United States* (New York: Oxford Univ. Press, 1985), pp. 14–15.
3. Ibid., pp. 12–45, especially p. 13.
4. Ronald Dale Karr, "Brookline Rejects Annexation, 1873," in *Suburbia Re-examined*, ed. Barbara M. Kelly (New York: Greenwood Press, 1989), pp. 103–10.

5. Sam Bass Warner, Jr., *Streetcar Suburbs: The Process of Growth in Boston, 1870–1890*, 2nd ed. (Cambridge, MA: Harvard University Press, 1978), p. 165.

6. Ibid., p. 164.

7. Ibid., p. 165.

8. For a vivid description of the black migration to the urban North that occurred since the 1940s, see Nicholas Lemann, *The Promised Land: The Great Black Migration and How It Changed America* (New York: Vintage, 1991), especially pp. 3–58.

9. Robert Fishman, *Bourgeois Utopias: The Rise and Fall of Suburbia* (New York: Basic Books, 1987), pp. 184–87.

10. Joel Garreau, *Edge City: Life on the New Frontier* (New York: Doubleday, 1991); and Peter O. Muller, "The Transformation of Bedroom Suburbia into the Outer City: An Overview of Metropolitan Structural Change since 1947," in *Suburbia Re-examined*, pp. 39–44. Of course, not all suburbs have prospered. Inner-ring, blue-collar suburbs have begun to exhibit some of the same social and fiscal problems typical of central cities—even while edge cities have prospered. See Scott Minerbrook, "A Tale of Two Suburbs," *U.S. News and World Report* (November 9, 1992): 32–40.

11. Paul E. Peterson, "Introduction," in *The New Urban Reality*, ed. Paul E. Peterson (Washington, DC: Brookings Institution, 1985), p. 1.

12. Carolyn Teich Adams, "Philadelphia: The Slide Toward Municipal Bankruptcy," in *Big City Politics in Transition*, ed. H. V. Savitch and John Clayton Thomas, Urban Affairs Annual Reviews, vol. 38 (Newbury Park, CA: Sage Publications, 1991), pp. 29–46; Carolyn Adams, David Bartelt, David Elesh, Ira Goldstein, Nancy Kleniewski, and William Yancey, *Philadelphia: Neighborhoods, Division, and Conflict in a Postindustrial City* (Philadelphia: Temple Univ. Press, 1991); Neal R. Peirce, "Philadelphia: A 1990s Omen for Cities," *National Journal*, September 22, 1990, p. 2287; and Michael deCourcy Hinds, "Philadelphia's Mayor Faces Tough Job," *The New York Times*, November 4, 1991.

13. John D. Kasarda, "Urban Change and Minority Opportunities," in *The New Urban Reality*, pp. 33–42.

14. John Hull Mollenkopf, *A Phoenix in the Ashes: The Rise and Fall of the Koch Coalition in New York City Politics* (Princeton: Princeton Univ. Press, 1992), pp. 44–68. Also see Saskia Sassen, *Cities in a World Economy* (Thousand Oaks, CA: Pine Forge Press, 1994), pp. 69–76.

15. Mollenkopf, *A Phoenix in the Ashes*, p. 47.

16. Sassen, *Cities in a World Economy*, pp. 78–82.

17. Banfield, *The Unheavenly City Revisited*, p. 26.

18. Clarence Stone, "The Politics of Urban Restructuring: A Review Essay," *Western Political Quarterly* 43 (March 1990): 219–31; the quotation appears on p. 222. Also see Michael P. Smith, *City, State, and Market: The Political Economy of Urban Society* (New York: Blackwell, 1988).

19. Kenneth T. Jackson, *Crabgrass Frontier: The Suburbanization of the United States* (New York: Oxford University Press, 1985), p. 204.

20. Quoted in Jackson, *Crabgrass Frontier*, p. 207.

21. Ibid., p. 208.

22. Citizens Commission on Civil Rights, *A Decent Home...A Report on the Continuing Failure of the Federal Government to Provide Equal Housing Opportunity* (Washington, DC: 1983), reprinted in *Critical Perspectives on Housing*, ed. Rachel G. Bratt, Chester Hartman, and Ann Myerson (Philadelphia: Temple University Press, 1986), p. 299.

23. Ibid., p. 301.

24. Dennis R. Judd, *The Politics of American Cities*, 3rd ed. (Glenview, IL: Scott, Foresman, 1988), p. 281.

25. Rachel G. Bratt, *Rebuilding a Low-Income Housing Policy* (Philadelphia: Temple Univ. Press, 1989), pp. 123–30.

26. Michael A. Stegman, *More Housing, More Fairly: Report of the Twentieth Century Fund on Affordable Housing* (New York: Twentieth Century Fund, 1991), p. 10.

27. Mark Schneider, *Suburban Growth: Policy and Process* (Brunswick, OH: Kings Court Communications, 1980), Chapter 2. Also see Anthony Downs, *Opening up the Suburbs: An Urban Strategy for America* (New Haven, CT: Yale University Press, 1973), chapters 1–3.

28. Thomas E. Bier and Ivan Maric, "IRS Homeseller Provision and Urban Decline," *Journal of Urban Affairs* 16, 2 (1994): 141–54.

29. For a discussion of the impact of federal transportation policy on urban areas, see Schneider, *Suburban Growth*, pp. 13–34 and 233–45.

30. Raymond A. Mohl, "Race and Space in the Modern City: Interstate–95 and the Black Community in Miami," in *Urban Policy in Twentieth-Century America*, ed. Arnold R. Hirsch and Raymond A. Mohl (New Brunswick, NJ: Rutgers Univ. Press, 1993), p. 102.

31. Arnold R. Hirsch, *The Making of the Second Ghetto: Race and Housing in Chicago, 1940–1960* (New York: Cambridge Univ. Press, 1983).

32. Robert Pear, "New York Admits to Racial Steering in Housing Lawsuit," *The New York Times*, July 1, 1992.

33. Jackson, *Crabgrass Frontier*, p. 191.

34. Patrick J. Ashton, "Urbanization and the Dynamics of Suburban Development under Capitalism," in *Marxism and the Metropolis*, 2nd ed., ed. William K. Tabb and Larry Sawers (New York: Oxford University Press, 1984), p. 63.

35. Joe R. Feagin and Robert Parker, *Building American Cities: The Urban Real Estate Game*, 2nd ed. (Englewood Cliffs, NJ: Prentice-Hall, 1990), p. 4.

36. Ibid., p.16.

37. Larry Sawers, "New Perspectives on the Urban Political Economy," in *Marxism and the Metropolis*, 2nd ed., ed. William K. Tabb and Larry Sawers (New York: Oxford University Press, 1984), p. 6.

38. David M. Gordon, "Capitalist Development and the History of American Cities," in *Marxism and the Metropolis*, 2nd ed., ed. William K. Tabb and Larry Sawers, p. 40.

39. Ibid., p. 41.

40. Quoted in ibid.

41. Judd, *The Politics of American Cities*, pp. 169–72.

42. David L. Clark, "Improbable Los Angeles," in *Sunbelt Cities: Politics and Growth Since World War II*, ed. Richard M. Bernard and Bradley R. Rice (Austin, TX: University of Texas Press, 1983), pp. 271–72.

43. David Brodsly, *L.A. Freeway* (Berkeley, CA: University of California Press, 1981), pp. 68–71.

44. Michael H. Schill and Richard P. Nathan, *Revitalizing America's Cities: Neighborhood Reinvestment and Displacement* (Albany, NY: State University of New York Press, 1983), p. 23.

45. Mortgage Bankers Association of America, *Report of the Redlining Task Force: Redlining—Solution Requires Unified Approach* (Washington, DC: no date, late 1970s), pp. 4–5.

46. David Listokin and Stephen Casey, *Mortgage Lending and Race: Conceptual and Analytical Perspectives of the Urban Financing Problem* (Piscataway, NJ: Center for Urban Policy Research, 1979), p. 173. For a more recent study that points to continued racial disparities in mortgage lending and insurance practices, see "The New Redlining," a U.S. News Investigative Report, *U.S. News & World Report*, April 17, 1995, pp. 51–58.

47. Leslie Wayne, "New Hope in Inner Cities: Banks Offering Mortgages," *The New York Times*, March 14, 1992. On the 1995 Republican bills to change the CRA, see "The New Redlining," pp. 51 and 56–58.

48. Martin Anderson, *The Federal Bulldozer: A Critical Analysis of Urban Renewal, 1949–1962* (Cambridge, MA: MIT Press, 1964), pp. 6–8; and Theodore J. Lowi, *The End of Liberalism* (New York: W. W. Norton, 1969), pp. 251–66.

49. This account of urban renewal politics in Chicago is primarily based on Hirsch, *The Making of the Second Ghetto*, pp. 100–70.

50. Roman A. Cybriwsky, David Ley, and John Western, "The Political and Social Construction of Revitalized Neighborhoods: Society Hill, Philadelphia, and False Creek, Vancouver," in *Gentrification of the City*, ed. Neil Smith and Peter Williams (Boston: Allen & Unwin, 1986), pp. 92–105 and 117–19.

51. Ibid., p. 105

52. Ibid., p. 119.

53. Carolyn Teich Adams, "Homelessness in the Postindustrial City: Views from London and Philadelphia," *Urban Affairs Quarterly* 21 (June 1986): 527–49; Charles Hoch and Robert A. Slayton, *New Homeless and Old: Community and the Skid Row Hotel* (Philadelphia: Temple University Press, 1989); Kim Hopper and Jill Hamberg, "The Making of America's Homeless: From Skid Row to New Poor, 1945–1984," in *Critical Perspectives on Housing*, ed. Rachel G. Bratt, Chester Hartman, and Ann Myerson (Philadelphia: Temple University Press, 1986), pp. 12–17; and Alan Finder, "SRO Hotels: Trying to Revive an Old Idea," *The New York Times*, February 9, 1990.

54. Joel Blau, *The Visible Poor: Homelessness in the United States* (New York: Oxford Univ. Press, 1992), pp. 34–47. Martha R. Burt, *Over the Edge: The Growth of Homelessness in the 1980s* (New York: Russell Sage Foundation, 1992), also observes the effect that urban economic restructuring has had on the surge in homelessness in the 1980s.

55. Peter Rossi, *Without Shelter: Homelessness in the 1980s* (New York: Twentieth Century Fund, 1989), pp. 34–36; and Burt, *Over the Edge*.

56. Blau, *The Visible Poor*, pp. 48–59 and 70–75.

57. Richard M. Bernard and Bradley R. Rice, eds., Introduction to their book *Sunbelt Cities: Politics and Growth Since World War II*, p. 12.

58. See ibid., p. 12; and two articles in the Bernard and Rice reader: Anthony W. Corso, "San Diego: The Anti-City," p. 329; and Clark, "Improbable Los Angeles," p. 283.

59. Virginia Mayer and Margaret Downs, "The Pentagon Tilt: Regional Biases in Defense Spending and Strategy," a publication of the Northeast-Midwest Institute, Washington, DC, January 1983, p. 9.

60. Ibid.

61. Richard S. Morris, *Bum Rap on America's Cities* (Englewood Cliffs, NJ: Prentice-Hall, 1980), pp. 147–52.

62. Ibid., pp. 76–77.

63. Joe R. Feagin, *Free Enterprise City: Houston in Political and Economic Perspective* (New Brunswick, NJ: Rutgers University Press, 1988), pp. 54–55, 63–71, 186–88, 203–04.

64. See two articles in the September 1993 *Northeast-Midwest Economic Review*, a publication of the Northeast-Midwest Institute (Washington, DC): "Coalition Leaders Protest Focus of NAFTA on Southwest," pp. 3ff.; and Eric Hartman and Allegra Cangelosi, "Borderline Case: NAFTA Plan Steers Clean-up Funds to Southwest Only," pp. 9–11.

65. Heywood T. Sanders, "The Political Economy of Sunbelt Urban Development: Building the Public Sector" (Paper presented at the annual meeting of the American Political Science Association, New York, September 2–5, 1994).

66. Ibid.

67. Bennett Harrison, "Regional Restructuring and 'Good Business Climates': The Economic Transformation of New England Since World War II," in *Sunbelt/Snowbelt: Urban Redevelopment and Restructuring*, ed. Larry Sawers and William K. Tabb (New York: Oxford University Press, 1984), pp. 51–62.

68. Roy Bahl, Bernard Jump, Jr., and Larry Schroeder, "The Outlook for City Fiscal Performance in Declining Regions," in *The Fiscal Outlook for Cities: Implications of a National Urban Policy*, ed. Roy Bahl (Syracuse, NY: Syracuse University Press, 1978), pp. 29–31.

69. John H. Mollenkopf, *The Contested City* (Princeton, NJ: Princeton University Press, 1983), pp. 242–53.

70. Virginia Marion Perrenod, *Special Districts, Special Purposes: Fringe Governments and Urban Problems in the Houston Area* (College Station, TX: Texas A&M University Press, 1984), pp. 86–115.

71. Robert Reinhold, "Sweeping Changes Weighed to Reduce Los Angeles Smog," *The New York Times*, December 19, 1988. Also see Jay Mathews, "California Plans War on Smog," *Washington Post*, March 18, 1989.

72. Anthony J. Mumphrey, Jr., and Pamela H. Moomau, "New Orleans: An Island in the Sunbelt," School of Urban and Regional Studies, University of New Orleans, Occasional Paper No. 4 (1982).

73. U.S. Department of Housing and Urban Development, *Pockets of Poverty: An Examination of Needs and Options* (Washington, DC: U.S. Government Printing Office, 1979).

74. Details of the Miami riots and the conditions that led up to them can be found in Bruce Porter and Marvin Dunn, *The Miami Riot of 1980* (Lexington, MA: Lexington Books, 1984); U.S. Commission on Civil Rights, *Confronting Racial Isolation in Miami* (Washington, DC: U.S. Government Printing Office, 1982); T. D. Allman, *Miami: City of the Future* (Boston: Atlantic Monthly Press, 1987), pp. 23–35; and Jeffrey Schmalz, "Disorder Erupts in Miami on 2nd Night after Fatal Shooting," *The New York Times*, January 18, 1989.

75. Neal Peirce, "Sunbelt-Frostbelt—Latest Developments" (Paper presented at the annual meeting of the Urban Affairs Association, Fort Worth, Texas, March 6, 1986).

76. Hilary Stout, "Jobless Aren't Migrating to Boom Areas: Great Disparity in Living Costs Is Major Deterrent," *Wall Street Journal*, February 24, 1989.

77. Peirce, "Sunbelt-Frostbelt—Latest Developments."

78. Carl Abbott, "Through Flight to Tokyo: Sunbelt Cities and the New World Economy, 1960–1990," in *Urban Policy in Twentieth-Century America*, ed. Arnold R. Hirsch and Raymond A. Mohl (New Brunswick, NJ: Rutgers Univ. Press, 1993), pp. 183–212.

79. Brian J. L. Berry, Susan W. Sanderson, and Joel Tarr, "The Nation's Most Livable City: Pittsburgh's Transformation," in *The Future of Winter Cities*, ed. Gary Gappert, Urban Affairs Annual Review, vol. 31 (Newbury Park, CA: Sage Publications, 1987), pp. 173–95. See also the debate between Marc V. Levine and Bernard L. Berkowitz over the nature of Baltimore's renaissance in the *Journal of Urban Affairs* 9, no. 2 (1987): 103–38.

80. John D. Kasarda, "Jobs, Migration, and the Emerging Urban Mismatches," in *Urban Change and Poverty*, ed. Michael G. H. McGeary and Laurence E. Lynn, Jr. (Washington, DC: National Academy Press, 1988), pp. 172–73.

81. See the contrasting points of view presented by Charles Murray, *Losing Ground: American Social Policy 1950–1980* (New York: Basic Books, 1984); William Julius Wilson, *The Truly Disadvantaged: The Inner City, the Underclass, and Public Policy* (Chicago: University of Chicago Press, 1987); and Lisbeth R. Schorr with Daniel Schorr, *Within Our Reach: Breaking the Cycle of Disadvantage* (New York: Doubleday, 1988).

82. T. D. Allman, "The Urban Crisis Leaves Town and Moves to the Suburbs," *Harper's*, December 1978, pp. 41–56. Eric H. Monkkonen, "What Urban Crisis? A Historian's Point of View," *Urban Affairs Quarterly* 20 (June 1985): 429–47, argues that substantial social problems remain even though cities have become better off financially. Also see Gregory R. Weiher, "Rumors of the Demise of the Urban Crisis Are Greatly Exaggerated," *Journal of Urban Affairs* 11, no. 3 (1989): 225–42.

83. *Whither or Whether Urban Distress* (Washington, DC: U.S. Department of Housing and Urban Development, 1979), p. 2.

84. All these terms have slightly different connotations. See Bruce London, "Gentrification as Urban Reinvasion: Some Preliminary Definitions and Theoretical Considerations," in *Back to the City*, ed. Shirley Bradway Laska and Daphne Spain (New York: Pergamon Press, 1980), pp. 77–92; and Neil Smith and Peter Williams, "Alternatives to Orthodoxy: Invitation to a Debate," in *Gentrification of the City*, ed. Smith and Williams (Boston: Allen & Unwin, 1986), pp. 1–3.

85. S. Gregory Lipton, "Evidence of Central City Renewal," in *Back to the City*, ed. Shirley Bradway Laska and Daphne Spain, pp. 53–58; and Brian J. L. Berry, "Islands of Renewal in Seas of Decay," in *The New Urban Reality*, ed. Paul E. Peterson (Washington, DC: Brookings Institution, 1985), pp. 86 and 95.

86. Dennis E. Gale, "Neighborhood Resettlement: Washington, DC," pp. 100–01; and Shirley Bradway Laska and Daphne Spain, "Anticipating Renovators' Demands: New Orleans," p. 120, both in *Back to the City*, ed. Laska and Spain; and Berry, "Islands of Renewal in Seas of Decay," pp. 72–76.

87. Mark Baldassare, "Evidence for Neighborhood Revitalization: Manhattan," in *Gentrification, Displacement and Neighborhood Revitalization*, ed. J. John Palen and Bruce London (Albany, NY: State University of New York Press, 1984), p. 91.

88. See the collection of articles in Shirley Bradway Laska and Daphne Spain, eds., *Back to the City*, particularly Phillip L. Clay, "The Rediscovery of City Neighborhoods: Reinvestment by Long-Time Residents and Newcomers," pp. 13–26. Also see Richard T. LeGates and Chester Hartman, "The Anatomy of Displacement in the United States," in *Gentrification of the City*, ed. Neil Smith and Peter Williams, pp. 180–181; Berry, "Islands of Renewal in Seas of Decay"; and Mario D. Zavarella, "The Back-to-the-City Movement Revisited," *Journal of Urban Affairs* 9 (1987), pp. 375–90.

89. Berry, "Islands of Renewal in Seas of Decay," p. 80; and Phillip L. Clay, *Neighborhood Renewal* (Lexington, MA: Lexington Books, 1979), p. 63.

90. LeGates and Hartman, "The Anatomy of Displacement in the United States," pp. 191–92; and Schill and Nathan, *Revitalizing America's Cities: Neighborhood Reinvestment and Displacement*, pp. 112–13.

91. Paul R. Levy, "Neighborhoods in a Race with Time: Local Strategies for Countering Displacement," in *Back to the City*, ed. Shirley Bradway Laska and Daphne Spain, p. 303.

92. Daphne Spain, "A Gentrification Research Agenda for the 1990s," *Journal of Urban Affairs* 14, 2 (1992): 128–29 and 131.

93. Ibid., p. 125.

94. Joyce Gelb and Michal Lyons, "A Tale of Two Cities: Housing Policy and Gentrification in London and New York," *Journal of Urban Affairs* 15, 4 (1993): 345–66.

95. Our gratitude goes to Bill Peterman for this observation.

96. Anthony Downs, *New Visions for Metropolitan America* (Washington, DC: Brookings Institution, 1994), pp. 45–59.

97. John D. Kasarda, "Urban Change and Minority Opportunities," in *The New Urban Reality*, ed. Paul E. Peterson (Washington, DC: Brookings Institution, 1985), pp. 33–68. Also see Richard V. Knight, "Knowledge and the Advanced Industrial Metropolis," in *The Future of Winter Cities*, ed. Gary Gappert, *Urban Affairs Annual Review*, vol. 31 (Newbury Park, CA: Sage Publications, 1987), pp. 196–208. A city can also use the arts to build its "amenity infrastructure" and thereby attract high-tech industries; see Williams S. Hendon and Douglas V. Shaw, "The Arts and Urban Development," in *The Future of Winter Cities*, pp. 209–17.

3

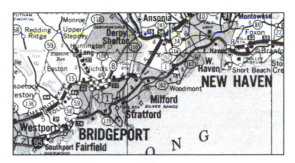

Who Has the Power? Decision Making and Urban Regimes

"Who has the power in local government?" This question is significant because it enables us to look behind the formal structures of local government and discern the roles of less visible political actors. We can ascertain if there are people and organizations behind the scenes who play an important role in the decision-making process.

Furthermore, an understanding of the decision-making process in local government can tell us how democratic or fair the city is in allocating its resources. If the political process appears to respond to a small number of influential business executives representing the corporate elite, then it is a relatively closed political system responding to the few. If, on the other hand, the system appears to be open and responsive to a range of diverse interests, then it is considered more democratic.

As we shall see, the question of "who holds the powers?" is a hotly debated topic in the field of urban politics. There is no agreement among academicians as to who has the power to get what they want in the local arena.

THE SOCIOLOGIST'S APPROACH:
THE DISCOVERY OF A POWER ELITE

After decades of field research, sociologists found that in the cities they studied, business elites controlled the decision-making process. In the late 1920s and early 1930s, two Columbia University sociologists, Helen and Robert Lynd, published their pioneering studies in the field of urban decision making. Their books, *Middletown* and *Middletown in Transition*, were the result of several years of field research in Muncie, Indiana.[1] By the time *Middletown in Transition* was published, it was clear from the Lynds' research that Middletown was controlled, in all important respects, by the "X Family." A business elite ran the community, and the X Family dominated that elite.

The Lynds' work inspired a new interest in power studies, not just in the power structures of local communities but also in the power structure of the nation as a whole. Over the years numerous power structure studies were undertaken. The possibility that the entire nation might be ruled by a *power elite* was advanced by researchers such as C. Wright Mills and G. William Domhoff.[2]

One of the most influential studies to arrive at elitist conclusions has unquestionably been *Community Power Structure*, Floyd Hunter's famous analysis of decision makers in Atlanta.[3] Published in 1953, the Hunter investigation has served as the archetype for a whole school of community power studies. Because of the overriding importance of Hunter's study of "Regional City" (Hunter's pseudonym for Atlanta), its main findings warrant summarization.

Hunter's first task was to find out who in Atlanta held power. In order to pursue this question, he employed the **reputational approach**. Hunter interviewed persons in prominent positions in four groups assumed to have power connections. These groups were business, government, civic associations, and "society." The leaders of these groups then provided Hunter with lists of persons presumed to have power in community affairs. Hunter then used a system of "judges" and self-selection to determine leadership rank; some forty persons in the top levels of power were identified from more than 175 names. Eleven of these top forty influentials were directly associated with the activities of large commercial enterprises. Seven more were in banking and investment.

These top leaders tend to have expensive offices, frequent similar social clubs, and reside in the best residential districts of the city. These persons are dominant economically and influential politically when they want to be. These leaders are apprehensive of social change. They accept the reports of planning experts but make sure that the reports gather dust in agency files. In short, the recommended programs are stopped before any implementation can be undertaken. On the most important issues, the policymakers are united, and this is a reason for their collective strength.

Hunter's overall conclusion is clear and unequivocal; Atlanta is a city dominated by a private business elite. It is a conclusion that he essentially reaffirms in his "revisit" to Atlanta published in 1980.[4]

Hunter's work triggered scores of decision-making studies by sociologists over the next few years. These studies of local government were remarkably similar in their methodology and findings. Using a reputational approach—asking people to identify who they think are the most important decision makers—they have almost without exception found an elitist governing structure heavily populated by prominent business executives. This pyramidal power structure is often referred to as the **power elite**.

A POLITICAL SCIENCE APPROACH:
THE DISCOVERY OF PLURALISM

The elitist model of local government has been challenged by a school of political scientists, who have charged that power is not as concentrated, nor decision making as closed, as the sociologists concluded. These political scientists attack the elitist theorists for an ideological blindness that predetermines their findings. These political scientists also attack the elitist studies for producing faulty conclusions as a result of faulty methodology.[5]

Nelson Polsby, for instance, sees more conflict in Middletown than the Lynds admit in their conclusions. Polsby further scores the Lynds for advancing nondisconfirmable propositions; whenever evidence is raised that the city's elite failed to get its way, the Lynds dismiss the issue in question as not important to the elite. Polsby also attacks Hunter for asking questions that presuppose the existence of an elite and for ignoring evidence that shows that Atlanta's decision makers were constrained in their operations. Polsby sees more heterogeneity and differences of opinion among Atlanta's top-identified decision makers than Hunter admits.[6]

More generally, the sociologists were attacked for confusing reputation with reality. By asking local experts to identify individuals they consider to be persons of power, the sociologists uncovered only those who in a community had the reputation for being powerful, not those who definitely exercised control over a city's affairs. Reputations could be based on misinformation and local mythology; those with the reputation for power might not possess anywhere near as much influence as the common wisdom attributes to them. According to Polsby and others in the school of thought that came to be known as *pluralism*, research based solely on reputations is insufficient to the task of studying community power. Instead, researchers must focus on behavior; they must investigate the making of important decisions in a community and document who in reality influences those decisions.

Of the many decision-making studies that have employed a behavioral methodology and come to a pluralist conclusion, *Who Governs?*, Robert Dahl's 1960 study of New Haven, Connecticut, has been the most influential.[7] Dahl begins by noting that in any American democratic political system—including that of New Haven—wealth, social position, and other political resources are unequally distributed. Yet to observe that people do not equally share power is not necessarily to imply that a power elite rules a community; it is only the beginning from which to study the distribution of power in a community.

Is power in a community concentrated in one set of hands? Or are different power resources dispersed among different sets of hands? As Dahl phrases it, it is necessary to discover whether "inequalities in resources of influence" are "'cumulative' or 'noncumulative'":

That is, are people who are better off in one resource also better off in others? In other words, does the way in which political resources are distributed encourage oligarchy or pluralism?[8]

According to Dahl, power inequalities were cumulative in New Haven society prior to industrialization; preindustrial New Haven was ruled by a closed elite set of **economic notables**. But industrialization and immigration acted to disperse wealth and voting power. New business entrepreneurs gained money; the immigrants possessed numbers, which was an important resource at the ballot box. As a result, New Haven was transformed from a system of elite domination to a system under which power resources were quite a bit more widely shared, albeit still unequally. **Pluralism** denotes this latter situation where many groups possess effective power resources.

Dahl studies the making of decisions in three key issue-areas: political nominations, urban redevelopment, and public education. Dahl observes that only a small number of persons or leaders have **direct influence** "in the sense that they successfully initiate or veto proposals for policies."[9] Such a finding might seem to indicate that New Haven was still ruled by an elite few. But Dahl finds that the larger citizenry, while refraining from direct political involvement, still retains considerable **indirect influence** as a result of democratic norms and the elections process.[10] As decisions in each of the three key issue-areas require the assent of local government officials and officials who pursue unpopular courses of action can be denied reelection, elections are a particularly potent weapon in ensuring that decision makers anticipate the public's concerns.

Dahl also finds that power is not concentrated in the hands of one small elite group. Instead, there is a **specialization of influence** under which different groups of leaders dominate decision making in different issue-areas. Of the fifty persons identified as leaders in the three issue-areas, only three "initiated or vetoed policies in more than one issue-area."[11] These were the two mayors, William Celantano and Richard Lee, and the redevelopment director, Edward Logue—public officials all subject to the indirect influence that voters possess. Leaders and subleaders did *not* come from a single homogeneous stratum of the community. On the contrary, they manifested considerable ethnic, religious, and economic diversity. Once again, Dahl finds no private business elite ruling New Haven.

Dahl also finds that all citizens possess some political resources. Usually citizens find politics unrewarding and choose not to use their power resources, letting these resources lie "slack" or idle. When threatened, however, these citizens can pull in these slack resources and exert influence on political leaders. Dahl cites a case of the developer who tried to construct metal frame houses that residents felt would be incompatible with the character of their neighborhood. Residents pulled in their previously slack resources and mobilized. As a result, the city halted construction of the controversial project.[12]

These findings add up to a rejection of the Hunter elitist thesis. No overt or covert elite of economic notables managed New Haven's affairs. Power was found to be located not in one small group but instead in several specialized groups. Different persons concerned with different issues were active in different issue areas. The citizenry itself possessed considerable influence as a result of its numbers at the ballot box and its ability to pull in slack resources. The result is a system of power unequally, but widely, shared—a system Dahl calls **pluralistic democracy**.[13]

THE ANTI-PLURALISTS AND THE NONDECISION CRITIQUE

Political science studies using the decision-making approach have repeatedly found that power in cities is pluralistic. Yet not all power analysts accept the methodology and conclusions of the pluralists. These analysts attack the pluralists for failing to prove that the public possesses sufficient indirect influence to constrain decision makers. These critics further charge that the pluralist method of studying only actual behavior ignores what cannot be easily seen; elites are not so dumb as to apply their pressure in full public view.

Critics of pluralism charge that effective power is not as widely shared or dispersed as the pluralists' theory asserts. Michael Lipsky, for instance, found that protests produced only the most marginal benefits for the poor. Protest leaders could not sustain their protest organizations or attract media attention for a prolonged period of time. The targets of protest action also possessed various means to deflect protest actions. These targets could dispense highly symbolic pronouncements as to what changes would be undertaken. But seldom were broad-scale changes ever implemented. In the end, protest did very little to change the real living conditions of the poor. Lipsky doubts that the poor, even when organized, are "effectively heard," as the pluralists insist.[14]

Michael Parenti reports similar conclusions from his study of Newark, New Jersey, when that city was still governed by white ethnic politicians. Citizens in a black ward, for instance, pulled in their slack resources in classic pluralist fashion to demand the installation of a new traffic light. Despite years of protests and the accumulation of hundreds of signatures, their efforts secured nothing. In a nearby white ward, however, residents were able to secure such a light in less than a month with fewer than fifty signatures.[15] For Parenti as well as for Lipsky, pluralism does not accurately portray the relative powerlessness of the poor. The poor are excluded from the pluralist interplay.

Pluralist theorists respond that while power is spread unevenly in American society, no group, not even the minority poor, is totally excluded. The election of black mayors, the increased number of minority appointments, and the advancement of black issue-concerns in both Newark and New York City all point to the power possessed even by the urban poor. No group gets everything that it demands in politics; yet, according to the pluralists, even the minority poor are heard.

The debate between the pluralists and elite theorists goes on and on.[16] The elite theorists do not even accept Dahl's conclusion as to the pluralistic nature of power in New Haven. In a more recent study, Domhoff has reexamined Dahl's old data and uncovered additional material that was unavailable to Dahl. According to Domhoff, Dahl was "factually wrong" in understating the power of both Yale University and the city's business institutions on the key redevelopment issue[17]:

> But whether we look at the origins of the local urban renewal program (in the Chamber of Commerce and Yale) or its eventual outcome (land for the expansion of Yale, the hospital, and the downtown business community), we must conclude, contrary to *Who Governs?*, that there is a power structure in New Haven, with Yale, the First New Haven National Bank and the Chamber of Commerce at its heart....[18]

Domhoff and others charge Dahl with having failed to detect the behind-the-scenes manipulations by the business community and the anticipation of business leaders' needs by public officials.[19]

More critical still are the criticisms made of the pluralists' insistence on studying only observable behavior in the making of key decisions in a community. This methodology, according to pluralism's critics, reveals only one "face" of power. Yes, power is exercised in the making of a decision. But power can also be exercised in a way that is not so easily observed if an elite can act to keep an issue from developing to the point that a decision must be made—that is, to use a very awkward phrase, if an issue can be kept among the ranks of a **nonissue** or **nondecision**. The pluralist method of focusing only on the making of decisions would miss this "other face" of power—the ability to keep an issue from developing on the urban agenda.[20]

Matthew Crenson has discovered that a corporation's reputation for power may be enough to suppress the development of certain issues in a community. Crenson has reported that Gary, Indiana, was relatively late in implementing air pollution controls because of the city's fear of offending U.S. Steel, the city's major employer. Yet, according to Crenson, had pluralists studied Gary, they would not have found any overt evidence of U.S. Steel's role, since the giant corporation did not actively or publicly lobby the mayor or the council. The point is that U.S. Steel did not have to engage in overt political activity. U.S. Steel's reluctance to install costly air pollution devices in the Gary mills was common knowledge. It was also common knowledge that should stringent regulations be imposed on U.S. Steel, the corporation had the ability to cut back production and employment in Gary by shifting operations to more modern plants located in other cities. According to Crenson, U.S. Steel was an "offstage influential" that did not have to exert a great deal of pressure publicly.[21] The presumption of U.S. Steel's power was sufficient to delay the imposition of strong air pollution controls.

The pluralists reject this nondecision critique.[22] For the pluralists, the nonappearance of a potential issue on the public agenda might simply mean that the public did not care deeply about the matter. Yet Crenson's study of the slow growth of air pollution controls in Gary shows that though it may be quite difficult, it is not necessarily impossible to document the existence of a nondecision.

SUNBELT CITIES: ELITE DOMINANCE AND RECENT TRENDS

Of course, no one power structure perspective can capably describe the distribution of power in all cities. One city differs from another. While one may be pluralist in makeup, another may be governed by a power elite. Hunter's finding that Atlanta was governed by a power elite does not necessarily imply that all American cities are governed by elites.

Yet Hunter's picture of private elite dominance may be generally applicable to the political styles of Sunbelt communities. One historian has observed that the "commercial-civic elite" has been the most influential group in the southern city, though the elite "did not preside over a monolithic community power structure."[23] This conclusion is reinforced by Peter Lupsha and William Siembieda, who observe, "A traditional aspect of politics in the Sunbelt has always been the close relationship between the private economic community and the public decision-making community."[24]

Nowhere has this close intermingling between the private and public sectors been as strong as in Houston. In Houston, the penetration of government by local business elites was so considerable that the borderline between business and government was no longer clearly discernible:

> As Houston grew during the 1950s and 1960s, the growth coalition held sway over local government. Oscar Holcombe, a land dealer and developer, was mayor for 22 of the years between 1921 and 1957. In 1981, the mayor was a developer; one-third of the city council was in real estate or closely related fields, and the planning commission was composed mostly of developers, builders, and others tied to the real estate industry field.[25]

The result in Houston was that the city invested considerable sums into the capital outlays demanded by business; also in response to business concern, tax rates and social services were kept at low levels. But Houston was not unique. Similarly strong business-government relationships could be found in the Citizen's Charter Association in Dallas, the Good Government League in San Antonio, the Phoenix 40, and Albuquerque, Memphis, Miami, Tucson, and New Orleans.[26]

The South's traditionalistic culture was not the only factor that helped produce this deference to established elites.[27] Elite dominance was also a product of the unique history of cities in the region. Unlike cities in the North where political machines dispensed specific benefits to gain the votes of larger numbers of immigrants and their families,

> Political organization in the Sunbelt cities has never been designed to accommodate mass demands or create services. It was designed to function as an adjunct to the business and economic community providing a mechanism for accommodating growth and development.[28]

Yet the power of business elites in Sunbelt cities has varied over time. The dominance of local commercial-civic elites and their brand of "business progressivism" was virtually unquestioned until the Depression of the 1930s.[29] But after World War II, returning veterans sought a new brand of civic-mindedness in local affairs; in the 1960s and 1970s, racial minorities and homeowner and environmentalist groups all presented further challenges to local elite dominance.

In San Antonio, for instance, the growth of that city's Chicano community has challenged the hold of the traditional governing elite.[30] Similarly in Houston, the growth in minority voting power has led to the election of mayors more willing to seek federal aid for job training and other people-oriented programs.[31]

Social change has even made contemporary Atlanta somewhat different from the business elite–dominated city of Hunter's Regional City:

> As Atlanta has grown from regional city to national metropolis its politics have also gone through two stages. From World War II to 1970 the white business power structure dominated. Since that time political and economic power have become separate entities, and the old forces increasingly have had to share influence with blacks, neighborhood groups, and the suburbs.[32]

The 1970s and 1980s saw the election of two black mayors, Maynard Jackson and Andrew Young:

> Much of the white business community resented Jackson's non-deferential, some would say abrasive, style. They charged him with reverse discrimination in his contracting and hiring practices, but the mayor rejoined that he was only giving minorities the just due that previous administrations (despite their progressive images) had denied them.[33]

Young attempted to pursue a course of economic development that entailed the building of bridges to his city's business community without sacrificing the concerns of the city's minority voters who helped elect him. Black electoral power altered the power structure in Atlanta. Yet, as we shall later discuss, downtown business interests maintained a privileged position in the governance of Atlanta despite the emergence of a black electoral majority.

The rapid growth of many Sunbelt communities brought with it new challengers to the traditional local power structures. As Philip J. Trounstine and Terry Christenson observe, "As cities grow, they diversify; elites can't command all the community's organizations; competition and pluralism increase."[34] In San Jose, for instance, the 1970s saw a coalition of homeowners and environmentalists confront that city's growth-oriented business elite as a result of traffic congestion, over-crowding, and the other obvious problems brought about by growth.[35]

Taxpayer associations, neighborhood and minority groups, and environmentalist organizations have all helped to make power in Sunbelt cities more pluralistic. Still, private power continues to exert great influence in these communities. Evidence from San Jose and Tampa serves as a case in point. Despite the pluralization of politics in San Jose, the names of private businessleaders and professionals still dominate any listing of community influentials. The increased cost of local election campaigns gives new prominence to big money contributors. The older locally rooted business elite no longer rules; but the decisions made by executives of national corporations who have sited facilities in the San Jose area are just as vital to the health of the city as were any of the decisions made by the older elite.[36] Similarly in Tampa, progressive Mayor Sandy Freedman, who was committed to affordable housing and nondiscrimination issues, was also obliged to support the construction of a convention center and the continued award of tax subsidies for development in Tampa's central business district.[37]

Recent studies of Florida cities confirm the pluralization of local politics in the Sunbelt. While growth interests continue to be extremely important, Sunbelt cities are not universally dominated by a cohesive elite that dictate policy. Instead, there is a range of municipal responses to growth pressures. In Orlando, city officials placed relatively strong design standards on new development. They also used development as a source of revenues for low- and moderate-income housing. In Fort Lauderdale, in contrast, development was pretty much allowed to pro-ceed on the private sector's terms. As a result, the construction of the Riverwalk esplanade, a new performing arts center, and other down-town facilities did little to help the city's low-income residents.[38] But even in Fort Lauderdale, there is no power elite. Instead, the situation is one more of "hyperpluralism," where rapid growth has overwhelmed city leaders and business interests are fragmented and disorganized. Busi-ness leaders have even met in an attempt to enhance their influence as they have complained that the city and county have been insufficiently responsive to growth needs.[39]

Downtown-led growth coalitions in the Sunbelt have faced new challenges from homeowners upset at increased congestion and the costs of servicing new development. In St. Petersburg, Florida, city voters have begun to question a downtown development strategy. The Suncoast

Dome failed to attract a major league baseball team and necessitated continued subsidies. Pier Park, a waterfront aquarium and marketplace similar to Baltimore's Harbor Place, was built despite its overwhelming defeat in a public referendum. The mammoth Bay Plaza development failed to attract shops, restaurants, offices, and other up-scale tenants. Voters, frustrated with the sums of money poured into these projects while neighborhood needs were ignored, finally elected a new mayor and council that proceeded to fire the city manager, indicating a reversal in the city's policies.[40]

Similarly, voters in suburban Tampa (Hillsborough County), upset by the prospect of having to pay still more taxes and fees to support growth, in 1990 elected new county commissioners who promised to reverse the promotional practices of the previous board. Suburban communities nationwide have begun to oppose growth projects because the fiscal payoffs of those projects have diminished over time, and such costs as increased traffic congestion have clearly emerged.[41]

ECONOMIC POWER AND "CITY LIMITS"

An examination of power in Sunbelt cities shows that neither elitist nor pluralist theory fully captures the distribution of influence in contemporary urban America. As a result, urban theorists have tried to get around the polarization of the elitism-pluralism debate. Elitism points to the influence that business leaders possess in certain policy areas, but it overstates business influence in other areas. Pluralism, on the other hand, fails to capture the degree of constraint that business does impose on economic decisions and other aspects of city affairs.

Paul Peterson, in his important work *City Limits*,[42] has attempted to paint a more complex portrait of urban power that points to the extensive influence that the business community possesses over a large range of city affairs. According to Peterson, municipal officials tend to give business leaders what they want even where the local business community does not comprise a vigilant, local elite. The **mobility of capital** gives the private sector its influence. The owners of a business can simply threaten to locate their facilities in another town or state; cities cannot afford the risk to their job and tax bases. Hence, whenever an important local decision has an impact on a particular development project or the city's business climate, municipal officials are reduced to anticipating what business wants. It is almost as if politics within the city does not matter; the city as a whole is led to act as if it had a **unitary interest** in pursuing continued economic development.

But business does not possess such influence in all aspects of city affairs. Peterson sees three types of city policies—developmental, redistributive, and allocation—only two of which business influence is felt. When it comes to **developmental policies** that can enhance the economic position of the city, governmental officials are led to anticipate business needs. In the second policy arena, **redistributive policies**, no city can afford to undertake a course of action designed primarily to serve the city's more disadvantaged residents. Should a city try to finance too much in the way of neighborhood projects, subsidized housing, or social services, it would be forced to raise taxes, reducing its competitiveness as an attractive site for commerce and industry:

> [T]he pursuit of a city's economic interests, which requires an efficient provision of local services, makes no allowance for the care of the needy and unfortunate members of the society. Indeed, the competition among local communities all but precludes a concern for redistribution.[43]

According to Peterson, city politics is quite different from national politics. The nation may decide on redistributive policy, but no city can jeopardize its business climate by raising taxes to support redistributive services.

But, as Peterson notes, not all issues in the local arena have a bearing on a city's competitive position or business climate. There are issues that are neutral in their economic effects. Business has no direct concern over these **allocation policies** which deal, for instance, with how municipal services such as library books and fire stations are distributed throughout the city. In this arena, cities do not need to follow the dictates of business. Instead, cities can allocate these services in response to a pluralist interest group struggle.

For Peterson, New York City's mid-1970s fiscal crisis only underscores the consequences that result if a municipality ignores "city limits" and attempts to initiate broad social welfare policy. New York was soon forced to scale back services. In the late 1970s and early 1980s, Mayor Ed Koch cut social services and instead concentrated on policies designed to promote economic investment in the city.[44] As a result, Koch's critics charged that the mayor catered too much to the needs of corporate investors and paid too little attention to affordable housing and programs for the poor.

Peterson's view of the limits of city politics has proven quite controversial.[45] His critics charge that cities are not universally reduced to acting as the agents of big corporations. Cities do not always favor local developmental policy over redistributive actions designed to serve low-income people and neighborhoods. There is no simple economic determinism as a city is led to anticipate business' needs. Instead, local politics remains important.

Certainly Peterson's assertion that "policies of benefit to the city contribute to the prosperity of all residents"[46] is overstated. The maximization of land values works to the benefit of the owners of land; neighborhood residents, in contrast, have a continued interest in fighting development projects that would displace them from their homes or destroy their neighborhoods.[47]

Even a city's business community is not unified in favor of new economic development. While businesses in the central city may benefit from new downtown growth projects, those in other sections of the community may find that they are paying higher taxes to support downtown growth. In Kalamazoo, Michigan, for instance, plans for center city revitalization stalled when the "larger community of business firms" objected to the costs entailed by higher taxes and the rerouting of traffic.[48]

Evidently, city politics is not so "groupless" or consensual as portrayed by Peterson's unitary interest theory. In many cities, community and neighborhood groups are active and oppose unabated development.[49] Should these forces prove powerful, it is in the political interest of elected officials to oppose, not support, new economic development projects. As political scientist Todd Swanstrom observes, the "political logic" may contradict the "economic logic" in a community.[50] This is especially true if the economic logic is much weaker than Peterson makes it out to be. Locally imposed taxes and regulations do not have nearly as much influence on the siting decisions by business as is commonly assumed.[51] Cities can often support housing and redistributive actions without risking an exodus of business.

The "economic logic" of Peterson's argument may also be flawed, as cities have obligations other than merely the pursuit of businesslike efficiency. Cities must maintain social order, which they can do only by promoting social justice and by working in accordance with norms of fairness. Peterson's insistence that cities pursue economic efficiency may impede their ability to perform this other, but quite critical, function of local government.[52]

Robert Waste charges that Peterson unfairly sees only three types of city policies when there are in fact many more. According to Waste, cities possess more autonomous power than Peterson suggests, as there is a wide range of city policy actions that do not affect development. Further, Peterson ignores the role of city leadership in defining and promoting political issues. A policy issue cannot always simply be fixed as "redistributive" or "developmental"; it often has dimensions of both. Is increased spending on education impermissible under Peterson's framework because it is a redistributive social welfare program? A creative mayor or policy entrepreneur can reframe or sell redistributive spending as aiding local economic development. Spending on education can be sold as a developmental policy that is necessary if the city is to have a quality labor force capable of attracting business in the future.[53] Day care programs, too, are not simply redistributive spending initiatives that require higher taxes imposed on business. Subsidized day care can also be portrayed as a developmental program that allows low-income mothers to work, thereby increasing the availability of low-cost labor in a community.[54]

Despite these criticisms, Peterson's theory remains important as it points to an extremely strong tendency in city affairs: Cities will tend to cater to the needs of the business community (and of tax-paying upper- and upper-middle income residents as well). City officials do exhibit a preference in spending for development projects as opposed to projects for other purposes.[55] However, development projects are more contro- versial than Peterson's notion of a unitary city interest may suggest. Neigh- borhood groups and more parochial businesses may even kill a particular development project. But the long-term bias of cities toward economic growth and developer interests cannot be denied.

SYSTEMIC POWER AND REGIME THEORY

Instead of trying to determine whether power structures in cities are generally elitist or pluralist, Clarence Stone asks a more important ques- tion: "Why, when all of their actions are taken into account, do officials over the long haul seem to favor upper-strata interests, disfavor lower- strata interests, and sometimes act in apparent disregard of the contours of electoral power?"[56]

Unlike Peterson, Stone does not feel that raw economic determinism universally draws a city to elite-driven economic projects. For Stone, the answer is that upper-strata interests control a disproportionate share of the resources that city decision makers value. As private powers decide where investments will be made, they often possess the ability to deter- mine the success or failure of a particular undertaking desired by city officials. While business leaders cannot command action from the city, they can often frustrate projects they dislike. And while city officials can resist the wishes of business leaders, they soon learn the importance of working with private interests.

Upper-strata private actors also possess the ability to confer honors and rewards for professional and career accomplishment. They can even bestow a sense of importance and grandeur on hard-pressed city officials. City officials often find themselves drawn to "power lunches" and dis- cussions of grandiose downtown development projects; less glamorous and more difficult proposals for neighborhood improvement and ghetto reclamation offer no equivalent sense of excitement and recognition.

For Stone, *power* is the ability to get things done. Private actors often control key resources that city officials need to govern successfully. As a result, they often occupy a privileged position in any **regime** or informal public-private governing arrangement for the city. In some cities, business cooperation is so crucial to the success of public projects that the busi- ness community can be seen to possess **preemptive power**; it can pro- tect its privileged position by parceling out selective benefits to political actors who chose to "go along."[57]

Regime theory points to the difficulties that political, community, and business leaders face in attempting to forge and sustain a govern- ing coalition. Regime theory also points to the difference between an

electoral coalition and a **governing coalition**. During the election, a mayoral candidate courts whoever's votes or support are needed for victory. But election does not guarantee the ability to govern or get important things done. Once in office, the mayor must build a new working, governing alliance. Oftentimes, he or she must seek cooperation from actors who were not participants in his or her election campaign. The mayor must woo whomever has the resources necessary for governance. The concept of a **regime** refers to the relatively durable alliances that can emerge among elected officials, their supporters, development interests, property owners, and professional bureaucrats in the day-to-day running of a city.

Regime Politics in Atlanta

Clarence Stone's study of the governance of Atlanta points to the importance of looking beyond elections and studying power in a city when attempts at governing begin. Atlanta has been traditionally governed by a downtown business elite that responded to change by forging a working coalition with middle-class black allies. There was nothing inevitable about the emergence of this corporate-oriented regime in Atlanta. It was the result of the strategic decisions of the white business community.

Atlanta's growing black population coupled with the suburban exodus of the white population all but assured an eventual black victory at the polls. Maynard Jackson (1973) and Andrew Young (1981) were the first two African-Americans elected mayor. Both, however, soon learned the value of working with the downtown business community—which was able to continue to exert its influence despite the emergence of black electoral power.[58]

Maynard Jackson was a political outsider who challenged Atlanta's traditional system of elite-led accommodation. He sought to make Atlanta more racially inclusive. Initially, he attempted to reshape the planning process to allow neighborhoods a veto over growth projects backed by the downtown elite. He insisted on strong affirmative action policies, awarding 20 percent of contracts on development projects to minority firms. He also sought to reform the police department. But major initiatives could seldom be realized without business support, and Jackson soon recognized the need for business cooperation if he was going to be able to complete a number of his desired projects. As a result, he eventually worked out a series of accommodations with the city's business elite, cutting back his support of the neighborhood planning system and giving business leaders greater access to city hall. Business leaders regarded Jackson as impertinent, but realized that they, too, needed to forge a cooperative working relationship with a city government that controlled resources critical to the health of their downtown establishments. As a result, a new reconciliation was reached. The city's traditional governing coalition was reconstituted, but on altered terms.

City business leaders found it more comfortable working with Jackson's successor, Andrew Young, who recognized that the support of neighborhood groups was insufficient to ensure the completion of new projects. Young sought the cooperation of business leaders in building a new Atlanta that would provide increased opportunities for its black citizens. A weakened neighborhood movement lay outside a city governing coalition of middle-class black leaders and white business interests who pursued unabated economic growth combined with new opportunities for minority businesses.

The tensions between Atlanta's neighborhood movement and the city's business elite and black middle-class growth coalition have persisted over time. For example, neighborhood leaders protested the city's plans to demolish houses and small businesses in a low-income part of the city in order to clear the site for a park that will serve as a gathering area for visitors to the 1996 Olympics, hosted by Atlanta.[59]

There is no unified governing elite in Atlanta with absolute power. Yet, despite the growth of black electoral power, business has emerged as a partner in the city's governing coalition. The different partners in Atlanta's governing regime have different goals, and business can be defeated. Yet, business concerns in Atlanta are usually taken into account.

Different Regime Types

While the business community controls key resources and hence occupies a privileged position in city affairs, there is no guarantee that a business-oriented regime will emerge in any particular city. In New York, a city that is substantially bigger and more diverse than Atlanta, the business community is less cohesive and enjoys a less dominant position in local affairs than the business community enjoys in Atlanta. In New York, the mayor, public sector officials, and other political groups offer a stronger counterweight to corporate elites.[60]

Different regimes or informal governing alliances have emerged at different times and in different cities. While a great many cities have corporate-oriented governing regimes, others do not. Other cities lack a governing regime because no stable, governing alliance has emerged.

Clarence Stone has identified three different types of regimes in the governing of cities.[61] A **corporate regime** (also called a **development regime**) promotes the interests of major downtown corporations. Equity concerns are slighted. A **caretaker regime** (also referred to as a **maintenance regime**), in contrast, will often fail to initiate large-scale development projects. In a caretaker city, government focuses on the provision of routine services as the small business community and homeowners alike both fear raising taxes and the disruption of established patterns of social interaction. The rarest regime type of all is the **progressive regime**, where a city responds to the demands of lower- and middle-class citizens and environmentalist groups in challenging growth.

In fact, there may be two variants of the progressive regime. A **middle-class progressive regime** that responds to the concerns of environmentalists and homeowners may be seen as progressive in its priorities as compared to the downtown growth coalition. But its policies will be quite different from those of a city with a **regime devoted to lower-class opportunity expansion** that seeks policies designed to aid the position of the poor and racial minorities. Harold Washington's relatively brief mayoralty in Chicago represents just such a lower-class progressive coalition. As we shall see, in San Francisco an incipient progressive regime of homeowners and environmentalists challenged high-rise office construction. But these activists failed to initiate policies that would provide new job opportunities and affordable housing for blue-collar workers and the poor.[62]

THE DEBATE OVER CITY POWER: THREE CASE STUDIES

The study of community power is an inexact science. Different urban observers have come to different conclusions in answering the questions: Who holds the power in city politics? and Exactly what influence does the business community enjoy in city affairs? A look at three different case studies will show how different urban analysts can come to different conclusions.

NEW YORK CITY: FISCAL CRISIS AND REBOUND

New York City's politics has almost always been described in terms of pluralist group interaction. Douglas Yates has even used the term **street-fighting pluralism** to denote the intensity of competition among various neighborhood and institutional groups in the city.[63] In fact, this pluralist competition can help to explain why New York went to the brink of default in 1975; at the same time that the city was losing much of its tax base to both the suburbs and the Sunbelt, New York mayors simply spent more to accommodate the demands of municipal labor unions, service providers, and neighborhood groups in order to gain their political support.

Yet this pluralist view of the roots of New York City's fiscal crisis ignores the role played by local and national financial elites in helping to bring about that crisis. New York's banks and other financial institutions encouraged, and profited from, continued borrowing by the city. The banks continued to lend money to the city until changes in the tax code and new investment opportunities made new write-offs more profitable than municipal bonds.[64]

It was the action of the banks themselves that directly precipitated the fiscal crisis. When credit to New York City began to appear overextended, the banks began to "dump" their portfolios of New York City bonds. Such a move signalled a lack of faith by the financial community in the creditworthiness of New York. Following the lead of the banks, no other actors were willing to extend New York the credit the city needed to pay off past debts that had become due and to provide the necessary funds to continue operations:

> So long as dealing in New York municipal securities had been a high-profit, low-risk venture for the city's banks, they had been quite happy to participate without asking too many embarrassing questions of city officials. But when the 11 major New York banks realized in the spring of 1975 that the outside world would shortly be able to figure out what the municipal government had been doing, they unloaded $2.7 billion in New York City securities that they owned. With the banks' flooding the market with old New York bonds at the same time the city was seeking to sell additional hundreds of millions in new municipal notes and bonds, the market in the city's securities collapsed.[65]

As New York journalists Jack Newfield and Paul DuBrul point out, "[I]t was the banks themselves that had overloaded the market."[66]

Despite their culpability in extending New York credit and in precipitating the crisis, financial elites in New York were still able to protect their interests and even enhance their power as a result of the crisis. Fifty-six thousand municipal workers lost jobs, and a wage freeze was imposed on public service workers as unions lost bargaining clout.[67] As fiscal crisis analyst Martin Shefter has affirmed, it was

> programs with predominantly black clienteles—youth services, addiction services, compensatory higher education—which have suffered disproportionately severe budget and personnel cutbacks. Moreover, personnel have been fired in disproportionate numbers from job categories—clerical, paraprofessional, and maintenance—heavily staffed by blacks and Puerto Ricans.[68]

In contrast, financial elites who willingly incurred risk when they lent the city money for profit were made to suffer virtually no penalty at all; they were repaid by the city every cent they were owed.

The creation of new institutions for the monitoring of the city's financial affairs, first the Municipal Assistance Corporation (known popularly as *Big MAC*), and later the Emergency Fiscal Control Board, further gave the city's financial community new influence over the city's taxing, spending, and development programs. The business community was able to gain such concessions as increased tax abatements, the revocation of the stock transfer tax, the offering of tax subsidies for gentrification, and the capital financing of economic development projects such as the new Convention Center.[69]

[handwritten margin note: RENOVATING OLD BLDGS. ETC. ?]

The fiscal crisis led city officials to pursue economic development with little regard for the social purposes of a project. Multimillionaire developer Donald Trump was given an estimated tax break of $120 million to convert the failing Commodore Hotel into the Grand Hyatt Hotel. He was given another $100 million in tax breaks to build the luxury condominiums of Trump Tower on Fifth Avenue.[70] Yet it is too simplistic to maintain that Trump dictated to city officials. The city denied Trump permission and development assistance to build what would have been the world's tallest skyscraper, the proposed 150-story Television City. Community groups had objected that such a structure would cast a shadow across Central Park and would bring too much congestion and automobile traffic to surrounding neighborhoods.

The influence of New York's business community increased and the power of municipal unions and minorities declined as a result of the fiscal crisis. Yet, this does not mean that a cohesive business elite ran New York City's affairs in the postfiscal crisis era. While the Emergency Fiscal Control Board (later just known as the Fiscal Control Board) dealt with the big budgetary numbers and set overall priorities, city officials still had the power to decide exactly what programs were funded and what combination of incentives were given each project. The bankers and developers were even defeated on numerous issues. As political scientist Robert Bailey reminds us, "[W]hile private economic influence was greatly enhanced, it was not omnipotent."[71] Also, in the midst of the economic boom that followed the fiscal crisis, the city regained autonomy.

From 1977 to 1989, New York City enjoyed a tremendous economic resurgence, gaining 150,000 jobs, almost 15 percent of its work force.[72] New York had transformed itself economically and politically. The industrial and port jobs the city lost to automation, to the suburbs, to the Sunbelt, and to overseas competitors were never recaptured. Instead, New York rebuilt its computer and telecommunications infrastructure and became an international headquarters city, a center of global finance and banking. However, side by side with New York's growing fortune was a new inequality; newer immigrant groups and a female-dominated clerical work force did not share fully in the prosperity enjoyed by those who held well-paid managerial and professional jobs.[73]

But it is too simple to portray business elites as having dictated the transformation of New York City. The business community—diverse, fragmented, and divided—lacked such extensive power. Instead, it was a political official, Mayor Ed Koch, who put together a dominant governing coalition, fusing business needs with those of the city's remaining conservative Italian and middle-class Jewish voters (and some of the more conservative elements in the black and Hispanic communities as well). Koch juggled this quite delicate coalition, often favoring business investment while at times raising taxes on business and opposing projects supported by the business community in order to appease his white ethnic voting base. Koch gave developers extensive financial support, tax exemptions, loans, grants, and zoning bonuses that allowed new buildings to exceed the local zoning code. Business influence was important but not dictatorial in New York; politics and public officials, too, counted.[74]

Koch served three 4-year terms as mayor. But in 1989, voters tired of Koch's more extreme public statements and elected the city's first African-American mayor, David Dinkins. Dinkins was elected by a multiracial coalition of blacks, Latinos, and liberal whites, especially Jews.[75]

Dinkins was a much different sort of mayor than Koch. Nonetheless, he was fiscally conservative and he faced new budget problems as a result of a new fiscal crisis precipitated by a real-estate slump and the inability of the city to contain the costs of servicing its large impoverished population.[76] Dinkins also did not attempt to cultivate community organizations as an independent political force in the city. As mayor he was unable to establish a progressive regime capable of governing the city.[77] His failure to curtail a riot in which a Jewish student was killed alienated the affections of part of the city's Jewish community. In 1993, Republican Rudolph Giuliani essentially reassembled the Koch conservative coalition and won the mayoralty. The business community was once again more fully incorporated into a conservative governing coalition.

SAN FRANCISCO: FROM MANHATTANIZATION TO AN ANTIREGIME

San Francisco, like New York, has been portrayed as a pluralist city where power is fragmented among different competing groups.[78] The increased clout of the city's gay and lesbian community only reinforces the view that San Francisco is a city fairly open to newly emergent political groups. Yet elite influence is clearly felt in what otherwise appears to be such a politically open city.

According to political scientists Chester Hartman and Rob Kessler, the building of the Yerba Buena Center (a large development project that includes the new Moscone Convention Center) was "an attempt by the city's ruling forces to expand the city's downtown boundaries, across 120-foot wide Market Street into the South of Market area, traditionally a low-prestige, low-rent area housing blue-collar workers and lower-income residents."[79] The center was to combine an indoor sports arena, exhibition hall, and new office and commercial facilities.

The project was supported by the convention industry and those downtown interests that would benefit from increased tourism, office construction, and real estate development. However, the operation of the convention center was likely to require a continuing subsidy. Estimates as to the number of jobs generated by the project were inflated in that construction of the office buildings at the center took away from construction that would have occurred elsewhere in the city. Construction at the site also displaced 723 businesses and 7,600 jobs.[80] Displaced residents from the South of Market area found themselves paying increased rents for housing in nearby overcrowded neighborhoods. Rising land values in the project area further fueled the gentrification and displacement processes.

Mayor Dianne Feinstein's concern for the health of the city's business district was reinforced by her dependency on downtown money for her election efforts. Her campaign war chest "came primarily from downtown corporations and big business."[81] This relationship was most clearly revealed in her successful campaign against a recall effort—a campaign where the $1,000 per contributor limit under San Francisco law was not applicable: "Nearly half a million dollars came in within a few weeks, almost all from large corporate contributions garnered at a February 14 fundraising dinner...."[82]

Yet not all observers agree that San Francisco is dominated by an elite-led growth coalition. The increased power of advocacy groups representing the concerns of racial minorities, gays, environmentalists, and those in need of affordable housing can be seen to attest to San Francisco's pluralistic makeup. These groups forced the adoption of plans and ordinances that controlled rents, limited condominium conversions, protected the city's stock of low-income residential hotels, and restricted the construction of new high rises downtown. In 1987 these groups helped elect a mayor, Art Agnos, who promised to protect neighborhoods even at the cost of questioning certain economic growth projects. One critic has charged that, far from being dominated by a progrowth coalition, San Francisco is ruled by neighborhood activists and antigrowth organizations that have throttled development with endless public hearings, environmental reporting, and procedural requirements.[83] This apparent shift in power in the city during the early days of the Agnos administration was reported by the *San Francisco Chronicle*:

> In the six months since Agnos has been mayor of San Francisco, he has slowly, systematically turned over the keys of City Hall to people who in the past often had the door slammed in their face.... Some old-time political players—the Chamber of Commerce, many labor unions, downtown business and development groups and even the Rev. Cecil Williams—are finding their keys to City Hall do not work anymore.[84]

San Francisco's progrowth regime collapsed in the 1970s and 1980s, as restrictive growth measures took their toll and businesses found new sites in the rapidly growing cities of the Silicon Valley and the South Bay. But Mayor Agnos was not always a dependable friend of antigrowth forces. As he attempted to govern the city and meet the needs of its diverse population, he needed to assemble the support of actors beyond those groups who had supported him in the election. In office, Agnos backed a number of major growth projects, including a major waterfront development project and a new ballpark for the Giants, who had threatened to leave the city for the South Bay. Many of his former grassroots supporters saw the mayor as a "progrowth wolf in slow-growth clothing."[85]

No truly progressive regime emerged in San Francisco. Instead, the forces of the "wild left" proved more adept at blocking projects they detested than at building a coalition capable of governing the city. Rather than building a progressive regime, the neighborhood and environmentalist forces in San Francisco remained a grassroots movement, what Richard DeLeon called an **antiregime**—a loose alliance of groups capable of blocking the big projects of the old growth coalition but unable to formulate workable, positive projects to reconnect the city with business, restore the city's economic base, and meet the jobs, social welfare, and housing needs of the city's poor and working class.[86]

Disappointed in the mayor's support for big growth projects, especially the China Basin ballpark, grassroots activists in the 1991 election showed no great love for Agnos. Frank Jordan, a conservative "ex-cop," won the mayoralty by promising to reverse the "anything goes" philosophy of San Francisco and take back the city's streets from panhandlers. In office, he cracked down on the homeless and began new initiatives to privatize municipal services.

DETROIT: THE CONTROVERSY OVER POLETOWN

Detroit, too, has been portrayed as a pluralist city where a number of interests contend for power. Automobile executives are challenged by union officials. The rise of black political power and the continued reelection of black mayors only further attest to the permeability of Detroit's influence structure. Yet in recent years Detroit has also lost both a substantial portion of its population and job base. This loss has given leaders in the automobile industry the ability to exert tremendous influence over Detroit on matters directly affecting corporate interests.

The building of a new General Motors assembly plant in Detroit's Poletown neighborhood serves as only the most notable case in point. In 1980 General Motors announced that it was closing two of its older Detroit factories with the intention of establishing a new, more modern, automated facility at a "greenfield" site in another part of the country. City officials quickly scrambled to find General Motors an acceptable alternative site and to meet GM's consequent demands regarding site preparation and tax abatements. The city, having already suffered a considerable loss of jobs and population, felt it could not afford to face the consequences of a GM pullout.

City officials offered GM nine possible sites; GM found suitable only the site in Poletown, the mixed black and Polish community adjacent to the old Dodge Main plant. The corporation resisted the pleas of area residents who sought to scale down the scope of site development in order to minimize the displacement the project would impose on the neighborhood. The city acquired homes under a "quick take" procedure; homes were demolished before final compensation in all cases could be arranged.

The costs, in both human and dollar terms, were substantial:

> This facility, the infamous "Poletown" plant, involved the destruction of a neighborhood. It was industrial urban renewal in a grand scale: within 18 months of the announcement of the project, 1,500 homes, 144 businesses, two schools, a hospital, 16 churches and an abandoned reinforced concrete automobile assembly plant whose demolition cost alone was estimated at $12 million were gone, and 3,438 citizens had to be relocated.[87]

The costs did not stop there. Site preparation costs were estimated at $200 million.[88] Court settlements, including interest and attorney fees, were likely to drive the costs of assembling the land much higher.[89] The city diverted Community Development Block Grant money from other neighborhood and downtown projects in order to help pay for the costs of site acquisition and preparation in Poletown.

The new plant added little municipal revenues that could be used to improve services for the people of Detroit. The plant was given a 50 percent tax abatement for a period of twelve years, thereby cutting in half the revenues the project was to bring to Detroit. Furthermore, under the tax increment financing plan for the project, property tax revenue derived from the plant could be used only to repay the initial loans on the project and to make further improvements in the project area: "[T]he municipal general fund and other taxing districts receive little of the benefits from the new investment."[90]

Nor was there any guarantee that GM would deliver all the jobs it had promised. Automation and robotics would reduce the number of jobs at the plant. Economic conditions in a competitive industry could conceivably force the company to employ only one shift, thereby halving the 6,000 jobs the company had said it would fill. This eventually is what happened. The agreement between GM and the city imposed obligations only on one side:

> Yet nowhere in the process does the city propose performance constraints to ensure net benefits before the project is actually undertaken. The people of the City of Detroit assumed all the expenses and took all the risks. GM managed to maintain the option of when and under what conditions the proposed plant would be completed, and to determine the level of employment at the plant when and if it began operating.[91]

There was not even an attempt to uncover just what tax subsidies GM needed to stay in Detroit. Instead, the city quickly acceded to the corporation's wish for the "maximum allowable tax abatement"[92] under state law! The "key issue was simply whether and how the city of Detroit could meet the stringent and inflexible demands of General Motors. There was, in a word, no policy discretion; there was only capitulation."[93] The power of General Motors had, in effect, made Detroit a "'company town' acting as effective advocate for the corporation."[94]

Overall, the Poletown project can be seen as a bad deal for the city. The project has not paid for itself. By 1996 the city of Detroit will have paid $100 million in excess of revenues and will still owe nearly $50 million. The city has even been forced to divert general fund revenues to help repay the bonds.[95] According to Bryan Jones and Lynn Bachelor, while the project may be defended as a "loss leader" strategy by serving "as a beacon to other industries that Detroit was a city that welcomed heavy industry," overall the model of industrial urban renewal used in Poletown "must be considered at best a questionable approach."[96]

The costs stemming from Poletown do not end there. Chrysler Corporation asked for a virtual carbon copy of the Poletown deal as it threatened to move and close its old Jefferson Avenue plant on the east side of Detroit. Economic conditions had changed as the automobile industry entered a period of prosperity, yet Detroit's poor taxpayers were asked to subsidize a new automotive plant. Although the evidence from Poletown showed that the city gave far more than it received in the previous deal with GM, the corporate regime in Detroit pursued an arrangement with Chrysler. The city further incurred additional costs in the environmental cleanup of the contaminated site.[97]

That GM exerted enormous influence in the Poletown case is undeniable. Yet in their book reviewing the Poletown controversy, Jones and Bachelor argue that local politics and leadership played more important roles in determining the outcome of this affair than is commonly assumed. While GM's demands and ability to build a new plant in another state confined the range of actions Detroit had at its disposal, it was still the city itself that decided to initiate action in response to the corporation's announced intention to leave. Detroit acted more quickly and with greater success than did other Michigan cities confronted with similar threats of lost automobile production.[98] Mayor Coleman Young proved to be an adept leader who got his bureaucracy to quickly formulate, and his city council to approve, a plan that would avert GM's departure. Who would invest in Detroit if GM were perceived to be abandoning the community?

There were also hidden beneficiaries to the choice Young had made. The media focused on the resistance by the white-dominated Poletown Neighborhood Council; ignored were the community's citizens, including a number of black citizens, who were more than pleased with the generous property settlements. Also unseen were the jobs that would be maintained in Detroit—jobs that would go to black workers as well as white workers. Mayor Young saw the controversy in racial terms: "In the mayor's mind the issue was zero-sum, part of a continuing black/white struggle."[99] The white residents of Poletown could not be given any more favorable treatment than had been received by black residents who had opposed earlier urban renewal efforts. As Jones and Bachelor sum up, "Paradoxically, by refusing to yield an inch to the 'little man' Coleman Young kept faith with the 'forgotten citizen' of Poletown: the black majority of the neighborhood."[100]

There was no simple economic determinism in the Poletown case. While the influence of GM was considerable, it was the city itself that decided on a plan of action. Jones and Bachelor use the phrase "creative bounded choice"[101] to denote both the private corporation's power and the latitude still possessed by city actors. According to Jones and Bachelor, "Business interests do not invariably dominate government policy even where a single industry dominates the community."[102]

Political leadership undoubtedly remains an important factor in city affairs, and economic determinism is too simplistic a way to look at city politics. Yet the lessons from Poletown must be primarily those of the considerable power possessed by the private corporation and the limitations that such power imposes on a city's course of action. Detroit rushed to judgment, giving in speedily and unconditionally to GM's demands.

WHAT THE THREE CASE STUDIES SHOW

The evidence in the community power debate is more than a bit ambiguous. In the three case studies reported above, both pluralist and elite theorists can find points of evidence that support their views of community power.

Pluralists can point to the fact that New York's mayors overspent in an attempt to mollify the demands of the city's pluralistic social structure—the diverse ethnic, minority, neighborhood, business, and municipal work force groups that all competed for power in New York City. Furthermore, after the crisis, elites could not unilaterally impose desired service cuts and economic development plans on the city; instead, these had to be negotiated with the city's elected officials. Mayor Koch proved to be a troublesome business ally, at times raising taxes and opposing their projects. The city also elected its first African-American, community-oriented mayor. Similarly, both the empowerment of new groups in San Francisco and the leadership exerted by Detroit's Coleman Young on behalf of his black constituents can be used to underscore the pluralist interpretation of power. Especially in San Francisco, where neighborhood and environmental forces have imposed numerous restrictions on new development, it is difficult to portray policy in the city simply as being dictated by the business community.

Elite theorists, on the other hand, can find evidence to support their point of view. They can point to the role played by the banks in New York City—both in extending the city's debt and in dumping their portfolios to precipitate the crisis. Elite theorists can also point out that, in the wake of the crisis, the city redefined its agenda so as to advance the interests of corporations and cut back the services given the poor, minorities, and neighborhood groups. Similarly, in San Francisco the pace of the economic transformation of that city has essentially continued despite the opposition and political victories of neighborhood groups and community activists. The city's Downtown Plan restricted growth in the central business district only when market forces would no longer support such growth. It also shifted growth to the South of Market area, just south of the old downtown, where property owners were given new and profitable development rights.[103] And in Detroit a neighborhood was destroyed to make way for a new General Motors plant—a plant that was given extensive subsidies and tax breaks without requiring any firm reciprocal commitment by the corporation.

The three case studies also underscore the notion of city limits in that cities are led to initiate policies favorable to new investment from the fear that possible investment will locate elsewhere. Clearly, business elites are not all powerful; they can be beaten back on specific issues or sets of issues. Yet, as the three studies show, overall, despite occasional setbacks, development favored by elites continues.

A Chicago case study further makes this point. Chicago's business community lost out in its desire for the city to host the 1992 World's Fair. Mayor Harold Washington refused to embrace enthusiastically the proposal, which gained little support from South Side community leaders. The city's business community was beaten on an important issue. Still, the city provided its corporate community with numerous benefits in the form of favors in a wide variety of subsidized growth projects.[104]

But the "city limits" thesis understates the importance of local politics. As regime theory suggests, in each of the three case studies, local elections and municipal political actors were important determinants of local policy. While business leaders occupied a privileged position in city affairs, there was nothing economically deterministic or automatic that led a city to cede to business interests. Mayors Koch, Giuliani, and Jordan formed corporate-oriented governing regimes; Dinkins and Agnos did not, even though they at times favored specific development projects. Koch, at times, even favored the demands of his white ethnic supporters and neighborhood groups in opposing certain development efforts. In Detroit, Coleman Young insisted that African-American concerns be respected in any such governing partnership. While Young proved to be a dependable business ally on the Poletown and Chrysler East Jefferson projects, he was a less dependable partner in other areas.[105] In all three case studies, city officials and community leaders alike found it difficult to sustain a workable governing alliance that was capable of getting things done.

CONCLUSIONS: A VIEW OF CONSTRAINED LOCAL POWER

As we have seen in this chapter, the debate over the nature of power in cities continues. Elite theorists believe that a relatively small group of corporate officials, local business leaders, and persons of high social status make the key decisions in a city. In contrast, the pluralists argue that power is more widely spread and that a great many people have the ability to form groups and influence city decision making. In turn, the antipluralists argue that relatively powerless citizens have a difficult time in organizing. Furthermore, antipluralists contend that powerful corporations can keep unwanted issues off a city's agenda, as was the case when the presence of U.S. Steel delayed the imposition of air pollution controls in Gary, Indiana. Local political systems are not as penetrable as the pluralists presume.

In part, the debate continues because the exact distribution of power varies from one city to the next. Power in one city might be highly structured, while in another it might be more widely spread. The debate also persists as there is no clear and convincing evidence as to what exactly is the shape of power in a particular city. Our review of politics in New York, San Francisco, and Detroit points to pieces of evidence that both pluralists and elite theorists can use to support their interpretations of urban power.

More recent attempts have been made to synthesize the evidence in the urban debate. While no closed-power elite exists in a great many American cities, a systemic view of power emerges nonetheless. While business elites can be beaten on specific issues, city officials act over the long haul to pursue development and provide tax incentives and other subsidies that favor upper-strata interests. Paul Peterson provides one very convincing explanation of why cities so often pursue policies favored by upper-strata interests: Cities must pursue continued development in order to maintain their job and tax bases.

Peterson provides us with a powerful insight when he argues that much can be gained by conceptualizing cities as *if* they had a unitary or consensual interest in pursuing "those policies which are in the interests of the city, taken as a whole." [106] Coleman Young, for instance, was led to the distasteful act of destroying Poletown in order to save Detroit as a whole. Contemporary city decision making remains highly constrained by private decisions and the mobility allowed corporate investment choices in a free market.

Cities are not in a strong position to challenge the claims made by business. Jobs often equate with votes, and local officials do not want to put themselves in the position of *not* supporting jobs for their cities. City officials also have no way to determine accurately whether a business is serious in its threats to move to another city or to locate a new facility elsewhere. Nor can municipal officials accurately assess just what concessions a business really needs to locate in a city. [107]

Yet, there is no simple economic determinism. Politics remains important, and some cities are willing to challenge the policy priorities of growth coalitions. Peterson clearly overstates the degree to which a city possesses a unitary interest in pursuing development. Citizens who are threatened by displacement, overcrowding, congestion, and higher taxes associated with continued development may at times be able to form political coalitions opposed to the demands of real estate developers and elite forces. Also, the business community itself is often divided. While some sectors of a business community receive the benefits of new growth projects, other sectors find that they are only paying new taxes or losing customers and services to the new development projects.

The notion of regime theory points to the difficulty that both city officials and private elites face in attempting to construct sustained, workable, governing alliances. City officials and business leaders need each other. Business leaders can often thwart the initiatives desired by city leaders. Municipal officials, in turn, control key resources essential to the good health of the business community, especially if businesses are not as free to pick up and relocate as the theory of capital mobility so often suggests.

In governing, mayors must seek to build effective governing coalitions. Electoral power is not enough to guarantee effective governance. As a consequence, governing coalitions by necessity will often include actors that were not a part of the electoral coalition that put a mayor in office. Regime theory points to the importance of these informal governing alliances or coalitions. The business community often occupies a privileged place, but not a dictatorial or command position, in such informal governing alliances.

Private institutions exert great influence in local affairs. Yet private elites do not simply dictate to city officials. Politics within a city and the leadership actions of city officials remain important. Government leaders choose which tasks they seek to accomplish and what alliances they will build in support of those tasks.[108] As we shall see in the next chapter, the formal structure of local government, too, helps to determine just whose interests are represented in city hall.

NOTES

1. Robert S. and Helen M. Lynd, *Middletown* (New York: Harcourt, Brace, 1929), and *Middletown in Transition* (New York: Harcourt, Brace, 1937).
2. C. Wright Mills, *The Power Elite* (New York: Oxford University Press, 1956); and G. William Domhoff, *Who Rules America?* (Englewood Cliffs, NJ: Prentice-Hall, 1967).
3. Floyd Hunter, *Community Power Structure* (Garden City, NY: Anchor Books, 1963). The book was originally published in 1953.
4. Floyd Hunter, *Community Power Succession: Atlanta's Policymakers Revisited* (Chapel Hill, NC: University of North Carolina Press, 1980).
5. Nelson W. Polsby, *Community Power and Political Theory* (New Haven, CT: Yale University Press, 1963). Also see Robert A. Dahl, "A Critique of the Ruling Elite Model," *American Political Science Review* 52 (June 1958): 463–69; and Raymond Wolfinger, "A Plea for a Decent Burial," *American Sociological Review* 27 (December 1962): 841–47.
6. Polsby, *Community Power and Political Theory*, pp. 21–24.
7. Robert A. Dahl, *Who Governs? Democracy and Power in an American City* (New Haven, CT: Yale University Press, 1961). Also see Raymond Wolfinger, *The Politics of Progress* (Englewood Cliffs, NJ: Prentice-Hall, 1974); and Polsby, *Community Power and Political Theory*, pp. 69–97.
8. Dahl, *Who Governs?*, p. 7.
9. Ibid., p. 163.
10. Ibid., pp. 100–103, 137–40, 163–65, and 311–25.
11. Ibid., p. 181.
12. Ibid., pp. 192–99.
13. Ibid., p. 305.
14. Michael Lipsky, *Protest in City Politics* (Chicago: Rand McNally, 1972).

15. Michael Parenti, "Power and Pluralism: View from the Bottom," *Journal of Politics* 32 (1970): 501–30.

16. In particular, see Robert J. Waste, ed., *Community Power: Future Directions in Urban Research* (Newbury Park, CA: Sage Publications, 1986).

17. G. William Domhoff, *Who Really Rules? New Haven and Community Power Reexamined* (Santa Monica, CA: Goodyear Publishing, 1978), p. 113 and Chapter 5. Also see Robert A. Dahl, "Rethinking *Who Governs?* New Haven, Revisited," in *Community Power: Future Directions in Urban Research*, ed. Robert J. Waste (Newbury Park, CA: Sage Publications, 1986).

18. Domhoff, *Who Really Rules? New Haven and Community Power Reexamined*, p. 113.

19. Ibid., pp. 107–113; and Matthew Crenson, *The Un-Politics of Air Pollution: A Study of Non-Decisionmaking in the Cities* (Baltimore: Johns Hopkins Press, 1971), pp. 108–109.

20. Peter Bachrach and Morton S. Baratz, "The Two Faces of Power," *American Political Science Review* 56 (December 1962): 947–52. Also see Bachrach and Baratz, *Power and Poverty: Theory and Practice* (New York: Oxford University Press, 1970), pp. 43–46.

21. Crenson, *The Un-Politics of Air Pollution*, pp. 55–82 and 107.

22. Richard M. Merelman, "On the Neo-Elitist Critique of Community Power," *American Political Science Review* 62 (June 1968): 451–60; Raymond E. Wolfinger, "Nondecisions and the Study of Local Politics," *American Political Science Review* 65 (December 1971): 1063–1980; and Geoffrey Debnam, "Nondecisions and Power: The Two Faces of Bachrach and Baratz," *American Political Science Review* 69 (September 1975): 889–99 (and pp. 900–07 for Bachrach and Baratz's reply and Debnam's rejoinder).

23. Blaine A. Brownell, "The Urban South Comes of Age, 1900–1940," in *The City in Southern History*, ed. Blaine A. Brownell and David R. Goldfield (Port Washington, NY: Kennikat Press, 1977), pp. 142–43.

24. Peter A. Lupsha and William J. Siembieda, "The Poverty of Public Services in the Land of Plenty: An Analysis and Interpretation," in *The Rise of the Sunbelt Cities*, ed. David C. Perry and Alfred J. Watkins (Beverly Hills, CA: Sage Publications, 1977), p. 185.

25. Arnold Fleischmann and Joe R. Feagin, "The Politics of Growth-Oriented Urban Alliances: Comparing Old Industrial and New Sunbelt Cities," *Urban Affairs Quarterly* 23 (December 1987): 216.

26. Lupsha and Siembieda, "The Poverty of Public Services in a Land of Plenty," p. 185.

27. Daniel J. Elazar, *American Federalism: A View from the States*, 3rd ed. (New York: Harper & Row, 1984), pp. 109–49.

28. Lupsha and Siembieda, "The Poverty of Public Services in a Land of Plenty," p. 187.

29. Brownell, "The Urban South Comes of Age, 1900–1940," p. 150.

30. David R. Johnson, "San Antonio: The Vicissitudes of Boosterism," in *Sunbelt Cities: Politics and Growth Since World War II*," ed. Richard M. Bernard and Bradley R. Rice (Austin, TX: University of Texas Press, 1983), pp. 235–54; and David R. Johnson, John A. Booth, and Richard J. Harris, eds., *The Politics of San Antonio: Community, Progress, and Power* (Lincoln, NE: University of Nebraska Press, 1983).

31. Fleischmann and Feagin, "The Politics of Growth-Oriented Urban Alliances," p. 216.

32. Bradley R. Rice, "Atlanta: If Dixie Were Atlanta," in *Sunbelt Cities: Politics and Growth Since World War II*, p. 44.

33. Ibid., p. 51.

34. Philip J. Trounstine and Terry Christensen, *Movers and Shakers: The Study of Community Power* (New York: St. Martin's Press, 1982), p. 40.

35. Ibid., pp. 99–108.

36. Ibid., pp. 127 and 162–92.

37. Robert Kerstein, "The Political-Economy of Urban Development in Tampa" (Paper presented at the annual meeting of the Urban Affairs Association, March 8–11, 1989).

38. Robyne S. Turner, "Growth Politics and Downtown Development: The Economic Imperative in Sunbelt Cities," *Urban Affairs Quarterly* 28 (September 1992): 3–21.

39. Ronald K. Vogel, *Urban Political Economy: Broward County, Florida* (Gainesville, FL: University Press of Florida, 1992), pp. 68–79, 101–07, and 113–17.

40. Platon N. Rigos and Darryl Paulson, "Public-Private Partnerships: When Things Fall Apart—The Case of St. Petersburg, Florida" (Paper presented at the annual meeting of the American Political Science Association, Chicago, September 3–6, 1992).

41. On the new opposition to growth in suburban Tampa, see three papers and articles by Robert Kerstein: "Suburban Growth Politics in Hillsborough County: Growth Management and Political Regimes," *Social Science Quarterly* 74 (September 1993): 614–620; "Growth Politics in Tampa and Hillsborough County," *Journal of Urban Affairs* 13 (1991): 55–76; and "Housing Policy in Tampa and Hillsborough County: 1937–1992" (Paper presented at the annual meeting of the Urban Affairs Association, Cleveland, April 1992). Mark Schneider, "Undermining the Growth Machine: The Missing Link between Local Economic Development and Fiscal Payoffs," *Journal of Politics* 54 (February 1992): 214–30, presents evidence on the mounting suburban opposition nationwide to new growth projects.

42. Paul E. Peterson, *City Limits* (Chicago: University of Chicago Press, 1981).

43. Ibid., pp. 37–38.

44. Ibid., pp. 206–12.

45. For an exchange between Peterson and his critics, see Heywood T. Sanders and Clarence N. Stone, "Developmental Politics Reconsidered," pp. 521–39; Paul E. Peterson, "Analyzing Development Politics: A Response to Sanders and Stone," pp. 540–47; and Sanders and Stone, "Competing Paradigms: A Rejoinder to Peterson," *Urban Affairs Quarterly* 22 (June 1987): 548–51. For an extensive detailing of the arguments critical of Peterson, see Clarence N. Stone and Heywood T. Sanders, eds., *The Politics of Urban Development* (Lawrence, KS: University of Kansas Press, 1987).

46. Peterson, *City Limits*, p. 147.

47. John R. Logan and Harvey L Molotch, *Urban Fortunes: The Political Economy of Place* (Berkeley, CA: University of California Press, 1987).

48. Heywood T. Sanders, "The Politics of Development in Middle-Sized Cities," in *The Politics of Economic Development*, ed. Clarence N. Stone and Heywood T.

Sanders, pp. 182–98 (the quotation appears on p. 192). The point that a city's business community is often divided and hence does not comprise a single monolithic elite was made much earlier by pluralists in the community power debate. See Wolfinger, *The Politics of Progress*, pp. 147–51.

49. John Clayton Thomas, *Between Citizen and City: Neighborhood Organizations and Urban Politics in Cincinnati* (Lawrence, KS: University of Kansas Press, 1986), pp. 1–21.

50. Todd Swanstrom, "Semisovereign Cities: The Politics of Urban Development," *Polity* 21 (Fall 1988): 96–110. Also see Kenneth K. Wong, *City Choices: Education and Housing* (Albany, NY: State University of New York Press, 1990), p. 147.

51. Ibid., pp. 88–96. Also see David I. Birch, "Who Creates Jobs?" *Public Interest* (Fall 1981): 3–14; and Ardeshir Anjomani, Jon Erickson, and Anthony Oji, "Major Factors Influencing Industry Location in Texas" (Paper presented at the annual meeting of the Urban Affairs Association, Baltimore, March 8–11, 1989).

52. William J. Grimshaw, "Revisiting the Classics: Political Order, Economic Efficiency, and Social Justice" (Paper presented at the annual meeting of the American Political Science Association, New York, September 1–4, 1994).

53. Robert J. Waste, "City Limits, Pluralism, and Urban Political Economy," *Journal of Urban Affairs* 15, 5 (1993): 445–55. Peterson, *City Limits*, p. 52, acknowledges that education policy is difficult to classify, as it spills over into more than one policy area.

54. Jeffrey R. Henig, "Defining City Limits," *Urban Affairs Quarterly* 27 (March 1992): 384.

55. Thomas Longoria, Jr., "Empirical Analysis of the *City Limits* Typology," *Urban Affairs Quarterly* 30 (September 1994): 102–13.

56. Clarence N. Stone, "Systemic Power in Community Decision Making: A Restatement of Stratification Theory," *American Political Science Review* 74 (December 1980): 978.

57. Clarence N. Stone, *Regime Politics—Governing Atlanta: 1946–1988* (Lawrence, KS: University of Kansas Press, 1989), p. 242.

58. The story of Atlanta under Jackson and Young in the 1970s and 1980s is told by Stone, *Regime Politics*, pp. 77–159.

59. "Plan for Olympic Park Spurs Atlanta Protest," *The New York Times*, November 21, 1993.

60. John Hull Mollenkopf, *A Phoenix in the Ashes: The Rise and Fall of the Koch Coalition in New York City Politics* (Princeton, NJ: Princeton Univ. Press, 1992), pp. 201–02.

61. Clarence N. Stone, "Summing Up: Urban Regimes, Development Policy, and Political Arrangements," in *The Politics of Economic Development*, ed. Stone and Sanders, pp. 272–73; and Clarence N. Stone, "Urban Regimes and the Capacity to Govern: A Political Economy Approach," *Journal of Urban Affairs* 15, 1 (1993): 18–22.

62. Richard Edward DeLeon, *Left Coast City: Progressive Politics in San Francisco, 1975–1991* (Lawrence, KS: University of Kansas Press, 1992), pp. 142–49.

63. Wallace Sayre and Herbert Kaufman, *Governing New York City* (New York: Russell Sage Foundation, 1960); Donald H. Haider, "Sayre and Kaufman Revisited: New York City Government Since 1965," *Urban Affairs Quarterly* 15 (December 1979): 123–45; and Douglas Yates, *The Ungovernable City* (Cambridge, MA: MIT Press, 1977).

64. Jack Newfield and Paul DuBrul, *The Abuse of Power: The Permanent Govern-ment and the Fall of New York* (New York: Penguin Books, 1977), pp. 45–46. Also see Richard S. Morris, *Bum Rap on America's Cities* (Englewood Cliffs, NJ: Prentice-Hall, 1980), pp. 51–66.

65. Martin Shefter, "New York City's Fiscal Crisis: The Politics of Inflation and Retrenchment," *Public Interest* 48 (Summer 1977): 111–12.

66. Newfield and DuBrul, *The Abuse of Power*, p. 41. For a parallel case as to the role played by the Cleveland financial community in bringing about that city's financial default, see the exchange between Davita Silfen Glasberg, "The Political Economic Power of Finance Capital and Urban Fiscal Crisis: Cleveland's Default, 1978"; Todd Swanstrom, "On The Power of Finance Capital Over Cities: A Rejoinder…"; and Glasberg's "Reply" in the *Journal of Urban Affairs* 10 (1988): 219–52.

67. Shefter, "New York City's Fiscal Crisis," p. 114.

68. Ibid.

69. Robert W. Bailey, *The Crisis Regime: The MAC, the EFCB, and the Political Impact of the New York City Financial Crisis* (Albany, NY: State University of New York Press, 1984), pp. 173–75.

70. Bernard J. Frieden, "The Downtown Job Puzzle," *The Public Interest* 97 (Fall 1989): 80–81; and Joe R. Feagin and Robert Parker, *Building American Cities: The Urban Real Estate Game*, 2nd ed. (Englewood Cliffs, NJ: Prentice-Hall, 1990), pp. 69–70.

71. Bailey, *The Crisis Regime*, p. 174. Also see Haider, "Sayre and Kaufman Revisited," p. 142.

72. Mollenkopf, *A Phoenix in the Ashes*, pp. 3–4.

73. Ibid., pp. 44–68.

74. Ibid., pp. 126–27, 142–47, and 201–02. Also see Susan S. Fainstein and Norman S. Fainstein, "New York City: A Manhattan Business District, 1945–1988," in *Unequal Partnerships: The Political Economy of Urban Redevelopment in Postwar America*, ed. Gregory D. Squires (New Brunswick, NJ: Rutgers Univ. Press, 1989), pp. 59–79.

75. Asher Arian, Arthur S. Goldberg, John H. Mollenkopf, and Edward T. Rogowsky, *Changing New York City Politics* (New York: Routledge, 1991), pp. 1–3 and 69–114.

76. Susan S. Fainstein, "The Second New York Fiscal Crisis," *International Journal of Urban and Regional Research* 16 (March 1992): 129–37.

77. Mollenkopf, *A Phoenix in the Ashes*, pp. 204–07.

78. Frederick M. Wirt, "Alioto and the Politics of Hyperpluralism," *Transaction* 7 (April 1970): 46–55.

79. Chester Hartman and Rob Kessler, "The Illusion and Reality of Urban Re-newal: San Francisco's Yerba Buena Center," in *Marxism and the Metropolis*, ed. William K. Tabb and Larry Sawers (New York: Oxford University Press, 1978), p. 154.

80. Ibid., p. 168.

81. Chester Hartman, *The Transformation of San Francisco* (Totowa, NJ: Rowman and Allanheld, 1984), p. 169.

82. Ibid., p. 174.

83. Dennis J. Coyle, "The Balkans by the Bay," *Public Interest* 91 (Spring 1988): 67–78.

84. Dawn Garcia, "Who Holds the Keys to Power in S.F. under Agnos?" *San Francisco Chronicle*, July 11, 1988.

85. DeLeon, *Left Coast City*, p. 12.

86. Ibid., pp. 7–8 and 132–33. Also see Richard E. DeLeon, "The Urban Anti-regime: Progressive Politics in San Francisco," *Urban Affairs Quarterly* 27 (June 1992): 555–79.

87. Bryan D. Jones and Lynn W. Bachelor, "Local Policy Discretion and the Corporate Surplus," in *Urban Economic Development*, Urban Affairs Annual Review, vol. 27, ed. Richard D. Bingham and John P. Blair (Beverly Hills, CA: Sage Publications, 1984), p. 245.

88. Ibid., p. 253.

89. Bill McGraw, "Poletown Land Costs Double, and Are Likely to Climb Higher," *Detroit Free Press*, March 1, 1988, pp. 1 and 11.

90. Jones and Bachelor, "Local Policy Discretion and the Corporate Surplus," p. 255.

91. David Fasenfast, "Community Politics and Urban Redevelopment: Poletown, Detroit, and General Motors," *Urban Affairs Quarterly* 22 (September 1986): 114.

92. Bryan D. Jones and Lynn W. Bachelor (with Carter Wilson), *The Sustaining Hand: Community Leadership and Corporate Power* (Lawrence, KS: University of Kansas Press, 1986), p. 129.

93. Jones and Bachelor, "Local Policy Discretion and the Corporate Surplus," p. 246.

94. Ibid., p. 260.

95. Bryan D. Jones and Lynn W. Bachelor, *The Sustaining Hand: Community Leadership and Corporate Power*, 2nd ed., revised (Lawrence, KS: Univ. of Kansas Press, 1993), pp. 215–16.

96. Ibid., p. 216.

97. Ibid., pp. 217–32.

98. Ibid., pp. 107–08 and 115–27.

99. Ibid., p. 161.

100. Ibid., pp. 161–62.

101. Ibid., p. 248.

102. Ibid., p. 254.

103. Hartman, *The Transformation of San Francisco*, pp. 236–60 and 273–79, especially p. 277.

104. Anne B. Shlay and Robert P. Giloth, "The Social Organization of a Land-Based Elite: The Case of the Failed Chicago 1992 World's Fair," *Journal of Urban Affairs* 9 (November 1987): 305–24.

105. Marion E. Orr and Gerry Stoker, "Urban Regimes and Leadership in Detroit," *Urban Affairs Quarterly* 30 (September 1994): 48–73.

106. Peterson, *City Limits*, p. 4.

107. Jones and Bachelor, "Local Policy Discretion and the Corporate Surplus," p. 265.

108. Stone, "Urban Regimes and the Capacity to Govern," pp. 1–2.

Community improvement districts - another form of special district

ex. Cumberland.
Town center in Cobb
Perimeter Mall in Dekalb

HOUSE BILL 489 - 1997? - requires cities and
counties to collaborate - combine
services.

4

Formal Structure and Leadership Style

School districts are special districts.

3 Forms of local govt. in GA.
1) municipalities (cities)
2) counties
3) special district

Many political issues are never effectively resolved at the local level because of the legal restraints imposed by state governments on local government powers. State constitutions, state laws, and state provisions for city charters all spell out the exact formal powers allotted municipalities. These documents define a local jurisdiction's spending obligations as well as its taxing and borrowing authority. State constitutions and state law even determine the formal structure of local government—whether a city has a strong-mayor, weak-mayor, council-manager (city manager), or commission system of government.

The formal rules and structure of government help to determine who gets what in the local arena. The different structures of local government have different biases. Groups who feel that a locality is not responding adequately to their needs will, at times, push for changes in the rules of operation of local government.

The reform movement, which gained power during the Progressive Era early in the twentieth century, brought one such set of changes that has had lasting influence on the structure and operations of municipal governments—and of the national and state governments as well (see "The Reform Movement and the Progressive Era" on pages 102–103). As we shall discuss in more detail in the next two chapters, the reformers were upset with the way political party machines had been running cities. The reformers sought the introduction of structural and electoral reforms to weaken the power of the machines and the interests the machines served. Among these reforms were the council-manager and commission forms of government, the direct primary, at-large and nonpartisan voting rules, and the introduction of civil service or merit systems for the protection of public employees.

Yet the victory of the reformers, while quite substantial, was not complete. In a great many cities reformed institutions coexist side by side

At-Large : not by districts

101

The Reform Movement and
the Progressive Era (1890–1920)

Urban reformers around the turn of the century sought "good government" to replace the partisanship and corruption of big city political machines. These civic activists sought to free municipal government from what they saw to be the parochialism of political party officials and their ethnic constituencies. The reformers wanted to create governments that would act in the public interest of the city as a whole.

The reformers thought cities could be run with businesslike efficiency. As far as possible, city affairs were to be directed by professionally trained managers. The reformers also favored the introduction of at-large and nonpartisan elections, open primaries, and the civil service or merit system hiring rules for government officials—all reforms intended to reduce the stranglehold over municipal affairs exerted by big city political machines.

But the search for good government during the Progressive Era was not confined to cities alone. Reform efforts at the local, state, and national levels were aimed at enacting social reforms, rationalizing government, and legislating antitrust laws to curb the power of big businesses. In part, the demand for reform was fueled by the revelations of the **muckrakers**. These crusading journalists exposed price-fixing by giant corporations, unsafe working conditions in factories, and corruption in city government. The muckrakers also reported the widespread poverty and misery of urban life during the industrial era. Lincoln Steffens' *Shame of the Cities*, published in 1904, and Upton Sinclair's *The Jungle* (1906) were only two of the more popular sensational books of this era. *The Jungle* shocked the public's conscience by revealing scandalously unsanitary conditions in the meat-packing industry in Chicago. These revelations soon led to the creation of the U.S. Food and Drug Administration. Curiously, the new federal regulations did not always hurt big business. The new food-processing regulations, for instance, drove some of the smaller meat-packing firms out of business, thereby consolidating the market position of the remaining giant corporations.*

In California the progressives came to power when a local prosecutor, Hiram Johnson, helped secure the conviction on bribery charges of Abraham Reuf, the boss of San Francisco. As was typical of a great many big city political machines of the era, officials in San Francisco had accepted **graft**, taking money in exchange for city favors. The trial gained great public attention when one prosecutor was shot in the courtroom and a witness was found dead in his jail cell. Johnson, a progressive Republican, won the governorship in 1910 on the basis of his fame from the trial and his ceaseless attacks against the power exerted by the Southern Pacific Railroad in California's affairs. Johnson was later elected U.S. Senator.

The progressives in California (and in other states in the American West) enacted the instruments of **direct democracy**— the direct primary, initiative, referendum, and recall. The initiative has proven to be an especially important and often used weapon by citizen groups in California. The progressives also amended the state constitution to make all local elections nonpartisan. They further undercut political party power by extending civil service protections and by scheduling local elections at an "off" time when no national or state offices were up for vote. The city manager form of government and at-large election of city council members were instituted in municipalities across the state. The result of all these reforms was to weaken the power of the mayoralty and to create the essential weak-party or "partyless" politics that so well characterizes California today.

The California progressives also succeeded in enacting numerous **social reforms,** including the establishment of workmen's compensation and the elimination of child labor. Wisconsin's Robert M. ("Fighting Bob") LaFollette was another prominent progressive who succeeded in instituting similar reforms in his state. LaFollette ran as the Progressive party's candidate for president in 1924, capturing 16 percent of the national vote. Many of the social reforms advocated by Johnson, LaFollette, and other Progressive Era politicians were later embraced by the national government during Franklin Delano Roosevelt's New Deal.

At the national level the progressive movement had reached its peak of power when more reform-minded forces bolted the Republican party in 1911 to endorse their own Progressive or "Bull Moose" party candidate for President, former President Theodore Roosevelt. Hiram Johnson was his vice presidential running mate. Party regulars and more corporate-oriented Republicans continued to support the incumbent President, William Howard Taft. The split in the Republican voting base resulted in the election of a Democrat, Woodrow Wilson, in 1912. Wilson's program as President embodied much of the progressive impulse to have government based on efficiency, rationality, and expertise.

In Chapter 6 we will discuss the nature and consequences of the reform movement in greater detail.

* Gabriel Kolko, *The Triumph of Conservatism* (New York: Free Press, 1963).

with numerous unreformed elements. Some cities have at-large and non-partisan elections but weak merit system protections for their employees; other cities have nonpartisan city council elections conducted on a district as opposed to a citywide basis. Some cities are more reformed in their structures and processes than are others.

In the modern American city, older machine patterns still persist despite the introduction of more modern reformed and postreform structures. As political scientist John Harrigan has observed, change in urban America has been incremental, not revolutionary, in nature: "Political change in the metropolis, then, does not mean that one form of political organization replaces a previous form. On the contrary, it means that several forms of political organization have evolved side by side."[1]

FORMAL VERSUS INFORMAL POWER

Knowledge of the formal powers and structure of local government alone, though, is rarely sufficient to a full understanding of how decisions are made. The distribution of legal power and authority recorded in the charter and laws affecting local government often does not reflect the pattern of actual influence in a community. Chicago, for instance, is formally a weak-mayor city under its city charter. Yet for two decades Mayor Richard J. Daley was able to amass considerable clout by centralizing power as head of the city and county Democratic machine.

The legal powers granted to local officials in city charters and state constitutions and statutes are often quite ambiguous, leaving cities with room for discretion. Court interpretation ultimately defines what scope of action the city has in such cases. In the 1960s and 1970s citizen groups were successful in securing court interpretations that tied up numerous freeway proposals and other projects that were seen to have adverse environmental consequences. Environmentalist and neighborhood groups so successfully used court action to stall New York City's proposed Westway project that the political climate shifted, and the city eventually abandoned this massive highway and economic development project.

Cities are also constrained in that administrative officials may not always follow through on orders issued by politicians. Bureaucrats are quite adept at using their civil service protections to insulate themselves from mayoral control.[2] Lower-level officials also have considerable discretionary power in interpreting guidelines and administering programs on a day-to-day basis. Political scientist Michael Lipsky has pointed to the great degree of discretion possessed by "street-level bureaucrats" who often work in the field insulated from direct hierarchical review. Although they formally are supposed to take orders from above, Lipsky says that these bureaucrats retain so much discretionary power that it would be fair to consider them, and not the city's elected officials, the primary policymakers in the urban political system.[3]

A city might even choose to forgo exercising a power which it is clearly legally granted. Also, cities lack the personnel and resources to enforce fully all the laws that are on their books. Cities possess legal authority and the threat of sanctions, but these are applied selectively and in varying degrees.

The intergovernmental system, too, is an influence that at times undermines local authority. Federal grants-in-aid to cities are almost always accompanied by rules and regulations that attempt to decrease the scope of local action. Over the years, federal laws and programs have also contained participatory requirements that encouraged the formation of citizen groups to challenge municipal authority.

As municipal powers are sharply limited, city leaders cannot rely on their formal authority alone to get things done. To be effective, a mayor or manager must also attempt to mobilize key actors through more informal coalition-building and leadership strategies.

DILLON'S RULE AND THE LIMITS OF CITY GOVERNMENT

The United States Constitution sets forth the basic distribution of governmental powers in the American system. The Constitution mentions only two levels of government. It assigns powers to the national government and the states; nowhere is there a mention of local governments. The legal assumption that results from this constitutional admission is that cities and other local governments fall under the jurisdiction of the states. No city, county, township, or other local subdivision of the state has an inherent right to exercise governmental powers. Instead, such powers must first be conferred on the local unit either by the state's constitution or by an act of the state legislature.

The legal position of municipal corporations and other local jurisdictions was given its classic formulation in 1868 by Iowa Judge John F. Dillon, a famous jurist and legal commentator. **Dillon's Rule**, the name by which this constitutional doctrine is usually identified, denotes a clear, hierarchical, superior-subordinate relationship between a state and its local governments. According to Judge Dillon, municipalities are "creatures of the states" and possess only those powers delegated to them by the states. Furthermore, as a state creates, it may destroy; any power it gives to cities it may abridge, amend, or take away. The state's power is so complete that "the Legislature might, by a single act, if we can suppose it capable of such great a folly and so great a wrong, sweep from existence all municipal corporations in a state."[4] Four years later, Judge Dillon even more clearly enunciated his view of restricted local government powers:

> It is a general and undisputed proposition of law that a municipal corporation possesses and can exercise the following powers, and no others:

First, those granted in express words; second, those necessarily or fairly implied in or incident to the power expressly granted; third, those essential to the accomplishment of the declared objects and purposes of the corporation—not simply convenient, but indispensable. Any fair, reasonable substantial doubt concerning the existence of power is resolved by the courts against the corporation and the power is denied.[5]

In 1903 and again in 1923, the United States Supreme Court upheld the principle established by Judge Dillon. Constitutionally speaking, local governments are subunits of the states. A state at its pleasure may modify or withdraw the powers it entrusts to its cities.[6]

There have been occasional challenges to Dillon's Rule, but most have not been successful. In recent years, though, a number of factors have served to give cities at least a modicum of insulation from state authority. Judge Dillon's assertion that any powers granted to the cities must be very strictly construed by the courts is counterbalanced in New Jersey, Michigan, New Mexico, and other states where constitutions and court rulings are explicit in declaring that provisions concerning local government powers be liberally construed. In these states local governments may perform a broad range of functions not expressly denied by state action. Also, the willingness of state legislatures to interfere in city affairs is often mitigated by the fact that elected state legislators often act as the voice of local constituencies. Considerations of practicality and fairness also act to limit the arbitrariness of states in dealing with their localities.

Still, whatever these modifications, Dillon's Rule remains the dominant doctrine of municipal law. Local boundaries are set by the state. Residents of Staten Island may have voted in 1993 to secede from New York City, but for actual secession to take place, approval by the state is still required. The powers of various local governing institutions, too, are determined by the states. New York Mayors David Dinkins and Rudolph Giuliani both had constant battles with the city's quasi-independent Board of Education and chancellor of schools. Both mayors sought measures to decrease the school system's independence, measures that would give the mayor increased appointive power over the board and the chancellor, or abolish the board entirely. But both mayors were rebuffed by a state legislature that refused to accede to their wishes.[7]

CITY CHARTERS

The specific powers allowed a city by the state are laid out in a **city charter**, roughly the equivalent of a city's constitution. Today there are several forms of city charters, all of which are drafted by state legislatures, except, as noted below, in the case of home rule cities.

Until about 1850, the normal practice was for the legislature to incorporate or charter a city by passing a special act. The legislature issued a **special act** or **specific charter** detailing exactly what structure and powers the new municipality was to have. But it soon became too cumbersome for the states to write specific charters of each individual city. As a result, the states today, for the most part, grant **general act** or **classified charters** that put cities into different categories or general classes (hence the name *classified*) according to population (although the assessed value of taxable property is sometimes used as well). Each state then imposes different structures, taxing and borrowing authorities, and service requirements on the different classes of cities. Larger cities are more likely to be granted a fuller range of governmental powers than are smaller incorporated towns and villages.

Even though the system of classes helps to protect a city against arbitrary treatment, a number of states still have been able to single out their major city for special action. If there is only one very large city in a state, all the legislature has to do is impose new obligations on its highest class of cities. In 1948, Louisiana Governor Earl Long, at war with the governing officials of his state's major city, began the "rape of New Orleans," limiting the city's powers and revenues while at the same time increasing the burden of expenses imposed on the municipality. A number of Louisiana's new statutes simply applied only to cities with a population of over 300,000—that is, only to New Orleans.[8] Baltimore, Boston, Chicago, Des Moines, and New York are among the other cities that states have singled out over the years for special treatment despite classified charter systems.

States can also target actions in an effort to help their major metropolitan centers. Oklahoma, for instance, passed legislation to allow the state's two largest counties to levy a sales tax for the purpose of constructing facilities for lease to the federal government. The hope was that either Oklahoma or Tulsa County would be able to win the site of a new Department of Defense record-keeping center.[9]

HOME RULE AND HOME RULE CHARTERS

The term **home rule** is open to a variety of interpretations. Generally, home rule can be seen as an attempt to give cities (and counties) greater leeway to undertake action of their own without first having to obtain expressed state permission.

The difference between a **home rule charter** and the charters that we have discussed thus far depends on who has the right to write and alter the provisions in this basic governing document. An ordinary city charter can be altered only by the state legislature (or by whatever state agency or charter commission the legislature has charged with this task). A home rule charter, in contrast, is drafted by the municipality (not the state) and grants the municipal corporation a high degree of independence in making its own charter changes and revisions.

Home rule cities are generally free to enact laws of their own, just so long as these local laws do not contradict existing state statutes and are not preempted by state action in the field. The idea is to give cities more control over their own affairs. Yet, as home rule charters are granted under the authority of a state's constitution or statutes, it is still the state that ultimately defines just which powers are a city's under home rule.

The concept of home rule is popular. As Table 4.1 reveals, forty-eight states presently give their cities at least some measure of home rule authority. (Alabama and Vermont are the two exceptions.) Home rule for counties is somewhat less popular, with thirty-seven of the fifty states providing some local autonomy to counties.

Yet, just how much power each city and county possesses under home rule varies from state to state. Only twenty-eight states allow **broad functional home rule** where cities are permitted broad governmental powers and a great deal of autonomy and discretion in carrying out local functions. Seventeen states allow cities what can be called **limited functional home rule;** local governmental powers are greatly circumscribed, and only limited local discretion is permitted. Localities with **structural home rule** also enjoy some autonomy to determine their form of government.[10]

As we have already noted, the courts in some states have taken an expansive view of the powers allowed local governments. Some cities have taken the opportunity to get into areas not always seen as traditional city functions. Morton Grove, Illinois, used home rule authority to enact local handgun control.[11] New York City and Seattle instituted the partial public funding of election campaigns, despite the fact that no expressed state authority had been given to either city to enact such a law.[12] Controversy has also arisen in municipalities that have attempted to enact rent control ordinances without any explicit authorization from the state legislature to do so.

Even cities that enjoy expansive home rule powers do not possess complete autonomy. Dillon's Rule remains the prevailing legal doctrine. Home rule cities, like all cities, are still constrained by the many general acts of the state legislature, including state-imposed taxing, borrowing, and spending limits and regulatory requirements.

In California, local governments have traditionally enjoyed broad functional home rule. But the changes brought about by Proposition 13 and other levy and borrowing limitations have abridged local autonomy. Home rule has a "hollow ring" to it when local governments have little real policy discretion because the state has effectively denied them much of their ability to raise revenue. With no real ability to raise property taxes and other own-source revenues, cities and counties in California have had to become increasingly reliant on state aid and state decisions in service provision.[13]

TABLE 4.1
Local Home Rule Powers (by State), 199'

State	Cities				State Grants Any Home Rule Authority to Counties	Local Home Rule over the Structure of County Government	Func. Home Rule Powers	Hom. Rule Powers
	State Grants Any Home Rule Authority to Cities	Local Home Rule over the Structure of Government	Broad Functional Home Rule Powers	Limited Functional Home Rule Powers				
Alabama	No				No			
Alaska	Yes			√	Yes			√
Arizona	Yes	√	√		Yes			√
Arkansas	Yes	√		√	Yes	√	√	
California	Yes	√	√		Yes	√	√	
Colorado	Yes	√	√		Yes	√	√	
Connecticut	Yes	√		√	No			
Delaware	Yes		√		No			
Florida	Yes	√	√		Yes	√	√	
Georgia	Yes		√		Yes	√	√	
Hawaii	Yes	√		√	Yes	√		√
Idaho	Yes		√		Yes	√	√	
Illinois	Yes	√		√	Yes	√		√
Indiana	Yes			√	Yes			√
Iowa	Yes	√	√		Yes		√	
Kansas	Yes	√	√		Yes			√
Kentucky	Yes	√	√		Yes		√	
Louisiana	Yes	√	√		Yes	√	√	
Maine	Yes	√		√	Yes	√		
Maryland	Yes	√	√		Yes		√	
Massachusetts	Yes	√		√	No			
Michigan	Yes	√		√	Yes	√		√
Minnesota	Yes	√	√		Yes	√		√
Mississippi	Yes	√	√		No			
Missouri	Yes	√	√		Yes	√	√	
Montana	Yes	√	√		Yes	√	√	
Nebraska	Yes				No			
Nevada	Yes			√	Yes			√
New Hampshire	Yes	√		√	Yes			√
New Jersey	Yes	√	√		Yes	√	√	
New Mexico	Yes	√	√		Yes	√	√	
New York	Yes	√	√		Yes	√	√	
North Carolina	Yes				Yes			
North Dakota	Yes	√	√		Yes	√	√	
Ohio	Yes	√	√		Yes	√		√
Oklahoma	Yes	√			No			
Oregon	Yes	√		√	Yes			√
Pennsylvania	Yes	√		√	Yes	√		√
Rhode Island	Yes	√		√	No			
South Carolina	Yes	√		√	Yes	√	√	
South Dakota	Yes	√	√		Yes	√	√	
Tennessee	Yes	√	√		Yes	√	√	
Texas	Yes	√	√		No			
Utah	Yes	√	√		Yes			√
Vermont	No				No			
Virginia	Yes			√	No			
Washington	Yes	√		√	Yes	√	√	
West Virginia	Yes	√	√		No			
Wisconsin	Yes	√	√		Yes	√	√	
Wyoming	Yes	√	√		No			
Total	48	40	28	17	37	24	21	14

Source: Adapted from Advisory Commission on Intergovernmental Relations, *State Laws Governing Local Government Structure and Administration* (Washington, DC: ACIR, 1993), pp. 20–23.

HE FORMAL STRUCTURE OF CITY GOVERNMENT

THE FORMS OF GOVERNMENT

In the United States there are three principal forms of city government: the mayor-council plan (with its weak-mayor and strong-mayor variants), the commission plan, and the council-manager plan. The mayor-council and the council-manager plans dominate. Very few communities have opted for the commission system.

A slight plurality of American communities appear to have adopted the council-manager form.[14] The council-manager plan dominates in mid-sized communities. It is particularly associated with local government in the Pacific Coast states. However, in the nation's largest cities and in small towns of population of 5,000 or less, the more traditional mayor-council arrangement still prevails. The mayor-council arrangement is fairly popular in the Mid-Atlantic and North Central states.

In this section we shall discuss the relative advantages and disadvantages of the various forms of government. In discussing these forms, however, it is important to remember that few cities today exactly match any of these types of government in their pure forms. Rather, most cities mix reformed and unreformed elements in the structure of their governments.

WEAK-MAYOR SYSTEM

The reformers of the Progressive Era scorned the weak-mayor/council form of government—a form still prevalent in many American cities today. From the beginning of this country's history until about 1870, mayors were truly quite weak.[15] They were given few administrative powers. They presided over council meetings, but generally they did not even possess the power to veto council action. The country still regarded its colonial experience under George III as sound enough reason to minimize and check executive power, even at the local level.

By 1850 an enormous increase in municipal functions had occurred. State legislatures responded by creating a series of boards and commissions with functional responsibility for policy in areas such as education and law enforcement. In many cases the members of these boards and commissions were made part of the local government, with their members directly elected by the local citizenry. In some cases boards and commissions were almost completely controlled by the states as their members were appointed by state officials. By 1870 a movement to curb the powers exercised by state legislatures was under way. New local charters were drafted, which for the first time provided for significant increases in the powers of the mayor.

The primary difference between weak-mayor and strong-mayor systems is the amount of administrative authority accorded the mayor. In the weak-mayor system the power of the mayor as the city's chief executive is quite limited. The mayor lacks the power to appoint and remove administrative personnel. In weak-mayor cities the mayor shares administrative power with a variety of other officials, including independently elected executive branch officials (such as the local prosecutor or the city's financial controller), council appointees, and numerous independent boards and commissions over whom he or she does not possess direct authority (see Figure 4.1). In some cities the members of these boards and commissions are elected by the voters. In others they are appointed by the city council. In still others they might be appointed by the mayor but subject to council confirmation. In many cities these board members are appointed to long, fixed terms of office that effectively remove them from direct control by the mayor. In certain states, local boards might be mandated by state law with their officials more responsive to gubernatorial than to mayoral direction.

In the weakest of weak-mayor cities, mayors find themselves without staff and without the power to veto council-passed ordinances. In Houston the mayor traditionally possesses no veto power. In some weak-mayor cities, the council or an independent budget director, not the mayor, is charged with the preparation and presentation of a budget. In Madison, Wisconsin, the mayor does not directly control the operations of such city agencies as the police, fire, and welfare departments. Personnel matters, including the appointment and dismissal of top agency administrators, are handled by the independent citizens' boards and commissions (i.e., the Police and Fire Commission and the Public Welfare Commission). The members of these commissions serve rotating fixed terms; in the absence of resignations, a mayor gets to appoint only one member a year to a commission.

Similarly in San Francisco, executive authority is "divided, dispersed, and decentralized."[16] While the mayor in San Francisco possesses some authority typical of a strong-mayor system, on the whole he or she faces a difficult situation in having to work with an independently elected assessor and city attorney and a variety of independent boards and commissions that enjoy considerable policymaking power. In other areas, it is the city's chief administrative officer (CAO), not the mayor, who has direct control over the city bureaucracy. Similarly, in fiscal matters the mayor shares authority with a city controller. Although the CAO and controller are both appointed by the mayor, they have considerable autonomy as they can be removed only by a two-thirds vote of the Board of Supervisors (the equivalent of the city council).

The weak-mayor city provides numerous safeguards against the potential misuse of executive power. The independent boards and commissions, and the presence of council checks, all serve to insulate departments from improper political encroachment by the mayor. Under the weak-mayor system, for instance, no parks superintendent will feel the need to hire summer park workers only from a list submitted by

FIGURE 4.1
Two Variations of the Weak-Mayor Structure

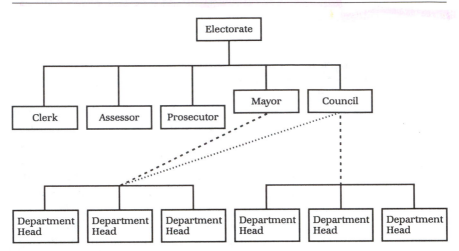

(a) The mayor does not possess total control over the executive branch but shares it with independently elected officials. Other departmental heads are subject to city council confirmation or are appointed directly by the council.

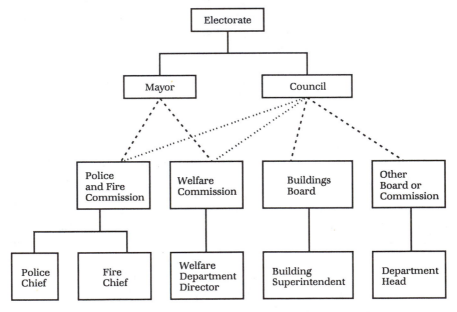

(b) Departmental heads are appointed not by the mayor but by independent boards and commissions. The members of these boards and commissions serve long, fixed terms and are appointed directly by the council or by the mayor, subject to council confirmation.

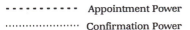

- - - - - - - - - -   Appointment Power

·····················   Confirmation Power

the mayor's office; protected by an independent parks commission that acts as a buffer between the superintendent and the mayor, the superintendent can feel free to run the city's parks according to professional norms.

Yet the disadvantages of the weak-mayor form of government are so considerable that reform and civic groups have routinely sought its replacement. Foremost among the objections is that the mayor is not given sufficient power to run the city. Just as no private business could be run efficiently without vesting significant power in the hands of its central executive, so too must sufficient power be vested in the head of the municipal corporation. Multiple executives and independent boards and commissions produce problems in coordination and direction. Such boards and commissions can also be dominated by amateurs who lack the training and understanding necessary to run city affairs competently.

Another problem in the weak-mayor form is that city voters do not know whom to blame when things go wrong. If parks services are not being adequately provided, is it the fault of the mayor, the parks superintendent, the independent parks commission, or the budget chief? In a strong-mayor system, in contrast, the lines of accountability are clear. Blame the mayor!

Of course, citizens in weak-mayor cities do in fact blame the mayor, the city's most visible elected official, when things go wrong—even when decisions were made by officials not directly under the mayor's authority. The weak-mayor system fails to give the mayor authority commensurate with the responsibility he or she bears.

On the whole, the weak-mayor form is seen to be inadequate to the task of governing large cities. The weak-mayor form is found mainly in smaller communities, particularly in the rural South, where the demands upon government are modest. On the other hand, Los Angeles, Minneapolis, and Seattle are notable large cities that have traditionally been governed by weak-mayor arrangements.

STRONG-MAYOR SYSTEM

Reformers believed that weak-mayor cities lacked the central executive authority necessary for the efficient running of a city's business. The reformers further believed that weak-mayor cities bred machine politics: In the absence of a strong executive, machines would emerge behind the scenes to help run the city.

As Figure 4.2 shows, under the strong-mayor structure the mayor is given substantial control over the workings of city departments. Like the American presidency with its right to appoint various cabinet and agency officials, the mayor in a strong-mayor city maintains the right to name the heads of the various municipal departments and agencies. In contrast with the weak-mayor system, the chief executive of a strong-mayor

FIGURE 4.2
Strong-Mayor Structure

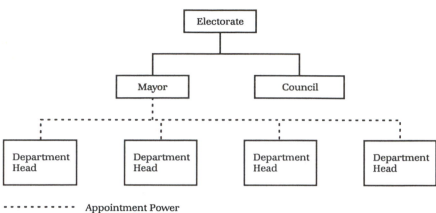

- - - - - - - - - -   Appointment Power

government does not contend for administrative power with a multitude of independently elected officials, council appointees, and citizen boards and commissions.

Of course, even strong-mayor charters do not grant unlimited power to the mayor. Most city charters include checks and balances on executive power. Councils often have the power to confirm the mayor's appointments as well as to limit his or her power to remove agency heads. Councils usually control the appropriations process, have the ability to restrict purchasing authority and contracting procedures, and can request audits and investigations of executive department activities. In cities where the mayor is given veto authority over city council actions, the council can vote to override the mayor's veto. Civil service systems also place great restraints on a mayor's executive power. Even a strong-mayor charter, then, does not automatically guarantee a mayor sufficient power for effective leadership. A number of strong-mayor cities have seen a succession of weak or uninfluential mayors.

The strong-mayor/council system is the dominant form of government in the nation's largest cities. Among those cities generally seen to be governed according to the strong-mayor form are Baltimore, Boston, Detroit, New York, Philadelphia, Pittsburgh, and St. Louis. The system appears to provide for the emergence of a leader who can mediate among the contending interests in a city. Giving the mayor sufficient power to hire and fire an executive team easily establishes accountability in the eyes of the voters, who can rightly blame the mayor for failures at city hall.

Yet many reformers soon found themselves dissatisfied with the strong-mayor system. Mayors could easily use their appointment powers to incur favors, repay political debts, and otherwise encourage patronage. Having department heads work directly under the mayor's thumb did not ensure administrators the protection needed for a truly professional, "scientific" administration. An administrator who failed to do the mayor's partisan bidding, even when such bidding ran contrary to the teachings and ethics of the administrator's profession, could too easily be fired.

Most of all, there was still no assurance that a mayor would be a trained administrator. Even in the nation's largest cities, the mayor may simply be a person who proved capable of surviving the local political obstacle course. The mayor may be a good campaigner, but he or she may not be skilled in the daily management of a city's affairs.

COMMISSION GOVERNMENT

Commission government probably originated in the Galveston, Texas, charter of 1901. The city government, which was operating under a mayor-council plan, had proved totally incapable of dealing with a disastrous flood during the previous year. At the request of a group of imaginative Galveston citizens, the Texas legislature granted the city a commission form of charter. Initially, the new government in Galveston proved so successful that it was widely imitated. Houston requested and received a similar charter in 1905.

The peak of popularity for the commission form of government was probably reached about 1917, when some 500 cities were operating under the plan. Since that time the number of adoptions has been small; Houston and other cities abandoned the plan as its disadvantages became apparent. As a result, only about 2 or 3 percent of all American cities are today governed by the commission plan. Its popularity has always been concentrated in small communities of less than 50,000 population. Tulsa and Portland are the nation's two largest cities with commission government.

Under the commission form of government, the same small group of persons (usually five to seven) who comprise the city council (referred to under the plan as the **city commission**) also act as administrative heads of the various city departments (see Figure 4.3). Normally, the commission members are chosen at large (not by districts) on a nonpartisan ballot. One commissioner is given the title of mayor. The title denotes only the titular head of the city; aside from presiding over meetings, greeting visiting dignitaries, and signing necessary federal aid forms, the mayor enjoys no more authority than any other commissioner.

By concentrating the powers of government in one set of hands, elected officials can respond quickly to the needs of the people. There is no checks-and-balances system to delay action.

Yet for most cities the disadvantages of the commission plan are overwhelming. Instead of providing quick action, the commission form often leads to deadlock. Each commissioner tends to represent only the narrow view of his or her own department; the plan creates no figure with the

FIGURE 4.3
Commission Structure

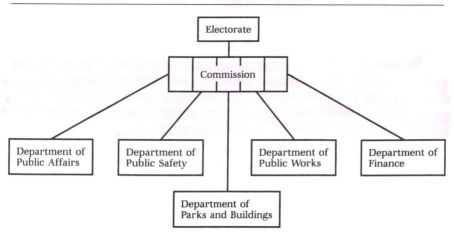

resources for effective leadership. There is little incentive for commission members to scrutinize carefully the budget requests of other departments, as such efforts are often rewarded by retaliation from other commissioners. Administrative reorganization proves difficult, as each commissioner acts to safeguard the interests and independence of his or her department. Voters also rarely take a candidate's administrative skills into great account when casting their ballots.

In recent years minority groups have also objected that the at-large election feature of the plan dilutes minority voting power. This was the basis of the challenge made against the commission plan of Mobile, Alabama, in 1980.[17]

COUNCIL-MANAGER (CITY MANAGER) GOVERNMENT

In 1908 Staunton, Virginia, became the first city to create the position of a general city manager with extensive administrative authority. After the success of Staunton's government became known, Richard Childs, president of the National Municipal League, a leading reform organization, began to promote the concept of council-manager government. The league's booklet, the *Model City Charter*, also extolled the virtues of the council-manager plan.[18] By 1920 over 100 cities had adopted the council-manager plan: it had become a critical component of the reform movement in local government.

Today, council-manager government is most commonly found in middle-sized cities with populations between 25,000 and 250,000. Small towns usually find it too expensive to hire a full-time, professional manager. Big cities are usually too diverse and heterogeneous to permit effective managerial direction. City managers are not allowed the autonomy to perform their jobs smoothly when substantial debate exists over just what policy goals a city should pursue. Though the nation's largest cities—New York, Los Angeles, Chicago, Houston, Philadelphia, and Detroit—all spurned the city manager form, the system has proven quite popular in Sunbelt cities. Dallas, San Diego, Phoenix, San Antonio, San Jose, Long Beach, Tucson, Fort Worth, Austin, Oklahoma City, Jacksonville, Charlotte, Memphis, Virginia Beach, and Miami Metro are all Sunbelt cities that have adopted the council-manager plan. Kansas City and Cincinnati also employ the city manager system of government.

Under the council-manager plan, the city council appoints a professionally trained manager, who is then given responsibility for running the daily affairs of the city (see Figure 4.4). Legislative policy making remains within the realm of the council; administration falls within the domain of the city manager. The manager is directly in charge of departmental heads and supervises their performance. The council retains the ultimate authority to dismiss or replace its appointed manager.

As with the commission plan, the council-manager plan provides for a mayor's office that is largely titular and ceremonial in nature; the mayor possesses no general administrative, appointive, or veto powers. Usually, the mayor is chosen by the council from among its own membership—although some council-manager cities retain direct city-wide elections for the mayor. The council itself is usually not large. Members are normally elected on a nonpartisan and at-large basis—although some cities retain district election or a system that mixes both at-large and district representatives.

Leadership in Council-Manager Cities

The line between policy formulation by the council and administration by the manager is never quite clear. The most successful managers have always been initiators of policy, even if only in subtle ways. A city manager must do more than simply direct the municipal bureaucracy; a city manager is also expected to function as an arm of the city council and to assist in the highest levels of policy development.[19] City council members look to the manager for leadership. Where councilmanic positions are only part-time, council members are quite dependent on the research, options, and policy advice presented by the manager. Yet the manager must be careful in exercising influence, for the manager serves at the pleasure of the council and may be discharged by the council at any time.

City managers do not always choose to play an aggressive role in policy making. Most see their role as that of an *expert adviser* whose job it is to provide information and recommendations to the city council. They spurn playing the alternative role of the *political activist* who attempts to build a power base in order to get the council to follow his or her policy leads.[20] One survey of city and county managers in North Carolina found

FIGURE 4.4
Council-Manager Plan

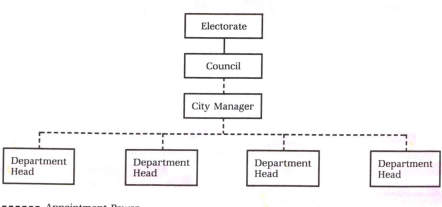

------ Appointment Power

that over half of the respondents preferred to confine their activities to administration, leaving policy matters to the councils.[21] The seeming ability of city managers to divorce policy making from administration may be the result of their professional training.

Yet, the separation between policy making and administration is not clear-cut. In clarifying policy options, developing choices, and deciding what information should be provided council members, managers influence policy. Also, just what matters fall under the headings of *policy* and *administration*? Jeffrey Pressman reported that Oakland, California, City Manager Jerome Keithley (1966–72) had a tendency to "define 'policy' and 'administration' in a manner in which 'administration' loomed very large and 'policy' loomed very small."[22] The city manager even argued that the mayor and council had no right to set a policy governing police officers' use of handguns:

> The manager's reasoning was clear. "A policy decision would be that policemen in Oakland should carry guns. Administrative decisions would be when they should carry guns, where they should carry guns, and how they should use those guns."[23]

A number of studies have reported the increased willingness of city managers to engage in policy-making activities. Policy-related activities are an unavoidable part of the city manager's job. The profession has accepted that its members by necessity will be involved in such policy-making activities as agenda setting, proposal development, and advocacy.[24] The older reform ideal of a city manager as an administrative expert insulated from the political process has given way to the vision of a dynamic executive leader who is capable of brokering community interests and building a policy consensus.[25]

Also, a new breed of city managers has emerged, who see an important role for themselves in policy making. Their concerns go beyond a simple managerial efficiency. They aid city councils in policy development. They also value citizen participation and the achievement of equity goals.[26]

One survey of over 1,400 suburban communities has found that a minority of city managers have acted as entrepreneurial leaders who propel dynamic policy change in response to citizens' demands and changed local conditions. These city managers are especially likely to seize the opportunity to act when local elected officials fail to initiate innovative policy.[27] Although activist managers are salespeople for new policies, on the whole they prefer to handle issues quietly, working behind the scenes.[28]

Managers are not purely neutral; their actions reflect their political ideology. Conservative managers tend to favor more fiscal prudence, whereas liberal managers opt for a more activist approach to social problems.[29]

Not surprisingly, the mayor and manager may wind up being competitors for influence. Even in a council-manager city, the mayor is still the most visible public official; he or she is expected to lead. The mayor's influence is enhanced in those cities where he or she is directly elected by the public. The mayor may accuse a city manager of improperly straying beyond matters of administration in attempting to influence the making of city policy. The manager, in turn, often sees the mayor and council members as overreaching their prerogatives in attempting to intrude into matters of administration that clearly fall under his or her domain.

James Svara has found out that the old policy-administration dichotomy no longer sufficiently describes the balance of activities between a city's elected officials and its manager. According to Svara, city councils are dominant in determining a city's overall **mission,** setting the city's general philosophy regarding taxing, spending, and growth. City managers and the council are both active when it comes to making specific decisions regarding **policy,** deciding just what programs will be initiated and services provided. City managers, however, dominate actual **administration** or implementation, the decisions regarding the daily workings of municipal programs. Council members tend to intervene in this administration only when required by oversight or when prompted by citizen complaints. Finally, broad issues of **management**—personnel, budgeting, purchasing, contracting, and data processing—are primarily left up to the city manager. In sum, overburdened, part-time council members retain their authority to determine the city's overall policy direction but leave the tasks of administration and management to the professional manager. The mayor can use the visibility of his or her office to provide guidance on policy issues and effective coordination even while ceding administrative and managerial matters to the professional executive.[30]

The relationship between the mayor and city manager varies from city to city and from personality to personality. In a number of cities, the relationship between the council and manager approximates the smooth working relationship of a private corporation's board of directors and its chief executive officer. In other cities the manager dominates passive councils. In still others the manager is victimized by an activist council or an ambitious mayor. In some cities a heated conflict may develop between the mayor and the manager.

Advantages of the Council-Manager Plan

The great advantage of the council-manager plan is the administrative strength it provides. A trained professional is hired to deal with the complex, increasingly technical problems of running a city. Administrative responsibility is centralized in the hands of one official. Professional standards are applied, and parochial and partisan concerns are resisted. The professionalism of city managers is evident in that the managers have developed a national organization with supportive conferences and publications. Successful performance brings with it recognition and career advancement; successful managers "move up" to bigger cities.

The council-manager plan also tends to produce governance based on cooperation rather than conflict. The council-manager plan predisposes actors to work together. Under the council-manager system, leadership roles are relatively specialized. As a result, there are generally fewer battles for power among officials in council-manager cities as compared to mayor-council cities. Cooperation is the result of shared goals and concentration of authority. The process by which a manager is chosen further contributes to the formulation of a shared mission. Selection by the council also helps to assure that the manager will be acceptable to a majority of the city's legislature.[31]

Criticisms of the Council-Manager Plan

The council-manager plan is also subject to numerous criticisms. First, the plan does not always work in reality as it does in theory. Some city councils, after one or two bad experiences with outside professionals, choose a local official to serve as manager, compromising professional training and competence. Also, a city council may not be able to dismiss a manager as easily as the council-manager model assumes. A municipality that gains a reputation as being a "bad" place for city managers to work will find itself at a disadvantage when competing to recruit a truly talented manager. Part-time council members may also be reluctant to undertake the time-consuming tasks involved in advertising for, screening, and interviewing new manager candidates.

In some cases, city managers cultivate important constituencies that make it nearly impossible to fire them. Miami Mayor Maurice Ferré learned this lesson too late when he dismissed city manager Howard

Gary, a black man. Ferré had won 97 percent of the black vote in the previous election. But in 1985, after his controversial firing of Gary, Ferré's support among black voters fell to a mere 10 percent. Xavier Suárez, the candidate Ferré had defeated two years previously, became the first Cuban-American to be elected mayor of Miami.[32]

One major criticism of the council-manager arrangement focuses on the question of responsiveness. Not having to face the public in a general election, a manager may not always be responsive to citizens' demands. A conservative manager may pursue tax stabilization and efficiency despite citizens' demands for new services. A corporate-oriented manager may pursue new business development and continued growth despite the objections of city neighborhoods opposed to the increased congestion and environmental destruction.

While an aggressive city manager can sometimes dominate policy making, in other municipalities the council-manager plan fails to provide for adequate political leadership. Writing in the 1960s, Jean Stinchcombe blamed Toledo's then-thirty years of experience with the city manager system for the absence of effective leadership in that city. In Toledo, mayors were amateur politicians who were for the most part content with performing the ceremonial aspects of their jobs. City managers "avoided public controversy or conspicuous leadership in order not to jeopardize the support crucial to their continued service and salary."[33] At long last, in the 1990s, a beleaguered Toledo abandoned elements of its "good government" past and strengthened the mayoralty.

Managerial government often is criticized for not being able to provide adequate leadership for the nation's largest cities, where municipal leaders face the difficult tasks of having to reconcile the conflicting demands of competing public groups. In such a setting, an elected mayor, not an appointed manager, is likely to have the public visibility and conflict orientation to engage in the far-reaching political campaign, public relations, and coalition-building activities necessary for leadership.

Modifying the Council-Manager System: The Case of San Diego and Other California Cities

The limitations of the council-manager model were most readily apparent in San Diego, the nation's second largest council-manager city. During his eleven-year (1971–82) tenure as mayor, Pete Wilson virtually "created" the office of mayor to deal with the emerging conflicts that the city manager could not resolve. The city manager's office had been the business community's line to a government that allowed for the boosterism and growth of the city. But newly active community and taxpayer groups were no longer pleased with unbridled growth.

When Wilson tried to walk a middle-line between booster and anti-growth factions, he came to find that the city's council-manager form of government was a "structural straitjacket" that severely limited his power.[34]

Wilson tried to reform the city charter, but voters overwhelmingly rejected the proposal to bring a strong-mayor system to San Diego.

Despite the charter reform defeat, Wilson succeeded in strengthening the power of the mayoralty. New rules in San Diego gave the mayor the right to name the members and chairs of the city council standing committees. Several new positions in the mayor's office, including a consultant for each council committee and an independent fiscal analyst, were created to give both the mayor and council new sources of information independent of those provided by the city manager. The mayor also gained the power to control what issues would go before the full council as well as the right to name appointments to various city boards and commissions.

According to Glen Sparrow, Wilson transformed the nature of city government in San Diego. Although San Diego still formally retained the council-manager structure, "knowledgeable people" recognized that Wilson was in charge. A succession of four city managers resigned, but Wilson found one who was willing to accept the heightened role that the mayor would play in policy and budget formation and downtown redevelopment. In San Diego, the mayoralty was strengthened, as "Leadership that is visionary, active, and responsible to the voters has become the preferred form."[35]

Pete Wilson left San Diego in 1982 to serve as U.S. Senator and later as governor. The mayors who succeeded him in office—Roger Hedgecock and Maureen O'Connor—were less effective leaders. They confronted a city manager and city council that acted to regain their prerogatives. The city manager assumed a new importance in the budget process, and the city council reduced some of the mayor's appointive powers. In the absence of city charter reforms to institutionalize the mayor's power, the gains that Wilson had made as mayor could not all be sustained. Executive leadership in San Diego proved quite ephemeral as mayoral power depended more on the personality and leadership style of each individual mayor than on the powers of the office. Wilson had the personality and vision for leadership, but in the years after he left San Diego, the city suffered from confusion, drift, and a lack of direction as the mayor, city manager, and city council all competed for power.

San Diego is not the only city to modify its form of government in the pursuit of more effective executive leadership. A similar modification of the city manager plan is also evident in other California cities. Oakland was once characterized by the leaderlessness of a local political system where, even in the explosive 1960s and early 1970s, a part-time, poorly paid, understaffed mayor was ill-equipped to challenge the business-as-usual priorities of a conservative city manager.[36] Since that time, a black-liberal coalition has come to power in Oakland and strengthened the problem-solving abilities of city government. The mayor now is well paid and serves full-time.

San Jose, too, has enhanced its mayoralty as the city began to confront the problems associated with rapid growth. San Jose, Sacramento, and Hayward all moved to the direct election of mayors. In these and other California cities, including Oakland, city managers were no longer regarded as "neutral"; city councils dismissed managers seen to be part of the old governing regime.[37]

A LESS SWEEPING REFORM: THE CAO

Reformers sought to introduce improved managerial competency even into municipalities where they could not get the council-manager plan enacted. In mayor-council cities they sought to embody administrative professionalism in the form of a **chief administrative officer (CAO)** who would serve as an adviser to the mayor. The chief difference between a CAO and a city manager is that the CAO reports to the mayor, not to the city council.

The exact powers and workings of the CAO position vary from city to city. The primary responsibilities of the CAO tend to be in the areas of budgeting, fiscal affairs, and personnel. In some cities, the CAO is charged solely with advising the mayor, handling whatever responsibilities the mayor chooses to assign. In other cities, the CAO is also given responsibility for supervising certain departments.

In some cities, the CAO is a permanent position that continues from administration to administration. Here the CAO represents a valuable source of institutional memory and continuity in city affairs; a new mayor has an insider from whom he or she can learn about the budget, the administrative processes, and the power realities within city hall. Sometimes, however, a newly elected mayor may distrust a CAO as being too closely tied to the policies of the outgoing administration.

In most cities the CAO is not a permanent position but is subject to mayoral appointment. The average tenure for CAOs is only two to three years.[38] In San Francisco and Los Angeles, however, the position is afforded some security in order to insulate the CAO against direct mayoral control and political interference. In Los Angeles, city council approval is required for the hiring and firing of a CAO.

San Francisco in 1931 was one of the first cities to install a CAO. Los Angeles, Philadelphia, Boston, and New Orleans are among the nation's larger cities to have positions that in many ways resemble a CAO. New York City formally abolished its City Administrator position in the 1970s only to create a new system of deputy mayors that embodies much of the original CAO concept.

Whatever the exact arrangement, the goal of the CAO plan is clear—to provide to mayors the technical competency and administrative expertise of a career professional. In some cities, the CAO has duties so extensive that they approximate those of a city manager. In Los Angeles, the duties of the office are so vast that in 1987 one national organization chose CAO Keith Comrie as its all-pro "city manager" of the year.[39] In most cases, however, the CAO is appointed by the mayor for reasons in addition to his or her professional qualifications.

Overall, the CAO position embodies less political independence and less of a professional orientation than does a city manager.[40] The CAO represents a compromise between the strong-mayor and council-manager forms of government.

CITY COUNCILS

Only in the largest cities in the United States is service on a city council a full-time, well-paid job. Only half of the nation's cities with a population of 500,000 and above hold weekly council meetings. In smaller communities, councils usually meet every other week or once a month.[41] Outside of the nation's largest cities, councils tend to be small, with, on the average, fewer than ten members. In contrast to the U.S. Congress and the great majority of state legislatures, most local councils do not organize along political party lines.[42]

Part-time, poorly paid councils may fit the grassroots ideal of a citizens' legislature. But such councils are often poorly equipped to handle the complex job of what, in many cases, is a big business—directing the affairs of a city. Council members are reliant on the work of adequate support staff, which in many cases is denied. Frequent turnover among council members also diminishes a council's ability to develop the necessary skills and knowledge to do their job.[43]

Amateurish, part-time legislators with little experience in government are in a poor position to challenge the reports and recommendations of the mayor, city manager, or department heads. They also lack the time necessary to oversee the performance of municipal agencies. As one local government commentator summarized, "[D]espite the idealized view of council members as rational, detached governors and merit-minded supervisors, in actuality many are befuddled policy makers, overly engaged implementors, and near-sighted overseers who ignore their supervisory role."[44]

Inadequate staffing does not fully explain the failure of city councils to keep a close watch over the municipal bureaucracy. Between 1959 and 1987, the central staff of the New York City Council was increased from 8 to over 120 without producing effective oversight.[45] Local legislators simply lack the motivation to engage in administrative oversight, an activity that receives little publicity and is seldom rewarded by voters.

But mayors and managers do not always succeed in dominating their city councils. Sometimes, city council divisions and fragmentation pose an obstacle to getting things done. In Philadelphia in the 1980s, an increasingly populist city council vetoed major development projects.

Neighborhood advocates were able to gain a sympathetic ear from council representatives elected from local districts. The overall result was to produce a political system that was incapable of mediating conflict or producing needed policy change.[46]

Especially in mayor-council cities, mayors will seek an "end run" around recalcitrant councils. In New York City, the council's legislative powers have been challenged by the ability of mayors to promulgate **executive orders** to create new agencies and programs. Under the city charter, New York's mayors have all powers not specifically delegated to other bodies. The courts will ultimately determine the exact scope of the quasi-legislative authority enjoyed by New York's mayors.[47]

On the whole, city council members do not serve lengthy legislative careers. Only about half of a newly elected council class will still be on the council five years later. Although council members seldom face defeat at the hands of voters, many choose to leave voluntarily as a result of the conflicts that council service poses with family life and business careers.[48]

Despite the evidence of substantial city council turnover, public opinion polls point to continuing interest in **term limitations.** Yet, as of the early 1990s relatively few communities—fewer than 5 percent—had instituted this procedure for their local councils.[49] One possible negative effect of term limitations is that they may "neuter" local councils by inhibiting the development of the political skills and governmental knowledge that accompany members' growing length of service.[50] Yet, as we will discuss further in Chapter 6, term limitations can also be viewed as part of a new reform movement designed to promote greater governmental responsiveness to the public.

What can be done to increase the quality of council performance? First, city councils need greater staff support if council members are to have an informed and independent voice in governmental affairs. Second, legislators must be offered modest but respectable compensation if they are to be expected to devote the considerable time necessary to do the public's business. Third, cities that have two-year terms for council members might consider shifting to four-year terms. Two-year terms do not make it more likely that incumbents will be defeated. Instead, frequent elections only pose an additional burden on part-time public servants, leading some of the more talented and capable council representatives to retire voluntarily from office.[51]

Women hold over 20 percent of the council seats in medium and large cities. While this figure falls far short of parity, it still represents a greater presence than women have achieved in the U.S. Congress. Women bear the brunt of family and child-care responsibilities, and it appears that service at the local level is less burdensome than the more extensive sacrifices required by national office. Evidence also seems to indicate that female council representatives devote more time to their legislative work than do men. Compared to men, women are also beginning to serve lengthier careers of council service. These trends point to the possibility that women may be emerging as a new force in city politics.[52]

MAYORAL LEADERSHIP STYLE

The study of formal governmental structure does not by itself reveal who has the power to run a city's affairs. As we have already noted, Chicago's Richard J. Daley and San Diego's Pete Wilson were two mayors who were able to provide effective leadership despite the relatively weak powers given to them under their city charters. Much more attention needs to be paid to an individual mayor's leadership style and not simply to the formal structures outlined in city charters.

THE DIFFICULT TASK OF MAYORAL LEADERSHIP

The formal powers and prerogatives of office are important to the mayor; they are the beginnings of influence. Writing in the 1970s, Jeffrey Pressman suggested that in order to exercise effective leadership, a mayor would first require several resources. These included sufficient staff and financial resources; municipal and mayoral authority over key program areas; sufficient remuneration to allow the mayor to serve as a full-time executive and to gain the respect of other officials and actors; and access to friendly media and political organizations that can be mobilized by the mayor to help achieve specific goals.[53] Direct election is another critical resource; mayors who are appointed by the city council cannot claim any great legitimacy in speaking for the community. In a great many cities, mayors are denied these preconditions of effective leadership.

The importance of a strong party organization to a mayor's power is underscored by a comparison of Chicago and New York. In the 1960s and early 1970s, Chicago's political machine organization allowed Richard J. Daley to constrain the demands of municipal workers for higher wages and benefits and to resist demands for new public spending. In New York, in contrast, in the absence of a strong party organization, mayors more readily acceded to the demands of these constituencies and the city teetered on the edge of bankruptcy.[54]

Today, Pressman's list of the preconditions of mayoral leadership would have to be broadened in recognition of the great influence that intergovernmental aid programs, regulations, and mandates have on local affairs. An effective mayor has to take on the role of **intergovernmental ambassador;** he or she must have sufficient time, budget, and staff support to lobby national, state, and regional actors.

City problems are so voluminous and complex, and mayoral powers so weak and limited in comparison, that some urban observers have proclaimed the modern city to be "ungovernable."[55] Social problems do not yield themselves to easy solutions. In major cities, the problem-solving capacity of municipal government is further undermined by excessive decentralization, too great a dependence on state and federal sources for program funding, and the inability of the mayor and the top administrative echelon to manage their bureaucracies. Douglas Yates examined urban politics in the 1960s and 1970s and found a never-ending spiral of demands and an unstructured free-for-all among contending city interests, which he labeled **street-fighting pluralism.** In such a hectic environment, mayors and other city decision makers "cannot easily plan for tomorrow's problems when they are fully occupied responding to today's, yesterday's, and last month's accumulated inventory."[56] Yates uses the metaphor of a "shooting gallery player" who "will frantically move from target to target" to describe the essentially reactive nature of city policy making.[57]

MAYORAL STYLE AND THE POSSIBILITY OF LEADERSHIP

The context of a city's politics does not by itself determine the possibilities for leadership. Leadership is also a product of a mayor's personality and style. Mayors with different personalities will assume quite different leadership orientations.

A Typology of Leadership Styles

John P. Kotter and Paul R. Lawrence have identified five different mayoral leadership approaches:

1. The **Ceremonial** mayor attempts few policy initiatives and is for the most part content to deal with the ceremonial aspects of the job.
2. The **Caretaker** mayor focuses on short-term issues and "what comes up." This mayor is essentially a troubleshooter who lacks a long-term vision or agenda for the city.
3. The **Individualist** is a mayor who attempts to make some changes in the city but goes about it through personal appeals instead of trying to build broader coalitions, alliances, or networks.
4. The **Executive** is a project-oriented mayor who attempts to get things done primarily by relying on his or her managerial skills and administrative authority.
5. The **Entrepreneur** has clear program goals and attempts to have a major impact on the city. The entrepreneur engages in a full range of public and coalition-building activities in order to amass broad community support for his or her program goals.[58]

Given the intractability of city problems and the street fighting observed by Yates, it is little wonder that effective leadership is relatively rare. Most big-city mayors observed by Kotter and Lawrence tend to be caretaker, ceremonial, and individualist mayors; very few were seen to be effective executives or entrepreneurs.

Yet such an overview understates the possibilities for mayoral leadership. Especially in council-manager cities, effective, but less conflict-oriented, leadership emerges. In the council-manager system, nonexecutive mayors act as a guiding force in city government. Effective mayors in such systems will often play the role of **coordinator** or **director.** They build a consensus on the city council and serve as a liaison with the city manager. They are team builders and facilitators who work cooperatively with both the city manager and city council in policy development. Instead of attempting to build a broad-based political coalition, they seek to strengthen, not supplant, other actors in the political system.[59] But even in council-manager cities, mayoral leadership will be inadequate if the mayor lacks the ability to get increasingly fractious and diverse council members to work together.[60]

Are Cities Ungovernable? Boston and New York Reexamined

Even in major, conflict-ridden cities, mayoral leadership may be more possible than the earlier generalizations admit. Yates' assessment may be unduly pessimistic as he overgeneralizes from the experience of New York City in the 1960s. Not all cities suffer the extreme fragmentation of governmental authority apparent in New York. Also, cities no longer suffer the degree in internecine conflict and "street fight" experienced by New York in the sixties.

An analysis of Boston mayors will serve as a case in point. Kevin White, first elected mayor in 1967 as a progressive moderate, survived Boston's street fight and the turmoil over school busing, gaining re-election until his retirement in 1983.[61] White adapted his style over time, playing the roles of reform-style individualist, city executive, entrepreneurial coalition-builder. In a number of ways he built his political power in the same manner as did the city's machine bosses of an earlier age.

White took advantage of neighborhood decentralization, building a system of little city halls to tie the mayor's office to the neighborhoods. His coalition of support extended beyond his ethnic Irish base; he dispensed highly symbolic appointments, lower-level jobs, and neighborhood projects to blacks, white liberals, and Italians.

White was able to centralize power as a result of the resources offered by the city's strong-mayor structure as well as the city's tradition of partisan politics. White enjoyed the advantages of a four-year term, extensive power over the budget, a large mayoral staff exempt from civil service, and the ability to name a large number of appointees on a "holdover" basis. But White saw these advantages to be an insufficient guarantee of leadership. He attempted to gain a new charter that would have centralized even more power in the mayor's hands. When the voters defeated this effort, White resorted to the creation of a machinelike political organization under which, for instance, public appointees were often expected to work in, and contribute to, the mayor's reelection efforts. As White saw it, whatever helped to build his power helped to further his policies. Over time, however, minority and neighborhood groups came to be suspicious of White's centralized power and connections to city developers.

White's successor, urban populist Raymond Flynn (1983–93), also proved successful, utilizing a quite different approach to governance. Flynn governed in different times. Unlike White, he could not depend on federal funds. Instead, he sought out public-private partnerships. He also acted to ensure that the benefits of economic growth would be shared by the city's disadvantaged residents. Flynn built an activist, progressive administration that attempted to meet the needs of the city's poor while at the same time providing a hospitable climate for the growth of business. He established a **linkage program** that forced downtown developers to contribute to a neighborhood housing fund. Flynn also bridged the city's racial tensions. He opposed school busing but fought to desegregate public housing. He won higher vote margins in black and Hispanic areas of the city than in white wards. Reelected twice, Flynn left office in the midst of his third term in order to become Bill Clinton's ambassador to the Vatican.[62]

Successful mayoral leadership was also exhibited in New York by a much different sort of mayor. In contrast to Ray Flynn's progressive politics, Ed Koch took New York City from the edge of bankruptcy and governed for twelve years by constructing a more conservative coalition.[63] Assuming the mayoralty in the wake of the city's fiscal crisis, Koch reestablished friendly ties with the federal government, whose continued program of seasonal loans the city required in order to get back on its feet. Koch essentially delivered on his promise to Congress that the city would balance its books, get its fiscal house in order, and countenance no fiscal gimmicks. Koch initially cut programs and even took on the municipal unions, delaying pay raises and negotiating "givebacks." He also brought numerous economic development projects, including a new convention center, to the city.

Koch's success did not come without costs. The mayor gave hundreds of millions of dollars of incentives and tax benefits to encourage private investment in the city—investment that spurred the city's land boom but aggravated the city's shortage of affordable housing. Spokespersons in the black community became increasingly critical of Koch's performance and his "shoot-from-the-lip" style. Koch denounced Jesse Jackson in New York's 1988 presidential primary, putting increased distance between himself and the city's black community.

Koch succeeded in governing the ungovernable city. He reoriented the city's policy direction. Yet, parts of the city, including the school system, remained beyond the mayor's reach. Well-publicized corruption exposés of machine-style patronage and corruption also hurt the mayor. The issuance of car-towing contracts in Queens was marred by payoffs. The Queens borough president, linked to the scandal, committed suicide.

By 1989, after three terms in office, even New Yorkers tired of the mayor's combative style. David Dinkins beat Koch in the Democratic primary and went on to become the city's first black mayor.

An Overall Assessment: What Prospects for Leadership?

Effective leadership in major American cities does not come easily. Yet, this does not mean that leadership is impossible or that cities are ungovernable.

A city's formal structure affects the prospects for leadership. Strong-mayor cities provide their executives with the resources that are the preconditions of leadership. In other cities, mayors face a more difficult job. In city manager systems, effective mayors will likely play the role of a coordinator or facilitator. They will take a more cooperative-oriented, as opposed to conflict-oriented, approach to leadership.

But formal resources and structure are only the beginnings of mayoral power. Effective mayors will skillfully build their influence; ineffective ones will waste their resources, producing little. Leadership style is a factor that helps to determine how effective or ineffective a mayor will be.

MINORITY MAYORS: BUILDING BIRACIAL (AND MULTIRACIAL) COALITIONS?

Effective leadership is especially difficult for racial minority mayors, especially if they must govern in quite polarized situations. Minority mayors face a difficult choice: Should they attempt to use city resources in an all-out effort to redress racial discrimination? Or should they moderate their approach and thereby seek to build and maintain biracial (and, in some cases, multiracial) coalitions?

COALITION-BUILDING OR RACIAL PARTISANSHIP? CLEVELAND AND GARY

Charles Levine's comparison of two of the first generation of big-city black mayors underscores the difficulty of the choice faced by minority mayors. Cleveland's Carl Stokes and Gary (Indiana) mayor Richard Hatcher were both elected in 1967. Given the racial polarizations of the time, Hatcher initially proved to be the more successful mayor.[64]

Stokes had put together a **biracial coalition** of black voters and white liberals to gain election in Cleveland. He attempted to be an entrepreneurial mayor who would lead by building a broad-based, executive-centered coalition that would embrace white as well as black interests. However, his programs were thwarted by the refusal of the city's white ethnic leaders to accede to his plans.

Hatcher, in contrast, acted as a stronger **partisan** of black interests. Stokes finally achieved a greater degree of policy success in Cleveland only after he abandoned his original attempt at consensus building and adopted Hatcher's more conflict-oriented leadership approach. In certain polarized situations a mayor can gain substantial policy achievements only by pursuing a strategy of conflict, with all its accompanying risks.

In many cities, minority mayors can seek to maximize policy change only at the cost of alienating crucial swing votes. Stokes' new conflict orientation resulted in heightened controversy that undermined the biracial alliance that had put him in office. When he chose not to run for reelection, the black candidate who ran as his designated successor was denied office by the voters, and a number of the gains that Stokes had made were rolled back. For two decades, African-Americans lost their handle on Cleveland's mayoralty—an office that would not again be won by a black candidate until Michael White in 1989 ran on the themes of neighborhood cooperation and racial harmony.[65]

COALITION-BUILDING IN SAN ANTONIO

Henry Cisneros' mayoralty in San Antonio shows that a racial minority mayor can successfully govern by forming a coalition that crosses racial lines.[66] Cisneros' 1981 election marked a decisive victory for his city's emerging Mexican-American community. Cisneros acted to ensure that his election did not usher in a new period of hostility between the city's Anglo and Latino communities. Instead, he sought to bridge relations between the two communities and forge a new sense of unity. Cisneros believed that job opportunities for the city's Latino population were dependent on the overall economic health of the city and its downtown. And that health, in Cisneros' eyes, was dependent on the city's ability to attract high-technology business. Cisneros was an outspoken advocate of both Chicano interests and the necessity for reforming cities to meet the needs of business in a high-tech society.

Cisneros was a broad-based coalition builder, but his formal power was limited by the city's classic council-manager system of government. Also, by the late 1980s, some of the bloom had worn off his mayoralty as activist community groups claimed he concentrated resources on the city's central business district to the neglect of the neighborhoods.[67] COPS (Communities Organized for Public Services), a neighborhood organization in the city's poorer Latino sections, was critical of a number of Cisneros' downtown development projects. Cisneros gained voter approval for the construction of a 65,000-seat domed stadium only after first suffering very bitter criticisms from civic groups who said San Antonio had more pressing needs. Newspaper stories also focused on Cisneros' personal life, including problems in his marriage and the health difficulties of his young son. In 1989 Cisneros declined to seek a fifth two-year term. He later became Bill Clinton's Secretary for Housing and Urban Development.

THE KEYS TO BIRACIAL COALITIONS: NEW YORK AND LOS ANGELES COMPARED

Why is it that biracial and multiracial coalitions emerge in some cities and not in others? Raphael Sonenshein's comparison of New York City and Los Angeles helps to identify some of the factors that work to facilitate, or alternatively to disrupt, the formation of a biracial coalition.[68]

A biracial coalition was a major factor in Los Angeles politics and helped produce the five-term, twenty-year rule of an African-American, Mayor Tom Bradley. In New York, in contrast, for a long period of time, no such biracial coalition emerged despite the city's liberal political tradition. Even when a multiracial coalition finally emerged in New York to elect David Dinkins mayor in 1989, the victory was short-lived. The coalition dissipated, and Rudolph Giuliani ousted the city's first black mayor after a single term in office.

Why is it that a strong biracial coalition emerged in Los Angeles and not New York? In New York, blacks and white liberals (especially the city's liberal Jewish population) were competitors for power. In New York, blacks could demand jobs in the schools or ownership of neighborhood stores only by denying Jews and white reformers positions they already held. Memories of the bitter intergroup conflicts of the 1960s also continued to act as a barrier to later attempts at intergroup bridge-building. In Los Angeles, in contrast, African-Americans and Jews were both outsiders. As neither group had a strong stake in Los Angeles' then-conservative municipal political system, both had something to gain from forming an alliance.

The quality of the local political leadership is another crucial factor that explains why a dominant biracial coalition was able to form in Los Angeles but not in New York. Tom Bradley was a "tough cop" who lived in a middle-class neighborhood. Even in the early stages of his political career, he built alliances with white liberal groups. He was not a street radical whose rhetoric and redistributional agenda offended potential white allies. In New York, in contrast, more divisive, ethnocentric leaders have emerged in many black and Jewish organizations.

But even in Los Angeles, biracial leadership, despite all its successes, had its costs. Critics charged that Bradley focused on the needs of developers and the building of a new glass-tower downtown, to the neglect of poorer neighborhoods. The outburst of violence in South Central only served as testimony to the extent that living conditions in the city's worst areas remained unchanged during the Bradley era.

Bradley also had a difficult time in balancing the competing demands of his diverse coalition members over his twenty years in office. Community activists wanted the revitalization of poorer areas of the city, not of the downtown. Business and labor backed new development, but west side environmentalists opposed it.[69] Racial minority groups also saw continued growth as the foundation of new jobs. And Bradley lost support among whites as he attempted to remove Police Chief Daryl Gates from his job. Over the years, Latinos and Asian-Americans had been integrated into the coalition, but their loyalty, too, was strained after the riots in the wake of the Rodney King verdict.

In the 1993 election that followed Bradley's retirement, the city elected conservative, Republican millionaire Richard Riordan as mayor. In his bid for the mayoralty, liberal City Councillor Michael Woo was unable to piece the multiracial coalition back together. Woo had built bridges to the African-American community; he was even able to bridge much of the conflict between African-Americans and Korean-Americans. But these ties now made him suspect among swing white voters and Latinos in the new racial polarizations of post-riot Los Angeles. Latino and Jewish areas, once centers of Bradley support, broke fairly evenly between Woo and Riordan. The issues of crime, violence, and civil unrest had made a difference. More moderate white voters joined an outpouring of conservative east side homeowners to give Riordan his victory.[70]

Although the city's population is two-thirds minority, "when it came to the voters, the image of a rainbow Los Angeles evaporated."[71] Nearly two-thirds of the city's electorate remained white as citizenship requirements, the young age of much of the Latino population, and racial differences in turnout rates all acted to deplete the ranks of minority voters. Given these figures, it is not surprising that the city's more moderate white and Latino voters were the pivotal force that decided the election outcome.

THE FUTURE OF BLACK AND HISPANIC MAYORS

The disintegration of the liberal, multiracial coalition in Los Angeles essentially follows the same pattern evident in other major cities where black mayors have been succeeded in office by whites. In Chicago, after Harold Washington's death, no black candidate could attract similar levels of support from the city's white liberal and Hispanic communities. Defections among these groups provided the margin of victory for Richard M. Daley, son of the legendary machine boss. Similarly in New York, moderate-conservative Rudolph Giuliani crossed racial lines in reaching out to Herman Badillo, a leader in the city's Puerto Rican community. Mayor David Dinkins lost his margin of victory as his inability to handle a number of racially explosive incidents, including the Crown Heights affair, led a number of his former Jewish and more moderate white supporters to defect to Giuliani.

Biracial and multiracial coalitions are difficult to sustain. In recent years, liberal biracial and multiracial coalitions have fallen on hard times. As of the early 1990s, New York, Los Angeles, Chicago, and Philadelphia were all governed by a "new breed" of conservative/moderate mayors—Giuliani, Riordan, Daley, and Edward Rendell—who used the crime issue and appeals to racial harmony, competency, and efficiency to build a triumphant conservative white/moderate white/Hispanic coalition.[72] A survey of school district elections reinforces the point: In city politics, Anglo-Latino electoral coalitions are more likely to be formed than black-Latino coalitions.[73]

Much of the recent controversy over the future of minority mayors concerns the extent to which African-Americans (and Latinos) should follow a **deracialization** strategy in their pursuit of city hall. Under deracialization, black candidates tone down their racial appeals and deemphasize their redistributional agenda; instead, they emphasize issues that cut across racial lines. Especially in cities where whites are in the majority, black candidates can improve their chances of winning by avoiding explicit reference to race-specific issues.[74] Where African-Americans do not comprise a clear majority of the electorate, "The new black politics must be broader in its appeal and both deracial and transethnic if it is to be successful."[75]

Seattle's Norman Rice, New York's David Dinkins, Los Angeles' Tom Bradley, and Charlotte's Harvey Gantt were all African-Americans who used a deracialized electoral strategy to win the mayoralty.[76] Even in cities in which there is a black majority and the candidates for office are black, deracialization may be a key factor in determining which candidate will emerge as the victor. In New Orleans in 1985, Sidney Barthelemy's appeal to white voters allowed him to beat William Jefferson, whose campaign had stronger roots in the poor, black sections of the city. In 1990, Barthelemy's cross-racial appeal proved crucial to his reelection. His margin of victory against a white liberal candidate came from a 23-percent white crossover vote that helped to compensate for a low turnout in the city's black community.[77] Similarly in Atlanta in 1989, in a race with only black contenders, Maynard Jackson used a deracialized campaign, stressing quality-of-life issues, to attract white votes and win a third nonconsecutive term as mayor.[78]

Does deracialization represent a pragmatic political strategy for blacks and Hispanics? Or is it a sell-out of the African-American and Latino communities? Much of the answer to these questions depends on whether or not deracialization in a political campaign leads to deracialization as a governance strategy.[79] Does moderation in the pursuit of a broad electoral coalition constrain the issues that a black or Hispanic mayor is willing to deal with upon winning office?

Advocates of the deracialization strategy argue that deracialization represents a maturation of black politics that allows blacks to win in communities where African-Americans are not the clear majority of the population. They further argue that a city's black community will receive little help from a black candidate who stresses racial consciousness but

I guess the most important thing is that they get elected! — regardless of what is best for the community!

cannot win office. In contrast, a candidate who campaigns on broader themes can, upon winning office, institute programs that will begin to address the socio-economic problems that plague the black urban community. The moderate rhetoric of a political campaign does not doom a black mayor to inaction on racial issues. In New Orleans, Sidney Barthelemy instituted a vigorous affirmative action and contract compliance program as mayor despite his deracialized campaigns for office.[80]

Was he lying during the campaign or at least hiding his true feelings?

Critics of deracialization argue, however, that campaign style does have a clear impact on governing style. They also argue that deracialization flies in the face of the historical context of black politics:

> Black politics is a group struggle for race-specific empowerment in order to exercise some degree of independence and self-determination. If campaign behavior is a predictor of governance style and behavior, then deracialization is an anathema to the essence of black politics.[81]

Another critic has surveyed the deracialization strategies and the election of black mayors and has concluded that "Black politics is not maturing and may be degenerating."[82] Once in office, moderate black mayors find themselves constrained by what white voters are willing to accept. The result is that black governing regimes at city hall "have generally pursued policies of fiscal conservatism and downtown development" rather than a more progressive or redistributive agenda.[83]

In Denver, Federico Peña (later to serve as Bill Clinton's Secretary of Transportation), a Hispanic, won office in a city where the minority population is relatively small. Like Los Angeles' Tom Bradley and Seattle's Norman Rice, Peña ran on a platform emphasizing managerial competence, economic development, improved policy-community relations, and homeowner and neighborhood—as well as minority—concerns. Peña's election in Denver did not signal strong minority political incorporation. He did not gain office as a result of Latino votes, and in office, according to one critic, his coalition was "dominated by white political and business elites."[84]

Do black and Hispanic mayoral candidates have to accede to the seeming dictates of deracialization? Not necessarily. It depends on the context of an election. Black mayors in communities with large African-American populations can emphasize racial themes just so long as they are also careful to garner a sufficient number of crossover votes to achieve victory. Birmingham's Richard Arrington and Chicago's Harold Washington were mayors who did not shrink away from issues of racial justice but who coupled racial issues with other reform themes that allowed them to win a relatively small, but crucial, percentage of the white vote.

Similarly, in New Haven (Connecticut) in 1989, John Daniels won an uncertain election, emphasizing his racial heritage, his neighborhood roots, and his ability to ease racial tensions. Daniels sought to mobilize a

This is Bullshit! learn the facts, take a 'stand, and do what is best for everyone!!! see top page 102

massive turnout in the city's black community and to build a progressive coalition that crossed racial lines. Daniels succeeded in assembling a winning multiracial coalition without taking a centrist or conservative stand to attract white voters.[85]

CONCLUSIONS

The formal powers and structure of local government vary from community to community in urban America. Power is distributed and exercised quite differently in different municipalities. This is especially true with respect to the powers given the mayor in relation to the council and the bureaucracy.

We have seen that much of the history of the development of local government in the United States was based on fears that Americans shared about strong executives. It took almost 100 years for cities to invest the office of mayor with enough power for there to be a strong-mayor form of government. The strong mayor had numerous strengths, especially in political leadership and appointive and budgeting powers. However, weaknesses were noted where mayors lacked essential administrative skills or ran the cities on a partisan basis.

An alternative to the strong-mayor form of government is the council-manager plan with its commitment to trained, professional administration. Governance under the council-manager arrangement emphasizes cooperation, not conflict. However, council-manager cities have often been charged with a lack of effective leadership. Many cities found it difficult to recruit well-trained managers, and some smaller cities found the plan to be much more expensive than a mayor-council or commission form of government.

The amount of influence a mayor exercises is not totally a product of the formal powers associated with the office. As we have seen, mayoral leadership is as much a product of an individual's skills and personal style as it is of the formal or legal powers of the office. Successful mayors can be found but success often comes at great cost, and the number of successful mayors is fewer than we would like to see. No matter what a mayor's leadership style may be, effective mayoral leadership is quite difficult to achieve, given the intractable nature of many urban problems and the highly dispersed structure of power in most big-city governments. Black and Hispanic mayors have a particularly difficult time in forging and maintaining cross-racial electoral and governing coalitions.

The restructuring of municipal government begun by the reformers of the Progressive Era continues to have a lasting effect on city governance today. In their move to rid the cities of the evils of machine politics, the reformers diminished the partisan-based resources that mayors could employ to enhance their influence. The reformers also set up allegedly "neutral" and "professional" administrative systems that insulated much of a city's affairs from direct political control. In the next two chapters we shall explore in more detail the politics of the machine and reform, and we'll see how the struggle between these two forces has shaped city politics.

NOTES

1. John J. Harrigan, *Political Change in the Metropolis*, 4th ed. (Glenview, IL: Scott, Foresman, 1989), p. 10
2. These issues are discussed in more detail in Chapter 6. Also see Theodore J. Lowi, "Machine Politics—Old and New," *Public Interest* 9 (Fall 1967): 83–92; and E. S. Savas and Sigmund G. Ginsburg, "The Civil Service: A Meritless System?" *Public Interest* 32 (Summer 1973): 70–85.
3. Michael Lipsky, *Street-Level Bureaucracy: Dilemmas of the Individual in Public Service* (New York: Russell Sage Foundation, 1980); and Lipsky, "Implementation on Its Head," in *American Politics and Public Policy*, ed. Walter Dean Burnham and Martha Wagner Weinberg (Cambridge, MA: MIT Press, 1978), pp. 390–402.
4. *City of Clinton v. Cedar Rapids and Missouri Railroad Company*, 24 Iowa 455 (1868).
5. John F. Dillon, *Commentary on the Law of Municipal Corporations*, 5th ed. (Boston: Little, Brown, 1911), vol. 1, sec. 237.
6. *Atkins* v. *Kansas*, 191 U.S. 207 at 220–21 (1903); and *Trenton* v. *New Jersey*, 262 U.S. 182, 67L Ed 93, 43 SCt 534 (1923).
7. Clifford J. Levy, "Criticizing Dinkins, Rivals Suggest Abolishing Board of Education," *The New York Times*, August 16, 1993; and Alison Mitchell, "Giuliani Presses to Get Role in Choosing Schools Chief," *The New York Times*, December 15, 1994.
8. Edward F. Haas, *DeLesseps S. Morrison and the Image of Reform: New Orleans Politics 1946–1961* (Baton Rouge, LA: Louisiana State University Press, 1974), pp. 124–28.
9. David R. Morgan and James T. LaPlant, "State Requirements Affecting Local Government Structure: The Case of Oklahoma" (Paper presented at the annual meeting of the American Political Science Association, Washington, DC, September 2–5, 1993).
10. Advisory Commission on Intergovernmental Relations, *State Laws Governing Local Government Structure and Administration* (Washington, DC: ACIR, 1993), pp. 17 and 20–21.
11. Advisory Commission on Intergovernmental Relations, *State Courts in the Federal System: Issues and Opportunities for State Initiatives* (Washington, DC: ACIR, 1989), p. 45.
12. Richard Briffault, "Taking Home Rule Seriously: The Case of Campaign Finance Reform," in *Restructuring the New York City Government: The Reemergence of Municipal Reform*, Proceedings of the Academy of Political Science, vol. 37, no. 3 (1989), ed. Frank J. Mauro and Gerald Benjamin, pp. 35–42.
13. Alvin D. Sokolow, "State-Local Relations in California: What Happens When They Take Away the Property Tax?" (Paper presented at the annual meeting of the American Political Science Association, Washington, DC, September 2–5, 1993).

14. Statistics in this section have been obtained from Tari Renner and Victor S. DeSantis, "Contemporary Patterns and Trends in Municipal Government Structures," *The Municipal Year Book 1993* (Washington, DC: International City/County Management Association, 1993), p. 59.

15. W. B. Munro, *The Government of American Cities* (New York: Macmillan, 1918).

16. Richard Edward DeLeon, *Left Coast City: Progressive Politics in San Francisco, 1975–1991* (Lawrence, KS: Univ. of Kansas Press, 1992), p. 21.

17. Heywood T. Sanders, "The Government of American Cities: Continuity and Change in Structure," *Municipal Year Book 1982* (Washington, DC: International City Management Association, 1982), p. 185. See also Chapter 6, "Reform Politics," in this book for a discussion of the legal status and effects of at-large voting rules.

18. For an analysis of this period in American urban history, see Richard S. Childs, *Civic Victories* (New York: Harper & Row, 1952); and John Porter East, *Council-Manager Government: The Political Thought of Its Founder, Richard S. Childs* (Chapel Hill, NC: University of North Carolina Press, 1965).

19. Eric Anderson, "Two Major Forms of Government: Two Types of Professional Management," *Municipal Yearbook 1989* (Washington, DC: International City Management Association, 1989), p. 30.

20. William F. Fannin and Don Hellriegel, "Policy Roles of City Managers: A Contingency Typology and Empirical Test," *Urban Affairs Quarterly* 13 (April 1985): 212–26.

21. James H. Svara, "The Complementary Roles of Officials in Council-Manager Government," *Municipal Yearbook 1988* (Washington, DC: International City Management Association, 1988), pp. 30–31.

22. Jeffrey Pressman, *Federal Programs and City Politics* (Berkeley, CA: University of California Press, 1975), p. 36.

23. Ibid.

24. Tari Renner, "Appointed Local Government Managers: Stability and Change," *The Municipal Year Book 1990* (Washington, DC: International City/County Management Association, 1990), pp. 41 and 49–53; David N. Ammons and Charldean Newell, "'City Managers Don't Make Policy': A Lie; Let's Face It," *National Civic Review* 77 (March/April 1988): 124–32; and Charldean Newell and David N. Ammons, "Role Emphasis of City Managers and Other Municipal Executives," *Public Administration Review* 47 (May/June 1987): 252.

25. John Nalbandian, "Tenets of Contemporary Professionalism in Local Government," *Public Administration Review* 50 (November/December 1990): 654–62. Also see Robert T. Golembiewski and Gerald T. Gabris, "Today's City Managers: A Legacy of Success-Becoming-Failure," *Public Administration Review* 54 (November/December 1994): 525–30.

26. Svara, "The Complementary Roles of Officials in Council-Manager Government," pp. 30–31; Nalbandian, "Tenets of Contemporary Professionalism in Local Government," pp. 659–61; John Nalbandian, "Reflections of a 'Pracademic' on the Logic of Politics and Administration," *Public Administration Review* 54 (November/December 1994): 535; and John Nalbandian, *Professionalism in Local Government: Transformations in the Roles, Responsibilities, and Values of City Managers* (San Francisco: Jossey-Bass, 1991).

27. Paul Teske and Mark Schneider, "The Bureaucratic Entrepreneur: The Case of City Managers," *Public Administration Review* 54 (July/August 1994): 331–40.

Also see David Morgan and Sheilah Watson, "Policy Leadership in Council-Manager Cities: Comparing Mayor and Manager," *Public Administration Review* 52 (September/October 1992): 438–46.

28. Teske and Schneider, "The Bureaucratic Entrepreneur," pp. 337–38.

29. Clifford J. Wirth and Michael L. Vasu, "Ideology and Decision Making for American City Managers," *Urban Affairs Quarterly* 22 (March 1987): 454–74.

30. James H. Svara, *Official Leadership in the City: Patterns of Conflict and Cooperation* (New York: Oxford Univ. Press, 1990), chap. 1; Svara, "Dichotomy and Duality: Reconceptualizing the Relationship between Policy and Administration in Council-Manager Cities," *Public Administration Review* 45 (January/February 1985): 221–32; Svara, "Mayoral Leadership in Council-Manager Cities: Preconditions vs. Preconceptions," *Journal of Politics* 49 (1987): 207–27; and Svara, "The Complementary Roles of Officials in Council-Manager Government." Also see David N. Ammons and Charldean Newell, *City Executives: Leadership Roles, Work Characteristics, and Time Management* (Albany, NY: State Univ. of New York Press, 1989), pp. 61–69.

31. Svara, *Official Leadership in the City*, pp. 51–58.

32. T. D. Allman, *Miami: City of the Future* (Boston: Atlantic Monthly Press, 1987), pp. 355–56.

33. Jean L. Stinchcombe, *Reform and Reaction: City Politics in Toledo* (Belmont, CA: Wadsworth Publishing, 1968), p. 98.

34. The story of the transformation of San Diego government under Pete Wilson is told by Glen Sparrow, "The Emerging Chief Executive: The San Diego Experience," *National Civic Review* (December 1985): 538–47. The quotation cited appears on p. 542. The description of San Diego's leadership problems in the post-Wilson years is taken from Glen W. Sparrow, "The Emerging Chief Executive 1971–1991: A San Diego Update," in *Facilitative Leadership in Local Government: Lessons From Successful Mayors and Chairpersons*, ed. James H. Svara (San Francisco: Jossey-Bass, 1994), pp. 187–99.

35. Sparrow, "The Emerging Chief Executive: The San Diego Experience," p. 546.

36. Pressman, *Federal Programs and City Politics*, p. 32.

37. Rufus P. Browning, Dale Rogers Marshall, and David H. Tabb, *Protest Is Not Enough: The Struggle of Blacks and Hispanics for Equality in Urban Politics* (Berkeley, CA: Univ. of California Press, 1984), pp. 201–02.

38. Svara, *Official Leadership in the City*, p. 180.

39. Ammons and Newell, *City Executives*, pp. 58–59.

40. Svara, *Official Leadership in the City*, pp. 180–84.

41. Renner and DeSantis, "Contemporary Patterns and Trends in Municipal Government Structures," p. 66.

42. Timothy Bledsoe, *Careers in City Politics: The Case for Urban Democracy* (Pittsburgh: Univ. of Pittsburgh Press, 1993), p. 32.

43. Ibid., p. 35.

44. Svara, *Official Leadership in the City*, p. 153.

45. David R. Eichenthal, "The Other Elected Officials," in *Urban Politics: New York Style*, ed. Jewel Bellush and Dick Netzer (Armonk, NY: M. E. Sharpe, 1990), pp. 92–93.

46. Carolyn Adams, David Bartelt, David Elesh, Ira Goldstein, Nancy Kleniewski, and William Yancey, *Philadelphia: Neighborhoods, Division, and Conflict in a Postindustrial City* (Philadelphia: Temple Univ. Press, 1991), pp. 146–53.

47. Eichenthal, "The Other Elected Officials," p. 96.
48. Bledsoe, *Careers in City Politics*, pp. 113–19 and 126–28.
49. Renner and DeSantis, "Contemporary Patterns and Trends in Municipal Government Structures," p. 66.
50. Bledsoe, *Careers in City Politics*, p. 181.
51. Ibid., pp. 18–82.
52. Ibid., pp. 46, 122, and 177–78.
53. Jeffrey L. Pressman, "Preconditions of Mayoral Leadership," *American Political Science Review* 66 (June 1972): 512.
54. Ester R. Fuchs, *Mayors and Money: Fiscal Policy in New York and Chicago* (Chicago: Univ. of Chicago Press, 1992).
55. Douglas Yates, *The Ungovernable City* (Cambridge, MA: MIT Press, 1977), p. 5.
56. Ibid., p. 86.
57. Ibid., p. 91.
58. John P. Kotter and Paul R. Lawrence, *Mayors in Action: Five Approaches to Urban Governance* (New York: Wiley Interscience, 1974).
59. Svara, *Official Leadership in the City*, pp. 81–121.
60. James H. Svara, "Mayoral Leadership and the Future of Council-Manager Government" (Paper presented at the annual meeting of the American Political Science Association, New York, September 1994).
61. Martha Wagner Weinberg, "Boston's Kevin White: A Mayor Who Survives," *Political Science Quarterly* 96 (Spring 1981): 87–106; and Barbara Ferman, *Governing the Ungovernable City* (Philadelphia: Temple Univ. Press, 1985).
62. Peter Dreier, "Ray Flynn's Legacy: American Cities and the Progressive Agenda," *National Civic Review* 82 (Fall 1993): 380–403; Peter Dreier, "Economic Growth and Economic Justice in Boston: Populist Housing and Jobs Policies," in *Unequal Partnerships: The Political Economy of Urban Redevelopment in Postwar America*, ed. Gregory D. Squires (New Brunswick, NJ: Rutgers Univ. Press, 1989); and Cynthia Horan, "Economic Success and Institutional Arrangements: The Changing Context of Development Politics in Boston" (Paper presented at the annual meeting of the American Political Science Association, New York, September 1–4, 1994).
63. Martin Shefter, *Political Crisis/Fiscal Crisis: The Collapse and Revival of New York City* (New York: Basic Books, 1985); and John Hull Mollenkopf, *A Phoenix in the Ashes: The Rise and Fall of the Koch Coalition in New York City Politics* (Princeton, NJ: Princeton Univ. Press, 1992).
64. Charles H. Levine, *Racial Conflict and the American Mayor* (Lexington, MA: Lexington Books, 1974).
65. Saundra C. Ardrey, "Cleveland and the Politics of Resurgence: The Search for Effective Political Control," in *Black Politics: Issues of Leadership and Strategy*, ed. Georgia A. Persons (New York: HarperCollins, 1993), pp. 109–27.
66. Kemper Diehl and Jan Jarboe, *Cisneros: Portrait of a New American* (San Antonio, TX: Corona Publishing, 1985), pp. 81–123.
67. For criticisms of both Cisneros' focus on economic development in San Antonio and Mayor Tom Bradley's economic development orientation in Los Angeles, see Henry Flores, "Structural Barriers to Chicano Empowerment," in *Latino Empowerment: Progress, Problems, and Prospects*, ed. Roberto E. Villarreal, Norma G. Hernandez, and Howard D. Neighbor (Westport, CT: Greenwood Press, 1988), pp. 28–35 and 39.

68. Raphael J. Sonenshein, *Politics in Black and White: Race and Power in Los Angeles* (Princeton, NJ: Princeton Univ. Press, 1993).

69. On the importance of organized labor to the Bradley coalition, see James A. Regalado, "Organized Labor and Los Angeles City Politics: An Assessment in the Bradley Years, 1973–1989," *Urban Affairs Quarterly* 27 (September 1991): 87–108.

70. Raphael J. Sonenshein, "Is This the End? Biracial Coalition in the 1993 Los Angeles Mayoral Election" (Paper presented at the annual meeting of the American Political Science Association, Washington, DC, September 1–4, 1994).

71. Ibid.

72. Ibid.

73. Kenneth J. Meier and Joseph Stewart, Jr., "Cooperation and Conflict in Multiracial School Districts," *Journal of Politics* 53 (November 1991): 1123–33.

74. Joseph P. McCormick II and Charles E. Jones, "The Conceptualization of Deracialization: Thinking Through the Dilemma," in *Dilemmas of Black Politics: Issues of Leadership and Strategy*, ed. Georgia Persons (New York: HarperCollins, 1993), pp. 66–84.

75. Huey L. Perry, "Exploring the Meaning and Implications of Deracialization in African-American Urban Politics," *Urban Affairs Quarterly* 27 (December 1991): 185.

76. On the election of Norman Rice, see Mylon Winn, "The Election of Norman Rice as Mayor of Seattle," *PS: Political Science and Politics* 23 (June 1990): 158–59.

77. Huey L. Perry, "The Reelection of Sidney Barthelemy as Mayor of New Orleans," *PS: Political Science and Politics* 23 (June 1990): 156–58.

78. Carol A. Pierannunzi and John D. Hutcheson, Jr., "Deracialization in the Deep South: Mayoral Politics in Atlanta," *Urban Affairs Quarterly* 27 (December 1991): 192–201.

79. Perry, "Deracialization as an Analytical Construct in American Urban Politics," p. 187.

80. Ibid., pp. 188–89.

81. Robert T. Starks, "A Commentary and Response to 'Exploring the Meaning and Implications of Deracialization in African-American Urban Politics,'" *Urban Affairs Quarterly* 27 (December 1991): 221.

82. David C. Smith, "Recent Elections and Black Politics: The Maturation or Death of Black Politics?" *PS: Political Science and Politics* 23 (June 1990): 160.

83. Ibid., p. 161.

84. Carlos Muñoz, Jr., and Charles P. Henry, "Coalition Politics in San Antonio and Denver: The Cisneros and Peña Mayoral Campaigns," in *Racial Politics in American Cities*, ed. Rufus P. Browning, Dale Rogers Marshall, and David H. Tabb (White Plains, NY: Longman, 1990), pp. 179–90. Also see Rufus P. Browning, Dale Rogers Marshall, and David H. Tabb, "Has Political Incorporation Been Achieved? Is It Enough?" in *Racial Politics in American Cities*, pp. 212–30.

85. Mary E. Summers and Philip A. Klinkner, "The Daniels Elections in New Haven and the Failure of the Deracialization Hypothesis," *Urban Affairs Quarterly* 27 (December 1991): 202–15.

5

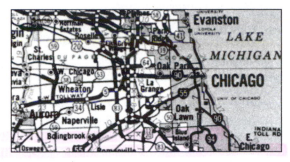

Machine Politics

> While California has a cosmopolitan population and an urban, industrial economy, it also displays virtually no signs of machine politics. The Governor has about as many patronage jobs at his disposal as the Mayor of New Haven. Californians who worked in John F. Kennedy's presidential campaign report the bemusement of Kennedy organizers from the East who came to the state with thoughts of building their campaign organization around public employees. These and other practices that are widely accepted in the East are abhorred on the West Coast. Paying precinct workers is commonplace in eastern cities. But when Jesse Unruh, a prominent California Democratic leader, hired some canvassers in the 1962 election, he was roundly denounced from all points of the political spectrum for importing such a sordid practice.[1]

Political machines are an important part of American urban history. Yet, as the above quotation indicates, states such as California have little experience with machine politics. *Machine politics* is a concept more characteristic of cities in the Northeast and parts of the Midwest than in the South or the West.

Throughout much of the nineteenth century and through the first half of the twentieth century, many large cities in the eastern part of the United States were controlled by political machines. Most notable were those of New York City, Philadelphia, Boston, Jersey City, and Albany. Still, machine politics was not confined solely to the cities of the eastern seaboard. For a number of years political machines dominated such midwestern cities as Chicago, Kansas City, and Cincinnati. Though even less common in the South and the West, political machines were also found in New Orleans, Memphis, San Antonio, Tampa, and San Francisco.[2]

Why should the student of urban politics study machine politics other than from an interest in urban history? First of all, machines and machine politics have not withered away.[3] While machines in a number of cities have ceased to exist, in other cities machine-style organizations continue, although in a severely weakened form. Patronage and machine-style exchanges can also be found in many cities with reformed governing

143

institutions. No observer can fully understand the nitty-gritty of urban political transactions without understanding machine politics.

Second, the political machine points to the importance of behind-the-scenes power in the running of cities. Chicago's Richard J. Daley derived his power not just from Chicago's weak mayoralty but also from his position as the head of the city and county Democratic organizations. In many cities the machine boss was not even the mayor but the behind-the-scenes organization official who dictated to the mayor. In New York, none of the famous bosses of Tammany Hall—not William Marcy Tweed, Richard Croker, John Kelly, Charles F. Murphy, or Carmine DeSapio—served as mayor. City government action was often just a public playing out of deals that had been cut in private.

Finally, reaction to the machine and its excesses gave us the reform movement. Reformed institutions such as the city manager plan and at-large and nonpartisan elections characterize the government of many cities today. Yet the nature of both the reform ideology and these reformed institutions cannot be fully understood without first considering just what the reformers were reacting against. Only by comparing the reformed city of today to the machine city of old can we truly understand the achievements, inadequacies, and biases of contemporary city government.

MACHINE POLITICS DEFINED

Political scientists Edward C. Banfield and James Q. Wilson offer the following definition of the political machine:

> A political machine is a party organization that depends crucially upon inducements that are both specific and material.... A machine like any other organization offers a mixture of material and non-material inducements in order to get people to do what it wants them to do.[4]

Machine politics is essentially an **exchange process**. In order to win elections, the political machine needed votes. The machine traded voters whatever was needed in order to get those votes. The machine gave its loyal supporters such **material benefits** as emergency assistance, food, housing, and jobs; it also fixed tickets, posted bail, and provided a host of personal services.[5]

The benefits the machine dispensed were also **specific** in that they could be denied to those who failed to support the machine. The machine rewarded its friends and punished its enemies. Citizens who refused to cast a ballot for the machine were denied certain city services; businesses which backed a machine's opponents were denied contracts with the city. Machine politics was closely associated with the **spoils system** whereby government jobs and benefits were dispensed only to followers of the winning party according to the old adage: "To the victors belong the spoils."

As we shall soon see, the machine did not rely on the dispensation of tangible benefits alone. It could also offer citizens such **nontangible benefits** as the sense of friendship between a ward or precinct committeeman and an urban resident. The importance of such friendship in cementing loyalty to the machine should not be discounted. Recently arrived immigrants found themselves all alone in a strange new land; often it was only the machine captain who came to their aid.

Machine politics also takes on the characteristics of a **brokerage system**. Persons or interests desiring some favor of political arrangement from the city came to the machine. The machine would then demand resources that it needed in return for dispensing the favor. For instance, a business requesting a specific zoning variance or construction contract might be expected to provide the machine with either cash contributions or a number of jobs that the machine could then dispense to its supporters. By "brokering" the requests of various groups in the city, the machine organization earned the obligations and votes that kept it in power.

Strictly defined, machine politics is the process of exchanging favors and inducements for votes. Over the years, however, the notion of the political machine has also come to imply a highly centralized and detailed organization capable of running a city from behind the scenes. Such characteristics were common to many, but not to all, political machines. Indeed, it is as highly disciplined centralized organizations that machines have suffered their most severe decline.

THE MACHINE AT WORK: CHARACTERISTICS OF THE POLITICAL MACHINE

The exact workings of political machines differed from city to city. Even in a single city, the structure and workings of the local machine evolved over time. In some cities the machine was tightly structured. In other cities and at other times, subunits of the machine contested for power. While political corruption is often associated with the urban machine, local political machines were not characterized by blatant corruption in all cities at all points in time. While the "classic" political machines can be identified by several characteristics, care must also be taken to note the variations of machine patterns.

The classic machine exhibited an element of **central control**. The boss and his associates made all the major decisions that had an impact upon the party. The chain of command of the Hague organization, which ruled Jersey City well into the late 1940s, illustrates the hierarchy inherent in the prototype machine:

> The nature of the leadership, as he [Hague] conceives it, leaves little room for the formation of policy anywhere except at the top of the organization; while the party workers keep the citizens in line by all the

> variety of means at the disposal of a well-built machine, the leader
> decides what is good for the people.[6]

City commissioners and legislators under Hague's control were expected to vote as they were instructed and to present a united front to the outside world: "Complete obedience is necessary from the bottom to the top; officials are not supposed to have ideas on public policies, but to take orders."[7]

This classic **hierarchical** or **pyramidal structure** was also reflected in the detailed territorial organization of many machines. Wherever possible, block captains (and in some cases even building captains!) were selected to minister to the needs of their constituents on a daily basis. This might include such services as providing food, shelter, or clothing to an unfortunate family. Block captains reported to, and took all their unsolvable problems to, the precinct captain who was charged with overseeing several blocks. The precinct captains, in turn, reported to ward leaders or chairmen, each of whom had responsibility for several precincts. The ward leaders reported directly to the boss or the boss's close assistants (see Figure 5.1). On election day all the captains and foot soldiers worked to turn out the vote for the organization's candidates.

Of course, not every machine exhibited such a clear, tight hierarchy. At times, political machines were marred by **factionalism** or factional in-fighting, as the loyalists of one machine politician sought power at the expense of rival machine factions. New York's Tammany Hall often saw a "reformed" machine faction at odds with more blatantly corrupt machine factions. Tammany leaders who sought a more disciplined organization feared that exposés of corruption would eventually lead to the machine's ouster at the polls.[8] Before the emergence in the 1950s of Richard J. Daley as the legendary boss of the Chicago machine, that city's Democratic political organization, too, was divided by factions competing for power.[9]

A second characteristic, as we have already discussed, involved the use of **material incentives**—jobs, housing, food, clothing, etc. The machine exchanged favors for votes; it also used these incentives to encourage and reward party workers so they would turn out the vote on election day. Victory at the polls allowed the machine to replenish its supply of rewards and to distribute them again at the next election. The cycle of rewards for votes, which generated more rewards, was crucial to the continued existence of the machine. The cycle continued as long as people put little or no value on their right to vote, or as long as the value of what the machine offered exceeded the value people placed on their vote.

In New York in the latter half of the nineteenth century, the notorious Tweed Ring in part earned the allegiance of voters by providing much-needed services. The Tammany machine delivered important emergency and social services in an era when no other institution was

FIGURE 5.1
Political Machine Organization Chart

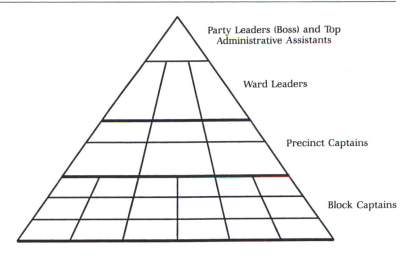

Party Leaders (Boss) and Top
Administrative Assistants

Ward Leaders

Precinct Captains

Block Captains

ensuring the adequate care of the people. For instance, "During the severe winter of 1870–71 Tweed spent $50,000 of his personal funds in his
own ward and gave each of the city's aldermen $1,000 out of his own
pocket to buy coal for the poor; the provision of those storied hods of coal
had yet to become institutionalized."[10] It is estimated that between 1869
and 1871 the city treasury gave about $1.4 million to the Roman Catholic
Church, $57,000 to the Protestant Episcopal Church, $25,000 to Jewish organizations, and lesser amounts to various Protestant denominations for
schools as well as charities. That the largest amount was given to Catholic
churches simply reflected the religious loyalties of most of the immigrants and the poor in New York City.[11] The Tweed ring also assisted in
the naturalization of many immigrants and organized a program of public aid to private charities.

The Tweed Ring even gained the support of elements in the business community. Of course, those business executives who objected to
taxation or who feared that the city's debt would jeopardize the repayment of municipal bonds regarded Tweed's schemes and payoff methods
as scandalous. Yet speculators such as Jay Gould, Jim Fiske, Cornelius
Vanderbilt, and John Jacob Astor all helped enrich themselves by reaching corrupt government officials to gain approval for their projects.[12]

Another characteristic of the machine was its **lack of ideology**. The
machine's only goal was to win elections by providing services to voters.
It was rarely concerned with the political ideology of people who needed
favors. If the machine could satisfy a need, it probably had won over a
voter, and that was an important source of power that surpassed the
political beliefs of the client.

Machines were also nonideological as they advanced no broad policy goals of their own. The machine's only objective was to win votes and maintain itself in power. To advance policy goals of its own was to risk making enemies and lose support. Hence, as Edward Banfield described, the early Daley machine in Chicago initiated no policies of its own in such important areas as urban redevelopment and housing. Instead, the organization chose the politically "safe" route of waiting for other actors and groups to reach a consensus. Then the machine assisted the parties to achieve their agreed-upon goals, earning the obligation of all concerned, a sort of "broker's fee." This entitled the machine to ask the various groups and special interests for favors at a later date.[13]

Latter-day critics have come to doubt claims that the machine was totally nonideological. All organizations embody a bias to some extent; they favor the demands of some people over others. As will be discussed throughout this chapter, the political machine was not a fair, neutral broker of the demands presented by all groups in the city. In cities with an Irish-dominated machine, the political organization was more willing to deliver services to the Irish and less willing to respond to the demands of East Europeans and racial minorities.[14] Political machines further embodied an ideological bias, as they were willing to respond to demands for individual services and group favors, but they were unwilling to respond to more politicized issues such as the demand for racial integration in schools and housing. The machine maintained an ideological bias against demands for redistributional policies, especially policies that threatened the ethnic constituency of the machine's leaders.[15]

Another characteristic of the political machine was its ability to develop close **personal relationships** with voters and to sustain them. These were the nonmaterial or nontangible rewards that the machine exchanged for votes. Block captains and district leaders were friends who provided needed services and help in emergencies. They also attended weddings, funerals, Irish wakes, and Jewish bar mitzvahs; they took note of as many birthdays and anniversaries as they possible could. The relationship between ward or precinct committeemen and district residents was a highly personal one that led to a great feeling of loyalty on the part of local residents. It was a feeling that the machine was able to convert into votes on election day.

George Washington Plunkitt, famed turn-of-the-century Tammany Hall district leader (or ward boss), bragged of his intimate knowledge of the people of his district:

> I know every man, woman, and child in the Fifteenth District, except them that's been born this summer—and I know some of them, too. I know what they like and what they don't like, what they are strong in and what they are weak in, and I reach them by approachin' at the right side.[16]

The personal knowledge Plunkitt gained then allowed him to attract the loyalty and votes of his district's residents:

> For instance, here's how I gather in the young men. I hear of a young feller that's proud of his voice, thinks that he can sing fine. I ask him to come around to Washington Hall and join our Glee Club. He comes and sings, and he's a follower of Plunkitt for life. Another young feller gains a reputation as a baseball player in a vacant lot. I bring him into our baseball club. That fixes him. You'll find him workin' for my ticket at the polls next election day. Then there's the feller that likes rowin' on the rivers, the young feller that makes a name as a waltzer on the block, the young feller that's handy with his dukes—I rope them all in by givin' them opportunities to show themselves off. I don't trouble them with political arguments. I just study human nature and act accordin'.[17]

Political machines gained a lot of attention for their **partisan favoritism** and, at times, for **corruption**. In many cities, the machine alternated between periods of corruption and periods where the excesses of machine officials were kept under tighter control.

The escapades of New York's Tweed Ring in the late 1800s are illustrative of the rapaciousness of the machine at its extreme. Tammany purchased the loyalty of its supporters by dispensing **job patronage**. The leaders of the machine were more concerned with their self-enrichment—taking huge payoffs or **graft**—than with the efficient running of the city. It was the excesses of the machine that fueled the fires of the reform movement and drove the machine, often only temporarily, from office. Tweed, himself, was quite different from most bosses of the era in that he "did not operate from offstage."[18] His visibility only added to the vehemence of the public reaction once newspaper accounts laid out the extent of the corruption.

The machine's tendency toward graft and the enrichment of its own officials is best seen in the words of George Washington Plunkitt, the Tammany district leader who became a millionaire through politics and who asked that his epitaph be written: "He Seen His Opportunities and He Took 'Em."[19] Speaking in the post-Tweed period, Plunkitt claimed that no Tammany official ever made a penny through "dishonest graft" by blackmailing saloon keepers or stealing from the public treasury. Instead, Tammany politicians made fortunes through insider knowledge and good business foresight—a process he labeled **"honest graft."** Plunkitt gave the following account of his political philosophy:

> Just let me explain by examples. My party's in power in the city, and it's goin' to undertake a lot of public improvements. Well, I'm tipped off, say, that they're going to lay out a new park at a certain place.
>
> I see my opportunity and I take it. I go to that place and I buy up all the land I can in the neighborhood. Then the board of this or that makes its plan public, and there is a rush to get my land, which nobody cared particular for before.

MAX GOLDIN @ GA DOT...!!!

> Ain't it perfectly honest to charge a good price and make a profit on my investment and foresight? Of course, it is. Well, that's honest graft.[20]

Plunkitt's protestations to the contrary, "honest graft" is not really very honest.

Yet machine politics was not always characterized by the extensive corruption or "rapacious individualism"[21] that marked the Tweed era. Too much corruption could lead to a public demand for reform that would oust the machine from power. As Martin Shefter, an expert on the history of machine politics in New York, points out, the payoffs of the Tweed era

> threatened the city's credit, shocked the moral sensibilities of a large segment of the community, and consequently mobilized into political activity a congeries of forces that, as the events of 1871 proved, were capable of overthrowing the entire system. The experience of the Tweed era indicated, then, that it is in the interest of patronage-seeking politicians as a class that municipal corruption be kept within reasonable limits.[22]

Tweed had developed the system of decentralized ward and precinct clubs as an effective way to get votes. Tweed's successors, John Kelly and Richard Croker, strengthened the power of the central party organization in order to control the excesses of corruption and avert a repeat of the public outcry that could drive the machine from power.

IMMIGRATION AND THE POLITICAL MACHINE

Patronage-based political machines existed in the nineteenth century American city even before the arrival of the massive waves of immigration from Eastern and Southern Europe.[23] An immigrant base was not necessary to the life of a political machine. Denver, Memphis, Kansas City, New Orleans, Nashville, and Richmond all had political machines at a time when the immigrant population comprised only a small portion of the total population in each city.[24]

Yet political machines would probably not have gained extensive power in so many cities were it not for the arrival of the immigrant on our shores. "It was the succeeding waves of immigrants that gave the urban political organizations the manipulable mass bases without which they could not have functioned as they did," notes urban historian Elmer E. Cornwell, Jr.[25] The machine in many respects dominated the lives of these immigrants through dispensation of jobs, housing, citizenship education, and numerous other favors.

Richard Hofstadter analyzed the importance of the immigrant to the political machine in his book *The Age of Reform*.[26] Hofstadter argued that up to approximately 1880, the United States could be characterized as rural, Yankee, and Protestant. However, industrialization and urbanization in the United States generated a new wave of immigration that lasted forty years, 1880 to 1920. The majority of these immigrants were from poor, rural settings. Their different backgrounds, religions, traditions, and customs made it very difficult for them to be assimilated into American society. In addition, the Yankee Protestants were bigoted and intolerant of the ethnic and religious backgrounds of the immigrants, which also slowed the process of assimilation.

The immigrants would have been important to the political organization solely by virtue of their sheer numbers. However, the immigrants of the 1880–1920 period were particularly well suited to fit into political organizations emerging in the large cities for three reasons.

First, the immigrants arrived with intense personal needs. There were virtually no private or government agencies to assist them in housing, employment, or starting a business. The block and precinct captains were only too happy to learn of new arrivals in their area who needed help. They assisted the immigrants to settle in their communities and to adjust to life in the United States. All they asked in return was the promise at some future date to vote for the candidates endorsed by the block and precinct captain.

Second, for the most part the immigrants were unfamiliar with the American political system. Concepts of representation and democracy were alien to them. Third, most of the immigrants were fleeing authoritarian political systems. They were accustomed to living under autocratic rule, where they had few freedoms but many regulations to guide them in their daily lives. This characteristic was of great value to the city political organizations that thrived on order, rules, discipline, and loyalty. For many new arrivals in this country the offer of material goods and services necessary to survive in exchange for a "negligible" item like a vote was a trade few could afford to pass up. It must have appeared to be one of the best bargains imaginable.

According to Hofstadter, the arrival of the immigrants brought a clash of political orientations that dominated urban politics for most of the twentieth century. The immigrants saw politics as a route for personal or family gain. The native Yankee Protestants, in contrast, believed that such parochial individual and family concerns had no place in politics. They saw politics in highly moralistic terms. They believed that government should pursue policies that gave benefits to the entire community, not just to machine politicians and organized immigrant groups.[27]

Recent debate on the subject, though, has called into question the assumptions that native Yankee Protestants had a "public-regarding" and the ethnics a "private-regarding" orientation toward politics. Each group may have been motivated to a great extent by its own private interest. The immigrants wanted and needed services. The native Protestants might simply have been unwilling to pay for projects and programs from which they drew no benefits.[28]

So long as immigration was a continuing process, it was possible for the machine to replenish its strength indefinitely. With the virtual cessation of large-scale European immigration during the 1920s, this important source of machine strength gradually dried up.

BLACKS AND THE POLITICAL MACHINE

In more recent years, two new streams of immigrants to the cities, blacks from the rural South and Hispanics, have added to the base of the political machine. In the 1950s and 1960s, it was Chicago's black wards that provided the city's Democratic machine with its most dependable source of votes. Yet, blacks and Hispanics felt that the city's Irish-dominated machine did not give them a full and fair share of benefits in exchange for their votes.[29] The machine could not respond to the demands both of its white ethnic base and of newly insurgent black and Hispanic voters. Ultimately, African-Americans and Hispanics would provide the votes that helped drive the Chicago machine from power. In 1983, African-Americans, Hispanics, and white liberals elected the city's first black mayor, Harold Washington, in a challenge to the candidates preferred by the machine's white ethnic factions.

The historical affinity of black voters for the political machine has been traditionally explained by the social welfare or economic exchange model of machine politics: Blacks, among the most poor and socially disorganized groups in the city, desperately needed the specific benefits the Chicago machine offered in exchange for their votes. But in recent years, this view has been subject to significant challenge.

Political scientist and Chicago political activist William Grimshaw argues that the conventional explanation of black support for the Chicago political machine is too simplistic. Blacks, Grimshaw argues, were motivated by a broader ideological concern for empowerment; they did not merely exchange their votes for simple economic favors. While some black voters supported the machine in exchange for individual benefits, other black voters, even poor black voters, cast their ballots in response to broader political concerns, especially civil rights and black empowerment.

In contrast to the expectations of the economic exchange model, blacks in Chicago did not always support the Democratic machine in overwhelming numbers. Large numbers of black middle-class voters voted Republican—for the party that freed the slaves. Black middle-class wards were not as supportive of the machine as were black lower-class wards.[30] From the late 1930s through the early 1950s, black support for the national Democratic party outdistanced black support for the local Democratic organization. African-Americans were not blindly voting on the basis of party loyalty; they could sophisticatedly distinguish between the policy orientations of the national and local Democratic parties. While black Americans favored the progressive New Deal policies of Democratic presidential candidates, they were reluctant to vote for the "raw deal" offered by Democratic mayoral and aldermanic candidates who represented the fears of white ethnics and maintained segregation in Chicago.[31]

It was not until the mid-1950s that Chicago's black wards gave overwhelming majorities to the Democratic organization's candidates. What explains the change? Conventional accounts argue that black Congressman William Dawson, the boss of Chicago's "machine within a machine" on Chicago's South Side, mobilized support for Richard J. Daley when Daley sought to unseat incumbent Mayor Martin Kennelly. The conventional explanation argues that Dawson helped "dump" Kennelly, as he was outraged by the moralistic mayor's interference with the "numbers" (or "policy") games and other South Side rackets from which Dawson profited.

However, Grimshaw argues that such an explanation is too simplistic. Grimshaw points out that concerns over racial matters, not just simple obedience to Dawson, led blacks to vote for Daley. Daley ran for mayor in 1955 as a progressive. Faced with the Daley challenge, Kennelly ran an explicitly racist campaign in an attempt to mobilize white ethnic votes. Kennelly argued that his dumping had been engineered by Dawson and if Daley were to be elected, city hall would be controlled by the likes of Dawson. Kennelly's racist appeals generated an enormous backlash against him in the city's black wards. Blacks gave an overwhelming margin of support to Daley in the 1955 mayoral election, not simply because they were interested in patronage or were told to do so by Dawson. Rather, Daley appeared to represent the more progressive candidate on racial issues. Blacks voted for Daley in 1955 when racial matters, not narrow economic self-interest, dominated. The city's black wards became the machine's new electoral stronghold.[32]

But Daley proved to be little more responsive to black concerns than was Kennelly. Dawson and other black officials inside the machine retained power just so long as they played politics within the boundaries sharply circumscribed by the larger machine's interests. They could distribute patronage, control the allocation of public housing units, profit from illegal gaming, and otherwise benefit from holding positions of power within their racially separated community. They could work for the machine and reinforce its power; they could gain substantial specific benefits by doing so. Blacks could not, however, push for integrated schools and housing. They could not propose courses of action that threatened the machines' white ethnic constituencies. Nor was the black submachine allowed to develop as an autonomous center of power. Daley felt that he could not trust the congressman and took the necessary steps to destroy the power of so-called Boss Dawson.[33]

The machine's constricted view of participation did not appeal to minority activists who wanted more from politics than just their own personal gain. Mike Royko relates the fabled story of Daley and one new black arrival to the city:

> Some jobseekers come directly to him [Daley]. Complete outsiders, meaning those with no family or political connections, will be sent to see their ward committeemen. That is protocol, and that is what he did to the tall young black man who came to see him a few years ago, bearing a letter from the governor of North Carolina, who wrote that the young black man was a rising political prospect in his state. Daley told him to see his ward committeeman, and if he did some precinct work, rang doorbells, hustled up some votes, there might be a government job for him. Maybe something like taking coins in a tollway booth. The Rev. Jesse Jackson, now the city's leading black civil rights leader, still hasn't stopped smarting over that.[34]

The limited ability of the machine to respond to black demands is most clearly seen in its response to the ghetto riots of 1966. Daley ignored black demands for workplace, housing, and school integration; instead, he responded only to black complaints that city workers had turned off fire hydrants children were playing in during the 100-degree temperatures:

> Now, there is a program, and Daley liked it. Give them water. He had a whole lake right outside the door. Even before the riots ended a few days later, City Hall had embarked on a crusade to make Chicago's blacks the wettest in the country. Portable swimming pools were being trucked in. Sprinklers were attached to hundreds of hydrants, and water was gushing everywhere.... One cynical civil rights worker said, "I think they're hoping we'll all grow gills and swim away."[35]

Why was the city so willing to respond with swimming pools while it ignored demands for integration? The answer is easy. Swimming pools did not threaten the city's white neighborhoods.

The swimming pool incident reveals an important truth about the workings of political machines. The machine is willing to broker only those demands, including demands from the black community, that are **distributional** in nature.[36] The machine thrives on distributional issues, whereby each community can be granted what it wants with no other community being made to feel that it is being deprived of service. By dispensing patronage, delivering emergency relief, and providing such particular services as neighborhood swimming pools, the machine earns the friendship of many and the animosity of none. In contrast, however, are issues that are **redistributional** in nature, whereby one group can get more of what it wants only by having other groups clearly see that they are being deprived of what they want. Racial integration is just such an issue; integration can be increased only at the cost of denying white ethnics the communities they want to preserve. Redistributional politics is anathema to the machine; in the redistributional arena the machine makes enemies as well as friends—enemies who might punish the organization in future elections. Hence, the Chicago machine spurned dealing with such redistributional issues as demands for increased racial integration. Forced to choose between its white ethnic and black constituencies, the machine's leaders chose their white ethnic roots.

African-Americans voted in response to both their new civil rights consciousness and the clear racial bias of Daley's policies. By the mid-1970s, the city's black wards could no longer be counted on to support the machine in city elections.

The Chicago machine, like a great many of the Irish-dominated big-city machines, was not willing to fully incorporate competing immigrant groups. Instead, the machine offered newcomers—Eastern Europeans and later blacks and Hispanics—only token and symbolic benefits and limited patronage and distributional benefits.[37] Steven Erie argues that the Irish machine was no "rainbow coalition" that dispensed economic benefits to diverse groups in order to build a multi-ethnic, electoral coalition. The machine had only a limited supply of benefits which it sought to conserve. Rather than spread benefits widely, the mature political machine sought to build a "minimal winning coalition" that preserved a disproportionate share of benefits for members of its own dominant ethnic group.[38]

Even Chicago's Poles were not fully incorporated into the Chicago machine, as the organization's Irish leaders sought to preserve the lion's share of benefits for members of their own ethnic group. As a consequence, Poles proved somewhat independent of the machine, and Polish-American Benjamin Adamowski provided a strong challenge to Daley in the 1955 and 1963 elections. Daley backed ally Roman Pucinski for a seat in the U.S. Congress in 1963 in an effort to contain the Polish revolt.[39]

African-Americans fared reasonably well under the Chicago machine only during periods of electoral competition and party factionalism, when black votes could help decide who would rule Chicago. But after Richard J. Daley consolidated his electoral position, black votes were expendable, and the machine reoriented itself more strongly toward the demands of its white ethnic and downtown business constituencies: "The Daley political machine functioned not as a *ladder* of political empowerment but as a *lid* blocking African-American political empowerment."[40] In Chicago, as Grimshaw points out, the fealty of black leaders to the latter-day machine was often the result of brute coercion, not the offering of positive inducements:

> For the black ward leaders, the machine was not the benign economic enterprise we find in the literature, where compliance is secured by material rewards. It was primarily a paramilitary organization, in which compliance was compelled through coercion.[41]

THE FUNCTIONS OF POLITICAL MACHINES

If machines performed no function other than to enrich themselves, it seems unlikely that they would have remained for so long on the political scene. In fact, as sociologist Robert K. Merton identified in his classic essay, such organizations served a variety of purposes that society—or some elements of society—wanted fulfilled. According to Merton, the machine satisfied the wants of "deprived classes" that were "not legitimately satisfied in the same fashion by the legitimate social structure."[42]

As has already been demonstrated, the machine served a **welfare state** function in providing important services to the immigrants and the needy. The machine extended such help before the welfare state became an institutionalized part of government. Not only did the machine provide much needed emergency assistance and relief, but it did so in a way that was more understanding and congenial than did the "impersonal, professionalized, socially distant and legally constrained welfare worker."[43]

Not all political machines, however, filled this welfare state function to the same degree. In the post–World War II era, many big-city machines relied on politically conservative ethnic groups for their support. While these more conservative machines distributed patronage, they were fiscally conservative organizations that sought to keep taxes low and resisted the expansion of services to minority groups.[44]

The machine also provided America's new arrivals with a highly symbolic **channel of social mobility**. The immigrants may have been barred by their lack of a proper birthright from debutante openings, society balls, and the upper rungs of the business world, but their numbers and the right to vote assured them of power in the political arena. Members of an ethnic group would take pride as "one of their own" advanced up the ladder of political power.

Yet, the mobility offered by the machine also can easily be overstated. As Steven Erie reports from his survey of the workings of big-city Irish machines, the mobility offered by the machine was limited. While the Irish machines could offer advancement to individual Irish politicians and contractors, they initially could not offer substantial group mobility. There were simply too few good-paying jobs to go around. Only the latter-day machines offered better-paying jobs. In fact, Erie argues that the political machine in the long run may even have acted to retard the economic advancement of the Irish. Secure in blue-collar patronage jobs, the Irish were slow to develop the entrepreneurial skills necessary for even greater economic mobility.[45]

The machine also provided **assistance to business**. While some businesses opposed the spending practices of the machine, others learned to live and work with the organization. While most upper-class New Yorkers objected to how the machine ran the city, even in the days of the Tweed Ring Tammany Hall had upper-class allies.[46] The machine provided cooperative business owners with "those political privileges which entail immediate economic gain."[47] For members of the business community who chose to work with the machine, the political organization offered security and predictability. The machine demanded from business both contributions and control over jobs that could be used as patronage. In return, the machine could offer business exclusive contracts, licenses, and other preferential treatments that would allow them to pursue growth, limit their competition, and maximize their profits.

In part, the machine offered cooperative businesses the advantages of **centralized power**. Before a business could expand or embark on a new, profitable venture, it might need a whole host of licenses, zoning variances, and various other inspections, permissions, and approvals from a myriad of city boards, agencies, and committees. Such fragmented authority posed a nightmare. But a behind-the-scenes agreement between a business owner and the party organization could assure that all needed clearances would be granted quickly.[48]

The centralization of power was also essential for **city growth**. Cities during the golden age of political machines were suffering severe population pressures. A growing city required new streets, sewers, housing, streetcar lines, and other facilities. Especially in weak-mayor cities, there was no formal authority capable of providing the necessary coordination. Once again, centralized power in the form of the political machine could make sure that all the necessary permissions were granted. New York's Tweed Ring in the 1860s gained the support of real estate owners, mortgage bankers, and other businessmen—and at the same time provided jobs for thousands of unskilled laborers and lined their own pockets via kickbacks—by pursuing an ambitious development program for upper Manhattan that entailed the construction of new streets, water mains, sewers, parks, and streetcar lines.[49] The city expanded, businesses profited, and the machine gained votes and prospered.

In some cities, the machine also responded to the needs of **racketeers, organized crime**, and **gambling**. In return for payoffs made to machine officials, the machine guaranteed that there would be no undue governmental interference in such activities.[50] The machine could even help eliminate a criminal organization's competitors. In Chicago in the 1940s, "Boss" Dawson protected the numbers game of a black cartel that contributed huge sums of money to black ward organizations. Any police officer who harassed the protected "policy wheels" (numbers games) was transferred. But when control of the city passed to a different machine faction, a powerful white crime syndicate used payoffs to other officials to move in on the turf of the black policy wheels. The police cracked down only on the policy wheels operated by blacks not affiliated with the organized crime syndicate. Wheels run by the white syndicate were allowed to keep spinning.[51]

Finally, Harold F. Gosnell, in his study of Chicago politics from the late 1920s to the mid 1930s, was struck by the **conciliating role** played by the Democratic machine. By dispensing both material and symbolic benefits, the machine helped to alleviate social conflict. Gosnell asserts: "Some of the submerged groups may not be so appreciative; but the fact remains that during the years 1930–36 the city was comparatively free from violent labor disputes, hunger riots, and class warfare."[52] While Chicago had plenty of trouble during the Great Depression, "on the credit side of the ledger should be placed the success of the bosses in softening the conflict."[53]

Left-wing and other social critics charge that political machines were too effective in this conciliating role. By individualizing politics and muting class antagonisms, the machines helped undermine any class-based action or Socialist party politics aimed at getting more extensive gains for the disadvantaged.[54] Steven Erie charges that the organizational maintenance needs of the Irish machine, including the need for the machine to placate a city's business community, introduced a "conservative strain" into an Irish-American urban leadership that saw labor-based parties as a threat to the machine's interests. The result was a failure of the machine to represent the needs of the working class more fully as "Irish bosses turned their backs on more radical forms of working-class politics. The machine ultimately tamed Irish voters as well as leaders."[55]

MACHINE POLITICS—SUNBELT STYLE

Machine politics was not as absent from the South as is commonly assumed. While the South lacked the concentrations of immigrants associated with the political machines of the eastern seaboard, notable statewide organizations in the South included the Byrd machine in Virginia, the Long organization in Louisiana, and the Talmadge organization in Georgia. Many rural areas found their county governments controlled by local political machines or **courthouse gangs**. The most infamous of all county machines was that of the Parr family in Duval, Texas. In 1948 Lyndon B. Johnson won that state's senatorial primary by a margin of only 87 votes. The vote in Duval County was 4,662 for Johnson, and a mere 40 for his opponent. Biographer Robert Caro asserts that Johnson stole the election.[56]

The corrupt practices of the local Texas machines were extensive, as revealed by Caro's description of machine activities on behalf of generating votes for Johnson in an earlier election:

> On Election Day, Mexican-Americans were herded to the polls by armed *pistoleros*, sometimes appointed "deputy sheriffs" for the day.... In some precincts, these voters were also handed ballots that had already been marked.... In other precincts, matters were managed less crudely: the voters were told whom to vote for, but were allowed to mark their own ballots; of course, the guards accompanied them into the voting cubbyholes to ensure that the instructions were followed.[57]

As Caro reports, similar corruption was evident in the San Antonio political machine.[58]

Machine politics did emerge in a few cities of the South, including New Orleans, Memphis, Charleston, Savannah, Augusta, Jacksonville, Chattanooga, Montgomery, and San Antonio.[59] Just as V. O. Key, Jr., identified race as the distinguishing factor of southern politics, race also proved to be a decisive factor in explaining the emergence and style of these Sunbelt urban machines.[60]

The Choctaw Club or Old Regulars of New Orleans was "a Democratic organization created in 1896 to wrest control of the city away from a coalition of reformers, Republicans, and blacks who had dominated municipal elections that year. Riding the rising tide of racism, the Choctaws eliminated the black vote in the Louisiana constitution of 1898 and thereby cut the electoral heart out of their opposition."[61] The Choctaws controlled city government from 1900 through the post–World War II era when Robert Maestri "presided over a machine that functioned much as it had a generation before. The Choctaws were meticulously organized on the ward and precinct level, held together by the glue of patronage, and experts in the techniques of electoral legerdemain practiced by most big-city machines."[62]

The most famous big-city organization in the South was the Crump machine in Memphis. Though the Crump machine's organization was typical of most machines and similar to that of the Choctaws in New Orleans, its relationship with the city's black community was vastly different from that of New Orleans' Old Regulars. Where the Choctaws had mobilized to resist the black vote, E. H. Crump realized that gaining black votes was the key to his continued power. In contrast to the states of the Deep South where blacks had such large numbers that whites denied them the vote, blacks in Tennessee posed less of a threat to white control and were allowed to vote in limited numbers. Crump permitted blacks a subordinate position in his machine:

> In Crump's view, which reflected accurately enough the opinion of white Mississippi and West Tennessee, the Negro was an inferior being. However, he could vote and his vote could be weighed in white disputes. And in Crump's view, the Negro had the right to expect a modicum of governmental care and service. The practice under Crump honored this expectation, but in an atmosphere of paternalism in which the black man had his "proper place."[63]

Crump dominated Memphis politics from the 1920s to the late 1940s. He maintained his power by keeping the machine free from corruption and by establishing a good relationship with the city's business community. He even provided an annual boat ride for orphans and shut-ins![64]

Crump's success is all the more amazing when one realizes that Memphis lacked the immigrant base usually associated with machine power. Ethnics constituted only 14 percent of the city's population. These ethnics were also relatively well-to-do small business owners, not the masses of immigrants who needed the fabled machine-provided services.

Crump succeeded by combining the votes of these ethnics with those of the city's black population. What could this well-to-do white group and poor black group have in common? According to urban specialist Kenneth Wald, the answer is nothing except for their "social marginality."[65] Both were outsiders in a southern community. As Wald reminds us:

> The ethnics, despite their impressive economic standing, were also treated as outsiders. When, for example, the Ku Klux Klan came to Memphis in the mid-1920s, it concentrated its verbal fire primarily on the "menace of Catholicism" and appealed for votes to put down the "Popish threat."[66]

By challenging the Klan in the municipal election of 1923, "Crump simultaneously appealed to blacks and white ethnics as a friendly ambassador from a hostile outside world."[67]

Wald's analysis points to the important role played by ethnic frictions in determining machine support. In Boston, for instance, Irish Catholics joined the Democratic party because they had been excluded from Boston society and the Republican party by native Yankee Protestants. It is the memory of such past ethnic tensions, often passed down in stories from one generation to another, that helps to explain why ethnic patterns of voting remain, despite the apparent assimilation or incorporation of these ethnic groups into the mainstream of American society. Voting loyalties, established as a result of the ethnic frictions of earlier times, also are passed down from one generation to the next.[68]

Tampa is another southern city where the votes of blacks proved crucial to the machine's success. In Tampa Nick Nuccio, the son of Sicilian immigrants, was able to gain power by fusing together the votes of Italians with those of the city's growing Hispanic and black communities. As a black newspaper publisher remembered, "He was the first public official who would come regularly to our meetings in our community— he was calling blacks 'mister' when most politicians were still saying 'boy' or 'nigger.'"[69] Once again, though, blacks were accorded only subordinate junior partner status for their contribution to the political machine. This was a pattern typical of big-city organizations in the North as well as in the South.

DECLINE OF POLITICAL MACHINES

The decline of political machines in American urban history was the result of a series of unrelated events that occurred over several decades. Each of these factors helped dissolve the important but fragile balance in the incentive-vote relationship between the political organization and its constituents.

Changes initiated by the reform movement (which will be discussed in the next chapter) took a long time to evolve. However, once they were adopted, a number of them adversely affected the political machine. One of the most damaging reforms from the standpoint of the machine was the use of **merit systems** to hire, promote, and fire local government employees. The **Pendleton Act**, passed in 1883, was the beginning of a civil service system at the national level. New York State adopted a similar law a decade later, and local governments began to implement them shortly thereafter. Today almost every city in the country uses the principles, if not the legal requirements, of a merit system for public employment.

The impact of this reform on political machines was devastating. Patronage, which was in many cases the key reward offered in exchange for votes, was eroded. Without jobs to offer, it became increasingly difficult for block and precinct captains to keep their voters satisfied. George Washington Plunkitt's vehement attack on the **civil service**, which he denounced as "the curse of the nation,"[70] can be understood only by recognizing the threat that this reform posed to the organization:

> The boys and men don't get excited any more when they see a United States flag or hear "The Star-Spangled Banner." They don't care no more for firecrackers on the Fourth of July. And why should they? What is there in it for them? They know that no matter how hard they work for their country in a campaign, the jobs will go to fellows who can tell about the mummies and the bird steppin' on the iron....
>
> Say, let me tell of one case. After the battle of San Juan Hill, the Americans found a dead man with a light complexion, red hair and blue eyes. They could see he wasn't a Spaniard, although he had on a Spanish uniform.... [T]hen a private of the Seventy-first Regiment saw him and yelled, "Good Lord, that's Flaherty." That man grew up in my district, and he was once the most patriotic American boy on the West Side. He couldn't see a flag without yellin' himself hoarse.
>
> Now, how did he come to be lying dead with a Spanish uniform on?... Well, in the municipal campaign of 1897, that young man, chockfull of patriotism, worked day and night for the Tammany ticket. Tammany won, and the young man determined to devote his life to the service of the city. He picked out a place that would suit him, and sent in his application to the head of department. He got a reply that he must take a civil service examination to get the place.... He read the questions about the mummies, the bird on the iron, and all the other fool questions—and he left that office as enemy of the country that he had loved so well. The mummies and the bird blasted his patriotism. He went to Cuba, enlisted in the Spanish army at the breakin' out of the war, and died fightin' his country.
>
> That is but one victim of the infamous civil service.[71]

Undaunted by the political bosses' complaints, the reformers succeeded in enacting civil service legislation and in changing many of the rules governing local politics.

Council-manager government and **at-large and nonpartisan elections** were some of the other devices used by the early twentieth-century reformers to erode the power of the political machine. Each of these reforms struck at the heart of the political machine. Council-manager government created the position of a professional, nonpolitical city manager who did not share the perspective of machine politicians. The system of at-large elections reduced the ward-based parochial interests that were at the center of the bargaining and vote trading arrangement of the political machine. As we shall see in the next chapter, at-large elections also worked against the representation of geographically concentrated ethnic groups. Nonpartisanship reduced citizens' reliance on the party cue necessary for disciplined machine voting. In the absence of party designations on the ballot, citizens tended to vote their preferences for individual candidates rather than for a party slate.

The **growth of the welfare state**, beginning with Franklin Delano Roosevelt's New Deal during the Great Depression and extending during Lyndon B. Johnson's Great Society of the 1960s, also undermined the power of local machines. The assistance offered citizens by the political machine paled when compared to the extensive range of services offered by an intergovernmentalized array of federal, state, and city programs. The hod of coal offered by the machine could not match the cash, housing, and food relief now provided by government agencies. Political party organizations were now being bypassed by state and federal programs. Unable to compete with the assistance provided by such programs as Social Security and Medicare, both machine politicians and reformers in New York in the 1960s set up storefront centers where they could help citizens apply for program benefits. The best the political organization could do was hope to take credit for the social welfare benefits now provided by the government.

As mentioned above, the lifeblood of many city machines was the successive waves of immigrants pouring into the country between 1880 and 1920. In the 1920s federal policy greatly **curtailed immigration**. The machine watched as earlier immigrants climbed the political, social, and economic ladder out of the ghettos and into middle-income and middle-class respectability. With no immigrants to replace the second- and third-generation immigrants of earlier times, the machine lost its natural supply of voters. As already noted, the arrival of blacks and Hispanics in the inner city succeeded in perpetuating the machine for only a limited period of time. Minority loyalty to the machine could only be maintained as long as minority members refrained from pressing issues of integration and racial justice.

World War II created many problems for the political machine. Jobs were plentiful, and salaries were good; prosperity continued through the postwar period. With **increased wealth**, voters were less dependent on those limited benefits the party organization could give; with **increased**

education citizens were less willing to trade their votes for the material and nonmaterial benefits provided by the machine. On top of this was the beginning of the **suburban boom**, as many once-loyal machine voters abandoned their city apartments and bought suburban homes made attractive by federal financing and insurance programs.

In more recent years, Supreme Court decisions further delivered a mortal blow to the few surviving strong, party organizations by placing new **limitations on patronage**. In the 1976 *Elrod v. Burns* decision, the Supreme Court limited a government's ability to fire a worker in a non-policy-making position on "the sole ground of his political belief."[72] An incoming administration could no longer simply discharge incumbent workers and replace them with loyalists who had worked for the party in the past election.

In the 1990 *Rutan* case, the Supreme Court extended the ban to partisanship in hiring and promotions. The court ruled that politically based hiring and promotions effectively deprived an individual of his or her First Amendment rights of freedom of speech, belief, and association. For Justice William Brennan, conditioning "employment on political activity pressures employees…to work for the election of political candidates they do not support" and is "tantamount to coerced belief." Brennan rejected the patronage contention that "to the victor belong the spoils" for a revised formulation that to the victor belong only "those spoils that may be constitutionally obtained."[73] Justice Antonin Scalia dissented, declaring that the patronage was a venerable American tradition and that the destruction of patronage would have severe repercussions in undermining the strength of political parties in government and in increasing the reliance of public officials on interest groups in electoral campaigns.[74]

Merit system rules and Supreme Court decisions are not self-implementing. As we shall see, local party organizations have found various ways to evade these restrictions and still utilize patronage hiring. Yet, the cumulative effect of these decisions is clear. While patronage will continue to exist, there will be less of it. The patronage armies are a thing of the past.[75]

One final factor contributing to the decline of the machines was a **change in both the mass media and social life**. The rise in television viewing made it more difficult for the block or precinct to establish and maintain a close personal relationship with local residents. Now if the machine captain comes to pay a visit, he or she is likely to be intruding on the family's television viewing. Further, no precinct leader today can hope to repeat Plunkitt's claim to know all the people in his district. Increased wealth and the availability of other forms of entertainment—movies, the theater, and weekend trips—also mean that citizens are no longer dependent on the political clubhouses for entertainment, picnics, dances, and sports. The political machine once filled an important social function that is now met by other institutions.

The rise of television has also changed the nature of the political campaign. Television provides viewers with an alternative source of information and voting cues, weakening the party organization's influence on voting behavior. In the age of television, patronage armies have yielded way to mass media campaigning and the raising of the vast sums of money required for television advertising. Public opinion pollsters, computer experts, direct mail specialists, and other professional campaign specialists have displaced machine politicians from key strategic electoral roles.

Younger voters have grown up without any sense of strong partisan allegiances or ties to the political machine. Today's electorate is more educated, independent, media-oriented, and prone to ticket-splitting. Low voting turnout rates characterize contemporary urban elections. Political parties no longer fill the functions they did in the past; the parties have lost out to competing institutions. In New York City, the decay of meaningful party organizations has been so pervasive that urban historian Richard Wade feels it is more accurate to talk about the city's new "No-Party System" as opposed to a party system.[76]

In Philadelphia, too, "party organizations have been reduced to administering elections" and no longer retain the functions served by the city's political machine in the past.[77] As late as the 1960s, Mayor James Tate was able to distribute patronage and money available through the War on Poverty. But the loss of federal funds in the 1970s and 1980s, coupled with the cutbacks in city spending, acted to limit the supply of job and contract patronage available in the city.[78]

THE CHICAGO MACHINE: HOW IT SURVIVED SO LONG

The Democratic organization in Chicago and Cook County survived the period that saw the decline of machine organizations in the nation's other great cities. The persistence of the Chicago machine was based on a number of factors. First, the machine maintained its stock of patronage. Government jobs were classified as temporary or seasonal to keep them exempt from civil service rules—even if seasonal jobs somehow lasted the full year or "temporary" employees somehow " 'stay temporary' for the rest of their lives."[79] Machine insider Milton Rakove believed that an educated guess would place approximately 30,000 patronage positions at the disposal of the machine.[80] Columnist Mike Royko estimated that Richard J. Daley controlled more than the twenty to twenty-five thousand jobs as a result of his twin positions as mayor and chairman of the Cook County Democratic party: "The Machine has jobs at racetracks, public utilities, private industry, and the Chicago Transit Authority, which is the bus and subway system, and will help arrange easy union cards."[81] As Rakove observed, "There are also many thousands of jobs in private industry throughout the Chicago metropolitan area which require the sponsorship of Democratic ward committeemen."[82]

Second, Daley maintained strong ties with the city's business community. The construction orientation and downtown business district renewal programs of "Dick the Builder" not only replenished the machine's stock of job and contract patronage but also earned him the endorsement of the city's business community and newspapers.[83] Daley was wise enough to recognize that the machine could no longer depend solely on the dispensing of patronage and other specific benefits to attract the support of the city's increasingly better-off and better-educated electorates. Hence, Daley shifted to building projects, such as the McCormick Place convention center, expressways, downtown parking garages, and the University of Illinois at Chicago campus that could be seen to provide "collective" benefits for specific groups in the city. Daley also realized that citizen support for the machine was conditioned upon his efficient delivery of city services. Chicago was proud of being "The City That Works!"[84] Bureaucrats and their professional standards played a more dominant role in determining the distribution of services in Chicago than was commonly assumed.[85]

Finally, Daley avoided the appearance of personal involvement in scandal. Patronage, influence peddling, and other aspects of corruption continue in Chicago to the present day. Yet as one of Daley's contemporaries observed, while his friends in public life may have enriched themselves, Daley himself was "unquestionably personally honest and has not accumulated a large fortune through graft and bribery."[86] Daley lived his entire life in an undistinguished bungalow in the working-class Irish Bridgeport neighborhood in which he was born. He also knew how to cut his losses. When it was revealed that Chicago police officers were involved in "boosting" goods from scenes of reported robberies, the revelations were too much for even the normally complacent citizens of Chicago to bear. It was the type of scandal that could drive the organization from office. But instead of being victimized by it, Daley came out smelling like a rose. He appointed a blue-ribbon commission to clean up the city's police department and brought in a new chief, the noted criminologist and University of California professor O. W. Wilson. Daley knew that it was better to suffer the short-term loss of control over the police department than to suffer the continuation of a scandal that might discredit his organization in the eyes of the voters.[87]

THE DECLINE OF THE CHICAGO MACHINE: FROM HAROLD WASHINGTON TO A NEW DALEY

In the 1970s and 1980s the Chicago organization suffered three particularly debilitating setbacks. The first came in the form of new limitations placed on patronage. The Supreme Court's 1976 ***Elrod v. Burns*** decision ruled that the newly elected Cook County Democratic Sheriff had acted improperly when he fired two noncivil service employees because they were not members of the Democratic party, did not support the party, and were not sponsored for their positions by the Democratic party. By protecting public employees from discharge on the basis of what they believe, the Court dealt the Chicago patronage system a serious blow. Patronage was further limited by the series of **Shakman consent decrees**.[88] The original Shakman decree was signed by Mayor Richard J. Daley in 1972 in response to a public lawsuit that charged the patronage system with denying the rights of voters and public employees. The city agreed not to fire workers for reasons of politics. Shakman III, signed by Mayor Harold Washington in 1983, was of even greater importance, banning the political hiring of most city workers. The Supreme Court's 1990 *Rutan* decision further narrowed patronage in hiring.

The second major shock to the machine was the death of legendary Mayor Richard J. Daley. No more would the county and city Democratic organizations be headed by the same man. No longer would factional warfare be averted by the dictate of "Hizzoner." Instead, in the 1979 election, Jane Byrne upset Daley's hand-picked successor, interim Mayor Michael Bilandic. Bilandic had been mortally wounded when Chicago was paralyzed by two major snowstorms. Not only did the trains not operate on time, but they failed to run altogether. Chicago citizens felt that this would not have happened had Mayor Daley still been alive. "The city that works" apparently no longer worked, and the city's voters vented their rage on Bilandic.

The city's black voters, in particular, were enraged when Bilandic, in an attempt to speed the flow of snowbound trains into the central business district, closed stations in the black areas of the south and west sides of town.[89] The snowbound train episode was an omen; **race** would be the last factor that would take down the Chicago machine.

The Chicago machine had exacerbated racial separation. The black population in Chicago was not concentrated solely in the original ghetto areas. Rather, city policy makers chose to build a "second ghetto," a "wall" of high-rise public housing apartment buildings that would keep blacks from spilling over into white ethnic neighborhoods.[90] Expressways were used as artificial barriers to contain minority neighborhoods: "The Dan Ryan [Expressway], for instance, was shifted several blocks during the planning stage to make one of the ghetto walls."[91] Aldermen were given the right to veto the placement of public housing units in their neighborhoods, thereby killing any chance for scatter-site housing. Assignments to public hosing projects were made on the basis of race; blacks would not be offered units in white buildings, and vice versa. And the city dragged its feet, virtually bringing to a halt the construction of new public housing units, rather than implement the Supreme Court's *Gautreaux* decision to disperse its public housing stock.[92]

Chicago's growing black population, comprising approximately 40 percent of the city's total population by the late 1970s, was no longer willing to accept such second-class status. Black defections from the machine had actually begun as early as 1975, the last election in which

Richard J. Daley ran. In 1979 five of the once dependable machine wards on Chicago's black South Side defected in the primary and voted for a black candidate, State Senator Harold Washington. In the general election they gave 63 percent of their vote to Jane Byrne against Daley's chosen successor, Michael Bilandic.[93] But once in office Byrne alienated the black community with her self-professed support of the machine, her appointments to the school board and the Chicago Housing Authority, and her refusal to accede to minority hiring demands in the city's Summerfest program.

In 1983 Harold Washington gained the Democratic nomination for mayor by triumphing over a white ethnic vote divided between Mayor Byrne and State's Attorney Richard M. Daley, the son of the late mayor. Until this time the Republican candidate, Bernard Epton, was presumed to have no chance to win in a city as heavily Democratic as Chicago; he was even slighted at a fundraising event by his own party's leaders. But now he was the beneficiary of a backlash vote of whites, who felt threatened by the possibility of a black mayor.

Washington promised to deliver a fair share of benefits to the city's South Side communities since the machine in the past had favored the North Side ethnic wards. By campaigning as a reformer who would end traditional machine practices, Washington threatened the self-interest of party organization officials. Little wonder that Vito Marzullo, legendary ward committeeman and dean of the city council (who died in 1990), endorsed the Republican candidate and expressed nothing but hostility toward Washington, whom he called "Buffalo Bill" and a "nitwit":

> Why do I have to support him [Washington]? After he got the nomination, you'd think we elected Mussolini and Hitler put together. This man here he want to do away with the patronage office. Do away with the power of the ward committeeman. What is this?[94]

Washington won a bitter general election, getting 51.8 percent of the vote. His opponent got 48.2 percent, a figure so amazing for a Republican mayoral candidate in Chicago that much of it must be attributed to the sudden salience of the racial factor.

The key to Washington's electoral success was threefold. Of greatest importance was the **mobilization of black voters**. In just the five months between the November 1982 gubernatorial election and the April 1983 mayoral election, over 92,000 new black voters were registered.[95] Even more striking was the **turnout** among black voters: "No black ward turned out lower than 73 percent. Washington captured close to 97 percent of the black vote."[96] Evidently, despite the common stereotype of black alienation and passivity in conventional politics, blacks can and will turn out to vote if they have a candidate who represents their concerns.

Second, Washington received over 50 percent of **the Hispanic vote**.[97] Finally, he also received the support of a narrow band of **Lakefront liberals**, that is, well-to-do whites who tended to favor liberal causes. The final two groups were crucial to his success, as black votes alone could not have put him over the top.

In government, Washington established a progressive, reform-oriented government. At the beginning, Washington was frustrated by the racial polarization that resulted in a "Council Wars" period during which the dominant, white, machine-oriented faction of the city council blocked virtually every one of the mayor's major policy programs. Washington did succeed in bringing long-excluded community and minority groups into the policy-making process. He sought a more equitable distribution of services to minority neighborhoods. He also sought a program to attract new blue-collar industrial jobs that were leaving the city as a result of increased land values and the pressures of gentrification.[98] He signed a Freedom of Information Order and banned hiring and firing on political grounds. Washington was a reform mayor whose sense of political reform was rooted in the experiences of the black community. It had less to do with classical reform's emphasis on businesslike efficiency and managerial culture and more to do with honesty in government, openness, and fairness.[99]

Washington won reelection in 1987, once again winning the three keys to victory: black mobilization, Hispanic support, and the votes of Lakefront liberals. This time even black captains in the machine had no choice but to support Washington or lose all credibility in their home constituencies. To the black community, the Washington candidacy had taken on the symbolic significance of a crusade. Washington also appealed to Lakefront homeowners, campaigning in the strategic Lakefront area and promising to construct a seawall to hold back a rising Lake Michigan—an issue of crucial importance to condominium owners in the area.

Later that year Harold Washington died in office of a heart attack. Jesse Jackson interrupted his presidential campaign in order to return to Chicago to try to maintain black unity in identifying Washington's successor. But the black community split. The white members of the City Council joined with only six of the eighteen black members to name Eugene Sawyer, a more machine-oriented black, as interim mayor. A great many blacks were outraged by the council's action and Sawyer's complicity, as they felt a candidate more in keeping with Harold Washington's action legacy should have succeeded to the office. Polls taken immediately after Sawyer's selection showed that the new mayor did not command majority support in the black community.[100]

In the 1989 special election following Washington's death, no black candidate could replicate the three keys to Harold Washington's success: black mobilization, support in the Hispanic community, and support from Lakefront liberals.[101] Instead of experiencing mobilization and unity, the black community was divided. Mayor Sawyer sought to defeat Richard M. Daley, son of the legendary Richard J. Daley, in the Democratic primary. Timothy Evans, knowing that Daley would triumph over a divided black vote, dropped out of the primary and ran in the general election on the newly formed, but woefully underfunded, Harold Washington Party ticket. Evans would not endorse Sawyer in the primary, and the schism and the factionalism remained through the general election. The antagonisms between the two black candidates split the black community and led to a sense of hopelessness, diminishing black turnout far below what it had been during the Harold Washington elections.

Also, Evans could not win sufficient votes from the swing Hispanic and Lakefront liberal communities. Evans was no Washington, who was capable of building a multiracial coalition. Instead, Evans' campaign was captured by the more militant or nationalist voices in the black community.[102]

Richard M. Daley, in contrast, sought to refashion his appeal in 1989 and broaden his electoral coalition. Daley was no longer running, as he had in previous elections, as the heir to his father's Democratic machine. Instead, in the 1989 election, Daley tried to project himself as a good-government reformer and the only candidate who could restore racial harmony in a bitterly divided Chicago. Daley made conspicuous stops in the black sections of the city, not so much with the hope of getting large numbers of black votes, but out of a need to cast an acceptable image to that swing group of more moderate and liberal white voters who could provide the margin of victory or defeat. In the most brilliant strategic move of the campaign, Daley appointed a black woman, Avis LaVelle, the well-known and highly respected city hall radio reporter, as his press secretary.[103] Once again, the message was racial conciliation. Daley also appealed to the city's Hispanic community, winning the key endorsement of 26th Ward Alderman (and later-to-be Congressman) Luis Gutierrez.[104] Daley's new reform image also proved effective in reaching into the Lakefront wards. According to one *New York Times* poll, 30 percent of Daley's voters in 1989 had voted for Harold Washington in 1987! Those voters making the switch were largely Lakefronters and Hispanics.[105] In 1993, Daley easily won reelection.

While machine politics in Chicago may be far from totally dead, the Democratic party is no longer the strong, centralized organization that it once was. While the transition is still far from complete, only elements of the classical machine remain. Black voters no longer follow the dictates of the machine. Washington's victory energized reform, no single figure now unites the city and county party organizations, and patronage has been limited by court order.

In office, Richard M. Daley did not attempt to revive the patronage army of his father but instead has resorted to **contract patronage**, rewarding political supporters with no-bid consulting contracts, legal work, and various other city favors.[106] While Daley has not rejected machine-style politics and the friends of his father, he has recognized the need to build a new coalition to ensure victory. Daley is ostensibly committed to open, accessible, and decentralized government. He is also committed to such reforms as privatization. Yet, under this mask of reform, Daley has extended the reach of the mayor's office, and government has become more recentralized and closed in the machine tradition. William Grimshaw has labeled the "part machine/part reform" politics of Richard M. Daley as "machine politics reform style."[107]

THE PERSISTENCE OF MACHINE POLITICS

Chicago is not the only city where strong elements of machine politics continue to survive. The O'Connell machine in Albany, New York, persisted well into the 1980s as a result of its reliance on patronage and a conservative politics of low spending and low taxes, which appealed to the city's homeowners.[108]

Dramatic examples of machine-style corruption and patronage are found in a great many cities. The administration of the school system in Hoboken, New Jersey, was marred by such extensive patronage, political interference, corruption, and mismanagement that in 1989 the state government took the unprecedented step of seizing control of the school district. In Atlantic City, New Jersey, the introduction of casino gambling has allowed new opportunities for machine-style exchanges. In the "City Hall for Sale" scandal of the late 1980s, city officials apparently received casino complimentaries, gambling credit lines, and other gifts and benefits in exchange for favorable zoning and planning considerations. Thirteen persons, including the mayor and other city officials, were arrested by the state police.[109] The machine politics of an earlier era in Atlantic City had reemerged in only somewhat altered form in the city's dealings with the casino industry.[110]

In New York, the reform movement has clearly not cleaned up all elements of machine-style politics. The "clubhouse" party organizations, the remnants of the old machine, remain and must be dealt with. In the late 1960s and early 1970s, even reform Mayor John Lindsay found that he had to rely extensively on the distribution of contract patronage in his attempts to build power and govern the city. In the 1980s, Ed Koch, another mayor with roots in the anti-machine reform movement, virtually abandoned the good-government reform tradition as he made even more extensive use of both contract and job patronage and sought an accommodation with the city's political clubhouse leaders. Koch dispensed jobs and contracts to gain the support of such borough machine leaders as Meade Esposito, Stanley Friedman, and Donald Manes. Koch also used control of a Talent Bank, nominally created to identify qualified minority job candidates, as a means of assuring mayoral approval of job appointees. Although the mayor denied it, the Talent Bank appeared to be a patronage mill.[111] The local political organizations dispensed contracts in classic machine fashion:

> In Queens, you had one-stop service, New York State Attorney General, Robert Abrams, observed. If you wanted a city contract, you went to [Queens County Democratic party leader and Borough President] Donald Manes. If you wanted a judgeship, you went to Donald Manes. If you wanted a job in government, if you wanted a cable franchise, you went to Donald Manes.[112]

Manes' suicide in 1986, after the revelation of his involvement in the improper award of automobile towing contracts, is only the most dramatic incident that points to the continued existence of machine-style politics in the modern city.

Ethnic politics is far from dead. Ethnic appeals still provide a valuable shortcut by which politicians can reach large blocks of voters. In the New York City 1993 mayoral election, Rudolph Giuliani won the mayoralty in part by repeating the ethnic appeals that characterized the machine era. He formed a partnership with Herman Badillo, the city's first Puerto Rican Congressman, in an effort to appeal to Hispanic voters who had backed Mayor David Dinkins in the previous election but were now increasingly dissatisfied with his performance in office. Badillo had made a brief entry into the mayoral race, but, in a classic example of ethnic ticket-balancing, dropped out to run for city comptroller on the ticket with the Italian Giuliani. Giuliani's campaign also used broadcast appeals by the noted actor Ron Silver to reach Jewish voters who were disenchanted by Mayor Dinkins' handling of the Crown Heights affair, where some observers charged that black-Jewish hostilities turned into an anti-Jewish "pogrom."

Political scientist Alan DiGaetano also points to the rise of a new form of machine politics, the **mayor-centered machine**. These newer versions of the machine are run under the direction of the mayor, not the political party. In part, federally funded programs allowed mayors to put together personal political organizations: "These mayor-centered machines are housed in city agencies not protected by civil service rules."[113] The agencies then provide the mayor with large numbers of political workers to canvass neighborhoods on election day. Federal aid also provided the mayors with resources that the mayor-centered organizations could use to mobilize both neighborhood groups and downtown development interests—the beneficiaries of many of the federal urban programs since the 1960s. Steven Erie stresses the importance of intergovernmental assistance—friendly national and state allies that provided cities with patronage resources—as crucial historically to the development of strong political machines.[114]

In Boston, Mayor Kevin White developed a mayor-centered organization by establishing "little city halls" in the neighborhoods and requiring city workers to work in political campaigns and donate part of their salary to his campaign effort.[115] In Detroit, Mayor Coleman Young employed Community Development Block Grants, CETA grants, Urban

Development Action Grants (UDAGs), and other federal monies to assist the city's majority black neighborhoods and to promote downtown growth. According to DiGaetano, "Detroit's business interests recipro-cated by donating large contributions to Young's campaign chest." [116]

But the power of such mayor-centered machines is limited, espe-cially when compared to the great urban machines of the past. When Coleman Young retired in 1993, the candidate of his legendary machine finished a distant third place in the primary. In the runoff election, the more independent Dennis Archer beat Young's preferred candidate, Sharon McPhail. Cutbacks in federal aid programs have also reduced the resources available to mayor-centered organizations.

Machine-style practices also exist in places where the classic urban political machines have never taken root. On the surface, Atlanta, with its system of nonpartisan elections and absence of mass patronage, would seemingly represent a rejection of machine politics. Yet, the city's busi-ness-dominated governing regime has been able, in classic machine style, to use selective incentives to reward its friends and punish its enemies, thereby helping to shape just which issues are allowed to enter the polit-ical arena. [117]

A SUBURBAN POLITICAL MACHINE

On occasion, political machines have appeared in the suburbs. In subur-ban New York City, the Nassau County, Long Island, Republican organi-zation has been described as "the last political machine." [118] This patronage-driven organization has dominated local politics in Hempstead, North Hempstead, Long Beach, Glen Cove, and Oyster Bay. Democrats have not controlled the county Board of Supervisors since World War I. Republican control of the Nassau County Executive was interrupted by the Democrats only in the 1960s. But even the power of this legendary Republican organization has lessened over the years, and Democrats made substantial inroads in the 1991 local Long Island elections.

The Nassau County Republican Organization has thrived on both job patronage and contract patronage. Though court rulings have had the effect of diminishing the organization's patronage army, the operations of the Nassau County Republican Party show that the Supreme Court rul-ings on patronage can still be evaded. The New York State Civil Service Commission is only a very weak watchdog when it comes to monitoring the affairs of local government. Civil service rules allow an appointing officer to pick from the three top-scoring candidates for a position; in Nassau County, any Republican candidate in the top three is almost always offered the job. If there is an insufficient number of candidates with pass-ing test scores, the appointing officer can hire someone else on a provi-sional basis—an appointment that can be made permanent if the person on the job passes the test at a later date. The Republican organization assures that there will be little competition for the jobs by restricting information about job openings and using outdated advertising lists. The organization can even assure that there will be no list of eligible job candidates by creating a new job title. Sometimes, misleadingly low salaries are announced so that only the organization's preferred candidates apply for the job—who are then hired and paid at much better rates.

New York Senator Alfonse D'Amato has emerged as the Nassau County machine's most prominent elected official. D'Amato rose through the ranks of the Long Island Republican organization, holding local party and elected offices. In the Senate he earned the nickname of "Senator Pothole" for his machine-style concern for the provision of local services. Throughout his career, D'Amato has also been accused of going along with the more seamy side of machine-style practices. He has been investigated for improprieties connected with his fundraising activities. In the HUD scandals in the 1980s, charges were made that friends of D'Amato got new HUD-assisted Island Park homes after somehow having put in their applications in advance of the legal opening of the process. Subsidized homes meant for the poor and racial minorities were allocated to politically connected, white, Island Park residents, including one of D'Amato's cousins.[119]

Both D'Amato's reputation and the reputation of the Nassau County machine were tarnished by the "one percent case." Local public employees were expected to contribute one percent of their salaries to the Republican party in order to get and keep their jobs. Employees who failed to make the expected contribution were also denied promotions and pay raises. In 1985 a jury found the Town of Hempstead and the Nassau County and Hempstead Town Republican organizations guilty of illegal activity and violating employees' rights. D'Amato's testimony during the trial and a letter that he had written during his days as Hempstead town supervisor indicate that he was aware of the one-percent practice.

CONCLUSIONS: MACHINE POLITICS EVALUATED

The common portrayals of the machine politician as a corrupt grafter and the reformer as a good guy in a white hat are clearly overplayed. The machines lasted as long as they did because they served functions and provided services that no other institution did. The machine offered social welfare and job benefits to those in need; it helped integrate immigrants into the American way of life; it provided businesses with necessary points of contact in city government to ensure that important transactions would receive orderly city approval; and it helped centralize power and abet city growth during this nation's period of rapid industrialization.

The achievements of the machine were substantial. Yet there is danger in this revisionism of overglorifying the machine. Many machine politicians were grafters only interested in their self-enrichment. The machine also bought votes, punished its enemies, and otherwise manipulated and corrupted the election process. City government has become a big business requiring trained professional management, which the machine politicians proved unable to provide. And the relationship between the machine and a city's black community is, indeed, a complex one. Both the Memphis and Chicago party organizations were willing to provide blacks with important, but limited, services. In return, the machine expected blacks to show fealty and accept subordinate status. In Chicago the white ethnic-based machine retarded integration; it was no fair broker of minority demands. It was willing to broker only those demands that advanced the machine's interests; it suppressed demands that threatened its ethnic constituency and jeopardized the organization's well-being.

Indeed, in contrast to the view that political machines are nonideological, the Chicago machine can be seen to have had an ideology that led it to spurn the redistributional demands of the city's minority citizens. Such a race-based ideology could be overcome only when blacks controlled the machine, as was the case in Detroit where Coleman Young used the new mayor-centered machine to help advance the position of that city's black residents.

From a more severe analytical perspective, even the machine's provision of welfare benefits and social services to the immigrants and urban poor can be criticized. According to this view, which we can label for convenience a **Marxist perspective**, the great urban machines acted as a conservatizing force in public affairs. By dispensing emergency relief, the machine bought off the anger that might have produced a demand for a more equitable sharing of the nation's wealth. By dispensing benefits through a specific exchange process, the machine individualized the political process and helped undermine any sense of class identity or collective action among the urban poor. The ward politicians taught the immigrants how to play politics American-style. In effect, the machine bought off the demand for change quite cheaply. By providing limited social welfare benefits, it averted mass disorder, maintained social control, and diminished the demand for a fundamental redistribution of results.

Yet this critique of machine politics may be just as overstated as was the above-mentioned view that portrays machine politicians solely as public-serving advocates of lower-class interests. The socialist critique is valid only to the extent that socialist politics ever had any real chance of taking root in the United States. Yet the enactment of socialism never had any real prospects in the United States. For immigrants arriving in this nation without a friend, for the social outsiders, and for the urban poor in need of jobs and emergency relief, the machine provided real and important benefits.

Centralized machine organizations have suffered severe decline. Today they dominate the political scene in only a very few cities. Even so, machine politics is not dead. Machine-style exchanges persist today and are quite widespread, but they are not as all-pervasive as they once were. The reform movement has gone a long way in cleaning up local politics, as we will see when we turn to the politics of reform in the next chapter.

NOTES

1. Raymond E. Wolfinger, "Why Political Machines Have Not Withered Away and Other Revisionist Thoughts," *Journal of Politics* 34 (May 1972): 394.
2. Boss Cox's Cincinnati is studied by Zane L. Miller, "Boss Cox's Cincinnati: A Study in Urbanization and Politics, 1880–1914," *Journal of American History* 54 (March 1968): 823–38, reprinted in *The City Boss in America*, ed. Alexander B. Callow, Jr. (New York: Oxford University Press, 1976), pp. 34–50. Good brief overviews of Boss Reuf's San Francisco and the Pendergast machine in Kansas City are provided by Dennis R. Judd, *The Politics of American Cities: Private Power and Public Policy* (Glenview, IL: Scott, Foresman, 1988), pp. 54–63.
3. Wolfinger, "Why Political Machines Have Not Withered Away."
4. Edward C. Banfield and James Q. Wilson, *City Politics* (New York: Vintage Books, 1963), p. 115.
5. William L. Riordan, *Plunkitt of Tammany Hall* (New York: E. P. Dutton, 1963), pp. 27–28 and 90–93.
6. Dayton David McKean, *The Boss: The Hague Machine in Action* (Boston: Houghton Mifflin, 1940), p. 270.
7. Ibid., p. 271.
8. Martin Shefter, "The Emergence of the Political Machine: An Alternative View," in *Theoretical Perspectives on Urban Politics*, ed. Willis D. Hawley and Michael Lipsky (Englewood Cliffs, NJ: 1976), chapter 2. Also see Terrence J. McDonald, "Introduction," in *Plunkitt of Tammany Hall*, ed. Terrence McDonald (Boston: Bedford Books of St. Martin's, 1994), pp. 6–13.
9. William J. Grimshaw, *Bitter Fruit: Black Politics and the Chicago Machine, 1931–1991* (Chicago: University of Chicago Press, 1992), pp. 11, 69–72, and 86–87.
10. Shefter, "The Emergence of the Political Machine: An Alternative View," p. 22.
11. John M. Allswang, *Bosses, Machines, and Urban Voters* (Port Washington, NY: Kennikat Press, 1977), p. 52.
12. Ibid., p. 30. The complex and changing relationship between the city's business community and the Tweed Ring is discussed by Shefter, "The Emergence of the Political Machine: An Alternative View," pp. 27–30.
13. Edward C. Banfield, *Political Influence* (New York: Free Press, 1961).
14. Steven P. Erie, *Rainbow's End: Irish-American and the Dilemmas of Urban Machine Politics, 1840–1985* (Berkley, CA: University of California Press, 1988).
15. Myron A. Levine, "Goal-Oriented Leadership and the Limits of Entrepreneurship," *Western Political Quarterly* 33 (September 1980): 401–403. Paul E. Peterson, *School Politics, Chicago Style* (Chicago: University of Chicago

Press, 1976), pp. 12–18, observes that brokerage is an accurate description of Daley's style only among those groups whose political perspectives he viewed to be legitimate.

16. Riordan, *Plunkitt of Tammany Hall*, p. 25.
17. Ibid.
18. Allswang, *Bosses, Machines, and Urban Voters*, p. 52.
19. Riordan, *Plunkitt of Tammany Hall*, p. 6.
20. Ibid., p. 3. There is some doubt as to whether Plunkitt's widely quoted comments on "honest and dishonest graft" are actually his own. The reporter, William Riordan, who interviewed Plunkitt was searching to write a book that would sell. It is possible that Riordan either prompted or even authored these and other famous Plunkitt quotations. See McDonald, "Introduction," pp. 1–2 and 28–29.
21. Shefter, "The Emergence of the Political Machine: An Alternative View," p. 21.
22. Ibid., p. 28.
23. Amy Bridges, *A City in the Republic* (Ithaca, NY: Cornell University Press, 1987), chapter 1.
24. Alan DiGaetano, "The Rise and Development of Urban Political Machines: An Alternative to Merton's Functional Analysis," *Urban Affairs Quarterly* 24 (December 1988): 250.
25. Elmer E. Cornwell, Jr., "Bosses, Machines and Ethnic Groups," *Annals* 353 (May 1964): 27–39.
26. Richard Hofstadter, *The Age of Reform* (New York: Vintage Books, 1955).
27. Hofstadter's view is essentially reinforced by James Q. Wilson and Edward C. Banfield, "Public Regardingness as a Value Premise in Voting Behavior," *American Political Science Review* 58 (December 1964): 876–87.
28. Timothy M. Hennessey, "Problems in Concept Formation: The Ethos Theory and the Comparative Study of Urban Politics," *Midwest Journal of Political Science* 14 (November 1970): 537–64.
29. Grimshaw, *Bitter Fruit*, chapter 5.
30. Ibid., p. 102.
31. Ibid., pp. 40–41 and chapters 3–5.
32. Ibid., pp. 42–44 and chapters 5 and 6.
33. Ibid., pp. 31–36 and chapter 4.
34. Mike Royko, *Boss: Richard J. Daley of Chicago* (New York: Signet, 1971), p. 26.
35. Ibid., pp. 154–55.
36. The typology that distinguishes among distributional, redistributional, and regulatory politics is presented by Theodore J. Lowi, "Distribution, Regulation, Redistribution: The Functions of Government," in *Public Policies and Their Impacts*, ed. Randall B. Ripley (New York: W. W. Norton, 1966), pp. 27–40, reprinted in *Readings in American Political Behavior*, ed. Raymond E. Wolfinger (Englewood Cliffs, NJ: Prentice-Hall, 1970), pp. 245–56.
37. Erie, *Rainbow's End*.
38. Ibid., pp. 9–10.
39. Tomasz Inglot and John P. Pelissero, "Ethnic Political Power in a Machine City: Chicago's Poles at Rainbow's End, "*Urban Affairs Quarterly* 28 (June 1993): 526–43.
40. Richard A. Keiser, "Explaining African-American Political Empowerment: Windy City Politics from 1900 to 1983," *Urban Affairs Quarterly* 29 (September 1993): 112.

41. Grimshaw, *Bitter Fruit*, p. 95.
42. Robert K. Merton, "The Latent Functions of the Machine: A Sociologist's View," pp. 71–82, of his book *Social Theory and Social Structure* (New York: Free Press, 1957), reprinted in *The City Boss in America*, ed. Alexander B. Callow, Jr. (New York: Oxford University Press, 1976), pp. 23–33. The quotation appears on p. 26.
43. Merton, "The Latent Functions of the Machine," p. 26.
44. Erie, *Rainbow's End*; and Rowan Miranda, "Machine Politics Without Political Machines: Implications for Urban Fiscal Policy" (Paper presented at the annual meeting of the American Political Science Association, Washington, DC, September 2–5, 1993).
45. Erie, *Rainbow's End*, pp. 240–43.
46. Martin Shefter, *Political Crisis/Fiscal Crisis: The Collapse and Revival of New York City* (New York: Basic Books, 1985), pp. 16–21.
47. Merton, "The Latent Functions of the Machine," p. 26.
48. Ibid. DiGaetano, "The Rise and Development of Urban Political Machines," pp. 242–67, disputes Merton's contention that political machines arose out of a need to overcome the decentralization of power in American cities. According to DiGaetano, a number of machines such as the Tweed Ring failed to centralize authority. In other cities machines emerged only after authority in the city had already been formally centralized. Still, it must be pointed out that even in a nominally strong-mayor city, a business owner or property developer may find it advantageous to deal with behind-the-scenes power brokers.
49. Shefter, *Political Crisis/Fiscal Crisis*, p. 17.
50. Merton, "The Latent Functions of the Machine," p. 27.
51. Grimshaw, *Bitter Fruit*, pp. 59 and 82–84.
52. Harold F. Gosnell, *Machine Politics: Chicago Model* (Chicago: University of Chicago Press, 1937), p. 183. While the Chicago machine's role in moderating violence and maintaining social control is clear, one author has observed that the 1940s was an era of racial violence in Chicago that remained "hidden" from view by the city's press. See Arnold R. Hirsch, *Making the Second Ghetto: Race and Housing in Chicago 1940–1960* (Cambridge and New York: Cambridge University Press, 1983), pp. 40–67.
53. Gosnell, *Machine Politics: Chicago Model*, p. 183.
54. Ira Katznelson, "The Crisis of the Capitalist City: Urban Politics and Social Control," pp. 214–29, in *Theoretical Perspectives on Urban Politics*, ed. Willis D. Hawley and Michael Lipsky (Englewood Cliffs, NJ: Prentice-Hall, 1976); and Paul Kantnor with Stephen David, *The Dependent City* (Glenview, IL: Scott, Foresman, 1988), pp. 130–38.
55. Erie, *Rainbow's End*, p. 8.
56. V. O. Key, Jr., *Southern Politics* (New York: Alfred A. Knopf, 1949), p. 274; and Robert A. Caro, *Means of Ascent: The Years of Lyndon Johnson* (New York: Knopf, 1990).
57. Robert A. Caro, *The Path to Power: The Years of Lyndon Johnson* (New York: Vintage, 1982), p. 721.
58. Ibid., pp. 718–20 and 736–37. The evolution of machine politics in San Antonio is described by John A. Booth and David R. Johnson, "Power and Progress in San Antonio Politics, 1836–1970," in *The Politics of San Antonio: Community, Progress, and Power*, ed. David R. Johnson, John A. Booth, and

Richard J. Harris (Lincoln, NE: University of Nebraska Press, 1983), pp. 3–27; and Dale Baum and Worth Robert Miller, "Ethnic Conflict and Machine Politics in San Antonio, 1892–1899," *Journal of Urban History* 19 (August 1993): 63–84.

59. Key, *Southern Politics*, pp. 397–98.

60. Ibid., p. 5.

61. Arnold R. Hirsch, "New Orleans: Sunbelt in the Swamp," in *Sunbelt Cities*, ed. Richard M. Bernard and Bradley R. Rice (Austin, TX: University of Texas Press, 1983), p. 121.

62. Ibid. Also see Edward F. Haas, *DeLesseps S. Morrison and the Image of Reform: New Orleans Politics, 1946–1961* (Baton Rouge, LA: Louisiana State University Press, 1974), pp. 7–25.

63. Lee S. Greene and Jack E. Holmes, "Tennessee: A Politics of Peaceful Change," in *The Changing Politics of the South*, ed. William C. Havard (Baton Rouge, LA: Louisiana State University Press, 1972), pp. 182–83.

64. Key, *Southern Politics*, pp. 63–64.

65. Kenneth D. Wald, "The Electoral Base of Political Machines: A Deviant Case Analysis," *Urban Affairs Quarterly* 16 (September 1980): pp. 8–9.

66. Ibid., pp. 18–19.

67. Ibid., p. 19.

68. See Wald, "The Electoral Base of Political Machines," pp. 21–22; and Michael Parenti, "Ethnic Politics and the Persistence of Ethnic Identification," *American Political Science Review* 61 (September 1967): pp. 717–26. For an explanation of how a changed economy, the decline of immigration, and the rise of the civil rights movement all led to the eventual decline of the Crump machine, see Alan DiGaetano, "Urban Political Reform: Did It Kill the Machine?" *Journal of Urban History* 18 (November 1991): 58–62.

69. Gary R. Mormino, "Tampa: From Hell Hole to the Good Life," in *Sunbelt Cities*, ed. Richard M. Bernard and Bradley R. Rice (Austin, TX: University of Texas Press, 1983), pp. 144–45.

70. Riordan, *Plunkitt of Tammany Hall*, p. 11.

71. Ibid., pp. 14–15.

72. *Elrod v. Burns*, 427 U.S. 347 (1976).

73. *Rutan v. Republican Party of Illinois*, 110 S. Ct. 2734 (1990). The Brennan quotations also appear in Anne Freedman, *Patronage: An American Tradition* (Chicago: Nelson-Hall Publishers, 1994), pp. 3 and 100. Freedman, pp. 1–8 and 109–111, reviews the *Rutan* decision.

74. Freedman, *Patronage: An American Tradition*, p. 6.

75. Ibid., chapter 5.

76. Richard C. Wade, "The Withering Away of the Party System," in *Urban Politics: New York Style*, ed. Jewel Bullish and Dick Netzer (Armonk, NY: M. E. Sharpe, 1990), pp. 290–94.

77. Bruce E. Caswell, "Machine, Reform, Interest, and Race: The Politics of the Philadelphia Fiscal Crisis" (Paper presented at the annual meeting of the American Political Science Association, Chicago, September 3–6, 1994).

78. Carolyn Adams, David Bartelt, David Elesh, Ira Goldstein, Nancy Kleniewski, and William Yancey, *Philadelphia: Neighborhoods, Division, and Conflict in a Postindustrial City* (Philadelphia: Temple University Press, 1991), pp. 27 and 152–53.

79. Royko, *Boss: Richard J. Daley of Chicago*, p. 70. Freedman, *Patronage: An American Tradition*, pp. 39–45, too, reviews the various means by which the Chicago machine was able to skirt civil service rules in hiring.

80. Milton Rakove, *Don't Make No Waves...Don't Back No Losers: An Insider's Analysis of the Daley Machine* (Bloomington, IN: Indiana University Press, 1975), p. 112.

81. Royko, *Boss: Richard J. Daley of Chicago*, p. 69.

82. Rakove, *Don't Make No Waves...Don't Back No Losers*, p. 112.

83. Royko, *Boss: Richard J. Daley of Chicago*, pp. 14, 23–24, and 100–01.

84. Ester R. Fuchs and Robert Y. Shapiro, "Government Performance as a Basis for Machine Support," *Urban Affairs Quarterly* 18 (June 1983): 537–50.

85. Kenneth R. Mladenka, "The Urban Bureaucracy and the Chicago Political Machine: Who Gets What and the Limits to Political Reform," *American Political Science Review* 74 (December 1980): 991–98.

86. Rakove, *Don't Make No Waves...Don't Back No Losers*, p. 48.

87. Royko, *Boss: Richard J. Daley of Chicago*, p. 48.

88. The battle over the Shakman decrees and its impact on patronage in Chicago are described by Freedman, *Patronage: An American Tradition*, chapter 2.

89. Grimshaw, *Bitter Fruit*, pp. 155–56.

90. Hirsch, *The Making of the Second Ghetto*.

91. Royko, *Boss: Richard J. Daley of Chicago*, p. 137.

92. *Hills* v. *Gautreaux*, 96 S. Ct. 1538 (1976). The complicity of the Chicago machine in public housing segregation is described by Hirsch, *Making the Second Ghetto*, pp. 212–75.

93. Voting trends in Chicago's black community in the 1975 and 1979 elections are reported by Michael B. Preston, "Black Politics in the Post-Daley Era," in *After Daley: Chicago Politics in Transition*, ed. Samuel K. Gove and Louis H. Masotti (Urbana, IL: University of Illinois Press, 1982), p. 88.

94. "This Daley Ward Boss Won't Back a 'Nitwit,'" *Washington Post*, April 10, 1983.

95. Michael B. Preston, "The Resurgence of Black Voting in Chicago: 1955–1983," in *The Making of the Mayor: Chicago 1983*, ed. Melvin G. Holli and Paul M. Green (Grand Rapids, MI: Wm. B. Eerdmans Publishing, 1984), p. 48.

96. Ibid., p. 49.

97. Ibid.

98. For an excellent collection of articles discussing Harold Washington's policy agenda, see Pierre Clavel and Wim Wievel, eds., *Harold Washington and the Neighborhoods* (New Brunswick, NJ: Rutgers University Press, 1991).

99. Grimshaw, *Bitter Fruit*, pp. 22–23 and 186–89. Also see Larry Bennett, "Harold Washington and the Black Urban Regime," *Urban Affairs Quarterly* 28 (March 1993): 423–40.

100. William J. Grimshaw, "Chicago Politics: What Next?" *Urban Affairs Quarterly* 23 (March 1988): 327.

101. Paul Kleppner, "Mayoral Politics Chicago Style: The Rise and Fall of a Biracial Coalition, 1983–1989" (Paper presented at the conference honoring Samuel P. Hays, Pittsburgh, May 1991); and Paul Kleppner and D. Garth Taylor, "Race and Ethnicity in Chicago Politics: The 1989 Mayoral Election" (Unpublished paper, date uncertain). Both papers are available at the Social Science Research Institute, Northern Illinois University.

102. Grimshaw, *Bitter Fruit*, pp. 203–04. More detailed analyses of the 1989 Chicago primary are provided by Paul M. Green and Melvin G. Holli, eds., *Restoration 1989: Chicago Elects a New Daley* (Chicago: Lyceum Books, 1991).

103. Paul M. Green, "The 1989 Mayoral Primary Election," in *Restoration 1989: Chicago Elects a New Daley*, ed. Paul M. Green and Melvin G. Holli (Chicago: Lyceum Books, 1991), pp. 11–12.

104. Ibid., pp. 19–20; and Jorge Casuso, "Hispanics," in *Restoration 1989: Chicago Elects a New Daley*, ed. Paul M. Green and Melvin G. Holli, pp. 70–73.

105. These figures are reported by Paul M. Green, "The 1989 General Election," in *Restoration 1989: Chicago Elects a New Daley*, ed. Paul M. Green and Melvin G. Holli, p. 51.

106. Freedman, *Patronage: An American Tradition*, pp. 69–70.

107. Grimshaw, *Bitter Fruit*, p. 206. See Grimshaw's larger discussion, pp. 206–24.

108. Alan DiGaetano, "Machine Politics in the Post-Industrial Era" (Paper presented at the annual meeting of the Urban Affairs Association, St. Louis, March 10–13, 1988); and Todd Swanstrom and Sharon Ward, "Albany's O'Connell Organization: The Survival of an Entrenched Machine" (Paper presented at the annual meeting of the American Political Science Association, Chicago, September 1987).

109. John Froonjian and Joseph Tanfani, "Trump Lawyer Threw Party for Usry While Seeking Approvals," *Press of Atlantic City*, August 8, 1989; and Joseph Tanfani and John Froonjian, "A.C. Probe Subpoenas All Casinos," *Press of Atlantic City*, August 9, 1989. Also see the newspaper's "Extra" edition, July 27, 1989.

110. George Sternlieb and James W. Hughes, *The Atlantic City Gamble* (Cambridge, MA: Harvard University Press, 1983), pp. 30–56 and 138–53.

111. John Hull Mollenkopf, *A Phoenix in the Ashes: The Rise and Fall of the Koch Coalition in New York City Politics* (Princeton, NJ: Princeton University Press, 1992), pp. 121–28; and Freedman, *Patronage: An American Tradition*, pp. 27–32.

112. Howard Kurtz, "Biaggi Influence-Peddling Trial to Open," *Washington Post*, August 24, 1987, quoted by Wade, "The Withering Away of the Party System," p. 283.

113. DiGaetano, "Machine Politics in the Post-Industrial Era."

114. Erie, *Rainbow's End*, pp. 9 and 201–08.

115. Kevin White's attempt to establish a mayor-centered machine is described by DiGaetano, "Machine Politics in the Post-Industrial Era," and also by Martha Wagner Weinberg, "Boston's Kevin White: A Mayor Who Survives," *Political Science Quarterly* 96 (Spring 1981): 87–106. Also see Barbara Ferman, *Governing the Ungovernable City* (Philadelphia: Temple University Press, 1985).

116. DiGaetano, "Machine Politics in the Post-Industrial Era."

117. Clarence N. Stone, *Regime Politics: Governing Atlanta, 1946–1988* (Lawrence, KS: University of Kansas Press, 1989), pp. 213 and 239.

118. The operations of the Nassau County Republican Party are described in great detail by Freedman, *Patronage: An American Tradition*, pp. 127–67. Our description here relies considerably on Freedman's account.

119. For a more detailed account of the allegations against D'Amato in the HUD housing scandals, see Nicholas Goldberg, "God's Chosen: The Fonz and His Buddies, " *New Republic* 202 (May 14, 1990): 13–16.

6

Reform Politics

Where the machine's political power and corruption became excessive, groups of individuals banded together in an effort to reform the system. Over time, the reformers succeeded in changing many of the rules of local political and administrative life.

The reforms helped clean up city politics and make city government more efficient. Yet the reforms also produced some unanticipated and undesirable effects. In some cities racial minorities and neighborhood groups began questioning the value of reform institutions. Knowing the origins of reform movements and who the reformers were, we can better evaluate the operation of reform institutions today.

THE REFORM MOVEMENT

The reform movement coincided with the loss of political power suffered by the old elite that had controlled northern cities prior to the Civil War.[1] Members of the elite group were "outgunned" by the new dominant class of business entrepreneurs wanting special favors from local government. The old elite was also outvoted by the new immigrant groups and the political machines. As a result, the old elite launched its appeals for municipal reform, calling for a politics that would serve the **public interest** instead of one that brokered various private interests.

During the Progressive Era the reform movement gained influence in municipal affairs as well as in state and national politics (see pages 102–103, "The Reform Movement and the Progressive Era (1890–1920)"). Attacking the political machines and their bosses on a variety of fronts, the reformers stressed **economy** and **efficiency** as the persistent catchwords of their movement. They firmly believed that they could do things better and cheaper, and they espoused four major concepts as ways to improve the quality of local government:

1. The public interest should be served.
2. Politics should be separated from administration.

181

3. Experienced administrators should be hired to manage local government that dealt with essentially technical problems.
4. Scientific management principles should be applied to local government.

In calling for a politics of the public interest, the reformers assumed that the tasks of local government were essentially technical in nature. Those citizens "best qualified to serve"—usually members of the old elite—would identify the public interest. Once policy objectives were determined, city governance became simply a matter of good administration left to qualified technicians. Politics was seen to be irrelevant at the local level; according to the reformers, there simply was no Democratic or Republican way to pave streets or pick up the garbage. Political parties at the local level were seen to be superfluous and evil; they would only introduce conflict and irrelevant, narrow partisan concerns. The reformers believed that the objectively identified citywide interest should take precedence over ward and neighborhood projects and narrow partisan interests.

The reformers also subscribed to the **scientific management** principles of Frederick Taylor, which were introduced into business in the early twentieth century.[2] Taylor, a mechanical engineer, spent much of his time trying to improve worker productivity. According to Taylor, scientific techniques could be used to uncover the single best way of performing any task. For the reformers, only professionally trained managers and administrators possessed the ability to discover and apply such principles to the running of city affairs. A city, too, could be run efficiently "like a business."

As can easily be seen, the reform model of politics values capable administrators more highly than it does successful local politicians. Good administrators possess the necessary training, technical expertise, and competency in such areas as accounting, budgeting, and city engineering to cope with the complexities of running a modern city. In contrast, popularly elected mayors and patronage appointees often lack essential administrative skills and abilities. Efficiency demanded that the city's executive branch be headed by a trained professional and staffed on the basis of **merit**, as defined by the newly emergent local government civil service systems.

The National Municipal League, founded in 1894, served as the intellectual center of the reform movement. Over the years, the league promoted a **Model City Charter** that emphasized nonpartisan elections, the city manager plan, and the short ballot.

The National Municipal League was notably successful in gaining adoption of its suggested reforms in smaller and middle-sized cities. While larger cities adopted features from the municipal program of the league, they never accepted the total program. The populations of larger cities were just too heterogeneous to govern themselves totally according to a plan that assumed a common citywide interest and the irrelevance of local politics. Even Los Angeles, with its reputation for being the nation's largest reformed city, retains the unreformed weak-mayor and district-based council structures.

The reform movement took various forms.[3] Citizen associations, such as the League of Women Voters, operated outside the party structure to review the records of elected officials and make recommendations on expenditures and taxes. In other cities, especially nonpartisan cities, candidate screening committees served to review prospective candidates and raise funds for the persons they endorsed. In the South, nonpartisan slating groups, such as the Citizen's Charter Association in Dallas and the Good Government League in San Antonio, were formed to represent the interests of the local business community. These groups, which dampened issue-oriented campaigns and muted minority voices by supporting the candidacies of only "safe" minority candidates, dominated politics in these cities through the 1970s.[4]

Occasionally reform movements assumed the form of an independent local party. One such was the Fusion party, which helped elect mayors of New York City in 1901, 1913, and 1933 by forming a temporary alliance with the Republicans. A more continuing type of local party is the independent good government organization, as exemplified by the City Charter Committee in Cincinnati.

In still other cities a blue-ribbon leadership faction emerged within a party to replace machine leaders with a reform-oriented elite. The Joseph Clark/Richardson Dilworth seizure of power in Philadelphia's Democratic party in the 1950s illustrates the blue-ribbon type of reform. Finally, issue-oriented intraparty reform clubs attempted to gain control from regular party officials. New York Mayor Ed Koch gained his start in politics with the Village Independent Democrats in that reform club's struggle to wrest power from the DeSapio organization.[5]

As political scientists Banfield and Wilson observe, the reformers "have in the main won their war for the adoption of particular measures of structural and other change."[6] All cities have adopted a good deal of the reform program. Yet Banfield and Wilson also report, "Although reform has won its war, victory has not yielded the fruits for which the reformers sought."[7] In general, modern city governments are a good deal more efficient and less corrupt than they used to be. At the same time, however, they continue to be plagued with repeated scandals over housing contracts, the award of city concessions, and patronage-plagued welfare and poverty programs.

Perhaps the most debatable assumption of the reform movement was that a common citywide interest could be identified. In fact, no such public interest can easily be ascertained. Different groups have different needs and different views as to what constitutes the public interest. What benefits one neighborhood may work to the disadvantage of another. Who can say with certainty what constitutes the public interest? Is it to provide improved public services, or is it to keep tax rates to a minimum?

Perhaps the reformers' failure to recognize this dilemma stems in part from the bias of their perceptions. The reformers assumed that their view of good government was necessarily the only correct view. They failed to see how their perceptions of the proper role of municipal government were colored by their own class position and self-interest.

THE SOCIAL BASE AND CLASS BIAS OF REFORM

The reformers were motivated by a desire to root out the corruption and parochialism of the political machine. Yet a good deal of hard evidence points to a class bias in the social base of the reform movement.

The work of historian Samuel Hays points to the class-based nature of the struggle between reformers and the machine. Hays found that there was very little involvement by small business operators, skilled and unskilled workers, or even white-collar employees in the reform movement. In the cities Hays studied, the reform movement was an attempt by upper-class professionals and the owners and managers of large businesses to redesign city government in order to take power away from the more numerous lower- and middle-class segments of the population. The reformers "wished not simply to replace bad men with good; they proposed to change the occupational and class origins of decision-makers."[8] Seen from this perspective, the reform movement was an elitist attempt to centralize and control decision making "rather than distribute it through more popular participation in public affairs."[9]

Yet the social elite did not dominate the reform movement at all times. Reform did not always have such a distinct upper-class tint. In 1901 a reform-oriented progressive, Tom L. Johnson, was elected mayor of Cleveland. Although a self-made millionaire, Johnson sought to regulate the profit making of private industries in order to provide better benefits for the working class.[10] He fought to preserve the three-cent fare in the private streetcar company; he established a municipal light plant to lower utility fees; and he municipalized garbage collection and street cleaning. Taxes were raised to pay for these and other extended public services. As a reformer, he limited patronage, hired experts, and used business methods in government.

Yet upper-class reformers soon reasserted themselves. As a result of his attacks on big business, "nearly all the 'right men' in Cleveland opposed Johnson. The Municipal Association, that bastion of good government reformers, attacked him. Johnson was considered a traitor to his class."[11]

According to Todd Swanstrom, in Cleveland "the radical roots of reform were killed off, leaving a spineless plant clinging congenially to big business."[12] The city's industrial elite sought to keep local politics "within safe and narrow confines."[13] It proposed a program of reforms that both enhanced efficiency and limited the influence of the city's ethnic working class. Cleveland adopted a system of nonpartisan elections, and in 1921 became the then-largest city in the nation to adopt the city manager form of government (which was repealed in 1931). An unsuccessful attempt was also made to introduce the at-large election of council members: "Opponents charged that this was an effort to disenfranchise foreign-born voters, especially Roman Catholics."[14] Reform in Cleveland in the post-Johnson era "was overwhelmingly financed and staffed by the business elite."[15]

Still, reform movements were not everywhere dominated by upper-class business interests. The New York reform movement in the 1950s and 1960s was initiated by young, idealistic, well-educated professionals who were upset by what they perceived to be the machine's ignoring of the public interest. The Democratic reform clubs crusaded against the power of Robert Moses, who, as New York City park commissioner and the head of the Triborough Bridge and Tunnel Authority and other bureaucratic agencies, destroyed neighborhoods and slighted environmental values. Moses had built expressways instead of enhancing mass transit; he had even attempted to encroach on the city's Central Park by building a parking lot adjacent to the Tavern on the Green.

The "advocacy professionals"[16] of New York's reform movement were also in favor of more extensive social services for the poor. Of course, the middle-class advocacy professionals were better-off financially than the city's population as a whole. Still this "reform vanguard" of social scientists, social workers, clergymen, and journalists was a far cry from the industrial elite that dominated the post-Johnson reform movement in Cleveland; they were no "mere mouthpiece for New York's business elite." In the 1960s social reformer and Republican mayoral candidate John Lindsay further fused the votes of racial minorities to the city's reform coalition.

It appears, then, that there are two types of reform movements—those centered in a city's conservative business elite and those rooted in visions of progressive social reform and the extension of government services to aid the needy. According to Melvin G. Holli, there is a need to differentiate **social reformers** from **structural reformers**.[17] Social reformers like Cleveland's Tom Johnson and Detroit Mayor Hazen S. Pingree (1890–97) placed their faith in the people and sought such populist reforms as reducing utility rates, extending government-provided relief and public services, and increasing the share of a city's tax burden borne by business. The New York reformers of the 1950s and 1960s for the most part fit within this social reform tradition.

In contrast, the structural reformers exhibited no equivalent faith in the judgment of the people; instead, they preferred that municipalities be ruled by educated, upper-class Americans and technical experts. Their concern was to introduce contemporary business practices into government and to limit, not extend, government welfare services.

As we have seen, reforms in the structure of city government and the election process were motivated to a great degree by the self-interest of elite groups. The class-based impact of these reforms is still felt today. As we shall soon discuss in detail, at-large elections diminish the influence of geographically concentrated ethnic and minority groups. Nonpartisan elections disproportionately reduce the turnout of lower-class citizens. Even voter registration requirements turn away a disproportionate number of less-educated, low-income voters.

Reformed government helps to insulate a city from the policy demands of lower-class citizens, although the extent of such discrimination is the subject of much debate. In their study of 200 cities, urban political scientists Robert L. Lineberry and Edmund G. Fowler found that reformed cities tend to spend less and tax less than unreformed cities. Even more significant was their finding that the ethnic, income, and education mix of a city's population has a greater influence on taxing and spending policies in unreformed as opposed to reformed cities: "[T]he more reformed the city, the less responsive it is to socio-economic cleavages in its political decision-making."[18] According to Lineberry and Fowler, "[T]he goal of the reformers has been substantially fulfilled, for nonpartisan elections, at-large constituencies and manager governments are associated with a lessened responsiveness of cities to the enduring conflicts of political life."[19]

Yet the discriminatory impact of reformed government may not be as great as it was initially assumed to be. More recent studies have called into question Lineberry and Fowler's finding that reformed institutions have worked against lower-class citizens. One study, for instance, has shown that cities that adopted nonpartisan, at-large election and city manager systems did not differ markedly in their spending patterns from cities that retained unreformed institutions.[20]

This point of view is confirmed by perhaps the most comprehensive study of the impact of nonpartisan and at-large election systems. As political scientists Susan Welch and Timothy Bledsoe observe, "The impact of political structure on policy views of council members appears to be quite small."[21] Reformed institutions do not produce spending and taxing outcomes that are so greatly different from those produced by unreformed institutions. Yet Welch and Bledsoe conclude in favor of the unreformed electoral systems:

> The fact that differences among electoral systems are not as night to day certainly does not mean that we should be satisfied with any system. Politics, after all, is usually incremental. If one system does a better job in providing representation for a whole community, even if that difference is only marginal, logic dictates that we should favor it assuming we believe that a democratic system should provide representation for all groups of citizens.... [A]mong the existing choices, district elections in a partisan system probably provide the fairest representation of all groups

and serve to structure political conflict and debate in the form most understandable to the average citizen.[22]

While the policy impacts of reform are difficult to measure exactly, they still may produce biases that are of critical importance in the urban arena. The contemporary history of greater Miami provides a case in point. The government of Metropolitan Miami-Dade County (popularly referred to as "Metro") was created with the institutions and values of the reform movement. Structurally, Metro has a council-manager form of government with nonpartisan, at-large elections. This structure of government was designed to promote decision making based on a communitywide public interest instead of neighborhood and local concerns. Candidates with a political neighborhood base often lack the support and financing for effective Metro-wide campaigns. As one commentator on the Miami scene has observed, "Metro's structure dissuades candidates from running as strong advocates of minority political interests."[23] The efficiency orientation of the Metro Commission, as well as its lack of responsiveness to minority demands in such areas as policing and economic development, may have been a contributing factor to the riots that plagued the city's black Overtown and Liberty City neighborhoods in the 1980s.[24] The riots fueled demands that both the city of Miami and Miami Metro switch from at-large systems to district elections, in effect abandoning the reformed electoral system that characterized Metro's government since its founding in the 1950s. Likewise in Los Angeles, reformed institutions have been charged with helping to create an insensitivity to the needs of the city's impoverished minority communities, an explosive situation that erupted after the 1992 Rodney King verdict.

THE REFORMS

The reform movement proposed numerous changes in the structure of municipal government and the conduct of local elections. Reformed government at the local level can be seen to embrace the three major remedies: the city manager system, at-large elections, and nonpartisan elections. The reformers also advocated the installation of civil service systems and a whole host of other measures designed to break the power of political party and machine organizations.

In Chapter 4 we evaluated reform proposals for the city manager and commission forms of government. In this chapter we shall identify and evaluate the remaining reform innovations that have had a lasting influence on the operations of city government.

AT-LARGE ELECTIONS—AND THE QUESTION OF MINORITY REPRESENTATION

One of the most widely adopted reform measures entails the use of at-large elections in which voters elect council members citywide instead of on a district basis. While a number of cities in recent years have moved away from strictly at-large voting systems due to the controversy that surrounds their use, they still remain popular. Approximately 60 percent of local governments use at-large voting systems, with another 30 percent of localities relying on **mixed or combination plans** under which some council members are elected at-large while others are chosen by district. Systems with no at-large voting component are relatively unpopular in the contemporary United States, with only 11 or 12 percent of all local governments electing council members solely from districts or wards.[25]

The reformers sought to rid the city of ward or district elections, which they felt allowed the machine to build a strong, decentralized political organization. The district council member, often with the aid of the ward and precinct committeeman (in those days it was almost always a committee*man*), could identify specific neighborhood services, such as the improvement of a neighborhood park or the installation of new curbs and gutters, that could be undertaken in order to gain votes.

The reformers felt that an at-large election system would force council members to focus on larger, citywide policy concerns rather than on the special interests of each separate neighborhood. The reformers also felt that at-large elections would help bring a higher quality member to the council; the reformers did not believe that persons of quality were scattered randomly through all wards in the city.

Despite these advantages, the system of at-large elections suffers from numerous disadvantages. Perhaps the most serious is the at-large system's tendency to discriminate against, or underrepresent, geographically concentrated ethnic and minority voting groups.

In large cities it is still quite common for people of similar socioeconomic backgrounds to live in the same general area. A large area of, say, black, Hispanic, or Polish people would likely be able to elect one of their own to the city council under a district or ward system. With all council elections conducted citywide in the at-large system, however, these minority groups are likely to find themselves outvoted by the city's majority population. Boston for many years had no black member on its school board due, in part, to the at-large basis of school elections in that city.

That at-large elections dilute minority voting strength is clear. Albert Karnig shows that, in at-large cities, blacks gain only 45.7 percent of the seats on city councils that they would have received had representation been an exact mirror of the population of the city. Blacks fare much better in cities with district elections; there they gain 77.2 percent of the seats they would have received on the basis of their percent of the population. This discrimination is especially severe in the South, where two-thirds to three-fourths of the municipalities have at-large voting rules. In at-large cities in the South blacks received only one-third (33.0 percent) of the council representation that was merited on the basis of their numbers.[26]

This assumes that blacks will always vote for blacks. Why can't people vote for the best candidate regardless of color!!!

Margaret Latimer found further evidence of the discriminatory effects of at-large voting systems in her study of fifty Alabama, Louisiana, and South Carolina cities. In cities with district elections, blacks gained 68 percent of the representation they would have had solely on the basis of their share of the population. In contrast, in cities with at-large elections, blacks gained a mere 18 percent of the council seats that was merited by their numbers![27]

By underrepresenting blacks, at-large elections are linked with a black community's sense of powerlessness and decreased sense of political efficacy.[28] In Auburn, Alabama, the change from at-large to district elections brought with it an increased black voting turnout. No similar increase in black turnout was observed in neighboring Opelika, which maintained its system of at-large elections. Apparently the district system stimulated, and the at-large system depressed, black voting turnout.[29]

At-Large Elections and the Voting Rights Act

In the years immediately following the Civil War, cities in the South used various procedures, including the adoption of at-large voting rules, to deny blacks an effective voice in public affairs. Mobile, Atlanta, Memphis, Chattanooga, and Nashville were only some of the cities in which "reformers" introduced at-large election statutes in an effort to exclude blacks from municipal and school office.[30]

In many areas of the South, blacks effectively gained the right to vote only as a result of the protection offered by the **Voting Rights Act (VRA) of 1965.** In the 1960s, advocates of civil rights feared that southern cities would once again turn to various structural reform measures in an effort to lessen the power of the new black voters. Indeed, a number of southern cities did switch to at-large elections in an effort to dilute black voting strength. In Georgia, twenty county governments and boards of education switched from district to at-large elections. Mississippi required that all county boards of supervisors and county school boards be elected at-large.[31] Section 5 of the Voting Rights Act had attempted to guard against such moves by requiring federal preclearance before a southern city covered under the act could switch to at-large voting rules. When cities persisted in making the change to at-large systems, the cases often went to court.

The challenge to at-large voting rules encountered an important setback in a case dealing with the reformed voting rules in the city of Mobile. Although blacks constituted 35 percent of Mobile's population, no African-American had ever been elected to the city council. A 1973 decision by the Fifth U.S. Circuit Court of Appeals ruled that the at-large electoral system in Mobile excluded blacks and was part of a demonstrated pattern of discrimination. Following the logic of the Court of Appeals ruling, Federal District Court Judge Virgil Pittman in 1976 ordered Mobile to convert to a ward-based election plan to enhance minority representation. Other cities in the South—including Dallas, Texas, and Montgomery, Alabama—had elected blacks to the city council almost immediately upon changing to district elections.[32]

But the Supreme Court in its 1980 *City of Mobile v. Bolden* decision ruled in favor of the city, reversing Pittman's order that Mobile institute district elections.[33] The Court ruled that, while at-large elections have the *effect* of underrepresenting black votes, the civil rights advocates failed to demonstrate that the at-large election system was introduced with the *intent* of diluting black voting power. The Court was not willing to strike down voting rules that may have been instituted for legitimate reasons but had the inadvertent consequence of lessening the impact of black voting strength. While civil rights attorneys could easily prove that at-large systems had the impact of denying black representation, they could not easily demonstrate that such voting systems were enacted for racial reasons, especially when the motives expressed by public officials were often cloaked in the good-government language of reform.

The setback, however, proved to be quite short-lived. In the wake of the *Bolden* decision, civil rights groups pressured Congress to rewrite the relevant sections of the Voting Rights Act. This the Congress did. In the **VRA Amendments of 1982** Congress made it clear that cases could be brought to court under the act whenever voting systems had either a discriminatory intent or result. Congress further weakened the "intent" threshold by stating that the "totality of circumstances" shall be sufficient evidence to prove the discriminatory nature of a nomination or election system.[34]

The Supreme Court, itself, moved away from a strict "intent" test and softened the effect of the *Bolden* decision by upholding a lower court ruling that forced Burke County, Georgia, to end its at-large system of elections. In Burke County, no black had been elected commissioner despite the fact that blacks constituted over 53 percent of the population. Such circumstantial evidence was seen as so overwhelming as to constitute sufficient evidence of discriminatory intent. In what has since become the controlling precedent, the Court in *Thornburg v. Gingles* (1986) went even further in eliminating the need to prove discriminatory "intent" in minority vote dilution cases.[35]

In recent years, many of the Voting Rights Act challenges to at-large voting systems concern attempts at major **annexations** (when a city incorporates a neighboring area into its borders) or the agreement of local jurisdictions to form new **metropolitan governing arrangements**. Many of these annexations and experiments in metropolitan governance have taken place in the South and are often accompanied by at-large voting rules that allow the city's white population, swollen by annexation, to continue to outvote a city's growing black or Hispanic population. Consequently, annexations are often challenged in court as violations of the protection offered minorities by the Voting Rights Act.

White residents often see annexation and the formation of new metropolitan governing arrangements accompanied by at-large election rules as nothing more than a commitment to good government principles. After all, why shouldn't they be allowed to modernize their government and pursue the larger collective interest of the region? Why shouldn't they be allowed to have at-large systems of representation that have gained widespread popularity throughout the country? But African-Americans often see more pernicious motivation underlying annexations accompanied by at-large voting rules. They know that, in the South, annexation has historically been a weapon to dilute the growing black voting power in cities.

In the Southwest, at-large elections coupled with annexations have had the effect of diluting Latino voting power. In San Antonio the city's business booster coalition had pushed an aggressive program of annexation. In 1976 the federal Department of Justice brought suit claiming that thirteen of the twenty-three annexations completed during the 1972–74 period violated the 1975 Voting Rights Act. The Department of Justice charged that the annexations, coupled with a system of at-large elections, had effectively diminished the voting power of the city's Mexican-American community. After much haggling the city relented and changed its charter to allow for the district election of ten council members; the eleventh, the mayor, was to be elected citywide.[36]

At-Large Elections: A Contemporary Assessment

Other objections to at-large elections go beyond the matter of race. At-large elections lead to voter disinterest and an increased number of incomplete ballots cast in an election. Voter interest in city council elections is, at least in part, spurred by localized campaign activity and the **ombudsman** or casework service provided by district councilpersons.[37] The voters are not likely to be familiar with a large number of the candidates competing in the many citywide races. Citywide candidates, in turn, are not likely to be greatly familiar with the particular problems of each ward or neighborhood.

At-large elections also increase the costs of both primary and general election campaigns, which may discourage potential candidates whose fund-raising capabilities are marginal. The heightened cost of campaigning citywide further increases the dependence of elected officials on financial contributions. Even campaign finance rules designed to limit political donations do not effectively control the ability of large campaign contributors to buy access to government. New York millionaire and developer Donald J. Trump testified that he had circumvented a state law that limits corporate contributions to $5,000; he simply made contributions through eighteen subsidiary corporations that had been established.[38] At-large and district elections reward different types of candidates. Only those who raise large sums of money can pay for the mass media

advertising necessary for a citywide race. Ward-based or district elections, in contrast, offer a good chance of victory to neighborhood candidates with grassroots organizations and politically active volunteers.[39]

Are at-large elections as biased against Hispanics and women as they
are against African-Americans? While Hispanics are clearly underrepresented on city councils relative to their population, the evidence as to
whether or not at-large elections exacerbates the representation problem
is somewhat ambiguous.[40] District elections may not be as politically
advantageous for Latinos as they are for blacks, as Latinos are not as
segregated residentially. Cities generally find it more difficult to create
politically safe Hispanic districts than to create safe black districts. In
Dallas, for instance, some Latino dissatisfaction with council redistricting
plans was simply the result of an inability to find sufficient concentrations
of Latino population around which safe council districts could be created.
Similarly, in Chicago in the 1990s, the city's first Hispanic congressional
district was created in the shape of a "C," with district lines snaking
around to create two separate areas of Hispanic concentration linked
together in a single district only by running the district's line along an
interstate highway (see Figure 6.1).

Still, district elections have, at times, been crucial to the election of
Hispanics. For example, district elections have been shown to aid the
election of Latinos to school boards.[41] Denver moved from an all at-large
to a district-based system of school elections some twenty years after the
switch had been made for city council elections. At the time, Denver's
school board did not have a Hispanic member, despite the fact that 40 percent of the city's population was Hispanic and that the city was able to
elect both Hispanic and black mayors.[42]

In Los Angeles in 1991, Gloria Molina became the first Hispanic in 115
years to be elected to the county's powerful five-member Board of
Supervisors. This occurred only after a federal judge, finding the then-all-
white, five-member board guilty of intentionally diluting the voting power
of the county's three million Hispanic residents, ordered the district map
redrawn. Before the remap created a Hispanic-dominated district, each of
Los Angeles County's five districts had been so big and diverse as to have
an effect equivalent to that of at-large elections—the large block of Anglo
voters (who constituted less than 50 percent of the population in multi-
ethnic Los Angeles County) outvoted the Hispanic minority.

When it comes to the election of women, at-large elections do not
seem to pose the same clear discriminatory barrier that confronts
blacks.[43] In fact, some studies show that female candidates fare slightly
better in at-large as opposed to district election systems. The reason for
the difference is simple: Women are the majority of the population; they
are not a spatially segregated minority discriminated against by at-large
voting rules. In some cases, however, female candidates may lack the
access to money to compete successfully on a citywide basis.

FIGURE 6.1
Chicago's Hispanic Congressional District

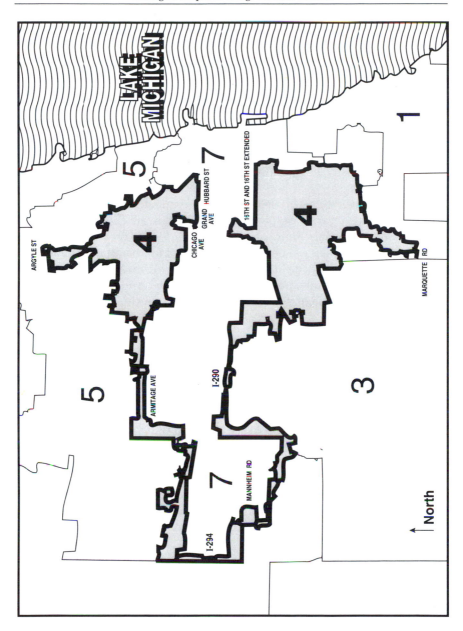

NONPARTISAN ELECTIONS

In **nonpartisan elections** candidates run for office without party designations next to their names on the ballots. Nonpartisanship has been one
of the lasting achievements of the reform movement. Approximately three-
fourths of local governments in the United States use the nonpartisan
ballot to elect local officials. Only in the Mid-Atlantic states is there a
strong tendency to use partisan elections for local government. In contrast, in the West, an area of traditional reform strength, virtually all local
jurisdictions have nonpartisan elections.[44] Further, nonpartisan elections
prevail in large as well as small cities. Boston, Cincinnati, Detroit, Los
Angeles, Milwaukee, San Francisco, Seattle, and numerous Sunbelt cities
all use nonpartisan elections. Even in Chicago, city council elections are
formally nonpartisan.

There appear to be different types of nonpartisan systems. In truly
nonpartisan cities, party organizations play little or no role in the election
process. Such is the case in most small cities and, to a great extent, in Los
Angeles. In other cities, parties are absent from the ballot but in fact play
a large role in slating candidates and turning out the vote. Chicago is a
good illustration of a city where active party activity lies just beneath the
surface of a nonpartisan system. Finally, there is the nonpartisan city
where parties disguise themselves behind other local organizations. Dallas
is an illustrative case in point.

The argument in favor of nonpartisanship has been discussed earlier
in this chapter in our review of the origins of the reform movement.
There are equally strong criticisms of nonpartisan elections.

First, the absence of party labels confuses voters. Party labels are
important cues which help voters find their preferred candidates in the
absence of other meaningful pieces of information.[45] A voter who considers himself a Republican knows that generally he prefers the Republican
candidate, and a voter who considers herself a Democrat knows that generally she prefers the Democratic candidate. But in the absence of party
labels, a voter who must choose from among a group of candidates whom
he or she knows nothing about will have no meaningful basis whatsoever
in casting a ballot. Voters will turn to whatever cue is available. Often, in
the absence of party labels, this cue turns out to be the ethnicity of a candidate's name. Nonpartisan systems encourage ethnic voting, as evident in
the historic success in Boston of candidates with obviously Irish or Italian
names. One survey of voters in council elections in Lexington, Kentucky,
found that in the absence of partisan cues and extensive media coverage,
voters focused not on citywide issues but primarily on candidates's personal qualities, background characteristics, name recognition, and concern for the district.[46]

Second, nonpartisanship aggravates the class bias in voting turnout.
Middle- and upper-class, better-educated people are self-starters when it

comes to politics. They have the ability to sort through the various candidates' issue positions, select a favored candidate, and go out and vote. In contrast, in the absence of party labels, lower-class, less-educated persons are likely to become confused and stay home rather than vote. Nonpartisanship systems further act to depress the activities of organizations of local party workers who work to bring lower-class citizens to the polls on election day.

The problem of skewed or distorted turnouts is exacerbated in many communities where nonpartisan elections for school boards and bond referenda are held at separate times from other elections. Reformers argue that the separate scheduling of elections allows voters to focus on the issues in the race at hand; candidates for offices such as a school board do not have to answer questions that arise from the races for other offices.

Yet in such isolated elections turnout is usually quite low, often running as little as 10 or 15 percent, and unrepresentative. Turnout is often so low as to give inordinate voting power to interest groups with a material stake in an issue. It seems quite likely that a large portion of the ballots in low turnout school elections and bond referenda are cast by teachers and other employees of the school system and members of their immediate families.

Third, nonpartisanship can encourage issue avoidance. Candidates in nonpartisan systems often seek election by playing up their name recognition, seeking the middle ground on issues, and avoiding to the extent possible the most controversial issues. In Oakland, California, in the 1960s, for instance, the city's nonpartisan council members and mayors were characterized as "shrinking violets" who preferred a businesslike approach to politics and ignored the issues of race and poverty even in the wake of that city's riots. Oakland's nonpartisan and at-large election system was incapable of bringing newly emergent social issues into the city arena.[47]

In Oakland, however, the government could not continue its pattern of issue avoidance in the face of sustained pressure from minority and neighborhood groups. Minority groups, dissatisfied with the city's unwillingness to address issues of fundamental concern to their lives, played a key role in pushing Oakland to a new system of district (albeit still nonpartisan) elections. Democrats came to dominate the nominally nonpartisan council elections in Oakland, San Jose, Sacramento, Stockton, and other northern California cities. In these formally reformed cities, the incorporation of minorities changed the nature of local politics. Local politics no longer fits the friends-and-neighbors pattern of nonpartisanship and more closely resembles the character of partisan systems.[48]

Finally, nonpartisanship destroys resources important to coalition building and effective governance. Once elected, there is no party discipline that might prove helpful in forging a governing consensus. An "each member for himself/herself" attitude may develop on the council. There are no party ties that a mayor can tap in attempting to develop an effective governing alliance. Council members view themselves as having been elected independently; they owe the mayor little.[49]

Voter Registration Requirements

Corrupt voting practices flourished in the days before personal voter registration. The machine relied on **repeaters**—voters who voted again and again in an election (hence, the slogan "Vote Early and Vote Often"). In some city elections, voter turnout even exceeded 100 percent! Requiring potential voters to register in advance of an election was a simple way to maintain a list of who was and who was not eligible to vote in each precinct.

But voter registration was more than just an attempt to clean up politics. It also represented "that old-stock nativist and corporate-minded hostility to the political machine, the polyglot city, and the immigrant which was so important a component of the progressive mentality."[50] When first introduced in the early 1900s, compulsory voter registration was required only for the residents of a state's larger cities. In Pennsylvania, for instance, the state legislature required personal registration in cities, but not in small towns or rural areas.[51] The political machine and the urban masses were the targets of voter registration laws.

The class bias of personal registration requirements is clear.[52] Less-educated, lower-income voters will tend to stay home as they find the act of registration a bit difficult to fathom. These tend to be voters who get excited during the last days of an election and find it impossible to vote, as the registration deadline has already passed. As the research of Raymond Wolfinger and Steven Rosenstone confirms, "Liberalizing registration provisions would have by far the greatest impact on the least educated."[53] Simply put, "[T]he costs of voting vary inversely with education. It is not surprising, then, that apparently trivial additions to the burden of registering raise the cost of voting above the threshold of many people."[54]

The adverse effects of voter registration requirements have been reduced over time. Court decisions have made local governments bring the registration cutoff date closer to the election, thereby enabling the registration of younger, more mobile voters and those voters who get excited about an election only as a campaign heats up. Certain states and cities are also experimenting with election day registration systems that would allow citizens to add their names to the voter rolls as they go to the polls to cast their ballots. **Motor voter** legislation allows citizens to register to vote when they renew their driver licenses. Still, voter turnout in this country would be higher, and the differences in turnout rates among various population groups would be reduced, if the United States were to follow the practice of many European nations where it is the responsibility of the government to maintain a current list of eligible voters.

DIRECT PRIMARY

The reformers found that political machines used closed party conventions to select their candidates, thus effectively shutting out the public from the nominating process. To counter this, reformers fought to institute the **direct primary**, which allowed citizens to directly choose who would be their party's candidates in the ensuing general election.

However, this reform, too, had a bias in helping to enhance middle- and upper-class power in local government. In nearly all elections middle- and upper-class voters participate at a greater rate than do lower-class voters. This class differential is greatest where voting turnout is the lowest. As party primaries generally have lower turnouts than general elections, middle- and upper-class voters will comprise an even more disproportionate share of the primary electorate than they do of the general election day electorate.

INITIATIVE, REFERENDUM, AND RECALL: THE INSTITUTIONS OF DIRECT DEMOCRACY

To open up the system still further and to weaken the grip of political parties on the political system, the progressive reformers proposed three institutions of direct democracy. The **initiative** permits a legally designated number of citizens to draft a piece of legislation or a charter amendment to be put before the voters in the next election. By this means citizens themselves can directly pass new statutes, bypassing party- or interest group–dominated state legislatures and city councils. The initiative has gained frequent use in California. Progressive reformers argue that the initiative allows citizens to bypass legislatures that are out of touch with the people.

The **referendum** is similar to the initiative except that the process begins with the passage of a piece of legislation by the council. The recently passed piece of legislation then goes on the ballot for the voters' approval or disapproval. The exact referendum process varies from city to city. Typically, citizens petition for a public vote on a bill that has already been passed by the council. Alternatively, the council members themselves can put a bill directly before the people.

The **recall** permits a prescribed number of voters to collect names on a petition requesting the removal from office of an elected official before his or her term expires. Should a sufficient number of valid signatures be gathered, the recall question is then put on the ballot; citizens can then vote whether or not to remove the official from office.

Advocates of the recall process argue that it forces elected officials to pay heed to the wishes of the people. Recall elections have become commonplace in numerous cities, including a number of small cities in California, Michigan, Washington, Alaska, Idaho, and Nebraska. Atlantic

City Mayor Michael Matthews was recalled in 1984; 1987 saw the recall of Omaha Mayor Mike Boyle. Cleveland's Dennis Kucinich and San Francisco's Dianne Feinstein were big-city mayors who successfully faced recall efforts.[55]

But the initiative and recall processes have been the subject of much recent criticism. Initiatives are often poorly drafted. The initiative procedure also bypasses the process of representative government that allows the compromise and balancing of concerns of many different groups of people. Often in the passion surrounding an initiative campaign, the ill effects of an initiative are not fully considered.

Such might very well have been the case in the 1978 statewide Proposition 13 initiative in California when the promise and symbolism of tax reduction carried the day. Voters did not fully understand how the lion's share of tax breaks would be enjoyed by corporations and other large property holders; nor did they recognize how the initiative would lead to service reductions, cutbacks in education spending, and tax inequities in California's communities.[56]

Recalls, too, have been criticized for intruding on responsible, representative government. Under the threat of a recall, an elected official is not too likely to respond to the needs of various groups in his or her community; instead, this representative will tend to be very responsive to the concerns of the active recall organizers. The intensity of their effort and their ability to mobilize votes in a low turnout election give the recall organizers influence beyond what may be merited by their numbers. In some communities recall efforts are begun any time a local official votes for a raise in taxes—even when a revenue increase is needed to maintain services or to get a community out of a tight fiscal squeeze.

Initiative and referendum campaigns are also quite expensive to mount. Affluent interest groups can even hire professional firms to garner the signatures necessary to get a measure on the ballot. Affluent groups can also buy substantial media time to present their views on an issue. The gambling industry spent lavishly on behalf of ballot measures authorizing casino gambling in Atlantic City, New Jersey, and a state lottery in California. At times, then, well-organized and financially well-heeled interest groups have been able to use the initiative and referendum processes to their advantage. The direct democracy ideal is compromised.[57]

While provisions for referenda are fairly universal in cities throughout the United States, the initiative and recall processes are much more a part of city government in the West than in the East. While initiatives and recall elections are allowed in about 90 percent of western cities, less than a third of Mid-Atlantic states permit these procedures.[58]

In Sunbelt cities, neighborhood and environmental groups have used the tools of direct democracy to counter development interests. In what Roger Caves has called **ballot box planning** or **electoral land use**

planning, voters in western cities—especially in California—and in such nonwestern areas as Cape Cod, Massachusetts, have used the initiative and referendum processes to decide important questions of growth and growth control. Frustrated over increased housing costs, pollution, and congestion, citizen groups have used the processes of direct democracy to counter the decisions made by local growth coalitions.

In San Diego in 1985, voters passed Proposition A, a local growth limitation initiative, after anti-growth forces had campaigned for the measure under the slogan: "No L.A.! Yes on A!" In the years that followed, San Diego residents voted on additional growth control measures placed on the ballot. Some were defeated amidst charges that massive spending by the development industry bought the election. San Francisco's 1986 Proposition M, which placed a cap on annual new construction and required developers to pay various linkage fees, has been characterized as the toughest growth limitation initiative passed by any major United States city. In Seattle, in 1989, citizen activists used Initiative 31—the Citizens's Alternative Plan—to limit the development of new office space downtown and thereby cap the skyscraper development and dynamic growth that was transforming the character of the city. Two years later the city council amended the plan to allow buildings to exceed the downtown height limit.[59]

The initiative and referendum devices are imperfect solutions to the problems of representative democracy. Discriminated-against groups can use the processes of direct democracy to get a government to address their needs. But groups who do the victimizing can equally use the initiative and referendum devices to promote exclusionary and discriminatory policies. In California in 1978, gay rights advocates defeated a ballot measure that would have allowed California schools to suspend any teacher who was accused of being homosexual. Similarly in Denver in 1991, voters defeated Ordinance 1, a ballot measure authored by the so-called Citizens for Sensible Rights that sought to exempt homosexuals from protection under the city's existing anti-discrimination policy.[60] In Oregon in 1992, a "'No Special Rights' Committee" campaigned for traditional family values and against the homosexual lifestyle in its literature that urged voters to pass Measure 9. According to Marcia Ritzdorf, such groups attempt to use the means provided by ballot box planning to control land use and thereby limit gays' and women's space.[61]

CIVIL SERVICE AND MERIT SYSTEMS

As we have already seen in this chapter and the preceding chapter on machine politics, the establishment of **civil service** or **merit systems** of municipal employment was one of the major goals of the reformers. Civil service rules spell out written job descriptions, determine the necessary qualifications for each position, and formalize a public recruitment system. While these merit rules do not completely eliminate patronage, they greatly reduce the number of jobs available for distribution by the political organization.

The arguments for efficiency and economy associated with the movement for a merit system were very persuasive, and city after city began to adopt these principles as standard personnel procedures. Yet, as we shall see both later in this chapter and in the next two chapters, the creation of civil service systems also produced many problems concerning the performance, accountability, and bias of civil servant actions. Simply put, the city bureaucracies became new power centers in urban politics as the merit system rules helped insulate these municipal agencies from direct political control.

Such insulation has not always proven to be for the good. The citizen participation, service decentralization, and privatization movements of the latter third of the twentieth century were all attempts to remedy the ill effects of the rigidities of merit system–protected bureaucracies.

CITY PLANNING COMMISSIONS AND DEPARTMENTS

The reformers believed that the machine made decisions on matters of city development purely on the basis of self-enrichment and partisan favoritism. The result was corruption, chaos, and the absence of orderly city growth. Instead, the reformers wanted city growth guided by scientifically rational planning principles, including concerns for efficiency and civic beauty.

Hence, the reformers sought to place development decisions in the hands of a group of nonpolitical professionals—the **city planning commission**. The commission was to be a group of prestige citizens who would make decisions on city growth and development in an objective manner. Alternatively, in other cities expert planners were hired as staff assistants to the executive and legislature. In many cities the planning experts and commissions did a much better job than the partisan-ridden process they replaced. Yet planning commissions and departments, as do all organizations, have biases of their own.

The 1950s and 1960s saw the beginning of citizen opposition to planning commissions that pursued highway development, downtown redevelopment, and urban renewal programs that uprooted residences and destroyed neighborhoods. Beginning in the 1970s community and taxpayer groups also objected to school overcrowding, environmental harm, and costs of continued growth. In short, citizens came to realize that they did not always agree with decisions made by nonpartisan planners. But these citizen groups generally lacked the expertise and staff resources to effectively challenge a city's plans.

One response in the planning profession has been to recognize the essentially political nature of planning. Some planners have called for **advocacy planning**, whereby planners would work for community groups, in effect becoming the "hired guns" of the community in its fight against city hall. Similarly, other professionals have called for **equity planning**, whereby planners working for the city would show a concern for neighborhood needs and preservation and not just for growth and downtown development. As director of city planning in Cleveland in the 1970s, Norman Krumholz took a strong advocacy stance in favor of the poor, distancing his planning department from the reformed principles of neutrality and objectivity that characterized planning in most cities. Krumholz used his experiences in Cleveland as a means of moving the entire planning profession in the direction of greater concern for equity.[62]

REFORM INSTITUTIONS AND THE SUNBELT

Sunbelt cities are generally characterized by reform institutions:

> [A] survey of fifty-nine large Western cities, most of which are in the Sunbelt, found 81 percent with a city-manager form of government, 95 percent using nonpartisan elections, and 75 percent selecting council members at large. A more inclusive sampling found nonpartisan elections in effect in 84 percent of Southern, border, and Western cities.[63]

Cities in the Southwest adopted reformed structures for the businesslike efficiency and other advantages that such structures allowed in the competition for government resources and economic development.[64]

One notable consequence was the access that reform institutions afforded booster or growth coalitions in many Sunbelt communities. In our chapter on the formal structure of city government, we have already observed the link between the city manager's office and the growth coalition in San Diego. That same link was also present in San Antonio, where the work of the city manager facilitated that city's aggressive growth and annexation strategies.[65]

San Jose, California, is another city where reform institutions, and the city manager's office in particular, have been linked to the politics of growth. Like San Antonio, San Jose in the 1950s and 1960s pursued an aggressive program of annexation to make available new sites for industrial and housing growth. Such a program was realized only with the active assistance of City Manager Anthony P. ("Dutch") Hamann. Hamann, a former business manager, was recruited for the city by the booster coalition and reflected the pro-growth orientations of that coalition. Hamann created a "Panzer division" in his office to seize potential sites for business development. Under his direction the city manager's office created a "paradise for developers" through lenient zoning, the provision of capital improvements, and the issuance of municipal bonds to subsidize the costs of new development projects.[66]

San Jose's system of at-large elections further "gave advantages to the well-known and affluent members of the business class who could secure newspaper support and raise the money necessary for a campaign."[67] The costs of campaigning at large further ensured that developers would have access to city hall: "Developers have always funded council campaigns, but with the cost of campaigns running $100,000 for a council seat and double that for mayor, candidates are even more dependent on them."[68]

Reform institutions in the Sunbelt created a political climate in which business leaders could prosper:

> Nonpartisan government, whether the weak mayor–council form, the commission system, or city-manager government is usually somnambulistic government. For, it is a form of government that fosters a quiescent, acquiescent citizenry, where only the business community and the property-owning middle class need be politicized.[69]

The desires and plans of growth leaders were seen to be the proper business of the city. Any opposition was thought to be *politics*, which was to be removed under reformed local government.[70] The reform movement created decision-making institutions, insulated from popular interference, with the authority to pursue infrastructure and economic development.[71]

Growth was not universally good for all residents of a city. Critics charged that Sunbelt cities subsidized business expansion by diverting funds away from projects that could have served older residential neighborhoods and poor people. In San Jose the rapid expansion of business on the city's rim even helped accelerate the decline of the city's downtown area, creating the need for urban renewal.

With the pluralization of interests in the Sunbelt, the reform institutions that helped facilitate growth came under attack. Minorities charged that at-large elections diluted their voting power. District council elections were revived not just in San Antonio and San Jose but also in Long Beach, Sacramento, Stockton, Oakland, Tacoma, San Antonio, Dallas, Fort Worth, El Paso, Albuquerque, Richmond, Montgomery, Charlotte, and Raleigh.[72] In cities such as San Diego, the power of the city manager's office came under attack.

The structural reforms of nonpartisan, at-large, managerial government enhanced the power of pro-growth forces in the Sunbelt. Yet another set of reforms—the initiative, referendum, and recall—provided the possibility of direct popular action that eventually brought an end to the period of unchallenged booster dominance in many Sunbelt cities. By the 1970s homeowner and community associations, taxpayer alliances, and environmental groups all began to oppose unfettered development. They recognized that continued growth brought traffic congestion, pollution, overcrowded schools, and a new demand for tax-supported services. These groups used the tools of direct democracy to stem—if not quite to reverse—the pro-growth policies of their local governments.

In San Antonio citizen groups used the referendum device to reverse a city council decision permitting the construction of a new shopping mall over the city's aquifer.[73] In San Jose an abortive 1962 recall effort against council members who supported Hamann's policies represented the first real challenge to that city's growth coalition. A 1973 initiative succeeded in prohibiting new residential development in areas where schools were overcrowded. The threat of an initiative even provided the impetus for the city council to place on the 1978 ballot a measure providing for the switch to district elections.[74] The ready availability of the initiative, referendum, and recall in Sunbelt communities means that "elites may have greater difficulty in trying to keep issues from getting out of the bag."[75]

One other force of change in the region is the increased empowerment of Hispanics as a result of the Voting Rights Act. In 1988 the Ninth Circuit Court of Appeals ruled that the system of at-large city council elections in Watsonville, California, "impermissibly dilutes the voting strength of Hispanics" in violation of the federal Voting Rights Act.[76] Although half the town's 28,000 residents are Hispanic, no Hispanic had ever been elected to Watsonville's city council.

The potential impact of the decision was quite far-reaching, given the concentration of Hispanics in the Southwest and the popularity of at-large elections in Sunbelt communities: "'We are looking at a number of other local governments—county boards, city councils, and school districts,' said Denise Hulett of the Mexican-American Legal Defense and Education Fund. 'We are looking at the entire state of California.'" In California over 400 of the state's 445 cities used at-large voting rules at the time of the decision. Cities such as nearby Salinas, where the 40,000 Hispanics of the Alisal neighborhood had never been able to elect one of their own to the city council, began to reexamine their voting rules in the wake of the Watsonville decision.

REFORM AND THE GROWTH OF BUREAUCRATIC POWER

The reformers sought to break the power grip the machines exerted on local government and make government more open and accessible to all citizens. Paradoxically, in trying to achieve this goal, the reformers instituted a number of changes in municipal government that had the opposite effect.

In professionalizing government, the reformers sought to limit government posts only to those best-qualified citizens who merited municipal appointment. The result was to exclude lower-class immigrants from municipal jobs and bureaucratic positions where decisions were made that affected their lives. The new reform structures were not especially responsive to lower-class citizens.

The reformers removed the government further from the people. Bureaucratic-client relations became strained as service providers were not representative of the people. In the 1960s and 1970s, much community resentment was directed by black and Hispanic city residents against white, middle-class municipal service providers. For instance, the police officer on the beat no longer lived in the neighborhood he or she patrolled; nor was the police officer necessarily a member of the predominant racial group in that neighborhood.

Yet citizen dissatisfaction with reform government crosses racial lines. Parents in white neighborhoods as well as in minority neighborhoods often express dissatisfaction with what they see to be a lack of effort or concern among teachers in a local school system. Protected by civil service, centralized bureaucratic structures have no need to be responsive to the people.

Nor were these civil service–protected agencies directly accountable to any higher authority. The consequence, according to political scientist Theodore Lowi, is that the modern reformed city is "well-run but ungoverned."[77] Each agency is free to operate efficiently by applying its own professional and technical standards to the work before it, but there is no certainty that the agency will respond to client needs or larger city concerns. Even mayors lack the power to fire civil service–protected officials who refuse to follow their policy directions. To use Lowi's words, city bureaucracies are "'islands of functional power' before which the modern mayor stands denuded of authority."[78]

Their power is so great that Lowi refers to the civil service–protected bureaucracies as the **New Machines**.[79] Agency independence is enhanced further still in those cities where the unionized municipal work force makes up a large portion of the campaign workers and votes any candidate needs to become mayor. A mayor who is elected with political debts to these groups will be in a weak position in attempting to impose discipline on them upon gaining office. New York's fiscal crisis in the 1970s resulted in part from the need of mayors to appease the city's electorally important mass membership bureaucracies.

Metropolitan and special service districts also show a lack of accountability to authority outside the agency. Reformers set up these special districts to allow the efficient provision of services across city/suburban boundaries. Established according to reform ideals, these metropolitan and special districts were to be autonomous organizations run in a nonpartisan manner. Most special districts and authorities collect taxes or user fees to finance their operations. Yet there is no certainty that these districts will respond to any directives other than their own narrowly defined determination of the public good.

Perhaps there is no more classic example of such independence than the refusal of the Port Authority of New York and New Jersey to help finance the region's decaying commuter rail system. The Port Authority operates the region's toll bridges, airports, and tunnels and maintains responsibility for the continued health of the port, including the provision of an adequate transportation network. The authority's commissioners resisted the pleas of governors and mayors to use the authority's considerable reserves to aid the region's decaying commuter rail system, despite the fact that many of the local rail systems were on the edge of bankruptcy. The commissioners' good business sense led them to look upon investment in rail transit as a losing proposition.

The authority refurbished the PATH rail tubes under the Hudson River, keeping its investment in mass transit to the minimum required by the political situation. Rather than devote larger funds to mass transit, the authority decided to construct New York's largest building, the 110-story twin towers of the World Trade Center. The advantages of such a massive construction project for authority officials were twofold; not only would the project aid the economic growth of the port district, but "a great part of its [the Authority's] excess revenues would be committed for many years to come, thus reducing pressure to divert these funds to mass transit."[80] Critics scored the project not only for draining funds for mass transit but also for drawing office development away from other areas in the city. The project also required continued subsidies. The larger goals of mass transit and decentralized office development were lost as the Port Authority, in a case of "bureaucratic egotism," chose to "meet the professional and personal goals of its own officials."[81]

The reform ideology's major failing was in its assumption that cities could be run by a **neutral specialist**.[82] The reformers sought to place expertly trained officials in the manager's office, the municipal bureaucracies, and the independent agencies. These experts were to make decisions according to professional criteria free from outside partisan influences.

What the reformers failed to realize, however, was that no matter how expert, these specialists could never be neutral. Even disciplined and dedicated public servants would continue to reflect the biases of their own class and personal backgrounds and the narrow perspectives of their professional training.

DO BLACKS AND WHITES HAVE DIFFERENT VIEWS OF REFORM?

"Reform" and "good government" mean different things to different people. To more traditional good-government reformers, upper-status aristocrats, and a city's business elite, reform has historically meant abiding by the principles of neutral competence, efficiency, and the respect for professional expertise. City operations were to be run in accordance with sound managerial principles.

In African-American communities, in contrast, reform politics is less based on an economic philosophy that emphasizes such goals as efficiency. Instead, black reform politics, strongly rooted in black churches, sees politics as a moral enterprise to be used in the pursuit of equity and fairness.[83] Earlier reform movements that stressed only the importance of businesslike efficiency had limited appeal in black neighborhoods, where the machine's promise of benefits was seen as more equitable than the decrease in services often promised by a reform victory.

In more recent years, as a result of the different racial perceptions of reform, white liberals have not always been willing to give their full support to African-American mayors generally characterized as agents of reform. Harold Washington's support in the pivotal Lakefront wards in Chicago may be more the result of the growing minority population of these wards; he gained only a "dismal level of support" in the liberal high rises that provided strong support for earlier reform candidacies in Chicago. White liberals may have feared the racial redistribution of services inherent in Washington's call for "fairness."[84] More traditional white reformers saw the mayor's Chicago First jobs program, which required city contractors to hire workers from Washington administration–approved lists, as a return to patronage politics.[85] Black reform forces, in contrast, dismissed the charges of "black patronage" as inconsequential. They applauded Washington's moralistic reform emphasis on fairness and equity, which led to new programs for the city's "have-nots."[86]

At-large elections, manager-council systems of government, and other reform institutions of the Progressive Era failed to create municipal governments responsive to the needs of a city's newly emergent minority populations. In many cities, minorities gained substantial political power in the local arena only after some of the institutions of reform were abandoned.

Rufus Browning, Dale Marshall, and David Tabb, in their study of ten northern California communities, report that "minority incorporation" in municipal affairs was strengthened in those cities (Oakland, San Jose, Sacramento, Stockton, and San Francisco) that switched from at-large to district elections. The impact of the 1977 switch to district voting in San Francisco was particularly dramatic. The first black woman and the first avowedly gay person, Harvey Milk, were elected to the Board of Supervisors. Milk, who had lost an earlier at-large bid, gained a seat by concentrating his efforts on mobilizing the gay population of San Francisco's Castro district. (Since then, San Francisco has flip-flopped back to at-large elections.) Minority incorporation in a city's affairs was also enhanced in those cities (Berkeley, Oakland, San Jose, Sacramento, Stockton, and San Francisco) where the power of elected officials was increased at the expense of the city manager.[87]

THE REFORM OF REFORM: THE RISE OF A NEW REFORM MOVEMENT

Reformed institutions that had proved so successful in correcting the municipal ills of an earlier time were now under attack for promoting government that was bureaucratized and unresponsive to the needs of a city's minority residents and neighborhood concerns. In Cincinnati two city managers vetoed funds for an additional community planning team: "Those vetoes come as no surprise given how city managers have traditionally championed the reform philosophy that is so unsympathetic to neighborhoods."[88] Nowadays neighborhood needs are seen to be valid and deserving of city response.

Dissatisfaction with reformed government eventually led minority and community activists to seek the "reform of reform."[89] The new reform effort sees district elections and increased mayoral and council power as the cures to governmental unresponsiveness. Federal government aid and spending requirements represent other ways of getting reformed local government to pay attention to community groups and neighborhood needs that it otherwise shuns.[90]

Measures ensuring citizen participation and government decentralization comprise still another broad-scale set of attacks on the insularity of the older generation of reform institutions—as we shall describe in the next chapter. A new generation of reform leaders has increasingly recognized the need to alter the older reform institutions. In Cincinnati, for instance, calls for increased neighborhood power have received endorsement from such bastions of reform as the League of Women Voters and the new city manager: "'Reform' was losing some of its traditional meaning in Cincinnati."[91]

Increased concern for neighborhood responsiveness and minority rights has led to the emergence of a **new reform movement** in cities. As seen in their concern for standards of ethics and campaign finance reform, contemporary reformers still seek the older ideal of structuring a city government free from corruption and insulated from the power of narrow special interests. But the new reformers spurn the ideal of centralized administration which dominated Progressive Era thought. Instead, the new reformers value decentralization and responsiveness to neighborhood and minority needs. They seek district elections and smaller council districts that will increase representativeness and citizen access to office. Much of this new reform agenda with its emphasis on participation was written into the structure of New York City's government as the city revised its charter in the late 1980s and early 1990s. The reform movement persists in American cities but with a new twist: "Democracy is now the primary goal; achieving efficiency is now secondary."[92]

City managers, too, have begun to abandon their norm of passive, professional neutrality for a heightened managerial activism consistent with the mission of finding solutions to problems entailing questions of racial fairness. More modern city managers have come to incorporate a concern for social equity in their vision of community's public interest.[93]

Even the good-government National Civil League (the modern-day version of the old National Municipal League) has revised its Model City Charter in response to the criticisms made against old-style reform. While the league still maintains the importance of the at-large principle, it has come to recognize that some cities will find it necessary to adopt district or mixed elections in order to increase the representation of racial minorities.[94]

Even where the new reformers have continued with the traditional reform goal of "cleaning up" politics, they have encountered great difficulty. Ethics laws are difficult to enforce, and corruption scandals continue to plague cities: "The conflict-of-interest provisions contain a lengthy list of 'shall nots,' many of which are ambiguous and vague." [95] Detailed conflict-of-interest laws and requirements for financial disclosure may also deter qualified persons from assuming positions in public service. In New York the Conflicts of Interest Board disqualified both the mayor and the city council president from voting on the renewal of the Time Warner cable television franchise because they had relatives who owned stock in Time Warner ventures. Council President Andrew Stein had difficulty in finding qualified appointees who lacked conflicts of interest, in the board's view. Even the presidents of Columbia University and New York University were disqualified from voting on the measure, as trustees of the universities were involved in Time Warner and the universities had received contributions from Time Warner's competitors.[96]

Campaign finance is equally hard to regulate. In 1985 New York City Mayor Ed Koch, fueled by contributions from investment bankers, real estate developers, trade union committees, and other interests with business before the city, spent nearly $10 per voter, for a whopping total of $7.2 million—four times what he spent in the previous election and over seven times the amount spent by runner-up Carol Bellamy.[97] Soon thereafter, the city enacted a new campaign finance law to eliminate such excesses, providing partial public funding to candidates who abided by spending limits. But while New York's campaign finance law limits a candidate's election spending, it does not, due to constitutional free speech concerns, control **independent expenditures** made by others on behalf of a candidate. In the 1993 election, the state Democratic party spent a half million dollars on radio and direct mail advertising in support of incumbent Mayor David Dinkins, although that money was not counted against Dinkins' allowable spending ceiling.[98]

TERM LIMITS

In the 1990s, the anti-incumbency mood that swept the nation led voters across the country to place limitations on the length of allowable service for elected officials. While these anti-incumbency measures were initially directed against members of Congress, soon citizens began to demand term limitations for state and local legislators.

Advocates of term limitations argue the virtues of returning to the **Jeffersonian ideal** of citizen-legislators. Term limitation measures, they argue, will break the stranglehold that special interests have had over legislators dependent on their financial support for a career in politics. While city councils experience a greater rate of personnel turnover than does Congress, the councils in a number of cities do have members who have enjoyed super-extended terms of office.[99]

Critics, however, counter that as a result of term limitations, city councils will lose their **institutional memory**, as those members with the greatest experience and knowledge of how a city attempted to cope with difficult problems are forced to leave office. Critics further argue that term limitation measures will only result in increasing the power of the bureaucracy, legislative staff, and special interest groups as inexpert, novice legislators become dependent on the information and studies provided by outsiders. Unlike Congress, local governments don't need term limitations because they already enjoy a substantial infusion of "new blood" each year; 47 percent of all council members in 1991 were serving their first term.[100] One study of San Mateo, California (just south of San Francisco), has also shown that term limitations do not necessarily end career politicians or ensure a citizen legislature. Instead, local legislators facing a cap on their service in one office simply seek higher office.[101]

Whatever the pros and cons of term limits, such measures have not yet been widely adopted by local governments. The term limitations movement is still in its infancy. According to 1991 data, only 8 percent of local jurisdictions have adopted term limits for their city councils; only 11 percent impose legal limits on the consecutive terms served by the mayor.[102] However, term limits have already proved somewhat popular in large cities; 40 percent of cities with population over 500,000 have adopted the mechanism. Small cities and towns, in contrast, exhibit virtually no inclination to impose term limits, perhaps as the part-time legislators in small jurisdictions pose no equivalent threat of the "professional" politician in bigger cities. Also, small jurisdictions have difficulty in finding qualified persons who are willing to take on the burden of public office as a frequently unpaid addition to their work and family responsibilities.

Statewide initiatives and referenda mandating limitations should increase the number of cities that place restrictions on service. In a number of cities, term limitations have been enacted by the citizen initiative process despite council opposition to the measure. In other cities, the council has put the measure up for referendum. In Los Angeles, term limits passed only with the retirement of Mayor Tom Bradley, who had beaten back an earlier term limitation effort. Western states, the heart of reform and direct democracy, have seen the most extensive adoption of term limits. However, the term limitation movement has begun to spread nationwide.[103] Cincinnati, Houston, Jacksonville, Kansas City, San Francisco, and San Jose are among the more populous cities to have imposed term limits on council members in recent years.

CONCLUSIONS

In light of recent attacks on reform institutions, it is easy to lose sight of the gains won by the reform movement. Its achievements were substantial. The reformers generally cleaned up the election process and protected the integrity of the ballot. They introduced a standard of fairness in the allocation of city jobs and services; as a result of reform, jobs and services were no longer allocated on the basis of whom you knew or for whom you voted. They reduced corruption and brought technical competence to city government.

The reformers also brought a new concern for the background, training, and experience of department heads selected for local government. The increased professionalism of city departments upgraded the quality of administration by increasing performance standards. Wherever cities continue to suffer from the ills of exaggerated partisanship and corruption, adoption of the first generation of reforms is still in order.

Yet all the achievements of reform came at a cost. The reforms lessened the power of lower-class and minority voting groups. Reforms also weakened city leadership and created relatively uncontrollable bureaucratic bastions of power. The professionalization of city agencies depersonalized administration. A sense of trust between urban service provider and client was broken.

No one wishes to return to the ills of the unreformed city. Yet where reform has yielded rigid local governments insensitive to the demands of the diversity of their citizens, a second generation of reforms is in order. Indeed, such a second wave of reform is already under way in a number of cities. A new generation of city managers and administrators has been schooled in the importance of administrative decentralization, citizen participation, and community relations. These topics will be taken up in our next chapter.

NOTES

1. The account follows generally from Edward C. Banfield and James Q. Wilson, *City Politics* (New York: Random House, 1963), pp. 138–50.
2. For a brief overview of Taylor's principles and the debate surrounding Taylorism, see Frederick W. Taylor, "Scientific Management," in *Classics of Public Administration*, ed. Jay M. Shafritz and Albert C. Hyde (Chicago: Dorsey Press, 1987), pp. 29–33; and George J. Gordon, *Public Administration in America* (New York: St. Martin's Press, 1986), pp. 187–89.
3. James Q. Wilson, "Politics and Reform in American Cities," in *American Government Annual, 1962–63* (New York: Holt, Rinehart & Winston, 1962), pp. 37–52.
4. Chandler Davidson and Luis Ricardo Fraga, "Nonpartisan Slating Groups in an At-Large Setting," in *Minority Vote Dilution*, ed. Chandler Davidson (Washington, DC: Howard University Press, 1989), pp. 119–43.

5. Edward I. Koch, *Mayor: An Autobiography* (New York: Warner Books, 1984), pp. 4–7.
6. Banfield and Wilson, *City Politics*, p. 148.
7. Ibid.; Alan DiGaetano, "Urban Political Reform: Did It Kill the Political Machine?" *Journal of Urban History* 18 (November 1991): 37–67, argues that the enactment of political reforms was insufficient in killing the urban machines. In many cities, the machine survived the introduction of structural reforms. Changes in a city's ethnic and racial make-up were also important factors that led to the decline of urban machines.
8. Samuel P. Hays, "The Politics of Reform in Municipal Government in the Progressive Era," *Pacific Northwest Quarterly* 55 (1964): 157–69, reprinted in *Readings in Urban Politics: Past, Present, and Future*, ed. Charles H. Levine and Harlan Hahn (White Plains, NY: Longman, 1984), pp. 54–73.
9. Ibid.
10. The story of the changing nature of reform politics in Cleveland is told by Todd Swanstrom, *The Crisis of Growth Politics: Cleveland, Kucinich, and the Challenge of Urban Populism* (Philadelphia: Temple University Press, 1985), pp. 36–53.
11. Swanstrom, *The Crisis of Growth Politics*, p. 47.
12. Ibid., p. 36
13. Ibid., p. 53.
14. Ibid., p. 50.
15. Ibid.
16. Martin Shefter, *Political Crisis/Fiscal Crisis: The Collapse and Revival of New York City* (New York: Basic Books, 1985), p. 22. The story of New York City's reform movement in the 1960s is told by Shefter, pp. 21–26 and 41–104. The quotations are from Shefter.
17. The distinction between types of reformers is made by Melvin G. Holli, *Reform in Detroit: Hazen S. Pingree and Urban Politics* (New York: Oxford University Press, 1969).
18. Robert L. Lineberry and Edmund P. Fowler, "Reformism and Public Policies in American Cities," *American Political Science Review* 61 (September 1967): 714.
19. Ibid., p. 715.
20. David Morgan and John Pelissero, "Urban Policy: Does Political Structure Matter?" *American Political Science Review* 74 (December 1980): 999–1006.
21. Susan Welch and Timothy Bledsoe, *Urban Reform and Its Consequences* (Chicago: University of Chicago Press, 1988), p. 101.
22. Ibid., p. 136.
23. Christopher L. Warren, John G. Corbett, and John F. Stack, Jr., "Hispanic Ascendancy and Tripartite Politics in Miami," in *Racial Politics in American Cities*, ed. Rufus P. Browning, Dale Rogers Marshall, and David H. Tabb (New York: Longman, 1990), p. 158.
24. Ibid., pp. 167–68.
25. Tari Renner and Victor S. DeSantis, "Contemporary Patterns and Trends in Municipal Government Structures," *The Municipal Year Book 1993* (Washington, DC: International City/County Management Association, 1993), pp. 67–68.
26. Albert K. Karnig, "Black Representation on City Councils: The Impact of District Elections and Socioeconomic Factors," *Urban Affairs Quarterly* 12

(December 1976): 229. Also see the exchange between Karnig and Leonard Cole following publication of Karnig's article. Susan A. MacManus and Charles S. Bullock, "Minorities and Women Do Win at Large!" *National Civic Review* 77 (May/June 1988): 231–44, show that Hispanics, blacks, and women have done quite well in at-large elections in Austin, Texas (a city which in 1980 was only 18 percent Hispanic and 11 percent black). These authors suggest that "the negativism attributed to reform structures may be waning. One reason for this change may be the growing tendency of whites to cross over and support minority candidates as the population becomes more educated and color/gender blind in their voting patterns" (pp. 242–43).

27. Margaret K. Latimer, "Black Political Representation in Southern Cities: Election Systems and Other Causal Variables," *Urban Affairs Quarterly* 15 (September 1979): 72.

28. Timothy Bledsoe, "A Research Note on the Impact of District/At-Large Elections on Black Political Efficacy," *Urban Affairs Quarterly* 22 (September 1986): 166–74.

29. Latimer, "Black Political Representation in Southern Cities," pp. 80–81.

30. J. Morgan Kousser, "The Undermining of the First Reconstruction: Lessons for the Second," in *Minority Vote Dilution*, ed. Chandler Davidson (Washington, DC: Howard University Press, 1989), pp. 32–33.

31. Chandler Davidson, "Minority Vote Dilution: An Overview," in *Minority Vote Dilution*, p. 11.

32. *Zimmer v. McKeithen*, 485 F. 2d 1287, 5th Circuit (1973).

33. *City of Bolden v. Mobile*, 446 U.S. 55, 100 S. Ct. 1490 (1980). See Chandler Davidson, ed., *Minority Vote Dilution* (Washington, DC: Howard University Press, 1989) for an analysis of the reasoning and impact of this case.

34. Welch and Bledsoe, *Urban Reform and Its Consequences*, p. 13; and Davidson, "Minority Vote Dilution: An Overview," p. 18.

35. *Rogers v. Lodge*, 458 U.S. 613 (1982); and *Thornburg v. Gingles*, 478 U.S. 30 (1986). For an overview of legislative and judicial action in the area of minority vote dilution, see Bernard Grofman, Lisa Handley, and Richard G. Niemi, *Minority Representation and the Quest for Voting Equality* (New York: Cambridge University Press, 1992), especially chapters 1 and 2.

36. Arnold Fleischmann, "Sunbelt Boosterism: The Politics of Postwar Growth and Annexation in San Antonio," in *The Rise of the Sunbelt Cities*, ed. David C. Perry and Alfred J. Watkins (Beverly Hills, CA: Sage Publications, 1977), pp. 164–65. For a more extensive discussion of the importance of district elections to the election of Hispanic council and school board members, see J. L. Polinard, Robert D. Wrinkle, Tomas Longoria, and Norman E. Binder, *Electoral Structure and Urban Policy* (Armonk, NY: M. E. Sharpe, 1994).

37. Michael V. Haselswerdt, "Voter and Candidate Reaction to District and At-Large Elections: Buffalo, New York," *Urban Affairs Quarterly* 20 (September 1984): 31–45. Polinard et al., *Electoral Structure and Public Policy*, p. 166, too, report that district elections tend to result in the election of council members with a decidedly neighborhood orientation.

38. Joyce Purnick, "Koch to Limit Contributions in Race," *The New York Times*, June 21, 1988.

39. Clarence N. Stone, *Regime Politics: Governing Atlanta, 1946–1988* (Lawrence, KS: University of Kansas Press, 1989), p. 84.

40. Rodney E. Hero, *Latinos and the U.S. Political System: Two-Tiered Pluralism* (Philadelphia: Temple University Press, 1992), pp. 141–42, summarizes the conflicting results of the studies attempting to research the impact of at-large systems on Latino representation.

41. Kenneth Meier and Joseph Stewart, Jr., *The Politics of Hispanic Education* (Albany, NY: State University of New York Press, 1991), cited by Hero, *Latinos and the U.S. Political System*, p. 141.

42. Susan Clarke and Rodney Hero, "The Politics of Education Reform in Denver" (Paper presented to the annual meeting of the Urban Affairs Association, New Orleans, March 4, 1994).

43. Susan A. MacManus, "How to Get More Women in Office: The Perspectives of Local Elected Officials (Mayors and City Councilors)," *Urban Affairs Quarterly* 28 (September 1992); 164–65 and 167 (footnote 2); and Susan A. MacManus and Charles S. Bullock III, "Women and Racial/Ethnic Minorities in Mayoral and Council Positions," *Municipal Year Book 1993* (Washington, DC: International City/County Management Association, 1993), p. 78.

44. Renner and DeSantis, "Contemporary Patterns and Trends in Municipal Government Structures," pp. 67–68.

45. Anthony Downs, *An Economic Theory of Democracy* (New York: Harper & Row, 1957), p. 234. See pp. 207–38 for Downs' discussion as to the "costs" to citizens of becoming informed and how voters thereby delegate analysis and evaluation to such other actors as interest groups and political parties.

46. Paul Raymond, "The American Voter in a Nonpartisan, Urban Election," *American Politics Quarterly* 20 (April 1992): 247–60.

47. Jeffrey L. Pressman, *Federal Programs and City Politics* (Berkeley, CA: University of California Press, 1975), pp. 40–42 and 129–47.

48. Rufus P. Browning, Dale Rogers Marshall, and David H. Tabb, *Protest Is Not Enough: The Struggle of Blacks and Hispanics for Equality in Urban Politics* (Berkeley, CA: University of California Press, 1984), pp. 34–36, 201–02, and 241–42.

49. See Eugene C. Lee, *The Politics of Nonpartisanship* (Los Angeles: University of California, 1960). Other important works on nonpartisan elections include Charles R. Adrian, "Some General Characteristics of Nonpartisan Elections," *American Political Science Review* 46 (September 1952): 766–76; Charles R. Adrian, "A Typology of Nonpartisan Elections," *Western Political Quarterly* (June 1959): 449–58; Carol A. Cassel, "Social Background Characteristics of Nonpartisan City Council Members," *Western Political Quarterly* 38 (September 1985): 495–501; and Susan Welch and Timothy Bledsoe, "The Partisan Consequences of Nonpartisan Elections," *American Journal of Political Science* 30 (February 1986): 128–39.

50. Walter Dean Burnham, *Critical Elections and the Mainsprings of American Politics* (New York: W. W. Norton, 1970), pp. 79–81.

51. Ibid., pp. 81–85.

52. Stanley Kelley, Jr., et al., "Registration and Voting: Putting First Things First," *American Political Science Review* 61 (June 1967): 359–79.

53. Raymond E. Wolfinger and Steven J. Rosenstone, *Who Votes?* (New Haven, CT: Yale University Press, 1980), p. 79.

54. Ibid.

55. The details reported in this paragraph were obtained from Charles M. Price, "Electoral Accountability: Local Recalls," *National Civic Review* 77 (March/April 1988): 118–23.

56. David O. Sears and Jack Citrin, *Tax Revolt: Something for Nothing in California* (Cambridge, MA: Harvard University Press, 1982); and Terry Schwadron and Paul Richter, *California and the American Tax Revolt: Proposition 13 Five Years Later* (Berkeley, CA: University of California Press, 1984).

57. An excellent review of the arguments pro and con regarding the contemporary use of the initiative, referendum, and recall is provided by Charles G. Bell and Charles M. Price, *California Government Today: Politics or Reform?* 3rd ed. (Chicago: Dorsey Press, 1988), pp. 86–111.

58. Renner and DeSantis, "Contemporary Patterns and Trends in Municipal Government Structures," pp. 68–69.

59. Roger W. Caves, *Land Use Planning: The Ballot Box Revolution*, Sage Library of Social Research Volume 187 (Newbury Park, CA: Sage Publications, 1992). For a review of the various ballot measures limiting growth in San Francisco, see Richard Edward DeLeon, *Left Coast City: Progressive Politics in San Francisco, 1975–1991* (Lawrence, KS: University of Kansas Press, 1992).

60. Amy Downs, "Citizen Sponsored Initiatives: Filling the Legislative Vacuum on Discrimination Issues," *National Civic Review* 80 (Fall 1991): 413–16.

61. Marcia Ritzdorf, "Regulating Space: Gender, Family Values, and Zoning" (Paper presented at the annual meeting of the Urban Affairs Association, Indianapolis, Indiana, April 23, 1993).

62. Pierre Clavel, *The Progressive City: Planning and Participation 1969–1984* (New Brunswick, NJ: Rutgers University Press, 1986); and Norman Krumholz and John Forester, *Making Equity Planning Work: Leadership in the Public Sector* (Philadelphia: Temple University Press, 1990).

63. Philip J. Trounstine and Terry Christensen, *Movers and Shakers: The Study of Community Power* (New York: St. Martin's Press, 1982), p. 44.

64. Amy Bridges, "Winning the West to Municipal Reform," *Urban Affairs Quarterly* 27 (June 1992): 494–518.

65. Fleischmann, "Sunbelt Boosterism," pp. 165–66.

66. Trounstine and Christensen, *Movers and Shakers*, pp. 89–97.

67. Ibid., p. 84.

68. Ibid., p. 107.

69. Peter A. Lupsha and William A. Siembieda, "The Poverty of Public Services in the Land of Plenty: An Analysis and Interpretation," in *The Rise of the Sunbelt Cities*, ed. David C. Perry and Alfred J. Watkins (Beverly Hills, CA: Sage Publications, 1977), pp. 185–86.

70. Fleischmann, "Sunbelt Boosterism," p. 165.

71. Bridges, "Winning the West to Municipal Reform," pp. 514–15.

72. Trounstine and Christensen, *Movers and Shakers*, p. 109; and John J. Kirlin and Dale Rogers Marshall, "The New Politics of Entrepreneurship," in *Urban Change and Poverty*, ed. Micahel G. H. McGeary and Laurence E. Lynn, Jr. (Washington, DC: National Academy Press, 1988), pp. 172–73.

73. Fleischmann, "Sunbelt Boosterism," p. 164; and Sidney Plotkin, "Democratic Change in the Urban Political Economy: San Antonio's Edwards Aquifer Controversy," in *The Politics of San Antonio: Community, Progress, and Power,*

ed. David R. Johnson, John A. Booth, and Richard J. Harris (Lincoln, NE: University of Nebraska Press, 1983), pp. 157–74.

74. Trounstine and Christensen, *Movers and Shakers*, pp. 100–03.

75. Ibid., p. 169.

76. Details of the Watsonville case and its potential impact were taken from Susan Yoachum, "Hispanics Win Fight in Court: At-large Elections Are Ruled Discriminatory," *San Jose Mercury News*, July 28, 1988.

77. Theodore Lowi, "Machine Politics—Old and New," *Public Interest* 9 (Fall 1967): 86.

78. Ibid., p. 87.

79. Ibid., p. 86.

80. Michael N. Danielson and Jameson W. Doig, *New York: The Politics of Urban and Regional Development* (Berkeley, CA: University of California Press, 1982), p. 317–18.

81. Ibid., pp. 316–21. The story of the World Trade Center and the Port Authority's ignoring of mass transit needs is also briefly told by John J. Harrigan, *Political Change in the Metropolis*, 4th ed. (Glenview, IL: Scott, Foresman, 1989), p. 266.

82. Lowi, "Machine Politics—Old and New," p. 85.

83. William J. Grimshaw, "Race and Reform: Minority Empowerment and the White Liberal Question" (Paper presented at the annual meeting of the American Political Science Association, Chicago, September 2–5, 1993).

84. Ibid.

85. John Camper and Mitchell Locin, "Patronage Seen in Hiring Plan," *Chicago Tribune*, January 22, 1987.

86. William J. Grimshaw, *Bitter Fruit: Black Politics and the Chicago Machine, 1931–1991* (Chicago: University of Chicago Press, 1992), pp. 186–88.

87. Browning, Marshall, and Tabb, *Protest Is Not Enough*, pp. 201–02.

88. John Clayton Thomas, *Between Citizen and City: Neighborhood Organizations and Urban Politics in Cincinnati* (Lawrence, KS: University of Kansas Press, 1986), p. 75.

89. Ibid., pp. 87–88. See also David B. Tyack, "Needed: The Reform of a Reform," in *Urban Politics and Public Policy: The City in Crisis*, ed. Stephen M. David and Paul E. Peterson (New York: Praeger Publishing, 1976), pp. 225–47.

90. Pressman, *Federal Programs and City Politics*, pp. 137–55.

91. Thomas, *Between Citizen and City*, p. 78.

92. Gerald Benjamin and Frank J. Mauro, "The Reemergence of Municipal Reform," in *Restructuring New York City Government: The Reemergence of Municipal Reform*, ed. Frank J. Mauro and Gerald Benjamin, *Proceedings of the Academy of Political Science* (1989): 11. Also see Douglas Muzzio and Tim Tompkins, "On the Size of the City Council," pp. 83–96 in the same volume.

93. John Nalbandian, "Tenets of Contemporary Professionalism in Local Government," *Public Administration Review* 50 (November/December 1990): 654–62.

94. James H. Svara, "The Model City and County Charters: Innovation and Tradition in the Reform Movement," *Public Administration Review* 50 (November/December 1990) : 688–92.

95. Frank Anechiarico and James B. Jacobs, "The Continuing Saga of Municipal Reform: New York City and the Politics of Ethics Law," *Urban Affairs Quarterly* 27 (June 1992).

96. Ibid., pp. 594–95.
97. John Hull Mollenkopf, *A Phoenix in the Ashes: The Rise and Fall of the Koch Coalition in New York City Politics* (Princeton, NJ: Princeton University Press, 1992), pp. 92–95. Arnold Fleischmann and Lana Stein similarly found that development interests were prominent contributors in citywide races in St. Louis and Atlanta. Interestingly, city races were not "closed" affairs, as contributions often came from suburban and national sources outside the city. See their "Ties That Bind: Campaign Money, Local Politicians, and Urban Development" (Paper presented at the annual meeting of the American Political Science Association, Washington, DC, September 2–5, 1993).
98. "Campaign Finance Chicanery" (editorial), *The New York Times,* October 13, 1993.
99. John Clayton Thomas, "The Term Limitations Movement in U.S. Cities," *National Civic Review* 81 (Spring/Summer 1992): 155–73.
100. Victor S. DeSantis and Tari Renner, "Term Limits and Turnover Among Local Officials," in *Municipal Year Book 1994* (Washington, DC: International City/County Management Association, 1994), pp. 36–42.
101. John David Rausch, "Testing Legislative Term Limitations: The San Mateo Board of County Supervisors as Laboratory," *National Civic Review* 82 (Spring 1993): 149–56.
102. The data in this paragraph is from DeSantis and Renner, "Term Limits and Turnover Among Local Officials"; and Renner and DeSantis, "Contemporary Patterns and Trends in Municipal Government Structures," p. 66.
103. John Clayton Thomas, "The Term Limitation Movement in U.S. Cities" (Paper presented at the annual meeting of the Urban Affairs Association, Indianapolis, April 24, 1993).

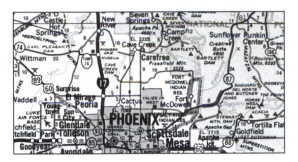

7

Citizen Participation and Decentralization

As we have seen in the preceding chapter, the reform movement placed decision-making power in the hands of professionally trained administrative officials who too often ignored the concerns of neighborhoods and the individual citizen. Urban renewal projects tore down good housing structures as well as bad, displacing people from their homes. New highway connector projects divided neighborhoods and displaced still more people. By the 1960s, racial minorities charged white middle-class-dominated police departments, public school systems, county welfare agencies, and a whole host of other public sector agencies with being insensitive to their needs. *Citizen participation* and *decentralization* were proposed as possible cures to the ills of a city government that had become insensitive, bureaucratized, and remote.

The disadvantaged are not the only residents who have a stake in citizen participation and decentralization. Middle-class citizens, too, need the means to make city officials more responsive to their concerns. Parents of college-bound children are often quite unhappy with the performance of local school systems. Environmentalist organizations from New York to Seattle initiated direct action to halt the construction of new highways that were deemed harmful to the local ecology.[1]

CITIZEN PARTICIPATION AND CLASSICAL THEORY

The idea of citizen participation is as old as democracy itself, surfacing even during the era of the Greek city-states, when it was believed that everyone should be allowed to participate in decision making. This concept is sometimes referred to as **primary democracy** or **face-to-face democracy** and is practiced in relatively small political jurisdictions where all citizens can have a voice in decision making. In cities and suburbs today, neighborhood organizations offer the best possibility for face-to-face citizen interaction.[2]

217

In ancient Greece citizen participation was practiced with great enthusiasm. It was rumored that in the city of Corinth, when the senate met, any citizen of the city could come forward and propose a piece of legislation. If it passed that same day, the citizen who proposed the bill would be rewarded with a sumptuous banquet in his honor, including food, drink, and entertainment. However, if the proposed piece of legislation failed to pass the senate, the person proposing it was brought to the public square, where one of his hands was chopped off. This unique system had two great benefits: First, it markedly improved the quality of the legislation that was introduced; and second, it drastically reduced the amount of legislation the senate had to consider.

Except for the New England town meetings and citizen group associations, our government has never functioned as a primary democracy. Because of our size and numbers, we have a **republican form of government** in which elected representatives speak and vote for their constituents. But today, many citizens question just how well elected officials represent their needs. This has led to a search for new techniques for citizen involvement in the political and administrative decision-making process.

There are various definitions of **citizen participation.** Edgar and Jean Cahn view citizen participation in terms of citizens having enough information to participate in initial decisions on the allocation of resources and creation of institutions that will affect their lives.[3] Sherry Arnstein gives a more complete definition of citizen participation as

> ...a categorical term for citizen power. It is the redistribution of power that enables the have-not citizens, presently excluded from the political and economic processes, to be deliberately included in the future. It is the strategy by which the have-nots join in determining how information is shared, goals and policies are set, tax resources are allocated, programs are operated, and benefits like contract and patronage are parceled out. In short, it is the means by which they can induce significant societal reform which enables them to share in the benefits of the affluent society.[4]

THE WAR ON POVERTY AND THE URBAN RIOTS: THE ROOTS OF CITIZEN PARTICIPATION PROGRAMS

Although urban renewal and a few other federal programs in the 1950s had perfunctory requirements for citizen participation and consultation, the new emphasis on citizen participation began to a great extent with the War on Poverty in the 1960s. The culmination of this concern for empowering poor people occurred in 1964, during the Johnson administration, with the passage of the Economic Opportunity Act. Title II-A of the act authorized the **Community Action Program (CAP)** and required the **"maximum feasible participation"** of the poor in locally developed community action programs. Local **community action agencies (CAAs)** were charged with involving the poor as much as possible in implementing programs in their communities.[5] The riots of the mid-1960s only served to reinforce the view that the poor themselves needed to be involved in shaping the actions and institutions that affected their lives.

In the 1960s citizen participation became a rallying cry for urban residents who sought to open up the whole structure of government and thereby redistribute power and authority. But bureaucrats and citywide elected officials, in contrast, viewed citizen participation as a more static concept. They did not necessarily wish to redistribute power. Instead, local officials often saw citizen participation as a tool to appease communities and as something that had to be undertaken only in order to satisfy federal guidelines.

Problems often arose as federally funded citizen organizations developed programs that city officials opposed. Inexperienced personnel frequently failed to administer programs in a competent manner. In an extreme case a Chicago neighborhood gang was able to obtain poverty funds to develop youth programs in a church. Later it was alleged that gang members were using federal money to buy weapons. Mayor Richard J. Daley was incensed. Daley and other mayors around the country objected that the federal government was using public money to help poor communities challenge the decisions of duly-elected officials.

In 1967 Congress responded to these concerns by passing the **Green Amendment,** named after Congresswoman Edith Green of Oregon. The Green Amendment gave local government officials the option of taking control of community action agencies, provided that a third of the board members represented the poor. In this way Congress hoped to eliminate some of the more distasteful programs and return much of the responsibility for oversight to mayors and council members. Community activists objected that this new centralized control undermined the citizen participation. In Chicago, Daley used the program as a new source of patronage to reward his allies; he shut out those community activists who were highly critical of the city's performance.[6]

But few cities even needed to exercise their option under the Green Amendment. The Office of Economic Opportunity had already sought to minimize controversy by having its field representatives approve local programs that were acceptable to governmental leaders and established private welfare agencies. These programs fell short of the autonomy desired by community activists.[7]

It was evident from the War on Poverty programs that formal mechanisms for involving citizens were not living up to even minimal expectations. Neighborhood residents were asked to elect representatives to serve on community action boards. The turnouts were dismal: Philadelphia

(2.7 percent), Los Angeles (0.7 percent), Boston (2.4 percent), Cleveland (4.2 percent), and Kansas City, Missouri (5.0 percent).[8]

Defenders of citizen groups responded that the stakes entailed in such community elections were not sufficient to justify larger participation. Furthermore, the low turnouts were the natural results of poor scheduling of meetings and lackluster efforts to spread information and promote attendance. Tacking notices on trees or sending them home with schoolchildren represented totally inadequate ways of communicating with neighborhood residents. Roland C. Warren sums up the disenchantment with the early antipoverty elections:

> Never again should we ask the slum residents of 150 American cities to come out to endless rounds of frustrating meetings, to be lectured on what a splendid opportunity they have to improve their neighborhoods if they will only participate responsibly in decision making; never again should we expect them to jump through the same old participation hoops, with the help of the same old professional people at their elbows telling them why this or that innovation is impractical; never again should we promise them the improvement of conditions of living in 150 cities for 575 million dollars a year. It is an insult to their own intelligence and integrity.[9]

EXPANDING CITIZEN PARTICIPATION:
ONCE AGAIN, THE FEDERAL ROLE

The federal government's insistence on citizen participation went beyond the "maximum feasible participation" provisions written into the Community Action Program. The Model Cities Program similarly called for "widespread citizen participation." While Model Cities programs were centralized in city hall, neighborhood organizations were given the opportunity to approve or veto grant proposals that affected their area. Citizens elected Model Cities Commissions that became the negotiating agent between the city and the residents.

During the 1970s federal requirements for citizen participation began expanding at a rapid rate. In program after program agencies administering federally assisted programs were required to "hold hearings," "involve citizens," or "seek consultation with affected parties." Citizen participation mechanisms were required by a wide range of federal legislation, including the Coastal Zone Management Act (1972), the Federal Water Pollution Control Act Amendments (1972), the Regional Development Act (1975), the Resource Conservation and Recovery Act (1976), the Housing and Community Development Act (1974), and the Headstart Economic Opportunity and Community Partnership Act (1974), to name only a few.

The federal mandate for citizen involvement reached its peak in the General Revenue Sharing program of the 1970s. The General Revenue

Sharing Act initially required some *39,000* units of local government to inform citizens about their planned uses of shared revenue. Cities issued public notices and held public hearings and open meetings to discuss spending plans. But in a great many cities citizen groups complained that citizen participation did not go far enough, as city councils merely informed the public of spending decisions that had already been made. To remedy this, the 1976 reauthorizing legislation strengthened the participation requirements, mandating both a public hearing early in the process and a budget hearing later in the process after all points of view had been presented.[10]

There was a virtual explosion of citizen participation requirements in the 1970s. According to a 1979 Advisory Commission on Intergovernmental Relations report, 155 of the 498 federal grant programs available to state and local governments required some form of citizen participation. These 155 programs accounted for over 80 percent of federal grant expenditures in Fiscal 1977.[11]

THE INSTITUTIONALIZATION OF CITIZEN PARTICIPATION REQUIREMENTS AND THE REPUBLICAN COUNTERATTACK

As compared with the 1960s, citizen participation efforts in the late 1970s and 1980s were less political and less conflictual. Citizen participation became an institutionalized, expected aspect of city politics.

The modification of citizen participation was a response to a changed urban environment. New York City's financial crisis of the mid-1970s was followed quickly by disclosure of similar ills in Cleveland, Detroit, and Philadelphia; neighborhood groups recognized that there just was not going to be lots of money available to respond to citizens' demand for services.[12] The high interest rates and inflation of the Carter years, the economic recession of the initial Reagan years and the Bush years, and the aid cutbacks under Republican administrations all acted to limit city resources and thereby depress the demand for new services.

Forced to confront a situation of diminished resources, city officials placed a new emphasis on management techniques.[13] New and sophisticated tools were introduced to evaluate program performance. This dispassionate assessment combined with a sense of fiscal "limits" to reduce citizen pressure.

In the 1980s the federal rules and regulations governing citizen participation were also weakened. The Reagan administration saw federal regulations for citizen participation as unnecessary, expensive, and undemocratic. Reagan sought to limit the costs and "red tape" burden that he felt federal regulations imposed on local action. Reagan further believed that as local elected officials were the duly chosen representatives of local populations, their decisions should not be second-guessed by the federal government or by groups favored by federal regulations. Reagan believed that citizen participation requirements were tools that were used to empower liberal, elite, activist groups, not the general public.[14]

A Democratic-controlled Congress kept in place most of the citizen participation requirements of federal aid programs. Yet, Congress was often forced to modify the requirements. And even where the requirements were maintained, federal bureaucrats during the Reagan era did not closely monitor local efforts at citizen participation.

Yet, despite all these changes, citizen participation continued. As urban political scientist John Clayton Thomas has shown in his study of Cincinnati, community organizations have become regular participants in local politics. For the most part these groups have adopted a negotiations approach as opposed to conflict tactics. Their presence has even been welcomed by "guerrillas" in the bureaucracy and by a new breed of public officials willing to accord citizens a wider role in policy making.[15]

Dayton, Ohio, is a city where participation has been incorporated into the decision-making process for years. Dayton has the reputation of being a city of neighborhoods with active and assertive community leaders. In one case, Dayton decided to fight the drug trade by blocking off a number of streets with barricades to make it impossible for drug buyers to drive through and make quick illicit purchases. The barriers also had a second advantage of helping to create a car-free environment in which young children could play. The idea for this program came from the citizens who, after meeting about the problem, designed a solution and sold it to the relevant local government officials.[16]

THE LEVELS OF CITIZEN PARTICIPATION

Citizen participation can be seen to run along a continuum from voting to violence, with a number of variations in between. Letter writing, interest group activity, organizing community groups, testifying before the city council, lobbying, picketing, nonviolent demonstrations, and sit-ins and other obstructionist tactics are all variants of citizen participation.

Sherry Arnstein has attempted to sort out the various meanings of the concept according to an eight-rung **ladder of citizen participation** (see Figure 7.1). She categorizes the bottom two rungs of the ladder, *manipulation* and *therapy*, as **nonparticipation.** The middle three rungs indicate degrees of **tokenism** which she labels *informing, consultation,* and *placation.* The top three rungs indicate various degrees of genuine **citizen power** including *partnership, delegated power,* and *citizen control*[17]:

1. Under **manipulation,** citizens are appointed to advisory boards and committees where they are educated or "coopted" into accepting the rationale behind the local officials' plan for action. Citizens are given the appearance or rituals of participation; however, they are denied any real influence over the course of events.

FIGURE 7.1
Eight Rungs on a Ladder of Citizen Participation

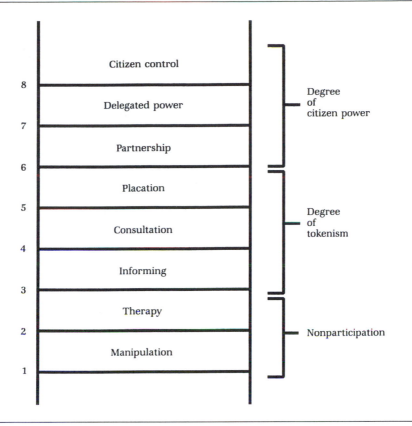

Source: Sherry R. Arnstein, "A Ladder of Citizen Participation," *Journal of the American Institute of Planners* 35 (July 1969): 217.

2. In **therapy,** powerlessness is seen to be synonymous with an illness. Citizens are brought together to discuss ways of altering their behavior instead of changing the behavior of public officials whose actions have helped to cause the problem at hand. Public housing tenant meetings that focus solely on modifying tenants' behavior and attitudes are a good example of this quite limited conceptualization of citizen participation.

3. Under **informing,** citizens are made aware of programs and their rights, responsibilities, and options in a one-way flow of information from government officials to citizens. A governmental agency may merely inform the audience by holding a "dog and pony" show that allows little genuine audience participation. As the information is presented too late in the policy-making process to

[handwritten margin note: MAYBE THAT IS WHAT THEY NEED!!!]

allow citizens an effective response, there is no real prospect for bargaining or compromising. Model Cities planning meetings in the 1960s often reflected this approach.

4. **Consultation** can be an important component of citizen participation. Citizen opinions are solicited through surveys, hearings, and neighborhood meetings. However, if no process is established for incorporating these views into policy decisions, consultation may prove superficial. Many of the early urban renewal programs used this approach to citizen participation.

5. Under **placation,** some poor residents of the community are picked to sit on police, education, housing, or health boards. These people are not accountable to their constituents and are likely to be outvoted on any of the boards where they sit.

6. Beginning with **partnership,** we move to the more significant forms of citizen participation. Under partnership, power is shared among citizens and local officials. Neither partner can act without the other or alter arrangements unilaterally. In effect, both citizens and administrators have possessed a mutual veto over proposed actions. One form that partnership can take is to give citizens and city officials equal representation on a decision-making board.

7. Under **delegated power,** citizen boards have actually gained the authority to make certain decisions. They possess a degree of autonomy in certain specified program areas.

8. Finally, under **citizen control**, residents exercise final authority over a program, including making the ultimate decisions that affect how the program is to be run. Neighborhood development corporations in which access to funding sources is unimpeded provide good examples of citizen control.

The Arnstein typology is important because it shows that not all forms of participation entail real power sharing. Bureaucrats and city officials are generally more willing to utilize those forms of participation toward the bottom of the ladder. Citizens are brought into the process, are given limited access and the illusion of decision-making power; they are thereby led to accept the agency's goals and plans as legitimate. In many cities, community action programs neutralized potential critics by giving activist citizen leaders positions on community boards or jobs with local action agencies. In other cities, however, neighborhood leaders determined that it was more important for them to remain outside the government so that they would not be compromised in their efforts to represent the views of community residents.

Arnstein's ladder is rooted in the experiences of the conflict-oriented 1960s; it portrays citizens and bureaucrats as engaged in a struggle over power. But might bureaucrats and citizens at times willingly join in cooperative efforts at improved service delivery? Hence, Desmond Connor has proposed a "new ladder" of citizen participation that represents "a systematic approach to preventing and resolving public controversy about specific policies, programs, and projects...."[18] Connor's ladder emphasizes *education, information,* and *feedback and consultation.* When these routes are exhausted, community leaders can then resort to *joint planning, mediation,* and *litigation.* Connor's hope is that cooperative efforts will result in the ultimate goal, the *resolution/prevention* of problems.

CITIZEN PARTICIPATION TODAY:
A SURVEY OF LOCAL PROGRAMS

Dayton, as we have observed, is one of several cities to have demonstrated the value of having strong neighborhoods, with active citizens, in constant touch with city hall. Portland (Oregon), St. Paul (Minnesota), and Birmingham (Alabama), too, have had much celebrated citizen participation efforts.[19] Other cities have begun to study the citizen involvement strategies that have worked so well in Dayton. Among the new converts are San Antonio, Phoenix, Richmond, Indianapolis, Santa Clarita, California, and Minneapolis.[20]

In a number of cities citizen participation has been regularized in the form of citizen or neighborhood advisory commissions. In New York City, community boards have been institutionalized to a degree that would surprise cynics.[21] In Washington, DC, too, citizen advisory committees have been built into the city decision-making process in certain policy areas. The Washington and New York case studies show how the concept of citizen participation has evolved over time as it has become a regular feature of city politics.

WASHINGTON, DC: ADVISORY NEIGHBORHOOD COMMITTEES

In 1976, the District of Columbia created a system of advisory neighborhood commissions (ANCs). Within the district there are 299 ANCs, each comprised of about 2,000 residents. Each district elects an unpaid representative who speaks for the residents at ANC meetings. In the November 1994 election, 96 district seats were contested by two or more candidates; 148 seats had but one candidate; the remaining 55 seats were uncontested. The District of Columbia allocates about $1.2 million to assist the ANCs in their work.

How effective are the ANCs? The verdict is mixed. Some organizations see the ANCs as ineffective and wasting the taxpayers' money. Others find this attempt at grassroots democracy in a large urban setting healthy and refreshing. The degree of activity and effectiveness of ANCs has varied widely in the city. Some have been very influential in achieving community goals; others have been fairly dormant or have failed to clearly articulate neighborhood concerns.[22] For the most part the ANCs have managed to keep a low profile, thereby not threatening any elected politicians.

The ANCs' greatest strength appears to be in the zoning process, as opposed to controlling the dispensation of social services. If an ANC supports a request for a zoning change, it is likely to be approved rapidly; similarly, if an ANC opposes a new zoning request, there will often be time-consuming delays. The American University, which is situated in an upper-middle-income neighborhood, found that the combination of local citizen associations and ANCs could be a formidable opponent in zoning politics. The university wanted to develop a revised master plan that included a new law school and a performing arts center. Both proposed additions to the campus, however, raised the prospects of increased traffic and parking problems in the surrounding residential neighborhood. In the recent past the ANCs had worked successfully with the university as it built a new athletic center on campus. Because the ANCs knew enough about zoning politics to understand the value of their support to the newest university zoning request, a period of protracted negotiations ensued as the university sought and won the support of the community for its new master plan. After several zoning board hearings the plan was finally passed.

NEW YORK AND MINNEAPOLIS: WHO PARTICIPATES?

New York City has experimented with a wide variety of citizen participation and decentralization mechanisms over the years. There were many efforts, with mixed results. The initial school decentralization plan for the Ocean Hill–Brownsville section of Brooklyn proved especially volatile, and the school system in the 1960s was shut down by a series of teacher strikes in the conflict that ensued.

Despite the controversy that surrounded earlier participatory efforts, decentralization and citizen participation were institutionalized beginning in the mid-1970s as part of New York's governance in the post-reform era. The new governing regimes that emerged in New York during this period needed community-based involvement in city affairs to help establish their legitimacy.[23]

New York's community board system, with its appointed membership and its advisory powers, represents a moderate form of decentralization.[24] While some board members are dissatisfied with the boards' authority, the modern system of community boards still gives citizens real influence in decisions affecting land use, the city budget, and service delivery. Board recommendations have been seriously considered by other city agencies. As a result, community boards have been able to insist that developers scale back a project's size, rehabilitate a local subway station, or include increased parking or other amenities in their plans in exchange for a positive board vote.

Still, there is much uncertainty as to exactly how much power the community boards actually wield. This is likely to remain a persistent issue throughout the 1990s. A real positive sign, however, is that the level of conflict between citizens and the city government does seem to have diminished.[25] Despite the objections of critics that the board system does not go far enough, New York's system of community boards has opened city decisions in land-use, budgeting, and other areas to greater public scrutiny: "The days of unquestioned citywide dominance of public policy are clearly over."[26]

The fact that extensive citizen participation efforts have continued in cities across the country despite substantially reduced funding and the loosening of federal mandates suggests that citizen participation offers urban governing regimes substantial benefits.[27] In New York, community groups were pragmatic actors focused on neighborhood improvements; they did not constitute a larger social movement. Community groups served to buffer the city's governing regime from unmitigated citizen demands. The community board system may also have even served to deflect local activists from more politicized mobilization efforts.[28]

Economic incentives may also be leading municipal officials to institute formalized mechanisms designed to increase citizen involvement in policy making. Carmine Scavo surveyed the citizen participation efforts in cities with over 100,000 population (with the exception of New York, Chicago, and Los Angeles). Scavo found that cities with extensive citizen participation efforts also tended to be cities that were trying to attract or retain middle-class residents. Citizen participation programs show geographically mobile, tax-paying residents that a city cares. Participatory efforts can be viewed as part of a strategy designed to attract and retain citizens who contribute to a city's tax base.[29]

A review of the extensive neighborhood planning efforts in Minneapolis reveals that community participation mechanisms are often dominated by white, middle-income homeowners. In Minneapolis as well as New York, citizen participation has taken on a middle-class character in promoting concerns for service provision and preserving neighborhood attractiveness.[30]

THE CHANGING STYLE OF CITIZEN PARTICIPATION: FROSTBELT AND SUNBELT

As community groups became regular actors in city politics, they increasingly focused their efforts on specific neighborhood improvements and the delivery of such important services as housing. In doing so, community groups became "more modest in their aims and less threatening to established power."[31]

By the 1970s and 1980s, a number of groups that had earlier followed the confrontational tactics of social activist Saul Alinsky refined their approach to embrace a new focus on service delivery. Alinsky advocated a model of community **organizing** that would bring new power to relatively powerless groups.[32] But his confrontation tactics became less relevant as community organizations gained a "piece of the action" and assumed new responsibilities in running neighborhood programs.

According to Alinsky, the successful organizer must seek out issues that are a source of grievance to a community. He or she must rub these wounds raw, mobilizing the community to attack the target of the protest action. The organizer must skillfully choose tactics that will mobilize the community and disorient and intimidate the target. Organizers need not worry about the ethics of their tactics. According to Alinsky, any tactic that brings about a more just society for the have-nots is morally justifiable.

In the 1960s The Woodlawn Organization (TWO) in Chicago successfully used Alinsky-style tactics to take on a number of targets. TWO dramatically publicized which merchants were shortchanging neighborhood residents. TWO also transported ghetto residents downtown to browse in major department stores, thereby scaring off middle-class customers and ultimately convincing store managers to alter their personnel hiring and promotion policies.[33]

But by the 1970s TWO shifted its focus "From Protest to Programs," as its own slogan phrased it. Like a number of other Alinsky-style organizations, TWO became less concerned with protest activities and more concerned with providing services that would improve the life of community residents—for example, building low-income housing and running day-care centers, dental clinics, and other neighborhood programs.[34]

In New York's South Bronx, the Banana Kelly Community Improvement Association (named for the curved block on Kelly Street) similarly took on new management and service responsibilities as it acquired distressed properties and ran low-income housing cooperatives. Where Banana Kelly once rallied against landlords, the association in effect became the landlord who must now collect overdue rents and somehow find the money to make necessary repairs.[35]

Baltimoreans United in Leadership Development (BUILD) is another community-based organization in the Alinsky tradition that has had to balance protest activities with a new service orientation. With the core of its membership in forty-five to fifty churches in the African-American community, BUILD sought to reinvigorate local black activism and gain power for the poor. BUILD has used Alinsky-style confrontation tactics to fight bank redlining and unfair auto insurance rates. But in more recent years BUILD has shifted its attention to education and human resource programs and has sought a cooperative working relationship with the Greater Baltimore Committee, an organization representing some 1,000 of the city's top businesses. BUILD leaders realize the advantages in establishing a partnership with business leaders that control money and rewards such as jobs that can be promised to high school graduates with good attendance records and good grades.[36]

In Sunbelt cities, too, citizen groups have changed their style. Where once Sunbelt groups were relatively quiescent, recent years have seen neighborhood organizations pose new challenges to local elites.

In Chapters 3 and 5 we reported how community groups confronted elite decision makers in such cities as San Diego and San Jose. In other Sunbelt cities, citizens used the referendum and initiative processes to check the power of government. Phoenix voters, for instance, repeatedly turned down proposals initiated by former Mayor Terry Goddard for development, expanded mass transit, and a new baseball park. Voters even put on the ballot and passed a measure requiring a referendum on any recreational facility or sports arena costing in excess of $3 million—a move that effectively tied the mayor's hands.[37]

In Seattle, a city of half a million inhabitants, citizen activism has come to dominate politics. Citizen involvement grew as residents began to question whether economic growth was compatible with quality of life and environmental protection concerns. Yet there are costs to Seattle's extensive grassroots democracy. Critics in Seattle charge that the decision-making system is often marked by **NIMBY** ("not in my backyard") attitudes and paralysis, whereby local activism has been more successful at stopping projects than at positive, constructive building.[38]

The Phoenix and Seattle examples point to the middle-class sources of citizen activism in many Sunbelt communities. These community elements have pressed for environmentalism, good government, and homeowner concerns. In Tucson, for instance, college-educated men and women have led a strong neighborhood network in an effort to ward off the "Losangelization" of Tucson.[39]

But there is also a second source of the new neighborhood activism in the Sunbelt—the mobilization of groups that represent the region's growing minority populations.[40] In El Paso, for instance, a city with a population that is two-thirds Hispanic, EPISO (the El Paso Interreligious Sponsoring Organization) represents an activist, church-sponsored, grassroots, Alinsky-style organization.[41]

Sometimes the demands of minority-based organizations are consistent with those of middle-class groups. At other times, however, the divergence in style and goals of groups representing different population bases becomes quite clear.

San Antonio has witnessed vigorous activity from middle-class and minority citizen groups.[42] San Antonio is a city divided between its relatively well-off and expanding north side and its less prosperous west side, the home of much of the city's burgeoning Hispanic population.

In 1974, flood runoff from the Anglo neighborhoods inundated large sections of the flat west side. Neighborhood residents were incensed. Over twenty neighborhood groups formed a federation, Communities Organized for Public Services (COPS), to protest the underprovision of infrastructure and other services on the city's west side. Organized along the lines of the Alinsky model and building on the organizational base provided by local churches, COPS used confrontational tactics to win new investment in street repair and drainage projects. Over the years COPS has achieved numerous other important victories, including the adoption of a system of ward-based elections that maximized Mexican-American and black political power. COPS even clashed publicly with Mayor Henry Cisneros, a Mexican-American, over his plans to build a 65,000-seat domed stadium and convention center. COPS would not support a costly project that promised benefits to wealthy business executives and imposed new taxes on poorer San Antonians.[43]

While COPS is the most notable, it is not the only community group to play an important role in contemporary San Antonio politics. Professionals and middle-class citizens on the city's north side have mobilized to block new suburban development. The Aquifer Protection Association (APA) was formed to stop a proposed new shopping mall and related development that was to be sited over the recharge zone of the city's groundwater supply.

COPS at first kept its distance from the APA on the aquifer controversy. COPS initially was not enthusiastic about embracing the cause of a group whose members in the past had been unwilling to support increased spending for improvements in the poorer sections of town. Eventually, though, COPS joined in the fight and hoped that restrictions on fringe development would free up money that could be used to assist Hispanic neighborhoods. Limits imposed on suburban development could also act to channel new investment and jobs back downtown.

In Houston, The Metropolitan Organization (TMO) used the pressure of a mass membership "accountability meeting" to convince Mayor Kathryn Whitmire to sign a compact with TMO. Whitmire agreed to meet with TMO's leadership once a month and to attend future TMO mass meetings. On the whole, though, TMO has proven less effective in Houston than COPS is in San Antonio. Minorities comprise a smaller percentage of the population in Houston than in San Antonio; and tensions among African-Americans, Hispanics, and poor whites in Houston have acted to impede the development of a strong grassroots coalition.[44]

In the poor and gang-ridden neighborhood of East Los Angeles, the shift from neighborhood organizing to service delivery has led to a schism among community groups. The United Neighborhood Organization (UNO), church-sponsored and community-based, was formed after neighborhood activists charged that The East Los Angeles Community Union (TELACU) had abandoned its citizen participation roots. TELACU, a community development corporation, depended on professional and technocratic skills in its contacts with funding agencies. Citizen participation only served to slow down and jeopardize the search for new program moneys. As one TELACU official said, "Who cares about an organization that doesn't maximize citizen participation if in the end the job gets done?"[45]

UNO emerged after Bishop Juan Arzube visited San Antonio in 1975 and observed COPS' effective use of mass meetings to pressure city council members into action. Ernie Cortes, who had put together COPS, was hired as UNO's principal organizer. Cortes built on citizens' cultural heritage, including their attachments to the church, in building a grassroots organization. Home-to-home interviews by UNO organizers confirmed the view that the organization's first priority should be to combat the exorbitant automobile insurance rates that East Los Angeles residents were paying as a result of redlining by auto insurance companies. UNO secured a 37-percent reduction in auto insurance rates for East Los Angeles. The organization then turned its attention to fighting education, housing, transportation, and gang violence problems.

What does a review of the activities of these community groups reveal? It reveals, first, the continued vitality of community groups; second, the continued importance of both conventional and unconventional participation strategies to people who would otherwise be excluded from urban decision making; and third, the tendency for community groups to change their style over time as they gain acceptance from bureaucrats and the media, and as they attempt to provide services to a larger organizational base.

Alinsky-style organizing continues. Yet, on the whole, neighborhood groups over time have become more institutionalized and less confrontation-oriented. This moderation in approach has at times enabled poor people's groups to join in coalitions with other citizen and neighborhood organizations. However, as the San Antonio experience shows, these alliances often prove quite ephemeral.

MAKING CITIZEN PARTICIPATION WORK

Berry, Portney, and Thomson have attempted to find the keys to successful citizen participation by examining five cities—Birmingham (Alabama), Dayton, Portland (Oregon), St. Paul, and San Antonio—that have extensive and noteworthy community participation programs.[16] They discovered that the neighborhood programs in these five cities are markedly different from the flawed citizen participation efforts of the 1960s.

While citizen participation in the 1960s did achieve notable successes in such areas as training a new generation of blacks to enter city politics, on the whole these earlier participatory efforts are generally regarded as a failure. Why did they fail? In part, city officials, threatened by the new programs, wanted them to fail. But that is only part of the answer. Berry and his colleagues further argue that these early programs provided average citizens with no real opportunity for face-to-face interaction and no real control over government programs. As the power given citizens was so limited, there was no compelling reason for poor people to participate: "The legacy of the 1960s and 1970s is that public involvement failed because the public did not care to participate."[47]

THIS SEEMS VERY OPTIMISTIC TO ME. I WOULD GUESS THAT THEY DIDN'T PARTICIPATE DUE TO APATHY, LAZINESS (AND) JUST NOT "GIVING A DAMN"!!! LET'S NOT GIVE THEM SO MUCH CREDIT!!!

So, what are the keys to building effective local participation programs? First, real powers must be turned over to the citizen bodies. These bodies cannot simply be planning or advisory boards. Only if neighborhood bodies possess authority to allocate some significant goods and services will citizens see participation as worthwhile.

Second, the city must employ the necessary rewards and sanctions to make sure that administrators interact with neighborhood groups. Otherwise, administrators will resist the loss of their power.

Third, citizen participation must be initiated citywide. Participatory programs implemented in only a certain few neighborhoods are seen as unfair and discriminatory. They will lack the widespread public support to sustain them against the assaults that will be made by those who are threatened by participation.

Fourth, cities must provide neighborhood organizations with the staff and financial resources so that these associations can engage in substantial outreach to bring residents into the process. They must have the ability to communicate with every neighborhood resident on an ongoing basis. Participation efforts that lack such financial backing likely will not succeed. Finally, the neighborhoods that each community organization serves must be small enough to promote face-to-face contact.[48]

THE CONTINUING DEBATE OVER CITIZEN PARTICIPATION

Over the years, citizen participation has gained legitimacy, yet it continues to have powerful enemies. While some city officials see the advantages in citizen and neighborhood partnerships, others do not wish to have their scope of decision making narrowed by citizen activism. Other officials object that participation markedly slows the process of government decision making. Furthermore, officials are never quite sure if the views presented by highly vocal citizens are representative of those of the community they claim to represent.

The debate over community participation continues. The major arguments advanced for developing a meaningful citizen participation (CP) program can be summarized as follows:

1. CP is consistent with democratic theory. It increases the number of people in the decision-making process and helps assure that government officials are more aware of and responsive to citizen concerns.
2. CP mechanisms help develop community leaders who otherwise might not emerge.
3. CP mechanisms help create political and social networks essential to building a community.
4. CP is psychologically rewarding for those who participate. It reduces feelings of powerlessness and creates a sense of efficacy.

5. CP makes local government appear more legitimate to neighborhoods and city residents, as people believe they have access to government and that public officials are listening to their point of view.
6. CP increases citizens' acceptance and enthusiasm for a program, thereby increasing the chances of successful service intervention. By bringing citizen involvement in service production, CP also improves the efficiency of service delivery.

The surveys taken by Berry and his colleagues confirm that increased participation leads to a heightened sense of community, a greater sense of governmental legitimacy, and increased trust in government. The authors caution, however, that citizen participation activities cannot, in and of themselves, overcome deep-seated and long-held feelings of community problems.[49]

The major arguments against CP are:

1. CP tends to heighten parochial concerns to the detriment of city-wide concerns. Neighborhood action can even be exclusionary, not just parochial.
2. CP is never completely representative of the range of community interests. It can never be said with any certainty that citizen activists represent a community's point of view. Even in cities with noteworthy programs for citizen involvement, it is middle-class citizens, not the poor, who take greatest advantage of the new participatory opportunities.[50]
3. CP increases competition and conflict among community factions.
4. CP is lengthy and time-consuming. It slows down the process of government, retarding service delivery and project completion, thereby frustrating government officials and citizens alike.
5. Under the best of circumstances, CP is likely to have only marginal impact on such broad concerns as the physical planning and development of the city.

In Chicago, Save Our Neighborhoods/Save Our City (SON/SOC), a coalition of citizen groups from the white ethnic "bungalow belt" communities on the city's northwest and southwest sides, shows the exclusionary dangers inherent in citizen participation. SON/SOC sought home-equity insurance, neighborhood watches, and restrictions on real estate practices in an effort to stabilize the decline of their neighborhoods. While some SON/SOC members acted solely from an urgency to protect their property values and their neighborhood, others were clearly racist. SON/SOC failed to build a sense of community across neighborhoods and across racial and class lines.[51]

Citizen participation derives its force from the democratic values inherent in the process. Whatever the flaws and imperfections of participative mechanisms, we can expect continued efforts to enhance citizen democracy.

DECENTRALIZATION

Decentralization is an attempt to devolve decision making closer to the people. In very important ways, decentralization is similar to citizen participation, as both reforms attempt to increase the citizen's voice in city decision making. Since a number of decentralization strategies entail increased citizen participation, at times the two concepts overlap.

The decentralization movement began out of a feeling that too many decisions in city government were being made in central offices downtown by officials who were unaware of, or insensitive to, the needs of residents in the neighborhoods. The decentralization movement sought to locate government offices and focus decision making out into the neighborhoods. Government was to be made more visible and more accessible.

Henry J. Schmandt defines **decentralization** as an institutionalized arrangement that "involves the allocation of authority and responsibility to lower territorially based echelons of the established bureaucracy or to geopolitical levels lower than the large municipality or school district."[52] Decentralization occurs when authority is yielded to agency field offices or to citizen organizations in the neighborhoods.

In many jurisdictions, municipal officials responded to calls for the decentralization by asserting that law enforcement, fire protection, education, and other services were already decentralized. Evidently, the concept of decentralization meant something quite different to public officials than it did to neighborhood groups. Public officials saw decentralization simply as a matter of devolving certain processes and responsibilities to field offices. Citizen groups, in contrast, wanted to alter who exercised decision-making power in the urban political community.

TYPES OF DECENTRALIZATION

One way to better understand the large variety of decentralization mechanisms is to categorize the range of decentralization possibilities according to how much power is devolved.[53]

GOEGRAPHICAL DECENTRALIZATION

Geographical decentralization occurs when a local governmental official decides to locate a branch or field office closer to the clients being served. For example, the agency may lease an abandoned store that contains only few staff people, whose main function is receiving complaints and passing them along to the responsible departments. The field office staff has no real discretion to exercise political or administrative power on their own.

These neighborhood offices are usually city grievance centers or complaint centers. Citizens entering the office fill out forms describing their complaints and are told that they will hear from the appropriate agency in the near future. If they receive a quick response and serious efforts are made to redress their grievances, then word will quickly spread through the community and other clients will begin to use the office. However, if citizen complaints go unanswered, or if responses are less than satisfactory, community interest in the services provided by the field office will soon decline.

This model of decentralization has the advantage of trying to take government to the people. The storefront and neighborhood offices give citizens new and more convenient sites at which to register for services or complain about service mistreatment. Yet, because complaints are merely fielded and then passed downtown, there is no real devolution of authority. Final decision-making power remains in the hands of central office bureaucrats who may be out of touch with local citizens and insensitive to neighborhood needs.

ADMINISTRATIVE DECENTRALIZATION

Administrative decentralization involves the transfer of several people to a field office. These can be either from a single government agency or from several agencies. The major difference between this and geographical decentralization is that administrative decentralization vests administrative discretion in the hands of field employees. Under administrative decentralization field employees do not merely forward complaints downtown; instead they possess some real discretionary power in program implementation and the allocation of benefits. Under administrative decentralization, for instance, a parole officer is empowered to decide whether or not a parolee should be allowed to travel out of the state for a short period of time to attend a relative's funeral. Likewise, a vocational rehabilitation officer may be given substantial discretion in determining the selection of applicants to a program.

Little city halls and multiservice centers are two well-known examples of administrative decentralization. **Little city halls** were initiated in the 1960s and 1970s by Boston Mayor Kevin White and New York Mayor John Lindsay and since have been replicated in a number of other cities. In the little city hall arrangement, agency branch offices are located in an easily identifiable neighborhood facility; the mayoral appointee in charge of the center is empowered to make a range of administrative decisions on the spot. The goal of this program is not only to improve service delivery in the neighborhoods but also to allow the mayor to build the support of neighborhood residents. The establishment of little city halls was also one of the recommendations suggested by the National Advisory Commission on Civil Disorders.[54]

Multiservice centers usually occupy large facilities and provide a fairly complete in-house array of services to a specific neighborhood. Residents can easily identify where they must go to apply for services.

With multiple agencies housed under the same roof, the referral of citizens and coordination of services are also improved. In the late 1960s and early 1970s, Baltimore, Chicago, and a number of other cities established multiservice centers, some of which were very successful in meeting citizen needs.

Administrative decentralization provides a speedier approach to service delivery, as compared to the time delays that occur under the geographical approach where additional paperwork is processed and sent downtown. Administrative decentralization also assures that increased decision-making power is vested in the hands of people who, located in the community, are more likely to know and understand a community's needs. Yet under the administrative approach, final authority is still retained by city officials who may not yield to neighborhood concerns. In the little city hall plan, it is the mayor's appointee who retains final authority; in the multiservice center, it is a decentralized bureaucratic employee.

POLITICAL DECENTRALIZATION

Political decentralization implies a shift in power and authority from city or county agencies to recognized community groups. Elected and/or appointed officials of a community participate with public officials in the development and implementation of policy. Under political decentralization there is an implied parity of power between the community and the city. Neither can impose its programs on the other; occasionally, there is even an explicit veto power granted to the community. An example of this sharing of power occurs when a local community-group screens candidates for principal of the local school and the superintendent selects one of the three candidates recommended by the community board.

Political decentralization is characterized in theory by negotiation, cooperation, and consensus building, as opposed to a conflict orientation. Yet conflict at times can break out. As political decentralization seeks to alter power relationships in a city, many actors require time to adjust.

COMMUNITY CONTROL

The last category in the typology is the one in which there is the greatest shift in power from the government agency to the community group. Under community control a community-selected subunit of government is given the authority to make policy, allocate resources, and veto unwanted governmental intrusions. It exercises a great deal of autonomy over a specific territorial unit. One such instance of community control occurred in the late 1960s when Washington, DC, created an independent school in the Adams-Morgan area and endowed it with power to hire its own teachers, determine its own curriculum priorities, purchase its own supplies, and establish its own local school board. A similar experiment was initiated later in the southeast part of the city.

Ideally such a unit should raise its own revenues from which to allocate resources in making policy decisions. Unfortunately, few if any inner-city areas have the wealth to provide a tax base sufficient for service delivery. Milton Kotler, who wrote one of the first books on neighborhood government with a prescription for community control, left the issue of finances ambiguous. Kotler suggested funding from three sources—taxation, foundations, and gifts—none of which can be expected to provide an adequate source of funding for large-scale neighborhood governments over time.[55] Hence, few inner-city communities can be expected to gain fiscal as well as political autonomy. In fact, community control may truly exist only in the incorporated middle-class suburban community. These suburbs exercise the financial and political autonomy that is sought, but rarely attained, by lower-income, minority communities.[56]

The typology presented above helps explain some of the conflict over decentralization. Local government officials prefer to minimize any shift of power away from their agencies; they prefer the geographical and administrative forms of decentralization. Community groups, in contrast, usually insist on the more extensive devolution of power inherent in political decentralization and community control.[57]

THE POLITICS OF NEIGHBORHOOD GOVERNMENT AND COMMUNITY CONTROL

As we have already seen, attempts at neighborhood government or community control arrangements face strong opposition from bureaucrats and other citywide interests. In his book, *Neighborhood Democracy*, Douglas Yates examined the results of seven decentralization experiments in New York and New Haven. Community control was not achieved in any of the experiments he examined.[58]

Perhaps the most publicized decentralization effort ever was the attempt in 1968 by the New York Board of Education to establish three experimental school districts that were to be controlled by local residents. One of these districts was in the impoverished Ocean Hill–Brownsville section of Brooklyn. Conflicts quickly arose. The new local community board began hiring community residents who were not members of the United Federation of Teachers to work in the schools. The district also sought to reshape its work force by transferring teachers to other schools. The teachers' union objected, and when a negotiated settlement could not be reached, the teachers went on strike. Police officers had to be called in to quell disturbances and to maintain law and order. New York was rocked by repeated citywide teacher strikes as the union and the community board fought over one issue after another.[59]

The Ocean Hill–Brownsville controversy showed just how difficult it was to introduce the more radical forms of decentralization. Still New York has continued to pursue important, although less visible, forms of decentralization. Most significantly, the city charter revisions of 1975 formalized decentralization by creating fifty-nine community boards with advisory powers over land use issues, capital expenditures, and service delivery matters. The result, as we mentioned in this chapter's section on citizen participation, has been a "measured decentralization" which community activists see "as only 'the first step' in what should be an ongoing process of devolving political power to communities."[60]

In middle-class, white neighborhoods, board members believe that New York's community board decentralization mechanism has been sufficient to allow neighborhoods to introduce their concerns into decision making. Minority activists, in contrast, argue that a greater political decentralization is still needed. As one study of New York's community board system has shown, "Poor and minority community districts do not fare as well as middle class, predominantly white communities in securing their local budget priorities."[61] The city's 1989 charter revisions made a number of changes in an attempt to assist community boards in lower-income neighborhoods.

The **community development corporation (CDC)** is one form of decentralization that has received a more favorable reception than have other approaches to neighborhood government.[62] Under this approach the government charters a corporation to be controlled by local residents. The corporation assumes authority over designated economic development and physical rehabilitation activities in a community. The CDC's major concern is with assisting local entrepreneurs and stimulating job creation. The corporation may also contract with governmental agencies to administer such programs as health clinics, day-care centers, and social service intake centers. Los Angeles' TELACU and New York City's Bedford-Stuyvesant Corporation are two prominent examples of this developmental approach to neighborhood government.

Yet even here the devolution of power is short of true community control. As the TELACU case in East Los Angeles demonstrated, sometimes a CDC's responsiveness to neighborhood citizens is diminished by its need to cultivate its government and nonprofit foundation funding sources. The municipal service bureaucracies also ultimately determine just what services and responsibilities are delegated in the management contracts. These bureaucracies can even abrogate the management contracts in cases when they feel the CDC has been grossly inefficient or incompetent.

Even in those rare cases when neighborhood residents succeed in achieving a fair degree of community control, some of the traditional problems of organizational life soon reemerge. Bureaucracy is essential to any organization's existence; bureaucratic standards provide an accepted way of accomplishing tasks. Community groups often find this out the hard way. Thinking that their newly won powers will help them eliminate or reduce bureaucracy, community residents are often shocked to find that they must recruit staff, set pay scales, prepare job descriptions for employees, establish criteria for personnel evaluation and promotion, and maintain personnel and financial records.[63] As the neighborhood organization grows and expands, it becomes more bureaucratic.

THE DEBATE OVER DECENTRALIZATION

Advocates of decentralization generally argue that:

1. Decentralization will improve communication between citizens and government officials by establishing a two-way feedback system so that information flows freely in both directions.
2. Decentralization will improve the responsiveness of service delivery systems. By bringing government closer to the people, neighborhood concerns will be heard and government officials can better determine the quantity and quality of services needed. Power will be redistributed to subunits in the city.
3. Decentralization will improve city-community relations by making people feel that government is closer to them and more willing to listen to their concerns.
4. Decentralization is democratic and fits in with notions of grassroots democracy. Citizens know their neighborhood government officials and can gain greater access to them.

Yet a number of empirical studies have drawn mixed conclusions about the validity of these generalizations. Douglas Yates, for instance, found little evidence that decentralization decreased feelings of powerlessness among community leaders.[64] Richard Cole, on the other hand, has found that such participation increases trust and confidence in government.[65]

Critics of decentralization argue that:

1. Decentralization is inefficient. The professional expertise of departmental experts can be overridden by lay citizens. Furthermore, economies of scale are lost as service decisions are made on a neighborhood as opposed to a citywide basis.
2. Decentralization exacerbates racial and ethnic tensions and might lead a majority in a neighborhood to ignore the concerns of a minority. The polarization of the Ocean Hill–Brownsville controversy is often cited as a case in point.
3. Decentralization will result in lower standards of service. New opportunities for corruption might also appear as the vestiges of backroom ward politics reemerge.

The troubles of community school boards in New York City in the late 1980s illustrate some of the problems that can plague decentralization. Over a third of the thirty-two local school boards that control the hiring of elementary and junior high school administrators were accused of corruption and mismanagement. Teachers often saw political ties to elected school board members and their powerful political friends as the key to promotion.[66] In 1990, the chancellor of public schools, Joseph Fernandez, sought to rid the system of patronage and raise the quality of public education by exercising greater central review over hiring decisions made by local boards. Community activists charged that Fernandez was seeking to undermine decentralization. Fernandez' successor, Ramon C. Cortines, too, found it necessary to abridge decentralization, announcing plans to take over six schools where failing local leadership, in his words, amounted to "educational corruption."[67]

Yet advocates of decentralization counter many of the criticisms made against decentralization. They observe that expertise does not always lead to superior decision making; it was the alleged experts of the departments who produced the highway planning and urban renewal disasters that destroyed neighborhoods. Moving decision making into the field might sensitize bureaucrats to neighborhood needs and improve the quality of their decisions. On a great many issues neighborhood residents do not need sophisticated training to evaluate the program choices that directly affect their lives.

Advocates of decentralization also argue that economies of scale do not exist for all services. Some services might cost less if they were administered flexibly by field offices or in direct response to community demand. Policing, social work, and education are some areas where services can be better provided on a small scale than by large bureaucratized organizations. Corruption, waste, and inefficiency characterize centralized as well as decentralized systems. Moreover, decentralization does not necessarily increase racial polarization. Such tensions already exist in a community and are not created by community control. Improved minority access to services might even increase citizen satisfaction and thereby reduce tensions.

CONCLUSIONS: CITIZEN PARTICIPATION AND DECENTRALIZATION TODAY

Much of the acrimony that surrounded the citizen participation efforts and decentralization experiments of the 1960s and early 1970s has faded and been replaced by a more cooperative spirit. The nation has undergone a minor revolution; cities and counties across the nation have adopted reforms stressing some degree of participation and decentralization. Also, a new generation of professionalized bureaucrats has been schooled as to the legitimacy of client participation. Bureaucrats now recognize that decentralization helps improve communications, reduce lead time in providing services, and increase responsiveness to citizens by bringing government closer to its clients. Middle-class as well as lower-class residents have an interest in decentralization and citizen participation measures that will make city decision making more responsive to their needs.

Bureaucracies have been more willing to accept the lower rungs of citizen participation as opposed to those participative mechanisms that entail genuine power sharing. The same goes for decentralization. Where decentralization has been introduced, it has been primarily that of the administrative model as opposed to the political type. *(REAL POWER)*

Citizen participation and decentralization continue to provide the basis for reform in a number of important policy areas. Both Dade County (Miami), Florida, and Chicago have commenced major efforts to improve school performance by decentralizing their school systems. In Miami, budget decisions are made at the school level, giving the principal and teachers more power to determine the allocation of resources.

In Chicago, the rules governing the school system were rewritten in 1989 to introduce local control in an effort to give parents and community representatives a new ability to shake up the performance of that city's much troubled schools. Each of the 595 public schools is governed by an eleven-member council consisting of the principal, six parents, two members of the community, and two teachers. In high schools, a non-voting student also serves on the council. Teachers do not dominate the councils. Potential board members are invited to training sessions at which they are taught the basic techniques of budgeting and school management.

The Local School Councils were given unprecedented powers. Each council has the power to hire a principal and decide whether or not to renew his or her contract. Each school was also given discretion on how to spend a lump sum of money under a locally adopted school improvement plan.[68] School decentralization in Chicago proceeded with an immediacy of purpose, and personnel and control of critical resources were transferred to the schools.[69]

Still, despite school decentralization's radical intentions, the early results of school reform in Chicago were uneven at best. Initial survey results indicated that parents and school council members were generally satisfied with the direction of the changes. Teachers, however, were less enthusiastic.[70] School principals were not always responsive to the new community school councils. Also, not all factions of the community possessed the organizational skills or sense of urgency to be able to win policy changes through the system of local school elections and council deliberations. In some instances, reform efforts got mired in conflict.[71] By itself, decentralization was insufficient to offset the many problems that plagued Chicago schools.

Citizen participation and decentralization also represent key elements in a new approach toward managing troubled public housing
projects. Frustrated by the lack of responsiveness of large citywide
housing authorities, tenants in a number of public housing projects
in St. Louis, Chicago, Boston, Jersey City, Cleveland, New Orleans, and
Washington, DC, have turned to resident management.[72] **Resident
management** allows tenants in an individual building or group of
buildings to select their own management board. These tenant boards
can then direct budgets and repairs to where they are most needed
and ensure that service personnel complete repair and maintenance
projects as directed. Resident management should also act to increase
citizen vigilance in keeping drug sales out of the projects and protecting public spaces against vandalism.

Yet resident management does not work well in all public housing
projects. The success of resident management may well be dependent
upon the strength of tenant leaders as well as the technical assistance and
level of funding given to the tenant groups.[73] Also, in many cities the local
housing authority will be reluctant to yield authority and budgetary power
to tenant organizations. Recent proposals by the Clinton administration
indicate a willingness to devolve management to the tenants wherever
possible and to increase flexibility in management everywhere through
deregulation. Yet budget cuts may undermine the success of tenant self-
management organizations.

Decentralization is also an important tool in fighting the difficult
problems posed by AIDS (acquired immunodeficiency syndrome) and
homelessness. Community-based care can provide more humane treatment to AIDS victims at less cost than does institutionalized care. Decentralized approaches in dealing with AIDS also allow for wide-ranging
experimentation in finding new ways to deal with this complex health
and social problem.[74]

In dealing with the homeless, a program of decentralized shelters
permits displaced persons to stay in the familiar and supportive confines
of their communities as they deal with such problems as the loss of a
job, substance abuse, marital tensions, and family breakup that brought
about their homelessness. Decentralized sites provide the homeless
with a sense of normalcy as clients attempt to reestablish themselves.[75]

Decentralization and community organizations are also essential if
the needs of women, especially lower-income women, are to be effectively represented in the city arena. The population near city downtowns
is often dominated by women. Their neighborhoods, busy during the
day, are often abandoned, isolated, and dangerous at night. Women in
these neighborhoods need assured physical safety, access to transportation, and adequate day care. Yet these needs have been ignored in cities
like Houston and Dallas, where corporate leaders and their city hall allies
have dominated decision making. In contrast, in Orlando and San Diego,

participatory mechanisms have allowed women to insist that a greater emphasis on transportation, crime prevention, affordable housing, and the preservation of residential neighborhoods be included in development plans.[76]

Citizen participation and decentralization add to the democracy of local government. But few local governments have successfully dealt with the management problems posed by these reform mechanisms. The most serious problem remains largely unsolved: how to devolve meaningful administrative authority to field offices and power to citizens while at the same time retaining a substantial element of policy-making and oversight control. This issue is one of the critical problems facing local government managers in the 1990s.

NOTES

1. The new literature on using citizen participation to improve service delivery is extensive. Jeffrey Berry, Kent Portney, and Ken Thomson, *The Rebirth of Urban Democracy* (Washington, DC: Brookings Institution, 1993), pp. 34–39, discuss how advocates embraced participatory requirements as a means of empowering middle-class citizens even after early participatory programs aimed at the urban poor proved somewhat disappointing. Coproduction and other means of reforming service delivery will be discussed in further detail in Chapter 8.
2. Berry, Portney, and Thomson, *The Rebirth of Urban Democracy*, p. 10.
3. Edgar S. and Jean Camper Cahn, "Citizen Participation," in *Citizen Participation in Urban Development*, ed. Hans B. Spiegel (Washington, DC: NTL and National Education Association, 1968), pp. 218–22.
4. Sherry R. Arnstein, "A Ladder of Citizen Participation," *Journal of the American Institute of Planners* 35 (July 1969): 216.
5. For a discussion of the politics surrounding the creation of the Economic Opportunity Act, see Daniel Patrick Moynihan, *Maximum Feasible Misunderstanding* (New York: Free Press, 1969); and John C. Donovan, *The Politics of Poverty* (New York: Pegasus, 1967).
6. In Chicago, the machine's control over the local CAA was quite substantial, yielding a situation that Greenstone and Peterson have labeled *minimum feasible participation*. See J. David Greenstone and Paul E. Peterson, *Race and Authority in Urban Politics: Community Participation and the War on Poverty* (Chicago: University of Chicago Press, 1976), pp. 19–24. It is interesting to note that not many local governments acted upon the Green Amendment. In the first six months only about 5 percent of the eligible CAAs were placed under city hall control.
7. Berry, Portney, and Thomson, *The Rebirth of Urban Democracy*, p. 33.
8. Lillian Rubin, "Maximum Feasible Participation: The Origins, Implications and Present Status," *Poverty and Human Resources Abstracts* (November/December 1967).
9. Roland C. Warren, "The Model Cities Program: Assumptions-Experience-Implications" (Paper presented at the Annual Forum Programme, National Conference on Social Welfare, Dallas, May 17, 1971).

10. As a result of the pressure to make budgetary cutbacks, the revenue-sharing program was not reauthorized by Congress in 1986.

11. Advisory Commission of Intergovernmental Relations, *Citizen Participation in the American Federal System* (Washington, DC: ACIR, 1979), chapter 4.

12. Martin Shefter, "New York City's Fiscal Crises: The Politics of Inflation and Retrenchment," *Public Interest* 48 (Summer 1977): 95–127. Also see Douglas Yates, "The Mayor's Eight-Ring Circus: The Shape of Urban Politics in Its Evolving Policy Arenas," in *Urban Policy Making*, ed. Dale Rogers Marshall (Beverly Hills, CA: Sage Publications, 1979), pp. 42–44 and 52–53.

13. See Charles H. Levine, Irene Rubin, and George G. Wolohojian, *The Politics of Retrenchment: How Local Governments Manage Fiscal Stress* (Beverly Hills, CA: Sage Publications, 1981); and Irene S. Rubin, *Running in the Red: The Political Dynamics of Urban Fiscal Stress* (Albany, NY: SUNY Press, 1982).

14. Berry, Portney, and Thomson, *The Rebirth of Urban Democracy*, p. 40.

15. John Clayton Thomas, *Between Citizen and City: Neighborhood Organizations and Urban Politics in Cincinnati* (Lawrence, KS: University of Kansas Press, 1986), chapters 1, 2, and 7.

16. Rob Gurwitt, "A Government That Runs on Citizen Power," *Governing* (December 1992): 48–54.

17. Arnstein, "A Ladder of Citizen Participation," pp. 216–24. The following discussion relies heavily on Arnstein, pp. 218–23.

18. Desmond M. Connor, "A New Citizen Participation Ladder," *National Civic Review* 77 (May/June 1988): 250.

19. Berry, Portney, and Thomson, *The Rebirth of Urban Democracy*.

20. Gurwitt, "A Government That Runs on Citizen Power," pp. 48–54.

21. Robert F. Pecorella, "Measured Decentralization: The New York City Community Board System," *National Civic Review* 78 (May/June 1989): 207.

22. Lenneal J. Henderson, "Neighborhood Power in the Capitol: Advisory Neighborhood Commissions in Washington, DC," *National Civic Review* 78 (May/June 1989): 209–15.

23. Robert F. Pecorella, *Community Power in a Postreform City: Politics in New York City* (Armonk, NY: M. E. Sharpe, Inc., 1994), p. 123.

24. Ibid., p. 170.

25. Ibid., chapters 6–7. For a more detailed analysis of citizen satisfaction with urban services, see W. E. Lyons, David Lowery, and Ruth H. DeHoog, *The Politics of Dissatisfaction: Citizens, Services and Urban Institutions* (Armonk, NY: M. E. Sharpe, Inc., 1992), chapter 2.

26. Pecorella, *Community Power in a Postreform City*, p. 195.

27. Susan S. Fainstein and Clifford Hirst, "Neighborhood Organizations and Community Planning: The Case and Context of the Minneapolis Experience" (Paper presented at the annual meeting of the American Political Science Association, New York, September 2–4, 1994).

28. Susan S. Fainstein and Norman I. Fainstein, "The Changing Character of Community Politics in New York City: 1968–1988," in *Dual City: Restructuring New York*, ed. John Hull Mollenkopf and Manuel Castells (New York: Russell Sage Foundation, 1991), pp. 315–32, especially pp. 327–28.

29. Carmine Scavo, "The Use of Participative Mechanisms By Large American Cities," *Journal of Urban Affairs* 15 (1993): 93–109, especially pp. 96 and 108.

30. Fainstein and Hirst, "Neighborhood Organizations and Community Planning: The Case and Context of the Minneapolis Experience."

31. Fainstein and Fainstein, "The Changing Character of Community Politics in New York City: 1968–1988," p. 315.

32. Saul D. Alinsky gave the clearest description of his organizing rules in his *Rules for Radicals* (New York: Vintage Books, 1971).

33. Charles Silberman, *Crisis in Black and White* (New York: Vintage Books, 1964), pp. 308–55.

34. Clarence N. Stone, Robert K. Whelan, and William J. Murin, *Urban Policy and Politics in a Bureaucratic Age*, 2nd ed. (Englewood Cliffs, NJ: Prentice-Hall, 1986), pp. 148–49. Also see Robert Bailey, Jr., *Radicals in Urban Politics: The Alinsky Approach* (Chicago: University of Chicago Press, 1974), pp. 61–62; and James G. Cibulka, "Local School Reform: The Changing Shape of Educational Politics in Chicago," in *Research in Urban Policy Volume 4: Politics of Policy Innovation in Chicago*, ed. Kenneth K. Wong (Greenwich, CT: JAI Press, 1992), p. 159.

35. David Gonzalez, "In the South Bronx, the Grass Roots Grow Up and Are the Establishment," *The New York Times*, January 7, 1993. For a more general discussion of the importance of community development to South Bronx revitalization, see William Clairborne, "Reclaiming the South Bronx, From the Grass Roots," *Washington Post*, November 8, 1992.

36. Marion Orr, "Urban Regimes and Human Capital Policies: A Study of Baltimore," *Journal of Urban Affairs* 14, 2 (1992): 173–87.

37. Former Arizona Governor Bruce Babbit (Address delivered to the annual meeting of the National Civic League, Denver, Colorado, October 25, 1989).

38. Margaret T. Gordon, Hubert G. Locke, Laurie McCutcheon, and William B. Stafford, "Seattle: Grassroots Politics Shaping the Environment," in *Big City Politics in Transition*, ed. H. V. Savitch and John Clayton Thomas (Beverly Hills, CA: Sage Publications, 1991), pp. 216–34. Also see Derek Shearer, "In Search of Equal Partnerships: Prospects for Progressive Urban Policy in the 1990's," in *Unequal Partnerships: The Political Economy of Urban Redevelopment in Postwar America*, ed. Gregory D. Squires (New Brunswick, NJ: Rutgers University, 1989), pp. 289–307.

39. Sallie A. Marston, "Urban Growth, Neighborhoods, and the Changing Dynamics of Political Arrangements" (Paper presented at the annual meeting of the Urban Affairs Associations, Baltimore, March 8–11, 1989).

40. Carl Abbott, *The New Urban America: Growth and Politics in Sunbelt Cities*, rev. ed. (Chapel Hill, NC: University of North Carolina Press, 1987) pp. 215–18.

41. Robert E. Villareal, "EPISO and Political Participation: Public Policy in El Paso Politics" (Paper presented at the annual meeting of the Western Political Science Association, Anaheim, California, March 26–28, 1987). Also see Donald C. Reitzes and Dietrich C. Reitzes, *The Alinsky Legacy: Alive and Kicking* (Greenwich, CT: JAI Press, 1987), pp. 129–31.

42. For details on community organizing in San Antonio, see Abbott, *The New Urban America*, pp. 232–41; Sidney Plotkin, *Keep Out: The Struggle for Land Use Control* (Berkeley, CA: University of California Press, 1987), pp. 121–45; David R. Johnson, John A. Booth, and Richard J. Harris, eds., *The Politics of San Antonio: Community Progress and Power* (Lincoln, NE: University of Nebraska Press, 1983), especially Joseph D. Sekul, "Communities Organized For Public Service: Citizen Power and Public Policy in San Antonio," pp. 175–90; Joseph D. Sekul, "The Free Rider Myth and Institutional Mobilization" (Paper presented at the annual meeting of the Urban Affairs

Association, Baltimore, March 8–11, 1989); and Reitzes and Reitzes, *The Alinsky Legacy*, pp. 117–26.

43. Lisa Belkin, "Vote Today in San Antonio Is About a Lot More Than a Stadium," *The New York Times*, January 21, 1989.

44. Reitzes and Reitzes, *The Alinsky Legacy*, pp. 126–29.

45. Curtis Ventriss and Robert Pecorella, "Community Participation and Modernization: A Reexamination of Political Choices," *Public Administration Review* 44 (May/June 1984): 226. Also see Reitzes and Reitzes, *The Alinsky Legacy*, pp. 35–41.

46. Berry, Portney, and Thomson, *The Rebirth of Urban Democracy*. Also see Sallie Marston, "Citizen Action Programs and Participatory Politics in Tucson," in *Public Policy for Democracy*, ed. Helen Ingram and Steven Rathgeb Smith (Washington, DC: Brookings Institution, 1993), pp. 119–35.

47. Berry, Portney, and Thomson, *The Rebirth of Urban Democracy*, p. 21. Also see pp. 22 and 34–39.

48. Ibid., pp. 47–51, 61–63, and 295–99.

49. Ibid., pp. 254–55.

50. Ibid., pp. 81–87; and Fainstein and Hirst, "Neighborhood Organizations and Community Planning: The Case and Context of the Minneapolis Experience."

51. Larry Bennett, *Fragments of Cities: The New American Downtowns and Neighborhoods* (Columbus, OH: Ohio State University Press, 1990), pp. 111–27 and 138.

52. Henry J. Schmandt, "Decentralization: A Structural Imperative," in *Neighborhood Control in the 1970s*, ed. George Frederickson (New York: Chandler Publishing, 1973), p. 19.

53. Howard H. Hallman, *Neighborhood Government In A Metropolitan Setting* (Beverly Hills, CA: Sage Publications, 1974), chapter 7.

54. *Report of the National Advisory Commission*, pp. 32–33; and Eric Nordlinger, *Decentralizing The City: A Study of Boston's Little City Halls* (Cambridge, MA: MIT Press, 1972).

55. Milton Kotler, *Neighborhood Government : The Local Foundation of Political Life* (Indianapolis, IN: Bobbs-Merrill, 1969), pp. 52–54.

56. David C. Perry, "The Suburb as a Model for Neighborhood Control," in *Neighborhood Control in the 1970s*, pp. 85–89.

57. This typology has been analyzed with respect to the Service Area System in Washington, DC. See Bernard H. Ross and Louise G. White, "Managing Urban Decentralization," *Urban Interest* 3 (Spring 1981): 82–89. Also see Henry J. Schmandt, "Municipal Decentralization: An Overview," *Public Administration Review* 32 (October 1972): 573.

58. Douglas Yates, *Neighborhood Democracy* (Lexington, MA: D. C. Heath, 1973), pp. 28–31.

59. See Mario Fantini and Marilyn Gittell, *Decentralization: Achieving Reform* (New York: Praeger Publishers, 1973); Mario Fantini, Marilyn Gittell, and Richard Magat, *Community Control and the Urban School* (New York: Praeger Publishers, 1970); and Maurice Berube and Marilyn Gittell, *Confrontation at Ocean Hill–Brownsville* (New York: Praeger Publishers, 1969).

60. Pecorella, "Measured Decentralization," pp. 202 and 204. Also see Pecorella, *Community Power in a Postreform City*, pp. 155–59.

61. Robert F. Pecorella, "Community Input and the City Budget: Geographically Based Budgeting in New York City," *Journal of Urban Affairs* 8 (Winter 1986): 58–59. Also see Pecorella, "Community Governance: A Decade of Experience," in *Restructuring The New York City Government: The Reemergence of Municipal Reform*, ed. Frank J. Mauro and Gerald Benjamin, Proceedings of the Academy of Political Science 37, no. 3 (1989): 97–109; and Pecorella, "Measured Decentralization."

62. Howard W. Hallman, *Neighborhoods: Their Place in Urban Life* (Beverly Hills, CA: Sage Publications, 1984), pp. 22–27 and 237–38. For a comparison of the developmental model to other models of decentralization, see Schmandt, "Decentralization: A Structural Imperative," pp. 17–35.

63. For a discussion of these problems, see Bernard H. Ross, "The Management of Neighborhood Organizations," *South Atlantic Urban Studies* 4 (1979): 32–42.

64. Douglas Yates, *Neighborhood Democracy* (Lexington, MA: Pegasus, 1970), pp. 102–07.

65. Richard Cole, *Citizen Participation and The Urban Policy Process* (Lexington, MA: D. C. Heath, 1974), pp. 106–11.

66. Joseph Berger, "Decentralization Has Lead Some School Boards Into a Political Quagmire," *The New York Times*, December 13, 1989.

67. Sam Dillon, "Testing Powers, Cortines Taking Over Six Schools," *The New York Times*, April 29, 1994.

68. Barbara Page Fiske, ed., *Key To Government in Chicago and Suburban Cook County* (Chicago: University of Chicago Press, 1989), pp. 133–34.

69. Marilyn Gittell, "School Reform in New York and Chicago: Revisiting the Ecology of Games," *Urban Affairs Quarterly* 30 (September 1994): 136–51.

70. Joe Reed, "Grassroots School Governance in Chicago," *National Civic Review* 80 (Winter 1991): 38–39.

71. Cibulka, "Local School Reform: The Changing Shape of Educational Politics in Chicago," pp. 145–73.

72. Daniel J. Monti, "The Organizational Strengths and Weaknesses of Resident-Managed Public Housing Sites in the United States," *Journal of Urban Affairs* 11 (1989): 39–52; and William Peterman, "Options to Conventional Public Housing Management," *Journal of Urban Affairs* 11 (1989): 53–68.

73. Michael A. Stegman, *More Housing, More Fairly* (New York: Twentieth Century Fund Press, 1991), pp. 81–89 and 120–22.

74. Walter J. Jones and James A. Johnson, "AIDS: The Urban Policymaking Challenge," *Journal of Urban Affairs* 11 (1989): 95–96 and 98–99.

75. Michael J. Lang, "Urban Homelessness and Local Shelter Policy: A Case Study" (Paper presented at the annual meeting of the Urban Affairs Association, Baltimore, March 8–11, 1989).

76. Robyne S. Turner, "Concern for Gender in Central-City Development Policy," in *Gender in Urban Research* (Urban Affairs Annual Review 42), ed. Judith A. Garber and Robyne S. Turner (Thousand Oaks, CA: Sage Publications, 1995), pp. 271–89.

8

Urban Bureaucracy and Service Delivery

THE URBAN BUREAUCRACY PROBLEM

In an effort to rescue government from the clutches of the machine, the reformers sought to professionalize the bureaucracy by instituting a civil service system and establishing standards for employment based on experience and training. A new corps of local government experts would manage the city and service delivery.

But by requiring experience and training or education as a prerequisite for holding a job, the reformers were changing the nature and composition of local bureaucracies. Many of the first- and second-generation immigrants did not have the educational or experiential qualifications to fill the civil service jobs. The result was a growing middle-class composition of service providers in such areas as schools, planning, urban renewal, and welfare. In many cases, the actions of these public officials were influenced by the biases of their middle-class upbringing. By the mid-1960s many big-city agencies were composed of administrators very different in age, race, and attitude from the clients they were serving, who were younger, poorer, and from minority groups.

The reform movement also changed the nature of the linkage between an urban service agency and its clients. The machine had an interest in making sure that bureaucrats provided the services citizens wanted; the citizens would then vote for the machine.

The nature of this relationship changed dramatically as the early twentieth century reforms were instituted and administrators were no longer beholden to the machines for their jobs. The strong ties linking the citizen, the political organization, and the service bureaucracy were unraveled. Power was centralized in a merit-system-protected bureaucracy that became distant from the citizens it was supposed to serve.

Administrative power began playing an increasingly important role in local politics.

According to Theodore Lowi, "The legacy of reform is the bureaucratic city-state."[1] The urban service bureaucracies have become the "new machines" with the power of running cities. Protected by civil service rules and other reform measures, agency heads are extremely powerful and semiautonomous. Also, as a large share of their budgets comes from federal and state sources, agency heads are not subject to direct control by elected municipal officials. The growth in agency power has posed new problems of **accountability**: To whom do these municipal departments answer? As Lowi observes, "Bureaucratic agencies are not neutral; they are only independent."[2]

SOURCES OF BUREAUCRATIC POWER

It could be argued that appointed administrators and career bureaucrats wield more power in making and implementing policy than any other group of actors involved in local political life. However, the size and impact of bureaucracy vary from city to city.

Why do bureaucracies have power? First of all, much of the legislation passed by local elected bodies is skeletal in nature and requires bureaucratic agencies to develop rules, regulations, and guidelines so that the policies can be implemented. This delegated authority to the bureaucrats carries with it a great deal of administrative **discretion**, or the leeway for administrators to decide just how a general law will be applied to a specific situation.

Second, bureaucrats are regarded as the repositories of **expertise**—the specialized body of knowledge concerning the programs assigned to their agencies. Administrators have helped to draft the legislation for a new program, formulate the program's administrative guidelines, and monitor and evaluate the program in operation. As elected officials and appointed department heads come and go in local government, career bureaucrats also help to provide the administrative and program continuity. These bureaucrats retain both the institutional and programmatic memory necessary to keep government functioning.

Third, bureaucrats are often active in **mobilizing outside client groups** to support their activities. These outside groups have a vested interest in the programs of the agency. When bureaucrats sense they are not able to exert enough pressure to influence the important actors on resource allocation decisions, they often quietly pass the word to client groups that external pressure might be welcome and appropriate.

Fourth, bureaucrats have learned the art of **delay**, or prolonging the decision-making and consultation process, thus slowing everything to a standstill. In a process that moves haltingly to begin with, delay can often be fatal to a proposed program or administrative reform.

CHARACTERISTICS OF BUREAUCRACY

In his writings on bureaucracy, the German sociologist Max Weber developed a set of characteristics that help to describe these large-scale organizations. To Weber, bureaucracy represented an important way to organize large groups of people to accomplish specific tasks.

Weber had mixed feelings about bureaucracies. He found them to be efficient and a much-needed way for society to organize action. However, he was also aware that bureaucracies were protective of their power and secretive in their command of important information.

Weber believed that the "ideal type" bureaucracy was characterized by the following patterns:

1. Hierarchy
2. Recruitment and promotion based on competence, not patronage
3. The use of written rules and regulations
4. Fixed areas of official jurisdictions
5. Development of a career system
6. Impersonality in the performance of one's duties[3]

Yet some of these very same characteristics of the ideal bureaucracy have led to a number of the problems commonly associated with bureaucratic organizations today.

Hierarchy connotes a pyramidal relationship among people that defines their role and influence in the organization (see Figure 8.1). There are large numbers of workers at the bottom of the pyramid and progressively fewer workers at each level as you go up the organizational hierarchy. The few direct the many by issuing directives and orders.

While Weber recognized the importance of an agency's **written rules,** hierarchy is also apparent in the many **unwritten or informal rules and customs** that guide agency practices. It does not take a new employee long to determine just which practices are approved by his or her supervisor. A worker quickly determines whether the unwritten rules of a particular office tolerate such personal items as plants, radios, and pictures. Informal rules in organizations are handed down from veterans to newcomers; newcomers are socialized into the agency's mores even when these informal codes of conduct contradict official agency policy.[4] Informal rules constrain an official's behavior and help determine how an agency allocates services to the public.

Rules and regulations have their place in all bureaucratic organizations. However, when carried to extremes, rules and regulations become burdensome and provide obstacles to good service performance. Workers can become attached to the process, and conformity to the rules can become a goal in and of itself. When overconformity to the rules becomes the norm, clients complain that the bureaucracy is insensitive to their individual needs.

FIGURE 8.1
The Pyramidal Structure of a Municipal Bureaucracy

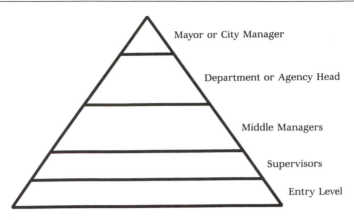

Mayor or City Manager

Department or Agency Head

Middle Managers

Supervisors

Entry Level

Bureaucrats can also use rules as a protective shield. They can hide behind them whenever they are confronted with an unusual or extraordinary request for service. A bureaucrat who sticks closely to the rules significantly reduces his or her chances of getting into trouble.

The literal application of rules can create problems. For instance, rules against loitering in shopping centers exist to enhance the shopping environment and reduce petty crime. But teenagers feel harassed and discriminated against by police who too strictly enforce these rules. Similarly in New York City, police faced a disruptive and potentially violent situation when they attempted to remove the homeless from Tompkins Square Park on the edge of Greenwich Village. Strict enforcement of park rules would return the park to the residents of the neighborhood. But it also created the potential for a violent confrontation with the homeless who lived in the park.

Another characteristic of bureaucratic organizations is **specialization**, whereby each worker concentrates his or her efforts on only a narrow portion of the agency's tasks. There is specialization of knowledge so that different people are working on different components of a complex program or an issue. There is also specialization by function. Within each department there are specialists working on different aspects of the department's work. In a health department there are specialized units for mental health, prenatal care, disease control, and outpatient care.

One disadvantage of this division of labor or specialization is that it leads to parochialism. Each division sees problems from its own narrow vantage point; few officials have the broader view as to how the agency overall is performing its mission. Specialization often precludes a bureaucrat from dealing in a holistic way with the "total" client.

The norm of **impersonality** demands that bureaucrats treat all clients equally; the personal opinions or feelings of the bureaucrat do not enter into the process. Impersonality contributes to bureaucratic impartiality and neutrality in the provision of services, but at a cost. Bureaucrats are often discouraged from being sensitive to a client's individual needs, as the bureaucracy is intentionally structured to allow large numbers of people to be processed in the most expeditious manner possible.

STREET-LEVEL BUREAUCRACY

The importance of bureaucracy at the local level is magnified by the fact that its employees are in daily contact with the clients they serve. This contact places unusual demands and burdens upon local bureaucrats.

It is too easy to look at the Weberian hierarchy of a bureaucracy and assume that only the top administrators make the important policy decisions and that low-level bureaucrats just complete tasks as they are told. According to Michael Lipsky, quite the opposite is often true. In many ways the people at the bottom of the bureaucracy have the power to decide whether and how services are to be dispensed to citizens:

> There are many contexts in which the latitude of those charged with carrying out policy is so substantial that studies of implementation should be turned on their heads. In these cases policy is effectively "made" by the people who implement it.[5]

Lipsky uses the term **street-level bureaucrats** to refer to "those men and women who in their face-to-face encounters with citizens, 'represent' government to the people."[6]

The ranks of street-level bureaucrats include police officers, teachers, housing inspectors, judges, welfare workers, and other service providers who regularly interact with clients or citizens. The work of these employees is characterized by several factors that differentiate them from bureaucrats who serve at a greater distance from the public.

First of all, street-level bureaucrats often serve **nonvoluntary** clients who are dependent upon agency action for the provision of vital services. In some cases clients have no alternative sources to turn to for support. Other bureaucrats like court officials, the police, and building and health inspectors have the authority to intrude directly on people's lives. Clients cannot "vote with their feet" and penalize an agency for poor service by going to another provider of assistance. As a result, Lipsky states, "Street bureaucrats usually have nothing to lose by failing to satisfy clients."[7]

Street-level bureaucrats also possess a high degree of independence or **discretion** in making decisions. Their actions in the field are not easily reviewed by superiors in the organization.

Street-level bureaucrats also often operate under conditions of severe job **stress**—stress that does not typically characterize the jobs of employees who perform more routine jobs such as processing drivers' licenses. Lipsky observes three sources of stress among street-level bureaucrats:

1. **Inadequate resources.** Street-level bureaucracies lack sufficient resources to do their required tasks. Police forces are under-staffed, welfare workers face caseloads that preclude individual-ized assistance, and class sizes are too big for effective teaching. Under these conditions street-level bureaucrats often make hasty decisions, using limited information in order to process people and problems as quickly as possible.

2. **Physical and psychological threat and challenges to authority.** Many street-level bureaucrats either work under or think they work under conditions that are physically or psychologically dan-gerous. Some, like police officers, fear death, while others, like social workers, housing inspectors, and teachers, either travel through hostile neighborhoods or work in threatening settings. Alternatively, sometimes the fear can be just of losing control or of being overwhelmed by the job.

3. **Contradictory or ambiguous job expectations.** Many bureau-crats are unsure of what is expected of them in the performance of their jobs. Besides the formal rules and regulations, there are also pressures for action imposed by elected officials, superiors, coworkers, clients, media, and friends. Each of these groups ex-pects the bureaucrat to perform a somewhat different version of the job. Teachers, for instance, are expected to respond to both slow learners and gifted children. Welfare workers are expected both to help the needy and to guard the public purse. Often these demands are mutually exclusive. To perform one well is to slight the other.[8]

In order to deal with the stress accompanying their jobs, street-level bureaucrats develop **defense mechanisms** to reduce threats they face in their jobs. They also develop **coping strategies** in response to the prob-lems of inadequate resources and ambiguous expectations. Street-level bureaucrats develop routines and stereotypes which help them to simplify their work tasks; they use shortcuts in decision making, **categorizing clients** and **reading cues.** Police officers scour communities looking for tell-tale signs that a crime has been committed—broken glass, open doors, or the "wrong" type of person walking down a residential street late at night. Teachers allocate their time to students after first categorizing them by their behavior, dress, and records of performance in past classes. But what may seem to the street-level bureaucrat to be an efficient allo-cation of resources on the basis of expert judgment might to a citizen appear to be an act of discrimination.[9]

The quantity and quality of services that a citizen receives are to a large measure determined by street-level bureaucrats. According to Jeffrey

Manditch Prottas, the decisions of street-level bureaucrats are particularly important in **slotting** or determining just how citizens are categorized in their initial dealings with a public agency. As Prottas observes, the

> public service bureaucracy does not distribute goods among clients, but distributes clients among goods. The work of the bureaucracy consists of categorizing and processing people as a precondition to their receiving benefits—not unlike an ordinary factory where materials are processed as a precondition to their sale. In this sense, the clients of a public service bureaucracy play the role of the organization's raw material: the real work of the employees is remolding clients to define their relation to the agency as consumers.[10]

It is often difficult to change the initial categorization or determinations that an agency makes; how a client is first slotted or labeled may determine all future treatment and response that an individual receives from an agency.

Limited resources and personnel also force agencies to limit or **ration** the services delivered to clients. Agency personnel may make citizens fill out intricate and confusing forms, apply for welfare assistance in full public view, come back for return visits, or otherwise intimidate or stigmatize clients, thereby reducing the demands on the agency for service. Agencies can also refuse to alter their routines in response to citizens' demands for new services.[11]

Agencies impose "costs" on clients as a means of rationing services.[12] Clients can be made to wait a long time before receiving services; they may even be required to come back for a second interview. A number will tire of waiting or will be unable to keep their return appointment; as a result they will not avail themselves of services to which they are entitled.

An agency's virtual monopoly over information helps to preserve its prerogatives in decision making. While some clients may possess adequate information to work the system to their advantage, others lack the elementary information needed to request service and gain entry to the system. An agency's rules and regulations can also prove to be unfathomable to clients. Decisions can be couched in professional jargon not easily understood by the agency's clients or the citizenry at large.

The resulting **mystification** of agency rules and procedures means that both clients and the public will often lack the understanding necessary to challenge an administrative decision. A parent, for instance, may be unable to understand, and therefore challenge, the logic by which school professionals justify assigning a student to one set of classes as opposed to an alternative program. Similarly, in the late 1960s planning agencies repeatedly made their master, sector, and function plans available to the public in ways that made it barely understandable to citizens what was being presented to them. Only when citizen groups hired their own planners did they develop the capacity to interpret and challenge these plans. In pressing their rights to service, clients often need the assistance of advocacy groups and trained professionals and paraprofessionals to help guide them through the morass of an agency's procedures.

As noted above, street-level bureaucrats enjoy a considerable degree of **autonomy** in the performance of their duties, since it is extremely difficult for the central office of each agency to constantly monitor the activities of this scattered network of employees, many of whom move from place to place in the performance of their jobs. Many street-level bureaucrats perform their jobs in the field, completely isolated from direct supervisory review; these include teachers in classrooms, outreach social workers in the home, police officers in patrol cars, and housing inspectors in individual apartments. Better monitoring of the activities of street-level bureaucrats could be achieved, but at a very high cost to the agency.[13]

Of course, it would be a mistake always to look upon street-level bureaucrats as causing problems in service delivery. While the conditions of job stress often lead to bureaucratic shortcuts and defensive reactions not always in the interests of the client, at times street-level bureaucrats act as "heroes" and provide client-serving action beyond expectations. Such was the case in the implementation of special education reform in Massachusetts. The Massachusetts program sought to mainstream developmentally disabled children into regular classrooms. But the program also made teachers' jobs more difficult. Teachers were expected to give individualized treatment in the classroom to an even greater range of students than they had before. They also had to cope with new demands for lesson preparation as well as with endless meetings with parents, administrators, legal staff, and special education and support personnel. The fact that the program worked as well as it did was a tribute to the dedication of a great many of the teachers involved.[14]

Lipsky has observed that the urban service bureaucracies are increasingly populated by **new professionals** dedicated to responding to client needs, not simply following agency rules. The problem, however, is one of "keeping new professionals new" and committed to client service despite the arduous demands of their daily work settings. **Peer support** and appreciation may be a crucial element in keeping these new idealistic recruits client-oriented.[15] Bureaucrats who feel that their efforts are recognized and valued by peers are less likely to "burn out" on the job.

PROFESSIONALISM AND URBAN BUREAUCRACY

A final characteristic of contemporary urban bureaucracy is increased **professionalism**—which denotes more than the fact that an employee has had some advanced training or higher education. Professionalism also implies an accepted set of methods or code of conduct and practices that has been developed and utilized.[16] The professional is inner-guided and committed to a higher service ethic; a professional will behave in a much different way than does an ordinary bureaucrat.

The concerns of professionals also extend beyond the specific local jurisdiction in which a member may work. Professional associations provide the local administrator with new program ideas and valuable continuing education and technical assistance.

The growth of the urban service professions and professionalism over the last twenty to thirty years has been enormous. Education, engineering, and social work are among the urban service fields that have witnessed the highest degree of professionalization. Employment in these fields usually requires a college degree and state certification; higher education is often required for job advancement. In contrast, police officers and firefighters comprise a group of semiprofessionals. Educational standards and in-service training in these fields have increased, but not to the extent apparent in the more clearly established professions. On the bottom end of the ladder are such occupations as highway workers and municipal clerical help, where low pay, the lack of advanced education, and high turnover rates have hindered the development of professionalism.

While increased professionalism is often seen as good, professionalism can also create new problems in agency-client relations. A professionalized urban service agency may intimidate potential clients from requesting services.[17] Professionals are also guided by norms that are a product of their background, education, and peer influences; their orientations, however, may not be shared by an agency's clients. Professionalism thus may decrease responsiveness to citizens, as some professionals deem it more desirable to follow the norms established by their peers in the profession than to "give in" to citizen demands.

A professional's concern for career advancement, too, may lead to service patterns that are not always in the interest of the client. For instance, many bureaucrats screen potential clients in a selection process know as **creaming.** They serve those agency clients who appear most likely to be able to respond to the agency's professionalized services. The professional can thereby show a demonstrated pattern of success that can be used to justify enhanced program funding or the individual's prospects for promotion. But the cost of creaming is that clients with the greatest need will be ignored.

THE NEW IMPORTANCE OF SERVICE DELIVERY

The primary purpose of urban bureaucracies is to deliver public services to citizens. The way bureaucrats deliver a service often determines how that service will be viewed by clients and whether or not a program will meet its stated objectives. The success or failure of most urban programs rests with bureaucrats.

Questions of urban service delivery have come to occupy increasingly important positions in the urban arena. Douglas Yates summed up the new importance of service delivery in the urban politics of the post-1960s:

> After a decade of protest and demands for participation and community control, urban government appears to be entering a new era. Now that the "urban crisis" has been discovered, debated, and in some quarters dismissed, government officials and academic analysts alike have increasingly come to focus on "service delivery" as the central issue and problem of urban policy-making.[18]

EFFICIENCY, EFFECTIVENESS, AND EQUITY

Three criteria used with great frequency in assessing service delivery are efficiency, effectiveness, and equity. **Efficiency** measures are concerned with costs. How can a unit of government maximize its output from a specific allocation of resources? What is the cost of each unit of goods or services an office, agency, department, or city as a whole produces? Efficiency measures tell us how much it costs to collect one ton of garbage, keep a police officer on the beat, treat a drug overdose patient in an emergency room, or operate a city bus on a per-mile basis. Efficiency measures do not tell us how well we do any of the above—just how much it costs to perform the service; efficiency measures tend to ignore issues of equity or fairness. Since the budget process plays such a paramount role in local government, it is not surprising to find that local officials often think in terms of efficiency criteria.

Effectiveness measures are concerned with objectives, with how well problems are being solved. Effectiveness measures are goal-oriented and focus on analyzing outcomes as opposed to the costs of service delivery. Is a governmental agency meeting its objectives? Are health care services readily available? Have elementary school test scores improved? Has crime been reduced in the central business district? Are public housing units all receiving heat and hot water?

The third term, **equity**, denotes fairness. But this concept presents difficult problems for guiding urban service delivery because there are competing definitions of fairness. In their study of Oakland, California, Frank Levy, Arnold Meltsner, and Aaron Wildavsky suggested three different approaches to the concept of equity.[19] First, equity could mean **equal opportunity** under which all citizens would receive the same level of service regardless of their level of need or the amount of taxes they paid. Trash collection, snow removal, and environmental protection are services that cities generally tend to provide in accordance with this principle of equity.

A second interpretation of equity is labeled **market equity.** Under this definition citizens receive services in rough approximation to the amount of taxes they pay. The more taxes a citizen pays, the higher the level of service he or she should receive, just as if the service had been purchased on the private market. In this system there is no adjustment for need.

When citizens in well-to-do or gentrifying neighborhoods demand an increased allocation of services as a result of the taxes they pay, they are voicing a demand for market equity. Metropolitan fragmentation can also be defended as promoting market equity. Residents in upper-middle-class suburbs generally enjoy better service levels as a result of the money they pay in taxes.

A third standard of equity is that of **equal results.** Under this type of equity, agencies are instructed to allocate resources so that citizens are in approximately equal status after funds have been expended and services provided. Persons with greater needs are given proportionately more services. Most social service and public welfare programs reflect this redistributional version of equity.

Finally, a fourth possible definition of equity, one not raised in the Oakland study, can be called **equal access.** Under this definition equity is achieved when poor people and minorities are empowered, and the political and administrative processes are opened up to allow all interested parties equal access to the decision-making process. Political bargaining then determines the results that each group receives. Some groups will win and some will lose, but all will have had an equal chance to influence the political and administrative processes.

WHO GETS WHAT? THE IMPORTANCE OF BUREAUCRATIC DECISION RULES

What determines how services are allocated by city governments, and what types of equity (or inequity) characterize the municipal arena? Is there a conscious effort by those in power to discriminate against certain groups or geographical areas in the city? Or are differences in levels of service better explained by a subtle or unconscious bias unintentionally imposed on the service delivery system?

One popular view of urban services can be called the **underclass hypothesis.** The underclass hypothesis suggests that poorer and minority neighborhoods are discriminated against in service delivery. The underserving of disadvantaged neighborhoods could be the result of racial and class biases; it could also simply reflect the lack of power of the poor in the political arena.

But a competing hypothesis emerges. Urban services may not always be characterized by a consistent pattern of discrimination against the urban poor and racial minorities. Instead, there may be unpatterned inequalities in municipal service delivery that simply reflect the internal **administrative decision rules** and procedures that agencies use to guide their actions.

In recent decades, the study of urban politics has pointed to the importance of these internal decision rules. According to this point of view, the level of services a community receives is not the result of conscious discrimination but is largely determined by decision rules made within the agency. These rules are seen by the bureaucracy to promote efficiency, effectiveness, and fairness. Occasionally citizen groups may succeed in stimulating a bureaucracy to become more responsive by altering its service delivery rules. However, this is not likely to happen very often.[20]

Is it underclass discrimination or bureaucratic decision rules that determine who gets what in city politics? In his study of San Antonio, Robert L. Lineberry found no consistent pattern of underservice based on race.[21] He offered a less conspiratorial hypothesis. Instead of focusing on political, racial, ethnic, and class factors, the **ecological hypothesis** sees age, population density, the state of housing disrepair, and other relevant criteria as determinants of what services are provided a neighborhood. Services are distributed in response to need and demand:

> The private Santa Claus delivers his largesse in rough correspondence to family incomes. The public Santa Claus is not much more equal in his allocation, but his largesse is only weakly related to socioeconomic status. Ecological factors carry us somewhat further than considerations of power and status. Age and density of neighborhoods are, on the whole, more closely tied to their service levels than are the class, racial and political characteristics of their residents.[22]

Lineberry also found some evidence to support the importance of bureaucratic decision rules. Bureaucrats generate formal and informal rules to cope with the complexities and conflicts inherent in their jobs. These rules and regulations provide guidelines for action that routinize work and make service delivery predictable.

Lineberry's conclusions about service delivery in San Antonio are consistent with the earlier findings of Levy, Meltsner, and Wildavsky in Oakland. In the Oakland study the authors found little evidence to support the popularly held view that urban services were consistently provided at lower levels to low-income communities and at higher levels to high-income communities. This pattern was observed in some cases, but not in others. In other service areas there was no evidence that any one group enjoyed favored treatment.[23]

A number of studies have confirmed the importance of a bureaucracy's decision rules as well as ecological factors in determining the allocation of services. For example, the importance of bureaucratic rules can be seen in the operations of municipal sanitation departments. The sanitation department in one city might decide on the seemingly egalitarian rule of picking up refuse from each and every household once a week. But the sanitation department in another city might try to keep all neighborhoods equally clean; hence, it might decide to send its trucks more frequently to those neighborhoods where more garbage is generated.[24] The point, quite simply, is that the bureaucracy's internal rules, not a neighborhood's racial or social class composition, appear to have the greatest impact in determining patterns of service delivery in a city.

Yet, the work of Lineberry and others is not universally accepted. The authors of at least one competing study suggest that it would be premature to reject the underclass discrimination hypothesis. According to these authors, earlier studies incorrectly observed that poorer districts suffered no discrimination—only because poorer neighborhoods located near central business districts appeared to receive police and fire protection and other services that a city provides to its daytime work force. Figures on service delivery in such downtown residential neighborhoods are artificially inflated.[25]

POLITICAL FACTORS:
ANOTHER INFLUENCE ON URBAN SERVICE DELIVERY

So far we have observed the importance of ecological factors and a bureaucracy's decision rules in determining how services are distributed. Yet in many cities suspicions persist that disadvantaged communities suffer from an underallocation of services.

Just what influence do citizen and neighborhood groups have when they apply pressure on government to change or improve services? Bureaucracies are often unwilling to make major changes in service delivery in response to citizen pressure. Can active citizen groups force a bureaucracy to change its usual way of doing things?

Bryan Jones looked at the enforcement of building codes in Chicago in an attempt to determine if organized community groups and locally based political parties could affect service delivery. Consistent with other studies, the bureaucracy's internal decision rules proved to be important. He also found that the influence of the Chicago machine's ward-based political party organization was felt at all stages of the political process affecting service delivery. In contrast, he discovered very little evidence to indicate that organized community groups had any impact on service delivery in the city: "Community organizations, with their small paid staffs and volunteer labor, cannot provide the day-to-day incentives that are necessary to keep government agencies constantly in touch with citizens."[26] Similar studies in other cities have repeatedly shown evidence of bureaucratic decision rules dominating the allocation of urban services in such areas as parks, libraries, housing inspections, schools, and street maintenance.[27] Bureaucratic rules and professional norms, not political forces, appear to be the important factors in determining the allocation of services in a city.

However, more than one study has come to the opposite conclusion. A reexamination of Chicago parks data shows that bureaucracies are not insulated from politics; politics plays an important role in determining the allocation of park land and park facilities in Chicago.[28] A study of 140 school districts, too, has found that political factors, such as electoral impacts, have much stronger influence on urban service patterns than the bureaucratic decision rules, as the earlier research implied. Simply put, in important, visible service areas like education, political factors affect urban service delivery. Residents can mobilize and affect the decisions of urban bureaucracies.[29]

COPRODUCTION AND NEIGHBORHOOD-BASED SERVICE DELIVERY

Alternating periods of inflation and economic stagnation, coupled with the federal aid cutbacks beginning in the Reagan-Bush years, played havoc with local government budgets and led cities to search for innovative ways to reduce the costs of service delivery. In a number of cities— including Philadelphia, Cleveland, Seattle, Kansas City, Indianapolis, Jersey City, Denver, and Minneapolis—dynamic mayors recognized that, as substantial increases in federal aid were not forthcoming, service improvement would have to come through better local service delivery.

COPRODUCTION

One alternative available to local officials is called **coproduction,** in which citizens work jointly with government in the provision of desired services. The quantity and quality of services available to neighborhood residents are determined by the efforts of both service providers and clients. Citizens who complain about high crime rates, dirty streets, or unacceptable reading levels in the schools have the option of working to improve service. For example, citizens fearful of rising crime rates have begun street patrols and neighborhood watch programs to monitor activity in their communities.

One recent coproduction success story occurred in the Park Slope section of Brooklyn, where harassed and angry residents decided to fight back against the rising tide of muggings, burglaries, and drug dealing. Led by long-time resident Terri Asch, the community instituted an informal block watch program. Unfortunately, it took the criminals only a short time to work around this minor inconvenience. Terri Asch then founded the North Slope Alliance, which blended the talents and resources of twelve block associations.

Working closely with local police in its precinct, the alliance put its first private patrol car on the street, keeping watch on the community. The cost was about $600 per week, paid from collections raised by the alliance. Each brownstone was assessed $1 per night. In a few months the alliance raised enough money to fund three patrol cars, each working sixteen hours a day. Initial reports indicate the patrol cars thwarted four felonies in progress, apprehending the criminals and calling the police on their car radios to come and make the official arrest.[30]

Coproduction is also evident in a number of smaller actions. Homeowners help make their areas safer by turning on outside lights when the sun sets. Neighborhood cleanliness is not a result of just trash collections by the sanitation department. Local communities engaging in organized antilitter efforts and community clean-up days invariably are cleaner than communities where no similar efforts are made. Neighborhood associations similarly can "adopt" and take care of a local park. Parents who volunteer to assist in remedial reading or math programs in the schools are helping to coproduce an important service that can improve the quality of their children's education.[31] Active involvement by citizens not only improves service levels but also produces financial savings for local agencies.[32]

Some critics, though, charge that coproduction is a "rip-off" where citizens supply the time and labor, in addition to their tax dollars, to improve service quality. Coproduction may also serve to exaggerate class-based inequities in service provision, especially if only upper-status people have the time and motivation to volunteer as well as the money to donate in order to supplement public service provision.[33] Despite this criticism, coproduction can be defended, as it allows citizens to decide how and when to participate and just what needs they would like met. As Rick Wilson points out:

> [C]oproduction is a broad form of citizen participation, directly impacting on service delivery, while simultaneously satisfying such traditional participatory functions as enabling citizens to express their preferences, inducing official and producer responsibility, and serving as an instructive information-gathering device for citizens.[34]

Coproduction has already proved to be an important element in the community fight against AIDS. Traditional public health facilities are incapable of handling the growing caseload. Patients in the later stages of the illness have difficulty in getting to out-patient clinics, and hospital care, especially extended care, proves expensive. Further, private nursing homes and convalescent care facilities are reluctant to admit AIDS patients. San Francisco has attempted to meet these problems by using volunteer and existing nonprofit and community organizations in the gay community for public health education, risk-reduction strategies, home-based health care, psychological counseling, and long-term care. Such cooperative community-based efforts provide a caring alternative to hospitalization and add to both the cost efficiency and effectiveness of service delivery. "Estimates are that the cost of care for an AIDS patient in San Francisco is only half that of care for a similar patient in New York City."[35]

NEIGHBORHOOD-BASED SERVICE DELIVERY

Another set of options relates to the establishment of a neighborhood-based service delivery system. To achieve this, local governments devolve power to neighborhood organizations that in turn deliver services to local residents. Neighborhood organizations can develop their own service delivery system under contract with city or county government. Alternatively, they might choose to purchase services from other political jurisdictions or contract with private firms for the purchase of services.[36]

Neighborhood delivery of services and other forms of decentralization (which we reviewed in Chapter 7) have often been proposed as a panacea that will solve the many ills that plague urban service delivery. However, few of the more extensive proposals for neighborhood-based service delivery have been enacted, and the few that have been enacted are only moderately successful.

CONTRACTING AND PRIVATIZATION

Some of the more far-reaching or radical attempts to reform urban service delivery have centered around **privatization** efforts that seek to make public sector operations more like those of the private sector. Where possible, private sector action can even substitute for government action. Conservatives and Republicans have traditionally called for privatization, in their efforts to limit government. But increasingly, privatization is viewed by local managers in nonideological terms simply as a means of making scarce public resources go further.[37]

Privatization is based on the distinction that can be made between providing and producing public services:

> [T]o provide a service is to decide that a service shall be made available and to arrange for its delivery. This is an integral part of a local government's policy making process. To deliver a service is to actually produce the service. Although a local government may decide to provide a service, it does not necessarily have to be directly involved in its delivery.[38]

A government may choose to have a government agency produce a service; alternatively, it can choose to utilize private sector firms or nonprofit agencies to deliver services in the public interest.

Among the most significant of the privatization strategies available to local government is **contracting with private and nonprofit intermediaries** for the provision of public services. Contracting implies a legal relationship between two parties in which one agrees to deliver a good or a service and the other agrees to pay a stipulated price for that good or service. Local governments have contracted with private and nonprofit sector organizations for the provision of services in such diverse areas as trash collection, drug abuse counseling, recreational activities, office maintenance, ambulance service, jail administration, and the operation of shelters for the homeless. As we shall see in Chapter 11, intergovernmental service contracts are also quite common.

ARGUMENTS FOR CONTRACTING

Privatization is the subject of a heated political debate. There are numerous arguments for and against contracting government services. Proponents argue as follows:

- Contracting encourages **competition** that reduces costs and improves efficiency. Contractors must be efficient in the performance of their work; otherwise they will lose the city's business to a competitor firm that submits a lower price for completing the contract.
- Contracting allows the government to circumvent the ills and rigidities of civil service. Protected by civil service regulations, public sector workers are too often unconcerned with the performance of their jobs or with their responsiveness to clients. Workers in private businesses, in contrast, must perform effectively and respond to clients' wishes, or else they will lose their chances for promotions and perhaps even their jobs. Similarly, workers in voluntary and nonprofit agencies exhibit a commitment and caring attitude that is too often absent among many government employees.
- Contracting permits certain economies available to the private firms that are not otherwise readily available to government. Private sector firms usually enjoy greater flexibility in assigning work tasks to employees and even in transferring a worker from one division in an agency to another. Private sector firms may also take advantage of their ability to hire part-time employees. In addition, they may pay workers less than the prevailing wage in government.
- Contracting permits the introduction of successful private sector management systems into the production of public services. To mention just one example, greater incentives can be offered to the top managers in private firms than would be permitted in government by civil service and merit-system protection rules.
- Contracting can reduce large, initial capital outlays for infrastructure, equipment, and training.
- Contracting also allows the government the flexibility to expand services only as needed without adding to the size of the permanent work force. Once a task is completed, the government can simply let a contract expire.

In Florida counties, contracting decisions are driven mainly by a desire to reduce production costs and run the county according to businesslike principles. Local growth pressures also led counties to look to contracting as a means of providing necessary services while keeping taxes down.[39]

ARGUMENTS AGAINST CONTRACTING AND PRIVATIZATION

Opponents of contracting also have persuasive arguments. They believe:

- Contracting often costs more when all of the hidden costs are calculated. Some of these involve monitoring the contract, evaluating the work to be performed, turnover time, and training new employees.
- Contracting procedures often encourage firms in the private sector to lowball costs when initially bidding to win a service contract. In subsequent years, costs then rise dramatically to cover the true cost of producing the service.
- Contracting might encourage some contractors to cut corners and deliver inferior quality in an attempt to maximize profits.
- Contracting lengthens the accountability cycle, thereby making evaluation more difficult and increasing the opportunities for corruption. Contracting reduces the local government's ability to make changes rapidly in response to client demands. Contractors can also refuse to alter services in response to public demand, citing the terms and limits of their contract.
- Contracting can reduce the expertise of government employees. Should the contract be terminated, it would be difficult for local government to resume providing the service.
- The public sector has the more successful record of affirmative action hiring. Contracting with private firms might reduce the number of women and minorities in the work force.
- Contracting is antiunion. Unionized municipal work forces could lose their jobs to nonunion firms. Even unionized contractors will have to show restraint in salary demands or work stoppages; otherwise, the city can award the next contract to a competing firm.[40]

Advocates of privatization point to the inadequacies of publicly provided services. Upper-status residents often find local government services so lacking that they privately purchase services necessary to meet their needs. A private community can hire its own security guards to patrol the streets as a deterrent to crime; an individual family can choose to pay tuition at a private school so that a child can receive the education the parents feel is necessary. Lesser-privileged groups rarely have the resources to purchase better services than those provided by municipal government.

Opponents of privatization, though, reject this crude critique of the public sector. They note that many public employees are highly qualified, energetic, and dedicated public servants. They further charge that the privatization ideologues have unfairly contrasted the worst of the public sector with a highly idealized portrait of the way private business works. The pressures of competition do not guarantee that private service delivery will be lean and trim. Firing or transferring a worker, especially a senior worker, in the private business world is not as easy as the privatization ideology would have us believe. Not unlike government, the performance of private business firms, too, is often marred by waste, payoffs, skimming, and corruption. Finally, in the pursuit of profits, private sector firms contracted by the city may sacrifice important public values.

PRIVATIZATION: WHAT THE EVIDENCE SHOWS

In recent years a number of studies have compared public and private agency provision of services. In his study of numerous cities, E. S. Savas has repeatedly found that private trash collection firms offer similar or better services at lower cost than does government. For instance, private firms working in the city collected trash at less than half what it cost the New York City Sanitation Department to pick up the same volume of rubbish. Municipal sanitation in New York costs more for several reasons. Since municipal sanitation workers are unionized, they receive higher pay and more fringe benefits than do nonunion workers. Unions also make it difficult for the city to implement productivity measures and cost-cutting techniques that might reduce the size of its work force. Finally, civil service–protected workers and public monopolies do not have any incentives to be efficient, since their clients have few, if any, service alternatives and they do not have to compete with others to retain their jobs.

Savas and others have examined other cities and found similar gains from privatization in such areas as fire protection, licensing, and inspection services.[41] In the early 1980s the U.S. Department of Housing and Urban Development funded a study that compared contracting with direct service production in eight local government services in the Los Angeles metropolitan area.[42] The eight services were street cleaning, janitorial services, residential refuse collection, payroll preparation, traffic signal maintenance, asphalt overlay construction, turf maintenance, and street tree maintenance. For all services except payroll preparation, the practices of private contractors led to cost savings. Private contractors:

1. Require more work from their employees for equivalent salaries, but with less liberal vacation benefits.
2. Use the least qualified personnel available to perform each specific task.
3. Use part-time employees whenever feasible.
4. Require program managers to be responsible for both labor and equipment availability.
5. Allow first-line supervisors to hire and fire personnel.
6. Use less labor-intensive approaches to produce each service.[43]

The New Wave of Local Government Contracting

Surveys indicate that local governments are becoming more involved in contracting.[44] Cost savings are the primary reason that local government looks to the private sector for help. Cities also resort to contracting when they lack the necessary municipal staff and facilities to deliver services.[45]

In Chicago, Mayor Richard M. Daley has done the unthinkable by reducing the size of the city's work force. Daley, like some other big-city mayors, has had to ask: "What are the legitimate functions cities can afford to perform for their constituents?" Not surprisingly, most cities find that over time they have taken on more and more services that historically have been provided by the private sector. Daley moved to privatize such services as fleet maintenance, tree stump removal, window cleaning, parking garages, abandoned car removal, golf course management, and drug addiction treatment.[46]

Daley initiated these privatization measures as a cost-cutting response to municipal fiscal distress. For Chicago, this was a major change in the way the city provides services. Old-line, machine-oriented mayors, including Richard M. Daley's father, had maintained a large municipal work force as a supply of job patronage. Progressive Mayor Harold Washington sought to give black and Hispanic citizens job opportunities that they had been historically denied. However, as a result of court rulings and settlements, municipal jobs no longer offer Richard M. Daley the patronage opportunities they provided his predecessors. Critics suggest that privatization offers Richard M. Daley a new "pin-stripe patronage"—contracts that the mayor can steer to his backers—that circumvents the restrictions on job patronage imposed by both court rulings and the Shakman decrees.[47]

In sum, Daley has initiated a relatively moderate, very selective contracting process. Political power concerns limit the extent of privatization. Daley has for the most part resorted to contracting for new city services, but he has been reluctant to contract existing services where municipal unions are strong and privatization efforts would displace existing city workers.[48]

Another big-city mayor, Ed Rendell of Philadelphia, has resorted to contracting in response to the severe fiscal pressures that his city faces. Upon coming to office, Rendell found himself faced with a $250 million municipal deficit and a terrible bond rating. He immediately began working with the city council and the unions on plans to privatize services and shrink the size of the municipal work force. Rendell was so upset with the condition of the nationally known Philadelphia Museum of Art that he put guard services and custodial and maintenance services up for public bid. Private companies won the contracts and the quality of services improved; in addition, the city saved several million dollars.[49]

Rendell's ability to turn around a city, thought by some to be the worst managed in the country, has not gone unnoticed. New York Mayor

Rudy Giuliani and Los Angeles' Richard Riordan both contacted Rendell to learn as much as possible about what is working in Philadelphia.[50]

In New York, Mayor Giuliani has looked to contracting as part of a strategy designed to diminish the fabled power and insularity of the school custodians' union. Over the years, the school custodians have been charged with a number of abuses. In the early 1990s, New York's school custodians received as much as $80,000 a year, worked second jobs, and routinely put relatives on the payroll. School custodians, pointing to the powers they possessed under the contract to open school buildings, often were unresponsive to the requests of parents, teachers, and community activists to use school facilities. They even imposed additional fees on groups who sought to use buildings after school hours for remedial classes and recreation. Giuliani sought to pressure the school custodians to accept a new contract that would allow the city to introduce private custodial services into half the city's schools. Giuliani hoped that privatization would both bring about new economies and pressure the school custodians to better performance in the remaining schools.[51]

Giuliani also attempted privatization efforts in a number of other service areas. But his reforms were not always enthusiastically greeted. New York's city council questioned whether privatization would truly produce the service improvements and cost savings that Giuliani claimed. Minority council members, in particular, saw Giuliani's privatization efforts as being misguided by a sense of fiscal efficiency that ignored the service needs of the city's poor.[52]

Even smaller communities have seen the advantages in privatization. In Sonoma County, California, Sheriff Mark Ihde turned to contracting when he found himself spending increasing amounts of time on activities not directly related to law enforcement and corrections. Ihde oversees fifty contracts that cover such services as inmate transportation, food services, helicopter services, and most importantly the privatized medical service, which has saved the county about $370,000 in its first year. Prior to privatizing health services, Ihde says he had no way to control prisoner medical costs.[53]

Many cities, though, are reluctant to convert more services to private contracts as a result of employee opposition, fear of corruption, and obstacles envisioned to active citizen participation.[54] Critics charge that privatization will decrease public control over services and substitute the private sector's profit-making ideology for public values. In some cities, there is little interest in privatization because private firms are reluctant to become entangled in the government rules and regulations that accompany contracts.[55]

Still, despite these deterrents, there is little doubt on one score: As cities search for more economical and effective ways of providing services, privatization efforts will continue. In many areas, private firms can provide services at a higher level and a lower cost to citizens.

THE PRIVATE MANAGEMENT OF PUBLIC SCHOOLS?

One very interesting controversy in privatization relates to the decision of some cities to turn over the day-to-day management of their schools to private sector firms. These firms were to debureaucratize schools in order to allow teachers and administrators more leeway to introduce innovative teaching tools. These firms were also to introduce new managerial techniques and share in any cost savings that were realized.

The privatized management of public school operations has been quite limited. Miami was the first city to contract with a private firm, the Minneapolis-based Educational Alternatives, Inc. (EAI), to run a public school.[56] In 1992 Baltimore signed a five-year contract that allowed Educational Alternatives to run nine of its schools. In 1994, Bridgeport (Connecticut) turned over all thirty-two schools in its much-troubled system to the same private management company. In EAI schools, each student is given an individualized learning plan. Principals and other administrators are relieved from such chores as maintenance and repairs, which are contracted to EAI's partners.

Privatization of public education has severe critics. Privatization efforts are often motivated by an anti-union animus that sees public labor organizations as an obstacle to educational reform. Consequently, teacher unions have opposed the new privatization efforts. They charge that the new managers will not only change the established way of doing things but will also attempt to breach tenure and other job protections. The Baltimore Teachers' Union was the most notable opponent of school privatization in that city. The actions of EAI, after taking over operations of the Baltimore schools, reinforced these fears. In Baltimore, EAI hired nonunion custodians; it also hired college students as teacher aides, at $7 an hour, to replace $13-an-hour union members.[57]

In Bridgeport, provisions in the contract for tenure protection (at least in the short run) did little to assuage fears of teachers and other personnel concerning the possible loss of job rights. Although Educational Alternatives, Inc., agreed to honor the existing union agreement, teachers feared layoffs and a loss of bargaining power at the expiration of the contract.

Neighborhood groups have been mixed in their reception to private school management. Some welcome the introduction as a first step to improving a failing system of urban schools. But in Baltimore, BUILD, the local activist community organization, opposed privatization out of concern that for-profit schools would reinforce capitalist, not community, values.[58]

SCHOOL CHOICE: VOUCHERS, TAX CREDITS, AND MINISCHOOLS

Proposals for the privatization of education go beyond contracting with private managerial firms. Critics of public education argue that present-day schooling is so bad that radical restructuring is necessary. They propose a variety of **school choice** plans that will increase the ability of parents to exercise greater options in their children's education.

Under a system of **vouchers,** students would receive a certificate that they could use to purchase education at the school of their choice. A system of **tax credits,** in contrast, would offer substantial tax advantages to those families that choose to purchase a private school education. Tax credits, in effect, subsidize the cost of a private education; a family's tax bill is partially reduced as a result of credits earned by the money spent on school tuition. Alternatively, some advocates of choice argue that reform can be offered within the public school system through a system of specialized schools or **minischools,** each with its own distinctive curriculum. As we shall see, critics of each method respond that in many ways the various choice plans will exacerbate the classist and racial inequalities in education.

THE ARGUMENTS FOR CHOICE PLANS

Advocates of privatization argue that public schools just cannot perform, and that vouchers and tax credits must be offered to allow students a way out. According to this argument, public school teachers are overly protected by tenure and unionization; their creativity and spirit for innovation are further stifled by a seniority-ridden system of promotion and overloaded educational bureaucracy, with its accompanying rules and regulations. Parents with sufficient money have already opted out of a failing public school system and have sent their children to private and parochial schools. The middle class and the poor are trapped in underperforming public schools that are moving increasingly toward custodial care as opposed to genuine education.

Advocates of vouchers and tax credits further argue that increased choice can promote racial integration. As vouchers and tax credits allow students to attend schools outside their local district, wherever students share a common interest—whether in science, the performing arts, or another discipline—there is the basis for sustained, voluntary integration. Appropriate controls over admissions can also be used to avoid the prospects of segregation.

Some choice advocates argue for a system of vouchers and tax credits that would allow children to choose schools (including private schools) and curricula to match their interests.[59] But other advocates reject vouchers and tax credits and instead seek only to increase the choices available within the public school system.

Among the strongest advocates of increasing choice within the public school systems are John Chubb and Terry Moe, who argue that public school systems suffer from two overwhelming problems. First, public schools are too bureaucratic; and second, the political institutions that govern the system tend to inhibit innovation.[60] Citywide rules and civil service and union protections often act to inhibit creative, innovative approaches in public education. Hence, Chubb and Moe want public schools run more flexibly, like the better private schools. While they would like to see additional options offered to students and parents, they do not necessarily want the public school system privatized; they recognize some of the dangers that vouchers and tax credits pose for public education. Their goal is to restructure the governance of schools and increase the number of schools that participate in choice programs.[61]

Arguments Against Choice Plans

Opponents argue that school vouchers and tax credits are very dangerous plans that will only exacerbate class and racial segregation in education. They charge that, for the most part, only middle-income and upper-middle-income families will have the additional money beyond the value of the vouchers and tax credits necessary to pay for private school tuition. Those who lack the additional money to "add on" to vouchers will have no choice but to attend whatever schools are left after other students have made their choice to leave the system. These schools will be drained of the best students and teachers. The poor, in effect, will be consigned to what will be the dumping ground of an increasingly segregated, lower-class, and underfunded public school system.

Critics also raise a number of other objections against vouchers and tax credits. They point out that well-to-do families whose children are already attending private schools would receive the financial benefits entailed by vouchers and tax credits, thereby diluting the pool of money available for the education of more needy students. To the extent that more children leave the public schools, there will be less support for tax increases and bond referenda to improve public education. Some critics also charge that vouchers and tax credits that aid parochial schools violate the constitutional requirement of the separation of church and state.[62]

A 1992 report by the Carnegie Foundation, a leading educational research group, raised new doubts as to the desirability of choice plans. The Carnegie Foundation acknowledges that "extending educational options is an idea whose time has come." Yet, the foundation was troubled by the fact that the movement toward school choice has been guided more by ideology than by evidence, that "many of the claims for school choice have been based more on speculation than experience."[63] The Carnegie Foundation reviewed school choice efforts nationwide and came to the conclusion that choice plans generally have worked to the advantage of the children of better-educated parents and do not necessarily result in improved student performance.

The Carnegie Foundation further warns that, inasmuch as choice programs often require substantial investments of public money, in the absence of appropriate safeguards choice plans can exacerbate the gap between rich and poor school districts. In Massachusetts, school choice caused fiscal havoc in the financially troubled city of Brockton, from which 135 students transferred to the tiny neighboring district of Avon. While the students who made the switch were pleased with their decision, "The picture is far grimmer for the 14,500 students left behind in Brockton."[64] The students who transferred took with them nearly $1 million in state aid, compounding the impact of other state budget reductions and helping to account for a layoff of 200 Brockton teachers.[65]

MILWAUKEE'S LOW-INCOME SCHOOL VOUCHER EXPERIMENT

Further evidence regarding the effects of school vouchers can be gained by reviewing the experience of the city of Milwaukee. In 1990, the state of Wisconsin enacted the first school voucher program in the nation. The program was intended for students in the Milwaukee public schools whose families had household incomes no greater than 1.75 times the poverty line. Targeted at low-income students, the program sought to avoid the criticism that vouchers were a subterfuge designed to aid well-off families. To further avoid charges of classism and creaming, schools accepting voucher students were barred from discriminating in admissions on the basis of a student's prior educational or behavioral record. Private schools that accepted a former Milwaukee public school student received state aid (approximately $3,200 in the 1994–95 school year) per student in lieu of tuition. To avoid the question of separation of church and state, only private, nonreligious secular schools were eligible to participate in the program. The Milwaukee program is a moderate-sized program that in 1995 was capped at 1.5 percent of the student enrollment in the city—limited to approximately 1,450 participants per year.[66]

Early evidence from the Milwaukee program indicates mixed results. The choice program has attracted students who performed very near the bottom in terms of academic achievement. It has enhanced the options of poor parents, especially poor African-American parents, dissatisfied with the Milwaukee public schools. Yet, while the overall educational climate in the "choice" schools was encouraging, students exhibited little clear improvement on standardized tests.[67] And despite the safeguards, there also appears to be evidence of "creaming" among the poor families who exercised choice, draining students who had more active and better-educated parents from the public schools. Also, approximately half of the students in the program chose not to reenroll for the second year, indicating a number of problems with the choice plan.[68]

The Milwaukee plan was also devised to provide the least possible oversight of private schools in an effort to liberate schools from onerous regulatory strings. The "dangers of this regulatory vacuum," however, quickly became apparent when, in the first year of the program, one school, the Juanita Virgil Academy, which had admitted sixty-three "choice" students, was shut down in the middle of the school year amid charges of mismanagement, lack of books, overcrowding, and poor discipline: "The Juanita Virgil fiasco confronted Milwaukee with the stark reality that when marketplace ideas fail, children suffer."[69]

Wisconsin Governor Tommy Thompson has proposed expanding the voucher plan and allowing parochial schools to participate. But, overall, the Carnegie Foundation found that the Milwaukee plan "has failed to demonstrate that vouchers can, in and of themselves, spark school improvement."[70] While a few students who were able to leave the public schools were pleased with their decision, there was no evidence that these students made significant academic gains or that public schools undertook great improvements in response to the competition offered by the choice alternative. Further, the foundation found that private schools received important subsidies from their teachers, in terms of their low salaries and limited benefits.[71]

THE DEBATE OVER EAST HARLEM'S SCHOOL DISTRICT 4

As we earlier observed, not all choice plans entail vouchers or privatization. Sometimes, choice can be increased within the public school system through the creation of minischools. In the mid-1970s Community School District 4 in New York City's East Harlem offered parents a choice of elementary and junior high schools that students could attend. By the late 1980s fifty-two different schools were created in twenty buildings. The distinguishing feature of the East Harlem plan was that it gave teachers great autonomy to shape the educational program in each school.[72] The District 4 experiment was credited with enabling teacher innovation, increasing school attendance, raising test scores, reducing instances of violence, and facilitating parental control.[73] Advocates of school choice applauded the results obtained in District 4 and held it out as model for the nation.[74]

Harlem's District 4 represents constrained choice. The schools in District 4 are still public schools subject to government rules, political pressures, and public unionization. While defenders of the public schools argue that such constraints are necessary to protect against the dangers of choice, advocates of choice plans argue that vouchers, tax credits, and other more free-market plans can permit the establishment of even more innovative schools free from governmental intrusion.

Critics argue that the results of School District 4 have been oversold. While education in District 4 is undeniably better than what it was before, it is not clear that choice made the difference. Because the administrators of District 4 aggressively pursued outside money, and at one time received more federal funding per pupil than any other district in the country, the improved scores may be the result of new money, not of school choice. When East Harlem began to face the same acute tight money situation that confronted the rest of New York City's schools, the pace of innovation slowed, students received fewer enrichment activities, and the district lost good teachers to schools in suburban Nassau and Westchester counties.[75]

Improvements in reading and other educational scores may also represent the impact of small class sizes, new ways of scoring tests, and the influx into the schools of "good," well-behaved kids from outside the district. To the extent that this is true, the choice arrangements did not improve education for students who already lived in the district. The heightened scores also represent the fact that, given the large number of applicants to attend District 4, certain District 4 schools were quite selective in their admissions.[76]

In sum, East Harlem's District 4 provides an improved education and a path out of the *barrio* for some students, but only at the cost of diverting resources, including good students and parents, from neighboring districts. District 4 schools are in many ways successes. Yet, School District 4 does not provide convincing evidence that choice, as opposed to increases in school spending and selectivity in admissions, made the difference.

SCHOOL CHOICE: PUBLIC OR PRIVATE BENEFITS?

While choice and competition can be used to bring improvements to education, the enthusiasts of school choice have greatly overstated the success of vouchers and similar arrangements. Also, as Jeffrey Henig has argued, market-based plans for education are not always appropriate for public education; they must be kept in their place.[77] School choice emphasizes only the *private* benefits of school, ignoring the traditional role the public schools have played in socializing the nation's future citizens by promoting democracy, community, and *the public good*.[78]

School choice does allow children with special needs choices outside the neighborhood school. Competition may generate market forces that lead public schools to "shape up"—although the evidence here is still less than clear. What is clear is that choice by itself provides no panacea or magic bullet that will remedy the ills of urban education. Overall, choice arrangements can be viewed profitably as only one weapon in a broader arsenal of educational reform strategies.[79]

The Reagan and Bush administrations supported the concept of choice and the expanded use of vouchers and tax credits, not just in education but in the area of housing as well.[80] Both Bush and Reagan faced a difficult time in getting their proposals through a Democratic-controlled Congress. President Clinton, while affirming the virtues of choice, did not share the enthusiasm of his two Republican predecessors for using vouchers and tax credits to create new competition for the nation's public schools.

CONCLUSIONS

The reform movement had a major impact on the structure and operation of local government. By professionalizing and centralizing local government, the reformers took decision making away from the political organizations that in a number of ways were accountable to elected officials and responsive to the people.

Today, bureaucracy and bureaucratic decision rules are important determinants of local services. The distribution of urban public services is to a great extent characterized as one of unpatterned inequalities, even if these inequalities do not always fit the pattern of conscious underclass discrimination. Street-level bureaucrats, too, exercise considerable discretionary power and often make decisions not in the best interests of their clients. Bureaucrats are often criticized for waste, inefficiency, and a lack of responsiveness to citizen demands. Change in bureaucratic service delivery systems will be slow but necessary if we are to increase the quality of life in urban America.

Coproduction, neighborhood-based systems, privatization, contracting out, and the increased use of vouchers, tax credits, and choice systems have all been proposed in an attempt to improve the efficiency and effectiveness of urban service delivery. Sometimes these alternative service delivery techniques are implemented at the expense of equity concerns and concern for broad-scale citizen participation and the public good. The test for urban managers in the 1990s will be to design and to pilot new ideas for greater efficiency and effectiveness in delivering urban services.

NOTES

1. Theodore J. Lowi, "Machine Politics—Old and New," *Public Interest* (Fall 1967): 86.
2. Ibid.
3. H. H. Gerth and C. Wright Mills, eds., *From Max Weber: Essays in Sociology* (New York: Oxford University Press, 1946), pp. 196–204.
4. Joseph Wambaugh has written several novels about police officers, depicting this type of behavior. See *The Blue Knight, The New Centurions*, and *The Black Marble*, all available in paperback. To date no exciting novel has been written about sanitation workers.
5. Michael Lipsky, "Standing the Study of Public Policy Administration on Its Head," in *American Politics and Public Policy*, ed. Walter Dean Burnham and Martha Wagner Weinberg (Cambridge, MA: MIT Press, 1978), p. 397.
6. See Michael Lipsky, "Toward a Theory of Street-Level Bureaucracy," in *Theoretical Perspectives on Urban Politics*, ed. Willis Hawley et al. (Englewood Cliffs, NJ: Prentice-Hall, 1976) p. 196.
7. Michael Lipsky, *Street-Level Bureaucracy: Dilemma of the Individual in Public Services* (New York: Russell Sage Foundation, 1980), p. 55.

8. Lipsky, "Toward a Theory," pp. 198–201. Also see Lipsky, *Street-Level Bureaucracy*, chapters 3–6.

9. Lipsky, "Toward a Theory," pp. 201–04; and Lipsky, *Street-Level Bureaurcacy*, chapters 7–10. Also see Jeffrey M. Prottas, "The Power of the Street-Level Bureaucrat in Public Service Bureaucracies," *Urban Affairs Quarterly* 13 (March 1978): 285–313.

10. Prottas, "The Power of the Street-Level Bureaucrat in Service Bureaucracies," p. 289.

11. Lipsky, *Street-Level Bureaucracy*, pp. 87–116. Also see Jeffrey Manditch Prottas, *People-Processing: The Street Level Bureacrat in Public Service Bureaucracies* (Lexington, MA: D. C. Heath, 1979), chapter 8.

12. For a discussion of the costs of services to clients, see Lipsky, *Street-Level Bureaucracy*, pp. 88–94; and Jeffrey Manditch Prottas, "The Cost of Free Services: Organizational Impediments to Access to Public Services," *Public Administration Review* 41 (September/October 1981): 527–32.

13. See Prottas, "The Power of the Street-Level Bureaucrat in Public Service Bureaucracies," pp. 288–89. Also see Lipsky, *Street-Level Bureaucracy*, pp. 15–25 and chapter 4. Also see a more recent analysis of police supervision in John Brehm and Scott Gates, "Donut Shops and Speed Traps: Evaluating Models of Supervision on Police Behavior," *American Journal of Political Science* 37 (May 1993), pp. 555–81.

14. Richard Weatherly, *Reforming Special Education: Policy Implementation from State Level to Street Level* (Cambridge, MA: MIT Press, 1979); and Richard Weatherly and Michael Lipsky, "Street Level Bureaucrats and Institutional Innovation: Implementing Special Education Reform," *Harvard Educational Review* 47 (May 1977): 171–97.

15. Lipsky, *Street-Level Bureaucracy*, pp. 204–06.

16. See Robert K. Merton, "Bureaucratic Structure and Personality," in *Social Theory and Social Structure*, ed. Merton (New York: Free Press, 1957); and W. Richard Scott, "Professional Employees in a Bureaucratic Structure: Social Work," in *The Semi-Professions and Their Organization*, ed. Amitai Etzioni (New York: Free Press, 1969), pp. 119–22.

17. Frances Fox Piven and Richard A. Cloward, *Regulating the Poor: The Functions of Public Welfare* (New York: Pantheon Books, 1971), chapters 4 and 5.

18. Douglas Yates, "Service Delivery and the Urban Political Order," in *Improving Urban Management*, ed. Willis D. Hawley and David Rogers (Beverly Hills, CA: Sage Publications, 1976), p. 147.

19. Frank Levy, Arnold Meltsner, and Aaron Wildavsky, *Urban Outcomes: Schools, Streets and Libraries* (Berkeley, CA: University of California Press, 1974), pp. 16–17.

20. York Wilbern and Lawrence Williams, "City Taxes and Services: Citizens Speak Out," *Nation's Cities* (August 1971): 10–23. Also see Wayne Hoffman, "The Democratic Response of Urban Governments: An Empirical Test with Simple Spatial Models," in *Citizen Preferences and Urban Public Policy*, ed. Terry N. Clark (Beverly Hills, CA: Sage Publications, 1977), pp. 29–50. Also see Sharp, *Citizen Demand-Making*, chapter 6.

21. Robert L. Lineberry, *Equality and Urban Policy. The Distribution of Municipal Services* (Beverly Hills, CA: Sage Publications, 1977), chapter 3.

22. Lineberry, *Equality and Urban Policy*, p. 147.

23. Levy, Meltsner, and Wildavsky, *Urban Outcomes*, chapter 3.

24. Bryan D. Jones, Saadia R. Greenberg, Clifford Kaufman, and Joseph Drew, "Service Delivery Rules and the Distribution of Local Government Services: Three Detroit Bureaucracies," *Journal of Politics* (May 1978): 332–68.

25. Frederic N. Bolotin and David L. Cingranelli, "Equity and Urban Policy: The Underclass Hypothesis Revisited," *Journal of Politics* 45 (1983): 209–19.

26. Bryan D. Jones, "Party and Bureaucracy: The Influence of Intermediary Groups on Urban Public Service Delivery," *American Political Science Review* 75 (September 1981): 699; also see p. 689.

27. See Kenneth R. Mladenka and Kim Hill, "The Distribution of Job Benefits in an Urban Environment: Parks and Libraries in Houston," *Urban Affairs Quarterly* 12 (1977): 73–93; Pietro Nivola, "Distribution of a Municipal Service: A Case Study of Housing Inspection," *Journal of Politics* (1978): 59–81; and Kenneth R. Mladenka, "The Urban Bureaucracy and the Chicago Political Machine: Who Gets What and the Limits of Political Control," *American Political Science Review* 74 (December 1980): 991–98.

28. David H. Koehler and Margaret T. Wrightson, "Inequality in the Delivery of Urban Services: A Reconsideration of the Chicago Parks," *Journal of Politics* 49 (February 1987): 80–89.

29. Kenneth J. Meier, Joseph Stewart, Jr., and Robert E. England, "The Politics of Bureaucratic Discretion: Education Access as an Urban Service," *American Journal of Political Science* 35 (February 1991): 155–77.

30. Eric Pooley, "Fighting Back Against Crack," *New York Magazine*, January 23, 1989, pp. 38–39. This article also contains success stories of coproduction for the upper west side of Manhattan and Queens.

31. For a discussion of coproduction of services, see Roger B. Parks et al., "Consumers as Coproducers of Public Services," *Policy Studies Journal* 9 (Summer 1981): 1001–11. Additional articles by Charles H. Levine and Jeffrey L. Brudney can be found in a special issue of *Public Administration Review* (March 1984).

32. Richard C. Rich, "Equity and Institutional Design in Urban Service Delivery," in *The Politics and Economics of Urban Services*, ed. Robert L. Lineberry (Beverly Hills, CA: Sage Publications, 1977), p. 128. Also see Stephen L. Percy, "Citizen Coproduction: Prospects for Improving Service Delivery," *Journal of Urban Affairs* (Summer 1983): 203–10; and Roger Ahlbrandt and Howard Sumka, "Neighborhood Organizations and the Coproduction of Public Services," *Journal of Urban Affairs* (Summer 1983): 211–20.

33. Charles H. Levine, "Citizenship and Service Delivery: The Promise of Coproduction," *Public Administration Review* 44 (March 1984): 184; and James M. Ferris, "Coprovision: Citizen Time and Money Donations in Public Service Provision," *Public Administration Review* 44 (July/August 1984): 328.

34. Rick K. Wilson, "Citizen Coproduction as a Mode of Participation: Conjectures and Models," *Journal of Urban Affairs* 3 (Fall 1981): 40.

35. Anne Elder and Ira Cohen, "Major Cities and Disease Crises: A Comparative Perspective" (Paper presented at the annual meeting of the Midwest Political Science Association, Chicago, April 14–16, 1988). Also see P. Arno, "The Nonprofit Sector's Response to the AIDS Epidemic: Community-Based Services in San Francisco," *American Journal of Public Health* 76 (1986): 1325–30.

36. Rich, "Equity and Institutional Design in Urban Service Delivery," pp. 134–36. Also see Marla Anderson, "Neighborhood-Based Service Delivery," *Management Information Service Report* 15 (Washington, DC: International City Management Association, 1983).

37. Bruce W. McClendon, *Customer Service in Local Government* (Chicago: American Planning Association, 1992), p. 104.

38. Carl F. Valente and Lydia D. Manchester, *Rethinking Local Services: Examining Alternative Delivery Approaches* (Washington, DC: International City Management Association, 1984), p. xi. Also see Ted Kolderie, "The Two Different Concepts of Privatization," *Public Administration Review* (July/August 1986): 285–91; and Ronald J. Oakerson, "Local Public Economies: Provision, Production, and Governance," *Intergovernmental Perspective* (Summer/Fall 1987): 20–25. See Donald F. Kettl, *Sharing Power: Public Governance and Private Markets* (Washington, DC: The Brookings Institution, 1993).

39. J. Edwin Benton and Donald C. Menzel, "Contracting and Franchising County Services in Florida," *Urban Affairs Quarterly* 27 (March 1992): 436–56.

40. For an overview of the arguments for and against contracting, see Donald Fisk, Herbert Kiesling, and Thomas Muller, *Private Provision of Public Services: An Overview* (Washington, DC: Urban Institute, 1978), pp. 7–8; Steve H. Hanke, ed., *Prospects for Privatization* (New York: Academy of Political Science, 1987); E. S. Savas, *Privatization: The Key to Better Government* (Chatham, NJ: Chatham House, 1987); and David R. Morgan and Robert E. England, "The Two Faces of Privatization," *Public Administration Review* 48 (November/December 1988): 979–87. An analysis of the role of unions in privatizing sanitation services can be found in Timothy Chandler and Peter Feuille, "Cities, Unions and the Privatization of Sanitation Services," *Journal of Labor Research* 15 (Winter 1994), pp. 53–77.

41. See E. S. Savas, "Municipal Monopolies versus Competition in Delivering Urban Services," in *Improving the Quality of Urban Management*, p. 483; and Roger Ahlbrandt, "Efficiency in the Provision of Fire Services," *Public Choice* 16 (Fall 1973): 1–15; and E. S. Savas, "How Much Do Government Services Really Cost?" *Urban Affairs Quarterly* 15 (September 1979): 23–42. Also see Savas, *Privatization: The Key to Better Government;* and Werner Z. Hirsch, *Privatizing Government Services: An Economic Analysis of Contracting Out by Local Governments* (Los Angeles: Institute for Industrial Relations–UCLA, 1991).

42. Barbara Stevens, ed., *Delivering Municipal Services Efficiently: A Comparison of Municipal and Private Service Delivery* (New York: Ecodata, 1984). Also see Eileen Brettler Berenyi and Barbara J. Stevens, "Does Privatization Work? A Study of the Delivery of Eight Local Services," *State and Local Government Review* 20 (Winter 1988): 11–20.

43. Stevens, *Delivering Municipal Services*, pp. 10–20.

44. Lori M. Henderson, "Intergovernmental Service Arrangements and the Transfer of Functions," *The Municipal Yearbook* (Washington, DC: International City Management Association, 1985), pp. 194–202.

45. *Privatization in America* (Washington, DC: Touche Ross, 1987), p. 5.

46. Charles Mahtesian, "Taking Chicago Private," *Governing* (April 1994): 26–31.

47. Rowan A. Miranda, "Privatization in Chicago's City Government," in *Research in Urban Policy*, volume 4, ed. Kenneth K. Wong (Greenwich, CT: JAI Press, 1992).

48. Ibid., pp. 40–41 and 50.

49. Jacob Weisberg, "Philadelphia Story," *New York Magazine* (May 2, 1994): 30–31.

50. Ibid., pp. 30–31. Also see Neal Peirce, "The City of Philadelphia Tries Reinvented Government," *County News* (June 6, 1993): 14; and Ben Yagoda, "Mayor on a Roll: Ed Rendell," *The New York Times Magazine* (May 22, 1994): 26–29.

51. Alison Mitchell, "Giuliani Warns Custodians They May Lose School Jobs," *The New York Times*, May 13, 1994. Also see John C. Fager, "School Custodians' Dirty Tricks," *The New York Times*, December 18, 1992. The actions of New York city school custodians have been so questionable that CBS aired an exposé on "60 Minutes."

52. Jonathan P. Hicks, "New York Council Votes for Role on Privatization Efforts," *The New York Times*, May 13, 1994.

53. "Sonoma County Sheriff Finds Privatization a Better Deal," *Governing* (July 1994): 41.

54. Patricia S. Florestano and Stephen B. Gordon, "Private Provision of Public Services: Contracting by Large Local Governments," *International Journal of Public Administration* (1979): 307–27; and Florestano and Gordon, "A Survey of City and County Use of Private Contracting," *Urban Interest* 3 (Spring 1981): 22–30.

55. *Privatization in America*, pp. 6–8. Also see Hanke, *Prospects for Privatization*, pp. 124–63.

56. William Celis 3d, "Unusual Public School Aiming to Turn a Profit," *The New York Times*, November 6, 1991.

57. William Celis 3d, "Hartford Seeking a Company to Run Its Public Schools," *The New York Times*, April 19, 1994.

58. Marion Orr, "The Politics of Urban Education Reform in Baltimore" (Paper presented at the annual meeting of the Urban Affairs Association, New Orleans, March 2–5, 1994).

59. A strong case for school vouchers is made by John E. Coons and Stephen D. Sugarman, *Education by Choice: The Case for Family Control* (Berkeley, CA: University of California Press, 1976). Coons and Sugarman propose a tightly regulated voucher system that does not allow parents to use their own wealth to supplement the vouchers. This proposal is quite different from the more unregulated voucher proposals advanced by other advocates of privatized schooling.

60. John E. Chubb and Terry M. Moe, *Politics, Markets, and America's Schools* (Washington, DC: Brookings Institution, 1990), p. 26. Other arguments for increased choice in public schools can be found in Kenneth R. Godwin, "Using Market-Based Incentives to Empower the Poor," in *Public Policy for Democracy*, ed. Helen Ingram and Steven Rathgeb Smith (Washington, DC: Brookings Institution, 1993), pp. 163–97. Chubb and Moe may have overstated their charge that bureaucratic public school governing structures produce ill effects on education. A study of Florida schools found no clear problems resulting from democratic school governing structures. See Kevin B. Smith, "Policy, Markets and Bureaucracy: Reexamining School Choice" (Paper presented at the annual meeting of the Midwest Political Science Association, Chicago, April 17, 1993).

61. Chubb and Moe, chapter 6.

62. For a review of the debate over vouchers and tax credits, see Thomas James and Henry M. Levin, eds., *Public Dollars for Private Schools: The Case of Tuition Tax Credits* (Philadelphia: Temple University Press, 1983). For a cogent argument that the virtues of choice plans have been oversold, see Jeffrey R. Henig, *Rethinking School Choice: Limits of the Market Metaphor* (Princeton, NJ: Princeton University Press, 1994).

63. Ernest L. Boyer, "Foreword" to The Carnegie Foundation for the Advancement of Teaching, *School Choice: A Special Report* (Princeton, NJ: Carnegie Foundation, 1992), p. xv.

64. Carnegie Foundation, *School Choice: A Special Report*, p. 58.

65. Ibid.; also see Susan Chira, "Research Questions Effectiveness of Most School-Choice Programs," *The New York Times*, October 26, 1992.

66. This section's review of the early history of the Milwaukee school choice program is largely based on John F. Witte and Mark E. Rigdon, "Private School Choice: The Milwaukee Low-Income Voucher Experiment" (Paper presented at the annual meeting of the American Political Science Association, Chicago, September 3–6, 1992); and Kimberly J. McLarin, "In Test of School-Voucher Idea, the Sky's Not Falling but Neither is Manna," *The New York Times*, April 19, 1995.

67. Carnegie Foundation, *School Choice: A Special Report*, p. 70; and McLarin, "In Test of School-Voucher Idea."

68. Witte and Rigdon, "Private School Choice: The Milwaukee Low-Income Voucher Experiment."

69. Carnegie Foundation, *School Choice: A Special Report*, p. 67.

70. Ibid., p. 73.

71. Ibid., p. 71.

72. Ibid., p. 40.

73. Edward B. Fiske, "The Alternative Schools of District 4: Accolades and Better Attendance Are Not Enough," *The New York Times*, October 1, 1989; and Manhattan Institute for Public Policy Research, *Model for Choice: A Report on Manhattan's District 4*, Education Policy Paper Number 1 (New York: MIPR, 1989). Also see Chubb and Moe, *Politics, Markets, and America's Schools*, pp. 212–15.

74. Seymour Fliegel with James MacGuire, *Miracle in East Harlem: The Fight for Choice in Public Education* (New York: Times Books, 1993).

75. Carnegie Foundation, *School Choice: A Special Report*, p. 42.

76. For studies that question the evidence normally used to document the success of School District 4, see David L. Kirp, "What School Choice Really Means," *The Atlantic Monthly* (November 1992): 119–32; Billy Tashman, "Hyping District 4," *The New Republic* (December 7, 1992): 14–16; The Carnegie Foundation, *School Choice: A Special Report*, pp. 38–46; and Henig, *Rethinking School Choice*, pp. 131–32 and 142–44.

77. Henig, *Rethinking School Choice*, chapter 9.

78. Carnegie Foundation, *School Choice: A Special Report*, pp. 83–84.

79. Henig, *Rethinking School Choice*, pp. 199–209.

80. The Bush administration's support of different approaches to school choice as attempted in Minnesota, Boston, New York City, and Seattle is described by Carol Steinbach and Neal R. Pierce, "Multiple Choice," *National Journal*, July 1, 1989, pp. 1692–95.

9

Suburban Politics and Metropolitan America

The 1970 census revealed that the United States had become a nation of suburbs. For the first time more than half of the population of America's metropolitan areas was located in suburbs. But as suburbia grew, it was also altered.

This chapter will describe the changing face of suburbia, which is no longer a string of elite bedroom communities. Never entirely accurate to begin with, this stereotype has no validity today. Instead, suburbia encompasses a quite heterogeneous mix of upper-class, middle-class, and working-class communities; residential and industrial suburbs; exclusive dormitory communities and declining inner-ring suburbs; the office and shopping centers of growing "edge cities"; and even far-flung exurban communities that have sprouted at some distance from the metropolitan center.[1]

We will attempt to identify the political attitudes and concerns that shape suburban politics. Two particularly important sets of issues, those concerning school finance and local land use, will be discussed in detail. Finally, we will take a brief look at the future of metropolitan America as suburbanization continues and older political boundaries lose some of their meaning.

A DIVERSITY OF SUBURBS

The image of suburbia in the 1950s was that of an almost exclusively white, middle-class, commuter community near a larger city. Both the literature and popular films of the period, including *Peyton Place* and *The Man in the Gray Flannel Suit*, attacked suburbia for its alleged sterility, boredom, and pressures toward conformity and middle-class success.[2] But even at the time, a number of scholars recognized that this stereotype was not entirely accurate. Bennett Berger's study of the "working-class suburb" of Milpitas, California, then a semirural community just north of

San Jose, identified many aspects of suburban life that defied the conventional portrait.[3]

Much of the 1950s assault on suburbia is clearly dated. With the continued decentralization of diverse populations, jobs, and educational and cultural opportunities, in many ways life in the suburbs can no longer be considered to be "sub" to life in the central city. In fact, Joel Garreau sees the concentrations of office towers, shopping gallerias, college campuses, research parks, and entertainment complexes as dynamic **edge cities,** new centers of concentrated economic activity in the United States.[4]

As suburban populations expanded, a new cosmopolitanism emerged to challenge the provincialism of old. Many suburbs, including communities in southern California's affluent Orange County, are culturally and ethnically diverse and have witnessed growing racial and cultural antagonisms.[5] Feminist scholars criticize suburbs for their social stratification and a "private patriarchy" not supportive of the rights of gays and independent women.[6] Yet, larger suburbs allow a degree of anonymity and lifestyle diversity unimaginable in smaller communities.

On the whole, citizens in suburbia express great satisfaction with their communities. Social commentators, however, continue to point to the environmental consequences of suburban sprawl and to important aspects of community life still missing in many suburbs.

A brief look at the Detroit metropolitan area underscores the diversity of suburbs. Well-to-do communities such as Birmingham, Bloomfield Hills, and the Grosse Pointes have employed their land use and zoning controls to bar all except the most "pricey" and attractive residential and retail development. Yet, not all suburban communities attempt to wield their powers to curtail residential and commercial development; some actually encourage growth. Southfield and Troy have welcomed so many new office towers that these suburbs have virtually been transformed into "satellite downtowns." Auburn Hills has seen an even more spectacular rate of growth, as leaders in this community have aggressively sought high-technology jobs and housing for a technologically competent work force. Auburn Hills rezoned land, created an industrial park and a tax increment financing district, and financed major industrial improvements—all in response to the demands of a growth coalition of property entrepreneurs, bankers, the automobile industry, and officials of both the state government and suburban Oakland University. Professional basketball's Detroit Pistons even moved to the Palace at Auburn Hills, about twenty miles from their old downtown arena.[7] As this overview of the Detroit area underscores, there is no typical suburb.

THE CHANGING FACE OF SUBURBIA

According to the 1950s point of view, people moved to the suburbs for reasons of family. Suburbia was seen as a good place to raise children; it offered back yards, good schools, and relative physical safety.

But the demography of both suburbs and the American population has changed over time. The American population has grown older; divorce is now more prevalent; couples tend to delay marriage. And while family life remains an important aspect of suburban life, suburbia is no longer a place dominated solely by traditional two-parent families and "familism."[8]

The population of the suburbs has clearly aged. The earlier genera-tion of suburban homeowners is now quite a bit older; their children have grown up and, in many cases, have left home. In other cases, elderly citizens have moved to the suburbs in order to escape the social ills of big-city life. The increased number of apartments and condominiums in the suburbs has helped to make suburbia more available to the aged.[9] On the other hand, older citizens in the suburbs still suffer isolation as a re-sult of the unavailability of mass transit, the distances to shopping, and the relative paucity of senior citizen centers and other group facilities.[10]

Feminist studies of the city argue that suburbia fails to provide an ideal supportive environment for women. During the earlier years of sub-urban development, suburban life was criticized as a result of the isola-tion suffered by women who stayed at home. Today, women have entered the work place. But suburban development patterns do not meet the needs of working women and single mothers. Local zoning ordinances preserve the tranquil, residential ambience of suburban neighborhoods by keeping out shops, supermarkets, and other facilities. These ordi-nances make it more difficult for working women to balance career and family responsibilities, as busy women are denied access to stores and services conveniently located in their neighborhoods. Similarly, local or-dinances that restrict child care facilities to commercial zones serve to di-minish the ability of a mother to find nearby, family-based child care run in private homes.[11] The lack of public transportation and the distances involved in suburbia further put the burden on "Mom's taxi," as it must shuttle children to various activities.[12]

MINORITY SUBURBANIZATION AND RESEGREGATION

For years, relatively few African-Americans lived in suburbia, and those who did were concentrated in very few communities. Inner-ring sub-urbs like East Chicago Heights (Illinois) and Yonkers (New York) evidenced a high percentage of minority population as a result of spillover from the central city.

However, the 1980 and 1990 censuses showed a sizable increase in minority suburbanization. During the 1970s alone the number of African-Americans living in the suburbs of the nation's thirty-eight largest met-ropolitan areas jumped from 2.3 million to 3.7 million—an increase of 60 percent in just ten years![13] In the Chicago metropolitan area, the number of suburbs without a single black household dropped from twenty-three in 1970 to just four in 1980.[14] The all-white suburb was a vanishing institution. For many affluent minority families, housing discrimination and central city ghettoization seemed like elements out of the past.[15]

The figures presented even better news for Hispanics. In 1980, for instance, 37 percent of Hispanics lived in suburbs, as compared to the 20.5 percent of the black population.[16] Hispanic suburbs could be found in the southwestern United States, Florida, and southern California.[17] Still, despite these gains, both Hispanics and African-Americans continue to be underrepresented in the suburbs.

MINORITY CONCENTRATION AND THE DANGER OF RESEGREGATION

As the suburban population of blacks and Hispanics tends to be concentrated in a relatively small number of communities, the integration of the suburbs has been very uneven. Nearly one-tenth of the total increase of black suburbanites came in a single county—Prince Georges County, Maryland, which had become a virtual extension of inner-city Washington, DC![18] The greater Washington, Los Angeles, St. Louis, and Atlanta areas account for much of the black suburban gain. In other metropolitan areas, there was relatively little minority penetration of the suburbs. Despite gains in suburbanization, the black urban population continues to be concentrated in central cities: Detroit (central city 63 percent black; suburbs 4.5 percent black); Chicago (40 percent black; suburbs 5.6 percent black); Kansas City (27 percent black; Missouri suburbs 1.3 percent); and Gary, Indiana (71 percent black; suburbs 7.8 percent black).[19]

Even where minority suburbanization has proceeded, blacks and Hispanics have tended to gain access to a suburbia far different from the suburbia of whites. Racial minorities tend to be concentrated in the more aging, distressed, and decaying communities of suburbia. They disproportionately reside in what the Rand Corporation has labeled **disaster suburbs,** including East St. Louis (over 96 percent black), Camden (the distressed New Jersey city just across the river from Philadelphia), and Compton (an extremely poor southern California community where the population is three-fourths black and over 95 percent black and Hispanic combined).[20] These distressed suburbs are not all that different from the central city. African-Americans and other minorities gain very little from residence in declining, inner-ring suburbs at a time when job growth and superior educational resources are increasingly to be found in ever-more-distant, predominantly white **exurbs.**[21] Whites have fled to those communities located on the fringes of the metropolis, places where there are relatively few blacks.[22]

Even though a bit dated, figures from 1980 clearly show that in the Chicago region blacks for the most part gained access to a suburbia different from that of whites. From 1970 to 1980, over half of the growth in black suburban population was absorbed by nine established black communities. The city's racial ghetto had simply expanded across the city's borders to already established black suburbs. In contrast, north and northwestern suburbs, including Forest Park (4.7 percent black), Schaumburg (1.3 percent black), and Skokie (0.7 percent black) received few new minority residents and remained overwhelmingly white.[23] Cincinnati, Cleveland, Detroit, Los Angeles, and Miami are other metropolitan areas where suburban segregation remains high.[24]

In a number of cases, minorities have moved into inner-ring suburbs that are integrated only for the moment. These communities will resegregate as racial transition proceeds and whites seek refuge in more racially homogeneous settings.[25]

Racial Steering and Discrimination

What accounts for the racial imbalance of suburbia? Contrary to widely held belief, it is not the result of differences in buying power and socioeconomic status between blacks and whites. The "Myth of Black Households' Insufficient Income for Suburban Housing" does not stand up to critical examination.[26] Large numbers of black households have the ability to buy or rent homes in the suburbs; African-Americans live in the suburbs at a level below what their buying power would suggest.

Buying power alone does not determine residential location. In Kansas City, blacks and whites of equal income, education, and professional status live in *different* areas.[27] In the St. Louis area, the socioeconomic difference between blacks and whites explains less than 15 percent of the segregation among suburbs.[28] Likewise, if economic factors alone explained residential location, each of Chicago's suburban counties would contain three to eight times the number of black families already living there.[29]

Nor is suburban segregation explained by differences in housing preferences between whites and blacks. Some black families do seek the safety of predominantly black suburbs out of the fear that their children will be unwelcome in the schools in white communities.[30] But survey after survey shows that African-Americans, on the whole, prefer to live in mixed, as opposed to all-black, neighborhoods. Both African-Americans and whites value neighborhoods with high-quality, single-family, detached homes.[31]

Neither differences in buying power nor in housing preferences adequately explain residential separation: "The 'nature of the beast' is race, not class."[32] Racial discrimination is a key contributor to the continuing imbalances, as one survey of the current situation observes: "[T]he residential separation of different racial/ethnic groups is due significantly, though not exclusively, to past and present discriminatory actions in the housing market."[33]

How can discrimination in real estate and rental transactions continue in the face of **fair housing laws** that make it illegal? Real estate brokers and housing finance officers act as "gatekeepers" whose actions help to determine the racial makeup of communities. **Racial steering,** illegal under federal law, has been greatly reduced over the years. Yet, despite the prohibitions of the law, realtors and lenders can still guide or steer nonwhite home seekers to neighborhoods that are already integrated or are on the road to becoming minority dominated.

The enforcement of fair housing laws is rare. Few local governments vigilantly monitor actions in this area. Moreover, the Reagan administration greatly cut the funding of federal fair housing efforts. Although the Clinton administration gave renewed emphasis to fair housing enforcement by the Department of Housing and Urban Development, the federal government has committed only a minuscule portion of the resources needed to monitor discrimination in housing markets across the nation.

Housing discrimination today also occurs in subtle ways that are difficult to detect. Realtors may show racial minorities fewer homes in predominantly white neighborhoods than they show prospective buyers who are white. Or realtors may present minorities with less information about how a financing package for a home in a desirable area can be arranged. Yet, how is the victim to know that discrimination is occurring when he or she does not know how many homes are being shown, or what information is being provided, to other home buyers? It is clear that effective fair housing enforcement cannot rely solely on victim-initiated lawsuits.[34]

Corrective action also requires an **audit** of a community's housing practices to find out whether or not steering has taken place. Discrimination by realtors, lending institutions, and landlords can be uncovered by a process know as **paired testing,** where white and minority individuals who pose as home seekers are matched according to important income and family characteristics. The experiences of these matched applicants are then compared as they seek assistance from realtors and landlords in their feigned efforts to buy or rent a home.

PROMOTING STABLE INTEGRATION: INTEGRATION MAINTENANCE IN SHAKER HEIGHTS, CLEVELAND HEIGHTS, AND OAK PARK

Although whites profess support for living in communities that are racially balanced, genuine support for residential integration is low. There is much scholarly debate over the exact minority population percentage that constitutes the **tipping point** of a community—the point at which whites, observing an influx of racial minorities, quickly leave. According to conventional wisdom, when a community's population becomes 20 to 30 percent black, white flight ensues and racial resegregation occurs. Andrew Hacker believes that, in most communities, the white exodus begins much sooner, when a community's population reaches only 9 or 10 percent black.[35]

In some cases the racial transition of a suburb can be particularly rapid and dramatic. In the early 1900s East Cleveland was the premier suburb of the city of Cleveland. Its population was overwhelmingly white, affluent, and business-oriented. But in the 1960s whites began to flee as East Cleveland faced an "invasion" of African-Americans from the central city's east side. By the 1980s East Cleveland's population was over 90 percent black; over 40 percent were below the poverty line.[36]

While a great many suburban communities have used their zoning and land use powers in ways that have made it difficult for minorities to enter a community, only a handful of suburbs have been willing to make a commitment to sustaining stable integration. These few communities have sought to initiate the programs necessary to calm white fears, maintain high-quality service levels, and promote racially balanced schools and neighborhoods.

The rapid resegregation and decline of East Cleveland spurred two more progressive east side suburbs to initiate positive action in order to avert a similar fate. Shaker Heights and Cleveland Heights represent possibly the two most notable instances of voluntary efforts by suburban communities to maintain a stably integrated population.

Facing the prospects of the suburb's racial transition and resegregation, the city council of Shaker Heights banned "For Sale" signs on property in an attempt to prevent the sort of **blockbusting** tactics that realtors had used to promote fear and **panic selling** in East Cleveland.[37] More integrated-minded community associations also sought to assure that this suburb of some 30,000 people would continue to be attractive to white home buyers. The Shaker Heights Housing Office lobbied realtors to show homes to prospective white buyers. The office also provided some small financial assistance to white buyers who were willing to move into parts of the city that were becoming increasingly African-American.

The housing office was criticized for initially focusing its efforts on attracting white prospects. In 1969 the office modified its practices to assist black home buyers as well, encouraging them to move into the unintegrated sections of the suburb. Financial assistance is given to blacks and whites who move into neighborhoods where they are underrepresented. Whites get small low-cost loans if they move into neighborhoods that are over 50 percent black; blacks get assistance if they move into areas that are 90 percent or more white. The office also seeks to identify housing opportunities for African-Americans in other Cleveland suburbs that have not been as open to blacks. The office will even provide small loans to black families who move to virtually all-white suburbs.

The Shaker Heights Board of Education supported integration, instituting a voluntary busing and magnet school plan so that the racial makeup of a school's population would not be an important factor in a home buyer's selection of a neighborhood. Enrollments in the elementary schools are racially balanced. There is only one city school for fifth and

sixth graders, one middle school, and a single high school. The city's reputation for quality schools has been a continued attraction to both white
and black residents alike.

Overall, the Shaker Heights model has shown that race-conscious
programs can stabilize the racial makeup of a suburb's population and
prevent resegregation. The city's nonwhite population, which stood at
only 1 percent in 1960, was 14.5 percent in 1970, 24 percent in 1980,
and just over 30 percent in 1990. No "tipping point" was reached despite the growth of Shaker Heights' minority population. Instead, the
actions of community leaders helped to ensure the continued white demand for housing in a stably integrated community.

Yet, the suburb's success in promoting integration has been uneven.
The population of certain neighborhoods, especially those bordering
Cleveland, is increasingly African-American, while the suburb's more
exclusive areas have remained less diverse. Also, classes in the high school
are not racially balanced, as black and white children pursue different
curricula.

The Shaker Heights approach is also controversial. Some critics
charge that it is racist, that it gives disproportionate assistance to whites,
and that it limits black in-migration out of a racist fear that something is
wrong with a suburb that becomes "too black." One black realtor attacked,
"When a city will pay to get blacks to move to another community, it sends
a powerful message."[38] Yet, supporters of the program respond that their
actions have averted massive white flight and maintained a stably integrated community.

Cleveland Heights has undertaken what may be a stronger pro-
integration position than Shaker Heights—upgrading the city's housing
stock, initiating legal action against realtors found to engage in racial
steering, and adopting a nine-point fair housing plan. A Heights Fund
rewards home buyers for pro-integration moves. While seeking to attract
young white home buyers, the housing service in Cleveland Heights also
shows black prospects the entire city. While the suburb has maintained an
integrated population that in 1990 was 37 percent black, parts of the community have become predominantly black, and enrollment in the city's
schools surpassed 60 percent black (with some schools having a student
body that was 80 percent or more nonwhite).[39]

Two Chicago suburbs, Park Forest on the city's South Side and Oak
Park immediately to the city's west, have integration maintenance programs similar to those of Shaker Heights and Cleveland Heights. In Oak
Park, local activists initiated positive steps in support of racial diversity
after they saw the quick racial transition of Chicago's Austin community
just across the suburb's border. In 1960, no blacks lived in Austin; by the
mid-1980s the area was predominantly black.[40]

Civil rights groups generally applauded Oak Park's pro-integration
programs, programs that allowed it to avoid the resegregation experienced

in Austin. Yet, Oak Park's success has been mixed. The city's population is not equally integrated throughout; African-Americans are concentrated in the suburb's eastern housing tracts that border Chicago. Oak Park, like Cleveland Heights, may only be serving to retard, not halt, the process of resegregation.[41] Activists in the black community have also criticized what they view as an attempt by the suburb to limit the size of its black population.

The constitutionality of local **affirmative marketing** practices that fall short of constituting explicit numerical quotas was upheld by the federal appellate court in a case dealing with Park Forest, Illinois. In the **South-Suburban Housing Center case,** the court ruled that race-conscious efforts to steer whites and blacks to pro-integration moves are constitutionally permissible—although realtors have no obligation to participate in affirmative marketing plans.[42] The court also ruled that restrictions on "For Sale" signs and other forms of property listing and advertising, too, are constitutional.

Whatever the success or problems with these suburban efforts at retaining racial diversity, they are all the more notable for their rarity. Very, very few suburbs have been willing to undertake the strong, activist steps necessary to promote stable integration. In some suburbs a commitment to integration will lead communities to participation in a regional **fair share plan**, under which they agree to permit the construction of a limited number of subsidized or otherwise affordable housing units. But in most suburbs, even this quite-limited step at integration proves politically impossible.

THE POLITICAL ATTITUDES OF SUBURBIA

Because suburbia denotes a set of quite diverse communities, it is perilous to generalize about the attitudes of people living there. Still, certain attitudes have historically been associated with suburbia, even though they are not found in equal force in every suburban community.

ANTI-CITY ATTITUDES AND THE INSISTENCE ON SUBURBAN AUTONOMY

Much of the political attitude of suburbia is based on a belief in the inherent superiority of suburban life to central-city life. Suburban residents see their communities as re-creations of small-town life, with all its virtues, in the midst of a growing, modernized, and increasingly dangerous urban United States. Suburbs are portrayed as the renaissance of the Jeffersonian agrarian ideal. Suburbanites tend to view their communities as outposts of virtue as contrasted to the venality, corruption, and welfarism of central cities. Even suburban political systems are seen to embody "good government" notions of nonpartisanship and grassroots democracy. The initial wave of suburbanites yearned politically "to shed the disreputable habits of the big city" or otherwise to rid themselves of "the shame of the cities."[43]

The residents of suburbia see their homes and lifestyles as "the American dream," a reward for their work and efforts. They will defend what they regard as hard-earned sanctuaries and the ideals of home, family, and property.[44] As a result, suburbanites have been insistent on maintaining the political autonomy of their communities. They resist metropolitan reform proposals that would draw them back into facing the financial and social problems of the central cities (and of the more distressed suburbs as well).

The sensitivity to questions of local independence is particularly pervasive in the Sunbelt, where growing suburban areas risk being annexed by larger cities. (In the Frostbelt, suburban communities are assured independence as a result of strict state rules on annexation and by their long tenure as incorporated entities.) In the Sunbelt, battles for control over sewer lines, water supply, and fire protection services are often seen as a prelude to a fight over suburban independence. Threatened by aggressive annexation programs, suburbs in a number of Sunbelt states prefer to keep their distance from central cities.[45]

THE GRASSROOTS IDEAL

Suburbanites value the relatively small-scale, participant nature of their government. They believe that government closest to the people governs best. In smaller communities, city councils are seen as friends and neighbors, people who reflect community values. Smaller governments also allow greater responsiveness; a citizen with a problem does not need to find a path through a maze of impersonal bureaucratic functionaries. Citizens in suburbs can also run for public office without having to arrange the support of political party leaders as well as the degree of financing required in bigger cities.

Yet, the grassroots ideal often proves to be a less than accurate description of contemporary politics on the city's rim. Voter turnout for local elections in many suburban communities is also quite low. Nonpartisan electoral systems and the scheduling of elections during off years both diminish turnout. Citizen interest and participation in local affairs is discouraged by the consensus character of local politics that turns elections into issueless contests in many suburban communities.

Only when it comes to "the special issues of public schools" have studies consistently found suburbanites to exhibit the high degree of activity expected under the grassroots ideal.[46] In other issue areas suburban residents tend to be more passive, trusting decision making to the experts of public officialdom. More recently, however, a new grassroots activism has emerged on matters relating to growth, land use, and environmental protection.

The growth in size of many communities has diminished some of the grassroots nature of suburban politics. Many suburbs are so large that elected officials no longer have a close personal relationship with the citizens they serve. A citizen may not even know whom in city hall to contact in case of a complaint. Some suburban governments have become as large, professionalized, bureaucratized, and bewildering as are the governments of medium-sized cities.

In larger suburbs, a prospective candidate can no longer rely on face-to-face campaigning to win public office. Instead a candidate must raise substantial sums of money for a mass media campaign. Suburban campaigns in larger communities are often marked by the work of paid campaign consultants and fundraisers. In the larger suburbs of the Northeast, candidates will also find it important to get the backing of local party leaders.[47]

NONPARTISANSHIP

In contrast to national and state elections, contests for suburban offices generally are conducted on a nonpartisan basis. In suburbs where public affairs is often seen to be a matter of "doing what is best" for the community, partisan concerns and philosophies are considered to be irrelevant. Political party organizations are viewed as an aspect of big-city politics best left behind.

Yet, the exact nature of suburban nonpartisan systems varies from community to community. The term *nonpartisanship* may even obscure the true characteristic of governance in a number of suburban communities. While some suburbs retain strict adherence to the nonpartisan ideal, in other suburbs nonpartisanship is nothing more than a thin veneer that covers the behind-the-scenes operations of political parties. In other communities, civic associations organized by a business-led elite have filled the void left by the absence of political parties. In these communities, nonpartisanship has helped to enhance the power of the local elite and insulate it from challenge from below.[48]

The suburban political ethos deplores partisan activity and conflict, and instead strives for a politics based on consensus. Part-time, amateur legislators rely on the reports and recommendations of professional experts—the city manager, the finance director, and other professional administrators.[49]

Yet, in some suburban communities, activist citizens and their school board and city council allies are not at all deferential to professional administrators. Montgomery County (Maryland), Fairfax County (Virginia), and Marin and San Mateo Counties (California) are only a few of the places where residents have challenged plans for subsidized housing, school curriculum reform, highway construction, and the development of new Metro rail systems. The growing diversity of suburban populations

also makes it increasingly difficult for communities to paper over conflicts. Suburbs face new problems; they cannot return to an idealized,
small-town politics of the past.[50]

SCHOOLS AND TAXES

The quality of the local schools is one of the major reasons residents offer
in explaining their preference for the suburbs. Perceptions of quality are to
a great extent linked to school financing and sometimes to race as well.

SCHOOL FINANCE REFORM

In recent years, state aid has come to exceed local-based funding for
schools. Yet, the money that a school district has available is still greatly a
function of local resources. Districts rich in property evaluation can generate significant money for schools even though property taxes are relatively low. Poorer districts often cannot produce equivalent revenues even
if they tax their citizens at much higher rates!

Examples from some of the more famous school finance reform
court cases underscore the fact that property-poor districts cannot produce the same monies for education available in wealthier districts. In
California in the early 1970s, Baldwin Park, a low-income community
near Los Angeles, taxed itself at double the rate of exclusive Beverly Hills,
yet was able to spend only $595 per student as compared to $1,244 per student spent in the wealthier suburb. Similarly, in Texas in 1968, residents
in San Antonio's very poor Edgewood district (which was 96 percent nonwhite) could raise only $37 per student and, with state aid, wound up
spending $231 per child. In contrast, the predominantly white and wealthy
Alamo Heights section of the city, incorporated as a separate district,
raised $412 per student from local sources and, with state aid, spent a
total of $543 per pupil.[51]

The California figures were the basis of a lawsuit that precipitated a
wave of educational finance reform actions that swept across the nation.
In *Serrano v. Priest* (1971) the California Supreme Court ruled that
extreme disparities among districts in the wealth available for education
denied residents of poorer districts the protections guaranteed by both
the federal and state constitutions.[52]

However, the school finance reform movement was dealt a serious
setback when a divided United States Supreme Court, in a 5 to 4 vote,
ruled in a Texas case, *Rodriguez v. San Antonio Independent School
District* (1973), that using local property taxes as a basis to fund schools
was *not* a violation of citizens' equal protection rights guaranteed by the
Fourteenth Amendment of the United States Constitution.[53] According to
the Court, education is not a **fundamental right**, as it is not explicitly

mentioned in the Constitution. When it comes to education, the Fourteenth Amendment does not require the full equality of resources, but only that schools provide students with the minimal skills necessary to participate in the political process. The Court was also unwilling to order the equalization of school monies because experts disagreed as to the importance of school spending in determining children's learning and future life chances. Some educators argued that the influence of students' parents and peers, not levels of spending, were the critical influences on education.

SCHOOL FINANCE TODAY: THE BATTLE SHIFTS TO THE STATES

In the wake of the *Rodriguez* decision, it was left up to state courts and state legislatures to tackle the problem of school finance.[54] Citizens aggrieved by inequalities in school funding would now have to bring suit on the basis of state law and the state constitutions, not the U.S. Constitution.

The California Supreme Court reheard the *Serrano* case in the wake of the *Rodriguez* decision, but nonetheless still ruled that California must reform its means of funding schools because great disparities in school funding violated provisions in the state's constitution, even if they did not violate the U.S. Constitution. In California, Texas, New Jersey, and a whole host of other states, decisions based on state constitutional guarantees for an "efficient" system of education forced state legislatures to take more equalizing action.

Greater levels of state assistance, prompted by court intervention, have helped to lessen, but not eliminate, the disparities between school districts. In California in the early 1990s, state efforts brought all but 5 percent of local school districts to within $300 of each other in terms of per student spending. Still, inequalities persisted. The poorest districts in the state spent less than $3,000 per pupil while the richest spent over $7,000. As we shall soon see, California may have attained greater parity only as the result of an "equalizing down" process that put a lid on local school spending. In Texas in the early 1990s, district spending ranged from $3,190 to $11,801, sparking a continued fierce battle over further finance reform.[55]

States have increased both the **basic aid** given to all districts and the **equalization aid** given to poorer districts. The states, though, have generally been reluctant to take further steps toward equalization, as they fear that any tax increase will incur the wrath of voters. Representatives of wealthier districts are also unwilling to pay new taxes to support increased spending in other districts. Consequently, it has often taken action by a court to force a reluctant state legislature to act. The New Jersey Supreme Court even shut down the schools in the state for a brief period of time in order to force the legislature to enact an income tax to fund a state school aid package.[56]

School finance reform continues to promote heated controversy. In New Jersey, a school finance program that narrowed the gap between richer and poorer districts was assailed by the residents of affluent sub-urban districts facing the loss of hundreds of millions of dollars in state aid. The tax increases and redistributional elements of the plan were a factor in Governor Jim Florio's reelection defeat at the hands of Christine Todd Whitman. But Governor Whitman, too, was forced to turn her attention to school finance reform when the New Jersey Supreme Court in 1994, for the fourth time in twenty years, ruled that the state must undertake still greater action to equalize spending between richer and poorer districts.[57]

In 1992, Texas was one of twenty-three states facing lawsuits as a result of school finance issues.[58] The legislature was unwilling to raise taxes, and the state supreme court struck down a number of school finance reform proposals for failing to provide adequate funds. Faced with a threat by the court to shut down the state's schools if it continued to drag its feet, the legislature turned the issue over to the voters. But the voters, by an almost 2-to-1 margin, defeated a 1993 proposed constitu-tional amendment that would have created larger school districts, merg-ing richer and poorer communities together. Voters objected to the "Robin Hood" aspects of the plan, as well as to the loss of local control in the larger districts.[59] Governor Ann Richards' strong advocacy of the amendment and other school finance reform efforts was a factor in her 1994 reelection loss to George W. Bush.

In some cases, change efforts have gone beyond finance reform. In Kentucky, court action led not only to finance reform but also to a restructuring of the state's entire school system that gave the state greater responsibility for the performance of local schools.[60] Chelsea, Massachusetts, an extremely poor and minority-dominated community located just north of Boston, in 1988 signed a contract turning over the operation of its schools to Boston University. The university's task was to energize the city's flagging schools by introducing new teaching and managerial approaches and raising new monies from public and private sources. This was the first time that a private institution was given the au-thority to manage an entire public school system. Since then, Baltimore and Hartford have turned over the operations of city schools to private contractors. However, critics charge that these moves diminish public accountability and undercut the job protections afforded teachers.[61]

THE TAXPAYER REVOLT

As events in the early 1990s in California, New Jersey, and Texas have shown, the movement to reform school finance has come face to face with a second strong movement. A nationwide taxpayer revolt has limited the ability of local communities, suburbs included, to fund their schools.

Perhaps the most significant political event in the taxpayers' rebellion was the 1978 passage of **Proposition 13** by voters in California. Rising property taxes had squeezed family incomes. The more desirable residential areas, especially in southern California suburbs, had witnessed a dramatic rise in the valuation of houses, with reassessments in some communities doubling a homeowner's tax obligation in just three or four years. Voter outrage was further fueled by the revelation of a substantial state surplus. At a time when local property taxes were rising through the roof, the state had been sitting on money that it could have used to fund services or pay for property tax relief.

Proposition 13 rolled back property taxes to their prior levels and sharply limited any annual increase that could be levied on a property owner. Proposition 13—and the other tax and spending limitation measures that followed—was a "revolt of the haves." It gained its greatest support among the well-to-do and middle-aged who stood to gain substantial tax savings as a result of the measure's enactment.[62]

The taxpayers' revolt soon spread to other parts of the country. Massachusetts' Proposition 2½ was only the most famous of the state-imposed taxing and spending limitations enacted at the time. Taxpayers revolts flared up on the local level as well. In Prince Georges County, Maryland, TRIM curtailed the ability of elected officials to pay for local services. Certain local communities also exhibited what can be labeled **recall fever,** with community groups immediately organizing a petition drive calling for an election to remove from office any public official who voted for a tax increase.

In California, the new taxing and spending limitations took their toll on the state's system of education. The state's economic downturn with the end of the Cold War only compounded difficulties. Once the national leader in per pupil spending, California fell to twenty-sixth place just eight years after Proposition 13; by the early 1990s, California had fallen to forty-sixth. In terms of class size, California ranked dead last, with the largest class sizes in the nation.[63] The taxing and spending limitations have acted to "equalize down" school spending, bringing a new level of mediocrity to education.

The limitations on taxing and spending especially constrained the ability of school districts to respond to the pressures created by California's growing Latino and Asian populations. Community after community also turned to **user fees,** including fees for participation in sports and extracurricular activities—charges that were challenged in the state courts.[64]

Numerous communities found it impossible to issue bonds in order to build new classrooms. As a result, California communities have tried to generate new money through **developer fees** and **access charges** levied on new homes.[65] Impact fees have also become popular in Florida, Oregon, and other states where communities have had to cope with the expenses brought about by rapid growth. But such developer fees add substantially to the cost of buying a home, decreasing housing afford-ability and discriminating against newcomers who must pay these charges in addition to their normal property taxes. A 1991 survey of localities in California, Florida, Oregon, and Washington revealed that impact fees added about $12,000 to the cost of a two thousand square foot house.[66]

In 1994, Californians, tired of taxes and faced with new economic problems, voted for **Proposition 187,** an initiative barring the provision of all, except emergency, services to illegal aliens. The measure, at least as it applied to education, was immediately challenged by local school dis-tricts who cited their responsibilities under prior U.S. Supreme Court rulings.

RACIAL INTEGRATION

To what extent are suburbs required to participate in school busing arrangements or other plans to bring about school integration? Appar-ently, under the Supreme Court's 1974 *Millikin v. Bradley* ruling, in a case that dealt with a metropolitan plan to desegregate Detroit's schools, not very much.[67] According to the Court, interdistrict school busing— that is, the busing of students across district lines—is not required even if such an arrangement is the only means by which the racial imbalance of central city schools can be reduced.

In what has become know as the **intent to discriminate doctrine,** it is not enough for advocates of desegregation efforts to show that there is a severe racial imbalance in school populations in the metropolis. Instead, a suburb can be forced to participate only if it can first be proved that the suburb, by its own actions, purposely acted to maintain racial segregation. Advocates of integration can easily demonstrate the racial imbalance between city and suburban schools; however, they cannot so easily prove that a racial intent underlies the imbalance. Suburbs argue that they are not motivated by racial intent, that they simply desire to maintain the advantages of local control and neighborhood schools.

School busing is not popular, and wherever possible districts have looked for room to narrow or abandon busing efforts. In a 1991 case involving Oklahoma City's schools, the Supreme Court gave districts that had been found guilty of past discrimination new leeway to alter or end desegregation efforts. School districts found guilty of past discrimination could end desegregation efforts if they had for a "reasonable" period of time undertaken actions to remove the "vestiges" of *de jure* discrimination "to the extent practicable." The Court's decision apparently even allows re-segregation to occur if a neighborhood school assignment plan is not seen to be designed with a discriminatory intent.[68]

A 1992 decision further limited the scope of metropolitan desegrega-tion plans, even where "white flight" to the suburbs had undermined court-ordered attempts to integrate central-city schools. In this case, involving DeKalb County, Georgia, the Court effectively ruled that districts have no obligation to remedy patterns of school segregation resulting from residential patterns that are the result of private choice.[69]

Without suburban participation, there are simply not enough white students in majority-minority cities to desegregate central-city schools. As a result, in a number of cities the focus of change efforts has shifted from desegregation to central-city educational enrichment programs. But, as we have already seen, suburban resistance to finance reform acts to limit increased investment in inner-city education.

HOUSING AND LAND USE

Problems of housing and land use are generally in the forefront of suburban political controversy, as they determine the style of life in a community. Local zoning and land use ordinances determine just which types of housing and which economic activities will be permitted in a community and exactly where they will be located.

ZONING AND SUBURBAN EXCLUSION

Communities can be described as **exclusionary** if they use their zoning ordinances and related powers in an attempt to restrict entry by people who are less well-off and maybe of a different race than existing community residents. Exclusionary zoning denies suburban opportunities to low- and moderate-income people.

Of course, not all zoning is equally exclusionary in its effects. Zoning also serves important community purposes. It can be used to protect property values, to safeguard the environment by preventing overdevelopment, and to implement a city plan that confines nuisance and commercial activities to certain areas while preserving the residential character of neighborhoods. The cost of not having effective land use controls was most dramatically shown by the deadly fire that swept homes in the Oakland Hills in the San Francisco Bay region. In the absence of strong land use restrictions, residential developments in attractive but hazardous woodland and hillside areas, with flammable decorative trees and shrubbery and narrow roads that bar easy access by fire trucks, are the "fires of the future."[70] Even citizens in Houston, Texas, the only major city in the United States to have no zoning regulations whatsoever, have recently voted on the need for zoning controls to interject some order on helter-skelter, haphazard patterns of land use.[71]

Even so, in suburbs, especially more exclusive suburbs, zoning has been used as an exclusionary tool, not just a means of guiding appropriate land uses. The motivations behind exclusion are varied. Some suburbanites want to ward off traffic congestion, crime, and other ills that would accompany the continued growth and "citification" of their communities. Other suburbanites seek to protect property values by preserving the attractive character of their communities. Suburban residents often have substantial equity invested in their homes, and they fear that the changing social composition of a community may adversely affect the price when they decide to sell.

The motivation behind exclusion is also related to taxes. By determining the mix of land uses in a community, zoning directly affects servicing and taxing requirements in a suburb. Better-off residents object that they are the ones who pay increased taxes to subsidize costly services, including education, when low- and moderate-income newcomers occupy rental units and low-valued homes that generate little in taxes.[72]

Of course, suburban exclusion often reflects racist and nativist, as well as classist, sentiments. Just northeast of Los Angeles, the San Gabriel Valley has become a major destination for upwardly mobile, working-class Chicanos, Chinese, and Vietnamese. Monterey Park, San Gabriel, Arcadia, and Alhambra, as well as other suburbs in the valley, have seen a backlash of community groups organized in a slow-growth attempt to limit the influx of non-Anglos.[73]

Robert Wood criticizes the false or incomplete sense of community that prevails in suburbia. Instead of genuine spirit of community, there is only a more limited sense of **fraternity** that "may be less than admirable, with overtones of exclusiveness, narrowness, provinciality and clannishness."[74] This fraternity in suburbia results from a homogeneity and intolerance enforced through the zoning and other legal powers of government; it is not a genuine or "voluntary brotherhood" where the common bonds of every person are "freely recognized and freely defined."[75] Similarly, sociologist Robert Bellah and his research colleagues attack more socially segmented suburbs as constituting nothing more than **lifestyle enclaves** for people of similar backgrounds and preferences.[76]

THE TECHNIQUES OF SUBURBAN EXCLUSION

There are a variety of means by which a suburb can limit the housing opportunities available to poor, working-class, and, in many cases, even middle-class families. Communities can refuse to approve the construction of subsidized housing units within their borders. Alternatively, they can restrict or bar altogether the construction of multifamily housing. One study of the New York area found that over 99 percent of the undeveloped land zoned for residential use was zoned for single-family dwellings, thereby excluding persons who can afford only rental apartments and condominiums.[77] Even where the construction of multifamily apartments is permitted, a community can keep large, poor families out by restricting the number of units that can be built with more than two bedrooms.

Most commonly, a suburb can make itself "off limits" even to moderate-income residents by driving up new home prices through

large-lot zoning—requiring that homes be built on no less than a half acre, one acre, or even two acres of land. Costs of home ownership can also be raised by **minimum room space requirements** beyond that demanded by reasons of health and safety. Suburban governments can further require the use of more expensive construction technologies and materials—that, for instance, homes be built piece by piece on site instead of by use of preassembled modular components, or that copper pipes be used instead of less expensive plastic pipes. And, as we have already observed, suburban municipalities can also add thousands of dollars, in **developer fees and access charges**, to the price of new homes whose owners are made to pay the full cost of new street, sewer, and school construction—despite the fact that these services are provided other residents of the community out of local property taxes.

Exclusionary suburbs may also seek to limit the land available for new construction through **sewer and water line moratoria** that ban the extension of service to developable areas. They may also seek to have the state designate certain areas as **agricultural preserves** or protected **green-space areas**.

Suburban jurisdictions can also defeat development projects by constantly **shifting development standards**. As a developer meets one set of conditions, new and even more expensive conditions are imposed. And once a developer fails to meet conditions, building permits are withdrawn. A developer may challenge the local government's action in court, but judicial action often takes quite a bit of time and can be very expensive. As delay itself, often combined with inflation, drives up the costs of construction, developers will tend to avoid communities where the likely imposition of costly delays makes development a bad gamble.[78]

Even in "free-market" greater Houston, renowned for its lack of zoning, new development is not totally unfettered. The majority of the other thirty-three cities in Texas' Harris County do have zoning. Houston itself regulates land development through municipal enforcement of private deed restrictions. The city also guides development through its capital investment program, a comprehensive planning process, and subdivision regulations that apply to newly developing areas.[79] Homeowners in the emerging Houston "new town" of Clear Lake City also succeeded in restricting the development of high-density, multifamily housing by pressuring the municipal utility district to restrict water and sewer extensions.[80] State law also gives Houston the **extraterritorial power** to limit new development in areas lying outside its boundaries but contiguous to the city.

BEYOND ZONING: LIMITED-GROWTH AND NO-GROWTH

In its most extreme form, exclusion takes the form of **limited-growth and no-growth ordinances** that strictly regulate the number of new residential units that can be constructed in a community each year. Ramapo, a town in Rockland County about thirty-five miles outside New York City, gained fame for its eighteen-year plan to slow down and phase in new residential growth. Developers had to submit their proposals, which were evaluated against the stringent criteria of the municipality's capital improvement program. The municipality would issue a special permit for new residential development only in those cases where the required municipal services were already available and a particular proposal was judged as meritorious. The court upheld Ramapo's action, holding that a community has a rational basis for phasing in growth where its physical and financial resources are inadequate to provide the essential facilities and services that a substantial increase in population would require.[81]

A similar growth plan that, too, survived challenge in the courts was implemented by Petaluma, California, a community lying to the north of San Francisco. Where Ramapo had only implied a sharp limitation on the number of new units that it would allow to be built each year, Petaluma imposed an explicit annual quota of a mere 500 units. Each year, the city chooses the winners in an annual competition among housing claimants.[82]

Boulder (Colorado), Livermore (California), and Boca Raton (Florida) are among the more notable cities to have adopted growth limitation strategies, placing a moratorium on new construction or otherwise devising plans to slow down or phase in new development. Although the Boca Raton effort to place an annual cap on new construction was struck down by the courts, in most communities growth management regulations persist because they are not even challenged in the courts.[83]

A recent trend has seen the rise of **ballot-box planning**, where citizens use the tools of direct democracy to place restrictions on land use. In San Francisco and in numerous southern California communities, from the Los Angeles–San Bernandino area to Carlsbad and Oceanside in San Diego County, citizens have taken advantage of the initiative and referendum processes to limit the issuance of building permits and otherwise restrict new construction.[84] While seemingly simple and democratic, the use of the initiative and referendum in the land use arena is also the subject of much criticism:

> Rezoning by initiative or referendum can be seen as an end-run around carefully enacted procedures for zoning decisions. No hearings are needed, no reports of professional planners, no amendments and compromise, no testimony by the affected landowner, and no city council members are held accountable for a controversial decision.[85]

The subtleties and trade-offs entailed in any land use decision are ignored when voters cast their ballots on a growth limitation measure in response to simplistic, emotional presentations, as was the case when a San Diego ballot campaign urged "No L.A.—Yes on [Proposition] A."[86]

Although ballot-box planning is particularly popular in the West, other parts of the country have also seen a new willingness of citizens to vote for growth controls. Citizens on Massachusetts' Cape Cod were given the opportunity to vote on plans for a development moratorium. In Portland, Maine, local citizens overwhelmingly approved a measure to preserve the city's waterfront for marine uses, limiting new residential development and the threat of "creeping condominiumism."[87]

The states, too, have become important actors in urban growth management and policies designed to protect agricultural land from urban development. Hawaii, California, Oregon, Vermont, New Jersey, and Florida have all taken important actions in these areas.[88] In Florida, in an effort to protect the Everglades and other environmentally fragile areas, the state strengthened its growth management efforts, requiring localities to develop comprehensive plans and to permit new development only in cases where the supporting infrastructure is available. Still, localities, convinced of the benefits of new development, have not always fully abided by the growth management vision. In fast-growing cities, the growth machine has not sought to slow the pace of growth but instead has pressed for new infrastructure to accommodate new development.[89]

THE LEGAL STATUS OF EXCLUSIONARY ZONING AND GROWTH MANAGEMENT

The Supreme Court upheld the constitutionality of zoning in the case of *Village of Euclid, Ohio, v. Ambler Realty Co.* (1926).[90] In **the Euclid case,** as it is commonly known, the Court found that zoning was a legitimate expression of the state's **police powers** to protect the public welfare. According to *Euclid*, a municipality clearly has the right to use its zoning powers to bar the construction of apartment buildings and thereby protect its people against the increased noise, congestion, and the general change in a community's character that would ensue.

Advocacy groups for the poor and racial minorities argue that exclusionary zoning is discriminatory. Yet, not all discriminations are barred by the Constitution. Discrimination on the basis of income is constitutionally acceptable; discrimination on the basis of race, however, is not. For the courts to strike down a community's zoning ordinance, it must first be proved that the intent to discriminate was racial, not economic, in nature.

The case of **Black Jack, Missouri**, in the early 1970s, provides an example of the courts' willingness to strike down zoning ordinances where the racial intent seems rather clear. A church-sponsored organization had obtained approval from the U.S. Department of Housing and Urban Development to construct some moderate-income housing in this unincorporated area just north of St. Louis. Local residents responded by swiftly mounting a drive to incorporate their community. One of the first acts of the new municipality was a zoning ordinance that outlawed the construction of multifamily housing. An advocacy group filed suit, challenging that the zoning ordinances were blatantly discriminatory and in violation of the 1968 Fair Housing Act. The Supreme Court in 1974 affirmed a lower court ruling that struck down the Black Jack zoning ordinance.[91] The racist sentiment expressed in the debates over incorporation and the timing of the incorporation coincidental with the church group's attempt to build the subsidized housing units may well have convinced the court that race was a factor in the zoning decision. But civil rights advocates won only a pyrrhic victory; the town houses were never built, as the delays inflated the costs of construction and allowed the federal government to withdraw the government subsidies.

Of much greater significance is the Supreme Court's 1977 decision in **the Arlington Heights case** that upheld the exclusionary zoning ordinance of a well-to-do, overwhelmingly white suburb northwest of Chicago.[92] Once again a church group had attempted to build subsidized housing units in a suburban area. But this time residents of the area did not need to incorporate a new municipality in order to pass zoning laws to bar the new development. Arlington Heights was already an incorporated city with zoning laws that prohibited multifamily housing in much of the suburbs.

According to the Court, a community may enact zoning restrictions where there is no **intent to discriminate** on the basis of race. A community may use zoning ordinances for such reasonable purposes as the preservation of a peaceable environment, the promotion of an orderly pattern of land development, and the protection of local property values. The *Arlington Heights* ruling stated that it is not enough for plaintiffs to show that a community's zoning laws have the discriminatory *effect* of helping to exclude blacks from the community, concentrating African-Americans in the central city and more impoverished inner-ring suburbs. Plaintiffs must also establish that such regulations were enacted with a racially discriminatory *intent*. As already noted in our discussion of school integration, while the racial imbalances in a metropolitan area can easily be demonstrated, an *intent to discriminate* is not so easily proven. A suburb's legal counsel can always argue that respectable purposes, such as the preservation of the integrity of the locality's land use plan, guided its actions.

For most suburbs the relevant precedent is *Arlington Heights*, not *Black Jack*. Their exclusionary zoning statutes are already on the books, and they are under no affirmative obligation to change them in order to accommodate plans for class or racial integration.

The legal status of exclusionary zoning seems secure. The only real constraint on local power here stems from the courts' concern that government not use its zoning power in such a way as to deny certain pieces of land all economic value, effectively constituting an expropriation or the **taking** of a piece of property without paying owners fair compensation. Hence, in 1972 the U.S. District Court for northern

California struck down zoning regulations by the affluent Silicon Valley suburb of Palo Alto that blocked new home development in the foothills because the local ordinance effectively denied owners any economically feasible use of their property. The city had to resort to an alternative route to block the housing development. In an out-of-court settlement Palo Alto bought the land and eventually built a new park that was open only to city residents.[93]

Two 1987 Supreme Court decisions again raised the issue of due compensation, casting doubt on limits-to-growth measures that effectively deny landowners the use of their property. In *First English Evangelical Lutheran Church of Glendale v. County of Los Angeles,* the Court ruled against a county action that had prohibited the church from constructing any buildings on its recently flooded campgrounds. In telling the county to pay compensation if its actions were in effect to deny the church all reasonable use of property, the Court recognized that the logic of its decision "will undoubtedly lessen to some extent the freedom and the flexibility of land-use planners and governing bodies of municipal corporations when enacting land-use regulations."[94]

In **the Nollan Case** (*Nollan v. California Coastal Commission*), the state coastal commission had sought to protect public beachfront access by denying the Nollans permission to build a shorefront home unless the couple first granted an easement across their property for public access. The Court ruled that the government could not restrict development in order to coerce the expropriation or taking of land for public use; it would have to pay for it.[95]

Some commentators expected these Supreme Court decisions to open the "floodgates of litigation," challenging local land use and zoning regulations. In New York, for instance, the owners of a single-room occupancy (SRO) hotel successfully used the *Nollan* precedent to challenge a municipal law that placed a moratorium on converting SRO's to other uses—a law that tried to prevent homelessness by preserving the supply of housing available to the poorest of the poor.[96] Still, the fears of a widespread challenge to local land use controls seem greatly exaggerated: "[T]he threshold for finding a taking remains as lofty as ever—the landlord must still demonstrate a complete deprivation of the use of property."[97] Exclusionary zoning will continue.

IS THERE AN ENVIRONMENTAL PROTECTION HUSTLE?

In his provocatively entitled book *The Environmental Protection Hustle,* Bernard Frieden relied on case studies of San Francisco Bay communities to argue that exclusionary zoning and limited-growth ordinances have greatly contributed to a housing affordability crisis. Young people, newly marrieds, the inner-city poor, and minorities were all victimized as zoning and other home-building regulations restricted supply and drove up the cost of housing.

Frieden argues that environmentalists have become the unwitting allies of suburban exclusionists who have disguised their elitist and classist land use preferences in the more respectable language of environmentalism—contending that the land use regulations are necessary to protect valuable green space and unique natural areas. Environmentalists rallied against plans to construct 2,200 affordable town home and condominium apartment units in the Mountain Village development in the foothills outside Oakland. The compromise that was finally negotiated changed the social class of the project but did little to protect environmental values. The compromise agreement allowed the building of a smaller number (no more than 300) expensive estate homes. But where the original plan devoted 480 acres of open space to public use, no public recreational space was dedicated under the new plan. Similarly, in nearby Marin County, exclusionary motives were also evident when residents, declaring the need to protect access to the beautiful Pacific coastline, blocked new home building but then enacted restrictions that made it all but impossible for persons outside the immediate community to visit the preserve.[98]

Frieden is not alone in his attack on exclusionary zoning and the ill effects of land use overregulation. David Dowall estimates that in the Bay Area the combined effects of local land use controls, excessive subdivision improvement requirements, delay costs, and developer fees and charges are to add between 18 and 34 percent to the price of a new home.[99]

While Frieden clearly describes the exclusionary basis of much of the support for suburban land use controls, his critics point out that he gives inadequate weight to legitimate environmental concerns. The Palo Alto foothills and Marin coastline are beautiful areas that need to be protected for future generations. Frieden understates the dangers of continued growth, especially given the political power possessed by property developers and their growth coalition allies. Also, the Bay Area's high housing costs, generally the highest in the nation, are due more to other factors, including the area's attractiveness, than to restrictions on growth. All the same, Frieden has pointed to the growing conflict in a number of suburban communities between environmentalism and the need for affordable housing.

OPENING UP THE SUBURBS: *MOUNT LAUREL* AND CHALLENGES TO SUBURBAN EXCLUSION

Given the growth of suburban power in the national and state legislatures, it is unrealistic to expect that these bodies will undertake effective action to "open" the suburbs. Pro-integration solutions are more likely to be imposed by state judicial intervention.

But corrective action through the courts is tortuously slow. Housing advocates lack the resources to challenge the exclusionary practices of community after community. Even when a substantial investment of time, money, and energy gains a rare judicial victory, open housing forces have succeeded in altering the housing practices in only a single community. As the federal courts have been unwilling to question exclusionary actions, open housing advocates must go to state courts to challenge that exclusionary practices violate the provisions of state constitutions and state law.

NEW JERSEY'S *MOUNT LAUREL* DECISIONS

One notable open housing victory was gained in New Jersey when the state supreme court in a single decision struck down the exclusionary practices of a broad range of communities throughout the state. The 1975 decision was the first in a series of controversial rulings that have come to be know as **the *Mount Laurel* decisions.**

In *Southern Burlington County NAACP v. Township of Mt. Laurel* (usually referred to as *Mount Laurel I*), the court ruled that the land use regulations in developing communities must ensure that affordable housing can be built within their borders.[100] The court ruled that New Jersey's state constitution required the equal protection of poor people—the requirement for affordable housing is included within the state constitution's general welfare clause. The court ruled that not only Mount Laurel township, a New Jersey suburb of Philadelphia, but similar communities across the state had the responsibility to ensure that their land use regulations allow for the construction of a "fair share" of a region's need for low- and moderate-income housing units.[101]

The initial decision produced little new housing for low- and moderate-income families. Suburban communities dragged their feet and rezoned as few parcels of land as possible. Even in Mount Laurel township, not a single new affordable home was built to implement the court's decision. Consequently, eight years after its initial ruling, the court went much further. In *Mount Laurel II*, the court imposed on all communities in the state, no matter their stage of development, an affirmative obligation to provide affordable housing.[102] The court streamlined the procedures by which exclusionary zoning ordinances could be challenged and even threatened that trial courts would directly change zoning ordinances where municipalities failed to meet their constitutional obligation.

Finally, in *Mount Laurel III* (1986), the court upheld the legislature's creation of a Council on Affordable Housing, a statewide regulatory body designed to replace the courts in resolving exclusionary zoning cases.[103] The new law also allowed a municipality to transfer up to half of its fair share obligation by paying for subsidized housing in needy communities in the state. The activist New Jersey Supreme Court had forced the governor and legislature to take positive action on this difficult issue in order to avert the possibility of still more court intervention.

While the *Mount Laurel* decisions led to an alteration in local zoning practices and the construction of thousands of additional affordable housing units, their effects should not be overstated. Communities rezoned as little land as possible and avoided giving direct assistance to developers of low-income housing. Also, during troubled economic times, little was built. As a result, in many communities, no new, affordable units were built despite the affirmative obligation placed on them by the court. Other communities changed their zoning ordinances only to allow for the construction of more luxury condominiums, town houses, and garden apartments.[104] Housing opportunities were created primarily not for the poor but for "young people whose life-time income profile is middle class but whose current wealth does not allow home ownership."[105] Only court-imposed setasides led to the construction of units for those of "very low income."

A significant number of suburbs also exercised their option under *Mount Laurel III* to transfer up to 50 percent of their fair share obligation to other municipalities. These suburbs usually contracted with older cities such as Newark, Paterson, and Jersey City to help pay for the construction of lower-income housing within the latter's borders. Such transfers did little to integrate suburbs either economically or racially. They did, however, add to the stock of low-income housing in the state. These transfers of funds were also welcomed by fiscally distressed cities.[106]

Even analysts who approved of the shift in policy goals recognize that "the right to exclude lower-income households is being traded."[107] *Mount Laurel* has become more a means of subsidizing housing in troubled cities than a tool for opening the suburbs.

OTHER INCLUSIONARY EFFORTS

Montgomery County (Maryland) and Orange County (California) are among the few local governments to have initiated **inclusionary programs,** relaxing zoning ordinances, modifying building codes, and providing financial assistance to developers in an effort to encourage the construction of more affordable dwellings.[108] A municipality's award of **density bonuses** allows a developer to build a greater number of units than local ordinances normally permit, thereby allowing each unit to be sold or rented at a reduced cost. Developers are allowed to build at higher-than-normal densities in mixed-income projects where they agree to set aside a certain number of units for low- and moderate-income people.

Some states have also initiated limited inclusionary actions. Under Massachusetts' Anti-Snob Zoning law, the state can invalidate local land use controls that unreasonably interfere with the construction of low- and moderate-income housing. Offending municipalities can even be denied development-related assistance. However, the requirements of the law have not been aggressively enforced. Rhode Island and Connecticut have adopted similar laws. In Connecticut, state law allows a special housing judge to overturn the decisions of local zoning officials where health and safety concerns do not outweigh the need for afford-able housing. The hope is that the law will eventually lead Connecticut's more unaffordable commuter suburbs to approve the construction of apartments.[109]

In Oregon, local zoning must gain state approval. The state requires that municipalities permit manufactured housing, ease subdivision requirements, and grant density bonuses to promote the development of lower-income housing.

California imposes similar planning efforts on its municipalities. But cities vary greatly in their response to this mandate. The state's housing laws merely require localities to prepare plans for affordable housing, not that they actually build the units. Seventy-nine percent of California cities failed to comply fully with the requirement that they adopt a hous-ing plan. Approximately 30 percent of cities in California have either quite dated plans or no housing plan at all. In other cities, even in progressive communities like Santa Monica, legal action by nearby homeowners has blocked the construction of low- and moderate-income rental units.[110]

At the federal level, the Clinton administration has tried to promote a "Move to Opportunity" program, challenging violations of fair housing practices that restrict residential mobility. But even here, federal action remains limited. Inclusionary action, if it is to come at all, will be brought about primarily as the result of state and local efforts.

Yonkers (New York): A Window into the Future?

The successes of inclusionary efforts should not be overstated. They are relatively few. *Euclid* and *Arlington Heights* constitute the prevailing doc-trine. As we have said, unless found guilty of *de jure* segregation, a suburb faces no obligation to change local ordinances that preserve the charac-ter of its community.

Yonkers (New York), a city of nearly 200,000 persons just across the New York City border, does not fit the mold of an elite, bedroom com-munity. Yonkers has a large population of the poor and racial minori-ties. It is a financially troubled city that faces many of the same economic and social problems that confront other urban centers.

Yet, in the 1980s and 1990s, Yonkers became a national symbol of suburban resistance, as for a dozen years the city fought desegregation. Even though Yonkers has a large minority population, parts of the city re-main predominantly white and quite exclusive. For a half dozen years, city officials even refused to comply with a court-imposed desegregation order. Prompted by the furious protests of outraged citizens, the city spent over $15 million in legal fees challenging the court's ruling. Federal

District Judge Leonard Sand eventually imposed crippling fines on the council and its members in order to force their compliance.

Judge Sand found Yonkers guilty of intentional segregation in its housing patterns, locating public housing in one end of the city in order to preserve the exclusive character of other areas. He ordered the city to build 800 units of affordable housing, to be dispersed throughout the city, for families earning between $27,900 and $66,960 a year. After years of fighting, the NAACP and the Justice Department finally agreed to a city plan to build 709 condominium and cooperative units. The city would also offer mortgage assistance, giving first priority to those who live in public and subsidized housing. Only 115 units, however, were to be new construction in the mostly white east and northwestern sections of the city.[111]

The Yonkers case reveals the depth of passion that underlies resistance to pro-integration rulings. Yonkers resisted, even though the income limits for the housing guaranteed that most units would not go to the poor. Twelve years of heated conflict and aggressive court action produced little real integration.

Suburbanites are willing to allow the construction of more affordable housing that will be occupied by their own children as they reach adult age. Suburban communities also need a supply of housing that will be occupied by nurses, teachers, police officers, and other essential service workers. But they remain generally unwilling to amend their zoning ordinances to make their communities accessible to a broader socioeconomic spectrum of new residents.

CONCLUSIONS: THE IMPACT OF SUBURBAN AUTONOMY AND METROPOLITAN FRAGMENTATION

The concept of a metropolitan area denotes economic and social interdependence. Central cities provide warehousing, distribution, manufacturing, and other economic and systems maintenance functions needed by all communities in the metropolitan area. They also provide housing for a region's low-wage workers. Despite the decentralization of new activities to the suburbs, central cities also continue to be educational, cultural, and entertainment centers.

No suburb is an island unto itself. Suburbs are not free-standing, socioeconomically balanced communities. Rather, they are only "slices of the metropolitan complex" that use their zoning and related powers to control the social fabric of their communities.[112]

Local autonomy has produced a system of **metropolitan fragmentation** whereby the metropolitan area is divided into many smaller jurisdictions with no government possessing the power to look out for the good of the entire region. No local jurisdiction is required to look at the effects of its actions on other jurisdictions. Few suburbs are willing to alter land use, housing, and school arrangements when such alterations impose new costs on existing residents.

The consequences of suburban autonomy and metropolitan fragmentation are numerous. They can briefly be summarized as follows:

1. **Racial imbalance in the metropolis.** One clear consequence of metropolitan fragmentation is racial separation. Despite the recent increase in the suburbanization of racial minorities, metropolitan areas remain greatly unbalanced in terms of race. Racial minorities are concentrated in central cities. The suburbs, themselves, too, show a distinct racial imbalance. While some jurisdictions are predominantly black, Hispanic, or Asian, others remain more exclusive and overwhelmingly white.

   Racial imbalance is even greater when it comes to the schools in a metropolitan area. As the minority population of a community reaches a tipping point, white families seek refuge by moving to the suburbs or in some cases by moving to even more far-off suburbs. Those whites who remain behind in increasingly minority-dominated communities tend to be the elderly, newly marrieds without children, and parents who pay to send their children to private and parochial schools. As a result, the population of central-city and inner-ring suburban schools becomes blacker and browner more quickly and more extensively than does the population of these communities as a whole.

   The *Millikin* decision and more recent court rulings have placed sharp limits on any interdistrict school busing plan. The combined effects of the *Millikin* and *Rodriguez* decisions have been effectively to return metropolitan schools to a system of "separate but unequal."[113]

2. **Income and resource imbalance in the metropolis.** Zoning ordinances and related land use restrictions allow suburbs a certain selectivity when it comes to their residents and commercial activity. The result is that the central city and the more distressed suburbs become the repository for persons and functions unwanted by other communities in the metropolis. The governments of central cities and declining suburbs serve a disproportionate share of people in need of costly housing, health, income support, social service, and compensatory education programs. At the same time, these jurisdictions are denied the tax base needed to provide these services, as high-valued housing and new commercial activities are increasingly located in the suburbs. Oftentimes, it is the middle-income suburb that has the greatest difficulty in providing services because it lacks a strong tax base but still has large numbers of people in need of support.[114]

3. **The protection of privilege.** Suburbanites are able to use exclusionary zoning ordinances and land use restrictions to maintain

the relatively uncrowded, comfortable nature of their communities. These tools also protect fiscal privilege; compared to central-city residents, suburbanites often pay lower tax rates for better-quality schools and a generally higher level of services.

4. **Increased business power.** Metropolitan fragmentation also affords considerable advantages to business owners and corporations. Not only can owners seek business locations in low-tax communities, they can also threaten to move their facilities from one jurisdiction to another. Such threats can coerce tax concessions and other favors from municipal officials who do not wish to see the flight of desirable businesses and jobs over the local border.

5. **The impact of suburbs on central cities.** Central-city residents are burdened by having to pay for services that benefit suburbanites. In what can be labeled the **exploitation hypothesis,** suburban commuters to central cities benefit from central-city fire and police protection and street repaving but pay no property or income taxes to support these and other services. Automobile commuting imposes still other costs on central-city residents in terms of the environmental harm and neighborhood destruction that results. Suburbanites also benefit from city-run parks, zoos, and museums where costs of operation are not fully covered by admission charges and user fees.[115] Where states allow cities to levy income taxes on commuters, such tax rates by law are kept quite low. As one comparative study of city spending concluded, "[T]he suburban population, by its daily use of central city facilities, substantially raised the costs of municipal services."[116]

6. **Problems of housing affordability and homelessness.** Suburban zoning regulations and land use restriction decrease housing supply and inflate to cost of housing. In many communities, especially in the nation's more expensive metropolitan areas, housing affordability has become a concern of the middle class, not just of the poor.

The refusal of most suburbs to accept subsidized units within their borders accounts, at least to some degree, for the housing shortage faced by the poor. Exclusionary ordinances further constrict the supply of housing in a metropolis—by driving up prices and by driving new construction to the outer edges of the region. Prospective home buyers who seek bargains and shorter commuting times are led to look for gentrifying areas, buying housing units in the central city and displacing the urban poor in the process.[117] Well-to-do suburban areas, including Westchester County, New York, and Silicon Valley, south of San Francisco, have also had to confront new problems of family homelessness. In communities where the price of housing, including rental units, is extremely high, any disruption in a family's income—brought about by marital breakup, job dismissal, or ill health—can result in homelessness.[118]

7. **The lack of rational land use planning and commitment to environmental values.** Each suburban jurisdiction has the autonomy to pursue whatever level of growth it finds to be in its self-interest. A suburb that desires an expanded tax base can promote the building of a new shopping mall or industrial park, even if the development exacerbates traffic problems in other neighborhoods or leads to vacancies in existing developments in nearby jurisdictions. Suburbs that restrict growth also act to drive new development farther out to the periphery of the metropolitan area. The result is increased sprawl, the destruction of agricultural land and green space, and increased pollution resulting from extended automobile commutes.

8. **Problems in service provision.** The division of the metropolitan area into numerous autonomous jurisdictions produces numerous problems in service delivery. First is a problem of coordination across political borders. Comprehensive transportation planning is impeded as bus and rail service may simply stop at the borders of a community where residents are unwilling to pay for service. Even the efficient provision of emergency medical services may be thwarted by metropolitan fragmentation; one community's ambulance service may not be permitted to cross a political boundary to aid a person in another community where the local service is slow in responding to a call for help.

    Metropolitan fragmentation can also lead to an expensive duplication of services as each community insists, for instance, on having its own fire station, hospital, or CAT scan equipment. Such services could be provided more cheaply had communities chosen to share facilities. Where communities refuse to cooperate, citizens are denied the advantages of **economies of scale,** where cost savings can be realized by the larger-scale provision of a service. Instead, citizens are left to pay the quite expensive costs posed by empty hospital beds and high-technology equipment not used to its full capacity. At least one study of spending in Illinois has confirmed that higher levels of fragmentation in metropolitan areas are associated with the higher costs of government.[119]

Numerous commentators have recognized the inadequacy of having antiquated, small, autonomous jurisdictions attempt to govern large, economically integrated metropolitan areas. Neal Peirce has called for a new level of thinking, whereby citizens and decision makers recognize that metropolitan areas now represent **citistates** that cross the political boundaries of old.[120] People in a metropolitan area will need to plan and work together if they are going to be able to meet the new challenges brought about by increased global economic competition and preserve the quality of urban life. Urban economist Anthony Downs, too, has observed that both suburban prosperity and the national interest require that suburban residents recognize the interdependence of urban communities:

> But the long-run welfare of suburban residents is still closely linked to how well central cities and their residents perform significant social and economic functions in each metropolitan area. The belief among sub-urbanites that they are independent of central cities is a delusion. So is the belief that central cities are obsolete. Both fallacies have conse-quences dangerous to America's economic and social health.[121]

But just what are the prospects for implementing reforms and cre-ating arrangements that will bring more cohesive regional action? This is the subject of our next two chapters.

NOTES

1. For an earlier work on the diversity of suburbs, see Frederick M. Wirt et al., *On the City's Rim: Politics and Policy in Suburbia* (Lexington, MA: D. C. Heath, 1972), pp. 35–48.
2. Three good examples of the more scholarly sociological 1950s literature on suburbia are William H. Whyte, Jr., *The Organization Man* (New York: Simon & Schuster, 1956); David Riesman, *The Lonely Crowd* (Garden City, NY: Doubleday, 1957); and J. Seeley, R. Sim, and E. Loosley, *Crestwood Heights* (New York: Basic Books, 1956). For a good overview of the commentary on suburbia during this period, see David Popenoe, *The Suburban Environment: Sweden and the United States* (Chicago: University of Chicago Press, 1977), chapter 1.
3. Bennett M. Berger, *Working-Class Suburb* (Berkeley, CA: University of California Press, 1960).
4. Joel Garreau, *Edge City: Life on the New Frontier* (New York: Doubleday, 1991). Also see Peter O. Muller, "The Transformation of Bedroom Suburbia into the Outer City: An Overview of Metropolitan Structural Change since 1947," in *Suburbia Re-examined*, ed. Barbara M. Kelly (New York: Greenwood Press, 1989), pp. 39–44.
5. Rob Kling, Spencer Olin, and Mark Poster, "The Emergence of Postsuburbia: An Introduction," in *Postsuburban California: The Transformation of Orange County since World War II*, ed. Kling, Olin, and Poster (Berkeley, CA: Univ. of California Press, 1991), pp. 20–22. For a provocative description of racial conflict in Orange County, see Mike Davis, "Behind the Orange Curtain," *The Nation*, October 31, 1994, pp. 485–90.
6. Lynn M. Appleton, "The Gender Regimes of American Cities," in *Gender in Urban Research*, *Urban Affairs Annual Review* 42, ed. Judith A. Garber and Robyne S. Turner (Thousand Oaks, CA: Sage Publications, 1995), pp. 44–59.
7. Alan DiGaetano and John S. Klemanski, "Restructuring the Suburbs: Political Economy of Economic Development in Auburn Hills, Michigan," *Journal of Urban Affairs* 13, 2 (1991): 137–58.

8. Hugh A. Wilson, "The Family in Suburbia: From Tradition to Pluralism," in *Suburbia Re-examined*, pp. 85–93.

9. Michael Gutkowski and Tracey Field, *The Graying of Suburbia* (Washington, DC: Urban Institute, 1979), pp. 1–17.

10. Popenoe, *The Suburban Environment*, especially pp. 138–39 and 165–86.

11. Marsha Ritzdorf, "Land Use, Local Control, and Social Responsibility: The Child Care Example," *Journal of Urban Affairs* 15, 1 (1993): 79–91.

12. Appleton, "The Gender Regimes of American Cities," pp. 53–55.

13. U.S. Department of Commerce, Bureau of the Census, *Standard Metropolitan Statistical Areas: 1980* (Washington, DC: Government Printing Office, 1981).

14. John F. Kain, "Housing Market Discrimination and Black Suburbanization in the 1980s," in *Divided Neighborhoods: Changing Patterns of Racial Segregation, Urban Affairs Annual Review* 32, ed. Gary A. Tobin (Newbury Park, CA: Sage Publications, 1987), p. 87.

15. Gary Orfield, "Minorities and Suburbanization," in *Critical Perspectives on Housing*, ed. Rachel G. Bratt, Chester Hartman, and Ann Myerson (Philadelphia: Temple Univ. Press, 1986), p. 222.

16. John E. Farley, "Segregation in 1980: How Segregated Are America's Metropolitan Areas?" in *Divided Neighborhoods*, p. 106.

17. For a description of politics in one southern California suburb as a Latino majority began to emerge, see Lisbeth Haas, "Grass-Roots Protest and the Politics of Planning: Santa Ana, 1976–88," in *Postsuburban California*, pp. 254–80.

18. W. P. O'Hare, R. Chatterjee, and M. Shukur, *Blacks, Demographic Change, and Public Policy: Migration Trends and Population Distribution in Metropolitan Areas*, report prepared for the U.S. Department of Housing and Urban Development (Washington, DC: U.S. Government Printing Office, 1982), cited in Orfield, "Minorities and Suburbanization," p. 224.

19. Farley, "Segregation in 1980: How Segregated Are America's Metropolitan Areas?" pp. 106–07.

20. *San Francisco Examiner*, August 10, 1982, cited by Orfield, "Minorities and Suburbanization," p. 222.

21. George C. Galster, "Black Suburbanization: Has It Changed the Relative Location of Races?" *Urban Affairs Quarterly* 26 (June 1991): 621–28.

22. *Standard Metropolitan Statistical Areas: 1980*. Also see Lowell W. Culver, "Changing Settlement Patterns of Black Americans, 1970–1980," *Journal of Urban Affairs* 4 (Fall 1982): 36–42.

23. Kain, "Housing Market Discrimination and Black Suburbanization in the 1980s," pp. 68 and 84–87.

24. Thomas A. Clark, "The Suburbanization Process and Residential Segregation," in *Divided Neighborhoods*, pp. 134–35.

25. John E. Farley, "Metropolitan Housing Segregation in 1980: The St. Louis Case," *Urban Affairs Quarterly* 18 (March 1983): 347–59; Robert W. Lake, *The New Suburbanites: Race and Housing in the Suburbs* (New Brunswick, NJ: Center for Urban Policy Research, 1981), pp. 238–39; and Elizabeth D. Huttman and Terry Jones, "American Suburbs: Desegregation and Resegregation," in *Urban Housing Segregation of Minorities in Western Europe and the United States*, ed. Elizabeth D. Huttman (Durham, NC: Duke Univ. Press, 1991), pp. 335–66, especially pp. 348–54.

26. Huttman and Jones, "American Suburbs: Desegregation and Resegregation," pp. 343–43.

27. Joseph T. Darden, "Choosing Neighbors and Neighborhoods: The Role of Race in Housing Preference," in *Divided Neighborhoods*, pp. 16–20.

28. John E. Farley, *Segregated City, Segregated Suburbs: Are They Products of Black-White Socioeconomic Differentials?* (Edwardsville, IL: Southern Illinois University, 1983) cited by Darden, "Choosing Neighbors and Neighborhoods," p. 16.

29. John F. Kain, "The Extent and Causes of Racial Residential Segregation" (Paper prepared for a conference on "Civil Rights in the Eighties," Chicago Urban League, June 15, 1984, Tables 1 and 2). This paper is cited by Gary Orfield, "Ghettoization and Its Alternatives," in *The New Urban Reality* (Washington, DC: Brookings Institution, 1985), p. 168.

30. Huttman and Jones, "American Suburbs: Desegregation and Resegregation," pp. 348–54.

31. The various surveys of black and white housing preferences are summarized by Darden, "Choosing Neighbors and Neighborhoods," pp. 25–30; and Kain, "Housing Market Discrimination and Black Suburbanization in the 1980s," pp. 77–82.

32. Darden, "Choosing Neighbors and Neighborhoods," p. 17.

33. Joe T. Darden, Harriet Orcutt Duleep, and George C. Galster, "Civil Rights in Metropolitan America," *Journal of Urban Affairs* 14, 3/4 (1992): p. 470. Douglas S. Massey and Nancy A. Denton, *American Apartheid* (Cambridge, MA: Harvard Univ. Press, 1993), detail the history of discriminatory actions in the housing market by both the government and the private sector.

34. George Galster, "Racial Discrimination in Housing Markets During the 1980s: A Review of the Audit Evidence" (Paper presented at the annual meeting of the Urban Affairs Association, Baltimore, March 15–18, 1989), p. 15.

35. W. Dennis Keating, *The Suburban Racial Dilemma: Housing and Neighborhoods* (Philadelphia: Temple Univ. Press, 1994), pp. 11–13; and Andrew Hacker, *Two Nations: Black and White, Separate, Hostile, Unequal* (New York: Ballantine, 1992), pp. 35–38.

36. Mittie Olion Chandler, "Homogeneity and Conflict: A Case of Political Conflict in a Black Suburb" (Paper presented at the annual meeting of the Midwest Political Science Association, Chicago, April 15, 1989); and Keating, *The Suburban Racial Dilemma*, chapter 5.

37. The history of Shaker Heights presented here relies greatly on Keating, *The Suburban Racial Dilemma*, chapter 6; and Isabel Wilkerson, "One City's 30-Year Crusade for Integration," *The New York Times*, December 30, 1991. Also see Donald L. DeMarco and George C. Galster, "Prointegrative Policy: Theory and Practice," *Journal of Urban Affairs* 15, 2 (1993): 141–60.

38. Wilkerson, "One City's 30-Year Crusade for Integration."

39. Keating, *The Suburban Racial Dilemma*, chapter 7.

40. Keating, *The Suburban Racial Dilemma*, pp. 211–17; and William Peterman, "Twenty Years of Racial Diversity in Oak Park, Illinois" (unpublished).

41. Richard A. Smith, "Creating Stable Racially Integrated Communities: A Review," *Journal of Urban Affairs* 15, 2 (1993): 129–31.

42. *South-Suburban Housing Center v. Greater South-Suburban Board of Realtors*, 935F. 2d, 112 S.Ct. 971 (1972). Also see Kermit J. Lind, "Recent Legal

Developments Affecting Residential Integration Programs" (Paper presented at the annual meeting of the Urban Affairs Association, Cleveland, Ohio, May 2, 1992); and Keating, *The Suburban Racial Dilemma*, pp. 226–36.

43. Robert Wood, *Suburbia: Its People and Its Politics* (Boston: Houghton Mifflin, 1958), pp. 153 and 53, respectively.

44. Gwendolyn Wright, *Building the Dream: A Social History of Housing in America* (Cambridge, MA: MIT Press, 1981), pp. 240–61 and 271–72.

45. Carl Abbott, *The New Urban America: Growth and Politics in Sunbelt Cities*, rev. ed. (Chapel Hill, NC: University of North Carolina Press, 1987), p. 213.

46. Wood, *Suburbia*, pp. 186–97.

47. For a description of partisan politics in New York's suburban Nassau County, see Anne Freedman, *Patronage: An American Tradition* (Chicago: Nelson-Hall, 1994), pp. 127–67.

48. Wirt et al., *On the City's Rim*, pp. 148–59.

49. Wood, *Suburbia*, pp. 162–66.

50. Robert N. Bellah et al., *Habits of the Heart: Individualism and Commitment in American Life* (New York: Perennial Library/Harper & Row, 1985), pp. 8–13 and 170–85.

51. Jonathan Kozol, *Savage Inequalities* (New York: Crown, 1991), pp. 214 and 220.

52. *Serrano v. Priest*, 5 Cal. 3d 584, 487 (1971).

53. *Rodriguez v. San Antonio Independent School District* 411 U.S. 1 (1973). Also see Kozol, *Savage Inequalities*, pp. 214–19.

54. Richard Lehne, *The Quest for Justice: The Politics of School Finance Reform* (White Plains, NY: Longman, 1978), pp. 194–97.

55. Kozol, *Savage Inequalities*, p. 221–25; and William Celis 3d, "A Texas-Size Battle to Teach Rich and Poor Alike," *The New York Times*, February 12, 1992.

56. The New Jersey early action on school finance reform is described by Lehne, *The Quest for Justice*.

57. Robert Hanley, "New Jersey School-Aid Law Assailed," *The New York Times*, November 1, 1990; and Jerry Gray, "Gap Narrows for New Jersey School Districts," *The New York Times*, October 12, 1994.

58. Celis, "A Texas-Size Battle to Teach Rich and Poor Alike."

59. Sam Howe Verhovek, "Texans Reject Sharing of School District Wealth," *The New York Times*, May 3, 1993.

60. William Celis 3d, "In Test of Kentucky Education Law, State Takes Over Harlan District," and "Kentucky Trying to Find Money to Better Schools," both in *The New York Times*, February 5, 1992.

61. Lee A. Daniels, "Doubts Abound on Boston U. Plan to Run Schools," *The New York Times*, August 10, 1988; "Boston U. Plan to Run Schools Facing Delay," *The New York Times*, December 6, 1988; Edward B. Fiske, "An Impoverished Urban District Hands Its Schools Over to Boston University to Run," *The New York Times*, August 16, 1989; and Susan Chira, "The Lessons Learned When College Officials Run Public Schools," *The New York Times*, July 11, 1990.

62. David O. Sears and Jack Citrin, *Tax Revolt: Something for Nothing in California* (Cambridge, MA: Harvard University Press, 1982), pp. 220–21.

63. Peter Schrag, "California Screamin'," *New Republic*, June 23, 1986, pp. 14–16; and Kozol, *Savage Inequalities*, p. 221.

64. Terry Schwandron and Paul Richter, *California and the American Tax Revolt: Proposition 13 Five Years Later* (Berkeley, CA: University of California Press, 1984), pp. 37–38.

65. Lillieanne Chase, "Funny-Money Classrooms," *Golden State Report* (September 1986): 33–35.

66. Alan A. Altshuler and Jose A. Gomez-Ibañez, with Arnold M. Howitt, *Regulation for Revenue: The Political Economy of Land Use Exactions* (Washington, DC: Brookings Institution, 1993), pp. 124–25.

67. *Millikin v. Bradley*, 418 U.S. 717 (1974).

68. See three articles in the January 16, 1991, *The New York Times*: Linda Greenhouse, "Justices Rule Mandatory Busing May Go, Even If Races Stay Apart;" Amy Stuart Wells, "Asking What Schools Have Done, or Can Do, to Help Desegregation;" and "Excerpts from Court Decisions on Desegregation."

69. "Guidance on School Desegregation," editorial, *Washington Post National Weekly Edition*, April 13–19, 1992.

70. Jane Gross, "Politicians, Amid Ruins, Talk of Laws," *The New York Times*, October 23, 1991; and Robert Reinhold, "Building on Sand: Pain Repays Reckless California," *The New York Times*, October 28, 1991.

71. Sam Howe Verhovek, "'Anything Goes' Houstonians May Go the Limit: to Zoning," *The New York Times*, October 27, 1993.

72. Robert C. Wood, "Suburbia: The Fiscal Roots of Political Fragmentation and Differentiation," in *Metropolitan Politics: A Reader*, 2nd ed., ed. Michael N. Danielson (Boston: Little, Brown, 1971), pp. 92–102.

73. Mike Davis, *City of Quartz* (New York: Random House, 1990), pp. 206–09.

74. Wood, *Suburbia: Its People and Its Politics*, p. 275.

75. Ibid., p. 275.

76. Bellah et al., *Habits of the Heart*, pp. 72–74.

77. Michael N. Danielson, *The Politics of Exclusion* (New York: Columbia University Press, 1976), p. 53.

78. The critical importance of delays as an exclusionary technique that creates paralysis and drives up costs is described by Bernard J. Frieden, *The Environmental Protection Hustle* (Cambridge, MA: MIT Press, 1979), pp. 60–71; and David E. Dowall, *The Suburban Squeeze: Land Conversion and Regulation in the San Francisco Bay Area* (Berkeley, CA: University of California Press, 1984), pp. 122–29.

79. J. Barry Cullingworth, *The Political Culture of Planning: American Land Use Planning in Comparative Perspective* (New York: Routledge, 1993), p. 229.

80. Dowall, *The Suburban Squeeze*, pp. 192–93.

81. *Golden v. Planning Board of the Town of Ramapo*, 285 N.E. 2d 291 (1972). Also see Cullingworth, *The Political Culture of Planning*, p. 125.

82. *Construction Industry Association of Sonoma County v. City of Petaluma*, 424 U.S. 934 (1976). Also see Cullingworth, *The Political Culture of Planning*, pp. 125–26; and Frieden, *The Environmental Protection Hustle*, pp. 32–36.

83. Cullingworth, *The Political Culture of Planning*, p. 126.

84. Roger W. Caves, *Land Use Planning: The Ballot Box Revolution* (Newbury Park, CA: Sage Publications, 1992); and Richard Edward DeLeon, *Left Coast City: Progressive Politics in San Francisco, 1975–1991* (Lawrence, KS: Univ. of Kansas Press, 1992).

85. Jon E. Goetz, "Direct Democracy in Land Use Planning: The State Response to Eastlake," *Pacific Law Journal* 19 (1988): 833–34. This article is reprinted in

Land Use and Environment Law Review—1989, ed. Stuart L. Deutsch and A. Dan Tarlock (New York: Clark Boardman, 1989), pp. 203–54.

86. Ibid., p. 821.

87. Caves, *Land Use Planning: The Ballot Box Revolution*, pp. 72–134. The "creeping condominiumism" remark appears on p. 133.

88. Cullingworth, *The Political Culture of Planning*, pp. 133–55.

89. For a more detailed description of Florida's efforts to strengthen its controls over local land use, see Robyne S. Turner, "New Rules for the Growth Game: The Use of Rational State Standards in Land Use Policy," *Journal of Urban Affairs* 12, 1 (1990): 35–47.

90. *Village of Euclid, Ohio, v. Ambler Realty Co.*, 272 U.S. 365 (1926). For an assessment of the impact of *Euclid* and zoning on communities in the United States, see Charles M. Haar and Jerold S. Kayden, eds., *Zoning and the American Dream: Promises Still to Keep* (Chicago: APA Planners Press, 1989).

91. *U.S. v. City of Black Jack, Missouri*, 508 F. 2d 1179 (1974). A more extensive overview of the Black Jack case is presented by Dennis R. Judd, *The Politics of American Cities: Private Power and Public Policy*, 3rd ed. (Glenview, IL: Scott, Foresman, 1988), pp. 185–90.

92. *Arlington Heights v. Metropolitan Housing Development Corporation*, 429 U.S. 252 (1977).

93. Frieden, *The Environmental Protection Hustle*, pp. 107–18.

94. 107 S.Ct. 2378, p. 2389, quoted in Lee P. Symons, "Property Rights and Local Land-Use Regulation: The Implications of *First English* and *Nollan*," *Publius: The Journal of Federalism* 18 (Summer 1988): 85. Our discussion of *First English* and *Nollan* relies heavily on Symons, pp. 90–95.

95. 107 S.Ct. 3141, 97 L. Ed. 677 (1987).

96. *Seawall Associates v. City of New York*, 542 N.E. 2d 1059 (N.Y. 1989). Also see "Stoned by *Seawall*: New York Decision Impedes Legislative Solutions to Affordable Housing Shortage," *University of Miami Law Review* 45 (1990–91): 467–530.

97. Symons, "Property Rights and Local Land-Use Regulation," p. 93.

98. Frieden, *The Environmental Protection Hustle*, pp. 23–24, 38–41, and 52–59.

99. Dowall, *The Suburban Squeeze*, pp. 133–34.

100. 67 N.J. 151, 336 A. 2d 713 (1975). Our discussion of the various Mount Laurel decisions borrows heavily from Harold A. McDougall, "From Litigation to Legislation in Exclusionary Zoning Law," 22 *Harvard Civil Rights–Civil Liberties Law Review* 623 (1987): 623–63. The McDougall article is reprinted in *Land Use and Environment Law Review—1988* (New York: Clark Boardman, 1988): 203–43.

101. The evolution of the *Mount Laurel* decisions is described by Cullingworth, *The Political Culture of Planning*, pp. 66–71.

102. *Burlington County NAACP v. Township of Mount Laurel*, 92 N.J. 158, 336 A. 2d 390 (1983).

103. *Hills Development Co. v. Township of Bernard*, 103 N.J. 1, 510 A. 2d 621 (1986).

104. Alan S. Oser, "Court Ruling on Zoning Weighed," *The New York Times*, April 4, 1975; and Charles Strum, "Fair Housing Buys Trouble in New Jersey," *The New York Times*, January 11, 1992.

105. Mark Alan Hughes and Peter M. VanDoren, "Social Policy Through Land Reform: New Jersey's Mount Laurel Controversy," *Political Science Quarterly* 105 (Spring 1990): 111.

106. McDougall, "From Litigation to Legislation in Exclusionary Zoning Law," pp. 637–41; and Hughes and VanDoren, "Social Policy Through Land Reform," pp. 108–11.
107. Hughes and VanDoren, "Social Policy Through Land Reform," p. 109.
108. Kevin Sullivan, "Housing Plan Passes, 5–4, in Montgomery: Affordable Units Allowed in Wealthy Neighborhoods," *Washington Post*, September 23, 1992; and Henry G. Cisneros, *Regionalism: The New Geography of Opportunity* (Washington, DC: U.S. Department of Housing and Urban Development, 1995), pp. 18–19.
109. George Judson, "Housing Law Disputes Zoning Boards' Power," *The New York Times*, November 5, 1991.
110. Morris Newman, "The Struggle to Provide Affordable Homes: In Santa Monica, Neighborhood Politics Prevails," *The New York Times*, March 8, 1992.
111. Lynda Richardson, "Yonkers Reaches Agreement On a Plan for Desegregation," *The New York Times*, April 15, 1992.
112. Wood, *Suburbia*, p. 71. Also see Anthony Downs, *New Visions for Metropolitan America* (Washington, DC: Brookings Institution, 1994).
113. Kozol, *Savage Inequalities*.
114. Mark Schneider and John R. Logan, "Fiscal Implications of Class Segregation: Inequalities in the Distribution of Public Goods and Services in Suburban Municipalities," *Urban Affairs Quarterly* 17 (September 1981), pp. 30–31.
115. Bennett Harrison, *Urban Economic Development: Suburbanization, Minority Opportunity, and the Condition of the Central City* (Washington, DC: Urban Institute, 1974), pp. 114–17.
116. John D. Kasarda, "The Impact of Suburban Population Growth on Central City Service Functions," *American Journal of Sociology* 77 (May 1972): 1123.
117. Todd Swanstrom, "No Room at the Inn: Housing Policy and the Homeless," *Journal of Urban and Contemporary Law* 35 (1989): 91–92 and 99–100.
118. Lisa W. Foderaro, "Westchester's Far-Flung Homeless," *The New York Times*, July 11, 1989.
119. Drew A. Dolan, "Local Government Fragmentation: Does It Drive Up the Cost of Government?" *Urban Affairs Quarterly* 26 (September 1990): 42.
120. Neal R. Peirce, with Curtis W. Johnson and John Stuart Hall, *Citistates: How Urban America Can Prosper in a Competitive World* (Washington, DC: Seven Locks Press, 1993).
121. Downs, *New Visions for Metropolitan America*, p. 52.

10

The Politics of Metropolitan Government

METROPOLITAN FRAGMENTATION AND THE CALL FOR METROPOLITAN GOVERNMENT

As we have seen, one of the chief problems of government in metropolitan areas is **fragmentation**. Each metropolitan area is divided into a large and diverse number of overlapping governmental units: municipalities, counties, towns, authorities, and special districts, including school districts, community college districts, water and sewer districts, library districts, and park districts. Even without being aware of it, citizens in the metropolis are likely receiving public services from several different local governmental bodies.

Such multiple responsibility for service provision often leads to chaos and confusion. With so many governments, effective, coordinated action and service delivery are not always possible. Nor can citizens easily see where their tax money is going or who is to blame for service inadequacies.

As a result, some urbanists have called for a system of **metropolitan government** to rationalize governmental structure and service delivery in the metropolis. Under metropolitan government a number of important decision-making powers would be taken away from the existing local governments and given to a new centralized metropolitan body capable of acting in the interest of the metropolis as a whole.

Yet the establishment of a metropolitan government possessing significant authority has been realized in only a few urban areas across the United States. Incorporated suburban governments refuse to sacrifice their autonomy for the ideal of establishing a new centralized regional governing institution. In most metropolitan areas, cities and suburbs cooperate with one another only on a limited and, to a great degree, a voluntary basis.

As we shall see in this chapter and in Chapter 11, interlocal cooperation has taken a wide variety of forms. Informal cooperation, intergovernmental contracting, and the creation of special districts are only among the most popular mechanism that contiguous suburbs have resorted to in an attempt to improve the provision of schooling, water supply, sewage disposal, transportation, and other services to their citizens. This variety of cooperative solutions allows suburbs to enhance service delivery without threatening their autonomy.

But critics charge that the vast variety of interlocal cooperative arrangements compounds certain problems of governing metropolitan regions. For instance, the increasing resort to special districts and independent authorities has shifted broad areas of public policy-making responsibility to the relatively invisible and insulated program specialists who populate the boards and agencies of these special districts and service areas.[1]

Interlocal cooperation can also be time-consuming and cumbersome. For instance, the orderly development of a new Washington, DC, metropolitan area subway system was delayed for many years as various local governments in the region debated the number and location of stations to be built, the financial contribution to be required of each local participating jurisdiction, and the fares to charge riders.

Critics further point out that local jurisdictions will cooperate only to the extent they find it convenient to do so. Rarely will effective joint action emerge for dealing with such controversial and politically sensitive issues as public housing construction, school integration, and public welfare provision. A city or suburb can even withdraw from a voluntary arrangement that threatens its interests. The results of this can be less than desirable for the region. In the greater San Francisco area, for example, the trains of the Bay Area Rapid Transit (BART) system do not serve the entire metropolitan area since a number of local jurisdictions chose not to participate in the construction of the new system.

Many urbanists, then, continue to call for the establishment of strong, centralized, metropolitan governments. But as we shall see, the political opposition to metropolitan government remains so strong that, in all but a few cases, the enactment of truly effective regional governing structures remains an impossibility.

THREE FORMS OF METROPOLITAN GOVERNMENT

Proposals for metropolitanwide governments entail boundary changes that alter power relationships. Suburban residents and local officials generally do not want to cede power to new regional governing institutions. Americans are also a generally conservative people who prefer their existing fragmented and flawed governmental arrangements instead of the great changes that might be brought about by more comprehensive reform. As a result, metropolitan government is not easy to achieve.

Yet a number of major metropolitan areas, including Jacksonville, Nashville, Baton Rouge, Lexington (Kentucky), Indianapolis, Miami, Portland, and Minneapolis/St. Paul, do have some form of metropolitan government. Special circumstances help to explain how centralized regional governments were established in these areas despite widespread opposition to their enactment.

In this chapter we will identify three variations of metropolitan government: city-county consolidation, the two-tier plan, and the Portland Metropolitan Service District and the Twin Cities Metropolitan Council three-tier plan. As the movement toward metropolitan reform has greatly slowed in recent years, we will also look at the debate over whether or not the goal of establishing metropolitan governments is really worth the effort.

City-County Consolidation: Nashville, Jacksonville, and Indianapolis (Unigov)

Under **city-county consolidation**, a county and the cities within it merge to form a single governmental unit. The county, in effect, becomes the government of the entire metropolitan region as other local governments are eliminated. In some cases existing local governments are allowed to keep their identities after consolidation, but their powers are lessened as increased authority is transferred to the enhanced countywide unit. The achievement of consolidation usually requires state legislative approval as well as approval at the polls by voters in both the central city and the noncentral-city areas of the county.

City-county consolidation is not a new phenomenon. (See Table 10.1.) Philadelphia, Boston, and New Orleans achieved city-county consolidation in the nineteenth century. In New York City consolidation was realized in 1897 when the five local counties (more commonly referred to as *boroughs*) merged to form a single city. Interestingly, in recent years the residents of one of these boroughs, Staten Island, have sought to secede from the city.

Our attention here will focus on more contemporary efforts toward consolidation. While consolidations in a number of smaller urban areas have been realized, the great majority of all consolidation plans never gain enactment. Three important consolidation efforts that did succeed were in Nashville-Davidson County, Tennessee (1962); Jacksonville-Duval County, Florida (1967); and Unigov in Indianapolis-Marion County (1969). Why did city-county consolidation plans in these areas succeed while consolidation efforts in so many other areas failed?

Nashville

A consolidation proposal for Nashville-Davidson County failed in 1958 when it received only 48-percent support from the electorate.[2] However, between 1958 and 1962 the city of Nashville initiated an aggressive annexation campaign, acquiring a substantial portion of land (some fifty square miles) in Davidson County. As a result, by 1962 many county voters

TABLE 10.1
City-County Consolidations

Year	City-County	State
1805	New Orleans-Orleans Parish	Louisiana
1821	Boston-Suffolk County	Massachusetts
1821	Nantucket-Nantucket County	Massachusetts
1854	Philadelphia-Philadelphia County	Pennsylvania
1856	San Francisco-San Francisco County	California
1874	New York (Manhattan)-New York County	New York
1984	New York-Bronx and Staten Island	New York
1898	New York-Brooklyn and Queens Boroughs and Richmond County	New York
1904	Denver-Arapahoe County	Colorado
1907	Honolulu-Honolulu County	Hawaii
1947	Baton Rouge-East Baton Rouge Parish	Louisiana
1952	Hampton and Phoebus-Elizabeth City County	Virginia
1957	Newport News-Warwick City County	Virginia
1962	Nashville-Davidson County	Tennessee
1962	Chesapeake-South Norfolk-Norfolk County	Virginia
1962	Virginia Beach-Princess Anne County	Virginia
1967	Jacksonville-Duval County	Florida
1969	Indianapolis-Marion County	Indiana
1969	Carson City-Ormsby County	Nevada
1969	Juneau and Douglas-Greater Juneau Borough	Alaska
1970	Columbus-Musckogee County	Georgia
1971	Holland and Whaleyville-Nansemond County	Virginia
1971	Sitka-Greater Sitka Borough	Alaska
1972	Lexington-Fayette County	Kentucky
1972	Suffolk-Nansemond County	Virginia
1975	Anchorage, Glen Alps, and Girdwood-Greater Anchorage Borough	Alaska
1976	Anaconda-Deer Lodge County	Montana
1976	Butte-Silver Bow County	Montana
1984	Houma-Terrebonne County	Louisiana
1988	Lynchburg-Moore County	Tennessee
1992	Athens-Clarke County	Georgia

Source: National Association of Counties, Research Department (March 1994).

came to see that their choice was between annexation by the city or joining with the city to form a new and more professional countywide government with a new metropolitanwide mayor and council. Many residents of Nashville's growing suburbs also needed new services and looked to consolidation to increase the provision of city-type services they had been doing without.

One of the major features of the Nashville-Davidson County plan was the creation of two service and taxing zones. A general services district serves the entire county, while a second district—the urban services district—provides intensified police protection, street lighting and cleaning, and other services. Over the years new suburban areas have been added into the urban services district. Overall, the creation of metro in Nashville-Davidson County has led to a kind of rising revolution of service expectations and has led to the upgrading, professionalization, and equalization of service delivery throughout the county.

Jacksonville

In Jacksonville-Duval County, Florida, the metropolitan reform movement was triggered by public concern over criminal indictments of numerous public officials. Waste, fraud, and inefficiency marked the delivery of public services under the old central-city government. Jacksonville even faced the possible loss of accreditation of its public schools. Reorganization was perceived as a means of getting rid of corrupt and incompetent officials and bringing good government and improved services to the area.

Yet, two and a half decades later, we can see that promised benefits of metropolitan reform have not been fully realized in Jacksonville. City-county consolidation did not eliminate corruption, increase efficiency, or bring new growth to the old city. City-suburban inequalities actually worsened in the years following reform. In many ways, the stated rhetoric accompanying reform covered ulterior motives. A Chamber of Commerce–dominated business elite used the vehicle of city-county consolidation to throw out the old political crowd that ran the central city government. Jacksonville reformers used the language of reform to justify consolidation. They avoided public discussion of the adverse impact that consolidation would have on the power of the city's black community.[3]

Unigov: Indianapolis/Marion County

The 1969 creation of **Unigov,** or the merger of Indianapolis with Marion County, was the first consolidation of a major large city and county to occur in the United States without a popular referendum since the formation of greater New York in 1897.[4] The history of Unigov illustrates how metropolitan reform efforts are motivated by considerations of political power as well as by a desire to improve metropolitan governance. Ordered by the Indiana state legislature, the consolidation was aided by a number of special circumstances.

First was a unique political alignment of forces under which Republicans controlled the mayor's office, the governorship, and the state legislature. Unigov came into existence largely as a result of the leadership efforts of then-mayor of the city of Indianapolis, Richard Lugar, who sold state Republicans on the political gains to be realized from Unigov's creation. The creation of Unigov allowed suburban Republicans to vote for the area's mayor, offsetting demographic trends that were acting to make the "old city" more and more Democratic.

Democrats charged that the move was a blatant power grab; they referred to the consolidation not as Unigov but as "Unigrab." Election results since then have underscored the truth in these charges. In 1975 Republican William Hudnut was elected Unigov's mayor, having lost the old central city by 17,500 votes and having carried the suburbs by over 31,000 votes. In 1979, Hudnut, the popular incumbent, won reelection by carrying both the city and the suburban portions of the metropolitan area—as Lugar had done before him. But the Republican bias that characterized Unigov's creation would soon reemerge. In 1991 Republican Stephen Goldsmith was elected mayor by a countywide marge of 30,000 votes despite having lost the old city by nearly 15,000 votes.[5]

Second, state legislative action in creating Unigov was facilitated by the absence of a strong home rule tradition in Indiana. The city of Indianapolis lacked its own legal charter. A tradition of direct state intervention in the city's affairs also helped legitimate the state legislature's action in creating Unigov. The willingness of the state to act without a public referendum may well have been crucial to Unigov's success.

Finally, potential opposition to the effort was muted as a number of governmental jurisdictions and critical services were left out of the unification plan. School districts were allowed to maintain their independence, thereby salving the fears of suburbanites in this most politically salient service area. To have included the schools in the plan would have raised prospects of racial integration and would have meant the instant death of the reform measure. Similarly, a number of cities, townships, and special districts and boards, as well as the county itself, were allowed to continue to exist as legal entities despite the consolidation. The creation of Unigov posed as little threat as possible to existing municipal officeholders. In total, over 100 separate taxing units exist in the area despite the Unigov consolidation.[6] As we can see, despite its name, Unigov does not really produce unified government.

Unigov's primary success was in creating a system of strong, regional leadership. Unigov created a single, countywide chief executive and combined the city and county councils into a single body. Even though governmental integration is incomplete, Unigov gave the regional executive and central policy-making council dominant power over what is arguably the strongest regional planning and economic development department in the country.[7]

Unigov has done well on bricks-and-mortar issues, allowing the city of Indianapolis to pursue an aggressive strategy of promoting public-private partnerships for economic growth. It has given both the mayor and the Department of Metropolitan Development the ability to steer investment from the urban rim to the downtown. For example, Unigov officials convinced the developers of Market Square Arena to locate the new sports facility in the center of the city rather than on the interstate. Unigov's officials also helped persuade the Lilly Endowment (the Eli Lilly Company is the only Fortune 500 firm located in the area) to pay part of the costs of the downtown Hoosier Dome.[8] The ability of the mayor and Department of Metropolitan Development to enhance the position of the central city is evident in the actions they undertook to convince American United Life (AUL) to abandon plans for a suburban headquarters facility and instead build a $55 million, 38-story office tower (the largest in the state) on a two-block site in the central business district, bringing an anticipated 1,500 employees downtown.[9] Unigov's ability to speak for the region and market the entire area also helped Indianapolis to win the 93-city competition for a $1 billion United Airlines maintenance facility and its promise of 6,400 jobs over ten years.

But while Unigov has been successful in promoting economic growth, it has done less well in human services.[10] Nor has Unigov equalized taxing and service provisions throughout the county. Not only do numerous local governments continue to exist, Unigov's structure has allowed for the creation of special service districts and special taxing districts, thereby leading to different service and taxing levels in different parts of the county. Consolidation also has not been particularly successful in tapping suburban revenues for city needs, especially as schools were kept out of the metropolitan arrangement. The creation of Unigov has also diluted the black voting base in the central city.[11]

Metropolitan reform has brought a new sense of policy direction and professionalism to Indianapolis. It has placed new leadership power in the hands of the metro mayor and has increased the faith of the business community in Indianapolis. But Unigov has succeeded in forging public-private partnerships for growth only at the costs of preserving Republican dominance over the old city and diminishing the influence of the central-city, African-American community.

City-County Consolidation: An Assessment

What can be concluded from a review of city-county consolidation efforts throughout the country?[12] First of all, consolidation is quite difficult to achieve, and consolidation efforts generally fail. Existing officeholders are likely to oppose it. Suburbanites fear that consolidation will diminish the quality of their services or raise their taxes. Minorities in the central city fear that consolidation will diminish their political power. As a result, voter approval for reorganizations through multiple referenda is most difficult to get. In the Indianapolis case, Unigov had to be imposed on voters from the outside, by the state legislature.

Second, the consolidation of multicounty areas is a virtual impossibility. All adoptions that have succeeded occurred in single-county metropolitan areas. Where a metropolitan area is so large that it spills beyond the borders of a single county, city-county consolidation may be considered no more than subregional government.

Third, an important impetus to reform exists where growing suburban areas desire improved service levels or where reorganization is perceived as a means of getting rid of corrupt or incompetent local officials. Such was the case in Nashville, in Jacksonville, and to a lesser extent in Indianapolis. In established suburbs, in contrast, residents will resist joining with the central city from fear that new governmental arrangements will increase taxes or lead to racial integration.

Fourth, city-county consolidation is to a great extent a regional phenomenon. With the exception of Unigov, there have been no major contemporary consolidations in the Northeast or North central states. Reorganizations that have succeeded are generally in the South. In part, this was due to the traditional one-party political systems and the general absence of competing local governments in southern counties. More recent years have also witnessed an increase in the number of consolidation efforts involving small cities in the West.[13]

Fifth, even where consolidations are adopted, they are most often incomplete. As we described above, Unigov is a very partial reorganization. Numerous local governments also remain in existence in various other consolidations, including Jacksonville-Duval, Nashville-Davidson, Baton Rouge–East Baton Rouge (Louisiana), Lexington-Fayette (Kentucky), and Carson City–Ormsby (Nevada). In the mid-1990s, Charlotte and Mecklenberg County (North Carolina) were considering consolidation, but five smaller cities in the county were likely to opt out of the plan.

Finally, city-county consolidation efforts can be viewed as part of the power struggle in urban politics. Consolidation has been used by city business elites to seize power away from the old political gang that ran city hall. In Indianapolis, Unigov was used by Republicans to maintain their control over city hall and the economic development of the region. City-county consolidation has also diluted the power of central-city minority groups.

Overall, prospects for future city-county consolidation are quite dim. As Vincent Marando concludes, "Metropolitan reorganization via consolidation is not a dead issue, but it is certainly not very healthy."[14]

THE TWO-TIER PLANS OF TORONTO AND MIAMI

Under **two-tier restructuring**, two levels of government are established in a metropolitan area. Areawide functions are assigned to an areawide, or metropolitan, government with boundaries that encompass all the individual local government units. More localized functions, however, are left to the existing municipalities; there is no consolidation or merger of governments. A variation of this restructuring is commonly called the **federation plan**; local governments retain their existence, but in effect are represented in a new federation that handles areawide concerns. Metropolitan Toronto and Winnipeg are two prominent examples in Canada of the federation plan; their local unit members are referred to as *boroughs*.

The chief advantage of the two-tier design lies in its ability to provide a metropolitan government to deal with regional problems while allowing the diverse municipalities to cope with their own local problems. Ideally, metropolitan efficiency is achieved without sacrificing local political identity and participation.

Despite these theoretical advantages, it is easy to see the barriers that work against the adoption of the plan in the United States. At the outset there is the question of which service and regulatory responsibilities will be assigned to which level of government. It is never quite clear if an issue is entirely local in scope or has implications that affect neighboring jurisdictions. Second, elected officials and the electorates of the various municipalities are likely to fear the concept of a "big" metropolitan government. Local voters will be reluctant to abandon local control over such areas as zoning, taxation, and the schools. The federation systems in Toronto and Winnipeg were imposed by legislation passed by the provinces (the Canadian equivalent of the American states), not by local referenda.[15]

Metro Toronto

According to Frances Frisken, "The name Metropolitan Toronto is virtually synonymous in North America with effective metropolitan administration."[16] This federation of the city of Toronto and twelve (now five) suburbs was established in 1954 because local jurisdictions proved unable to provide the sewer and water facilities, transportation system, and planning and environmental safeguards necessitated by the area's rapid growth. Metropolitan Toronto was to aid both the suburbs and central city alike, providing rapidly growing suburbs with basic public services and assisting the city of Toronto by establishing the necessary planning systems to stem city overcrowding, traffic congestion, and deterioration.[17]

The success of Metro Toronto is readily apparent in the region's development of a relatively balanced transportation system. The shift away from expressways to a greater investment in both rapid transit and bus routes was made possible only as regional planning and transportation were clearly upper-tier responsibilities. The metropolitan government aggressively pushed the extension of bus routes and rail lines in order to meet its twin missions of upgrading suburban service and providing the infrastructure necessary to maintain a strong central-city economy.[18]

Metro Toronto has also made impressive strides in other areas of public works, including the construction of new water and sewage facilities, a baseball stadium, and a regional parks system. Centralization has also brought about the upgrading of the police force. Critics, however, charge that the physical construction and fiscal needs of the area dominated Metro Toronto's early years to the disadvantage of housing and social concerns.

Of course, Metro Toronto has not always made decisions that have worked to the advantage of the central city. Only nine of the thirty-four Metro Council wards lie inside the city of Toronto.[19] This minority position has put the city at a disadvantage in political battles over who will pay the cost of public works projects. Consequently, the city of Toronto is the greatest contributor to the region's mass transit system, with a fare structure that in effect has central-city riders subsidize the more lightly used suburban lines. Still, it can be argued that the development of mass transit has clearly contributed to the city's growth and prosperity.[20]

Miami Metro

In the United States, Metro Miami–Dade County, established in 1957, is the only important example of a two-tiered system. Metro's creation was a response to the area's extraordinary population growth and the resulting new pressures for planning and municipal services.

The creation of Metro Miami was facilitated by a number of special circumstances.[21] At the time of Metro's formation, many of the residents of Dade County's suburbs were émigrés from the North and were not long-time residents of the region; as a result, they had little time to develop strong attachments to their communities or strong resentment against the city of Miami. Second, Miami's downtown business leaders were able to use exposés of public corruption in the city to show the unsatisfactory nature of existing government arrangements; they praised the quality of the county's government by comparison. These downtown business interests were joined by "good government" organizations and the *Miami Herald* in the campaign for metropolitan reform.

Finally, there were no strong competing forces that opposed reform, other than some local government officials who feared a loss of their power. Even here only about twenty jurisdictions were involved in Metro's creation; there were relatively few entrenched politicians with whom to deal. Miami also lacked strong political parties and labor unions, which might have found their interests adversely affected by reorganization. Furthermore, during this period Miami lacked a large, potently organized minority community that might have looked upon metropolitan reorganization as an attempt to dilute its power. At the time of adoption, blacks constituted only 6.8 percent of the registered voters in Miami, and the great waves of Hispanic migration were yet to arrive.

Yet the implementation of the two-tiered plan in Metro Miami–Dade County has not always been easy. The wealthier communities in the county opposed the plan from the beginning, seeing it as an attempt by the city of Miami to tap into their resources. In 1960 a number of the more wealthy communities—Miami Beach, Surfside, Golden Beach, Bal Harbour, and North Bay Village—attempted to secede from the county. The exact division of powers between the two levels of government also remained a long drawn-out and complicated affair. By 1961 some 600 lawsuits challenging Metro's authority had been filed with the courts. A referendum that same year sought to end Metro's control in such areas as water supply, sewage, transportation, and planning. Voters defeated this move; but over the years some amendments were passed curbing the powers of the county manager.[22]

Population changes in the region have led to new criticisms of Miami Metro. African-Americans, Hispanics, and white neighborhood groups haved criticized a seemingly distant Metro government as being irresponsive to their needs.[23] For a long time, African-Americans and Hispanics also complained that Metro's at-large system of electing members of the Metro Commission acts to diminish their voting power. But the Metro Commission and Miamians in public referenda repeatedly rejected measures to change the system, by instituting district elections and enlarging the size of the Metro Commission in order to ensure greater black and Hispanic representation.

Discontented with their lack of influence in the countywide Metro Commission, leaders in the predominantly poor, black Liberty City section of Miami in the 1980s sought to incorporate their area as "New City," an independent municipal government with its own police force and other governing powers: "The bottom line is self determination for Black folks...The [Metro] commissioners in charge of the area now live in Miami Beach and North Miami and they take care of those areas."[24] But this effort, too, was rejected by the Metro Commission. The lack of black power on the Metro Commission was also clearly visible in 1981 when the commission bowed to the protests of white homeowners and reversed its earlier decision to build 120 units of low-income housing in the affluent West Kendall section of southwest Dade County.[25]

Miami's at-large system of elections was at long last changed in 1992 when a federal district court judged ruled that Metro's at-large electoral system was an impermissible violation of the Voting Rights Act, as it diluted the voting power of minority groups. The federal judge ordered a new system of district elections and enlarged the commission from 9 to 13 members. The ruling had the potential of radically altering the balance of power in the county. At the time of the court's ruling, Anglo whites had 7 seats, and Hispanics and blacks had one seat each on the at-large commission. Under the new arrangement, Hispanics had a majority of the population in 7 districts, and blacks and Anglo whites had a majority in 3 districts each. Now it was non-Hispanic whites, who made up approximately a third of the county's population, who charged that they were underrepresented in the new voting plan.[26]

The powers of Miami Metro have gradually been strengthened over time. Metro has brought notable achievements in such areas as highway construction, countywide land use planning, improved social services, and the professionalization of government. Dade voters have also approved the creation of a more powerful county chief executive beginning in 1996.

But Metro still falls short of the idealized vision of metropolitan government. For the half of the county's population that lives in unincorporated areas, there is no two-tier system; the county is the sole municipal service provider. Metro Miami also possesses no authority to coordinate growth and services in neighboring Broward County (Fort Lauderdale) and other neighboring areas in the sprawling, multicounty, metropolitan south Florida agglomeration.[27] The history of Miami Metro has also been marked by severe conflict and debate. Older conflict lines between wealthier residential communities and poorer areas have been joined by newer divisions of ethnicity and race.

THREE-TIER PLANS: PORTLAND AND THE TWIN CITIES

The **three-tier reform** is a rarely used approach that tries to deal with the problems of multicounty areas. It derives its name from the fact that it keeps the existing county and municipal levels of government but simply seeks to add an areawide coordinating agency with some real power on top. The three-tier reform is a plan for limited metropolitan government that seeks to avoid the hostility that often greets more comprehensive unification efforts. The two most prominent examples of this approach are the Greater Portland (Oregon) Metropolitan Service District and Twin Cities (Minneapolis–St. Paul) Metropolitan Council.

Portland (Oregon)

The Portland Metropolitan Services District was established by the state legislature in 1970. In a 1978 referendum, voters gave the district (commonly referred to as Metro) responsibilities for waste disposal, zoo administration, and designated other services in the three-county area. In 1992, Portland-area voters approved a new home-rule charter to affirm Metro's primacy in regional planning, giving the district new powers to manage the area's growth. Metro is unique, as it is the only directly elected regional government in the United States.[28]

In recent years, some of the Portland District's most notable achievements have been in the areas of land use control and environmental protection. Local land use and zoning regulations must comply with the framework set by Metro. The metro district is also charged with developing an affordable housing plan under which each of the twenty-four cities and towns in the three-county region must accept a proportionate share of low- and moderate-income housing. Portland planners have sought to concentrate new development in the city and thereby protect the surrounding countryside—to "build up" as opposed to "build out."

Initially, the list of service responsibilities given Metro was small. But over time the district's responsibilities have been expanded to include recycling, transportation planning, regional air and water quality programs, and the construction and operation of the Oregon Convention Center. Although Metro is in many ways a model of multicounty regional government, still, in Portland, regional government has been used to deal primarily with physical infrastructure and quality-of-life concerns, not questions of social policy and racial equity.[29]

The Twin Cities

The Twin Cities Metropolitan Council was created by the Minnesota state legislature in 1969 to deal with the problems brought by the capital area's rapid growth.[30] Members of the Metro Council are not popularly elected; instead, they are appointed by the governor. Also, the sixteen districts cross municipal boundary lines. The Metro Council is to represent the region's interest, not the parochial interest of local constituencies.

The Metropolitan Council develops long-term plans for the metropolitan area and oversees the actions of other municipal and regional bodies in such areas as sewers, waste management, the protection of open space, and the development of sports facilities.[31] Unlike other metropolitan planning agencies, the Twin Cities Metropolitan Council possesses real power. The Metropolitan Council has the authority to levy a property tax and to issue bonds to support its activities; it is not dependent on the voluntary contributions of local governments. Further, the council can pursue federal grants. In 1974, the Metropolitan Transit Commission and the Metropolitan Airport Commission were placed under the council's direction, giving the council a virtual veto power over new projects in these areas. The Metro Council demonstrated genuine muscle when it vetoed a proposed light-rail transit project and a second airport for the region. The council is also the region's housing authority and over the years has taken on certain human services activities as well.

Of particular importance is the Metropolitan Council's power to develop a Metropolitan Development Guide, in essence a "binding plan" that controls public and private land development activities in the region.[32] The council designates certain areas for concentrated development, thereby protecting rural and agricultural acreage and reducing the prospects of urban sprawl.

As the review agency of federal sewer, water, and road-building dollars, the council possesses a "carrot" that it can offer to communities that accept subsidized housing.[33] By 1986 the suburban share of all subsidized housing units in the region had risen to 40 percent, up from 10 percent in 1970. Data from the mid-1980s further show that over three times the amount of Section 8 new construction dollars was spent in the suburbs than in the central cities of Minneapolis and St. Paul combined.[34] Still, the more affluent communities of the "fertile crescent" south and west of the city have been able to use exclusionary zoning codes to preclude low-income housing.[35]

One other important aspect of metropolitanism in the Twin Cities area is **regional tax base sharing**, which assures each municipality a share of the revenue generated from new development, no matter where in the region growth takes place.[36] Under the state's **fiscal disparities law,** 40 percent of the new value of all new construction (since 1971) is placed in a pool for redistribution to localities on the basis of population and need.

Tax base sharing has mitigated some of the local competition for growth. It has also aided the region's poorer communities, reducing tax base disparities among communities in the Twin Cities area from a ratio of about 20:1 to about 4:1.[37] But in recent years, tax base sharing has not worked to the advantage of the central cities. By 1983 Minneapolis had become a net "loser" or "giver" to the assessed value pool as a result of all the new construction taking place inside the city. St. Paul, too, has become a net loser under the act which has served to transfer funds to already built-up suburbs and to growing suburbs with little industry.[38]

Tax base sharing is controversial. Communities that lose revenue under the plan continue to challenge the fiscal disparities law in court, and state legislators from "giver" communities continue to propose the law's repeal.

In its early years, the Twin Cities Metropolitan Council was highly regarded as a model of metropolitanism. But by the 1980s, this optimism gave way to a period of disappointment when the council was bypassed on major development decisions, including the building of the Metrodome sports stadium, a new basketball arena, a World Trade Center skyscraper, and a new racetrack.[39] The council even approved the Mall of America, with its amusement park, office space, and eventual 600 to 800 stores on a site in suburban Bloomington (the vacant site of the former Metropolitan Stadium), despite possible adverse effects that the new giant mall would have on central-city retailing, other suburban regional malls, and beltway traffic congestion. Given the project's huge size and importance to the region's economy, the megamall likely would have been built even had the Metro Council opposed it.[40] Minnesota's governor, too, had endorsed the project, and members of the council were dependent on the governor for reappointment.[41]

The Metro Council has not been able to control the pace of suburban development. Newly developing and fast-growing suburbs often refuse to cooperate with it.[42] And the bulk of job growth has taken place in the suburbs, not in the region's two central cities.[43] While the council has been able to steer much development to close-in suburbs, growth has also begun to appear in exurban communities located beyond the reach of the metropolitan authority.

In 1993 and 1994, a series of proposals before the state legislature sought to strengthen the Metro Council. But the legislature narrowly refused to provide for the direct election of the council, a move that would have enhanced Metro's public legitimacy and leadership potential. The state has given the Metropolitan Council new operating responsibility for running—not just planning—metropolitan transit. The council was also given new authority in the area of waste control. The state created a new executive figure, the Metropolitan Chief Administrator, a sort of regional city manager. As the position was appointive, however, there was little likelihood that the new administrator would be able to demonstrate the degree of regional leadership shown by Unigov's elected mayor.[44]

In summary, the creation of the Twin Cities Metropolitan Council, enacted without public referendum, was the product of the good-government orientation of Minnesota's citizens and its state legislature. Despite its ups and downs, the Metropolitan Council is a body that is working, and its powers have expanded over time. Yet, in the opinion of former St. Paul Mayor George Latimer, neither the Metropolitan Council nor the fiscal disparities law could be enacted in Minnesota today.[45] The council represents a controversial model that is not likely to be copied by other metropolitan areas in the United States.

IS METROPOLITAN GOVERNMENT DESIRABLE? POLYCENTRISM OR THE PUBLIC CHOICE ALTERNATIVE

There exists a sharp debate between two schools of thought regarding the desirability of metropolitan reform. **Metropolitanists** seek a consolidation of some or all of the local governments in the metropolitan area in order to provide more uniform resource and service distribution over a wide range of communities. As we have seen, the more comprehensive forms of metropolitan reorganization are quite difficult to realize. Yet a second school of thought questions whether the achievement of more comprehensive metropolitan government is really worth the effort. These **polycentrists** favor the status quo, whereby a multitude of autonomous governments continue to exist in a metropolitan area. The polycentrists believe that a multicentered or polycentric metropolis can better serve its citizens. Each local government can provide a different set and level of services as demanded by its constituents.

Arguments for Public Choice

The polycentric model of governance, often referred to as the **public choice** approach, is an attempt to use economic or market theories to explain metropolitan patterns.[46] The polycentrists believe that different persons desire different services from government. No one centralized government can satisfy the diversity of citizens' tastes. Instead, public satisfaction can be maximized if each citizen in a metropolitan area is to be allowed a choice of communities in which to reside:

> Polycentric models are primarily concerned with maximizing the options of the citizens to satisfy their preferences for public goods by making residential choices from a selection of governments with different combinations of services and taxes.[47]

Some citizens are willing to pay more while some are willing to pay less for the public provision of such services as education, housing, mass transit, and recreational and cultural activities. According to public choice theory, citizens who prefer a high standard of public services can choose to live in one community; citizens who prefer lower rates of taxation can choose another community of residence. The multiplicity of local governments provides a market mechanism similar to that in which consumers shop for products and compare brands in a competitive system.

When the priorities of individuals or families change, they can "vote with their feet" by moving to another community with a different standard of education, policing, public amenities, and taxation. Here, too, it can be argued that the market model of public choice is working; the multitude of communities allows citizens choices that increase their satisfaction.

Public choice theorists reject the metropolitanists' argument that large, regional governments necessarily achieve economies of scale. The polycentrists argue that metropolitan government is not necessarily more economical or efficient. In fact, the polycentrists argue, large, metropolitan government can become highly centralized, bureaucratized, and inefficient, creating **diseconomies of scale**. Large governmental bodies can also prove quite difficult for citizens to access; citizens cannot even easily locate the persons they need to speak to when they seek to register a complaint or request the provision of a new service.

Public choice theorists argue that different types of services are best administered on different scales of production. The present metropolitan area allows different services to be delivered on different scales. Intergovernmental cooperative arrangements permit large-scale service provision when necessary. Intergovernmental contracting, joint service agreements, and the creation of special districts and authorities all take advantage of the economies of scale that exist, when, for instance, a project entails large capital expenditures. Yet in service areas that have a more human dimension to them—such as the more personal social services, education, law enforcement, and recreation—large-scale government may prove too inflexible to accommodate the variety of people's tastes. In such cases smaller units of government can tailor service provision to citizens' preferences. Citizens, for instance, tend to prefer school systems run on a small-scale or community basis, as they feel such localized systems will be more responsive to their demands and complaints.

In summary, the major arguments advanced for the polycentric approach can be summarized as follows. First, a greater variety of citizens' wants and desires can be satisfied if constituents are given a choice of jurisdictions in which they can reside—each with a different service and taxation "package." Second, smaller political jurisdictions provide greater access to governmental officials and, as a result, possibly better representation of constituent wishes. Third, smaller political jurisdictions are better suited to provide services requiring interpersonal relationships. Fourth, competition among jurisdictions produces innovation and a greater incentive for local governments to improve efficiency and monitor costs. The greater the number of governments in a metropolitan area, the more the number of new techniques that will be tried. A successful innovation introduced by one jurisdiction will likely be noticed and copied by neighboring localities. Finally, even in the polycentric metropolis, larger-scale service provision and coordinated action can be realized as a result of the variety of existing intergovernmental cooperative arrangements.

CRITICISMS OF PUBLIC CHOICE

Critics of polycentrism counter that the public choice or market economy model paints in highly idealized terms how most persons go about selecting a place to reside in the metropolis. First of all, when citizens choose a place to live, they do not really look at the service and taxation packages of various communities nearly to the extent that the public choice theorists allege. The space afforded by a dwelling, its price, and its proximity to the workplace are more important factors in the selection of a house than are the services and amenities offered by a community.[48] A study in Kentucky found that residents of the highly fragmented Louisville urban area do not appear to be any better informed about local tax and service packages than were residents of the consolidated Lexington–Jefferson County area. Nor do Louisville area residents show any greater level of satisfaction with local tax-service packages as compared to residents of the consolidated Louisville area.[49] People apparently do not choose housing on the basis of local tax-service packages to the extent portrayed by public choice theory.

Second, not everyone possesses a totally free choice of residence in the polycentric metropolis. Exclusionary zoning regulations enacted by suburbs can limit housing availability and drive up the price of accommodations. For racial minorities, the poor, and even for younger workers and newly married, actions of various governments in the polycentric metropolis may restrict housing choice.[50] Metropolitan housing markets are not yet free from barriers. To the extent that public choice theory is valid at all, it is a model that describes a market mechanism open primarily to middle-, upper-middle-, and upper-income residents, and not to the poor or racial minorities. As such, polycentrism is an ideology that defends the class exclusions and race-based inequities in the metropolis. It is a model that gives choice to some, but restricts the choice afforded others.

Third, polycentrism tends to exacerbate parochialism. In the fragmented metropolis each jurisdiction can pursue its own economic good to the detriment of the economic health of others. If an already thriving suburb can gain new commercial development, it will do so, despite the jobs and businesses that such development will likely draw away from its more impoverished neighbors. Each jurisdiction need not be concerned with **externalities** or **spillovers**—the effects of its actions on neighboring communities. Whatever metropolitan cooperation is obtained under polycentrism will be quite limited in scope. Jurisdictions will cooperate only when it is to their mutual advantage. There will be little resource sharing to solve the more deeply entrenched problems of urban poverty and racial imbalance.

Fourth, the school of public choice focuses on short-term concerns to the exclusion of long-term considerations. Public choice theorists tend to evaluate the performance of the public service delivery system at one point in time, looking at short-term efficiency measures and citizen satisfaction. But metropolitan governments can initiate actions, such as measures to curb urban sprawl, that will in the long run control costs. Metro Toronto's construction of a new mass transit system both aided the region's economic development and added to citizen satisfaction.[51]

Polycentrism recognizes the advantages of small-scale government. It also takes note of the economies of scale that can be provided by voluntary metropolitan cooperative agreements. However, polycentrism does not seek to correct the vast ills that result from metropolitan fragmentation. Overlap and duplication continue to exist, as do the more serious problems of fiscal and racial imbalances among political jurisdictions in the region. For the critics of polycentrism, more comprehensive metropolitan reform is needed.

GOVERNING THE GREATER ST. LOUIS AREA: A CASE IN POINT

The difference between the public choice and metropolitanist points of view is most clearly revealed in the debate over the adequacy of governmental arrangements in the metropolitan St. Louis area. A major Reagan-era study by the Advisory Commission on Intergovernmental Relations (ACIR) used a public choice perspective to argue that the suburban Missouri part of the greater St. Louis area is being effectively governed under polycentric arrangements.[52]

According to the ACIR, the presence of numerous small governments in the St. Louis area allows for high levels of citizen representation in policy making and responsiveness of government to citizen concerns. The presence of multiple jurisdictions also creates opportunities for **public entrepreneurship** whereby local officials seek out new or innovative ways of more efficiently providing services. Furthermore, ACIR's quantitative analysis found that economies of scale do not exist in many service areas. Contrary to the metropolitanist viewpoint, large-scale government does not always bring with it savings in costs.

Of even greater significance still is ACIR's contention: "It is possible to have a form of metropolitan *governance* in the absence of a metropolitan *government*" (emphasis in the original).[53] Over the years a quite intricate web of interlocal cooperative arrangements has been created in the St. Louis area.

On the negative side the ACIR study admits that voluntary cooperation does not adequately address the needs of the area's most distressed communities. Voluntary cooperation is not readily forthcoming when problem solving requires resource sharing. As a result of metropolitan fragmentation, some St. Louis County residents are relatively well-off and bear a relatively low tax burden for the services they receive. In contrast, the residents of poorer communities can tax themselves at much higher rates and still obtain less in the way of services. The residents of the area's most disadvantaged communities tend to be racial minorities.

In sum, the ACIR concludes that the St. Louis County model of fragmentation with overlap and coordination provides a viable alternative to the ideal of metropolitan government. Yet even here the ACIR conclusion is qualified: "A complex metropolitan area that has performed well in terms of service responsiveness and in finding efficient ways to deliver services may not perform equally well in assisting distressed communities."[54]

The ACIR's conclusions proved particularly controversial. Two citizen groups released major plans attacking the governmental structure's shortcomings. The Board of Freeholders' report, for instance, cast doubt as to the ACIR's conclusion that citizens were for the most part well served by the existing governmental arrangements. The freeholders' plan especially attacked the inadequacy of services provided to the approximately 400,000 residents in unincorporated areas of St. Louis County. The more wealthy areas of the county had already been incorporated or annexed; the poorer residential areas were left for the county to take care of despite its diminishing resources. Emergency medical services were not sufficiently provided throughout the county. As one review of the Board of Freeholders' study concludes, "The Board's plan clearly is at variance with the ACIR report conclusions that everything is working fine as is and that the St. Louis solution is a model to be emulated elsewhere in the nation's metropolitan areas."[55]

RACIAL MINORITIES AND METROPOLITAN REFORM

Before leaving the question of metropolitan reform, we must return to the debate over the impact that metropolitan reform would have on minority group power, especially on black power. It is fair to generalize that, in most cases, African-Americans and other racial minorities have been very suspicious of plans for metropolitan reorganization.

As black populations began to increase substantially in central cities, control of many of these governments passed into the hands of black elected and appointed local officials. Proposals for metropolitan reorganization threaten to undermine the developing black political power base (and in some Florida and southwestern cities the developing Hispanic political power base) by diluting its voting strength over a broader geographical and population base. Attempts at consolidated governments in metropolitan areas almost always reduce the percentage of racial minorities in the new electorate as compared to the prior central-city electorate. In Jacksonville the percentage of the electorate that was black dropped from 44 to 25 percent as a result of reorganization; in Indianapolis the drop was from 27 to 17 percent, and in Nashville from 38 to 20 percent.[56]

Metro Miami's at-large election system, an inherent part of its philosophy of promoting the public good, for three decades worked against minority interests in the region. Minority candidates working from neighborhood political bases found it difficult to gain the financial backing and the broad public support necessary for a successful metrowide race.[57] After the 1980 riots the predominantly black Liberty City area sought to incorporate in order to establish greater local control over police and service delivery. The Metro Commission blocked the move, saying it would not be cost-effective. Similarly, the commission failed to respond to the demands of a middle-class black neighborhood where residents objected to the construction of a nearby stadium for the Miami Dolphins.[58]

Black opposition to proposals for a metropolitan consolidation was evident as early as the 1950s. Repeated efforts to reorganize both Cleveland and St. Louis met with opposition from black leaders and then from black voters. In the 1960s reorganization efforts in both Nashville and Tampa, the latter of which proved unsuccessful, were confronted with strong opposition from blacks. In Nashville over 55 percent of the black voters, and in Tampa over 90 percent, voted against reorganization.

During this period, however, black opposition to consolidation was not universal. Specific safeguards granted to the black community helped generate black support for certain reorganization plans. In Jacksonville-Duval County in 1967, 59 percent of the blacks voted for consolidation; in Lexington-Fayette County in 1972, 70 percent of black voters approved.[59] In the Jacksonville case, black leaders threw their support behind the plan, as they were involved in the drawing of district lines and hence were virtually guaranteed that the black community would receive three seats on the new consolidated government council. In Lexington, too, district lines were drawn in such a way as to virtually guarantee blacks two or three seats on the new council.[60] In Miami the growing number of Latin and black voters led to new demands for, and the eventual institution of, district elections.

Despite the dilution of racial minority voting strength that metropolitan reorganization might bring, some advocates of metropolitan government have argued that metropolitan reform will aid minorities. They point out that blacks and Hispanics are gaining control over fiscally weakened central cities that have both a population with many needs and a severely limited tax base. These advocates argue that minorities and the poor will be better off if new metropolitanwide governments are created that can draw upon regional wealth to combat inner-city problems.[61] They are especially prone to approve metropolitan government plans that include district election systems that guarantee a degree of minority-elected representation.

Advocates of black and Hispanic power, however, counter that minority groups are unlikely to win control over these resources in a predominantly white metropolitan area government. They believe that in many metropolitan areas a metropolitan government would be controlled by a majority coalition of whites from both the suburbs and the central city. Racial minorities, who had waited so long to gain control over central-city governments, would once more find themselves in subservient status in the new metropolitan arrangements. Rather than accept continued colonial status, racial minorities would be in a better strategic situation if they controlled the government of central cities, with the substantial corporate resources that remain inside each city's borders.[62]

There is no clear evidence on the question of whether African-Americans and other racial minorities fare better in a fragmented metropolis or under a system of metropolitan government. Yet, at least one study points to the benefits that metropolitan government brings to African-Americans who live in relatively poor, predominantly black suburbs. Citizens in Green Acres, Kentucky, a black spillover community just outside the borders of the preconsolidation city of Lexington, received a higher level of governmental services and showed less dissatisfaction with those services as compared to black citizens who lived in Newburg, a similar suburb in the nonconsolidated Louisville area. The black citizens of Newburg did not benefit from the "public choice" offered by a fragmented metropolis; their community lacked the tax base to provide good quality municipal services. In contrast, the black residents of Green Acres had access to the high level of services provided by the Lexington-Fayette County consolidated government.[63]

CONCLUSIONS: POLITICAL POWER
AND METROPOLITAN REFORM

As we have seen throughout this chapter, future prospects for comprehensive metropolitan reform plans are not very good. Except when special circumstances facilitate their creation, the achievement of one-tier, two-tier, and three-tier governments in most American metropolitan areas remains a political impossibility. Too many powerful interests oppose the creation of metropolitan government.

Suburbanites fear that a new metropolitan government vested with land use powers will ultimately change the social composition of their local communities. Similarly, they fear that new metropolitan governing arrangements will raise their taxes as they will have to help pay for services delivered to others. They prefer the grassroots ideal of small-scale government—and the tax advantages that oftentimes accompany it—over any claims of a more equitable or efficient metropolitan ideal.[64] The dual referenda requirement of most states gives these suburbanites the power to veto consolidation efforts of any significant size.

Suburban residents are not the only ones who oppose metropolitan reform. Suburban business interests enjoy the tax advantages that result from location in a suburb and may be suspicious of any proposal for change. Racial minorities in central cities tend to oppose new metropolitan arrangements as a dilution of their power. Elected officials and local bureaucrats, in both the central city and suburbs alike, fear that the creation of a new consolidated metropolitan government might result in a dilution of their power and might even cost them their jobs.

But suburbanites and businesses are not always threatened by metropolitan reform. Under certain circumstances, suburban residents and business owners actually benefit from and demand reorganization. The Nashville-Davidson County plan was created as residents in poorly developed suburban areas wanted the services the city could provide. As we shall see in the next chapter, cities like Houston continue to expand outward, as such expansion meets the needs of developers and residents of the urban fringe.

Given the strong constellation of powers that usually opposes metropolitan reform, it takes a unique situation and the organization of a countervailing coalition to bring about reform. As we have seen, an exposé of corruption in local government can sometimes set the stage where metropolitan reorganization can be presented as a "purification ritual" that will cure the city of its vices.[65] In Miami-Dade County the city's major newspaper joined with the good government coalition in a campaign to bring about reform.

Outside power is often necessary to bring about metropolitan reform. The residents of the Toronto, Indianapolis, and Minneapolis–St. Paul Twin Cities areas all had new metropolitan arrangements imposed on them from above by state (or provincial) governments. Whether or not the enactment of a metropolitan government could be repeated in any of these areas today is problematic.

Wholesale metropolitan reform represents an impossible dream. Perhaps the best that can be hoped for is an intermediate level of reform. Glen Sparrow and Lauren McKinsey have observed that metropolitan consolidation efforts are rejected at alarmingly high rates as they have been presented as "all-or-nothing" approaches. They suggest that given such intense opposition, metropolitan reformers would do better to follow an incremental approach to service transfers, by initially proposing that only a limited number of functions be combined. Those services chosen for consolidation should be the least symbolic or politically sensitive; they should also possess the greatest potential for economic savings. Only after the initial reorganization has been accepted and gains familiarity in the community can further service transfers and reforms be attempted.[66]

Voluntary, cooperative solutions do provide certain benefits. They increase communications among jurisdictions, they enable joint problem solving, and they save money by realizing economies of scale. As public choice theorists point out, a wide variety of interlocal cooperative arrangements do presently exist in the metropolis. Even in the absence of a centralized metropolitan government, metropolitan *governance* still takes place. We will now turn to an analysis of these more commonplace forms of intergovernmental cooperation.

NOTES

1. Stanley Scott and John Corzine, "Special Districts in the Bay Area," in *Metropolitan Politics: A Reader*, 2nd ed., ed. Michael N. Danielson (Boston: Little, Brown, 1971), pp. 203–05.
2. Details of the Nashville-Davidson County consolidation are taken from Brett W. Hawkins, *Nashville Metro* (Nashville, TN: University of Vanderbilt Press, 1966); Brett W. Hawkins, "Public Opinion and Metropolitan Reorganization in Nashville," *Journal of Politics* 28 (May 1966): 408–18; and Daniel R. Grant, "A Comparison of Predictions and Experience with Nashville 'Metro,'" *Urban Affairs Quarterly* (September 1965): 35–54.
3. Bert Swanson, "Three Morality Plays and Three Subliminal Themes of Urban Reform: Consolidation in Jacksonville, Florida" (Paper presented at the annual meeting of the Urban Affairs Association, Indianapolis, Indiana, April 22–24, 1993).
4. C. James Owen and York Willbern, *Governing Metropolitan Indianapolis: The Politics of Unigov* (Berkeley, CA: University of California Press, 1985), provide an excellent overview of the politics surrounding the creation of Unigov and the operation of the new government in its early years.
5. William Blomquist, "Metropolitan Organization and Local Politics: The Indianapolis-Marion County Experience" (Paper presented at the annual meeting of the Midwest Political Science Association, Chicago, April 9–11, 1992).
6. Ibid.
7. Owen and Willbern, *Governing Metropolitan Indianapolis*, pp. 1–2.
8. C. James Owen, "Indianapolis Unigov: A Focus on Restructured Executive Authority" (Paper presented at the annual meeting of the Urban Affairs Association, Indianapolis, April 22–24, 1993); and William H. Hudnut III, "Indianapolis: From No-Place to Show-Place to ???" (Speech at the annual meeting of the Urban Affairs Association, Indianapolis, April 22, 1993).
9. Owen, "Indianapolis Unigov: A Focus on Restructured Executive Authority."
10. Sam Jones, Indianapolis Urban League, "Indianapolis: From No-Place to Show-Place to ???" (Remarks at the annual meeting of the Urban Affairs Association, Indianapolis, April 22, 1993).
11. Blomquist, "Metropolitan Organization and Local Politics"; and William Blomquist and Roger B. Parks, "UNIGOV: Local Government in Indianapolis and Marion County, Indiana," paper 93–U05, Center for Urban Policy and the Environment, Indiana University School of Public and Environmental Affairs, Indianapolis, March 1993.
12. For a review of consolidation efforts from 1949 to 1976, see Vincent L. Marando, "City-County Consolidation: Reform, Regionalism, Referenda and Requiem," *Western Political Quarterly* 32 (December 1979): 409–21. Also see Vincent L. Marando, "The Politics of City-County Consolidation," *National Civic Review* 64 (February 1975).
13. Parris N. Glendening and Patricia S. Atkins, "City-County Consolidations: New Views from the Eighties," *The Municipal Yearbook 1980* (Washington, DC: International City Management Association, 1980), pp. 68–72.

14. Marando, "City-County Consolidation: Reform, Regionalism, Referenda and Requiem," p. 420.

15. Three classic studies of the Toronto government are Frank Smallwood, *Metro Toronto a Decade Later* (Toronto: Bureau of Municipal Research, 1963); Harold Kaplan, *Urban Political Systems: A Functional Analysis of Metro Toronto* (New York: Columbia University Press, 1967); and Albert Rose, *Governing Metropolitan Toronto: A Social and Political Analysis, 1953–1971* (Berkeley, CA: University of California Press, 1972). On Winnipeg, see Meyer Brownstone and T. J. Plunkett, *Metropolitan Winnipeg: Politics and Reform of Local Government* (Berkeley, CA: University of California Press, 1983).

16. Frances Frisken, "Planning and Servicing the Greater Toronto Area: The Interplay of Provincial and Municipal Interests," in *Metropolitan Governance: American/Canadian Intergovernmental Perspectives*, ed. Donald N. Rothblatt and Andrew Sancton (Berkeley, CA: Institute of Governmental Studies Press, 1993), p. 153.

17. Frances Frisken, "The Contributions of Metropolitan Government to the Success of Toronto's Public Transit System: An Empirical Dissent from the Public-Choice Paradigm," *Urban Affairs Quarterly* 27 (December 1991): 272.

18. Ibid., pp. 268–92.

19. Frisken, "Planning and Servicing the Greater Toronto Area," p. 165.

20. Frisken, "The Contributions of Metropolitan Government to the Success of Toronto's Public Transit System," p. 289.

21. The creation of Metro in greater Miami is described by Edward Sofen, *The Miami Metropolitan Experiment* (Bloomington, IN: University of Indiana Press, 1963).

22. Raymond A. Mohl, "Miami: The Ethnic Cauldron," in *Sunbelt Cities: Politics and Growth Since World War II*, ed. Richard M. Bernard and Bradley R. Rice (Austin, TX: University of Texas Press, 1983), pp. 82–83.

23. Raymond A. Mohl, "Miami's Metropolitan Government: Retrospect and Prospect," *Florida Historical Quarterly* 63 (July 1984): 24–50.

24. Spokesperson for the New City Political Action Committee, quotation excerpted from Mohl, "Miami's Metropolitan Government," p. 48.

25. Mohl, "Miami's Metropolitan Government," pp. 48–49.

26. Larry Rohter, "Miami Court Decision Shifts Political Power to Minorities," *The New York Times*, December 25, 1992.

27. Ibid., p. 50; and Ronald K. Vogel and Genie N. L. Stowers, "Miami: Minority Empowerment and Regime Change," in *Big City Politics in Transition, Urban Affairs Annual Review* 38, ed. H. V. Savitch and John Clayton Thomas (Newbury Park, CA: Sage Publications, 1991), pp. 121–22.

28. These and other details of the evolution of Portland's Metro are taken from David Rusk, *Cities Without Suburbs* (Washington, DC: Woodrow Wilson Center Press, 1993); David Rusk, "Suburban Renewal," *The New York Times*, September 8, 1993; J. Linn Allen, "Dividing Line: Portland, Ore.'s unique approach to growth management sets it apart," *Chicago Tribune*, October 9, 1994; and Henry G. Cisneros, *Regionalism: The New Geography of Opportunity* (Washington, DC: U.S. Department of Housing and Urban Development, 1995), pp. 21–22.

29. H. V. Savitch and Ronald K. Vogel, "Comparing Regional Governance in the United States" (Paper presented at the annual meeting of the American Political Science Association, New York, September 2, 1994).

30. The evolution of the Twin Cities Metropolitan Council is described by Robert E. Einsweiler, "Metropolitan Government and Planning: Lessons in Shared Power," in *The Metropolitan Midwest: Policy Problems and Prospects for Change*, ed. B. Checkoway and C. V. Patton (Urbana, IL: University of Illinois Press, 1985), pp. 285–301; John M. Levy, *Contemporary Urban Planning* (Englewood Cliffs, NJ: Prentice-Hall, 1988), pp. 264–72; John J. Harrigan and William C. Johnson, *Governing the Twin Cities Region: The Metropolitan Council in Comparative Perspectives* (Minneapolis: University of Minnesota Press, 1978); and John J. Harrigan, *Political Change in the Metropolis*, 4th ed. (Glenview, IL: Scott, Foresman, 1989), pp. 347–51.

31. Judith A. Martin, "In Fits and Starts: The Twin Cities Metropolitan Framework," in *Metropolitan Governance: American/Canadian Intergovernmental Perspectives*, ed. Donald N. Rothblatt and Andrew Sancton (Berkeley, CA: Institute of Governmental Studies Press), pp. 206 and 214.

32. Einsweiler, "Metropolitan Government and Planning," pp. 292–93.

33. Martin, "In Fits and Starts: The Twin Cities Metropolitan Framework," pp. 229–30.

34. Joanne Vail and Rosanne Zimbro, *1986 Subsidized Housing in the Twin Cities Metropolitan Area* (Minneapolis: Metropolitan Council, 1986), quoted in Martin, "In Fits and Starts: The Twin Cities Metropolitan Framework," p. 230.

35. John J. Harrigan, "Governance in Transition: Regime Under Pressure in the Twin Cities" (Paper presented at the annual meeting of the American Political Science Association, New York, September 2, 1994).

36. Metropolitan Dayton, Ohio, also has experimented with a form of regional tax base sharing.

37. Remarks of James L. Hetland, Jr., former chairperson of the Metropolitan Council, to the annual conference of the National Civic League, Denver, Colorado, October 27, 1989.

38. Ibid.; and Martin, "In Fits and Starts: The Twin Cities Metropolitan Framework," p. 228.

39. Harrigan, "Governance in Transition: Regime Under Pressure in the Twin Cities;" John J. Harrigan and William C. Johnson, "Trouble in River Cities: Metropolitan Governance under Attack" (Paper presented at the Midwest Political Science Association, Chicago, April 12, 1986); and Amy Klobuchar, *Uncovering the Dome* (Prospect Heights, IL: Waveland Press, 1986).

40. Martin, "In Fits and Starts: The Twin Cities Metropolitan Framework," pp. 233–36.

41. Harrigan, "Governance in Transition: Regime under Pressure in the Twin Cities."

42. Martin, "In Fits and Starts: The Twin Cities Metropolitan Framework."

43. Harrigan, "Governance in Transition: Regime under Pressure in the Twin Cities."

44. Ibid.

45. Remarks of George Latimer, former mayor of St. Paul, Minnesota, to the annual conference of the National Civic League, Denver, Colorado, October 27, 1989.

46. The most important application of the public choice model to urban political life is found in Vincent Ostrom, Charles Tiebout, and Robert Warren, "The Organization of Government in Metropolitan Areas," *American Political Science Review* 55 (December 1961): 831–42. Other classic works on this

subject include Robert L. Bish, *The Public Economy of Metropolitan Areas* (Chicago: Markham, 1971); Robert L. Bish and Vincent Ostrom, *Understanding Urban Government: Metropolitan Reform Reconsidered* (Washington, DC: American Enterprise Institute, 1973); and Vincent Ostrom and Elinor Ostrom, "Public Choice: A Different Approach to the Study of Public Administration," *Public Administration Review* 31 (March/April 1971): 203–16.

47. Harlan Hahn and Charles H. Levine, eds., *Urban Politics: Past, Present and Future* (White Plains, NY: Longman, 1984), p. 28.

48. Peter H. Rossi, *Why Families Move* (Beverly Hills, CA: Sage Publications, 1980), pp. 204 and 223.

49. W. E. Lyons and David Lowery, "Governmental Fragmentation versus Consolidation: Five Public-Choice Myths About How to Create Informed, Involved, and Happy Citizens," *Public Administration Review* 49 (November/December 1989): 533–43.

50. Bernard J. Frieden, *The Environmental Protection Hustle* (Cambridge, MA: MIT Press, 1979).

51. Frisken, "The Contributions of Metropolitan Government to the Success of Toronto's Public Transit System," especially pp. 269–70 and 288–89.

52. Advisory Commission on Intergovernmental Relations, *Metropolitan Organization: The St. Louis Case* (Washington, DC: ACIR, 1988); and Roger B. Parks and Ronald J. Oakerson, "St. Louis: The ACIR Study," *Intergovernmental Perspective* 15 (Winter 1989): 9–11.

53. Parks and Oakerson, "St. Louis: The ACIR Study," p. 10.

54. Ibid., p.11.

55. Donald Phares, "Governmental Reorganization in the St. Louis Area: The Board of Freeholders' Plan" (Paper presented at the annual meeting of the Urban Affairs Association, Baltimore, March 16–18, 1989). Also see Donald Phares, "Reorganizing the St. Louis Area: The Freeholders' Plan," *Intergovernmental Perspective* 15 (Winter 1989): 12–16; Donald Phares, "Bigger Is Better, or Is It Smaller? Restructuring Local Government in the St. Louis Area," *Urban Affairs Quarterly* 25 (September 1989): 5–17; and Donald Elliott, "Reconciling Perspectives on the St. Louis Metropolitan Area," *Intergovernmental Perspective* 15 (Winter 1989): 19.

56. ACIR, *Substate Regionalism and the Federal System: The Challenge of Local Governmental Reorganization* (Washington, DC: ACIR, 1974), p. 103.

57. Christopher L. Warren, John C. Corbett, and John F. Stack, Jr., "Hispanic Ascendancy and Tripartite Politics in Miami," in *Racial Politics in America's Cities*, ed. Rufus P. Browning, Dale Rogers Marshall, and David H. Tabb (White Plains, NY: Longman, 1990), p. 158.

58. Ibid., pp. 167–68.

59. ACIR, *Substate Regionalism and the Federal System*, pp. 101–04.

60. Ibid.; and Dale Rogers Marshall, Bernard Frieden, and D. W. Fessler, *The Governance of Metropolitan Regions: Minority Perspectives* (Washington, DC: Resources for the Future, 1972). Also see Tobe Johnson, *Metropolitan Government: A Black Analytical Perspective* (Washington, DC: Joint Center for Political Studies, 1972).

61. Willis D. Hawley, "Blacks and Metropolitan Governance: The Stakes of Reform" (Paper published by the Institute of Governmental Studies, University of California, Berkeley, 1972).

62. Frances Fox Piven and Richard A. Cloward, "What Chance for Black Power?" *New Republic*, March 30, 1968, pp. 19–23.

63. Ruth Hoogland DeHoog, David Lowery, and William E. Lyons, "Metropolitan Fragmentation and Suburban Ghettos: Some Empirical Observations on Institutional Racism," *Journal of Urban Affairs* 13, 4 (1991): 479–93.

64. See Robert C. Wood, "Suburbia: The Fiscal Roots of Political Fragmentation and Differentiation," pp. 92–102; and Charles R. Adrian, "Suburbia and the Folklore of Metropology," pp. 270–76, both in *Metropolitan Politics: A Reader*, 2nd ed., ed. Michael N. Danielson (Boston: Little, Brown, 1971).

65. Scott Greer, "The Morality Plays of Metropolitan Reform," in *Metropolitan Politics: A Reader*, pp. 263–64, 2nd ed., ed. Michael N. Danielson (Boston: Little, Brown, 1971).

66. Glen Sparrow and Lauren McKinsey, "Metropolitan Reorganization: A Theory and Agenda for Research," *National Civic Review* 72 (October 1983): 494–95.

11

Metropolitan Governance: The Politics of Regional Cooperation

As we have just seen, the creation of a full-fledged metropolitan government is a virtual impossibility in most urban areas. Yet, as public choice scholars argue, the intergovernmental cooperative arrangements that do exist in any metropolitan area are so extensive that they can be perceived as constituting metropolitan *governance* in the absence of a full-fledged metropolitan government.

In this chapter we will describe the variety of arrangements for interlocal cooperation and governance in the metropolitan area. We will also see how global and interregional competition has led localities to enter into new cooperative arrangements in the pursuit of economic development.

Yet, the new move toward regionalism is quite incomplete. Regional cooperation is for the most part voluntary. Federal and state law requires cooperation in only very narrow service areas such as higher education, antipollution efforts, and health and transportation planning. In all other areas, local governments cooperate with one another only to the extent that they find it in their mutual interest to do so.

Intergovernmental cooperation is more likely to occur when the social distance between communities is small. Perhaps this explains why, as we shall see, the aggressive use of annexation and extraterritorial powers constitutes a major approach to metropolitan government in the Sunbelt, particularly in the Southwest, that is for the most part lacking in the North.

The works of Roscoe Martin and David Walker have provided a framework that will allow us to understand the vast variety of metropolitan accommodation and government reform plans.[1] Walker has identified seventeen forms of interlocal cooperation, which he has ranked from easiest to hardest according to how politically difficult each is to achieve (see Table 11.1). In Chapter 10 we already described the "tough trio" of the more comprehensive metropolitan reform plans: the one-, two-, and three-tier plans for metropolitan government. In this chapter we will describe the less comprehensive but more commonplace means of regional cooperation.

THE EASIEST MEANS OF METROPOLITAN COOPERATION

We begin by describing those arrangements that are most easily achieved.

INFORMAL COOPERATION

Informal cooperation represents the desire on the part of officials from two or more local governments to cooperate to improve service. It might entail nothing more than the sharing or exchanging of information; or it may entail an unwritten agreement whereby one jurisdiction is allowed to use equipment owned by another. Informal cooperation is clearly the most pragmatic, and probably the most widely practiced, approach to regionalism. However, what can be accomplished through informal collaboration is greatly limited. Such collaboration rarely requires fiscal actions "and only rarely involves matters of regional or even subregional significance."[2]

Informal cooperation is widely practiced. It is an especially important means of intergovernmental cooperation in those metropolitan areas that cross state or international borders. For instance, officials in El Paso, Texas, a city of a half million people, clearly recognize that the health of their city is intricately tied to that of Ciudad Juárez, its million-person Mexican neighbor. Yet national boundary lines and the intricacies of international diplomacy often preclude the possibility of formalized cooperation. As a result, each working day a county truck from the American side crosses the international bridge and sprays an eighteen-mile-long open sewage ditch that would otherwise provide a fertile breeding ground for disease-carrying mosquitoes. In another effort Mexican children who break the law in El Paso are sent home to Mexico, where a social worker hired by the Texas Youth Commission makes sure that they go to school. This program saves Texas taxpayers approximately the $70 a day that it would cost to house such offenders in juvenile facilities in Texas. Cooperative efforts like these are largely informal: "There are no treaties involved in the low-level diplomacy, and little Federal input. Only some of the joint programs are officially written down. Many are based on handshakes between local officials [in El Paso]...and their counterparts in Juárez." As one Mexican official described the agreement, "It is informal and extra-governmental."[3] Of course, more extensive projects, such as the construction of a new international bridge, require more formalized agreements.

Similarly, the city councils of San Diego, California, and Tijuana, Mexico, have met in joint sessions to discuss problems of mutual interest.

House Bill 489 — requires cities & counties to consolidate — put on back burner with beginning of GRTA

TABLE 11.1
David Walker's Seventeen Regional Approaches to Service Delivery

Easiest

HB489

ARC

1. Informal cooperation
2. Interlocal service contracts
3. Joint powers agreements → *NOT ALLOWED IN GA.*
4. Extraterritorial powers
5. Regional councils/councils of governments
6. Federally encouraged single-purpose regional bodies
7. State planning and development districts *predecessors of ARC*
8. Contracting (private) *privatization of water in Atlanta*

Middling

GRTA

9. Local special districts — *schools*
10. Transfer of functions
11. Annexation
12. Regional special districts and authorities
13. Metro multipurpose district — *grta also regulates land use planning*
14. Reformed urban county — *resemble city govt.*

Hardest

15. One-tier consolidations *Athens—Clarke County*
16. Two-tier restructuring *Miami — Dade Co.*
17. Three-tier reforms — *regional govt. other than the city & county*

Source: David B. Walker, "Snow White and the 17 Dwarfs: From Metro Cooperation to Governance," *National Civic Review* 76 (January/February 1987): 16.

Cumberland, Perimeter, Town Center → community improvement districts; they can collect taxes; all around shopping centers

San Diego has come to realize that its economic and social good health is in many ways tied to the fate of the mushrooming Mexican metropolis, with well over a million people, just on the other side of the border. San Diego residents, for instance, are victimized by untreated effluent from Tijuana that washes up on California beaches.

But the extent of joint action that is needed goes beyond mere informal cooperation. Already a light rail system has been built to connect the downtowns of the two cities. Local officials have also proposed to build a new international airport that would straddle the border. There is even a proposal to establish a transnational border authority to promote infrastructure investment, economic development, and other matters of joint benefit.[4]

Yet cooperation between the two cities for the most part remains limited to informal understandings. The U.S. Constitution bars state and local governments from negotiating their own formal agreements with foreign nations; and the city often finds it quite difficult to get the federal government to pay attention to local problems and go through the intricate task of negotiating more formal accords with Mexico.[5]

INTERGOVERNMENTAL SERVICE CONTRACTS AND THE LAKEWOOD PLAN

Interlocal Service Contracts

Interlocal service contracts are legally binding agreements entered into by two (or more) governments under which one government agrees to provide a service that the other pays for upon receiving it. Smaller jurisdictions are able to obtain a service that they could never hope to provide for themselves except at a very high cost. The purchasing jurisdiction can also choose the exact quantity and quality of the service it is willing to pay for. For instance, in a service agreement with a county for police protection, a municipality can specify that exact level of patrol and backup services it desires.

Local jurisdictions tend more to enter into service agreements with counties than with other municipalities. Some of the services most commonly contracted out are jail and detention home services, sewage disposal, water supply, fire prevention, tax assessing, computer and data processing, police training, libraries, and animal control. Contracting is frequently used in the West (especially the Pacific Coast states) and is less popular in the Northeast (see Table 11.2).[6]

The Lakewood Plan

One very interesting example of intergovernmental contracting is the **Lakewood Plan**, where Los Angeles County offers a large menu of services to local governments. The Lakewood Plan offers such a wide range of services that a participating jurisdiction can choose to provide few services of its own and instead purchase all or nearly all of its services from the county. It takes its name from the city of Lakewood, the first suburban community to incorporate after Los Angeles County's enactment of the plan in the mid-1950s. The plan's enactment helped to produce a rash of municipal incorporations in Los Angeles County, with new cities choosing not to create their own municipal service bureaucracies but instead to contract most of their services from the county.

One advantage of the Lakewood Plan and service contracting in general is the greater efficiency that is offered as the result of the **economies of scale** in service provision. For a large number of services, cost savings can be realized in large-scale production that cannot be gained in small-scale production. For instance, capital investment is minimized if, instead of having each community construct its own police and fire stations, a few centrally located facilities are built to serve the entire area. A city can often contract for policing, fire protection, and other services from the county for less than it would cost to directly provide the service itself.

Efficiency is also obtained as a **competitive market** is created. There is no requirement that a local government buy a service from the county; it can also choose to provide the service itself or else purchase it from an alternative provider. As municipalities secure services from a variety of sources, they can seek the best possible quality and lowest price.

Yet, despite these gains in efficiency, the Lakewood Plan is also the target of severe criticism. Some critics have argued that the Lakewood Plan gives too much power to the county and thereby diminishes local control. The county, as the dominant service provider, has great influence

TABLE 11.2
Intergovernmental Service Contracts, by Regions

Geographic Region	Percent of Cities with Contracts*	Percent of Counties with Contracts[+]
Northeast	38%	35%
North Central	53	50
South	49	54
West	72	75

*1,639 cities responding to survey.
[+]430 counties responding to survey.
Source: Adapted from Lori M. Henderson, "Intergovernmental Service Arrangements and the Transfer of Functions," *Municipal Year Book 1985* (Washington, DC: International City Management Association, 1985), p. 196, Table 3.2.

over the quality, price, and style of service delivery. As Richard Cion observes, the result for cities is "a gross restriction of their freedom of action in all fields save one. While left with the ability to control their own land-use patterns, Lakewood Plan communities are unable to set independent policy in other areas."[7]

The Lakewood Plan also has exacerbated metropolitan fragmentation by serving as a catalyst for previously unincorporated areas to form new municipal governments and thereby resist possible annexation by neighboring municipalities. Lakewood itself incorporated in order to escape possible annexation by the city of Long Beach.

The new incorporations have provided attractive sites for "white flight" from Los Angeles. The new suburbs have also used their zoning and land use powers to exclude low-income, service-demanding, renter populations. The result has been the creation of a number of low-tax, **minimal cities** that exacerbate racial and class stratification in the region. In very exclusive Rancho Palos Verdes, just outside of Long Beach, incorporation allowed that community's wealthy homeowners to limit new development and preserve the area's estate-like character.[8]

As Gary J. Miller makes clear in his extensive study of Lakewood Plan communities, concern for increased efficiency in service provision was *not* the dominant motivation behind Lakewood Plan incorporations. Instead, the establishment of new cities was driven more by concerns for local power and the protection of economic privilege. The primary purpose of the Lakewood Plan incorporations was "to limit the property tax burden on homeowners and businesses and to limit the expansion of governmental bureaucracies and social welfare programs."[9] Lakewood Plan incorporations created new suburbs, attractive to residents and businesses, weakening the tax bases of older cities such as Compton, which found it increasingly difficult to provide services to their low-income and minority populations.[10]

Major industries took advantage of the rules of incorporation associated with the plan in order to escape the higher levels of taxation they would have to pay if their property were to be annexed by larger cities. The city of Industry, California, was created as a tax shelter for the railroad yards, factories, and warehouses within its borders. When incorporated, the town included only 624 residents. In order to meet the minimum population of 500 required for incorporation, the city had to count the 169 patients and 31 employees of a local psychiatric sanitarium. Similarly, the city of Commerce represents an enclave where incorporation acted to shield railroad and industrial property from the higher rates of taxation that would have resulted had this area been annexed by a rapidly growing neighboring municipality. Likewise, Santa Fe Springs was created to insulate local industry from control by citizens in neighboring Whittier and South Whittier. The city of Dairy Valley was a newly created tax island of agricultural land holdings which later changed its name to Cerritos, only after farmers sold their acreage to developers for high profits.[11]

JOINT POWERS AGREEMENTS

Under **joint powers agreements** two or more units of local government formally agree to work together in the financing and delivery of a service. A joint powers arrangement was proposed as part of the cooperative effort by communities on San Francisco's South Bay to lure the baseball Giants to a new stadium in Santa Clara. A joint powers authority for the proposed South Bay stadium was to include representatives from Santa Clara, Sunnyvale, San Jose, and Santa Clara County. But the Giants' management recoiled in horror at what they saw to be the unworkable bureaucratic entanglements of such a complicated governing arrangement.[12]

A variation of the joint powers agreement is **parallel action**, whereby two or more governments pursue their agreed-upon commitments separately, even though the results are designed to benefit both parties.

EXTRATERRITORIAL POWERS

Extraterritorial powers are allowed cities in thirty-five states. Under these powers, certain cities in a state are given authority outside their boundaries over some of the actions of contiguous unincorporated areas.

Texas state law grants cities the right to regulate subdivisions on unincorporated land lying adjacent to the city. The city of San Antonio has used these powers to prevent the incorporation of new suburban municipalities and to prevent land in the surrounding area from being annexed by competing municipalities.[13] San Antonio and numerous other Texas and Sunbelt communities have used their extraterritorial powers in order to preserve land for future annexation.

Houston has been able to increase its tax base and capture suburban growth as a result of the extensive extraterritorial and annexation powers it possesses. Texas state law gives the city extraterritorial jurisdiction that extends five miles from its corporate limits. Houston's extraterritorial jurisdiction is larger than the state of Rhode Island; it covers in excess of 2,000 square miles and includes the entirety of Harris County and parts of six neighboring counties. Houston has used this authority to annex land with voter approval, to prevent new incorporations, and to create special utility districts for new development. As a result of the broad powers that it possesses under state law, Houston in the 1970s was able to capture nearly 90 percent of the region's population growth within its borders and its extraterritorial jurisdiction, thereby preventing these areas from forming new suburbs. Only 10 percent of the region's growth occurred in independent suburbs. Houston's extraterritorial powers also extended the area under the influence of the city's business leaders.[14]

COUNCILS OF GOVERNMENTS (COGS) AND REGIONAL PLANNING COUNCILS

A **council of governments (COG)** brings together, on a voluntary basis, the top elected officials of municipalities in a metropolitan area. These officials, or their representatives, meet on a regular basis to discuss problems of mutual interest and to share information and ideas. Originally, COGs were also involved with the preparation of comprehensive plans for regional growth and development. But over the years, as the weakness of the COG approach has become apparent, COGs have had to shift away from metropolitan planning and instead have focused on other activities demanded by their members.

The Growth, Decline, and Adjustment of COGs and RPCs

Early COG efforts in the 1950s included the New York Metropolitan Regional Council; the Washington Metropolitan Conference (since replaced by the Washington, DC, Metropolitan Council of Governments); the Puget Sound Government Conference in Seattle; the Mid-Willamette Valley Intergovernmental Cooperation Council in Salem (Oregon); the Association of Bay Area Governments (ABAG) in greater San Francisco; and the forerunner of the present-day Southeast Michigan Council of Governments (SEMCOG) in the greater Detroit area.

In the 1960s, federal action spurred the creation of COGs as federal grants provided money for regional planning studies and the professional staffing of regional organizations. In a further attempt to promote regionalism, the Office of Management and Budget's Circular A–95 required that local governments submit certain applications for federal money to regional clearing houses for their comments as to how the program would affect metropolitanwide concerns. The A–95 metropolitan review responsibility was lodged with both COGs and **regional planning councils (RPCs).** RPCs are metropolitan planning agencies staffed by professional officials, but without the round table of elected officials on top that characterizes the COG approach. By the 1970s over 100 federal programs required that grant applications be reviewed by regional organizations. These federal initiatives accelerated the creation of COGs (see Table 11.3). Whereas 126 COGs existed nationwide in 1963, the number jumped to 253 in 1970 and 670 in 1980. The Reagan administration, however, reduced both federal requirements and funding for regional planning. As a result, by 1990 the number of COGs had shrunk to fewer than 450.

The COG approach was initiated with great hopes. Yet the weaknesses of COGs soon became apparent.[15] First, COGs are only advisory in nature. They possess no substantial legislative power or authority. Member governments need not follow COG recommendations. Even federal officials, when dispensing aid, can choose to ignore a COG's recommendations.

Second, COGs are voluntary organizations from which members can withdraw at any time. This potential threat hangs over each COG as it attempts to deal with metropolitan issues. In both Cleveland and Washington, DC, member governments, upset at the council's action, have withdrawn from the local COG for short periods of time.

Third, COGs have few independent sources of revenue; they are dependent to a great extent on the financial contributions of their members as well as on federal grant-in-aid programs. In order to avoid antagonizing council members and prompting their withdrawal, COGs have tended to debate only safe or bland issues, or those issues that can gain unanimous support. They tend to avoid such controversial social issues as school and housing integration. Even in their review of federal aid applications, COGs tried to avoid alienating members; COGs largely took on the roles of boosters, uncritically commenting on proposals in attempting to maximize the chances of their members' receiving federal aid.

Fourth, many COGs are quite understaffed. The Washington, DC, Metropolitan COG has the reputation of being one of the nation's best; it is one of the few that have had the resources to attract quality professional personnel and engage in a substantial array of social as well as physical planning activities.

Fifth, the one government–one vote rules of many COGs give disproportionate power to smaller jurisdictions at the expense of central cities and larger suburbs. In the late 1960s, for instance, the city of Cleveland felt that it was being discriminated against since it had 25 percent of the area's population but only 6 percent of the votes in Northeast Ohio Areawide Coordinating Agency (NOACA). Cleveland withdrew its support from NOACA and was suspended for nonpayment of dues.[16]

Finally, COGs are heavily dependent upon federal funding. Reductions in federal support are not generally compensated for by increased local contributions, as few localities see COG operations and regionalism as major priorities.

The Reagan administration reduced the federal monies available for COGs and regional planning. As part of its deregulation efforts, the administration greatly relaxed the federal A–95 review requirements, thereby further undercutting COGs. Primary responsibility for performing the

TABLE 11.3
Growth of Councils of Government (COGs)

Year	Number of COGs
1950	23
1963	126
1967	216
1970	253
1980	670
1990	435 (est.)

clearing-house role was moved to the states. As a consequence, 125 of the 660 regional councils shut their doors. Other COGs, however, were able to adjust and adapt. Some solicited greater contributions from state and local governments. Others increased the level of their service activities, providing a new range of consultation and technical assistance services to their members.[17]

For the faithful, COGs represent the only broad forum for the discussion of regional concerns in many urban areas. While they are far from perfect, they do provide an institution that initiates debate over metropolitan concerns and plans for regional needs.[18] Yet their weaknesses are obvious. An activist council, such as the Washington, DC, Metro COG, may attempt the bold step of initiating a plan for suburbs to take their fair share of housing construction for lower-income persons in the region. Yet Washington Metro COG has succeeded in persuading suburban governments to make only very small additions to the supply of affordable housing in their jurisdictions available to disadvantaged citizens.

Regionalism, Political Power, and the Environment:
The San Francisco Bay Region and Southern California

Regional planning is often suggested to offset the extreme governmental fragmentation of the San Francisco Bay area with its 9 counties, 98 cities, and 721 special districts. Environmentalists have proposed strengthening regional institutions in an effort to stem the area's rapid growth.

But other environmentalist organizations see dangers in enhanced regional planning, especially if regional councils are given the authority to override local governments that implement growth controls. They believe that commercial elites, banks, and other members of the growth coalition endorse regional planning efforts because they have the resources to influence decision making at the regional level.[19]

In southern California, the 1988 planning report *L.A. 2000: A City for the Future* was the manifesto of a "new regionalism" that sought to enhance the power of regional planning agencies in an effort to build "a congregation of livable cities." Proponents saw the plan as an attempt to balance development with environmental concerns. However, other environmental activists feared the influence that developers would have at the regional level.[20]

A COG, the Southern California Association of Area Governments (SCAG), has played an important planning role in the new regionalism. SCAG has joined with other regional and subregional agencies in an attempt to find new means of coping with the region's extensive air pollution problem.

Yet SCAG possesses only planning and coordination responsibilities and lacks any real governing or implementation power. The greater Los Angeles area's response to the rapidly growing problem of air pollution provides a vivid illustration of both the potential and weakness of the COG approach.

The South Coast Air Basin had repeatedly failed to meet federal clean air standards. The federal government's Environmental Protection Agency threatened to impose limitations on new construction if the region itself did not commence action to correct the situation. In 1989 the South Coast Air Quality Management District (AQMD) and SCAG adopted a plan that included a number of drastic steps to curtail that region's ever-growing smog problem. The plan entailed a switch to cleaner-burning fuels. The plan even envisioned numerous changes in the lifestyles of southern Californians, including levying fees in supermarket parking lots and bans on the sale of barbecues that require starter fluid, bias-ply tires, and certain chemicals in underarm deodorants. A major part of the plan also sought to reduce automobile commuting by bringing new jobs closer to the residential developments that have sprung up in the inland regions of the state. Businesses in the region would also have to develop plans to reduce commuting by their work force or face the possibility of fines.

The plan drew support from citizens dissatisfied with the region's slow progress on the air pollution problem. However, the plan was also bitterly opposed by the cities of coastal Orange County, which feared the loss of jobs and tax revenues. Some proponents of continued economic development objected that permits could be denied to new factories or shopping centers that sought locations on the coast. Representatives from poorer and minority-dominated communities expressed the fear that the plan would curtail economic development in the region, thereby lessening job opportunities for citizens who still needed the benefits of economic growth. Others objected to the intrusiveness of the regulations that sought to alter southern California lifestyles and driving habits. The trucking industry vociferously objected to SCAG's call for plans to relieve freeway congestion by eliminating truck traffic during rush hours—a plan that had previously been used to avoid monumental traffic jams during the Los Angeles Olympics.

Given the controversy surrounding the plan, SCAG and the other regional bodies were not able to implement important pollution-reduction steps. Nor is there even a guarantee that SCAG and the Air Quality District will even cooperate successfully in developing the detailed measures needed to carry out the plan. AQMD sets the performance standards that have to be met. SCAG, in contrast, has tried a more consensus-oriented approach of bringing various concerned parties to the table to decide just what specific measures will be taken. SCAG also realizes that the region is too large to have one central agency develop the necessary implementation measures. Hence, SCAG has attempted to establish subregional cooperative associations in such areas as the San Fernando Valley, the San Gabriel Valley, and the Riverside area. Each association will decide just what specific steps are best taken to reduce pollution in its own subregional area.[21]

COGs and the Future of Regionalism

COGs no longer serve as the vehicles for comprehensive metropolitan planning, as their federal backers in the 1960s had envisioned. Yet, despite their limitations, COGs represent a viable vehicle for less comprehensive but still important ventures in regional planning and cooperation.

Those regional councils that have survived have done so by avoiding political enemies and adapting to a changed political environment. They have turned away from expansive regional planning and instead have concentrated on providing research and services to their member local governments.[22] In North Carolina, for instance, the removal of the federal A–95 planning requirements led regional councils to seek out new missions as defined from below by member jurisdictions. Regional councils in North Carolina assist member governments in securing grants. They also provide members with such services as managerial and planning assistance.[23]

On the whole, COGs remain very weak mechanisms of metropolitan coordination and cooperation. Like the United Nations, they can debate, discuss, and suggest; but they seldom have the power to enforce action on any of their members.

Regional planning in the United States has been insufficient to cope with urban ills. Even in the Seattle metropolitan area, renowned for its extensive planning efforts to preserve the area's environment, planning has not been able to stop a pattern of urban sprawl and spread development that is beginning to fill in the open spaces between towns. As urban journalist Neal Peirce observes, the "bottom line" in Seattle's planning is not hard to figure out: "Beyond some elementary environmental controls, don't get in the way of development. Let 'er rip."[24]

One recent federal action, however, has given new credence to regionalism. The **Intermodal Surface Transportation and Efficiency Act (ISTEA,** or, as it is commonly pronounced, "Ice Tea") seeks to promote the integrated development of transportation in order to preserve environmental quality. The act requires that governments in a metropolitan area designate Metropolitan Planning Organizations to carry out specified highway and mass transit planning functions. The act also provides federal funding to help pay for these activities.[25]

FEDERALLY ENCOURAGED SINGLE-PURPOSE REGIONAL BODIES

Federally encouraged single-purpose regional bodies are planning agencies that have been established over the years as a result of federal aid requirements in such areas as economic development, job training, metropolitan transportation, and the provision of assistance to Appalachia. As noted above, the federal ISTEA planning requirements represent an important federal impetus to regional cooperation in the area of transportation planning.

In the Los Angeles region, the federal Clean Air Act spurred the creation of the Air Quality Management District (AQMD) because states were required to develop plans for improving air quality in areas where pollution exceeds acceptable levels.[26] AQMD and other regional bodies in the greater Los Angles area gained increased power as a result of federal and state requirements. The AQMD has more than a thousand employees and an annual budget authority of over $100 million. Its authority in pollution control extends over the greater Los Angeles air basin, a four-county region with more than 10 million residents. AQMD's actions involve it in land use planning and other measures to reduce traffic congestion. It is a federally encouraged, state-created district that has become involved in the basic decisions of local government.[27]

STATE PLANNING AND DEVELOPMENT DISTRICTS

State planning and development districts (SPDDs) were established as states sought to get some control over federal spending in metropolitan areas. In the 1980s SPDDs took on the responsibilities for the regional clearing-house function as a result of Reagan's modification of the A–95 review requirements.

CONTRACTING WITH THE PRIVATE SECTOR

Contracting with the private sector follows the same logic as intergovernmental service contracts; only here municipal governments enter into agreements with private sector firms, not with other governmental jurisdictions, for the provision of specified services.[28] A private sector firm can take advantage of economies of scale that would not exist if a service had to be produced solely within the confines of an individual city's boundaries. Yet, the authorizing legislation for private sector contracting is not easy to obtain; only twenty-six states permit such local contracting.[29] Public sector unions, in particular, oppose private sector contracting from fear that municipalities will issue such contracts in order to circumvent union protections and undermine municipal work force wage structures.

Municipalities also contract with nonprofit organizations. Local governments use nonprofits most frequently for the delivery of health and human services and cultural and arts programs. In recent years, for example, Pittsburgh has increasingly relied on contracts with nonprofits for cultural and arts programs in an attempt to have suburban users share some of the burden of supporting these services.[30]

THE MIDDLING SIX

Martin and Walker identify six other approaches to metropolitan service delivery that are a bit more difficult to achieve than the easiest eight. Each of these middling six means of structural and procedural reforms represents "a more stable way to effectively align governmental and service delivery boundaries" without asking regions to turn to metropolitan government.[31]

SPECIAL DISTRICTS

The increased demand for urban services has led to the growth of special districts across the country. **Local special districts** are units of government that provide a single specific service or a related set of services. The overwhelming number of special districts provide a single service: Of the 33,131 special districts that existed in 1992, over 91 percent performed a single function such as drainage and flood control, solid waste management, fire protection, or housing.[32]

Special districts have proved to be quite flexible means of providing services. Special district boundaries can cross-cut municipal, county, and even state lines. District size can vary with the service provided and the needs that are identified. In Cook County, Illinois, for instance, the Metropolitan Sanitary District of Greater Chicago, the Forest Preserve District of Cook County, and the Suburban Cook County Tuberculosis Sanitarium District are all very large creations that provide a single service or a set of related services. Special districts for libraries, fire protection, and parks and recreation are much narrower in the geographical areas they serve. In many cases special districts are even formed within a city or village to provide services not offered by the municipality.[33]

Illinois, New York, California, Pennsylvania, and Washington contain over 30 percent of the nonschool special districts in the nation. At the same time, other urban states—Connecticut, Ohio, Massachusetts, and Michigan—contain very few special districts.

In at least one aspect, Walker's ranking or scale (Table 11.1) is misleading. Special districts, which Walker lists among the middling six, are so commonplace that they can be ranked among the more easy-to-achieve forms of intergovernmental cooperation. Since the late 1980s, there has even been rapid growth in the creation of special districts. As noted, there are over 33,000 in the United States. In fact, special districts outnumber counties, municipalities, and townships (see Table 11.4). Furthermore, as each special district tends to provide only a single service or two, they

TABLE 11.4
Scope of the Subnational System:
Number of Governments in the United States

Type of Government	1962	1967	1972	1977	1982	1987	1992
Total	91,237	81,299	78,269	80,171	82,688	83,328	86,743
U.S. government	1	1	1	1	1	1	1
State governments	50	50	50	50	50	50	50
Local governments	91,186	81,248	78,218	80,120	82,637	83,277	86,692
Counties	3,043	3,049	3,044	3,042	3,041	3,042	3,043
Municipalities	18,000	18,048	18,517	18,856	19,083	19,205	19,296
Townships	17,142	17,105	18,991	16,822	16,748	16,690	16,666
School districts	34,678	21,782	15,781	15,260	15,032	14,850	14,556
Special districts	18,323	21,264	23,885	26,140	28,733	29,490	33,131

Source: U.S. Bureau of the Census.

can be seen to pose a much narrower attempt at metropolitan coordination than do the COG and regional council approaches.

The growth in the number of special districts over the years is due to the presence of economies of scale. Left to their own, local governments often lack the size or the ability to provide required services at a satisfactory level of quality and at a reasonable cost. Special districts enable local governments to spread the costs of purchasing equipment or constructing new facilities over a large taxpaying area. One other primary reason for their rapid proliferation is that special districts help local governments circumvent legal restrictions on legislative taxing and borrowing imposed by state constitutions or state legislation.

Special districts are administratively and fiscally autonomous governmental bodies. They set their own budgets and raise their own revenues. Some special districts, such as independent school districts, have the authority to levy taxes. Others rely on user fees or charges.

Critics charge that special districts compound many of the problems of metropolitan fragmentation. Many special districts are too small in size to achieve economies of scale in service provision. The creation of special districts also multiplies the number of independent governments in the region, exacerbating problems of coordination. In the New York City region alone, there are 2,191 units of local government; over one-half are special districts (716) and school districts (661).[34] Furthermore, by enabling suburbanites to secure needed services, the creation of special districts also forestalls the need to enact more comprehensive metropolitan reform plans.

Special districts also constitute relatively "invisible" and unaccountable units of government.[35] The news media give little coverage to the meetings and actions of district boards. Very few urban citizens can name any of the officials who serve on these numerous boards. Most citizens are probably even only marginally aware of the existence of these single- and multiple-purpose governmental bodies. When annual property tax statements are mailed, few citizens realize just what portion of their tax bill has been levied by the officials of these low-visibility special district governments. Popular control over these district boards is muted further still, as most district board members are appointed to office and serve staggered terms in order to insulate them from partisan demands by elected officials.

According to Virginia Marion Perrenod, much of the growth in the number of special districts in recent years has been the result of the creation of **urban fringe districts**.[36] These fringe districts have expanded service provision to the periphery of the metropolitan area in response to suburbanites' demands. Unlike the usual special district which provides only one or two functions, urban fringe districts have become **junior cities**. In California, community service districts provide a variety of services, including water, sewage disposal, garbage collection, police and fire protection, street construction and lighting, library service, and recreation. In Texas, municipal utility districts provide water, drainage, sewage systems, garbage collection, firefighting, and parks and recreational services.

Perrenod has found that the creation of these water districts around Houston was the result of an implicit alliance between real estate developers and the city of Houston. Under Texas law water districts are given unlimited taxing and borrowing authority, powers that are denied to cities and counties in the state. As a result, these districts have the capacity to underwrite much of the costs of providing new infrastructure to areas ripe for residential and commercial development. Development is facilitated, and the area is later annexed by the city, with the city absorbing the debt that the annexed area had piled up.

Houston benefits in that it can annex these new areas—and the city's fleeing middle class—back into the city. Real estate developers profit as these districts are used to finance almost all the land development costs in a new project area. In many cases local democracy is undermined as the developers retain effective control over the administration and operation of the water district boards. Private interests make the key decisions in these districts with very little accountability to residents. In recent years such developments have been plagued by flooding and land subsidence and the revelation of shoddy construction practices.

The Houston experience points to the importance of private power in the creation of special districts. In Florida, the Disney Corporation, too, found that the creation of a special district afforded it significant privileges. In building Disney World, its first request to the state government was for the creation of a special district, the Reedy Creek Improvement District outside Orlando. The special district *is* Walt Disney World, a municipal government with the authority to regulate land use, provide police and fire service, lay sewer lines, and even build an airport (if it so desired) and issue bonds. The formation of its own independent local government meant that Disney was free to develop its project without having to fear the imposition of growth controls, impact fees, or other unwanted intrusions by neighboring local governments.

In 1994, a similar district was created by Dade and Broward Counties, giving Blockbuster Entertainment Corporation authority over 2,500 acres in order to build a new hockey arena, a new ballpark for the Florida Marlins, a new amusement park, and various other hotel, entertainment, and retail facilities. Like Disney, Blockbuster had in effect become its own local government. Under the new special district arrangement, Blockbuster gained the ability to levy its own sales taxes, issue tax-exempt bonds, annex and condemn property, and apply for federal grants.[37]

Special districts provide an excellent illustration of how private interests seek the creation of formal government institutions to enhance their power. Private developers have been very active in the creation of special districts that can raise huge sums of money to subsidize new commercial and residential development projects. These business entrepreneurs are especially interested in having special districts issue revenue bonds to fund infrastructure. Even the requirement for a public vote on the creation of a special district does not pose a formidable barrier to development interests; a developer usually can afford to subsidize the move of a few friendly people into a marginally populated urban fringe area. Active in the creation of a special district, developers also frequently serve on the district's board and dominate its decision making during the early years when the population of a newly created district is small.[38]

TRANSFER OF FUNCTIONS

A **transfer of functions** entails a permanent shift in the responsibility for providing a service from one jurisdiction to another that is better able to handle the service or realize economies of scale. Cities are most likely to shift service responsibilities to the county, though services are also shifted to COGs and to special districts. A significant use of the transfer mechanism occurred when Atlanta and Fulton County agreed to reassign service responsibilities between the two governments.[39]

Despite the increased use of this mechanism in recent years, a reassignment of functions is allowed in only about half of the states; and half of those require voter approval before any transfer is finalized. Furthermore, local political rivalries can stand in the way of a service transfer. In Pima County, Arizona, a virtual "sewer wars" was fought as city and county residents debated effluent rights (a valuable resource in arid Arizona) and user charges in a consolidated system.[40]

ANNEXATION

Annexation is the acquisition of additional territory to enlarge the existing governmental jurisdiction. Annexation occurs when a municipality extends its boundaries outward, thereby absorbing a neighboring area.

Annexations that take place are almost always of areas that are still unincorporated. This is because most states seek to protect the sovereignty of incorporated municipalities. When the annexation of an incorporated area is attempted, state laws usually require **dual referenda**—that is, citizens in both jurisdictions must approve of the proposed consolidation. This requirement greatly impedes the ability of older cities surrounded by already incorporated suburban municipalities to annex new land. In some rare instances, however, the dual referenda requirement can be circumvented, as annexation can be decided by special state legislative action, judicial determination, and the action of state boundary commissions. For very small annexations, local governments are sometimes given the authority to expand their boundaries without having to obtain the consent of the area to be annexed.

Many of America's largest cities achieved their present size as a result of annexations carried out toward the end of the nineteenth century. In 1854 Philadelphia used an aggressive annexation approach to expand its land area from 2 square miles to 136 square miles; the city has not expanded since then. In 1898 the most famous of all annexations occurred when New York City, then only 40 square miles in size, consolidated with Brooklyn, capturing over 240 new square miles of territory and one million new residents.[41] Such expansion was possible, as resistance to annexation had not yet reached its peak. Other cities were able to expand their boundaries, as the areas around them were relatively sparsely populated and few, if any, incorporated areas existed to defend suburban residents against central city annexations.

Los Angeles pursued an aggressive policy of annexation, increasing its territory in just ten years from 108 square miles in 1915 to 415 square miles in 1925. In a policy known to its neighbors as **Los Angeles water imperialism**, Los Angeles refused to supply water to outlying communities unless they accepted incorporation into the city. Municipal leaders "expanded the size of the city by forcing other communities to accept annexation or die of thirst."[42]

The prominence of annexation policies has varied from city to city and from region to region. Some cities such as Fort Worth (Texas), Omaha (Nebraska), and Shreveport (Louisiana) have shown a steady reliance over the years on annexation as a tool of expansion. Others such as Atlanta, Milwaukee, and Knoxville (Tennessee) pursued annexation during a single decade. Still others such as Detroit, Baltimore, and even Los Angeles have experienced little change in the boundaries over the last forty or more years. In the New England and Middle Atlantic states, there have been virtually no annexations in recent decades, as cities in these regions are fully surrounded by already incorporated areas.[43]

In recent decades, annexation has proven to be a dynamic instrument of city expansion in the Sunbelt. Texas, North Carolina, and California are the nation's annexation leaders, in terms of the total population involved in municipal annexations (see Table 11.5). Virtually all the largest annexations in the 1970s took place in the Sunbelt, with Houston the clear leader in annexing areas with an estimated total population of

208,000.[44] In the 1980s, the greatest annexations involved Sunbelt and Pacific rim cities: San Antonio (73,000 persons annexed); Portland, Oregon (54,000); Houston (50,900); and Charlotte (37,700). But even these sizable annexations were smaller than those that had taken place in the 1950s. Houston and Phoenix have been annexation leaders in every decade beginning with the 1950s. In recent years, North Carolina cities—Charlotte, Durham, Greensboro, Raleigh, and Winston-Salem—have been particularly aggressive in pursuing annexations.[45]

Annexation can be used as a tool by progrowth regimes. Where a city lacks a sufficient supply of developable land, annexation can be used to gain control over new land outside the city's borders. In the rapidly growing suburb of Auburn Hills (the home of the Detroit Pistons), city officials found that their aggressive pursuit of rapid high-tech and office development was being hampered by a shortage of nearby available housing. The city had been unable to attract residential development because it lay within the borders of the predominantly black Pontiac school district, which operates under a court-ordered school busing plan. To circumvent this problem, the city moved to annex three square miles of land from neighboring, unincorporated townships that lie outside the Pontiac school district.[46]

Cities pursue the annexation of relatively sparsely populated tracts of land in order to promote development—and, in some cases, to prevent development and protect the environment of surrounding areas. Houston took new land to the city's north in order to build a new international airport. Denver annexed more than 43 square miles, adding 40 percent to the city's land area, in order to acquire the land to build the nation's largest airport. Columbus (Ohio) and San Jose (California) are other cities that have annexed land that was undergoing development.[47] In Albuquerque land that was for the most part empty was brought into the city in the 1950s and early 1960s at the request of developers who hoped that the provision of city services would add to the marketability of their subdivisions.[48]

The success of annexation in the Sunbelt is the result of liberal state laws that facilitate annexations, including regulations that give cities extraterritorial power to keep nearby land unincorporated and available for annexation. In Oklahoma annexation laws are so permissive that a city can annex any piece of land it surrounds on three sides, with or without the permission of the property owners. Oklahoma City, acting under the urging of the local chamber of commerce, calculated land acquisitions so as to surround and capture many such land parcels. Oklahoma City proved so aggressive in acquiring neighboring land that neighboring Edmond itself annexed over fifty square miles of land in order to block further expansion by Oklahoma City. Other suburbs followed suit, allowing Oklahoma City little room for similar vigorous expansion today.[49]

The success of annexation in the Sunbelt is also due to the relatively small degree of socioeconomic differences between suburbs and central

TABLE 11.5
States Ranked by Estimated Population of Areas Annexed by
Municipalities, 1980–1986
(Top Ten States)

State	Population of Areas Annexed (in Thousands)	Rank
Texas	240.5	1
California	216.0	2
North Carolina	169.9	3
Florida	92.2	4
Alabama	73.2	5
Oregon	69.3	6
Louisiana	52.4	7
Nebraska	50.2	8
Arkansas	49.3	9
Arizona	46.5	10

Source: Adapted from Joel C. Miller, "Municipal Annexation and Boundary Change," *Municipal Year Book 1988* (Washington, DC: International City Management Association, 1988).

cities in this region as compared to the much larger differences between the older central cities and the more established suburbs of the Northeast. Annexations are most likely to occur in areas where the populations in both the central city and the surrounding suburban areas are of similar socioeconomic backgrounds, thus reducing many of the anxieties and apprehensions that result when people of diverse backgrounds and aspirations attempt to live together under one political system.

Annexation provides a relatively comprehensive answer to the problems of metropolitan fragmentation. Where annexation is permitted, a city's boundaries and service responsibilities are simply extended outward to encompass new areas of population growth. However, the dual referenda requirement means that the annexation of already incorporated areas proves next to impossible. As a consequence, annexation continues to be a viable metropolitan governance strategy only in the cities of the South, the Southwest, and the Pacific Rim.

The annexation of growing middle-class areas has been a key to the continued good health of Albuquerque, Charlotte, Houston, San Antonio, Columbus, and other **elastic cities.** Indianapolis and Nashville have similarly extended their borders through more comprehensive metropolitan reorganization plans. According to David Rusk, the former mayor of Albuquerque, by expanding municipal boundaries, elastic cities have been able to capture new development and thereby maintain a strong tax base and a favorable bond rating. In contrast, cities in the Northeast and North Central region—including Cleveland, Detroit, and Hartford—are hemmed in by already incorporated suburbs and unfavorable annexation laws. Unable to expand geographically, they have declined while the growth of new economic activity has taken place outside the city limits.[50]

The aggressive annexation policies of Sunbelt cities have led to a rash of municipal incorporations by areas on the city rim. Residents in previously unincorporated suburban areas have been led to form their own municipalities in an effort to stave off annexation efforts by the central city.[51]

REGIONAL DISTRICTS AND AUTHORITIES

Regional special districts and authorities are large areawide institutions that are usually established by state law. In some cases, interstate agreements create regional authorities that extend across state borders. In many cases these regional units can be seen as constituting a metropolitanwide version of the special district. The Bay Area Rapid Transit District, the Southern California Metropolitan Water District, the Massachusetts Bay Transit Authority, the Chicago Metropolitan Sanitary District, and the Seattle Port District are each charged with providing a single service for the region. Others, like the Port Authority of New York and New Jersey, possess broad powers in a number of service areas. The reach of the Port Authority extends way beyond maintaining New York's port; over the years, the Port Authority has also been involved in regional planning and building bus terminals, highways, and even the twin-tower World Trade Center skyscraper.

Regional authorities are difficult to set up. They require state enactment, and they also often face the opposition of local jurisdictions who fear a loss of power to the regional agency.

Even more critically, special authorities often represent relatively unaccountable islands of power. Just whom is served by these governing bodies with their considerable professional talent and financial resources? Regional authorities may represent the interests of financial and development elites. As Walker observes, these authorities "are frequently as accountable to bond buyers as to the localities and the citizen consumers."[52]

The creation of the Illinois Sports Facility Authority (ISFA) illustrates the power and potential of public authorities as well as the accountability problem such authorities pose. Despite the body's impressive name, the ISFA was really charged with a quite narrow purpose. It was not empowered to build sports facilities throughout Illinois or even throughout the Chicago region. Instead, it was charged with deciding on the exact site for and raising money to build only one stadium, a new ballpark on the south side of the city that would keep the White Sox in Chicago. The authority gave the baseball club its desired site; it built a new White Sox stadium directly across from aging Comiskey Park, which was then torn down. The creation of the ISFA gives the illusion that the final decision on the ballpark was the result of independent, professional judgment. In reality, the creation of the ISFA helped to legitimize a decision that seemingly had already been made. By creating the ISFA, the state government, the ball club, and their allies could do what the city of Chicago, responsive to the political clout of its black community, was unwilling to do. The ISFA displaced the residents and businesses of a poor, black neighborhood in order to build a new, subsidized stadium demanded by the White Sox.

As we recounted in Chapter 6, the actions of the Port Authority of New York and New Jersey, too, raise serious questions about the accountability and responsibility of authorities that have enormous independent revenue-raising capability. In the early 1970s, environmentalists and local officials wanted the Port Authority to turn away from its road-building orientation in order to invest part of its money in the region's ailing mass transit system. But the Port Authority resisted. It felt an obligation to its bondholders. It was also dominated by businesspersons who did not wish to invest the agency's money in a long-term losing proposition such as mass transit; like all authorities that raise money in the bond market, the leaders of the Port Authority felt that they should follow established business practices so as to receive the most favorable interest rates possible. The Port Authority assumed new responsibility for mass transit (including the takeover of a failing New Jersey railroad) only when virtually forced to do so by the states. Instead of making further investments in mass transit, the Port Authority chose to use much of its surplus funds to construct the World Trade Center in lower Manhattan.[53]

Despite its regionwide orientation, the Port Authority has proven to be a weak tool of metropolitan planning. As the only public regional planning agency in the greater New York–New Jersey–Connecticut region, the Port Authority is by default "the only planning game in town."[54] Yet the Authority has failed to act aggressively in the area of regional planning; instead of promoting interlocal cooperation in the region, the Authority has chosen to focus on highway building and other infrastructure projects. As the Authority derives revenues only from the projects it builds and operates, it has little incentive to pursue more extensive and less profitable planning efforts.

In recent years, more aggressive leadership has led the Authority to take a more active role in outlining a marketing strategy for the region designed to benefit the region as a whole. But the Port Authority enjoyed little success in getting localities in the region to join in a common economic development strategy. The Authority has been unable to overcome the parochial interests of state and local governments.

The failure of a regional "nonaggression pact" illustrates the weakness of the Port Authority in attempting to guide economic development. In 1991, the executives of the three states and New York City signed an Authority-authored agreement promising not to use negative advertising against one another or to offer incentive programs to lure businesses from one community to another. But "job wars" soon ensued as the various jurisdictions offered new tax incentives and other subsidies in an effort to lure corporations away from their neighbors. In a move that outraged New York City, the state of New Jersey offered to subsidize First Chicago Trust's relocation of over 1,000 jobs from its offices in lower Manhattan.[55]

In southern California, such bodies as the Orange County Transit Authority and the (Los Angeles County) Metropolitan Transit Authority have gained increased power in recent years. While these bodies do not serve the entire region, they nonetheless constitute narrow-purpose, sub-regional governments capable of tempering some of the parochialism of local governments.[56]

METROPOLITAN MULTIPURPOSE DISTRICTS

Metropolitan multipurpose districts are regional districts set up to provide a variety of services. The municipality of Metropolitan Seattle District is the most prominent example. Seattle's METRO was created in response to environmental and sewage problems in the region. While state statute initially gave METRO authority over sewage treatment and five other functions, METRO was also allowed to take on new functional responsibilities with voter approval. Voters approved METRO's assumption of new responsibilities in the area of transit.

But the metropolitan multipurpose district is rarely used, as it is among the most difficult regional reform plans to set up. Only four states authorize the creation of such broadly empowered districts. In recent years, even Seattle's fabled METRO has suffered as a result of the difficulties inherent in the arrangement. METRO's expanded authority was often opposed by King County, its rival for regional preeminence. METRO also faced legal challenge, as its governing body is not directly elected but consists of forty-five members appointed by the participating local jurisdictions. In 1990 a U.S. District Court finally ruled that, inasmuch as METRO provides more than one service function, it is a general-purpose local government, and its governing body must meet the constitutional standards of one person/one vote. As a result, King County renewed its efforts to absorb METRO's functions.[57]

STRENGTHENED COUNTY GOVERNMENT

The **reformed urban county** is often suggested as an institution that can provide improved services, particularly to the suburban and fringe portions of the metropolis. Suburban counties have had to modernize in the face of citizen demands for more improved and efficient service delivery.

Counties were once seen as America's "forgotten governments"[58]— backward, rural-oriented governments dominated by part-time commissions and ill-structured for effective action. But nowadays, these once-forgotten governments are no longer concerned only with such traditional county responsibilities as maintaining roads and the county sanitarium. Urban and suburban county governments have undertaken new responsibilities in social welfare, education, corrections, and environmental protection. Figure 11.1 documents the new concerns of the modern county. The top three spending categories in county budgets—health and hospitals, public welfare, and education—are all in the social service area.[59] One study has found that suburban counties spend a greater share of their budgets on redistributive services than do suburban municipalities.[60] County spending for corrections has also increased rapidly. County budgets have grown dramatically as a result of the counties' new service undertakings.[61]

Urban and suburban counties have sought to move away from the weakness of the traditional **county commission** governing arrangement, where part-time elected officials made the county's laws and supervised county departments. These part-time officials seldom had the time or professional ability to lead a growing county.

The reformed urban county has tried to correct this deficiency by providing a strong central executive who has the capacity to run the county effectively on a daily basis. Presently, about three-quarters of the nation's nearly 700 metro counties have either an elected chief executive or an appointed chief administrative officer.[62] The reformed urban county has taken three forms.

The most minimal reform is the **county administrator plan**, under which the part-time legislature hires a full-time chief administrative officer (CAO) to assist it in staff work, budget preparation, and the administration of its policies. The **county manager plan** places even more power in the hands of a professional executive who is authorized to coordinate a city's administrative affairs. The county manager plan is analogous to the city manager plan discussed in Chapter 4. Finally, the **county executive plan** is analogous to the strong-mayor system of government. Under this plan the voters directly elect an executive who is the political, administrative, and symbolic leader of the county. St. Louis County (Missouri); Nassau and Westchester Counties (New York); Wayne County (Michigan); and Baltimore, Montgomery, and Prince Georges Counties (Maryland) are all prominent examples of suburban counties that use the elected executive form of government.

Yet even the modernized county does not provide the perfect answer to the problems posed by metropolitan fragmentation. First of all, the powers and importance of counties vary from state to state. In some states, such as Maryland, counties possess an important range of powers. In other states, including the New England states where tradition has vested powers in towns, counties are not especially important units of local government.

Second, the reformed county can provide a valuable means of metropolitanwide integration of services only in the 140 or so single-county areas in the United States. In the more than 150 metro areas that contain multiple counties, enhanced county government represents only a subregional solution at best. In these multicounty areas, it may be somewhat silly to portray a strengthened county as having achieved metropolitan government.

FIGURE 11.1
Percentage Distribution of Total County Expenditures, 1991: The Prominence of Health,
Social Services, and Education

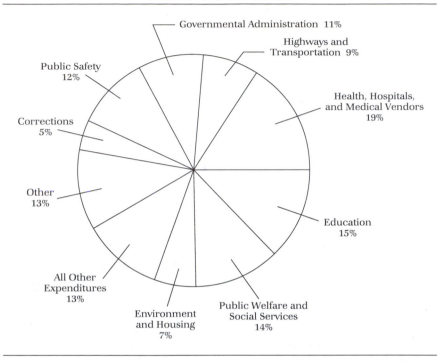

Governmental Administration 11%

Highways and
Transportation 9%

Public Safety
12%

Health, Hospitals,
and Medical Vendors
19%

Corrections
5%

Other
13%

Education
15%

All Other
Expenditures
13%

Environment
and Housing
7%

Public Welfare and
Social Services
14%

Source: Prepared from figures presented by U.S. Bureau of the Census, *Governmental Finances: 1990–91*, GAO/HRD-94-1 (USGPO), Appendix IV, p. 63.

THE PURSUIT OF ECONOMIC DEVELOPMENT: A NEW IMPETUS TOWARD REGIONALISM?

The new focus of local governments on economic development has, in some instances, served as a catalyst for regional cooperation. There is a growing recognition of the role that regions play in securing economic development, and that communities in an area often don't compete with one another but with communities in other regions.[63] Interlocal cooperation can increase the economic competitiveness of a region.

The marketplace values an integrated, total labor market.[64] A central city and its suburbs comprise a single, economic region. When cities and suburbs cooperate together, they can fashion a joint strategy in the interregional and global pursuit of new business. For instance, cities in Connecticut find it difficult to attract new business if workers often must live in more affordable communities fifty or more miles away! With intergovernmental cooperation, one city can provide the site for a new business, while a neighboring municipality can provide the new housing.[65]

Regional cooperation recognizes the economic interdependence of cities and suburbs in a global economy. Standing alone, no city or suburb can provide the airports, universities, land, transportation, material resources, and trained labor force demanded by businesses in a high-tech age.[66] Regional cooperation allows more aggressive planning in the pursuit of economic development. Public support for regional cooperation, even consolidation of governments, increases when metropolitan action is perceived to bring new economic benefits to a community.[67]

According to Allan Wallis, there have been three great waves of metropolitan reform plans.[68] The first wave emphasized the virtues of annexation, metropolitan unification, and the formation of full-fledged metropolitan governments. This emphasis on unification corresponded to the central-city–centered metropolitan economies of the industrial era. But, as we have seen in Chapter 10, in recent years such plans for comprehensive reform and consolidation have been hard to realize. The second wave of metropolitan reform sought incremental, cooperative arrangements to bring about greater governmental efficiency and protection of the environment in the midst of burgeoning suburbanization. With the drying up of federal planning funds, this wave of regional reform, too, has waned.

The third and most recent wave of metropolitanism focuses on regional cooperation for economic development. This wave is a response to the globalization of the postindustrial economy, where cities and suburbs often find that they must join together in efforts to bring jobs to their region. Oftentimes, economic development efforts are ad hoc attempts to find solutions to a particular economic problem. They are less structured than more formalized regional arrangements.

Urban journalist Neal Peirce has shown the inadequacy of thinking of cities solely as defined by their formal political boundaries. According to Peirce, **citistates** have grown beyond antiquated political borders. The "real city" is regional in scope. It recognizes the economic interconnections of the center city, inner suburbs, and outer suburbs. The term *citistate* denotes an intimately interconnected regional community with a shared work force and a shared economic and social future.[69] Peirce asks how American citistates can hope to compete for enterprise with their European or Asian counterparts that enjoy more extensive metropolitan governing and planning arrangements.[70] Citistates must form cooperative efforts if they are to marshall their internal strength and "find a profitable niche in the new world economy."[71]

The new regional cooperation is focused on *governance*, not *government*—on problem solving, not on building new governmental institutions.[72] More formal means of regional cooperation have been weak and inadequate to the task. As a consequence, formal cooperative arrangements need to be supplemented by the creation of **metropolitan partnerships** that cross borders for the common good.[73]

The active involvement of local chambers of commerce and other business groups, governmental officials, nonprofit organizations, and strong citizen associations is needed to forge partnerships that can produce regionwide solutions. Such metropolitan partnerships will require the support and financial backing of the business and non-profit sectors.[74] In Charlotte, the local university has been asked to play a leading role in efforts at regional cooperation, including the development of a regional marketing plan, as the university is seen to be a neutral third party with no turf to protect.[75]

Yet even the promise of shared economic benefits in a competitive global economy may be insufficient to promote extensive regional cooperation. The failure of the Port Authority of New York and New Jersey to get state and local jurisdictions to abide by an economic nonaggression pact points to the inherent difficulty of interlocal cooperation even in the economic development arena. In older metropolitan areas, in particular, postindustrial economic restructuring is generating even greater interlocal inequalities and differences that may serve to undercut the prospects of regional cooperation.[76]

The importance of social distance to new regional cooperation becomes all the more apparent if we contrast Denver's success in building a regional airport with St. Louis' failure to construct a similar facility. In Denver a regional alliance motivated by the promise of shared economic benefits mobilized on behalf of the project. But in St. Louis, in contrast, no unified regional leadership emerged. Illinois and Missouri each wanted the airport on their side of the border. The greater social distance between communities in the St. Louis area produced an entrenched parochialism that made it difficult for the region's leaders to form a workable coalition.[77]

The new vitality of regional cooperation may also represent a shift in power. In the greater San Francisco area, business and environmentalist groups formed Bay Vision 2020, an attempt to forge regional cooperation in such areas as economic development and landfill sitings. But San Francisco and Oakland opposed the effort as diluting minority and inner-city power.[78]

CONCLUSIONS: POLITICAL POWER AND THE FUTURE OF METROPOLITAN REFORM

In most metropolitan areas, full metropolitan government is no longer possible. As a consequence, urban advocates must recognize the potential offered by multiple regional institutions.[79] Regional cooperation is possible, and there exists a wide variety of vehicles for interlocal cooperation. Different regional agencies handle different aspects of the metropolitan problem.

Yet coordination of the actions of these agencies will at times prove difficult. Purely voluntary action will also likely ignore the more fundamental equality and racial problems plaguing the fragmented metropolis. Suburban residents can generally be expected to oppose metropolitan governing arrangements that will raise their taxes or diminish their control over local land use. The dual referenda requirement in most states further gives suburbanites an effective veto power over proposed annexations and more extensive metropolitan restructuring proposals.

Since the Reagan years, federal money and requirements in support of regionalism, too, have been reduced. ISTEA and the Clean Air Act, though, stand as notable exceptions—continuing federal inducements to regional planning and action. The states, with their powers to redraw boundaries, create new local governments and authorities, and redefine service boundaries, may have to take the lead if more extensive interlocal coordination is ever to be realized.

Intergovernmental cooperation is most likely to occur when joint efforts produce benefits for all participating parties. For instance, only coordinated, regional action can reduce air pollution, a problem that has no respect for municipal boundaries. Interlocal cooperation is also likely to be realized when economies of scale are well apparent.

Businesses have often been key actors in the politics of metropolitan governance. In many cases, suburban businesses, like suburban residents, opposed new metropolitan governing arrangements that threatened to raise taxes in order to pay for heightened service delivery in poorer jurisdictions. Yet, in other cases business leaders promoted metropolitan cooperation in order to advance their interests.

Regional reform measures are not initiated solely from a concern for increased service efficiency and economies of scale. Instead, private entrepreneurs have at times found it in their financial interest to promote initiatives associated with regionalism. In Los Angeles County, the Lakewood Plan allowed the creation of tax islands that shielded major areas of industrial property from annexation and taxation by larger jurisdictions. In Houston, extraterritoriality and annexation allowed developers to use the revenue powers of special districts to subsidize basic services and infrastructure improvements on the urban fringe. Regional planning commissions and authorities, too, have allowed developers and other business interests access that they do not enjoy in local city halls throughout the region.

As the United States entered the 1990s, a new trend in regionalism was evident as communities began to recognize the virtues of collaborative efforts in the intersectional and global competition for economic development. Entire metropolitan regions are competing with each other for desirable businesses. As a result, in some metropolitan areas a new mentality emerged. If a jurisdiction cannot attract a major new facility within its borders, it may still gain economic benefits by helping a neighboring community to win the location of the facility. The importance of these new regional partnerships was recognized by the good-government National Civic League, whose 1989 national conference was organized around the theme of "The New Metropolitan Reality: Collaborate or Decline."

Oftentimes, the new move toward regionalism occurs when businesses and citizen groups organize and press government to respond. In the greater Denver area, the forty local chambers of commerce pulled together to form the Denver Metropolitan Network in order to market the region to national corporations. When the city of Denver proved unable to gain the location of a new federal engraving and printing plant, it assisted the neighboring suburb of Aurora in its efforts to win the competition for the new facility. Similarly, when Sears, Roebuck & Co. announced its intention to move its offices out of its namesake landmark skyscraper tower in downtown Chicago, numerous communities in the greater Chicago area and the state of Illinois joined together in an effort to keep as many of the company's jobs as possible in the region. Sears finally settled on a new suburban campus in Hoffman Estates, in the region's northwestern suburbs.

In such areas as pollution control, economic development, and mass transit construction, new regional problem-solving efforts are being attempted. Some suburbs have even begun to cooperate with central cities in very limited school and housing integration plans. Yet, for the most part, voluntary intergovernmental cooperation has been lacking in education, social welfare, and other service areas where the shared benefits of joint action are not readily apparent. Even in the economic development arena, parochialism can win out over regionalism, as the continuing "job wars" between New York City and New Jersey attest. Paradoxically, regional cooperation and metropolitan *governance* (as opposed to metropolitan *government*) are alive and well, but still quite limited in what they can achieve.

NOTES

1. Roscoe C. Martin, *Metropolis in Transition* (Washington, DC: Housing and Home Financing Agency, 1963); David Walker, "Snow White and the 17 Dwarfs: From Metro Cooperation to Governance," *National Civic Review* 76 (January/February 1987): 14–28; and David B. Walker, *The Rebirth of Federalism: Slouching Toward Washington* (Chatham, NJ: Chatham House, 1995), Chapter 9.
2. Walker, "Snow White and the 17 Dwarfs," pp. 16–17.
3. Lisa Belkin, "Separated by Border, 2 Cities Are United by Needs," *The New York Times*, December 17, 1988. Details regarding El Paso–Ciudad Juárez cooperation are taken from the Belkin article.
4. Anthony W. Corso, "San Diego: The Anti-City," in *Sunbelt Cities: Politics and Growth Since World War II*, ed. Richard M. Bernard and Bradley R. Rice (Austin, TX: University of Texas Press, 1983), p. 342; and Bruce Stokes, "Boom at the Border," *National Journal*, July 29, 1989, pp. 1922–27.
5. Glen Sparrow and Dana Brown, "Black Water, Red Tape: Anatomy of a Border Problem," *National Civic Review* 75 (July/August 1986): 216.

6. Advisory Commission on Intergovernmental Relations (ACIR), *Intergovern-mental Service Arrangements for Delivering Local Public Services: Update 1983* (Washington, DC: ACIR, 1985), pp. 25–28. ACIR, *Substate Regionalism and the Federal System: The Challenge of Local Governmental Reorganization* (Washington, DC: ACIR, 1974), pp. 35–36.

7. Richard M. Cion, "Accommodation par Excellence: The Lakewood Plan," in *Metropolitan Politics: A Reader*, 2nd ed., ed. Michael N. Danielson (Boston: Little, Brown, 1971), p. 229.

8. Gary J. Miller, *Cities by Contract: The Politics of Municipal Incorporation* (Cambridge, MA: MIT Press, 1981), pp. 85–145; and Mike Davis, *City of Quartz: Excavating the Future of Los Angeles* (New York: Vintage Books, 1992), pp. 165–69.

9. Miller, *Cities by Contract*, p. viii. Also see chapters 1–5.

10. Ibid., pp. viii, 8–9, and 176–83.

11. Cion, "Accommodation par Excellence: The Lakewood Plan," p. 230; Miller, *Cities by Contract*, pp. 41–62; and Charles Hoch, "Municipal Contracting in California: Privatizing with Class," *Urban Affairs Quarterly* 20 (March 1985): 303–23.

12. Richard Edward DeLeon, *Left Coast City: Progressive Politics in San Francisco, 1975–1991* (Lawrence, KS: Univ. of Kansas Press, 1992), p. 111.

13. Arnold Fleischmann, "Sunbelt Boosterism: The Politics of Postwar Growth and Annexation in San Antonio," in *The Rise of the Sunbelt Cities*, Urban Affairs Annual Review, vol. 14, ed. David C. Perry and Alfred J. Watkins (Beverly Hills, CA: Sage Publications, 1977), pp. 158–62.

14. Robert E. Parker and Joe R. Feagin, "Houston: Administration by Economic Elites," in *Big City Politics in Transition*, ed. H. V. Savitch and John Clayton Thomas (Newbury Park, CA: Sage Publications, 1991), pp. 185–87.

15. John J. Harrigan, *Political Change in the Metropolis*, 4th ed. (Glenview, IL: Scott, Foresman, 1989), pp. 345–47, reviews a number of the charges that have been levelled against COGs. Also see Robert Weaver and Sherman Wyman, "Regional Councils and Their Managers: Profiles, Problems and Prospects" (Paper presented to the annual conference of the Urban Affairs Association, Vancouver, B.C., April 1991).

16. Advisory Commission on Intergovernmental Relations, *Regional Decision Making: New Strategies for Substate Districts* (Washington, DC: ACIR, 1973), pp. 83–86; and Frances Frisken, "The Metropolis and the Central City: Can One Government Unite Them?" *Urban Affairs Quarterly* 8 (June 1973): 395–422.

17. Walker, "Snow White and the 17 Dwarfs," p. 18.

18. A passionate defense of COGs is made by Nelson Wikstrom, *Councils of Governments: A Study of Political Incrementalism* (Chicago: Nelson-Hall, 1977).

19. Details of the debate over regionalism in San Francisco are taken from Richard Edward DeLeon, *Left Coast City* (Lawrence, KS: Univ. of Kansas Press, 1992), pp. 139–41. In making these observations, DeLeon cites Michael Peter Smith, *The City and Social Theory* (New York: St. Martin's Press, 1979), p. 273.

20. Davis, *City of Quartz*, pp. 82–83.

21. Remarks of Mark Pisano, executive director of the Southern California Association of Governments, and John Crowley, city director of Pasadena, to the annual conference of the National Civic League, Denver, Colorado, October 25, 1989.

22. Patricia Atkins and Laura Wilson-Gentry, "An Etiquette for the 1990s Regional Council," *National Civic Review* 81 (1992): 466–87; and Donald F. Norris, "Killing a COG: The Death and Reincarnation of the Baltimore Regional Council of Governments," *Journal of Urban Affairs* 16 (1994): 157–58.

23. James H. Svara, "Setting a Regional Agenda for Councils of Government in North Carolina" (Paper presented at the annual meeting of the Urban Affairs Association, Cleveland, April 1992).

24. Neal R. Peirce, with Curtis W. Johnson and John Stuart Hall, *Citistates: How Urban America Can Prosper in a Competitive World* (Washington, DC: Seven Locks Press, 1993), p. 87.

25. Norris, "Killing a COG," pp. 163–64.

26. Anthony Downs, *New Visions for Metropolitan America* (Washington, DC: Brookings Institution, 1994), pp. 174–75; and Peirce, with Johnson and Hall, *Citistates*, pp. 6 and 32.

27. Alan L. Saltzstein, "Greater Los Angeles: Politics Without Governance" (Paper presented at the annual meeting of the American Political Science Association, New York, September 1994).

28. Local government resort to private sector contracting is discussed by Patricia S. Florestano and Stephen B. Gordon, "A Survey of City and County Use of Private Contracting," *Urban Interest* 3 (Spring 1981): 22–29; Patricia S. Florestano and Stephen B. Gordon, "Public vs. Private: Small Government Contracting with the Private Sector," *Public Administration Review* 40 (January/February 1980): 29–34; Edward C. Hayes, "In Pursuit of Productivity: Brokering Services and Pay-for Performance in Scottsdale," *National Civic Review* 73 (September 1984): 390–94; and E. S. Savas, *Privatization: The Key to Better Government* (Chatham, NJ: Chatham House Publishers, 1987). Also see Werner Hirsch, *Privatizing Government Services* (Los Angeles: Institute of Industrial Relations, 1991); Roger Kemp, ed., *Privatization: The Provision of Public Services by the Private Sector* (Jefferson, NC: McFarland & Company, Inc., 1991; and Ted Kolderie, "The Two Different Concepts of Privatization," *Public Administration Review* (July/August 1986): 285–91.

29. Walker, "Snow White and the 17 Dwarfs," p. 20.

30. Ibid., pp. 16 and 20.

31. Rowan Miranda and Karlyn Andersen, "Alternative Service Delivery in Local Government, 1982–1992," *Municipal Year Book 1992* (Washington, DC: International City/County Management Association, 1994), p. 28.

32. Joseph F. Zimmerman, "Single-Purpose Governments on the Increase," *National Civic Review* 83 (Spring-Summer 1994): 209–10.

33. Donald F. Stetzer, "The Interaction of Special Districts and Local Government in Cook County, Illinois" (Paper presented at the "Conference on the Small City and Regional Community," University of Wisconsin–Stevens Point, Stevens Point, Wisconsin, March 30–31, 1978). For a more detailed description of the current mix of special districts and other forms of local government in the Chicago-Cook County area, see Barbara Page Fiske, ed., *Key to Government in Chicago and Suburban Cook County* (Chicago: University of Chicago Press, 1989).

34. Michael N. Danielson and Jameson W. Doig, *New York: The Politics of Urban Regional Development* (Berkeley, CA: University of California Press, 1982), p. 4.

35. Stanley Scott and John Corzine, "Special Districts in the Bay Area," in *Metropolitan Politics: A Reader*, 2nd ed., ed. Michael N. Danielson (Boston: Little, Brown, 1971), pp. 201–13.

36. Virginia Marion Perrenod, *Special Districts, Special Purposes: Fringe Governments and Urban Problems in the Houston Area* (College Station, TX: Texas A&M University Press, 1984). The reference to junior cities is from John C. Bollens, *Special District Government in the United States* (Westport, CT: Greenwood Press, 1957), p. 114, and is cited by Perrenod, p. 3.

37. For a description of the power gained by Disney, see Nancy Burns, *The Formation of American Local Governments: Private Values in Public Institutions* (New York: Oxford University Press, 1994), p. 31. The Blockbuster arrangement is described by Jill Conley, "Blockbuster Wins Own Quasi-Government in Florida," *County News*, September 26, 1994.

38. Burns, *The Formation of American Local Governments*, pp. 4–6, 14–15, 25–32, and 114–17.

39. Glen Sparrow and Lauren McKinsey, "Metropolitan Reorganization: A Theory and Agenda for Research," *Nationa Civic Review* 72 (October 1983): 491.

40. Keith J. Mueller, "The Politics of Functional Realignment: Consolidating Wastewater Management in an Urban County," *Journal of Urban Affairs* 4 (Winter 1982): 67–79.

41. Joel C. Miller, "Municipal Annexation and Boundary Change," *Municipal Year Book 1986* (Washington, DC: International City Management Association, 1986), p. 77.

42. David L. Clark, "Improbable Los Angeles," in *Sunbelt Cities: Politics and Growth Since World War II*, ed. Richard M. Bernard and Bradley R. Rice (Austin, TX: University of Texas Press, 1983), p. 274. Details of Los Angeles' annexation policy during this period are provided by Robert M. Fogelson, *The Fragmented Metropolis: Los Angeles, 1850–1930* (Cambridge, MA: Harvard University Press, 1967), pp. 223–28.

43. Miller, "Municipal Annexation and Boundary Change," *Municipal Yearbook 1986*, p. 77.

44. Joel C. Miller, "Municipal Annexation and Boundary Change," *Municipal Year Book 1986* (Washington, DC: International City Management Association, 1989), p. 77.

45. Joel Miller, "Annexations and Boundary Changes in the 1980s and 1990–1991," *Municipal Year Book 1993* (Washington, DC: International City/County Management Association, 1993), p. 104.

46. Alan DiGaetano and John S. Klemanski, "Restructuring the Suburbs: Political Economy of Economic Development in Auburn Hills, Michigan," *Journal of Urban Affairs* 13, 2 (1991): 150–51.

47. Miller, "Municipal Annexation and Boundary Change," *Municipal Year Book 1986*, p. 84; and Joel C. Miller, "Municipal Annexations and Boundary Changes, 1980–87," *Municipal Year Book 1990* (Washington, DC: International City/County Management Association, 1990), p. 75.

48. Howard N. Rabinowitz, "Albuquerque: City at a Crossroads," in *Sunbelt Cities: Politics and Growth Since World War II*, ed. Richard M. Bernard and Bradley R. Rice (Austin, TX: University of Texas Press, 1983), pp. 258–59.

49. Richard M. Bernard, "Oklahoma City: Booming Sooner," in *Sunbelt Cities: Politics and Growth Since World War II*, ed. Richard M. Bernard and Bradley R. Rice, p. 222.

50. David Rusk, *Cities Without Suburbs* (Washington, DC: Woodrow Wilson Center Press, 1993), pp. 9–12, 17–23, 29–38, and 41–44; and Henry G. Cisneros, *Regionalism: The New Geography of Opportunity* (Washington, DC: U.S. Department of Housing and Urban Development, 1995).

51. Platon N. Rigos and Charles J. Spindler, "Municipal Incorporation as a Defense Against Annexation: The Case of Texas" (Paper presented at the annual meeting of the Urban Affairs Association, Vancouver, B.C., April 1991).

52. Walker, "Snow White and the 17 Dwarfs," p. 22. For more extensive discussion of the accountability problems posed by public authorities, see Donald Axelrod, *Shadow Government: The Hidden World of Public Authorities and How They Control Over $1 Trillion of Your Money* (New York: John Wiley & Sons, 1992); and Beverly A. Cigler, "Reforming Municipal Authorities" (Paper presented at the annual meeting of the Urban Affairs Association, Indianapolis, April 21–24, 1993).

53. Michael N. Danielson and Jameson W. Doig, *New York: The Politics of Urban Regional Development* (Berkeley, CA: University of California Press, 1982), pp. 179–204 and especially 316–22. The power, independence, and lack of larger public accountability by the Port Authority in development decisions is also described by Jameson W. Doig, "Coalition-Building by a Regional Agency: Austin Tobin and the Port of New York Authority," in *The Politics of Urban Development*, ed. Clarence N. Stone and Heywood T. Sanders (Lawrence, KS: University of Kansas Press, 1987), pp. 52–73.

54. Bruce Berg and Paul Kantor, "The Politics of Avoidance and Conflict: The New York Region" (Paper presented at the annual meeting of the American Political Science Association, New York, September 1–4, 1994). Their use of the reference "the only game in town" comes from Annmarie Walsh and James Leigland, "The Only Planning Game in Town," *Empire State Report* (May 1983): 6–12.

55. Berg and Kantor, "The Politics of Avoidance and Conflict: The New York Region."

56. Saltzstein, "Greater Los Angeles: Politics Without Governance."

57. Walker, "Snow White and the 17 Dwarfs," p. 22; Allan D. Wallis, "Inventing Regionalism: The First Two Waves," *National Civic Review* (Spring-Summer 1994): 170–71; and Margaret T. Gordon, Hubert G. Locke, Laurie McCutcheon, and William B. Stafford, "Seattle: Grassroots Politics Shaping the Environment," in *Big City Politics*, ed. H. V. Savitch and John Clayton Thomas (Newbury Park, CA: Sage Publications, 1991), pp. 228–29.

58. Vincent L. Marando and Robert D. Thomas, *The Forgotten Governments: County Commissioners as Policy Makers* (Gainesville, FL: Florida Atlantic University/University Presses of Florida, 1977).

59. Victor S. DeSantis, "County Government: A Century of Change," *Municipal Year Book 1989* (Washington, DC: International City Management Association, 1989), p. 63.

60. Mark Schneider and Kee Ok Park, "Metropolitan Counties as Service Delivery Agents: The Still Forgotten Governments," *Public Administration Review* 49 (July/August 1989): 347.

61. DeSantis, "County Government: A Century of Change," p. 63.

62. Walker, "Snow White and the 17 Dwarfs," p. 23.

63. William R. Dodge, "Strengthening Intercommunity/Regional Governance: New Strategies for Intercommunity Problem Solving and Service Delivery" (Paper presented at the annual meeting of the National Civic League, Minneapolis, September 19–21, 1991); and John J. Kirlin, "Citistates and Regional Governance," *National Civic Review* 82 (Fall 1993): 371–79.

64. David Rusk, *Cities Without Suburbs* (Washington, DC: Woodrow Wilson Center Press, distributed by Johns Hopkins University Press, 1993), p. 86.

65. Allan D. Wallis, prepared comments presented at the annual meeting of the National Civic League, Minneapolis, September 19–21, 1991.

66. Hank V. Savitch and Ron Vogel, "Regional Patterns in a Post-City Age" (Paper presented at the annual meeting of the American Political Science Association, New York, September 1994). A revised version of this paper is also scheduled to appear in their forthcoming book *Regional Patterns in a Post-City Age*.

67. Patricia K. Edwards and James R. Bohland, "Reform and Economic Development: Attitudinal Dimensions of Metropolitan Consolidation," *Journal of Urban Affairs* 13 (1991): 461–78.

68. Wallis, "Inventing Regionalism: The First Two Waves," pp. 159–75; Allan D. Wallis, "The Third Wave: Current Trends in Regional Governance," *National Civic Review* 83 (Summer-Fall 1994): 290–310; and Allan D. Wallis, "Inventing Regionalism: A Two-Phase Approach," *National Civic Review* 83 (Fall-Winter 1994): 447–68.

69. Peirce, with Johnson and Hall, *Citistates*, p. 6.

70. Ibid., pp. 33–34.

71. Ibid., p. 292.

72. Dodge, "Strengthening Intercommunity/Regional Governance."

73. Peirce, with Johnson and Hall, *Citistates*, pp. 322–23.

74. Ibid., pp. 322–23; and Allan D. Wallis, "Governance and the Civic Infrastructure of Metropolitan Regions," *National Civic Review* 82 (Spring 1993): 131–37.

75. William J. McCoy and Michael Gallis, "Regional Approaches: The Charlotte Region" (Paper presented at the annual meeting of the Urban Affairs Association, Indianapolis, April 21–24, 1993).

76. Berg and Kantor, "The Politics of Avoidance and Conflict: The New York Region."

77. Alan V. Tucker, "The Politics of Airport Expansion in Denver and St. Louis" (Paper presented at the annual meeting of the American Political Science Association, New York, September 1–4, 1994).

78. Allan D. Wallis, prepared comments presented at the annual meeting of the National Civic League, Minneapolis, September 19–21, 1991.

79. Downs, *New Visions for Metropolitan America*, p. 182.

12

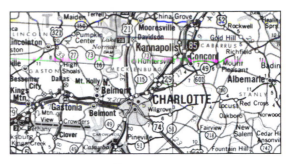

Intergovernmental Relations

Intergovernmental relations (IGR) has become one of the most important aspects of American politics in recent years. Local public officials exercise very few powers, implement very few programs, and provide very few services that are not in some way affected by decisions made in their state capital or in Washington, DC. Put another way, with the extraordinary growth in domestic spending by the federal government over the past sixty years, there are hardly any governmental functions that are not influenced by federal policy makers.

When it comes to intergovernmental programs, the dichotomy between **policy making** and policy **implementation** is often difficult to distinguish. Broad policy goals and objectives are legislated by Congress. Administrative agencies then develop rules and regulations to guide the states, counties, and cities charged with the responsibility of implementing or carrying out the programs.[1]

Just as local governments find it difficult to set policy goals and objectives without intrusions from the federal government, Washington officials find it equally burdensome to administer programs that rely on the cooperation of local officials. Most domestic programs receive some funding from the federal government, but the management of these programs is left to state, county, and local officials.

When it comes to intergovernmental programs, there is no simple hierarchical relationship within which the states and localities unquestioningly carry out the orders of the national government. State and local governments are not as powerless as a strict adherence to the policy-making/implementation hierarchy would imply. Instead, in deciding just how programs are to be implemented, states and localities possess a great deal of discretion to determine the exact shape and effects of federal government policy.

The American intergovernmental system is unique. It is comprised of complex and intricate financial, administrative, and judicial relationships that do not fit easily into a pattern. But it is essential for students of urban politics to understand the intergovernmental system since it often indicates how political power is distributed and exercised.

IGR AND FEDERALISM

Several years ago a student in an undergraduate seminar asked a guest speaker why he kept using the terms *IGR* and *federalism* interchangeably. The student found this confusing. The speaker responded that the two concepts have come to mean basically the same thing. Yet, there is a difference. As political scientists Michael Reagan and John Sanzone observe: "Federalism—old style—is dead. Yet federalism—new style—is alive and well and living in the United States. Its name is intergovernmental relations."[2]

According to Reagan and Sanzone, **old style federalism** (or, more simply, **federalism**) is a constitutional or legal concept that focuses on the source of powers and how they are divided among the different levels of government. Old style federalism emphasizes Supreme Court interpretations of the Constitution as to which powers belong at which level of government. In contrast, **new style federalism** or **intergovernmental relations (IGR)** is more pragmatic and action-oriented, and focuses more on federal-state-local power sharing and interdependence. Intergovernmental relations emphasizes the real working relationship—how the national, state, and local governments cooperate and interact on a daily basis.

Morton Grodzins of the University of Chicago was one of the first political scientists to reorient our thinking away from the formalistic, structural approach of federalism toward a view that stressed cooperation and sharing. Old style views could be termed **layer cake federalism**, as it saw each level having separate and autonomous powers. In contrast, intergovernmental relations can be termed **marble cake federalism**, as the different levels interact and share in the decision making and implementation of policies.[3]

There are several reasons for using the term *IGR* rather than *federalism*: (1) Federalism primarily implies a federal-state relationship, as cities are not mentioned in the Constitution; IGR, by comparison, encompasses federal-city and state-city relations as well; (2) Federalism implies a hierarchical set of relationships, not the more complex set of national-subnational interactions of IGR; and (3) Federalism is too legalistic a concept to describe the contemporary relationships among the different levels of government.[4]

Intergovernmental relations is also a much more inclusive term that covers actions on all levels of government, while federalism is more narrowly focused on the relationship of the central government to the states.[5]

For instance, the term *IGR* embraces how various states cooperate with one another and how various cities and suburbs cooperate with each other—important elements of intergovernmental cooperation that are missed under a formalistic study of federalism.

For purposes of this book we will use *IGR* to describe the political, administrative, and financial relationships among the many actors on the different levels of government. Whenever we discuss theoretical or judicial relationships between the federal government and another level, we will use the term *federalism*.

EVOLUTION OF THE IGR SYSTEM

Scholars differ markedly in their assessment of how the intergovernmental system has evolved in American history. Political scientist Deil Wright provides one guide that points to seven different periods in the history of intergovernmental relations in the United States[6]:

Conflict:	until 1930
Cooperative:	1930s–1950s
Concentrated:	1940s–1960s
Creative:	1950s–1960s
Competitive:	1960s–1970s
Calculative:	1970s–1980s
Contractive:	1980s–1990s

The *conflict* phase (up to 1930) was characterized by efforts to define appropriate spheres of action and jurisdiction among the different levels of government. For instance, during this period it was decided that the central government had the power to establish a national bank (*McCulloch v. Maryland*, 1819) but not to regulate child labor, which was a power reserved for states under the Tenth Amendment (*Hammer v. Dagenhart*, 1918). In *McCulloch*, Chief John Marshall viewed the relationship between the national government and the states as essentially one of conflict; the power of one level of government could expand only by thwarting the power and goals of the other. The Court served primarily as the referee in this often bitter and conflictive dispute over governmental powers. During this phase of intergovernmental relations, the states remained the dominant actors, despite the growth of central power in certain narrow areas.

The *cooperative* phase (1930–1950) was highlighted by a common concern for stabilizing and improving the economic life of the nation in the period of the Great Depression and World War II. The twin evils of economic depression and international conflict increased the need for cooperation among the different levels of government. The New Deal and its grants for health services, old age assistance, and dependent children—policy areas previously seen as reserved for the states—indicated a new shared approach to problem solving that stood in marked contrast to the conflict phase, when it was perceived that the different levels of government had distinctly different sets of problems to solve.

The 1940s–1960s are labeled the *concentrated* period because federal programs became increasingly specific and highly focused. New administrative rules and regulations were developed to ensure the attainment of program goals funded by narrow-purpose **categorical grants**. During this period, the federal government helped the states and localities to expand services and build new capital plant and infrastructure (in such areas as airports, hospitals, highways, waste treatment, and urban renewal).

As government expanded to meet the nation's postwar needs, there was a corresponding increase in the number of professionals required to manage the new programs. This new professional class was viewed by some observers as the beginning of a bureaucratic era labeled the **professional state**.[7]

The *creative* phase of IGR (1950s–1960s) derives its name from Lyndon B. Johnson's use of the term **creative federalism**; it denotes the increasingly varied and innovative vehicles of regulation and assistance adopted by a federal government decidedly intent on domestic problem solving. Johnson "creatively" expanded the boundaries of federalism to include new partnerships between the national government and the localities and between the national government and private industry. The expanded concept of partnership not only included federal, state, and local governments but also involved school districts, churches, businesses, and nonprofit organizations. This period was highlighted by increased attention to urban and metropolitan problems, with a specific focus on poor and disadvantaged residents. The new creative problem-solving arrangements were all consistent with the Johnson administration's goal of trying to end poverty.

The concept of creative federalism was implemented through an increase in the number and dollar amount of categorical grants, with their narrowly defined purposes and their accompanying rules and regulations. This changed the face of intergovernmental relations for the next generation by making the system much more complex and by establishing a whole new set of administrative and financial relationships which, prior to 1964, had not existed.[8]

By the fifth phase in Wright's typology, the *competitive* period (1960s–1970s), the number of grant-in-aid programs had grown to over 500. The different levels of government and program professionals in the different service areas all saw problems from different perspectives. Conflict resulted when each sought to pursue program goals that were slightly different (and in some cases greatly different) from those pursued by others.[9]

Program coordination became difficult, if not impossible. Program specialists at all levels often resisted attempts at control by such elected policy generalists as governors, mayors, and state and local legislators.

Tension and conflict escalated. Efforts to reform and stabilize the system took the form of reorganization, regionalization, and revenue sharing.

During the sixth phase in Wright's typology, the *calculative* period (1970s–1980s), governments began to calculate the costs as well as the benefits of their participation in specific federal aid programs. Wright suggests that this period began in 1975, when New York City was on the brink of bankruptcy. One major characteristic associated with this period was cutback management. Many state, county, and local governments were calculative in perfecting managerial techniques to assist them in making decisions to reduce or eliminate programs. These actions were taken in response to reductions in federal program funding, a weakened economy, and reduced revenues from taxes.[10]

During this period, state and local governments also began to calculate their self-interest in fighting for federal aid formulas that would provide them the greatest amount of federal assistance. This competition was popularly labeled **politics by printout**, as competing constituencies and interest groups would present computer printouts to their representatives in Congress, showing how their districts would fare under alternative aid formulas.[11]

A further characteristic of this period, according to Wright, was the tendency of states and localities to calculate the risk of noncompliance. Many state and local governments began asking themselves if they could afford to bear the costs associated with the federal rules and regulations that had multiplied over the years. Also, no local government was capable of meeting all the applicable grant rules and regulations. Just which rules would they meet, and which would they dodge? To some observers the intergovernmental system had become overloaded with an excess of program requirements that acted to impede the effective operation of programs.

In the final phase of Wright's history, the *contractive* period (1980s–1990s), the intergovernmental aid system is no longer expanding but rather is beginning to contract. First, steps to reform an overloaded federal system were initiated by President Reagan. Federal grant monies under Reagan in 1982 showed the first dollar decline since the Advisory Commission on Intergovernmental Relations began analyzing the grant-in-aid system. Presidents since Reagan have voiced their intention to continue to reform or shrink a bloated intergovernmental system.

The contractive process has not been confined to the national government alone. In numerous policy areas, cutbacks in federal aid led the states, too, to reduce the assistance they were able to provide local governments. In the late 1970s and 1980s, the growth of state aid to cities slackened (see Table 12.1). State aid diminished as a percentage of local government revenue.

Finally, Supreme Court decisions, too, have been involved in a contracting of local authority. In *Garcia v. San Antonio Metropolitan Transit Authority* (1985), the Supreme Court reversed an earlier ruling and sharply

TABLE 12.1
State Intergovernmental Expenditures to Local Governments, Selected Years 1954–1992
(Millions)

Fiscal Year	Total	Annual Percentage Change
1954	$5,679	
1964	12,968	8.6%[1]
1965	14,173	9.3
1966	16,928	19.4
1967	19,056	12.6
1968	21,949	15.2
1969	24,779	12.9
1970	28,893	16.6
1971	32,640	13.0
1972	36,759	12.6
1973	40,822	11.1
1974	45,940	12.5
1975	51,978	13.1
1976	57,858	11.3
1977	62,470	8.0
1978	67,287	7.7
1979	75,975	12.9
1980	84,505	11.2
1981	93,180	10.3
1982	98,743	6.0
1983	101,309	2.6
1984	108,373	7.0
1985	121,571	12.2
1986	131,966	8.6
1987	141,426	7.2
1988	151,662	7.2
1989	165,506	9.1
1990	175,096	5.8
1991	186,469	6.5
1992	201,313	8.0

[1] Average annual change from 1954 to 1964.
Source: Advisory Commission on Intergovernmental Relations, *Significant Features of Fiscal Federalism 1994* (Washington, DC: ACIR, 1986), p. 35, Table 45 (extracted).

limited just what powers local governments inherently possess—free from national government regulation—under federalism.

Cutbacks in aid and authority also led subnational governments to look at *contracting* in a different sense of the word. Increasingly, acting from a concern for efficiency, state and local governments have entered into contracts with private companies for the provision of services.

President Clinton's policy of **reinventing government** essentially represents an extension of the contractive period. His announced intention is to allow states and localities to do more with less. Working with limited resources, the federal government will relax program rules and regulations to permit states greater leeway to undertake innovative policy action.

Initially, Clinton sought to expand the national government's authority in certain domestic program fields, most notably in health care. But the extensive Republican victories in the 1994 mid-term congressional elections were seen as a sharp public rebuke to any of his continuing big-government orientations. Immediately after the Democrats' disastrous 1994 electoral showing, Clinton began to pursue his reinventing government strategy in earnest. He proposed to cut back the national government's role in such program areas as transportation. For a while, the President and his advisers even strongly contemplated eliminating the Department of Housing and Urban Development—a department that had suffered much criticism from state and local officials as a result of the confining nature of its program rules and regulations. But in response to the prodding of HUD Secretary Henry Cisneros, Clinton finally accepted a plan to dramatically shrink HUD—a plan that would eliminate 40 percent of its staff over five years and give subnational governments greater program discretion by consolidating all HUD grants into three broad performance grants. Cutbacks in governmental assistance programs imposed by the new post-1994 Republican Congress, too, represent a continuation of the contractive period.

CONSTITUTIONAL QUESTIONS

The evolution of the intergovernmental system shows that the meaning of federalism has changed over time. The power of the national government has grown. While critics sometimes argue that the growth of national government power is unconstitutional, a review of the Constitution and relevant court cases will make clear the basis for that growth.

The Constitution provided for certain powers to be delegated to the federal government. Most of these powers are found in Article 1, Section 8. Some of the **delegated powers** or **enumerated powers** listed for the national government include taxing, regulating interstate commerce, declaring war, entering into treaties, establishing post offices, and coining money.

In Article 1, Section 9, the Constitution lists certain powers that cannot be exercised by the national government. These include suspending the writ of habeas corpus, passing bills of attainder or ex post facto laws, and drawing money from the treasury unless it has been lawfully appropriated. Article 1, Section 10 lists several powers forbidden to the states. States are not allowed to enter into treaties, coin money, grant titles of nobility, impose duties, declare war, or pass bills of attainder or ex post facto laws.

The **Tenth Amendment** to the Constitution seeks to point out where the powers not delegated should reside. The Tenth Amendment reads:

> The powers not delegated to the United States by the Constitution, nor prohibited by it to the States, are reserved to the States respectively, or to the people.

In post–Revolutionary War America, power resided with the thirteen former colonies. In order to form a union of the separate states, it was agreed each would have to give up some of its powers to a national

government; these were the delegated powers. The powers not delegated were to remain with the individual states.

The Tenth Amendment would seem to give most powers to the states.
However, the Tenth Amendment and the delegated powers clause are
counterbalanced by Article VI, which is sometimes called the **supremacy
clause**. In this article the framers specified that the laws passed by Congress shall be the supreme law of the land and that judges throughout the
country shall be bound by these laws.

Article VI, which favors national power, and the Tenth Amendment,
which favors the states, appear to be in conflict. The Supreme Court,
however, has resolved this conflict in a way that has paved the way for the
increased scope of national government action—in essence, expanding
the power of the national government at the expense of the states. The
Court has done this by broadly interpreting the **elastic clause**, also called
the **necessary and proper clause**, that appears at the end of the enumerated powers listed in Article 1, Section 8. This clause gives the federal
government the right "to make all laws which shall be necessary and
proper for carrying into execution the foregoing powers..." The result is
a **doctrine of implied powers**, as the clause implies that the national
government has the authority to undertake a whole host of actions not explicitly listed or set out in the Constitution.

One of the earliest tests of this conflict came in the famous Supreme
Court case, already referred to, *McCulloch v. Maryland* (1819). In this
case the court upheld the right of the national government to establish a
bank, even though such a power was not explicitly stated anywhere in the
Constitution. This decision by Chief Justice Marshall had a profound effect on the intergovernmental system. Marshall ruled that the national
government possessed all those powers that could reasonably be implied
from the delegated powers:

> Let the end be legitimate, let it be within the scope of the Constitution,
> and all means which are appropriate, which are plainly adapted to that
> end, which are not prohibited, but consist with the letter and spirit of the
> constitution, are constitutional.[12]

By broadly interpreting the "necessary and proper" clause of Article I,
the Supreme Court established that actions of the national government
that appeared legitimate and were not strictly forbidden were within the
purview of Congress. The *McCulloch* case laid the foundation for the expansion of national government power.

Over the years the federal courts have been called upon on numerous
occasions to decide issues concerning the division of powers among the
different levels of government. While this division has shifted over time,
most constitutional theorists believe that the balance has only occasionally
tilted dramatically in favor of the federal government, and usually only
during times of crisis.[13]

This viewpoint, however, is disputed by David Walker, who sees the federal judiciary as greatly to blame for the rise of overloaded federalism. According to Walker, it is difficult to find a case where the federal courts have denied the federal government the power to spend for the general welfare; nor have the courts placed effective curbs on the coercive and quasi-regulatory conditions that usually accompany federal grants.[14] According to Walker, the Supreme Court was a one-sided "umpire" which for a long time distrusted subnational governments for being undemocratic and "controlled by racists, reactionaries, and/or rural folk."[15]

The Tenth Amendment has not posed any significant restraint on the power of the federal government since the late New Deal period. As Michael Reagan and John Sanzone observe, "[T]he Court came in 1941 to see the Tenth Amendment as simply stating a truism, 'that all is retained which has not yet been surrendered.'"[16]

Little wonder then that states were overjoyed when the Supreme Court, in a 5–4 decision in 1976, ruled that neither states nor their localities could be compelled by Congress to observe the federal minimum wage and maximum hour laws for their own employees (*National League of Cities v. Usery*). The Court stated that this law violated the sovereignty of each state government, and that Congress did not have the right to impair that sovereignty.[17]

The rejoicing at the state and local level was to be short-lived, however. In 1985 the Supreme Court reversed itself and in **Garcia v. San Antonio Metropolitan Transit Authority**[18] ruled that the principles applied in the *NLC v. Usery* case were both unsound and unworkable since the courts were not the proper entities to determine jurisdictional disputes of this nature between states and the federal government. Once again, the Court appeared to be saying that it would not use the Tenth Amendment to protect states and cities against federal government power.

Three years later the Supreme Court reaffirmed its Garcia decision in the case **South Carolina v. Baker**.[19] The South Carolina case dealt with a seemingly narrow question of federal and subnational authority in taxation: Does the federal government have the power to mandate exactly what form state and local bonds must take in order to earn federal tax-exempt status? The larger question, though, was whether the national government rules applied to the states and localities even when it came to financing, a matter crucial to subnational autonomy. According to the Supreme Court, the federal government clearly does possess such a right. According to the Court, there is no constitutional protection against federal taxation of the interest earned on state and local bonds. Consistent with the *Garcia* ruling, the court again ruled that the Constitution did not pose a limit to the actions of the national government. Should states and localities desire protection against actions by the central government, they must seek such protection through Congress and the political process, and not through court rulings.

South Carolina v. Baker continues the history of the judicial erosion of the Tenth Amendment. Justice Sandra Day O'Connor, a believer in a more literal interpretation of federalism, declared in her dissenting opinion that the Court's ruling was a threat to state and local government autonomy. According to O'Connor, the ruling also struck at the heart of the federal system. Similarly, political scientist Margaret Wrightson has observed that the decision is "wholly consistent with a philosophy of a supremely powerful national government and semi-sovereign states."[20] As Wrightson concisely summarizes, "American federalism has been construed by the Court as a political and administrative relationship rather than a constitutional one."[21] Former Advisory Commission on Intergovernmental Relations Chair Robert Hawkins, Jr., too, feels that the *South Carolina* decision may mark the end of federalism as we have traditionally known it. Federalism has been redefined to mean that whatever Congress decides is the way states and localities must operate in the intergovernmental system.[22]

What can be said to summarize this complex subject—the changing federal system? Overall, the American federal system can be seen to have evolved from a system of *dual federalism* to *cooperative federalism*.

Dual federalism implies a system of separate authorities under which the federal government and the state pursue separate goals and programs without sharing ideas, resources, or technical assistance.[23] Dual federalism is based on a reading of the Constitution that gives strong weight to the Tenth Amendment; it limits the federal government to its enumerated powers and reserves all else for the states. Cities are seen to fall under the domain of the states.

Yet, as we have already seen, the power of the Tenth Amendment has been counterbalanced by the elastic clause and to a great extent neutered by interpretations of the Supreme Court. While dual federalism is no longer representative of our intergovernmental system, some scholars believe the term did reflect earlier periods in American intergovernmental history. Walker, for instance, writes, "The period from 1789 to 1869, for the most part, reflected an adherence to these dual federal themes—constitutionally, politically and operationally."[24]

Cooperative federalism, in contrast, implies a strong sharing of responsibilities and goals by two or more levels of government. This can be federal-state, state-local, or federal-local. It is difficult to pinpoint precisely the beginnings of cooperative federalism since there is some evidence of common sharing of ideas, objectives, and resources among the levels of government throughout our history. *McCulloch* provided some of the constitutional framework for the expanded national government power implicit in cooperative federalism. However, the national government did not really begin to expand its authority until much later. Federal expansion in the form of trust-busting and utilities regulation came at the turn of the century. Still, it was not until the administration of Franklin D.

Roosevelt and the advent of the New Deal that the national government became involved in a broader range of affairs, and cooperative federalism became an accepted basis for the practice of IGR in the United States.[25]

CITIES AND STATES

Cities have always been active centers of commerce, finance, and culture. Hence, one of the most remarkable features of the U.S. Constitution is that cities are not mentioned at all.

Throughout the latter part of the eighteenth century and the first half of the nineteenth century, local governments staunchly resisted state pressures to centralize power. They continued to fight for power and authority that would allow them greater freedom to manage their own affairs. But, as we noted in Chapter 4, the issue finally was resolved by Judge John F. Dillon in his 1868 decision in *City of Clinton v. Cedar Rapids and Missouri River Railroad*. Judge Dillon declared that cities were to be regarded as the mere "creatures" of the states.[26] In 1903 and again in 1923, the U.S. Supreme Court upheld **Dillon's Rule** which established the subordinate constitutional position of cities to states.[27]

However, as we have also observed in Chapter 4, the relationship between cities and states is not nearly as rigid as a strict interpretation of these court rulings seemingly implies. Over the years states have legislated to grant their cities **home rule**, enabling them to have a great degree of autonomy over local affairs. This grant of power can be either broad or narrow. Under the broadest grant of power, the state even permits a city to draft its own charter.

Even though the states reign supreme within their borders, there has still developed a certain amount of local government autonomy. States are constrained by constitutional concerns for due process. State legislatures cannot be totally unpredictable and arbitrary in their dealings with cities. States are also concerned by more pragmatic considerations: They need local governments to solve problems effectively; otherwise, the problems are tossed back on the doorstep of the legislature. As political scientists Ann O'M. Bowman and Richard Kearney point out:

> One might think that against the backdrop of Dillon's Rule, states would ride roughshod over their cities and counties. Such an inference would be somewhat wide of the mark. Although states may have been a bit cavalier in their treatment of substate governments in the past, there is a growing realization that such behavior is self-defeating. Cities and counties may fail to produce effective political leaders or to develop their own solutions to local problems if they are overregulated. In other words, keeping local governments weak might seem a plausible tactic for states anxious to hoard power, but it simply spawns a continuing cycle of impotence. Eventually, cities and counties become burdens to the very government that determines their fate.[28]

The degree of autonomy permitted cities varies from state to state. As the Advisory Commission of Intergovernmental Relations concluded after having surveyed local governing authority, local autonomy is far from complete: "[I]n most states general-purpose governments in fact do fall short of possessing broad structural, functional, and financing powers—particularly the last." [29]

CITIES AND THE FEDERAL GOVERNMENT

Throughout most of the history of the United States, intergovernmental relations meant a relationship between the federal government and the states. But in the past sixty or so years the system has seen the rise of a third partner—the city.

Several factors help to explain the increased importance of cities in domestic policy. Most notably, as cities grew in population, their voting strength increased. By 1920 a majority of the country's population lived in cities, and national political officers began to pay greater attention to urban problems. Cities and their residents comprised an important constituency in the Democratic party.

The Great Depression of the 1930s also led to the emergence of the city as a key actor in the intergovernmental system. Many of the New Deal recovery programs were directed at the urban centers of the nation. Local agencies and officials were charged with the responsibility for implementing the new federally funded programs. The 1937 low-rent public housing program was the first federal program to give grants directly to the cities. By the end of World War II, the cities had clearly demonstrated that they could be entrusted with responsibility for federal programs.

As post–World War II urban America continued to grow, the federal government became more conscious of urban problems. After the war, new federal programs in the areas of highways (1956), slum clearance and urban renewal (1949), urban planning (1954), hospital construction (1946), waste treatment facilities (1956), and water pollution control (1956) all helped to forge strong federal-city links and to increase the prominence of the cities in the intergovernmental system.

The result was a new system of **direct federalism** based upon federal-city program relationships that bypassed the states. In effect, the national government treated cities and counties as if they enjoyed equal status with states. Lyndon Johnson's Great Society expanded direct federal-city relationships. By the late 1970s, between 25 and 30 percent of all federal aid bypassed state capitals. [30]

ROLE OF THE STATES IN URBAN AFFAIRS: HOW PROGRESSIVE?

The direct federal-city relationship grew at a time when states were generally unwilling and unable to provide sufficient assistance to cities in need. State governments, however, have changed greatly since the 1960s. Although there is still considerable debate concerning just how progressive the states are when it comes to dealing with the problems of cities, the states have, without a doubt, become increasingly important actors in urban affairs.

THE CHANGING NATURE OF STATE GOVERNMENT

In the mid-1960s, state governments lacked the revenue base, administrative structures, and political will to play an active role in aiding cities. Thirty-one states still operated under antiquated constitutions that had been drafted in the nineteenth century. Their governments were more suited to an agrarian, not an urban, society. The anti-urban bias of state governments was also the result of the **malapportionment** of state legislatures, where small towns and rural areas enjoyed greater representation than merited by their populations. As early as the 1920 census, population figures showed that the United States had an urban majority. But this fact was not reflected in an increase of urban power in state capitals; rural-dominated state legislatures refused to draw up new apportionment plans to give an increased number of seats to urban areas.

Malapportionment was brought to an end by a series of U.S. Supreme Court cases beginning with **Baker v. Carr** (1962).[31] *Baker v. Carr* dealt with the Tennessee House of Representatives, which had not been reapportioned since 1901 despite the dramatic shift in population in the state. Areas with the fastest growing population were grossly underrepresented. The Supreme Court ruled that gross malapportionment diluted a citizen's voting rights, depriving persons in underrepresented areas of the "equal protection of the law" guaranteed by the Fourteenth Amendment of the United States Constitution.

Baker v. Carr began a virtual **reapportionment revolution** where urban groups in state after state challenged their underrepresentation in state capitals. In **Reynolds v. Sims** (1964), the Court moved beyond its original *Baker v. Carr* ruling and endorsed the principle of **one person–one vote**.[32] Prodded by the federal courts, the states had little choice but to reapportion legislative seats strictly in accordance to population.

As a result, the rural stranglehold over state legislatures was brought to an end. Reapportionment helped to produce a new urban orientation in state legislatures. The new legislators from urban areas also sought to modernize state government, enhancing its capacity to solve contemporary problems.[33]

States adopted new constitutions or greatly revised and modernized their old ones. These new constitutions strengthened the powers of the governor, improved legislative capability, and extended home rule and new taxing authority to local governments.

The new administrative structure of state government provided for strong executive leadership. Many states increased the term served by governors from two years to four years. Half the states also reduced the number of independently elected state officials, thereby giving the governor more control over the executive branch through the exercise of his or her appointive powers. In addition, governors' salaries were raised, and governors were given enhanced budgetary authority and greater powers to reorganize the executive branch.

Dramatic changes were also made to strengthen state legislatures. In the early 1960s only twenty state legislatures met each year. By the mid-1990s forty-three of the state legislatures met annually; and in those states where legislatures met biannually, several were called into special session by their governors on a regular basis.

The state legislatures also took steps to professionalize their operations. In 1960 few states had a year-round professional staff for their key committees. By the 1990s most states provided their legislatures with professional staff. The legislatures also acted to increase their accountability, opening committee meetings to the public, recording roll call votes, strengthening requirements for the registration and disclosure of lobbying activities, and legislating against conflicts of interest.[34]

The reconstituted state governments began to take a closer look at the problems of cities and metropolitan areas. More than half the states opened a state department or office of community affairs. The states also responded to the growth of the federal grant-in-aid system. The National Governors' Association (NGA) in 1967 moved its headquarters to Washington, DC, giving the governors greater visibility in the nation's Capitol and reinforcing the impression that the states were ready to take a more active role in issues directly affecting them. The new offices of the NGA established better communication links with influential members of Congress and government agencies and monitored key legislative and administrative actions on a daily basis. Based in Washington, the association was also in a better position to notify state officials of likely federal action and mobilize state officials, when necessary, to put pressure on Washington decision makers.

The changed orientation of states towards cities is easily seen in a quick review of state aid to cities. In 1954, state aid to cities stood at slightly less than 42 percent of local own-source revenue. Ten years later, the figure, 43 percent, was essentially unchanged. By 1980, however, as the states showed a new commitment to their cities, this figure climbed to nearly 64 percent. The states had assumed new program responsibilities and become more active partners in the intergovernmental system. Even after Reagan's first-term budget cuts took their toll on state spending, state aid to cities still amounted to 55 percent of local own-source revenue.[35]

Still, the Reagan-era cutbacks in federal aid forced the states to reassess what they could afford to do. As Table 12.1 reveals, in the 1980s state governments began to cut back on what had been, until then, their rapidly escalating commitment to cities. The pace of increases in state aid slackened. Still, overall, state aid to local governments continued despite the fiscal pressures of the Reagan era. An analysis undertaken by the National Association of State Budget Officers (NASBO) reveals that the yearly increases in state aid to localities outpaced the growth in overall state spending. As NASBO executive director Gerald Miller observed, "It represents the states' increased commitment to local government." [36]

Clearly, the nature of state governments and their involvement in the intergovernmental system has changed dramatically over time. As the Advisory Commission on Intergovernmental Relations (ACIR) summarized:

> Just 20 years ago states largely deserved many of the criticisms directed their way including descriptions such as "antiquated" and "weak sisters." Those who looked at the state in the 1930s or even in the early 1960s and decided that they lacked the capability to perform their roles in the federal system because they operated under outdated constitutions, fragmented executive structures, hamstrung governors, poorly equipped and unrepresentative legislatures, and numerous other handicaps should take another look at the states today. The transformation of the states, occurring in a relatively short period of time, has no parallel in American history.[37]

POLITICAL CHANGE IN THE SOUTH

Nowhere has the modernization of state government been as apparent as in the South. In the past, state governments in the South had a poor reputation. Southern governments were underdeveloped, ill-equipped, and ill-disposed to undertake programs to combat urban and social ills. Numerous southern governors, including Arkansas' Orville Faubus and Alabama's George Wallace, gained national notoriety by blocking school integration and other progressive reforms. Wallace, in a futile attempt to stop integration, stood in the schoolhouse door and proclaimed "segregation forever." States were tarnished by an "Alabama syndrome,"[38] where federal officials were unwilling to entrust state governments with program authority. States, as a result, were denied a role in the War on Poverty:

> Any suggestion within the poverty task force that the states be given a role in the administration of the act was met with the question, "Do you want to give that kind of power to George Wallace?" And so, in the bill submitted by President Johnson to Congress, not only George Wallace but Nelson Rockefeller and George Romney and Edmund Brown and all the other governors were excluded from any assigned role.[39]

But southern politics was transformed by the civil rights movement, the Civil Rights Act of 1964, and the Voting Rights Act of 1965, all which led to the enfranchisement of black citizens. The growth of the black vote in the South meant that African-Americans could no longer be ignored in elections. Immediately, the black vote led to a lessening of racist rhetoric in political campaigns.[40] Candidates for office simply could not afford to alienate such a large block of voters. Even the symbol of segregationist sentiment, George Wallace, learned the importance of appealing to black voters. He won Alabama's governorship in 1982 only by securing approximately 90 percent of the black vote in the general election. Wallace openly courted black voters; he promised them more than did his conservative Republican opponent.[41]

Black voting rights is not the only factor that has changed the nature of southern politics. New population patterns also added to the region's moderation and new metropolitan orientation. The shift in population from countryside to city and, in some areas, the new population pressures brought by the shift to the Sunbelt have led southern state governments to show a new concern for urban problems. In Florida, for instance, the state government has been active in initiating new land use controls in an effort to minimize environmental degradation resulting from that state's population boom.

The result of all these trends has been the election of a new breed of more moderate and progressive southern politician, including, to name only a few, Bill Clinton in Arkansas, Jimmy Carter in Georgia, Lamar Alexander in Tennessee, Chuck Robb in Virginia, and Lawton Chiles in Florida. These officials saw the urgency of responding to urban problems and the needs of minority populations. Carter as governor even took the highly symbolic step of hanging a picture of Martin Luther King, Jr., in the capitol. The changing face of state politics was encapsulated in the 1989 election of L. Douglas Wilder as governor of Virginia. The one-time heart of the old Confederacy had elected the first black governor since Reconstruction.

THE STATES: A DISSENTING VIEW

Not everyone shares the perspective that the states have become modern, progressive governments interested in solving contemporary urban and social problems. Political scientist Gerald Houseman, for instance, sees the states as remote, unresponsive, corrupt, and too prone to act on behalf of elite interests. According to Houseman, the states "must get better" if they are to meet the needs of the "left-out groups" of American society.[42]

In the long run, reapportionment has not advanced the political power of central cities as much as it has enhanced the power of suburbs. As suburban areas have seen the greatest growth in population, they have gained the greatest power in state capitals. In recent years, declining central cities have lost population and representation. As a result, cities do not always fare well in state capitals.

In a number of states, a coalition of suburban and rural (or *outstate*) legislators remain wary of spending state resources on a few major cities. Instead of targeting money on distressed cities, these legislatures spread program funds around the state. Grants and other forms of assistance are distributed in a manner that does not adequately reflect local need. In a number of policy areas, legislators from suburban districts are no more willing to commit state resources to meet the problems of central cities than were the rural legislators who dominated state politics during the malapportionment era. In order to be competitive economically, states like Michigan have built suburban research and industrial parks—growth poles that have also had the effect of attracting development away from the central city.

Critics of the states point out that city resources are still seriously constrained by state-imposed restrictions on local taxing and borrowing. Few suburban state legislators are willing to authorize central cities to enact new commuter taxes or local tax-sharing schemes that would allow cities to tap the wealth of their suburban-based work forces. In an age of antitax sentiment, state legislators are reluctant to vote for new taxes for programs to help cities.

Critics of the states also point out that while the South has changed, it still remains the most conservative region in the nation. Southern states as a whole are generally reluctant to spend for public assistance and social services. Texas, for instance, refused to extend relief to the large number of job seekers from the North who came to the state during its economic boom of the 1970s. The Lone Star State also refused to enact an income tax or find other state revenue sources to fund school equalization. The more recent economic downturn in Texas has only added to the squeeze on state resources, further adding to the state's reluctance to initiate new educational and social welfare spending.

Federalism theorists Michael Reagan and John Sanzone have recognized the vast improvements that have been made in state structures over the years. Still, they are reluctant to give all states a greatly expanded sphere of power in the federal system. Not all states have exhibited sufficient responsibility in their past actions to be entrusted with extensive new program authority in implementing intergovernmental programs. Instead of simply returning power to the states, Reagan and Sanzone have proposed a system of **permissive federalism** under which "the state's share [of power] rests upon the permission and permissiveness of the national government."[43] Under permissive federalism, only those states that have shown a demonstrated record of action will be allowed substantially greater program flexibility and discretion.

ROLE OF THE STATES IN URBAN AFFAIRS: AN OVERALL ASSESSMENT

Over the years the states have made great strides in urban problem solving. Reapportionment brought an end to the era of rural dominance, and civil rights and voting rights changed the orientation of southern governments. Nationwide, the states reformed their tax structures to increase their own revenue-raising capacities. The nonstop economic boom of the mid-1980s further provided the states with revenue to respond to cities' requests. The states undertook numerous new and innovative actions in such policy areas as providing assistance to the homeless and reforming public education. New Jersey even took the unprecedented step of assuming control of the much-troubled Jersey City school system.

Still, certain doubts as to the urban orientation of the states remain. Variation among the states remains considerable. The impact of such variation is evident in the areas of homelessness and welfare policy. Despite increased state activity in support of the homeless, there are still serious service gaps in providing both shelter and meals to those in need. The less active states did not even make full use of the variety of federal programs available to support action in this policy area. In states dominated by rural legislators, little or nothing was done as homelessness was defined only as a big-city problem.[44] Similarly, in the policy area of welfare, some states have initiated innovative programs to provide welfare recipients with job training and placement opportunities. Other states, however, have used their discretion in a more punitive fashion in attempts to promote individual responsibility and cut welfare rolls.

A slowdown of the economy, further reductions in federal assistance to the states, and a taxpayers' revolt among state electorates have all acted to diminish the states' willingness to undertake costly urban actions. Further, a large proportion of state budgets is being spent on two big-ticket items, Medicaid and prisons. By the late 1980s the state share of Medicaid alone accounted for 11 percent of state spending. The danger is that state energies in the urban area may be diverted by the necessity of spending on prisons and health. Very little may be left over for other urban-oriented programs.[45]

FISCAL FEDERALISM: THE GRANT-IN-AID SYSTEM

Much of this federal assistance to subnational governments has taken the form of the cash *grant-in-aid*, which replaced the land grants initiated in the nineteenth century. The cash grant-in-aid system began to expand during the New Deal under President Franklin D. Roosevelt, and it would continue to expand over time. In 1932 only about $10 million in federal grants was given to cities. By 1960 federal aid to state and local governments reached $7 billion. Beginning in the 1960s, federal aid transfers expanded much further.

A **grant-in-aid** can be defined as money transferred by the federal government to state or local governments to be used for specific purposes, but subject to rules and guidelines established by law and by administrative regulations. The urban grant-in-aid allows cities to combat important problems with the technical assistance and financial support of the federal government.

Types of Grants[46]

Generally speaking, grants are either *formula grants* or *project grants*. A **formula grant** is distributed to all states and/or eligible local governments in accord with a formula written into law. The distribution of assistance can be based upon any number of factors, including population, per capita income, tax effort, or the number of senior citizens or school-age children in a jurisdiction. Recipient governments are entitled to the grants by virtue of the law; unlike other grants, they do not have to submit elaborate proposals and compete for available funds.

Project grants are designed to combat specific problems deemed important by Congress, but such grants are not distributed to all political jurisdictions. The authorizing legislation states the purposes of the grant and who can participate in the program, but eligible recipients must take the initiative in submitting a proposal to apply for the grant. In effect, potential recipients compete for the money. Federal administrators assess the proposals and make grant awards based upon legislative guidelines and the criteria publicized in the request for proposal notice.

Project grants are either *categorical grants* or *block grants* (see Table 12.2). **Categorical grants** are designed for very narrow and specific objectives that Congress has determined to be in the national interest. Categorical grants have been enacted for a variety of purposes, including, to name only a few, vocational education, child nutrition, reading programs in poverty-impacted school districts, public libraries, and urban parks development. A recipient government has only limited discretion in the use of categorical grant funds. A local government that receives, say, a categorical grant to upgrade its police communications equipment cannot use that grant for any other police or nonpolice purposes.

The intergovernmental grant system is quite complex. There is no one form of categorical grant; rather there are variations. Some categorical grants are formula-based; others follow the model of an *open reimbursement grant* under which the federal government agrees to compensate state and local governments for whatever program costs are incurred. This approach eliminates the need for both competition among jurisdictions and a congressionally determined formula.

Most federal aid programs take the form of categorical grants. But a relatively new form of federal aid, the *block grant*, was introduced in the late 1960s and 1970s and gained increasing popularity in the decades that followed (see Table 12.3). Under a **block grant**, the recipient community is given increased discretion as to how to use the assistance, which must still remain within the specified functional or service area. For instance, under the Comprehensive Employment Training Act (CETA), a very well-known block grant, local governments were given quite a bit of flexibility in designing local job-training efforts; they could not however, divert the money to housing, streets, or other areas of need.

TABLE 12.2
Selected Characteristics of Major Types of Federal Grants

Type of Grant	Recipient Discretion	Program Scope	Funding Criteria
Categorical			
a. Project	Lowest	Narrow-program	Federal administrative review
b. Formula	Low	Narrow-program	Legislative formula
Block	Medium	Broad-functional area	Legislative formula
General revenue sharing	High	Broadest-government operations	Legislative formula

Source: George E. Hale and Marian Lief Palley, *The Politics of Federal Grants* (Washington, DC: Congressional Quarterly Press, 1981), p. 12. Reprinted with the permission of Congressional Quarterly, Inc.

Beginning in 1966 with the Partnership for Health Act and continuing through the 1970s, Congress began to enact block grants in community development, manpower training, criminal justice, and social services. These grants were much broader in scope than categorical grants and often resulted from the consolidation of several existing categorical grants. Because far fewer strings are attached to such grants, local officials have much greater discretion in administering them. As a result of the flexibility that they allow, block grants are popular with the nation's governors and mayors. More recently, the nation's governors have urged the Clinton administration to make greater use of block grants, observing that they could get by with a small reduction in federal government assistance if they were also given new leeway to use program funds in ways that they see fit.

In 1972, the federal government initiated an even broader intergovernmental transfer of funds called **revenue sharing**. Revenue sharing funds were distributed by formula, with virtually no restrictions on how the money could be spent. But this program of no-strings money given to state and local governments lasted only for a decade, as the Carter administration reduced it, and the Reagan administration eliminated it entirely, in the face of new budgetary pressures.

EXPANSION OF THE GRANT-IN-AID SYSTEM

During the 1960s and 1970s, the grant-in-aid system expanded rapidly. Under the Johnson, Nixon, Ford, and Carter presidencies, the number of categorical and block grants increased and so did the dollars appropriated for them. In 1960 federal grant-in-aid outlays were about $7 billion, representing 7.6 percent of the total federal budget outlays and 14.5 percent of state and local budgets (see Table 12.4). By 1980, the last year of the Carter presidency, grants totaled $91 billion, amounting to nearly 16 percent of federal spending and 26 percent of state and local outlays.

TABLE 12.3
Number of Categorical and Block Grant Programs, Selected Fiscal Years, 1975–1993

	1975	1978	1981	1984	1987	1989	1991	1993
Block	5	5	5	12	13	14	14	15
Categorical	422	492	534	392	422	478	543	578
Total	427	497	539	404	435	492	557	593

Source: ACIR tabulation based on *Catalog of Federal Domestic Assistance, United States Code,* and federal agency contacts.

With the arrival of the Reagan administration, federal grants-in-aid fell to $88.2 billion in 1982, the first recorded decline since the ACIR began keeping records in the 1950s. By 1989, grants-in-aid were reduced to less than 11 percent of federal outlays and only 17 percent of state and local budgets. The Reagan administration had succeeded in reducing the prominence of federal grants in state and local budgets.

During the Bush administration, the grant-in-aid system once again expanded. In every year but one of the Bush presidency, the federal outlay for grants to state and local governments increased by double-digit figures. When Clinton came into office, grants totaled $178 billion and represented 12.9 percent of federal outlays.

These same trends are evident if we look at the number of federal grant programs. In 1960 there were about 130 federal grant programs available to state and local governments. By the time Lyndon B. Johnson left office in 1969, the number of grants had risen to 306. When Reagan took office in 1981, the figure was 539. The number of grants diminished as the Reagan administration consolidated a number of categorical grants into block grants and eliminated other federal programs. When Reagan left office in 1989, there were approximately 492 federal grant-in-aid programs.[47] Three years later, however, the General Accounting Office would count 593 separately funded federal grant programs. Despite the Reagan consolidations, the grant-in-aid system has continued to grow.

The grant-in-aid system expanded in response to the scope and complexity of the problems facing urban and metropolitan America. An effective fight against urban problems could not be undertaken in the absence of federal resources.

The federal government used its influence to help establish more uniform program and service standards across the nation. There are continuing differences in service and assistance levels from one state and one city to another, but federal action has succeeded in alleviating the gross inequalities of an earlier era. Federal grants have also led to an upgrading of local government by providing incentives for localities to

TABLE 12.4
Federal Grants-in-Aid in Relation to State and Local Outlays, Total Federal Outlays
and Gross Domestic Product
1955–1993
(Billions)

Fiscal Year	Amount	Percent Increase or Decrease (–)	As a Percentage of	
			Total State-Local Outlays	Total Federal Outlays
1955	$3.2	4.9%	10.2%	4.7%
1956	3.6	15.6	10.4	5.0
1957	4.0	8.1	10.5	5.2
1958	4.9	22.5	11.7	6.0
1959	6.5	32.7	14.1	7.0
1960	7.0	7.7	14.5	7.6
1961	7.1	1.4	13.7	7.3
1962	7.9	11.3	14.1	7.4
1963	8.6	8.9	14.2	7.7
1964	10.2	17.4	15.4	8.6
1965	10.9	7.9	15.1	9.2
1966	12.9	19.3	16.1	9.6
1967	15.2	16.9	16.9	9.7
1968	18.6	22.4	18.3	10.4
1969	20.2	9.1	17.8	11.0
1970	24.1	18.2	19.0	12.3
1971	28.1	17.1	19.7	13.4
1972	34.4	22.4	21.7	14.9
1973	41.8	21.5	24.0	17.0
1974	43.4	3.8	22.3	16.1
1975	49.8	14.7	22.6	15.0
1976	59.1	18.7	24.1	15.9
1977	68.4	15.7	25.5	16.7
1978	77.9	13.9	26.5	17.0
1979	82.9	6.4	25.8	16.5
1980	91.5	10.4	25.8	15.5
1981	94.8	3.6	24.7	14.0
1982	88.2	-7.0	21.6	11.8
1983	92.5	4.9	21.3	11.4
1984	97.6	5.5	20.9	11.5
1985	105.9	8.5	20.9	11.2
1986	112.4	6.1	19.9	11.3
1987	108.4	-3.6	18.0	10.8
1988	115.3	6.4	17.7	10.8
1989	122.0	5.7	17.3	10.7
1990	135.4	11.0	19.4	10.8
1991[r]	154.6	14.2	20.5	11.7
1992[r]	178.3	15.3	22.0	12.9
1993[e]	203.7	14.2	n.a.	13.8

(handwritten annotations: "REAGAN" next to 1981 row, "ERA" next to 1983 row)

n.a.—not available
[r]revised
[e]OMB estimate
Source: Extracted from ACIR, *Significant Features of Fiscal Federalism, 1994* (Washington, DC: ACIR, 1994), p. 36, Table 10.

take action in a number of program areas they otherwise might have ignored. Numerous federal programs have made remarkable headway in achieving stated goals, including Head Start, compensatory education, and special education programs; nutrition programs; Urban Mass Transportation Administration grants to aid urban public transit systems; programs for older Americans; and programs aimed at solving water pollution and solid waste disposal problems.

Despite much public mythology to the contrary, many federal programs do work. One major study of domestic aid programs has concluded that many of the criticisms are overstated. Intergovernmental conflict is most apparent during the early years of a program's operation. But as programs age and mature, conflict and confusion are replaced by more effective program coordination. Over time, program professionals begin to identify with program goals, understand federal regulations, and adjust to each others' expectations. The result is much greater policy success than is commonly perceived.[48]

Finally, the concept of cooperative federalism has been broadened and strengthened by the relatively new activity of local spokespersons on the Washington scene. Today mayors are frequent visitors to Washington; they have direct access to agency officials as well as to key senators and representatives who are responsible for policies affecting their cities. When the mayors are not in Washington, the big cities and urban counties rely heavily on their national associations to speak for them and to keep them informed about political and administrative decisions being made in Washington. Organizations like the U.S. Conference of Mayors, the National League of Cities (NLC), and the National Association of Counties (NACO) grew in importance in the 1960s and 1970s.[49] All these organizations have been active in trying to influence the Clinton administration's attempts to "reinvent" government. The local government associations in Washington are often referred to as **public interest groups (PIGs)**, and many observers feel that these organizations were largely responsible for the huge increases in both the number of grants and the dollars allocated to grants in the 1960s and 1970s.[50]

While the PIGs were instrumental in mobilizing their members to support a number of grant programs, they were also aided by other actors in the political arena. By 1980 approximately 30 states and 100 cities had opened their own offices in Washington. As more and more grant programs were proposed in Congress, specialized interest groups and associations also developed to push their own causes and interests. Congress, too, deserves a share of the responsibility for program expansion. Members of Congress sought to assure their reelection by working closely with both the public and special interest groups in promoting programs in their constituents' interests. Representatives and senators quickly became associated with specific issues, and many of them chaired the subcommittees responsible for authorizing the new programs. As everybody involved had something to gain from the process, grant-in-aid programs continued to expand.[51]

THE ISSUE OF UNFUNDED MANDATES

State and local governments have always complained about the various rules, regulations, paperwork requirements, and other program "strings" that accompany federal grants. But recently, states and localities have also complained about federal requirements that have been imposed without accompanying program money!

As the federal government began to tighten its purse strings, it increasingly sought means to accomplish program objectives without adding to the national budgetary deficit. One technique was to **mandate** or order action by state, county, or local governments without appropriating funds for the implementation of programs. The issue of **unfunded federal mandates** refers to those many instances where the federal government requires, but does not provide the financial assistance for, state and local action.

State and local governments complained of the costs imposed by unfunded mandates. They also complained that mandates distorted local budgetary priorities. Subnational governments had to reallocate revenues in order to comply with federally mandated rules and regulations. Tax revenues were diverted away from education and public safety as subnational governments paid the costs of complying with federal laws.

Few issues in the past twenty years have galvanized the public interest groups as quickly as the need to seek relief from unfunded federal mandates. Throughout most of the 1990s efforts have been undertaken to convince Congress to pass a mandate-relief bill.

The National Association of Counties (NACO) commissioned a survey by Price Waterhouse in 1993 to ascertain the costs incurred by counties in implementing twelve specific laws. More than 120 counties responded, indicating a total estimated cost of $4.8 billion for 1993 and an estimated cost of $33.7 billion from 1994 to 1998. Counties reported that unfunded federal mandates now account for 12.3 percent of locally based revenues.[52]

In 1993, the National League of Cities (NLC) launched a National Unfunded Mandates Day in Washington to call attention to the seriousness of the problem. This was expanded to a week in 1994. The National Conference of State Legislatures (NCSL) created a Mandate Watch List to identify the costs of compliance with both proposed and existing legislation.

Congress has not been unmindful of the serious and growing problem. After the Republican sweep in the 1994 midterm congressional elections, Congress made an unfunded mandates bill one of its priorities. Among the measures discussed in Congress was a requirement that there be a cost estimate for every new mandate, and that the government authorize specific funding sources—either through new taxes or reduced spending—to pay for any new mandate with a cost in excess of $50 million annually. Proposed legislation also required that a cost/benefit analysis be undertaken before a new mandate could be imposed. Environmentalists and civil rights activists vigorously protested that such a requirement would cripple new governmental action in important policy areas. While the legislation contained many exemptions and loopholes that would allow mandates in many areas to continue, it provided no such exemptions for environmental regulations.[53]

State and local governments generally welcomed the relief promised by the new unfunded mandates legislation. Yet, it should also be pointed out that while the states complained about the costs of mandates imposed by the federal government, they often themselves mandated costly actions by local governments. This even happens in states that nominally have legislation barring such action.[54] Local officials were especially wary that, in response to federal cutbacks, the states would impose yet additional service responsibilities on localities.

PICKET FENCE FEDERALISM

During the period of grant-in-aid expansion, the federal government assumed responsibility for a major share of intergovernmental program funding, but the administration and implementation of the programs were delegated to state, county, and local officials. One interesting consequence of this expanded partnership was the concept of **picket fence federalism (PFF)**.[55] PFF depicts the linkage among the different levels of government by functional category. PFF illustrates the complex relationship of national or subnational decision making and administrative units (see Figure 12.1).

The picket fence concept points to the existence of intergovernmental bureaucratic alliances of program specialists that can often resist control by legislators and other elected officials at each level of government. Since federal programs are funded and administered by functional agencies, the vertical slats in the fence represent the major program areas as they span the three levels of government. Functional specialists and program managers on all levels of government are linked by the enabling federal legislation, funding, program rules and regulations, auditing and reporting requirements, and evaluation procedures. Program by program, federal bureaucrats work on a continuous basis with their program counterparts in state and local governments.

Once a bill is signed into law at the national level, elected officials at all levels find themselves virtually excluded from policy decisions; daily operations and funding decisions for program implementation are conducted by national, state, and local bureaucrats, not elected officials. Subnational elected officials have not been able to counterbalance the powers federally funded programs have invested in state, county, and local bureaucrats. Citizens also often have found themselves at a disadvantage in trying to apply pressure to influence the administration of federally funded programs, with guidelines and regulations written in Washington.

FIGURE 12.1
Picket Fence Federalism: A Schematic Representation

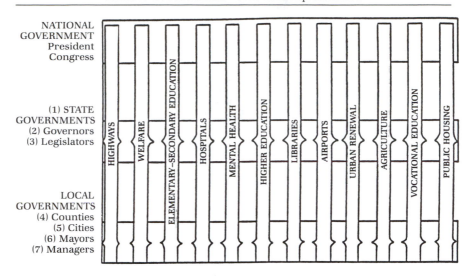

The Big Seven
(1) Council of State Governments
(2) National Governors' Conference
(3) National Legislative Conference
(4) National Association of County Officials
(5) National League of Cities
(6) U.S. Conference of Mayors
(7) International City Management Association

Source: Reprinted from Deil S. Wright, "Intergovernmental Relations: An Analytical Overview," *Annals of the American Academy of Political and Social Science* (November 1974):15.

The bureaucratic agencies that gained power under grant-in-aid programs are supported by the well-organized and influential special interest groups that helped to pass the legislation. They want to insure that the programs are administered in a manner consistent with their interests.

In recent years local elected officials have begun to exercise greater oversight over federally financed grant programs. In addition, the federal government has modified some of its funding approaches. More money is now allocated to state and local governments with fewer restrictions, giving elected officials greater discretion over how the money is spent. Still the system is heavily dependent upon bureaucrats for administrative and policy decisions.[56]

The Pennsylvania state legislature in 1976 made a much-publicized attempt to break the picket fence bureaucratic alliance and gain control over federal monies coming into the state. It passed two laws requiring that all federal funds coming into the state be deposited in the general fund and be subjected to the state appropriation process. It further required that all federal funds be appropriated to state agencies through specific line items in the state budget. Governor Milton Shapp opposed the legislation, as he was unwilling to see this power legislatively pass from the bureaucracy to the legislature. The governor went into court to have the two laws declared unconstitutional. Because the lower court and the Pennsylvania Supreme Court upheld the validity of the legislation and the U.S. Supreme Court refused to hear the case, the Pennsylvania legislature was permitted to claim the power to appropriate federal funds coming into the state.[57]

But few state legislatures carefully monitor either the amount or the administration of federal dollars and programs coming into their states.[58] The degree of oversight and assessment differs markedly from state to state. But as the United States enters a period of scarce resources and tightened budgets, state legislatures can be expected to show an increased interest in controlling how intergovernmental funds are used.

THE INTERGOVERNMENTAL SYSTEM: THE LOCAL VIEW

Not even the cities, which benefited greatly form the growth in the grant-in-aid system, have been delighted with all aspects of federal aid and technical assistance. One immediate problem concerned the question of centralization. As more and more power gravitated toward Washington, the role of the federal agency field office diminished in importance. Historically, units of local government worked more closely with federal field offices; municipal officials felt less confident in dealing with bureaucrats in Washington who have little familiarity with local problems and programs.

A second problem concerned local autonomy and federal control. Few local governments anticipated the extent to which federal rules and regulations accompanying grant assistance would require changes in local operations. Many local governments had to hire new staff just to comply with federal regulations and meet the federal reporting, auditing, and paperwork procedures. As governmental programs expanded, requirements began to overlap. A local government administering a mass transit grant had to comply with environmental quality regulations, civil rights laws, equal employment opportunity guidelines, and citizen participation requirements, as well as whatever transportation-specific concerns were written into the grant.

As grants became more plentiful in the 1960s and 1970s, the competition for them intensified rapidly. Jurisdictions sought to secure as many grants as possible, and questions began to arise about the efficacy of this whole competitive process. In a federal grant-in-aid system that had grown so large and so cumbersome, few local governments even knew about all the available grants. Also, instead of pursuing their own genuine priorities, local governments pursued federal funds, seeking "sure grants" while ignoring needs in areas where there was no grant money available. In effect, the grant-in-aid system provided a perverse set of incentives that rewarded the irrational grant-chaser rather than those local officials who sought to focus rationally on local objectives.

CONCLUSIONS

Federal-state-city relations have changed greatly over time. The more formalistic theory of federalism has yielded to a more dynamic view of intergovernmental relations. Federal program reach has increased. Cities have gained a new prominence under direct federalism. States have modernized their governing structures and revenue systems to become increasingly important actors in urban affairs.

Some people have criticized the rapid expansion of federal involvement and authority since the 1960s as being both undesirable and a violation of the strict construction of the Constitution, specifically the Tenth Amendment. The result has been to produce a system of overloaded federalism, top-heavy with federal rules and regulations. According to intergovernmental relations expert David Walker, the United States no longer has a working, cooperative system, but rather has an overloaded, dysfunctional system.[59]

Yet, not all observers are as critical of the new roles being played by the federal government and the states. Civil rights activists, environmentalists, and advocates of the poor have all welcomed the federal government's actions in working jointly with state and local governments to help solve contemporary social, economic, and urban problems. Over the years, Supreme Court rulings have legitimized the extended reach of the federal government and the rise of the new system of intergovernmental relations.

Overall, the expanded intergovernmental system with hundreds of grants has had many advantages:

1. It stimulated states, counties, and cities to recognize and act on some of the more pressing urban problems.
2. Federal programs assisted the truly needy with programs for the blind, disabled, unemployed, disadvantaged, and homeless. Federal dollars also assisted local governments in fighting problems that are national in scope—including poverty, job training, nutrition, housing, environmental protection, and health care.
3. Federal grant programs stimulated local economies by providing funds for highways, housing, hospitals, mass transit, job training, and numerous other projects.
4. Federal requirements encouraged citizen participation in local government. As a result of the conditions for receiving federal aid, local governments have had to open themselves up to new means

of citizen participation. Participatory requirements in federal programs have given both the middle class and the urban poor new channels of participation in local government.

5. Federal requirements also helped to ensure that subnational governments would respect the civil rights of minorities and the disabled.[60]

On the other hand, the new system of intergovernmental relations also has numerous disadvantages:

1. As the grant-in-aid system grew, the problems of accountability and control became much more complex. Federal programs increased functional specialization and functional hierarchies as depicted in *picket fence federalism*. Federal programs often resulted in the creation of semiautonomous and quasi-independent agencies, regional bodies, and authorities, increasing the waste and other problems posed by fragmentation and duplication.

2. Federal grant programs and their matching requirements often act to distort local priorities, leaving many pressing problems unattended. Local government budgets are skewed toward programs determined by federal officials. Categorical grants are targeted to narrow, specific issues usually demanded by active interest groups. These are not always the most pressing problems confronting local governments.

3. The number of federal programs today is so large that oversight has become extremely difficult and is often remiss. To compensate for this, federal agencies develop very specific program rules and require excessive reporting systems that antagonize local governments by adding to program costs and limiting program flexibility.

4. Federal programs and grants often constituted a hidden urban policy that had unexpected adverse effects on the health of local communities. As we have seen in preceding chapters, federal highway assistance, the programs of the Federal Housing Administration (FHA), and federal grants for hospitals and new sewage plants all greatly facilitated the exodus from cities to suburbs, inadvertently helping to produce the central-city poverty that too often exists today.

The problems inherent in intergovernmental partnerships are not easily resolved. Calls for increased program coordination can produce only limited results. In Connecticut, for instance, state and local officials and representatives of social service organizations met to decide how social service money would be spent in the wake of federal aid cutbacks. But as such extensive negotiation places great demands on participants' time, it cannot be used as a general approach to resolving intergovernmental disputes.[61] Federal, state, and local officials all have different perspectives on how programs should be run; disagreements will reemerge over time.[62]

Americans are upset with the waste, inflexibility, and intrusiveness inherent in intergovernmental programs. Since the late 1960s this has led to a call for a **New Federalism** to limit the federal government's role in domestic programs.

As we approach the twenty-first century, the expansion of federal grants to states and localities has yielded to a new sense of constraint imposed by limited resources. Expanding federal assistance has yielded the need to "reinvent government"—to find newer and better ways of organizing intergovernmental programs for more effective service without a massive transfusion of additional federal aid.

Yet, despite the continued criticisms of federal programs, there is also the recognition that central government power is needed to combat urban, social, and environmental ills and to protect the civil rights of minorities. This tension, and the alternating periods of expansion and contraction in national urban policy that results, is the subject of our next chapter.

NOTES

1. A. Lee Fritschler and Bernard H. Ross, *How Washington Works: The Executive's Guide to Government* (Cambridge, MA: Ballinger Publishing, 1987), p. 73.
2. Michael D. Reagan and John G. Sanzone, *The New Federalism*, 2nd ed. (New York: Oxford University Press, 1981), p. 3.
3. Morton Grodzins, "The Federal System," in *President's Commission on National Goals: Goals for Americans* (Englewood Cliffs, NJ: Prentice-Hall, 1960). The marble cake analogy was first used by Joseph E. McLean, *Politics Is What You Make It*, Public Affairs Pamphlet No. 181 (Washington, DC: Public Affairs Press, April 1952), p. 5.
4. Deil S. Wright, *Understading Intergovernmental Relations*, 3rd ed. (Monterey, CA: Books/Cole Publishing, 1988), p. 15.
5. Parris N. Glendening and Mavis Mann Reeves, *Pragmatic Federalism: An Intergovernmental View of American Government*, 2nd ed. (Pacific Palisades, CA: Palisades Publishers, 1984), pp. 12–13.
6. Wright, *Understanding Intergovernmental Relations*, chapter 3. The phases denote major characteristics of the period, which explains why there is some overlap.
7. See Frederick Mosher, *Democracy and the Public Service* (New York: Oxford University Press, 1968), chapter 4. Also see Herbert Kaufman, "Emerging Conflicts in the Doctrines of Public Administration," *American Political Science Review* 50 (December 1956): 1057–73.
8. For a discussion of this new approach, see Wright, *Understanding Intergovernmental Relations*, pp. 101–10.
9. Two good case studies of the conflict that develops among federal, state, and local officials in administering federal programs are provided by Jeffrey L. Pressman, *Federal Programs and City Politics* (Berkeley, CA: University of California Press, 1975); and Jeffrey L. Pressman and Aaron Wildavsky, *Implementation*, 3rd ed. (Berkeley, CA: University of California Press, 1984).

10. See Elizabeth K. Kellar, ed., *Managing with Less: A Book of Readings* (Washington, D.C.: International City Management Association, 1979). Also see Charles H. Levine, Irene S. Rubin, and George G. Wolohojian, *The Politics of Retrenchment: How Local Governments Manage Fiscal Stress* (Beverly Hills, CA: Sage Publications, 1981).

11. Wright, *Understanding Intergovernmental Relations*, pp. 90–99; Rochelle L. Stanfield, "Playing Computer Politics with Local Aid Formulas," *National Journal* (December 9, 1978): 1977; and Robert Jay Dilger, *Sunbelt/Snowbelt Controversy: The War over Federal Funds* (New York: New York University Press, 1982).

12. 4 Wheat 316 (1819).

13. Joseph Zimmerman, *Contemporary American Federalism: The Growth of National Power* (New York: Praeger Publishers, 1992), chapter 3.

14. David B. Walker, *The Rebirth of Federalism* (Chatham, NJ: Chatham House, 1995), chapter 7. See pp. 173–205 for Walker's view of the role played by the Warren, Burger, and Rehnquist courts in abetting the expansion of federal government power.

15. David B. Walker, *Toward a Functioning Federalism* (Boston: Little, Brown, 1981), p. 138.

16. Reagan and Sanzone, *The New Federalism*, p. 10. The quotation is from *U.S. v. Darby*, 312 U.S. 100, 1941.

17. *National League of Cities v. Usery*, 426 U.S. 833 (1976).

18. 464 U.S. 546 (1985).

19. *South Carolina v. Baker*, 108 S.Ct. 1935 (1988).

20. Margaret T. Wrightson, "The Road to *South Carolina*: Intergovernmental Tax Immunity and the Constitutional Status of Federalism," *Publius: The Journal of Federalism* 19 (Summer 1989): 51.

21. Ibid., p. 53.

22. Robert B. Hawkins, Jr., "An Ode to the 10th Amendment," *Governing* (July 1988): 74.

23. For an elaborate definition of dual federalism, see Edwin S. Corwin, "A Constitution of Powers and Modern Federalism," in *Essay in Constitutional Law*, ed. Robert McCloskey (New York: Alfred A. Knopf, 1962), pp. 188–89. Also see Zimmerman, *Contemporary American Federalism*, pp. 90–93.

24. Walker, *The Rebirth of Federalism*, pp. 67–68.

25. Morton Grodzins, *The American System: A New View of Government in the United States*, ed. Daniel J. Elazar (Chicago: Rand McNally, 1966); David B. Walker, *The Rebirth of Federalism*, pp. 24–26; and Daniel J. Elazar, "Cooperative Federalism," in *Competition Among States and Local Governments*, ed. Daphne A. Kenyon and John Kincaid (Washington, DC: The Urban Institute, 1991), chapter 4.

26. 24 Iowa 455 (1868).

27. *Atkins v. Kansas*, 191 U.S. 207 at 220–21 (1903); and *Trenton v. New Jersey*, 262 U.S. 182, 67L Ed 93, 43 S.Ct. 534 (1923).

28. Ann O'M. Bowman and Richard Kearney, *The Resurgence of the States* (Englewood Cliffs, NJ: Prentice-Hall, 1986), p. 136. Also see Zimmermann, *Contemporary American Federalism*, chapter 8.

29. *Measuring Local Discretionary Authority* (Washington, DC: Advisory Commission on Intergovernmental Relations, November 1980), p. 60.

30. Walker, *The Rebirth of Federalism*, pp. 111–13.

31. *Baker v. Carr*, 369 U.S. 189 (1962).

32. *Reynolds v. Sims*, 377 U.S. 533 (1964).

33. For a discussion of these changes, see ACIR, *State and Local Roles in the Federal System* (Washington, DC: Advisory Commission on Intergovernmental Relations, 1981). Also see ACIR, *The Question of State Government Capability* (Washington, DC: Advisory Commission on Intergovernmental Relations, 1985); David C. Nice, *Federalism: The Politics of Intergovernmental Relations* (New York: St. Martin's Press, 1987), pp. 88–911; and Bowman and Kearney, *The Resurgence of the States*, chapters 1–3.

34. *The Question of State Government Capability*, chapter 4. Also see Nice, *Federalism*, pp. 89–90; and Bowman and Kearney, *The Resurgence of the States*, chapter 3.

35. Advisory Commission on Intergovernmental Relations, *Significant Features of Fiscal Federalism 1985–86* (Washington, DC: ACIR, 1986), Table 45; and ACIR, *Significant Features of Fiscal Federalism 1989* (Washington, DC: ACIR 1989), vol. II, Table 10. It should be noted that these figures may overstate the fiscal commitment of state governments to local governments. Much of the state aid given to local governments is given to counties and school districts rather than to general-purpose municipal governments.

36. "State Aid to Locals Outpacing Overall Spending Growth," *Governors' Weekly Bulletin*, a publication of the National Governors' Association, January 5, 1990.

37. *The Question of State Government Capability*, chapters 2 and 15.

38. Ira Sharkansky, *The Maligned States,* 2nd ed. (New York: McGraw-Hill, 1978); and James L. Sundquist, *Making Federalism Work* (Washington, DC: Brookings Institution, 1969), p. 271.

39. Sundquist, *Making Federalism Work*, p. 271.

40. Earl Black, *Southern Governors and Civil Rights: Racial Segregation as a Campaign Issue in the Second Reconstruction* (Cambridge, MA: Harvard University Press, 1976).

41. Alexander P. Lamis, *The Two-Party South* (New York: Oxford University Press, 1984), pp. 88–91.

42. Gerald L. Houseman, *State and Local Government: The New Battleground* (Englewood Cliffs, NJ: Prentice-Hall, 1986), pp. 11–28 and 56–80. An important statement of the exact opposite view—that the states and a new breed of activist governors have taken the lead in innovative urban assistance and economic development programs—is provided by David Osborne, *Laboratories of Democracy* (Boston: Harvard Business School Press, 1988).

43. Reagan and Sanzone, *The New Federalism*, p. 175.

44. Martha R. Burt and Barbara E. Cohen, "Who Is Helping the Homeless? Local, State, and Federal Responses," *Publius: The Journal of Federalism* 19 (Summer 1989): 117–20 and 127–28.

45. Neal Peirce, "The New, New Federalism" (Remarks presented at the annual meeting of the National Civil League, Denver, Colorado, October 27, 1989).

46. For a discussion of the different types of grants, see Reagan and Sanzone, *The New Federalism*, pp. 57–60. Also see Dennis L. Dresang and James J. Gosling, *Politics, Policy and Management in the American States* (White Plains, NY: Longman, 1989), pp. 28–33; and Nice, *Federalism*, pp. 210–25. Also see Zimmerman, *Contemporary American Federalism*, pp. 115–26.

47. Advisory Commission on Intergovernmental Relations, *Significant Features of Fiscal Federalism, 1989* (Washington, DC: ACIR, 1989), Table 8 and ACIR Staff Data.

48. Paul E. Peterson, Barry G. Rabe, and Kenneth K. Wong, *When Federalism Works* (Washington, DC: Brookings Institution, 1986), pp. 131–32, 158–59, and 189–90.

49. For an analysis of the strategies and tactics of the public interest groups, see Charles H. Levine and James A. Thurber, "Reagan and the Intergovernmental Lobby," in *Interest Group Politics*, 2nd ed., ed. Allan J. Cigler and Burdett A. Loomis (Washington, DC: Congressional Quarterly Press, 1986), pp. 202–20; and Donald H. Haider, *When Governments Come to Washington: Governors, Mayors and Intergovernmental Lobbying* (New York: Free Press, 1974).

50. Aside from the three organizations mentioned above, the other members of the public interest group coalition are the International City Management Association (ICMA), the National Governors' Association (NGA), the National Conference of State Legislatures (NCSL), and the Council of State Governments (CSG).

51. For a discussion of this process and how it changed in the 1980s, see B. J. Reed, "The Changing Role of Local Advocacy in National Politics," *Journal of Urban Affairs* 4 (Fall 1983): 287–91. Also see Levine and Thurber, "Reagan and the Intergovernmental Lobby," pp. 209–20.

52. *The Burden of the Unfunded Federal Mandates: A Survey of the Impact of Unfunded Mandates on America's Counties* (Washington, DC: National Association of Counties, October, 1993). Also see *Federal Regulation of State and Local Governments* (Washington, DC: Advisory Commission on Intergovernmental Relations, 1993), chapter 5.

53. David Hosansky, "Loopholes May Diminish Power of Mandates Legislation," *Congressional Quarterly Weekly Reports* (March 4, 1995): 683–84.

54. Joseph Zimmerman, "State Mandate Relief: A Quick Look," *Intergovernmental Perspective* (Spring 1994): 28–30. Also see Zimmerman, *Contemporary American Federalism*, pp. 74–79.

55. See Terry Sanford, *Storm over the States* (New York: McGraw-Hill, 1967), pp. 80–81; and Wright, *Understanding Intergovernmental Relations*, pp. 83–86.

56. See Wright, *Understanding Intergovernmental Relations*, pp. 84–85, for a discussion of the modifications and reassessment of picket fence federalism.

57. For a discussion of *Shapp v. Sloan* (later changed to *Thornburg v. Casey*), see *Intergovernmental Perspective* 4 (Washington, DC: Advisory Commission on Intergovernmental Relations, Fall 1978): 5–6; and *Intergovernmental Perspective* 5 (Winter 1979): 28.

58. ACIR, *The Question of State Government Capability*, pp. 117–22.

59. Walker, *The Rebirth of Federalism*, pp. 4–13.

60. For further discussion of a number of these points, see Reagan and Sanzone, *The New Federalism*, pp. 60–65; and Nice, *Federalism*, pp. 57–60.

61. Donald E. Kettl, *Government by Proxy: (Mis?)Managing Federal Programs* (Washington, DC: Congressional Quarterly Press, 1988), pp. 66–69.

62. Pressman, *Federal Programs and City Politics*; and Pressman and Wildavsky, *Implementation*.

13

Federal Policy Toward Cities: From New Federalism to Reinventing Government

Richard M. Nixon became President in 1969, committed to changing the balance of power in the intergovernmental system. His **New Federalism** sought to reverse the flow of power from states and local governments to elected and administrative officials in Washington. The New Federalism sought to give power back to the states and localities.[1]

The New Federalism was an important idea that reshaped national-subnational relations, not just in the Nixon years but in the years that followed. Its influence was felt even in the Democratic Carter and Clinton administrations. Yet, it is doubtful that the federal government possesses the full extent of power alleged by critics. State and local officials maintain great discretionary power in the administration and implementation of intergovernmental programs. Federal agencies find it difficult to monitor joint programs that are administered by thousands of state and local jurisdictions. As a result, state and local officials possess a good deal of administrative latitude in program implementation.[2] Still, anti-Washington sentiment remains strong, as the costs of excessive federal intrusion are easily seen while the limitations of the central government's power are less easily recognized.

As we shall see, while the arguments against a top-heavy federal system are many, sometimes there are good reasons for keeping program authority in Washington. Democratic administrations have attempted to find an appropriate balance between national and subnational power in forging partnerships among the national government, the states, and the cities. Republican administrations, in contrast, have generally been more willing to devolve program responsibilities back to the states and localities. Both Democrats and Republicans alike, though, have had to respond to the strong popular sentiment to decrease the power of the Washington establishment.

In this chapter we trace the changing shape of federal urban policy efforts that have varied greatly from one presidential administration to another.

NIXON'S NEW FEDERALISM

Nixon's New Federalism was a reaction to the centralization of program authority that had occurred under Lyndon Johnson's Great Society. Johnson believed that the federal government could be used as a force to correct the inequalities of American society. Nixon, in contrast, used two innovative tools—general revenue sharing and block grants—in an effort to give power back to the states and localities.

THE BIRTH AND DEATH OF REVENUE SHARING, 1972–1986

The component of the New Federalism that received the greatest publicity was **general revenue sharing** (often referred to simply as **revenue sharing**). The program lasted for a little more than a dozen years and was terminated in 1986.

Revenue sharing was first proposed in the early 1960s by Walter Heller, President Kennedy's chairman of the Council of Economic Advisers. Heller's proposal was designed to return a portion of forecasted surplus federal revenues to the states with virtually no strings attached, thus giving the states flexibility to allocate these funds anyway they deemed necessary.

Because of American involvement in the Vietnam War and a host of congressionally enacted social programs, however, the projected surpluses envisioned by Heller never materialized. Still, the idea of no-strings-attached grant money proved appealing.

The advocates of revenue sharing argued that: (1) revenue sharing would provide the program flexibility that was obviously missing in the categorical grant-in-aid system; (2) no-strings funds would encourage greater innovation in programs; and (3) revenue sharing represented a reduction in the paperwork, auditing, and regulations that accompany most other federal programs.[3]

In 1972, revenue sharing was signed into law, and $30.2 billion in no-strings-attached money was made available to the states and general-purpose local governments over a five-year period. Renewed for four additional years in 1976, revenue sharing faced bitter political opposition beginning in 1980 as federal officials, confronted with mounting budget deficits, began to question the wisdom of sharing revenues with states, most of which had budget surpluses. The state portion of revenue sharing was terminated.

Throughout the 1980s President Ronald Reagan fought to eliminate revenue sharing, as he saw the program to be unnecessary and wasteful. He believed that revenue sharing encouraged overspending by inducing localities to undertake unnecessary projects that they would not normally choose to fund.

Budgetary pressures continued to take their toll, leading to the decision to phase out the program by 1986. As shared revenues were a sizable portion of local budgets (constituting almost 4 percent of city and county revenues),[4] the elimination of revenue sharing was a serious blow to more troubled cities and many smaller cities and rural counties that had limited alternative sources of revenue.

The short history of revenue sharing shows how new fiscal pressures have acted to limit federal urban spending, even forcing the termination of a once-popular program that gave funds to states and localities across the nation.

REVENUE SHARING EVALUATED

Revenue-sharing funds were not targeted to areas in need, but were given to all general-purpose governments, including such wealthier jurisdictions as Scarsdale, New York; Grosse Pointe, Michigan; and Palm Beach, Florida. Wealthier communities often used the new revenues to build tennis courts and expand their recreational facilities. At the same time, the mayors of more troubled communities complained about the inequities of a program that supported luxuries in wealthier jurisdictions at a time when declining cities had a difficult time finding money to support basic services.

Just how did local governments use their new discretion in spending shared revenues? In contrast to the expectations of revenue sharing's creators, the states and localities did not use shared revenues primarily to fund expanded or innovative problem-solving efforts. Quite the contrary. Instead, revenue sharing allowed state and local governments to stabilize or reduce taxes. By using federal funds to support existing services, localities could keep a lid on taxes. Local governments also tended to use revenue-sharing funds to support ongoing activities rather than to develop new approaches or programs.[5]

Overall, the experience of revenue sharing points to the dilemma of decentralizing power in the federal system. Revenue sharing gave local officials new flexibility, which they used to maintain existing services and stabilize taxes. Moreover, localities were not especially innovative in their use of these funds, nor were they generally willing to spend the money on social services targeted for the poor. Local governments were especially fearful that Congress would terminate the program, leaving them responsible for the new social service costs. Overall, the history of revenue sharing raises important concerns regarding state and local power.

BLOCK GRANTS

Block grants, Nixon's second alternative to categorical grants, proved to be a more permanent innovation than was revenue sharing. The use of block grants has had a lasting impact on the shape of the intergovernmental system.

Nixon's goal was to merge numerous, narrow categorical grants into larger, more broadly defined **block grants.** Categorical grants constrained state and local action by narrowly defining program purposes. The consolidation of numerous categorical grant programs into new block grants would allow states and localities greater discretion in deciding how to spend federal aid monies. Block grants gave recipient governments a much wider range of program choices, just so long as they remained within the broad functional area covered by the grant. The Democratic Congress succeeded in protecting numerous programs from consolidation, so Nixon did not get the complete package of block grants he wanted. Still, he was able to persuade Congress to add to the two block grants that were already on the books. During Nixon's second term, Congress passed both the Comprehensive Employment Training Act (CETA) in 1973 and the Community Development Block Grant (CDBG) program in 1974. The following year Congress approved Title XX of the Social Security Act.

In cases like the Community Development Block Grants, the Democratic Congress also compromised the block grant ideal by imposing more limitations (or "strings") on local use of the money than Nixon had desired. The Democrats added a provision ensuring that a portion of community development monies would be spent on low- and moderate-income communities. Other qualifications ensured the protection of civil rights and the participation by the poor in program decision making. Members of Congress were also wary of creating programs that ceded power to the discretion of state and local officials. Congressional incumbents preferred to protect categorical programs that favored key elements in their political constituencies. Despite these setbacks, Nixon's overall efforts at grant consolidation and program decentralization can generally be regarded as successful.

The Community Development Block Grant (CDBG) proved to be an especially popular program—and one of great importance to cities. But over the years, the CDBG program has been the target of budget-cutting pressure. For a number of years, the CDBG program was able to weather the political wars and preserve its status as the number-one urban aid program. In an era of budget cuts, CDBG funding increased four years in a row.

But a Republican-controlled Congress finally forced major reductions in CDBG spending. Republican-authored budget resolutions for fiscal 1996 proposed a 50-percent reduction in community development assistance, dropping annual CDBG appropriations from $4.6 billion to $2.3 billion. As had been the case with general revenue sharing, new budgetary stringency was forcing cuts even in popular programs that allowed great local flexibility.

THE LASTING IMPACT OF NIXON'S NEW FEDERALISM

The New Federalism of the Nixon administration, at best, receives mixed reviews. The most significant innovation of the New Federalism, revenue sharing, was short-lived. As we have observed, states and cities also did not always use shared revenues as creatively or responsibly as the program's more liberal advocates had hoped. Revenue sharing's importance also diminished over time as its funding levels were not increased to meet inflation. The program was eventually terminated as a result of national budgetary pressures.

The legacy of the Nixon New Federalism, then, is twofold. First, the New Federalism contained the idea that the federal aid system needed to be reshaped to enhance the flexibility allowed states and localities. This proved to be a powerful idea that has continued to influence the federal program mix after Nixon. Presidents Carter, Reagan, Bush, and Clinton all pursued program decentralization in accordance with the New Federalism ideal. Second, the use of block grants, rarely utilized before the Nixon presidency, has become a lasting and important feature of the intergovernmental aid system.

New Federalism emphasized program decentralization. Yet it would be misleading to speak of Nixon's years in office solely in terms of decentralization. During that time, Congress succeeded in greatly expanding the scope and funding of numerous domestic aid and entitlement programs. Also, while Nixon clearly sought to reshape the grant-in-aid system in order to give states and localities greater authority, he was not totally a decentralist.[6] He also sought to increase the central government's authority in important program areas. Nixon even proposed the nationalization of welfare—that the national government assume welfare responsibilities from the states. This was a remarkable and controversial proposal that would have revolutionized the American welfare system. But it did not gain congressional passage. However, the diary entries of Nixon Chief of Staff H. R. "Bob" Haldeman indicate that Nixon's commitment to the nationalization of welfare may well have been less than genuine.[7]

In short, the Nixon New Federalism is remembered primarily for its decentralist tendencies and its hallmark revenue sharing and block grant programs. However, the Nixon New Federalism also contained centralist elements that would clearly differentiate it from the more ideological antigovernment orientation of the Reagan New Federalism that would soon follow.

CARTER'S NEW PARTNERSHIP:
A FAILED ATTEMPT AT NATIONAL URBAN POLICY

Jimmy Carter promised a "New Partnership"[8] that would blend aspects of Johnson's Creative Federalism with Nixon's New Federalism, two program approaches that seemingly were quite contradictory. Carter wanted to focus federal program efforts on urban areas, targeting aid to cities in distress. Similar to Johnson, Carter proposed expanding the federal-local-private partnership, bypassing state governments where necessary. But Carter also spoke of fiscal restraints and of the need to reform categorical grant programs. Carter realized that the federal government did not by itself have the resources to solve urban problems. It would have to enter into partnerships with subnational governments, private businesses, neighborhood groups, and voluntary associations. These themes were all consistent with Nixon's New Federalism.

The concept of greater private sector involvement was especially appealing. In the privatist United States, business-siting decisions are made by the private sector, not the government. Carter proposed that the government work in partnership with the private sector to direct investment back toward declining communities. Many felt that the federal government had at long last begun to recognize the importance of private sector resources in solving urban problems.

THE FIRST-EVER NATIONAL URBAN POLICY

During his 1976 presidential campaign, Jimmy Carter promised the nation's mayors that he would be the first president ever to formulate an explicit national urban policy. Shortly after taking office, Carter created an intergovernmental Urban and Regional Policy Group (URPG) and charged it with the task of preparing a national urban policy report. The result was a "New Partnership to Preserve America's Communities" that emphasized three themes:

1. **Targeting** federal aid to troubled urban communities, as opposed to **spreading** federal funds across the country in order to satisfy political interests.
2. Using public funds to promote private investment in distressed communities. In contrast to previous Democratic administrations, the Carter policy emphasized **economic development** and job creation, not the provision of social services.
3. Reducing the administrative red tape and paperwork associated with federal grants.

Emergency fiscal relief was also offered to the nation's most hard-pressed communities.[9]

The early URPG discussions originally provided no role for the states in the new urban policy. A number of federal officials continued to see state governments as the enemies of cities. But the nation's governors lobbied hard for inclusion in the urban policy. The result was a belated and limited recognition of the role that the states could play in helping cities. Carter asked for a relatively paltry $400 million in incentive grants to encourage states to develop urban-oriented strategies. The amount was obviously insufficient to the task at hand.

The emphasis of the Carter urban policy was clearly on reversing the decline of economically troubled communities. The major pieces of the national urban policy were designed to bring new jobs and emergency fiscal relief to the nation's most distressed communities. His proposed **National Development Bank** was generally considered to be the centerpiece of the Carter urban policy. As private credit institutions were often unwilling to extend financing for new business ventures in distressed communities, Carter proposed the creation of a government institution to offer grants, loan guarantees, and other financial incentives to businesses that chose to locate or expand in economically depressed urban and rural areas.

A $1 billion program of Labor Intensive Public Works was intended to create 60,000 jobs and help cities repair their streets and infrastructure. A program of Targeted Employment Tax Credits was intended to encourage businesses to hire disadvantaged young persons, aged eighteen to twenty-four. For each eligible person hired, employers could reduce their tax obligation by $2,000 in the first year and $1,500 in the second year. Two billion dollars in Supplemental Fiscal Assistance over two years were offered to help economically troubled communities withstand the fiscal problems associated with high unemployment.

THE DEFEAT OF THE NATIONAL URBAN POLICY

The major pieces of the Carter urban policy were never enacted into law. The Targeted Employment Tax Credit was the sole major program initiative to gain congressional approval. Congress also approved the program's more modest initiatives in such areas as housing rehabilitation, urban parks, intermodal transportation, and social services. However, Congress dealt the urban policy a crippling blow by defeating nearly all the policy's big-spending items: local public works, supplemental fiscal assistance, state incentive grants, and the National Development Bank. In place of his proposed urban investment bank, Carter secured only a modest increase in funding for programs of the Economic Development Administration.

Rising fiscal conservatism in the face of mounting budgetary deficits helps to explain the urban policy defeat. But the reasons for failure go way beyond this simple explanation. Members of Congress are constituent-oriented. Sunbelt and suburban representatives were unwilling to vote for targeted programs that promised little in the way of benefits to their own districts. Key committee and subcommittee chairs from

Sunbelt states obstructed the enactment of the public works and fiscal assistance programs.

A national urban policy aimed at revitalizing decaying urban areas has a difficult time surviving a Congress increasingly dominated by representatives from suburban and Sunbelt districts. Members of Congress even forced changes in the Economic Development Administration (EDA) to ensure that virtually every congressional district would be eligible to participate in that agency's revitalization programs. Carter had sought to target EDA assistance. But instead of targeting, Congress broadened program eligibility requirements to the point that approximately 90 percent of the nation's population lived in areas defined as "distressed" and hence eligible to apply for assistance under the legislation.[10] A constituency-oriented Congress had reduced the concept of targeting to an absurdity.

WHY NATIONAL URBAN POLICY IS SO DIFFICULT TO ACHIEVE

To a great extent, the Carter urban policy was defeated by the same forces that had undermined the integrity of Lyndon Johnson's Model Cities Program. The Model Cities idea was based on the realization that fragmented government programs in such areas as housing, social welfare, education, and community development each dealt with only a part of the urban poverty problem. To fight urban poverty effectively, a comprehensive, coordinated, interagency assault is needed. The Model Cities program was intended to show what could be accomplished in riot-torn Detroit and a select few other demonstration cities by a coordinated, concentrated attack on all facets of the problem of urban poverty.

But Model Cities never gained enactment as it was originally conceptualized. Realizing that members of Congress would not vote for a program that denied benefits to their areas, the Model Cities Task Force broadened its proposal and urged the creation of 66 Model Cities around the nation. Congress spread the benefits further still, approving the award of nearly 140 Model Cities. Model Cities were set up to appease powerful members of Congress. As a result, Model Cities were created in such unlikely states as Maine, Tennessee, Kentucky, and Montana.[11] The spread of program assets meant that there was no critical mass of resources for a sustained, multipronged attack on urban poverty in any city. The idea of Model Cities as a coherent urban policy had been undermined.

It is no accident that the United States is a country lacking effective national domestic and urban policies. Whether the issue is health, transportation, housing, employment, energy, or the needs of cities, the fragmented and highly decentralized nature of the American political system makes it extremely difficult to legislate coherent and targeted national policies. Major policy initiatives are broken down into small, discrete proposals that are assigned to relevant congressional committees and subcommittees. In these smaller forums, members of Congress join with bureaucratic experts, lobbyists with a stake in the problem, White House staff, and state and local officials to evaluate and modify the proposed legislation. Different sets of committees, subcommittees, and related actors focus on different policy issues. Each different policy area is dominated by a different **policy subsystem** of political actors—members of Congress, mid-level bureaucrats, and active interest groups. Proposed legislation is often changed to reflect the rather narrow and parochial views of the members of the subsystems, not the national policy concepts advanced in the original legislation proposed by the President.[12]

THE CARTER URBAN POLICY:
NEW FEDERALISM VIOLATED, YET REAFFIRMED

The very idea of a national urban policy represented a reversal of the New Federalism attempts to minimize the central government's role in domestic affairs. Many Carter administration officials distrusted the states; they envisioned a direct federal-city relationship that would bypass the states in urban affairs.

The Carter administration's willingness to recentralize power in urban programs is also clearly seen in its handling of the Community Development Block Grant (CDBG) program. Under the Republican Gerald Ford administration, the Department of Housing and Urban Development (HUD) followed the decentralist tendencies of the Nixon block grant design; federal officials routinely approved local plans to spend CDBG money. Under Carter, however, HUD officials demonstrated an increased willingness to withhold funds in cases where local spending plans ignored the needs of a city's low- and moderate-income citizens. HUD, under Carter, was no longer willing to defer to local plans that devoted the bulk of community development money to parks improvements and new tennis courts. HUD, under Carter, had reversed the maximum decentralization thrust of the Nixon/Ford era.[13]

Yet, despite the heightened role played by the central government in urban affairs, in a number of ways the Carter urban approach was consistent with the spirit of New Federalism. Carter recognized that budgetary limitations imposed severe constraints on the scope of the federal government's involvement in urban problem solving. In fighting important domestic problems, the federal government would have to work in partnership with subnational governments, local and neighborhood organizations, and the private sector. Finally, there was the new priority given to economic development. The Carter urban policy contained little of the social spending emphasis of the federal programs of the 1960s. Instead, national efforts focused on increasing the numbers of jobs in, and bringing a new tax base to, cities.

Although Carter's urban policy and Reagan's New Federalism both embraced the principle of economic development, there was a difference. Carter pursued *local* economic development, seeking to reverse the decline of economically troubled communities. Reagan, in contrast, pursued *national* economic growth; he did not attempt to lure business back to troubled communities, communities that business had deserted as inefficient and unprofitable.[14]

REAGAN: THE NEW FEDERALISM AGAIN

Carter's initiatives, however disappointing, represent the high water mark of national urban policy in the United States. Presidents after Carter would not make cities the focus of national policy action. Ronald Reagan pursued a policy designed to strengthen national economic productivity. He did not favor costly urban and social programs that he believed sapped the United States' economic competitiveness. The government would reinforce, not contradict, market forces. Productive areas would grow; high-cost cities and states would have to relax the taxing, unionization, and regulatory burdens they imposed on business or face continued decline. As the *President's National Urban Policy Report* (1982) explained, the national government would no longer respond to symptoms of local distress with programs that tried to halt or slow, rather than accommodate, adjustment to the new national economy. The earlier June 1982 draft of the *Report* had even more bluntly declared, "Cities are not guaranteed eternal life."

Reagan had campaigned hard on the theme of reducing federal governmental spending and the intrusion of government into people's lives. His goal was to decentralize power by giving program authority back to the states.[15]

Reagan had an impact on the intergovernmental system in four different areas. First, he effected extensive cuts in domestic aid programs, particularly in his first budget. Second, Reagan consolidated many existing categorical grant programs into new block grants. Third, Reagan proposed to shape the federal system in accordance with New Federalism ideals. He proposed a "swap" of program responsibilities and funding sources. The federal government was to assume full responsibility for Medicaid, while the states would be given full responsibility, free from central oversight, for Aid to Families with Dependent Children (AFDC), food stamps, and a number of other programs. (Congress, however, rejected most of this far-reaching proposal.) Finally, Reagan sought an extensive program of regulatory relief to reduce the paperwork and regulatory burdens imposed on state and local governments.

THE REAGAN BUDGET CUTS

The most significant cuts in domestic spending were effected during Reagan's first year in office. Having been elected on a landslide victory, Reagan was at the peak of his power. He proposed budget cuts of about 14 percent in federal grants to state and local governments, and Congress was afraid to say no.

But Reagan's political clout quickly waned after his initial budgetary successes. As the nation soon entered a prolonged recession, with unemployment reaching its highest levels since the Great Depression, Reagan's popularity fell. Democrats, who made sizable gains in the 1982 midterm elections, solidified their opposition to Reagan's program.

Year after year, Reagan proposed reducing or "zeroing out" numerous urban and social programs. But Congress often acted to save threatened programs by placing them in mega-bills that included programs that Reagan could not afford to veto. Community Development Block Grants (CDBG), the Economic Development Administration (EDA), and the Small Business Administration (SBA) all survived Reagan's efforts to terminate them. Still, Reagan forced drastic reductions in spending for these programs as well as in grants for publicly assisted housing, wastewater treatment, and mass transit.[16] He also brought a virtual halt to the construction of new subsidized housing. Urban Development Action Grants (UDAG) survived numerous efforts at termination before finally falling victim to the budgetary axe during Reagan's last year in office.

Reagan's impact on cutting intergovernmental aid is evident in a quick review of spending figures. From Fiscal Year 1980 to Fiscal Year 1989, grants to state and local governments rose from $91.5 billion to $119.0 billion; but expressed in constant dollars (controlled for inflation), this represents a negative annual growth rate of 1.5 percent![17] In 1982 and 1987, grants to state and local governments were even reduced in terms of actual dollars spent! This was the first reported decline in intergovernmental spending since the Advisory Commission on Intergovernmental Relations started keeping data in 1955.

BLOCK GRANTS

Reagan proposed the consolidation of a number of categorical grants into block grants, but his use of block grants differed markedly from that taken by his Republican predecessors, Nixon and Ford. Under Nixon and Ford, block grants such as CDBG and CETA gave increased program control to cities. Reagan, in contrast, used block grants to give increased authority to the states. For Reagan, the primacy of states over cities was a constitutional matter; the Constitution allocates powers to the states but makes no mention of cities. The Reagan New Federalism was primarily a partnership between the federal government and the states, and there would be no direct federal-city relationship bypassing the states. Cities were left in the very tenuous position of being dependent on state-spending decisions.

The Reagan administration approached block grants with a different set of overall goals than did his Republican predecessors. Nixon officials saw block grants as a way to improve the administration of programs that were worth funding. In contrast, Reagan officials saw block grants "as an effective transitional device for weakening the 'Washington establishment' by providing a halfway house on the road to total federal withdrawal from affected policy areas."[18]

Reagan proposed cutting block grant spending levels, not increasing block grant funding as had occurred under Nixon. Reagan wanted to shrink the role of government in society, not increase the capacity of state and local governments to administer service programs. For Reagan, block grants were a means of restoring responsibility to government; state decision makers would have to ask if a program was really worth the cost of added taxes. Reagan felt that, forced to choose, state decision makers would opt to eliminate programs rather than raise taxes.

Congress followed a number of the Reagan reform efforts but did not give the President everything he wanted. Congress passed nine new block grants, consolidating seventy-seven categoricals that totaled to only $7.5 billion.[19] Overall, the number of categorical grants was reduced from 534 in 1981, when Reagan first came to office, to 422 in 1987. The new block grants accounted for approximately 10 percent of federal aid to state and local governments.[20] Reagan also broke much of the direct federal-city relationship. The power of federal agencies was curtailed, while the power of state officials was enhanced. Reagan had changed the nature of the federal system.

REGULATORY RELIEF

Reagan also gained substantial achievements in reducing the burden imposed on state and local officials by federal rules and regulations. Sometimes new legislation was introduced to cut the red rape accompanying federal aid. In other cases, Reagan officials used their administrative power to liberalize program rules without having to go through Congress. A Presidential Task Force on Regulatory Relief chaired by Vice President George Bush worked with state and local officials to identify potential areas of regulatory reform. The White House's Office of Management and Budget (OMB) was used to make sure that all federal agencies pursued the goals of regulatory and paperwork relief; an agency proposing new federal regulations would first have to get the approval of a reluctant OMB.

The Reagan record in providing regulatory relief was substantial. To provide just one instance of Reagan's impact here, the number of pages specifying how local governments were to spend their CDBG money was reduced from fifty-two to just two.[21] States and localities generally applauded the new freedoms they were allowed by the relaxation of federal rules.

Yet the Reagan administration did not always defer to the states and localities. The administration was willing to relax program rules only when it felt that state and local governments would use their newfound discretion to pursue conservative program priorities.[22] The Reagan administration, for instance, was not even willing to entrust local public housing authorities with such a minor matter as deciding what type of wood would be used in the construction of kitchen cabinets; instead, the Department of Housing and Urban Development mandated that cabinets be constructed of cheap particle board.[23]

A NEW AGE OF BUDGETARY LIMITATIONS AND PRAGMATISM: THE BUSH ADMINISTRATION

George Bush was less ideologically disposed against aiding cities than was Reagan. In contrast to Reagan, Bush was not wedded to the idea of shedding large areas of federal program responsibility. Bush's Secretary of Housing and Urban Development, Jack Kemp, was an activist who pushed for innovative urban problem solutions consistent with conservative, market-oriented ideology—enterprise zones, tenant self-management in public housing, and other strategies of citizen empowerment. Kemp's high-profile leadership was a breath of fresh air in HUD after eight years of agency inactivity under his predecessor, "Silent" Sam Pierce.

But Bush was unwilling to launch major new spending programs on behalf of cities. Nor was there any political will in Congress—faced, as it was, with the need to make further budget cuts—to restore general revenue sharing, urban development action grants, or any of the other programs that it had just painfully eliminated or reduced.

HUD further suffered as a result of the revelation of scandals in the agency under Secretary Pierce. HUD programs were marred by massive waste, fraud, and politicization. Contracts for the rehabilitation of housing had often been directed to political friends of the Reagan administration and not to areas where funds were needed most. This well-publicized scandal demoralized the agency and made both the President and Congress reluctant to fund a number of HUD programs. Secretary Kemp found that much of his time and energy was devoted, not to establishing a new housing agenda, but to cleaning up the agency in the wake of the scandal and fending off attacks from investigatory committees on Capitol Hill.

The need for deficit reduction and the enactment of new laws designed to impose budgetary discipline both acted sharply to constrain new spending efforts. The gigantic size of the budget deficits of the Reagan years, coupled with the budget reduction targets required by the **Gramm-Rudman-Hollings Deficit Control Acts** of 1985 and 1987, meant that not only was there little money for new programs, but that existing programs would be scrutinized for possible further cutbacks.

The **Budget Enforcement Act (BEA)** of 1990 established still stricter spending ceilings and "scorekeeping" rules to prevent some of the games that politicians had used to circumvent previous budget control efforts.

The act also set up **firewalls** that prohibited the use of savings in one substantive area to finance new spending in other areas. As a result, at least initially, funds freed by reductions in the defense budget at the end of the Cold War could not be raided to finance new urban and social programs. The BEA also set **pay-as-you-go** (also called **PAYGO**) procedures that prohibited Congress from launching new spending initiatives without first identifying specific tax increases or commensurate spending cuts in other programs that would be used to pay for the new programs.

The effect of all of these budgetary reforms has been to make the Congress and the President reluctant to launch new urban programs. The new budgetary procedures have also led to cuts in existing urban programs. To protect benefits for the elderly and the poor, Gramm-Rudman-Hollings and the BEA spending caps and firewalls forced disproportionate reductions in spending for mass transit, community development, job training, and local economic development.[24]

Budgetary limits also explain the disappointment of Bush's **Home Ownership and Opportunity for People Everywhere (HOPE)** program. HOPE sought to promote the empowerment of citizens and communities. Grants were to be given to help enable low-income people to buy public housing units and own a home of their own. Where home ownership was impossible, the program sought to encourage the formation of tenant organizations to take control of the management of public housing complexes, freeing tenants from reliance on unreliable public housing bureaucracies. But tenant organizations and potential homeowners needed costly training and financial support. Oftentimes, public housing units also needed extensive repairs.[25] The funding for the program was inadequate. As a result, HOPE fell far short of its empowerment ideals.

Bush had sought to rely on nonprofit associations, with their commitment and expertise, to build new, affordable housing. But here, too, budgetary constraints lessened what he had hoped to accomplish. Nonprofits and community groups can play a greatly expanded role in the construction of affordable housing only if government provides them with the necessary funds.[26]

Bush's New Federalism orientation was clearly apparent in other urban-related policy areas. Bush promised to be the "education president"; and he convened an "education summit" with the nation's governors and helped to bring the status of the nation's schools to the front burner of national attention. States were encouraged to institute innovative education programs and results-oriented reforms, but little in the way of new federal monies was offered. Likewise, Bush's war on drugs placed great burdens on state and local budgets, especially for law enforcement and prison construction.

In transportation policy, Bush declared the need for improved infrastructure if the United States was to be competitive in the global economy of the twenty-first century. But it was the states, not the federal government, that were urged to increase their spending to finance the effort. Bush's Secretary of Transportation Samuel Skinner claimed that "state and local governments have not provided a sufficient amount of infrastructure spending."[27] Illinois Republican Governor James R. Thompson amusedly parodied the President's most well-known election pledge: When it came to transportation, the message from Bush and Skinner to the states was: "Read my lips. Raise your taxes."[28]

"WASHINGTON ABANDONS CITIES"

Demetrios Caraley has succinctly summarized the urban policy approaches of the Reagan and Bush presidencies under a simple heading: "Washington Abandons Cities."[29] Caraley estimates that during the first ten years of the Reagan and Bush administrations, cities suffered a reduction of 46 percent of their federal aid, a loss of some $26 billion expressed in constant 1990 dollars. The authority of the Department of Housing and Urban Development (HUD) was sharply curtailed under Reagan. HUD's budget authority plummeted from $36 billion in fiscal 1982 to just $15 billion in fiscal 1989, Reagan's last budget year. Spending by HUD, which represented 7 percent of the federal budget in 1980, fell to just one percent by the time Reagan left office.[30] Appropriations for public housing under Reagan dropped by nearly three-fourths, from $30 billion a year to $7.8 billion in the last Reagan budget year. Reagan eliminated UDAGs and general revenue sharing and greatly reduced the funding of other urban aid programs.

Cities were forced to cope with dramatic reductions in federal aid. Los Angeles received $269 million in direct federal aid in 1981 but only $182 million in 1986, five Reagan budget years later. Baltimore received $220 million in direct aid in 1981 and only $124 million in 1986. Detroit lost over half its direct federal aid. Even Dallas saw its federal assistance fall from $54 million in 1981 to $30 million in 1986.[31]

Cities reacted by economizing and cutting services. But the burden of the Reagan aid cuts varied from city to city. Rochester, New York, had been heavily dependent on the lost federal revenues. The city had a declining population, a large stock of abandoned housing, and a deteriorating tax base. Faced with the Reagan cutbacks, Rochester was even forced to reduce its job training efforts and, for a time, eliminate subsidized day care for the poor. New York State increased its social welfare assistance but could not offset the federal aid reductions. Rochester's working poor were particularly hard hit by the cutbacks.[32]

In contrast, better-off cities were able to cope more easily with the Reagan aid reductions. In relatively wealthy Stamford, Connecticut, a city that was not heavily dependent on intergovernmental funds, the Reagan reductions had only a most modest effect on city services.[33] Similarly, in

Phoenix, continued population and job growth provided a tax base that allowed the city to expand services despite the Reagan aid reductions. The state of Arizona also enacted a state lottery and a temporary sales tax to provide new revenues to help offset the federal aid reductions. Overall, service retrenchment in this Sunbelt city was mild compared to that experienced by cities in other parts of the nation.[34]

As a result of the Reagan aid reductions, services once financed in part by a progressive federal income tax were increasingly supported by local property taxes, sales taxes, and user fees—all regressive instruments of taxation that placed a disproportionate burden of paying for municipal services on middle-class and low-income residents.[35] State aid did not come forward at sufficient levels to compensate for the federal cuts. The states had to cope with citizen antitax sentiment and a decline in the level of assistance that they received from the federal government.

Cities also responded to the Reagan aid cutbacks by postponing capital improvements. Mayors and councils had to respond to citizen demands for services needed at the moment; street resurfacing, scheduled bridge repairs, sewer improvements, and other capital projects could always be delayed another five or ten years. After all, these facilities were still in working order. But postponing scheduled maintenance and replacement has only added to an **urban infrastructure crisis** where preventive maintenance is not completed on schedule and where decaying facilities eventually break down. The result, in the long term, is more costly replacement and repair bills. Future generations will pay for the cost of infrastructure improvements that are forgone today. That, too, is a cost of the Reagan years.

CLINTON: STEALTH URBAN POLICY AND REINVENTING GOVERNMENT

No President of the United States came to the office better prepared in intergovernmental relations than Bill Clinton. Having served as governor of Arkansas for almost the whole decade of the 1980s, Clinton understood the complexity of program relationships among the federal, state, and local governments. He had also been very active in intergovernmental and urban issues as a result of his involvement in the National Governors' Association.

As a Democrat, Clinton was more willing to use government to help cities and disadvantaged people than were his Republican predecessors. Big-city mayors—including Richard Riordan in Los Angeles, Ed Rendell in Philadelphia, Mike White in Cleveland, and Rudy Giuliani in New York— all pressed the new President to develop and deliver new urban programs. In his first year, Clinton doubled expenditures for the homeless. He also awarded grants to thirty-two cities to turn around conditions in the nation's most severely distressed public housing projects. The Reagan and Bush administrations, in contrast, had "left in the pipeline" $6 billion in unspent public housing modernization money. Clinton also created a Community Reinvestment Fund (financed at only $60 million for 1994) to assist community development corporations, minority-owned banks, and other nontraditional lenders in the inner city. The new President also stepped up enforcement of fair housing laws, a policy area that had been virtually ignored by his Republican predecessors, doubling the budget for enforcement, cracking down on mortgage discrimination, and helping poor families "Move to Opportunity" in the suburbs. In a highly publicized move, HUD forced the integration of public housing in Vidor, Texas, after the local Klan vowed that they would continue to run off African-Americans who moved into the project.

But his experiences as governor also led Clinton to embrace notions of intergovernmental reform to give greater program leeway to the states and localities. Budgetary limitations, too, acted to ensure that there would be no return to the big-government approach of the Great Society.

URBAN POLICY BY NONURBAN MEANS

Budgetary concerns constrained Clinton's urban actions. Clinton had campaigned for the presidency as a "New Democrat," not a big-government liberal. He understood that the public had little tolerance for major new urban programs. He also knew that the public was increasingly concerned about the huge national budget deficits—a concern that was manifested in a sizable vote for Ross Perot in the 1992 election. The Budget Enforcement Act, too, virtually precluded the enactment of major new programs, inasmuch as the Congress could launch a new undertaking only by first identifying specific sources of revenue to offset the expenditure.

Consequently, Clinton's policy toward cities had two sometimes conflicting tendencies. First was his recognition that the national government had to play a more active role in urban affairs than was played under his Republican predecessors. The federal government had a role to play in building housing for the poor, preventing homelessness, and barring discrimination. In these and other areas, the national government had important responsibilities that it would not abdicate. The Clinton administration would try to aid cities, not abandon them to the forces of the free market.

But Clinton's policy also embraced a second broad principle, the ideal of **reinventing government** to make government perform better with less. Federal programs were to be surveyed with an eye for eliminating waste. Greater latitude was also allowed states and localities to experiment in areas such as welfare policy to come up with innovative program approaches of their own. Consistent with the New Federalism ideal, Clinton did not believe that all wisdom lay in Washington; he was willing to increase the program authority of the states and localities.

[handwritten margin note: got to make sure you keep getting that black vote!]

Clinton also learned from past experience the impossibility of enacting an explicit national urban policy as Carter had attempted. To announce a specific set of programs targeted on helping cities in need would only galvanize opposing forces. Clinton's first unsuccessful foray into the urban thicket only reinforced the perception that there was quite limited support in Congress for targeted urban programs. Congress balked at what appeared to be a set of social programs focused on heavily Democratic voting districts. Thereafter Clinton would attempt more modest and oblique urban aid efforts. Urban public interest groups began to show concern about the President's reluctance to act in this area.

Clinton essentially pursued urban policy without much new urban money. In an age where there was little public support for explicit urban policy, Clinton essentially followed the path of a **stealth urban policy,** of pursuing urban goals through "nonurban" program initiatives that were not perceived as targeting benefits on cities.[36] In the absence of legislative support for explicit urban policy, he sought targets of opportunity— tapping, for instance, Congress' willingness to fund Head Start, pass a new Crime Bill, and expand the Earned Income Tax Credit (EITC)—a program that provided additional income assistance to the working poor. These programs promised disproportionate benefits to urban populations. Under the expanded EITC program, a working mother with two children could receive up to $3,370 annually in income assistance. EITC's sliding scale of benefits even offered cash assistance to families earning up to $27,000 a year.

During his first two years in office, Clinton pursued a politically pragmatic course of action. Pro-urban policy pieces coexisted with his budgetary and reinventing government concerns.

THE CRIME BILL

For a number of years public opinion polls have documented the public's rising fear of crime. Whether or not violent crime has actually increased over the years, people are more and more concerned about it.

Not only are people scared, but they have adjusted their way of living to ensure their safety. People are reluctant to shop or dine out at night; home entertainment is becoming increasingly popular. They buy personal and home-protection systems and support taxes for additional police and prisons. In gang-ridden neighborhoods, children get shot on their way to school; teens at times avoid school from a fear for their personal safety. In big cities, the elderly, in particular, often have adjusted to the fear of crime by living isolated lives behind securely locked doors.

In the wake of this sentiment, the Clinton administration introduced a comprehensive crime bill that drew widespread support. The bill contained money for prisons and, according to its backers, one hundred thousand new police officers. The bill also mandated stiffer sentences for certain felonies. The "three strikes and you're out" approach, however, drew criticism from those who objected to the new costs to be imposed on states and cities who would bear the expense of imprisoning offenders found guilty of three such crimes.

However, the proposed legislation emphasized prevention as well as punishment. Crime prevention programs aimed at youth can represent a more cost-effective alternative than the $600,000 to $750,000 that it costs a state to imprison a three-time loser from age 40 to 75![37] Consequently, the Clinton bill contained money for such preventive programs as after-school and summer programs, drug rehabilitation centers, midnight basketball leagues, creative arts programs, and other programs that serve to provide teens with an alternative to drugs, gangs, and crime. The bill earmarked money for the establishment of drug courts, where offenders who accepted treatment would be allowed time off.

The crime bill was based on the concept of partnerships. The 100,000 new officers were to assist in **community policing,** working with the community in establishing goals.[38] The Clinton crime program also did not propose a one-size-fits-all solution. Consistent with New Federalism ideals, it gave recipients leeway to custom-design solutions to local problems.[39]

Initially, both houses of Congress passed the bill by wide margins. However, as the congressional conference committee met and both houses prepared to vote on a compromise package, Republicans raised new objections to the costs of the preventive measures. They did not want to give Clinton a major victory. Also, as part of their efforts to win a congressional majority in 1994, they continued to portray the Democrats as the root of a big-government, Washington establishment that threw money at problems with little care as to whether the money was effectively spent or not. Support for the revised bill eroded as critics argued that the Democrats had added numerous, irrelevant programs to the bill, including programs such as midnight basketball that had little demonstrated impact on reducing crime. According to the Republicans, midnight basketball and other social programs were simply bits of congressional **pork**—special projects that Democrats inserted in the bill to reward their urban constituencies. Whatever the controversy over the virtues of midnight basketball and other youth programs, other provisions, such as the decision to fund a research institute at a college in the district of a key member of Congress, clearly did fit the description of "pork." The National Rifle Association (NRA), too, opposed the bill, as it put restrictions on the sale of assault weaponry.

At one point, the Clinton administration was unable to muster a majority in the House on a procedural vote to bring the bill to the floor. The President, Vice-President Albert Gore, and other executive branch officials dropped what they were doing and began an all-out lobbying effort in both houses of Congress. The Crime Bill narrowly gained passage, only after some of the alleged pork was removed by making cuts in some of the social programs targeted for the inner cities.

Clinton had narrowly prevailed on an issue of importance to cities. The narrowness of the victory, however, only served to underscore the immense difficulty that the President would have in attempting to pass any program dedicated to funding inner-city programs. Programs focused on less salient issues than crime could be expected to have even less support in Congress.

The Republican victories in the House and the Senate in the 1994 midterm elections eroded still further whatever level of congressional support there was for urban programs. The new Republican majorities demanded that urban aid programs be cut, not expanded. Immediately upon coming to Washington, Republican members even began talking about rewriting the crime bill, shifting money from preventive to punitive programs, and withdrawing its prohibitions on assault weapons. Republicans also proposed refashioning the crime legislation as a block grant to allow the states greater leeway to spend the money in ways they deem best.

A number of local law enforcement agencies opposed the proposed block grant; they preferred the guarantee of 100,000 new police officers contained in the original legislation. Detroit Mayor Dennis Archer and other big-city mayors decried the efforts to undo the assault weapons ban. According to Archer, critics of the weapons ban had little familiarity with the extent of the devastation wrought by urban violence. President Clinton promised to stand firm, vowing to veto any changes contained in a revised crime bill.

THE 1994 CONGRESSIONAL ELECTIONS AND THE SHIFTING PROGRAM BALANCE

The sweeping Republican victory in the 1994 midterm congressional elections altered the terms of politics in the nation's capitol. In the face of both the voters' verdict at the polls and a new Republican congressional majority, Clinton fundamentally changed the balance of his programs as they affected cities. A new urgency was given to reinventing government and establishing the public perception of Clinton as a President seriously committed to cutting government and reducing its intrusion in people's lives. Much less emphasis was placed on continuing traditional federal urban policy tools.

In the wake of the election, the White House even considered eliminating the Department of Housing and Urban Development (HUD) in order to demonstrate its seriousness in changing government-as-usual in Washington. HUD Secretary Henry Cisneros successfully pressed for the department's preservation, but in return promised to dramatically restructure the agency, radically cutting staff, and to restructure programs to empower individuals and give localities and community groups greater freedom in spending federal aid.

HUD was to be reformed to give maximum discretion to local communities, yet national action would continue in such areas as fair housing, combatting lending discrimination, and promoting the mobility of poor families. However, the balance between national program actions and subnational flexibility had clearly shifted toward the latter. As Cisneros detailed:

> It's a difficult tension that we will have to negotiate. But clearly we come down on the side of flexibility and maximum discretion for local leaders who are closest to the problems...[40]

The tension between maintaining national program goals and maximizing local discretion, given the current prevailing public mood, can be seen in a review of Clinton's efforts to aid urban America in three areas: his plans for the reinventing or reorganization of HUD; the creation and evolution of local empowerment zones; and the Clinton proposals to reinvent and reengineer government.

REINVENTING HUD

The scandals at HUD during the Reagan years had hurt HUD severely. But these much-publicized instances of mismanagement were not the only reasons why the agency was held in such low esteem. Local officials also objected that the agency's maze of rules and regulations stood as a barrier to the effective performance of intergovernmental programs. They also complained of the costs and difficulties of having to apply for and administer so many different HUD programs. Other critics disliked HUD for continuing to support public housing programs that in many ways did not make the lives of the poor better. The reform of HUD was a Clinton priority.

In his first months in office, Secretary Henry Cisneros issued a report outlining "how HUD is clarifying its mission, consolidating and streamlining its operations, changing program design, restructuring its field organization, and developing better performance measurement systems to improve customer service and to restore public confidence in the Department."[41] According to Cisneros, HUD suffered from a high degree of micromanagement because Congress distrusted the department and consequently made it subject to overly restrictive rules. HUD, itself, placed too much time on refining program regulations and procedures and not enough time on promoting better performance. HUD would need to overhaul its procedures to provide a stimulus for innovative and entrepreneurial ideas. Cisneros promised to change HUD's core programs to make them more responsive to communities in need.[42]

Cisneros was poised to lead a revitalized HUD concentrating on six major missions: reducing homelessness, turning around conditions in public housing, expanding housing opportunities, opening housing markets, empowering communities, and bringing excellence to management.[43] But the Democrats' disastrous showing in the 1994 congressional elections changed the equation.

Political operatives in the White House were no longer willing to wait for reform. They argued that the Democrats lost so badly in 1994 because Clinton had strayed from the "New Democrat" message that two years earlier had won him the presidency. Upon coming to office, Clinton pushed a monumental and exceedingly complicated reform plan for national health care. As a result, the public no longer perceived him as a "New Democrat" but as a big-government liberal who was part of the Washington problem. White House advisers argued that Clinton could reclaim his reform image only by taking dramatic steps to clean up the mess in Washington. They recommended the elimination of HUD as one such dramatic step. Spending could be reduced by eliminating the department and many of its programs; other programs could be fundamentally reshaped or placed with other agencies.

HUD Secretary Henry Cisneros, however, argued the importance of maintaining a department focused on housing, communities, and the homeless. Cisneros convinced Clinton and staved off the department's execution. But the President gave Cisneros a "direct order": Change the way the department operates or face elimination. As Cisneros further recounted, "There is something about the prospect of elimination that focuses your attention."[44]

One month after the midterm election fiasco, President Clinton announced a major reorganization of HUD to reduce waste and inefficiency as part of his "Middle Class Bill of Rights." HUD would be substantially smaller and different. Plans called for consolidating over 60 categorical grants administered by the agency into just three, quite broad **performance-based grants** that would allow recipient jurisdictions much greater leeway in the use of program monies. While the performance-based grants in many ways resembled block grants, they attempted to maintain a commitment to national goals by requiring recipient communities to develop plans and performance indicators.

HUD Secretary Cisneros also promised a "dramatic transformation of public housing" where, as a "first step," block grants and deregulation would decentralize public housing management so that local housing authorities "can use funds interchangeably" without HUD's daily intrusion. He announced the ultimate goal of providing **certificates** or **vouchers** directly to public housing residents who could force the reform of public housing management by "voting with their feet."

Housing vouchers would give tenants the ability to leave unsatisfactory public housing. Local housing authorities would have to become more responsive to market forces. These authorities were to be given assistance only for a short term, for three to five years, to make repairs so that "a level playing field with market apartments" is established.[45] After that, voucher recipients would exercise their own choice of where to live. HUD's primary constituency would no longer be the bureaucratic local housing authorities but the residents themselves. Public housing as Americans know it would be phased out. HUD would also be downsized, losing possibly a third of its employees in the move toward efficiency.

Housing activists called the proposal "breathtakingly irresponsible."[46] They questioned whether the vouchers would be sufficient to provide low-income families with a real choice of housing in urban areas with more expensive housing markets. They further doubted that the plan provided adequate assistance to public housing projects. They also believed that the plan would lead to the further deterioration of public housing because funds for maintenance would be reduced, as there would be fewer tenants. They also argued that the plan effectively wrote off those housing projects that could be modernized and greatly improved with a small transfusion of public funds.

Cisneros' housing proposal exempted programs for the elderly and the disabled from conversion to vouchers. As Cisneros explained, seniors want security at this point of their life and feared the disruptions in their life that might accompany a voucher system. The HUD Secretary wanted to avoid a situation where all the tenants in a building for seniors would be forced to find new housing if the building were to lose its financial viability as a consequence of the decision by a few tenants to use their vouchers to seek housing elsewhere.

Housing vouchers were a far-sweeping and controversial idea. Cisneros recognized that problems inherent in any voucher plan would make it difficult to switch all public housing all the way to vouchers. As an intermediate step, HUD announced that it would offer incentives and new flexibility to those local communities that wished to experiment with voucher plans.

FROM ENTERPRISE ZONES TO EMPOWERMENT ZONES

The Debate over Enterprise Zones

The Reagan and Bush administrations advanced the idea of **enterprise zones** as an alternative to more traditional, bureaucratic urban programs. Johnson's Great Society and Carter's National Urban Policy had both attempted to revive depressed areas by concentrating governmental program efforts. In contrast, the Republicans sought to promote local revitalization by *withdrawing* government and thereby creating islands in which free enterprise could flourish. Business would be attracted to areas where taxes were kept low and governmental regulations were relaxed.

Enterprise zones have been enacted in the United Kingdom and in numerous countries in Asia. While the idea of enterprise zones has often attracted bipartisan support in the United States, many Democrats and poor people's advocates criticized that the Republican enterprise zone plan was more a tool for aiding business than for aiding the revitalization of cities. A proposal that targeted zone creation in troubled communities could be a valuable tool for local economic revitalization. In contrast, a program that lowered tax rates and regulatory burdens in vast numbers of communities across the nation gave little new comparative advantage to troubled communities. Under such a program, businesses would have no special incentive to locate in the country's most distressed communities or regions; they could locate in any of a vast number of communities and still receive a zone's tax and regulatory benefits.

During the Bush years, HUD Secretary Kemp urged the creation of enterprise zones across the nation. He argued that the reduction of taxing and regulatory burdens would, in effect, make the entire nation a zone of new entrepreneurial activity. Such widespread zone creation, though, promised little in the way of targeted benefits for cities.

The idea of cutting taxing and regulatory burdens as a means of encouraging business proved irresistible. In 1987, Congress passed an enterprise zone bill, but the legislation was largely symbolic, as it provided for no reduction in federal taxes for businesses that located in the zones. No zones were ever designated by HUD under the act. In 1992 George Bush vetoed as excessive urban aid and economic stimulus bills that contained provisions for enterprise zones.[47]

While the idea of national enterprise zone legislation floundered in Congress, the states picked up the ball and proceeded by creating enterprise zones of their own. Connecticut, New Jersey, Maryland, and Illinois were among the most active states in establishing them. By 1993, thirty-five states and the District of Columbia had created over 3,000 enterprise zones.[48] But as state legislation could not cut federal taxes and regulations, the state zones were only pale imitations of the enterprise zone ideal.

State enterprise zones have tended to lack a strong "urban" component. State enterprise zones have often been used to enhance a state's competitive economic position. The states have not targeted zone creation on distressed communities. Instead, they have established zones in those areas that are potentially attractive to mobile businesses. Nor have the states used enterprise zones as a tool to aid the start-up of smaller, more labor-intensive businesses and entrepreneurial ventures. Instead, state enterprise zone programs have provided a combination of tax breaks, loans, grants, regulatory relief, and other forms of development assistance—all in an attempt to snare much-prized big business.

State enterprise zones have been oversold.[49] Even where state enterprise zones have been successful, to a very great degree they have represented little more than a package of conventional state economic development incentives, relying on increased public spending and the use of governmental power to collect and allocate land as opposed to deregulation.[50]

The Democrats Revise the Concept: Clinton's Empowerment Zones

Clinton found the idea of enterprise zones attractive. He wanted to empower poor people and local communities. But his administration would not author a Republican-style proposal that gave tax and related benefits to business with little assurance that the poor would benefit as well. Instead, he sought to meld the Republican free-market approach with more traditional Democratic ideas.

As a result, the Clinton administration came up with a new Democratic variant of the enterprise zone idea. Clinton's **empowerment zone** proposal sought to maximize local responsibility in creating public-private partnerships aimed at rebuilding distressed communities. But the proposal was not strictly a market-oriented plan that provided capital incentives to business. Instead, the Clinton program saw an appropriate role for the government, including the federal government, to ensure that the benefits led to the greater public good. The federal government would award zones to those local governments that came up with the best plans for revitalizing their troubled communities. A Democratic proposal, empowerment zones targeted the bulk of the program's benefits on the nation's most distressed communities. Long-time advocates of the Republican enterprise zone plans, including the free-enterprise Heritage Foundation and former HUD Secretary Kemp, objected to the presence that the government would play in the Clinton proposal.[51]

Under the concept of empowerment zones, no revitalization plan was dictated by HUD to any city. Instead, each local community had to work with its private and nonprofit sectors to come up with its own plan for aiding a distressed community whose borders the local participants had set.

Rather than aid business on business's preferred terms, the Clinton approach sought to ensure that the benefits of new development were delivered to zone residents. Wage credits were to be given to business only for jobs given to persons who resided in the designated zones. The older Republican enterprise zone proposals, in contrast, had relied primarily on cuts in the capital gains tax and other incentives that rewarded capital-intensive business, with little assurance of job creation for the poor.

The Clinton empowerment zone concept was based on the realization that the withdrawal of government could not, by itself, reverse the decline of the nation's most distressed communities. Direct public spending and a plan of action were also needed to make these areas attractive to investment.[52] While the program offered tax breaks to businesses, it also offered $100 million in federal assistance to each of the six winners of the urban enterprise zone competition. This money was to provide for new social services and infrastructure to lure investment. Three rural empowerment zones were to each receive an additional $40 million. In a move that helped the program gain political passage, Clinton also proposed the designation of a number of smaller **enterprise communities.** These smaller communities would be given no additional federal aid, but they would be allowed expanded use of tax-exempt state and local bonds to help finance new development.

Urban empowerment zones were awarded to six cities: New York, Chicago, Atlanta, Detroit, Baltimore, and the Philadelphia/Camden bi-state area. Detroit was commended for having secured more than $2 billion in private sector commitments, including commitments from the automobile industry to hire and train zone residents, as well as commitments from banks to invest in home ownership and small business development in the zone.[53]

The Clinton administration was so pleased with the proposals that the various cities had developed that it expanded the number of awards beyond what had been originally envisioned. Los Angeles received $125 million and Cleveland $90 million in funds as **supplemental zones;** neither, however, received the federal tax credits for job creation given the other six urban zones. Los Angeles Mayor Richard Riordan, miffed at the awards, refused to participate in the President's announcement. The city that had expected to receive a full-fledged urban empowerment zone to aid its postriot rebuilding did not win an empowerment zone designation. According to HUD officials, Los Angeles simply had not submitted as good a plan as had other cities. Los Angeles officials in return complained that HUD officials had unfairly stressed the geographic compactness of zones, a criterion that rewarded older cities in the East and did not fit the needs of urban poverty in more spread cities in the West and the Sunbelt.

Boston, Houston, Kansas City, and Oakland (California) each received $25 million as **enhanced enterprise communities,** but, like Los Angeles and Cleveland, received none of the job-creation-oriented tax credits. Kansas City and Philadelphia-Camden were commended by the President for their regional cooperation in developing their proposals. The three rural empowerment zones were created in Kentucky, the Mid-Delta area of Mississippi, and the Rio Grande Valley in Texas. Dozens of rural enterprise communities were designated across the nation.

Not all urban activists greeted the creation of empowerment zones with great enthusiasm. Some saw them as too limited, as constituting a "bastard idea" and "a weak substitute for an urban policy."[54] Also, it remains to be seen just how empowerment zones would fare in the midst of the block grant consolidations and the new budget-cutting measures imposed by a Republican Congress.

REINVENTING GOVERNMENT

Early in his administration, President Clinton asked Vice-President Al Gore to head a task force on **reinventing government,** to assess what the federal government does, how well it does it, and how the costs associated with providing services can be reduced. The Vice-President presented his report to the President in September 1993.[55] One year later, he produced a follow-up report on the progress made toward achieving the expected goals.

A number of the proposals in the report relate directly to intergovernmental relations and urban affairs. Gore's report advised that the federal government restrict its use of unfunded mandates. The report further identified the cost savings that could be achieved by the consolidation of various categorical grants into a smaller number of more flexible block grants. The report also recommended the deregulation of public housing authorities who have a demonstrated record of managerial excellence.

To permit states and localities greater room for program experimentation and innovation, the report also recommended that all cabinet secretaries and agency heads be given the authority to grant subnational governments **waivers** from federal regulations and mandates. The Clinton administration notably followed this route of action in two quite important policy areas: health care and welfare. In Clinton's first two years in office, nine or so states were granted waivers from federal rules in order to experiment with new health approaches that might serve as a precursor to national health reform. Similarly, approximately thirty states were given waivers in the operation of their welfare systems in order to test the different approaches to reforming welfare by promoting work and parental responsibility.

Much of the intellectual roots of Clinton and Gore's efforts in this area can be traced to David Osborne and Ted Gaebler's popular book *Reinventing Government* that identified numerous ways by which government can be made less ossified and more entrepreneurial.[56] Reinventing government is a popular concept. Examples of government waste and extravagance are many. Government can be made more cost-efficient and entrepreneurial; government can be made to perform better.

On the other hand, the risks inherent in reinventing government are not always recognized. First, there is a sacrifice of the rule of law. The Gore report and the Osborne and Gaebler books both see laws and regulations as impediments to organizational behavior that are to be cast aside.[57] Yet, laws do serve public purposes. Laws also demand uniformity. Some welfare rights advocates have complained of the unfairness of welfare reform waivers that allow states to deny people benefits that they otherwise are deserving under law.

Reinventing government also understates the risks inherent in devolving authority to states and local governments that may do what is popular in communities at the price of ignoring justice and the needs of racial minorities, the disenfranchised, and the poor. Reinventing government sees states and localities as "laboratories of democracy."[58] The federal government can learn from states and localities, and the various locales can learn from one another. But while many communities are progressive and efficient, others are not. Federal rules and regulations can assure that the needs of the less powerful are respected in all communities.[59]

Reinventing government also overstates the advantages of making government more private-like. Private efficiency mechanisms are not always suitable for government. Often, things can be done more quickly and creatively at the cost of decreased accountability. Regulations do not always pose barriers that impede performance in the public interest. Regulations also serve to protect the public from the hazards of ill-conceived, individual action.

The 1994 fiscal crisis in affluent Orange County, California, serves as a case in point. The official charged with investing the county's receipts certainly was entrepreneurial; he invested the public's money in high-risk "derivatives" in order to gain a high rate of return. For a long time, his entrepreneurship was celebrated. But when the value of the investments sharply fell, municipalities in Orange County suddenly faced a cash crisis and were forced to reduce services, lay off public personnel, and face the prospect of new taxes.

CLINTON IN PERSPECTIVE

Bill Clinton attempted a number of pragmatic program steps designed to help communities in need. But his programs were buffeted by budgetary and political pressures. Critics charge that, even during his first two years in office, it was difficult to discern any coherence to his program. But Clinton was not the first President to have great difficulty in the area of urban policy. Clinton's defenders argue that the President had accurately read Congress and the electorate. The public was more interested in economic policy, health care, tax reductions, and welfare reform. Clinton had pushed urban policy as far as the public would allow.

CONCLUSIONS

Our review of the past three decades of federal urban policy has revealed a number of common themes. The first theme is the popularity of New Federalism, reinventing government, and similar anti-Washington reform efforts. Democratic and Republican administrations alike have recognized that the federal government cannot solve all the problems faced by states and localities. The age of the big-government solutions of the Great Society is over. More flexible solutions to local problems are called for. As a result, federal policy toward cities has come to see the need for a partnership arrangement among the different levels of government.

The essence of the continuing debate is over just which service responsibilities should be lodged at which level of government, and how much power should be accorded the different levels. Devolution to the states and localities maximizes flexibility and promotes efficiency by reducing redundancy and waste. Power at the central government level assures the protection of equity and civil rights concerns; citizens are treated the same no matter their place of residence or the policy desires of their immediate neighbors.

Second, all administrations have come to see the need to involve the private and nonprofit sectors in their actions. Even if it wanted to, the federal government cannot by itself reverse urban decline. The government does not create jobs or decide on their locations. Government must work hand-in-hand with the private sector to change the economic conditions of urban life. Republicans tend to see the virtue of free-market urban solutions. Democrats, in contrast, tend to believe that tax concessions and deregulation are insufficient to the task of reversing urban decline or ensuring that the poorest of the poor receive benefits from urban revitalization. They see a continuing role for government action and government spending programs—in such areas as education, job training, and infrastructure investment—to help create the conditions that can lead to urban recovery.

Third, we have learned that formulating and implementing a national urban policy is a very difficult process. The nature of the American political system makes it very difficult to enact national policy solutions in the face of major national problems. President Carter was the nation's only chief executive to even formulate a national urban policy. The program's major elements, however, were never enacted into law. The results were hardly a coherent, national urban policy.

Even President Reagan, who enjoyed numerous political successes in Congress during his first two years in office, suffered a stinging defeat when he proposed that the national and state governments sort out and "swap" program responsibilities. While Reagan succeeded in cutting and eliminating a number of major urban programs, he was also forced by Congress to accept the continuing existence of spending programs he disliked. Reagan cut domestic aid, but his cutbacks imposed great difficulties on more dependent cities. The federal government, in essence, washed its hands of responsibility for a number of urban problems. Still, the intergovernmental aid system as a whole survived the Reagan onslaught.

Bill Clinton, too, suffered at the hands of Congress. Clinton attempted a stealth urban policy, an urban policy by nonurban means. But Congress refused to pass his program for comprehensive national health care, a reform that would have alleviated the burdens placed on numerous state and local governments. Congress also spurned his urban aid and economic stimulus packages. And in the face of the Republican victory in the 1994 midterm elections, Clinton also found himself facing a Congress pushing a more radical welfare reform proposal than the one he thought desirable. The new Congress was also intent on forcing both major

reforms in HUD's operations and sizable cutbacks in such urban programs as CDBG and multifamily assisted housing. Cities dependent
on federal assistance would have to face increasingly difficult program
decisions.

Federal policy by itself cannot be expected to solve urban problems.
As a result of the New Federalism cutbacks, cities in recent years have
become increasingly reliant on own-source revenues. Our next chapter
covers the fiscal roots of the contemporary urban situation.

NOTES

1. David Walker, *Toward a Functioning Federalism* (Boston: Little, Brown, 1981),
   pp. 104–05. Also see Timothy Conlan, *New Federalism: Intergovernmental
   Reform from Nixon to Reagan* (Washington, DC: Brookings Institution, 1988),
   chapter 2.
2. For a discussion of where power resides in the intergovernmental system, see
   David C. Nice, *Federalism: The Politics of Intergovernmental Relations* (New
   York: St. Martin's Press, 1987), pp. 60–63. Also see Donald F. Kettl, *Government
   by Proxy: (Mis?)Managing Federal Programs* (Washington, DC: Congressional
   Quarterly Press, 1988), pp. 3–9.
3. For a discussion of the arguments for and against revenue sharing, see
   Michael D. Reagan and John G. Sanzone, *The New Federalism*, 2nd ed. (New
   York: Oxford University Press, 1981), pp. 85–92. Also see Glendening and
   Reeves, *Pragmatic Federalism*, pp. 249–50; Deil S. Wright, *Understanding
   Intergovernmental Relations*, 3rd ed. (Monterey, CA: Brooks-Cole Publishing,
   1988), pp. 153–62; and Timothy Conlan, *New Federalism: Intergovernmental
   Reform from Nixon to Reagan* (Washington, DC: The Brookings Institution,
   1988), pp. 65–70.
4. Thomas Muller, "The State Role in Revenue Sharing: A Fiscal Perspective,"
   in *Revenue Sharing with the States*, Hearings before the Subcommittee on
   the City, Committee on Banking Finance, and Committee on Urban Affairs,
   U.S. House of Representatives, 96th Congress, 1st Session, May 3, 1979, p. 2.
5. F. Thomas Juster, ed., *The Economic and Political Impact of General Revenue
   Sharing* (Washington, DC: Government Printing Office, 1976), p. 5; David A. Caputo and Richard L. Cole, "Revenue Sharing and Urban Services: A Survey,"
   Tax Review 34 (October 1973); Caputo and Cole, "General Revenue Sharing
   Expenditure Decisions in Cities over 50,000," *Public Administration Review*
   35 (March/April 1975): 136–42; and Richard P. Nathan and Charles F. Adams,
   Jr., *Revenue Sharing: The Second Round* (Washington, DC: Brookings Institution, 1977), pp. 27–32.
6. Conlan, *New Federalism*, pp. 76–91.
7. H. R. Haldeman, *The Haldeman Diaries: Inside the Nixon White House* (New
   York: G. P. Putnom's, 1994).
8. Jimmy Carter, "Address on Urban Policy to the United States Conference of
   Mayors," June 29, 1976.
9. *The President's National Urban Policy Report,* Washington, DC: U.S. Government Printing Office, August 1978, p. 5.
10. For an analysis of the legislative struggle over the 1978 national urban policy,
   see "How Urban Policy Gets Made—Very Carefully," *The New York Times*,

April 2, 1978, Section 4, p. 1; and "Carter Urban Policy: A Smorgasbord," *Congressional Quarterly Weekly Reports*, April 1, 1978, p. 782.

11. Bernard Frieden and Marshall Kaplan, *The Politics of Neglect* (Cambridge, MA: MIT Press, 1975). Also see Marshall Kaplan and Franklin James, eds., *The Future of National Urban Policy* (Durham, NC: Duke Univ. Press, 1990).

12. For a discussion of subsystem politics, see A. Lee Fritschler and Bernard H. Ross, *How Washington Works: The Executive's Guide to Government* (Cambridge, MA: Ballinger Publishing Co., 1987), chapters 6–8.

13. Richard P. Nathan and Paul R. Dommel, "Federal-Local Relations under Block Grants," *Political Science Quarterly* 93 (Fall 1978): 421–42; and Paul R. Dommel, "Social Targeting for Community Development," *Political Science Quarterly* 95 (Fall 1980): 465–78.

14. Myron A. Levine, "The Reagan Urban Policy: Efficient National Economic Growth and Public Sector Minimization," *Journal of Urban Affairs* 5 (Winter 1983): 17–28.

15. See President Reagan's inaugural address in *Weekly Compilation of Presidential Documents*, January 26, 1981. Also see Conlan, *New Federalism*, chapters 6–10.

16. Ellen Perlman, "Reagan's Last Budget," *City and State*, February 29, 1988, pp. 1 and 22. Also see *Nation's Cities Weekly*, May 30, 1988. A complete analysis can be obtained from the Executive Office of the President, Office of Management and Budget, *Historical Tables, Budget of the United States Government, Fiscal Year 1989* (Washington, DC: U.S. Government Printing Office, 1988).

17. Lillian Rymarowicz and Dennis Zimmerman, "Federal Budget and Tax Policy and the State-Local Sector: Retrenchment in the 1980's," Congressional Research Service, Report 88-600E, September 9, 1988.

18. Conlan, *New Federalism*, p. 160.

19. For a breakdown of the block grants, see David B. Walker, Albert J. Richter, and Cynthia Cates Colella, "The First Ten Months: Grants-in-Aid, Regulatory and Other Changes," *Intergovernmental Perspective* 8, no. 1 (Winter 1982): 8–12. Also see Richard P. Nathan, "The Nationalization of Proposition 13," *PS (Political Science)* 14, no. 4 (Fall 1981): 752–56. For an analysis of block grants in the Nixon and Reagan administrations, see Timothy J. Conlan "The Politics of Federal Block Grants from Nixon to Reagan," *Political Science Quarterly* 99, 2 (Fall 1984): 247–70. Also see Conlan, *New Federalism*, chapter 8.

20. Richard L. Cole, Delbert A. Taebel, and Rodney V. Hissong, "America's Cities and the 1980s: The Legacy of the Reagan Years" (Working paper of the Institute of Urban Studies, The University of Texas at Arlington, March 1990; presented at the annual meeting of the Urban Affairs Association, Charlotte, NC, April 19, 1990).

21. *National Journal*, October 3, 1981, p. 1785.

22. Conlan, *New Federalism*, p. 212. For a balanced view of the Reagan years, see *Federal Regulation of State and Local Governments: The Mixed Record of the 1980's* (Washington, DC: ACIR, 1993).

23. Harry Spence, director of the Boston Public Housing Authority. Testimony before the Subcommittee on Housing, U.S. Senate Committee on Banking, Housing and Urban Affairs, March 20, 1982.

24. Demetrios Caraley, "Washington Abandons Cities," *Political Science Quarterly* 107, 1 (1992): 1–30.

25. Michael A. Stegman, *More Housing, More Fairly: Background Paper on the Limits of Privatization* (New York: Twentieth Century Fund Press, 1991).

26. Carolyn Teich Adams, "Nonprofit Housing Producers in the U.S.: Why So Rare?" (Paper presented at the annual meeting of the Urban Affairs Association, Charlotte, NC, April 19, 1990).

27. John H. Cushman, Jr., "Bush Transportation Policy Assailed," *The New York Times*, March 9, 1990.

28. Ibid.

29. Caraley, "Washington Abandons Cities," pp. 1–30.

30. Carol F. Steinbach, "Shelter-skelter," *National Journal*, April 8, 1989, pp. 851–55.

31. Cole, Taebel, and Hissong, "America's Cities and the 1980s: The Legacy of the Reagan Years."

32. Sarah E. Liebschutz and Alan J. Taddiken, "The Effects of Reagan Administration Budget Cuts on Human Services in Rochester," in *Reagan and the Cities*, ed. George E. Peterson and Carol W. Lewis (Washington, DC: Urban Institute Press, 1986), pp. 131–54.

33. W. Wayne Shannon, C. Donald Ferree, Jr., Everett Carll Ladd, and Carol W. Lewis, "The Public Sector of Stamford, Connecticut: Responses to a Changing Federal Role," in *Reagan and the Cities*, ed. George E. Peterson and Carol W. Lewis, pp. 155–84.

34. John Stuart Hall, "Retrenchment in Phoenix, Arizona," in *Reagan and the Cities*, ed. George E. Peterson and Carol W. Lewis, pp. 185–208.

35. Cole, Taebel, and Hissong, "America's Cities in the 1980s: The Legacy of the Reagan Years."

36. Myron A. Levine, "Urban Policy in America: The Clinton Approach," *Local Economy* 9 (November 1994): 278–81. Kaplan and James, *The Future of National Urban Policy*, also argue the political necessity of pursuing national urban goals by "nonurban" policy tools.

37. Adele Harrel, The Urban Institute, "Crime Policy" (Paper presented at the annual meeting of the Urban Affairs Association, New Orleans, March 3, 1994).

38. Ibid.

39. For a description of mayors' concerns in this area, see Stephen Goldsmith and Kurt L. Schmoke, "Crime Control, City by City," *The New York Times*, December 19, 1992. At the time of the article, Goldsmith, a Republican, was mayor of Indianapolis and Schmoke, a Democrat, was mayor of Baltimore.

40. Remarks of HUD Secretary Henry Cisneros at the White House Press Conference on the Middle Class Bill of Rights, Washington, DC, December 19, 1994.

41. *The Transformation of HUD*, A Report to the Senate Appropriations Subcommittee on VA, HUD, and Independent Agencies, May 2, 1994, p. 1.

42. Ibid., pp. 20–23.

43. Ibid., pp. 4–5.

44. HUD Secretary Henry Cisneros, White House Press Conference, Washington, DC, December 19, 1994.

45. All quotations are from the remarks of HUD Secretary Henry Cisneros at the White House Press Conference on the Middle Class Bill of Rights, Washington, DC, December 19. 1994. Cisneros also explained HUD's proposed reforms of public housing in his testimony before the Senate Appropriations Subcommittee on VA, HUD, and Independent Agencies, May 19, 1995.

46. Michael Kane, director of the National Alliance of HUD Tenants, quoted in Guy Gugliotta, "Critics See Unstated Motive for Restructuring HUD," *The Washington Post*, January 13, 1995.

47. Marilyn Marks Rubin, "Can Reorchestration of Historical Themes Reinvent Government? A Case Study of the Empowerment Zones and Enterprise Communities Act of 1993," *Public Administration Review* 54 (March/April 1994): 162–63.

48. "Local Creativity a Key for Enterprise Zones," *The Washington Post*, June 1, 1993.

49. DeLysa Burnier, "Self-Regulating Urban Policy: The Paradox of Enterprise Zones" (Paper presented to the annual meeting of the American Political Science Association, Washington, DC, August 29–September 1, 1991); and Richard Elling and Ann Workman Sheldon, "Determinants of Enterprise Zone Success: A Four State Perspective," in *Enterprise Zones*, ed. Roy Green and Michael Brintnall (Newbury Park, CA: Sage Publications, 1991), pp. 136–54.

50. Robert Guskind, "Zeal for Zones," *National Journal*, June 3, 1989, p. 1359; and Mark Bendick, Jr., and David W. Rasmussen, "Enterprise Zones and Inner-city Economic Revitalization," in *Reagan and the Cities*, ed. George E. Peterson and Carol W. Lewis (Washington, DC: Urban Institute Press, 1986), pp. 97–129. There is a virtual consensus in the literature that state enterprise zones have resembled traditional economic development tools in the search for business. Still, more positive overall assessments of state enterprise zone programs are reported by Roy E. Green and Michael Brintnall, "Reconnoitering State-Administered Enterprise Zones: What's in a Name?" *Journal of Urban Affairs* 9 (1987): 159–70; and Margaret G. Wilder and Barry M. Rubin, "Targeted Redevelopment through Urban Enterprise Zones," *Journal of Urban Affairs* 10 (1988): 1–18.

51. Jeffrey L. Katz, "Enterprise Zones Struggle to Make Their Mark," *Congressional Quarterly Weekly Report*, July 17, 1993, p. 1882.

52. Assistant Secretary for HUD Andrew Cuomo, press briefing, Washington, DC, December 21, 1994.

53. President Clinton, phone call to recipients of Empowerment Zone awards, December 21, 1994.

54. Peter Marcuse, "Empowering New York," *City Limits* (March 1994): 20–21.

55. *Creating a Government that Works Better and Costs Less*. Report of the National Performance Review (Washington, DC: U.S. Government Printing Office, September 1993).

56. David Osborne and Ted Gaebler, *Reinventing Government: How the Entrepreneurial Spirit Is Transforming the Public Sector from School House to State House, City Hall to Pentagon* (Reading, MA: Addison-Wesley, 1992). Also see Carmine Scavo, "What Cities Can Do" (Paper presented at the annual meeting of the Urban Affairs Association, New Orleans, March 2–5, 1994).

57. Ronald C. Moe, "The 'Reinventing Government' Exercise: Misinterpreting the Problem, Misjudging the Consequences," *Public Administration Review* 54 (March/April 1994): 115. Also see Donald F. Kettl, *Reinventing Government: Appraising the National Performance Review* (Washington, DC: The Brookings Institution, 1994).

58. William A. Galston and Geoffrey L. Tibbetts, "Reinventing Federalism: The Clinton/Gore Program for a New Partnership Among the Federal, State, and Tribal Governments," *Publius* 24 (Summer 1994): 25. Also see David Osborne, *Laboratories of Democracy* (Boston: Harvard Business School Press, 1990).

59. R. W. Apple, Jr., "You Say You Want a Devolution," *The New York Times*, January 29, 1995.

14

Financing Urban America

Throughout this book we have discussed how power is distributed and exercised in urban policy making. We have seen how different actors are able to marshall resources to try and influence the outcome of a decision in their favor. Still, all the influence possible cannot turn straw into dollars. In other words, cities and counties need adequate revenues to finance programs.

This chapter explores the finance picture in urban America. Specifically, we are interested in how cities obtain revenues, decide on expenditures, seek out alternative sources of income, and function in a rapidly changing economic system. As we shall see, local governments often have a quite difficult time in finding the additional sources of revenue to pay for increasingly expensive city services. As the mid-1990s bankruptcy of Orange County, California, underscores, even relatively affluent localities have faced new and serious constraints in attempting to find the money to fund local services.

REVENUES AND INCOME

Local governments rely on a complex variety of income sources. Quite obviously, local governments levy taxes—property taxes, sales taxes, and income taxes—that raise fairly large sums of income. Local governments can also impose a large number of license fees, user fees, and "nuisance" taxes that generate increasingly important sums of revenues. The exact taxes and fees that a locality is permitted to levy vary from state to state. The vast majority of cities are greatly reliant on local property tax revenues. Yet, only half of the states permit municipalities to levy a local sales tax. As of the mid-1980s, a local income tax was permitted in only eleven states (Alabama, Arkansas, Delaware, Georgia, Iowa, Kentucky, Michigan, Missouri, New York, Ohio, and Pennsylvania); and in a number of these states only a handful of cities actually chose to levy the tax.[1]

451

But local governments do not depend on taxes alone for the money they need to operate. As we have already discussed in Chapters 12 and 13, localities are the recipients of large sums of intergovernmental grants. But the revenue picture does not stop here. Cities and other local jurisdictions also borrow money by issuing short-term tax anticipation notes and long-term bonds to creditors who will advance the sums necessary to help finance local projects.

In accounting, **revenue** is a narrower term than **income** and would exclude such items as funds borrowed through the issuance of notes and bonds.[2] In this chapter we will discuss the larger concept, income. We will trace contemporary patterns of both municipal revenue raising and borrowing. We will note the potential and limitations of each income source available to local governments.

THE TAXING POWER AND STATE-IMPOSED LIMITS

A tax is generally defined as a compulsory contribution for the support of government, exacted without regard for individual benefit. That is, you cannot refuse to pay a tax simply because you, as an individual, receive no particular benefit from it. Local governments possess only such taxing power as has been conferred on them by the states; local governments may only impose those taxes the states permit them to levy.

Over the decades there has been a feeling that state and local legislatures could not altogether be trusted to levy taxes wisely, and, as a result, all state constitutions impose certain limitations upon the taxing power of the states and their municipal corporations. Ordinarily these provisions take the form of exempting certain classes of property from taxation. It is common, for instance, to exempt from taxation all publicly owned property, as well as property used for educational, religious, or charitable purposes. Also, most states provide exemptions of one sort or another for veterans. Other forms of exemption include **homestead exemptions** (under which owner-occupied homes of lower income or elderly residents are wholly or partially nontaxable) and exemptions for certain kinds of industrial and agricultural properties. Because of these numerous exemptions, a very substantial proportion of real estate does not appear on big-city tax rolls. As a result, property tax revenues are severely diminished.

Local property taxes are also subject to state-imposed percentage or millage limitations upon the rates that may be imposed for specific purposes, such as new school construction, street repair, or recreation.[*] As an illustration, a municipality may be authorized to levy up to five mills on

---

[*]Millage is a tax rate expressed in mills per dollar. It is normally used in property taxation. A mill equals one-thousandth of a dollar; a ten-mill rate is a 1-percent rate. Usually property tax rates are expressed as per hundred or per thousand of assessed value.

each dollar of assessed valuation for street purposes, three mills for parks, two mills for health care, and so on. Most states allow local voters, through the use of referenda, to authorize taxes in excess of maximum rates. But some states set an overall limitation on property taxes. Under this plan the combined tax levies on a single piece of property may not exceed a designated maximum. Some states make it difficult to raise local taxes as they require that voters approve increases in millage even if there are no state-imposed limits. As we noted in Chapter 11, local governments attempt to circumvent such limitations by having services provided by special districts that are not subject to the tax limitations placed on general-purpose local governments.

Property Taxes

The property tax has been at the heart of urban finance for 200 years. About 30 percent of municipal general revenue comes from property taxes (see Figure 14.1). While most cities rely heavily on property taxes, Enid (Oklahoma) is a notable city that does not use a property tax at all.[3] Over the past few years, as we shall see, property taxes have been declining in relative importance as local revenue sources (see Tables 14.1 and 14.2).

There are numerous problems that result from the reliance of local governments on the property tax. Ideally, property taxes have two major characteristics. They are both universal and uniform.[4] That is, the taxes are levied on all forms of property (universality) and at the same rate (uniformity). Unfortunately, in the real world neither of these ideals has been maintained. As the different types of property multiplied, the concept of universality became unattainable. **Real property**—land and improvements—is the easiest to reach through taxation. But **personal property**—home furnishings, appliances, automobiles, and inventories and equipment at work—are harder to locate, since they have a lower degree of visibility coupled with a higher degree of mobility. Most taxation of tangible personal property is of items required to be registered with the state, such as cars, boats, mobile homes, and RVs.

Today, real and tangible personal property no longer represents a citizen's true wealth. Wealth also takes the form of cash, stocks, and bonds, all of which are classified as **intangible personal property**. But taxes on intangible personal property are difficult to enforce. For a long time, Ohio counties had an intangibles tax; but in Ohio, as in other states, the intangibles tax was evaded by many residents.

In recent years, state and local governments have largely given up the effort to tax intangibles and hard-to-locate household personal property. Most jurisdictions have abandoned the notion of universality and, instead, have concentrated their taxation efforts on real and tangible personal property. As a result, a significant portion of the wealth of the members of

FIGURE 14.1
General Revenue of State and Local Governments, 1992

State Governments
Total $605.3 Billion

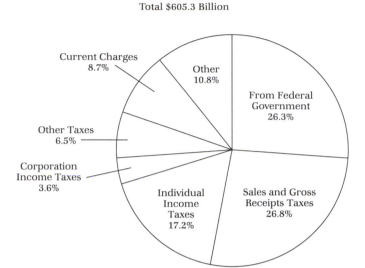

Current Charges
8.7%

Other
10.8%

From Federal
Government
26.3%

Other Taxes
6.5%

Corporation
Income Taxes
3.6%

Individual
Income
Taxes
17.2%

Sales and Gross
Receipts Taxes
26.8%

Source: U.S. Department of Commerce, Bureau of the Census, State Government
Finances, 1992, p. xiii.

Local Governments
Total $573.5 Billion

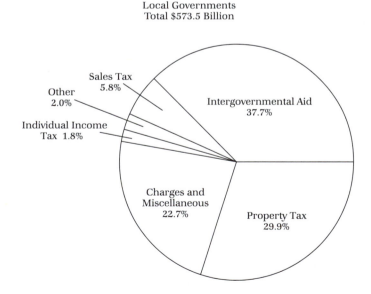

Sales Tax
5.8%

Other
2.0%

Intergovernmental Aid
37.7%

Individual Income
Tax 1.8%

Charges and
Miscellaneous
22.7%

Property Tax
29.9%

Source: Advisory Commission on Intergovernmental Relations, Significant Feature of Fiscal Federalism, 1994, Table 34, p. 67.

TABLE 14.1
Property Taxes as a Percentage of General Revenue, by Level of Government, Various Years

| Year | States | Local Governments | | | | | |
		All	Counties	Municipalities	Townships	School Districts	Special Districts
1962	2.1	48.0	45.7	44.2	65.3	51.0	25.0
1967	1.7	43.2	42.1	38.1	61.8	46.9	21.5
1972	1.3	39.5	36.5	31.3	64.9	47.3	17.3
1977	1.3	33.7	31.0	25.8	56.8	42.1	14.0
1982	1.1	28.1	26.6	21.4	52.1	35.8	9.5
1986	1.1	28.2	27.3	20.5	52.1	36.2	10.4
1991	1.1	29.9	28.1	22.9	55.8	37.2	11.3
1992	1.1	29.3	27.9	23.1	56.9	37.4	11.0

Source: U.S. Department of Commerce (1962, 1967, 1972, 1977, 1982), table entitled "General Revenue by Type of Government." For 1986 and 1991 data, see the Bureau of the Census, *Governmental Finance*, 1986 and 1991. 1992 data provided by the Bureau of the Census.

HALF OF BUDGET COMING FROM PROPERTY TAXES

TABLE 14.2
Property Taxes as a Percentage of Taxes, by Level of Government, Various Years

| Year | States | Local Governments | | | | | |
		All	Counties	Municipalities	Townships	School Districts	Special Districts
1962	3.1	87.7	93.5	93.5	99.3	98.6	100.0
1967	2.7	88.6	92.1	70.0	92.8	98.4	100.0
1972	2.1	83.7	85.6	64.3	93.5	98.1	94.9
1977	2.2	80.5	81.2	60.9	91.7	97.5	91.2
1982	1.9	76.1	77.2	52.6	93.7	96.8	79.6
1986	1.9	74.0	74.5	49.3	92.7	97.4	79.8
1992	2.0	75.6	74.3	52.6	93.0	97.4	67.6

Source: U.S. Department of Commerce (1962, 1967, 1972, 1977, 1982), table entitled "General Revenue by Type of Government." For 1986 and 1991 data, see the Bureau of the Census, *Governmental Finance*, 1986 and 1991. 1992 data provided by the Bureau of the Census.

any community is removed from the reach of local governments, which depend on property taxes as a major source of revenue.

Uniformity, too, has come into question. Most states began by requiring that all property be taxed at the same rate. Yet, legislators began to realize that the owners of industrial and commercial property generally can afford to pay more than individual citizens can. They consequently levied different tax rates on industrial and commercial property as opposed to purely residential property and tangible personal property. This arrangement is very productive in generating revenue. Still, most states insist on equity in taxation; they have maintained their constitutional or statutory requirements for uniform property taxes.

The property tax is a very unpopular tax.[5] As studies by the Advisory Commission on Intergovernmental Relations (ACIR) show, it proves to be the item most in trouble in our domestic revenue system. The ACIR called the property tax our "sick giant" and traced its problems to several "tax overburdens," including overassessment of property owned by individuals with average and below-average incomes, and the high costs of often inadequate administration.[6] The property tax can also be a **regressive tax**. The property tax paid by a low- or moderate-income homeowner often represents a greater percentage of that family's annual income than does the property tax paid by an upper-income household.

In many communities, especially in "property poor" jurisdictions, the property tax base does not provide adequate revenue to support much-needed city services. This is often the result of sectoral patterns of metropolitan development. Wealthy residential, commercial, and industrial property tend to be found in certain communities in the metropolis, while poorer people tend to be concentrated in others. In recent years, the real thrust for reform in the property tax has come from persons interested in the more equitable financing of schools.

It is often charged that persons who occupy rental units and who own no real property pay no property taxes. This is false. A good portion of property taxes are passed on to tenants through higher rents, except where rents cannot be raised for market reasons or where rent controls, as in New York City and a few other cities, prohibit immediate rent hikes. The gross injustice here is not that tenants do not pay property taxes, for in the long run they do. Rather, the injustice is that tenants do not turn out to vote in as strong numbers as homeowners on referenda dealing with proposed increases in the property tax.

Another central problem in property taxation concerns assessment. A **tax assessor** has the responsibility of determining the value of property for tax purposes. Under a well-administered tax system, the assessed valuation of all property in the taxing jurisdiction is divided by the amount of money to be raised through the tax, thus determining the tax rate. Then the actual tax on each piece of property is calculated, subject to the limitations on taxes established by state laws and the state constitution.

As we might expect, the levying of a property tax is rarely that simple. First of all, different jurisdictions assess on different bases. One city in a county might assess at 100 percent of market value; others might assess property as low as 25 percent for tax purposes. A tax rate levied by a county could impose greatly different levels of taxation on two equivalent pieces of property assessed at different levels in different parts of the county. To correct this, most states now provide for an equalization procedure to adjust for the differences in the assessed valuation levels in each assessment jurisdiction.

However, this does not solve all the problems. Within a single governmental unit, comparable parcels of land may still be assessed at different values. This is sometimes due to the failure of assessors to bring assessments up to date with changes in the market value of real estate in the area. No jurisdiction has the capacity to assess or reassess all the property within its borders each year. As a result, property that is assessed more recently often bears a higher tax burden than does older property in the same area. This undermines the concept of uniformity in taxation.

In other cases undeveloped land is seriously underassessed through pressure applied by owners, land developers, and real estate interests. These groups insist that tracts waiting for development be assessed as agricultural land and not as residential, commercial, or industrial property.

To remedy this problem, some local governments have adopted the policy of assessing all land at its highest usage level. But this, in turn, creates new problems. An old single-family dwelling in a central-city area may be reassessed at a much higher value when a zoning change indicates that the site may be profitably used for a high-rise apartment house or some other commercial development. Such reassessment may lead to a whopping increase in taxes that an owner cannot bear.

Land near suburban areas is virtually forced out of agricultural usage when taxes make it uneconomical to maintain it as farmland. Incredible as it may seem, citrus groves in southern California suburbs are assessed as potential residential developments in recognition of the huge profits that will be realized when the property is converted to such use. Such taxing practices virtually encourage the outward continuation of urban sprawl. Some states have tried to cope with this problem by providing special taxing categories to protect agricultural land, no matter where it is located. Further, some states allow agreements with owners that require them to keep land in agricultural use or as wetlands, in return for appropriately lower assessments.

Property tax reform is difficult to achieve since any change will raise taxes on some people while cutting the taxes on others. Most municipal governments also lack the full ability to control assessment and collection procedures, as these functions are usually performed on the county or township level. Reforms must come from the state legislatures, which to date have been unable to achieve a fully uniform and fair property tax system.[7]

SALES TAXES

To supplement the revenue resources of local governments, thirty-two states have authorized local sales taxes. Half of the states allow municipalities to levy a sales tax; a small number of other states allow counties and transit districts to impose such a levy.[8] This right has also been extended to school districts in Louisiana.

Over the past twenty years the use of local sales taxes has been on the upswing (see Table 14.3). Most states permit municipalities to piggyback the local levy onto the state sales tax, retaining the collection and administration at the state level. This reduces the costs of collection to local governments while producing maximum revenue for municipalities.

TABLE 14.3
General and Selective Sales Taxes as a Percentage of General Revenue,
by Level of Government

		Local Governments					
Year	States	All	Counties	Municipalities	Townships	School Districts	Special Districts
1962							
General	16.4	2.5	1.1	6.6	*	*	*
All	38.6	3.8	1.5	9.9	1.5	*	*
1967							
General	17.1	2.1	1.6	5.1	0.1	0.1	*
All	35.7	3.4	2.1	8.5	1.5	0.1	*
1972							
General	17.9	2.6	3.2	5.4	*	0.2	0.8
All	33.7	4.1	3.8	9.1	1.6	0.2	0.9
1977							
General	18.3	3.1	3.9	5.8	*	0.3	1.2
All	31.0	4.6	4.7	9.6	2.1	0.3	1.2
1982							
General	18.3	3.6	4.4	6.9	*	0.4	2.2
All	28.6	5.3	5.5	11.1	0.1	0.4	2.2
1986							
General	19.0	4.2	5.6	7.4	*	0.3	3.9
All	28.6	5.9	6.7	12.0	*	0.4	3.9
1991							
General	18.7	4.1	5.8	7.1	*	*	4.3
All	12.9	5.9	7.1	11.9	*	0.3	4.4

*Less than 0.1 percent.
General: includes state and local government general sales and gross receipt taxes.
All: includes state and local government selective excise taxes, general sales, and gross
receipt taxes.
Source: U.S. Department of Commerce (1962, 1967, 1972, 1977, 1982), table entitled
"General Revenue by Type of Government." For 1986 and 1991 data, see the Bureau of the
Census, *Governmental Finance*, 1986 and 1991.

Sales taxes, though, have one major fault; they are regressive, even
though items such as food and drugs are generally exempted. Sales taxes
impose a greater burden proportionally on lower-income groups than on
the wealthy, since the poor spend a greater proportion of their incomes
on purchases subject to taxation. Sales taxes applied to groceries, medi-
cine, and other necessities of life are particularly distressing. Many states
exempt the purchase of such items from taxation. Some exempt clothing
as well. These exemptions make the tax burden less regressive and nearly
"flat" in some cases.[9]

As the United States has moved further and further away from a manufacturing economy to one based on services, policy makers have begun
to consider the possibility of taxing services in order to preserve state
and local revenue streams. States including Florida and Massachusetts
introduced sales taxes on services, only to repeal them in the wake of
voter unhappiness. Opponents of taxes on services complain that sales
taxes are taxes on consumers and should not be levied on the components

TABLE 14.4
Individual Income Taxes as a Percentage of General Revenue,
by Level of Government, Various Years

Year	States	All	Counties	Municipalities	Townships	School Districts	Special Districts
			Local Governments				
1962	8.8	0.8	0.1	2.0	0.2	0.3	—
1967	9.4	1.6	0.1	4.2	0.4	0.3	—
1972	13.2	2.1	0.8	5.4	0.7	0.3	—
1977	15.1	2.2	0.9	5.1	1.1	0.3	—
1982	16.6	1.8	1.0	4.3	1.4	0.3	—
1986	17.1	1.8	1.0	4.5	1.3	0.3	—
1991	17.9	18.6	1.1	4.7	1.4	0.3	—

Source: U.S. Department of Commerce (1962, 1967, 1972, 1977, 1982), table entitled
"General Revenue by Type of Government." For 1986 and 1991 data, see the Bureau of the
Census, *Governmental Finance*, 1986 and 1991.

of production. Taxes on services can also severely damage a state's ability
to compete with neighboring jurisdictions.[10]

INCOME TAXES

Many cities have begun to look for other ways to tap the wealth within
their borders. Income taxes, which are so productive at the national level,
appear to be equally attractive on the state and local levels (see Table
14.4). As we already noted, eleven states allow some or all of their cities,
counties, and school districts to levy income taxes. In some cities, such as
Louisville, Columbus (Ohio), and Philadelphia, the income tax has provided nearly half of local tax collections—a consideration that increases
the tax's attractiveness.

There are some serious problems with a local income tax, however.
In areas where localities must collect and administer the tax, these costs
run particularly high. Also, the question of payment of local income
taxes by nonresidents has raised controversies in every city that has
adopted the income tax. Municipalities tax nonresidents who work
within their boundaries as a means of making suburbanites contribute
for the services the central city provides. However, suburban dwellers
(who may be heavily taxed within their own communities) feel that such
additional taxation for services they use only partially is unfair. In response to this complaint, state law often requires that nonresident taxes
be set at a lower rate than resident taxes. Also, nonresident taxes are imposed only on income earned in the city, not on total income. Therefore,
they are not as burdensome as they might be, especially considering
the benefits commuters usually derive from police and fire protection
and other city services. In any case, wherever enacted, a commuter tax
produces new antagonisms and does little to ease the already strained
relations among neighboring communities. Though income taxes add

appreciably to the funding of local governments, they do not appear to be politically feasible, long-run solutions to the revenue problems of a great many cities.[11]

One relatively new opportunity for state and local income taxes, though, has been created by federal tax reform. The Tax Reform Act of 1986 reduced the maximum tax brackets at the federal level to 33 percent. The act also indexed tax brackets to prevent "bracket creep" as the cost of living increased; taxpayers would not move into the next tax bracket unless their income increased proportionately.[12] By reducing the federal income tax burden, the act opened up opportunities for state and local governments to increase their own revenues through the imposition of new taxes.

OTHER TAXES AND LICENSING FEES

Most cities impose minor taxes and licensing fees to supplement their revenues. Many have adopted a wheel tax levied on automobiles driven within the city by residents or by commuters who work in the city. Other cities tax amusements, the occupancy of hotel rooms, and the sale of cigarettes and alcoholic beverages. Many areas also have licensing requirements for the sale of alcoholic beverages, the operation of taxicabs, and other services. These licensing requirements serve a dual purpose: They regulate these activities while producing new revenue for the city. Such taxes and fees, however, seldom provide a significant portion of local revenues.

USER FEES AND CHARGES

Another popular form of taxation is the imposition of charges or fees for services rendered. Only those who use a service pay for it. Most urban transit systems partially operate this way. Public utilities providing water, power, and sewage disposal also are financed, at least in part, on a user basis. Other improvements (streets, sidewalks, and street lighting, for example) are often financed by special assessments against property owners in the affected area.

User fees are attractive, as they appeal to our basic sense of fairness. The problem lies, though, in the inability of many people to pay the fees even though they need the services. Public transportation is a good example of this; those who need it most, namely, people with no other form of transportation available to them, are the ones least able to pay for it. Children from impoverished families would not be able to participate in extracurricular activities if these were to be financed on a user fee basis. Subsidies from general tax revenues are required for the continuation and equitable provision of such services.[13]

User fees are popular, as they are seen by many citizens to be a fair way of raising revenue. User fees are also paid by nonresidents who use a city's services. Conservatives also applaud the fact that user fees help stem the growth of government; by paying for services they use, citizens are discouraged from viewing services as "free." As a result, citizens are likely to demand better quality of service or the elimination of services that are not worth the charge. For this to happen, though, user fees must be set at the true price of the service provided; user fees that are set too low represent only token charges and encourage the overutilization of services, even shoddy services.[14]

In the early 1980s, state and local governments increasingly turned to user fees in the wake of federal aid cutbacks and the recession. Surveys by the Advisory Commission on Intergovernmental Relations indicate that taxpayers by a wide margin prefer user fees to raising the level of other taxes.[15] In a tight revenue situation, local governments have become increasingly reliant on user fees (see Table 14.5).

GAMBLING

States and cities have also begun to turn to government-sponsored gambling as a way to augment their resources. State lotteries often dedicate a portion of the proceeds to education. Recently, more and more cities have turned to casino and riverboat gambling in an effort to find new revenues. Where necessary, they have even sought out Indian tribes to sponsor gaming that would otherwise be prohibited by state law.

Opponents charge that the advocates of gambling often overstate the benefits and understate the costs of introducing gambling to a community. They point out that lottery revenue has not solved the education crisis. While lottery revenue certainly has helped schools, it is also undoubtedly true that the lottery funds have given state legislators new freedom to divert other revenues to nonschool purposes.

The benefits of casinos, too, are usually overstated, as casino gambling brings new costs as well as revenues to a community. Cities must increase police activities, build new convention centers, and make other necessary infrastructure improvements in order to support the casinos and the convention trade. High-paying casino jobs also attract talented workers away from a city's school and public health systems. Further, revenues from casinos and lotteries alike often fall short of expected projections as states and cities compete with one another for gambling dollars.

The initial chorus of opposition seems to have muted as more and more states and cities have realized substantial revenue gains from gambling. In Detroit, a public vote in support of casinos finally passed after a number of similar measures had gone down to defeat. The opening of a casino in Windsor (Canada)—just across the river from Detroit—probably had something to do with the change of public opinion in the city.

The degree to which gambling is good for a state or city is to a great degree dependent on how the proceeds of gambling are distributed. Just what percentage goes to the city and to the state? What percentage goes to

TABLE 14.5
User Charges and User-Associated Taxes as a Percentage of General Revenue,
by Level of Government, Various Years

Year	States	Local Governments					
		All	Counties	Municipalities	Townships	School Districts	Special Districts
1962							
Charges	7.1	10.6					
All	16.3	13.7	11.9	17.8	7.8	6.6	48.2
1967							
Charges	8.1	10.8					
All	15.7	13.3	12.3	16.7	8.6	6.9	44.9
1972							
Charges	7.9	10.5					
All	14.0	12.7	13.4	15.3	7.7	5.7	44.3
1977							
Charges	7.1	10.7					
All	11.8	12.6	14.0	14.6	6.6	4.7	39.0
1982							
Charges	6.4	11.4					
All	11.7	14.7	16.6	17.3	9.3	4.9	38.1
1986							
Charges	7.6	13.2					
All	11.9	15.5	17.0	19.0	10.5	4.6	38.5
1991							
Charges	8.6	14.4					
All	17.7	23.0	25.7	27.9	16.0	7.9	55.0

Source: U.S. Department of Commerce (1962, 1967, 1972, 1977, 1982), table entitled
"General Revenue by Type of Government." For 1986 and 1991 data, see the Bureau of the
Census, *Governmental Finance,* 1986 and 1991.

the gambling industry and, where appropriate, the sponsoring Native American tribes? What percentage of gambling proceeds are dedicated to making improvements in the casino district as opposed to being put in the municipal treasury to help pay for more general public services? The exact terms of a gambling agreement determine the extent to which gambling helps a city and its people and not just the state and the gambling industry.

INTERGOVERNMENTAL REVENUES

Intergovernmental assistance to cities takes various forms. By sharing tax revenues, for instance, states return to local governments a portion of some taxes collected within the local jurisdiction. An example of this is the popular motor fuel tax; a percentage of its revenue is given to local jurisdictions to maintain and improve local streets and highways.

Grants-in-aid are a response to the inability of local governments to rely on the property tax and other local taxes, charges, and fees to support an adequate level of municipal services. Over the years, both state governments and the federal government have tended to emphasize categorical grant programs, which are directed at ensuring the provision of certain specified service functions. Such grant assistance is usually given in policy areas where the consequences of local inaction are deemed to be most serious. However, critics charge that the narrowness of aid categories leads to program inflexibility that impedes the performance of local government. As intergovernmental grants often require matching funds from local governments, critics further charge that intergovernmental programs have allowed higher levels of government to gain too great an influence on local resource allocation. In some cases, this is definitely true. But as we discussed in Chapter 12, substantial subnational discretion remains. Grants-in-aid are not always accompanied by a loss of local policy control to the degree alleged by critics of federal programs.

Compared to cities, the federal and state governments possess superior revenue-producing capacities by virtue of their access to the progressive and more income-elastic income tax. The national and state governments can help to equalize the ability of local governments to meet the pressing demands of urban society. However, in recent years, large federal budgetary deficits and tight state budgets have reduced the willingness of these governments to fund housing, community development, mass transit, waste disposal, and other urban programs. As we saw in Chapters 12 and 13, intergovernmental assistance to cities decreased throughout the 1980s and 1990s. In the immediate future, it is not likely to increase in importance in local budgets.[16]

MUNICIPAL BONDS AND THE URBAN DEBT

As costs have increased and funds have become harder to find, urban governments are turning more and more frequently to borrowing in order to support their programs and pay for the growth of new facilities. Short-term obligations are called **tax anticipation notes (TANS)** and are usually repaid in 30 to 120 days from a city's normal revenues.[17] Cities engage in short-term borrowing in order to smooth out irregularities in revenue and expenditure cycles. Cities need money to pay workers, contractors, and suppliers today, yet property taxes may not be due for another month or so. Hence, municipalities borrow against expected revenues.

Most municipal loans, however, are for long-term, not short-term, purposes. They are used to finance capital expenditures such as the purchase of new road-building equipment or the construction of schools or a municipal auditorium. The payment cycle for these long-term bonds is usually over the "useful life" of the goods purchased or the facility constructed. The financial burden of constructing new facilities is not placed solely on the shoulders of present-day taxpayers; future residents of a city will help pay for facilities that they, too, will enjoy. This principle is often referred to as **intergenerational equity**.[18]

There are a variety of long-term borrowing instruments that a city can use to raise money. The most traditional are **general obligation bonds**, also called **full faith and credit bonds**, which impose a legal obligation on the city to appropriate funds in the future to repay the money borrowed. General obligation bonds are only one type of city indebtedness, yet they are often the only type restricted by the state.

Often approval through a public referendum is required before a city can issue general obligation bonds. Such referenda are not easily won. The referendum requirement has impaired local borrowing power, since many citizens vote no because they feel that bond repayment requires tax increases.

Faced with the need for still greater sums of money than those permitted under general obligation bonds, cities have increasingly turned to alternative long-term borrowing instruments. **Revenue bonds** are used to finance the construction of a particular project such as a bridge, parking garage, or civic auditorium. The holders of revenue bonds are repaid from revenues—tolls, user fees, and admission charges—derived from the project. In contrast to general obligation bonds, a city is under no legal obligation to commit future tax money to pay off this debt; rather, the expectation is that tolls and other revenues derived from the completed project will be sufficient to repay the holders of bonds. As the full faith and credit of a city is not put behind revenue bonds, this form of debt incurs a greater risk for lenders than do general obligation bonds. Consequently, cities usually find that they have to pay greater rates of interest on revenue bonds than on general obligation bonds.

Cities have identified still more creative approaches in their search for resources. Under **moral obligation bonds** a city declares a moral obligation to repay borrowed funds. There is no legal obligation for the city to commit revenues for the repayment of debt incurred under moral obligation bonds; nor, in contrast to revenue bonds, are there specific monies derived from a project that are set aside and dedicated to repayment.

Cities have also been able to skirt state borrowing restrictions through **lease-purchase agreements**, whereby a city agrees to the long-term lease of a facility that is built by the private sector. Such an agreement enables the municipality to make capital expenditures for assets and infrastructure improvements that seldom produce revenue. Leased arrangements also allow cities to avoid liability problems that accompany municipal ownership. Public sector leasing is a rapidly growing tool of local government finance.[19]

Investors favor municipal bonds only because the federal income tax exemption for interest earned on such bonds offsets the lower interest rates paid by municipalities to bond holders. If the exemption is ever eliminated, local governments will be forced to pay the going competitive rates of interest in order to borrow funds. Such a development would greatly increase the costs of municipal borrowing and would impede the ability of cities, counties, and school districts to undertake new projects.

Changes in the federal tax code have begun to cloud the future outlook for municipal bonds. The 1986 Tax Reform Act changed provisions regarding the alternative minimum tax to require that interest earned from "tax-exempt" municipal bonds be included in a person's income subject to the minimum tax. This change, in effect, makes these bonds taxable for that category of taxpayers who previously were the largest purchasers of tax-free bonds. The market for municipal bonds was adversely affected by the new minimum tax provisions. New restrictions were also placed on revenue bond usage.

A further threat to municipal borrowing comes from the Supreme Court's 1988 *South Carolina v. Baker* ruling that there is no constitutional requirement that municipal bonds be tax-free. This decision raised the possibility that Congress, should it choose to do so, could attempt to reduce annual federal budget deficits by eliminating altogether the tax exemption of such bonds. While many influential members of Congress declared the critical importance of preserving the tax-exempt status of municipal bonds, growing concern over the size of the annual federal budget deficit led others to look to the taxing of municipal bonds as a potential target of fiscal opportunity.

By the mid-1990s, budgetary "hawks" in both the new Republican congressional majority and conservative "think tanks" were proposing a major overhaul in the federal tax system. They sought to replace the federal income tax, with its multitude of loopholes and tax rates, with a more simplified **flat tax.** But many of the proposed flat tax plans had the potential of seriously disrupting municipal bond markets, as they offered investors no special tax advantage for buying municipal bonds. Should such a flat tax be passed, cities would find that they would have to pay higher interest rates in order to borrow money; they would be able to fund fewer projects.

Borrowing for Municipal Investment: The Case of Orange County

In the face of tight revenue constraints, some localities have sought to put municipal revenues into investments that earn a high rate of return. In some cases, municipalities have even borrowed money to invest in what they hoped would be high-yield investments. By earning money through investments, city financial officers attempt to support continued service provision without raising taxes. Such an investment strategy, though, is not without risk. Should the value of an investment decline, the municipality will have lost money and will find that it is forced to curtail services in order to repay creditors.

In December 1994, Orange County, California, filed for Chapter 9 federal bankruptcy protection, making it the largest municipality in the history of the United States to declare bankruptcy. Orange County already had lost nearly $2 billion from its investment pool and was in the process of auctioning off $1 billion of its most marketable securities. More than 180 other municipalities that had invested in this very interest-sensitive pool were attempting to recoup their investments and loans from the pool.

Orange County got into this financial debacle by accumulating about $12 billion in loans, which were used to pursue an aggressive, but high-risk investment strategy. Faced with state-imposed tax limitations and a constituency unwilling to support new taxes, the county sought to finance continued services by finding investments that paid high interest. But eventually a combination of heavy borrowing and sharply falling interest rates led to the projected $2 billion loss. The county filed for bankruptcy when it could not repay loans as they came due. The county closed library branches, cut school programs, reduced social programs and policing, and stopped testing for fecal coliform bacteria on its beaches. In a controversial move, county officials even proposed that the local sales tax be increased as part of the program to put the county's fiscal house in order. Voters, however, defeated the tax increase despite the urgency of Orange County's situation.

Orange County was not the only local government in the country to be affected by the rapid fall-off in interest rates. Cuyahoga County in Ohio reportedly lost $114 million when it was forced to sell bonds to cover falling interest rates. The investment pools in both the state of Texas and San Diego County, too, reported sharp drops in the market value of their portfolios, but neither appeared to be in danger of losses akin to those of Orange County.

In two important ways, the situation in Orange County stood in sharp contrast to New York City's fiscal default in the 1970s. First, Orange County was an area of affluence and growth; it had not suffered the degree of fiscal distress that New York City experienced in the 1970s. But this southern California area also contained strong antigovernment sentiment, as citizens in Orange County had the ability to pay more for government but most certainly did not wish to do so. State laws such as Proposition 13 also impeded the ability of the locality to find new revenues in the midst of the crisis. Second, Orange County did not seek arrangements that would permit it to repay the full debt owed to city bond holders. New York City had restructured its fiscal house and repaid all the money it owed in short-term debt. Orange County, in contrast, used its declaration of bankruptcy as a negotiating weapon in an attempt to strike a deal under which creditors would agree to accept less than the full amount owed. Such a strategy had the potential of raising borrowing costs for all municipalities and school districts, as Orange County showed investors that a municipal government felt no clear moral obligation to repay in full its debts to its bond holders. Municipal bond buyers would now demand higher rates of interest given the greater risks they occurred in the wake of Orange County's default.[20]

KEY ACTORS IN CITY FINANCE: A LOOK AT BIG CITIES IN CRISIS[21]

As we have already noted, cities routinely borrow money to construct capital facilities and to finance needed projects in the face of revenue constraints. The buyers and sellers of municipal bonds and municipal bond houses are key actors in affecting a city's fiscal health. Other financial institutions, such as Moody's, rate bond quality, thereby determining the creditworthiness of cities and the cost in interest that a city will pay on the issuance of a bond. Moody's, a nongovernmental institution, has been an important player in urban fiscal crises, determining the terms on which New York, Cleveland, and Orange County are allowed to reenter the bond market and borrow money.

A brief survey of New York, Philadelphia, and Washington, DC, will help to underscore the key roles played by various public and private actors alike in shaping a city's response to fiscal distress. In some cities (including Los Angeles in the mid-1990s), local officials have been able to lead. In other cities, local officials are constrained by the power of private sector and intergovernmental actors.

NEW YORK

As we have previously seen, changing demographic and economic patterns made it difficult for New York City to continue to provide services needed by its citizens. The administration of Mayor John Lindsay (1966–74) attempted to maintain social service program levels and cover projected revenue deficits by borrowing money on short-term notes. As these notes became due, they were refinanced at higher and higher rates. New York City also improperly used long-term borrowing in an effort to help finance the city's current operating expenses. Both city and state authorities acted to circumvent debt limitations by resorting to moral obligation bonds to finance housing, medical, and higher education facilities.[22] Private investors willingly cooperated as a result of the promised high returns.

All this came to a head as the Lindsay administration left office and Abraham Beame became mayor. As we reported in Chapter 4, the crisis was precipitated by the decision of Chase Manhattan Bank to "dump" its New York bond portfolio. New York then engaged in massive layoffs of civil servants and a lowering of standards of municipal services. But the city still could not meet its payroll or pay off its debts.[23]

As it turned out, the day before D (for Default) Day, the state imposed a temporary solution on New York City in the form of the Municipal Assistance Corporation (MAC). "Big Mac," as it was called, was set up to transform $3 billion in city short-term debt into state long-term debt. But strings were attached. Big Mac was to receive stock transfer and sales tax revenue (more than $1 billion) that previously had gone to the city. In addition, Big Mac was instructed to impose its own auditing procedures on the city and to audit city agencies. Exasperated by what it considered a long train of city fiscal abuses, the state of New York felt it necessary to force financial controls on New York City as a condition of assistance. The national government eventually offered loan guarantees so that New York would be able to reenter the bond market. But the federal government also set up the Emergency Financial Control Board (EFCB) to overlook the city's finances and to help put the city's fiscal house in order. To a great extent, Big Mac and the EFCB were established as private institutions and demanded that the city "clean up its act" and be run more like a business before they would be willing to buy city bonds once again.

Who were the key actors in this involved game? They included city, state, and federal officials, financial control boards set up by the state, and some important but less visible performers. The banks and the financial community were important, because they determined whether the city could borrow money through the sale of bonds. Moody's and its credit ratings helped to determine the interest that the city would have to pay on its bonds. The municipal pension fund managers were important, because they were under pressure to buy city bonds. If the city went broke, the pension funds of city workers would be jeopardized.

The business community and the bankers emerged with a city much more to their liking. For one thing, the city work force was smaller. Police, sanitation, and social service departments were anywhere from 13 to 20 percent smaller. Second, the unions were able to retain certain contractual gains, but found themselves agreeing to salary deferrals. This, too, pleased the business community which had found some of the union contracts very excessive.[24]

The bankers survived in good shape. Before the crisis, they had continued to market the city's bonds even though there were disturbing indications of the city's fiscal distress. When the city reached the legally allowed limit on general obligation bonds, the financial community advanced lending through the sale of the more risky moral obligation bonds. One can only surmise that the enormous commissions blinded them to the full extent of the emerging crisis.[25] As already noted, once indications of the forthcoming crisis began to surface, it was the bankers who precipitated it by refusing to market or buy the city's bonds. Later in the crisis, the bankers were able to influence Big Mac and the EFCB to achieve additional fiscal and management changes more to their liking. It seems that at every stage of the process the bankers were not only involved and concerned but were also able to exert influence to achieve their goals. Even the removal of political and fiscal autonomy from the city officials and its placement in the hands of two state-appointed boards did not seem to diminish the power of the banking community who, in the long run, continued to control the fate of the city. In reality, it did not matter what device—MAC or EFCB—was created; they would still have to come back to the business and banking communities for the ultimate approval, namely, the sale of the city's bonds.

New York's economy rebounded nicely during the 1980s under the administration of Mayor Ed Koch. Koch realized quickly that he had to gain the support of the business community if he was to stimulate economic development and growth, which would translate into jobs for New Yorkers. Koch and New York were helped by a growing national economy during the Reagan Administration. But a new (though somewhat less severe) fiscal crisis emerged during the administration of Mayor David Dinkins.

By the time Rudy Giuliani was elected mayor in 1993, the city was once again facing huge projected budget deficits. Giuliani immediately put a lid on expenditures and began looking for ways to increase revenues and to cut costs. Many basic programs in the city had to take cuts, and the unions were brought into negotiating sessions to defer or to give back hard-fought collective bargaining gains. There were buyouts and early retirements, but few other union workers lost their jobs. In exchange, job reassignment was used to increase productivity.

Giuliani also proposed contracting out and privatizing many city services that he deemed to be too expensive for the city to manage. Organized labor, which has historically opposed contracting and privatization, appealed to the city council. At this juncture the mayor and his administration entered into negotiations with Democratic leaders on the council over which functions of government could be privatized immediately and which functions would require city council approval for privatization to proceed.

Giuliani made New York City more efficient and businesslike. He instituted necessary reforms and uncovered new economies. But, according to his critics, the city became even less responsive to the needs of racial minorities, organized labor, and the poor as a result of the mayor's policies.

PHILADELPHIA

Much of what Giuliani inherited in New York was similar to the situation that Ed Rendell confronted when he was elected mayor of Philadelphia in 1991. Rendell was confronted with a $200 million budget deficit and a public housing authority that was so corrupt and badly managed that the U.S. Department of Housing and Urban Development, for only the fifth time in its history, took charge of the day-to-day operations of a public housing authority.

Rendell immediately set out to clean house, cut costs, and raise revenues. He developed a five-year fiscal strategy designed to cut the deficit and increase revenues without raising taxes or incurring layoffs or service cuts. Rendell involved the community, department heads, and city council members in all of his pre- and post-fiscal plan deliberations. Rendell sought to build a new consensus in turning Philadelphia around.

Rendell has had his share of difficulties in convincing city workers to buy into his plan. However, he has had much more success working cooperatively with a city council that has long had a reputation for undermining mayoral programs. Rendell was particularly successful in winning council support for his privatization efforts.

Rendell pulled Philadelphia from the brink of fiscal insolvency. He also energized the city with a new infusion of community spirit—even on such small matters as establishing festivals and celebrations to bring people downtown.

Giuliani and Rendell became friends, with the New York mayor openly talking with Rendell regularly about what is working in Philadelphia and what might be applied to New York. Richard Riordan, the Republican mayor of Los Angeles, too, talked frequently with Rendell and even visited the city to view some of the positive changes the Philadelphian has brought about.[26]

Washington, DC

In Washington, DC, there has been no fiscal recovery equivalent to the success achieved by Rendell in Philadelphia. In fact, the severity of the fiscal and social problems in the federal district have been so extreme that they led to the intervention of powerful actors absent from the Philadelphia scene.

In the midst of its fiscal crisis, the district was placed under a federally appointed control board that was given authority over every aspect of the city's financial affairs. The District of Columbia Financial Responsibility and Management and Assistance Authority was created by an act of Congress to ensure that the city undertook the necessary changes to balance its budget within a four-year period.

The district had always complained about its lack of autonomy, that it was in effect the last American federal colony. But in the wake of the fiscal crisis, the federal government became an even more important player than ever in the city's affairs. Low bond ratings had virtually precluded the city from borrowing. Without federal intervention, the city faced certain bankruptcy.

Advocates of the district hoped that the federal government would provide increased aid to help the city through its difficult times. But the new Republican Congress was reluctant to commit increased sums on urban spending, especially when that spending would benefit only one city—especially an overwhelmingly Democratic city! Many congressional actors were convinced that the district itself—through its wasteful practices and unpardonable bookkeeping practices—was responsible for its failures. The city's high murder rate and drug and gang problems further undermined the Congress' confidence in the local government. Many outsiders were particularly scornful of the managerial abilities and alleged misdealings of Mayor Marion Barry, who had been returned to office by the voters despite his past conviction on drug-related charges. They also blamed the mismanagement of previous Mayor Sharon Pratt Kelly, who failed to initiate strong attempts to control spending, as she attempted to extend services in order to win votes in her race against Barry. Yet Democrats and more moderate Republicans saw the necessity of providing the city with some help in order to stave off the ill effects that would result from extreme service cutbacks and bankruptcy in the nation's capitol.

The new fiscal control board was arguably the strongest of its type ever created. It was given much greater powers than those possessed by similar fiscal control boards in New York in the 1970s and Philadelphia in the early 1990s. The new financial responsibility authority in the district was given final say over all city budgets, contracts (including all labor contracts), and loans, as well as supervisory authority in such areas as the city jails and Medicaid system.

Despite the board's power and the further threat it posed to local autonomy, Mayor Barry welcomed its creation. He had little choice if he hoped to gain any heightened federal assistance as the city attempted to escape from its fiscal quagmire. According to some commentators, Barry also welcomed the federal board, as it gave him the political excuse to make the difficult program cuts that had to be effected in order to shrink the city's budget.

The influence of the Republican congressional majority and the business community assured that the focus of efforts would be on reducing the city's payroll, curtailing spending, and putting the city's fiscal house in order. There would be little effort to expand federal assistance or allow the city to tap the wealth of middle-class homeowners and businesses that had migrated to city's suburbs.

EXPENDITURE PATTERNS

How do local governments spend money? The local function upon which the most money is spent is education (see Figure 14.2). Highways, street maintenance and construction, and police and fire protection are other areas of traditional local service responsibility. Health and hospitals and social services have also been increasingly important areas in local budgets.

Cities spend more each year to provide the services demanded of them. Municipal expenditures have grown beyond increases required by population growth and inflation, and we can see that the increases continue to grow each year. Why are expenditures growing so rapidly at the urban level? There are several answers. One is the desire for program expansion on the part of planners and administrators in urban governments. This type of upward pressure on expenditure levels is to be expected at all government levels and serves only to mask the real reasons for rising expenditures.[27]

Pressure for the expansion of public services also comes from the private sector and not just from public sector employees. Increases in the population of metropolitan areas have put increasing pressure on existing governmental services and facilities, and have required an enormous expansion in expenditures just to stay even with demands. Technological changes, too, have led to demand for new public services. Industrial demands on public utilities have grown dramatically, requiring the construction of new facilities. Industrialization and technological developments have created demands for new public services, such as air and water pollution control, to keep the urban environment habitable.

Added to these burdens is the passage of time, the importance of which any automobile owner well knows. The older the equipment owned by the city, the higher are the costs for its maintenance in normal running condition. We can, in fact, expand that metaphor to consider the entire city as a car. As the central cities deteriorate, more and more money must be spent just to keep them minimally habitable. To return them to ideal conditions would take massive sums of money—just as it would cost an enormous amount, probably greater than the original cost, to restore an old automobile to mint condition.

Finally, citizens in urban society are no longer satisfied with the mere maintenance of old governmental service levels. Growth in national productivity and wealth has resulted in rising public expectations. Americans see "the good life" as one of increasing opulence, with expectations of governmental service changing accordingly. What we saw as "frills" yesterday are seen as necessities today, and so our expenditures must continually grow.[28] Citizens want a wider variety of services to choose from, not just more services.

Direct general expenditures by state and local governments have steadily increased. The combined totals rose from $51.9 billion in 1960, to $131.3 billion in 1970, to $367 billion in 1980, and to over a trillion dollars in 1992.[29] While this rise partly represents inflation, it mostly represents demands for new, improved, or extended services. As would be expected, the number of state and local government employees has also risen sharply—from 6.4 million in 1960 to over 15 million in 1992. Figure 14.2 illustrates the order of priorities in expenditures as established by state and local governments.

Do central cities spend more than suburbs? Comparisons of expenditures among municipalities can be very misleading as a result of variations in the governmental structure in urban areas. Comparisons of local government expenditures can be especially specious, as in some communities education is a city or county function while in other communities the schools are run by an independent district with its own separate budgetary authority.

Similar caution must be exercised when attempting to compare the expenditure patterns of jurisdictions within a metropolitan area. For instance, some observers claim that suburban governments are inherently more efficient than central-city governments, as suburban governments tend to spend less per capita than do central cities. However, this comparison often breaks down when the figures are examined in detail. Suburban government may appear more economical because the costs of education are not included in the suburban side of the ledger sheet, inasmuch as education in suburbia is usually provided by independent school districts. Further, in many cases central cities provide services to persons more in need of governmental service. Central cities may also be saddled with the costs of certain services, such as public transit or specialized

FIGURE 14.2
General Expenditure of State and Local Governments, 1992

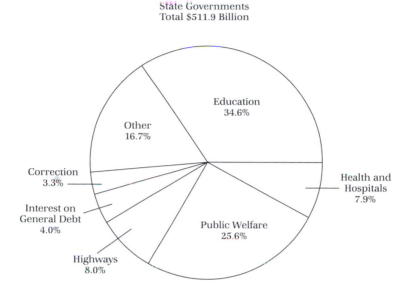

State Governments
Total $511.9 Billion

Source: U.S. Department of Commerce, Bureau of the Census, State Government
Finances, 1992, p. xiii.

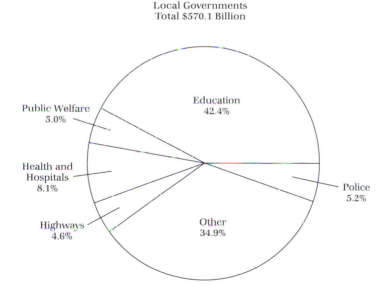

Local Governments
Total $570.1 Billion

Source: Advisory Council on Intergovernmental Relations, *Significant Features of Fiscal
Federalism, 1994,* Table 34, p. 67.

health care, not provided by many suburbs. Hence, the general picture of higher governmental costs in central cities and lower ones in the suburbs is a misleading and unfortunate oversimplification.

THE BUDGETARY PROCESS

Deciding how much money a particular city needs to raise and how available funds are to be spent lies at the heart of any urban political process. Taxpayers' organizations and real estate interests maintain antitax pressures on city councils, local governing boards, and other taxing agencies. Countervailing pressures are numerous, however, as citizen demands for municipal services continue to increase.[30] The bitter conflict engendered within the political process as a result may be relieved in part by the adoption of the **municipal budget**, or operating budget, which details the departmental programs and services for which money is expended on a day-to-day basis.

The responsibility for preparing the budget varies from community to community. In most cases, the executive (usually the mayor or the city manager) is responsible; in others the task falls on the city council, on a legislative committee, or on the executive in conjunction with a legislative committee. In larger cities the chief executive has assistance in the form of a budget (or finance) director, whose job it is to supervise the collection of data and actual formulation of the budget within the guidelines set by the chief executive.

Before the budget can be drawn up, it must be decided where the money will go. This process of setting priorities is probably the most crucial point in the entire budgetary process. Budget makers, like other decision makers, do not operate in a political vacuum. They respond to pressures and opportunities as they perceive them. Budgets determine just how much money will be allocated to different programs.

Not surprisingly, most variations among expenditure levels in American cities have been found to be associated with such population factors as socioeconomic status (SES), age, and mobility.[31] Communities with many low-income residents spend more money per capita on police protection, fire protection, water systems, housing and urban renewal, parks and recreation, and employee retirement programs than do communities on a higher socioeconomic level. The older the population, the more a city can be expected to spend on health care and hospitals, employee retirement, and parks and recreation.

An appropriation act may be of the lump-sum type, or it may be itemized. Under **lump-sum appropriations** each spending agency is granted its funds in a single amount. While this approach encourages flexibility, which is desirable, its successful execution depends on the ability of department heads and their financial officers to plan carefully and competently. In contrast, **itemized appropriations** details exactly how money is to be spent, item by item. It furthers administrative planning, but may result in undue rigidity. Generally, itemized or highly segregated appropriations are looked on with disfavor by fiscal experts.

One device they do favor in order to maintain administrative control while keeping a good deal of flexibility is the **allotment system**. Under this plan each department head is required to divide the total appropriation into four or twelve parts, depending upon whether the allotments are quarterly or monthly, based on the amount the department is expected to spend during each period. Expenditure controls are thereby established, in that the accounting officer will not approve expenditures during a particular quarter or month in excess of the allotment. Of course, the expenditure pattern may be revised from time to time if a crisis or unusual situation arises.

The most commonly used approach to preparing local budgets has been that of **incremental budgeting**. In the incremental approach each municipal department assumes that it will receive at least as much funding in the upcoming fiscal year as it did in the current one. The only decisions remaining relate to the size and purposes of any increase.

Incrementalism is a pervasive characteristic of budgeting for a number of reasons. First of all, incrementalism reduces the amount of information and time needed to prepare a budget. The existing programs or **base** of a budget are for the most part accepted as a given; critical attention is paid only to the proposed additions or increments contained in the budget. Second, incremental budgeting tends to minimize the amount of conflict inherent in the budgetary process. Old issues embedded in the budgetary base are not rehashed every time a budget is presented to the city council. Third, incrementalism encourages compromise and mutual adjustment among competing interest groups, departments, and city agencies. Each group acts to safeguard the programs that it feels are most important.[32]

The criticism of incremental budgeting is that existing programs are never critically scrutinized. Programs that have outlived their usefulness continue to receive funding, and money is not shifted in the budget to meet new priorities.

In recent years, many local governments have had to use **decremental budgeting** as opposed to incremental budgeting. Faced with tight budgets as a result of economic recession, the high costs of inflation, decreased federal grant dollars, and citizens' reluctance to raise taxes, most municipal departments can no longer assume that they will maintain the previous year's budgetary base. Instead, localities had to find new ways of economizing or impose program cutbacks from the existing budgetary base.[33] More and more cities and counties have also developed sophisticated accountability systems designed to assess program and departmental performance. Elected officials have been able to use new tools of performance measurement to help guide difficult decisions concerning the allocation of scarce resources.

CAPITAL BUDGETS

The **capital budget** details proposed capital expenditures and the means for financing them. It complements the regular budgeting process as a financial planning tool. A **capital expenditure** pays for the construction or purchase of a facility that is expected to provide services over a considerable period of time.[34] Rather than raising taxes to pay for a capital project, a local government can sell bonds to finance the project. The process is similar to the way we purchase a home by taking out a mortgage and making monthly payments instead of paying outright for the home at the time of purchase.

How does a municipality determine a plan for capital investment? A capital budget program is founded on economic base studies, land use reports, and population and migration studies. Data on existing industries, the city's economic history, and an analysis of economic development trends are contained in economic base studies. Land use reports reveal population densities and present inventories of property developments. Other reports assess migration trends and the characteristics, income, and talents of the local population.[35] These demographic studies help planners determine future needs for schools, streets, parks, and highways.

Capital projects require long-range planning. Decisions about capital projects are irreversible for an extended period, and without adequate consideration they could result in long-lasting and costly mistakes. Another justification for the capital budget is that, without special programming, important municipal expenditures would be postponed. Capital projects are also sporadic, and their tendency to be concentrated in short periods can be counteracted through the leveling effects of a planned schedule of bond offerings.[36]

For a while, municipalities found it difficult to gain voter approval of bond referenda, especially for the construction of schools. Business groups, parochial and private school parents, and childless couples formed coalitions to oppose new taxes. This trend, however, showed signs of reversing in the early 1990s in many areas of the country as citizens became more aware of local needs that resulted from prior bond rejections.

The advantage of capital budgeting is that it makes possible some measure of long-range planning. Capital and operating budgets may be distinct parts of the same budget document, or they may take the form of separate documents. The distinction between capital and operating expenditures has been made in the financial practices of large corporations for many decades. Local government has tended to imitate corporate practice in this and other fiscal areas.

CURRENT TRENDS AND PROBLEMS

The 1980s and early 1990s were a volatile time for local governments that sought to maintain service delivery levels while balancing local budgets.

Cities and counties experienced serious financial problems as a result of alternating periods of economic recession and high rates of inflation, coupled with a citizens' tax revolt and the decreased availability of federal aid.

Coping with Tax Limitations

In numerous cases, conditions of local fiscal stress were compounded by citizens' movements that enacted tax limitations. The nationwide movement to limit taxes received its greatest impetus in California with the passage of **Proposition 13** in 1978. This constitutional ballot measure, spurred on by a grassroots movement led by antitax crusaders Howard Jarvis and Paul Gann, essentially rolled back property taxes to 1975 levels and limited any annual increase to just 2 percent. It passed by a two-to-one margin. The next year saw a three-to-one victory for Proposition 4 (called the **Gann limit**), which placed a constitutional spending ceiling on all levels of government in California.

Emboldened by their success, Jarvis and his associates placed Proposition 9 on the ballot during the summer of 1980. "Jarvis II," as it was popularly called, would have cut state income taxes by 50 percent. Apparently, though, California voters did not want the severe fiscal austerity that would have resulted from such a radical move to limit state revenues; they rejected Proposition 9 by a substantial majority. Citizens' concern for school funding and the provision of other services had placed an outside boundary on the tax revolt. Yet the spirit of the tax revolt continued.

The tax revolt quickly spread to other states. By the early 1980s nineteen states had already passed some form of tax limitation. Proposition 2½ in Massachusetts probably had the most drastic effect. This amendment provided that the property tax level be reduced from 10 percent of its fair market value to 2½ percent. As a result, the city of Boston made immediate plans for 25-percent cuts in funds for the police and fire departments, 60 percent for the parks department, and 30 percent for the public works department.

How have local governments responded to voter-imposed tax limitations? As the Boston case shows, sometimes the result has been severe local service cutbacks. In California, the immediate impact of Proposition 13 was cushioned by the existence of a large state surplus; the state helped local governments by increasing aid for schools and other key services. The real constraints that Proposition 13 imposed on local service delivery, in effect, were delayed for a few years. Some California communities also held elections, as allowed under the Gann resolution, to authorize increases beyond the spending ceilings.

Localities have also responded to property tax restrictions by searching for new sources of revenue. In California some of the impact of Proposition 13 was ameliorated as localities imposed user charges for services.[37] One popular method of raising funds for new classrooms in

fast-growing school districts was for districts to levy fees on the developers of new subdivisions. In 1986 fees charged developers of new subdivisions ranged from a low of $150 per new home to a whopping $5,604 per
new home in Poway Unified School District in San Diego County.[38] Both
developers and new homeowners complained about the inequitable
nature of such charges.

Some tax limitation measures roll back the assessments faced by
established homeowners in a community, but not the assessments imposed on newcomers. Proposition 13, for instance, rolled back property
assessments to 1975 levels; but once a home was sold, it was reassessed at
current market value. As a consequence, a newcomer to a community
pays a higher tax rate on an equivalent piece of property than does an existing homeowner. Such a "welcome stranger" tax has faced increasing
challenge in the courts. The U.S. Supreme Court in 1989 struck down a
similar practice in Webster County, West Virginia, which systematically assessed newly sold property at higher rates than neighboring properties.
The Court held Webster County's practices to be in violation of the Equal
Protection Clause to the Fourteenth Amendment.[39] But the differential
taxing of resident and newcomer property in California has been upheld
by the courts.

HOME RULE IN TAXATION

States are beginning to answer the problems of localities with inadequate
property tax bases by allowing them to tax other forms of wealth. As we
have already seen, a number of states permit local income and sales taxes.
This developing trend toward increased home rule in taxation policy is
seen as beneficial by many tax experts. The personal income tax allows
government to tap a rich source of income. Yet, state and local income
taxes are generally a flat rate taxes, not the graduated type that forms the
base for the federal income tax. For the most part these state and local
income taxes are levied on gross income and make no allowance for exemptions. Most local governments that have a flat tax start with the federal
or state adjusted gross income, which already includes a number of credits, deductions, and exemptions.

COPING WITH MANDATES

Part of the frustration that led Massachusetts voters to approve Proposition
2½ stemmed from the state legislature's practice of adopting expensive
programs and then mandating that local communities pay for them,
essentially through their property taxes.[40] Massachusetts was not alone in
imposing mandates on its local governments. Throughout the 1980s more
and more states adopted this technique. Some local government officials
complained that mandates pose a bigger problem than do tax limitations.

Cities began to demand that states provide the necessary funds to accompany mandates for service provision. Cities, of course, also complain about the costs of federal mandates.[41]

The 1980s were also characterized by a dramatic increase in local government spending mandated by the courts. One such set of mandates had to do with jail and prison overcrowding. City after city was told to build more jails or release prisoners already incarcerated. Local political officials were caught between the high costs associated with new construction or releasing criminals before their time was up. Neither choice was particularly palatable to an elected official.[42]

In 1995 the federal government passed a law reducing its ability to impose future unfunded mandates on states and cities. The law did little to ease the costs of existing mandates on local governments. Cities claimed that similar legislation was needed at the state level to ensure that state capitols, too, would be restricted in their ability to impose costly new service responsibilities on municipalities.

TRENDS IN MUNICIPAL DEBT

The major trend in urban borrowing is the increased reliance on nonguaranteed debt. In the 1960s and 1970s, general obligation bonds accounted for about 60 percent of long-term municipal borrowing; but by 1982 nonguaranteed debt accounted for 59 percent of the total.[43] According to political scientist Elaine Sharp, cities have resorted to nonguaranteed debt as a way to escape debt limitation ceilings and voter approval requirements. In addition, cities have used industrial revenue bonds for economic development purposes.[44] In the wake of Proposition 13, California cities turned increasingly to the offering of nonguaranteed debt.[45]

Unlike traditional bonds backed by local property taxes and a city's full faith and credit, nonguaranteed bonds are often referred to as **junk bonds** because their repayment is dependent upon revenue derived from the successful completion of a project. Investors purchase these bonds, as they enjoy relatively high returns free of federal income taxes. Yet the purchase of these bonds can engender great risk. This risk became well apparent in the mid- and late 1980s when certain southwestern districts, in the midst of the oil patch crisis of the mid- and late 1980s, were having trouble paying off their debt. For instance, in the Houston area the Northwest Harris County Municipal Utility District No. 19 issued $2.6 million in bonds in 1982 to finance the water and sewer lines for a new housing development. The bonds were to be repaid from the tax revenues derived from the new homeowners. Five years later, "the utility district went bust, leaving investors holding the defaulted bonds."[46] The prospect of such defaults made the purchase of junk bonds in Texas a very risky venture. While cities in other states continued to issue debt, the market for junk bonds in Texas dried up to a great degree. A variation on this theme is found in our earlier discussion of the unwillingness of Orange County, California, to consider it the municipality's "moral obligation" to repay its debt in full.

In some localities new semiautonomous authorities with their own borrowing capacity have been created. These authorities can borrow to build schools, hospitals, airports, or a new stadium, thereby circumventing any debt limitations placed on the general purpose government. However, such off-budget borrowing presents great questions as to public accountability in exercising a city's power. Important borrowing and project decisions are often made by actors who are not fully visible to the public, who are insulated from the citizenry, and who at best are only indirectly controlled by elected officials.[47]

Two interesting examples of authorities with special powers are both located in the state of Florida. The Disney World project in Orlando has its own special district, with greatly enhanced powers, since the park was initiated in the 1960s. More recently the Blockbuster Entertainment Group has won permission from both Dade and Broward counties to create a sports, tourism, and special entertainment district. The new district is to house professional baseball and hockey teams, an amusement park, restaurants, a roller rink, movie theatres, dinner theatres, hotels, broadcasting facilities, and a championship golf course. In order to protect this investment, Blockbuster was given the authority to create its own special purpose government that will hold and exercise all of the traditional powers of a democratically elected government, including the right to issue tax-exempt bonds. Approximately 20,000 full-time jobs will be created at the project. In an era of high-stakes interstate competition, it is likely that more corporations will view the Disney and Blockbuster districts as models to emulate.[48]

CUTBACK MANAGEMENT

Perhaps the most serious problem facing local governments in the 1980s and 1990s was what Charles H. Levine called **organizational decline** or **cutback management**. Cutback management requires that an

> ...organization change toward lower levels of resource consumption and organizational activity. Cutting back an organization involves making hard decisions about who will be let go, what programs will be scaled down or terminated, and what clients will be asked to make sacrifices.[49]

Limits on tax revenues combined with large cuts in federal aid have forced local officials to make better use of available revenues. Local officials are learning to adjust to a shrinking revenue pie.

Reducing the size and scope of local government entails distinct difficulties. First, unlike growing organizations, declining organizations have no incentives to offer their personnel. This reduces the likelihood that proposals for change will be received favorably and creates the possibility of heightened political tensions, particularly between elected officials and public service unions. Second, public organizations have numerous built-in impediments to quick, effective management decision making. Civil service regulations, union contracts, and court orders on equal employment opportunity can all interfere with a rational plan for organizational shrinkage and adjustment.[50] Third, organizations undergoing budget and program cuts develop low morale which hampers the productivity necessary to overcome the cuts. Fourth, declining organizations become more conservative. Fewer risks are taken, and innovation and initiative wane.[51]

The hard choices to be made concern the strategy employed for reducing the size of the organization. The most frequently discussed issue is the "equity" versus "efficiency" approach to cutbacks. Under the **equity approach** each department is asked to take the same percentage cut, thereby eliminating charges of favoritism or political influence. This approach is preferred by most managers because it has an element of justice in it. It is easy to defend before client groups, and it requires little or no in-depth analysis to discriminate among programs.

The **efficiency approach** generates more problems, because it requires targeting those programs for cuts which, after analysis, appear to be most inefficient or expendable. Much staff time is required to assess each program's contribution to the overall mission of the department. Ranking programs and evaluating them economically, politically, and socially often leads to bitter infighting. In some cases the methodology used in the assessment becomes the subject of intense debate. Client groups also involve themselves in these deliberations, hoping to convince administrators that their programs are worthy of continued departmental funding.

Another important question concerns the extent of cuts to be made. Should organizations attempt to make small cuts each year, hoping that an adverse fiscal situation will soon reverse itself? Or should agencies resort to deep cuts early in the process and gamble that funding will be available in later years with which to rebuild the organization? Charles H. Levine points out that the deep-cut approach may make good management sense, but that the decremental (that is, small cuts) approach may be the only feasible political strategy available.[52] Several studies have begun to analyze the administrative and political processes involved in cutback management.[53]

The Clinton administration's plan of "reinventing government," which we discussed in Chapter 13, too, can be considered as an attempt at cutback management. Clinton charged Vice-President Al Gore with the task of conducting a thorough analysis of the major functions of each agency and to report back to the President on how we could create a government that works better and costs less. One year later, in September 1994, the Vice-President's report to the President showed remarkable progress in all facets of government efficiency. The Gore report focused on four major areas of analysis: cutting red tape; returning to basics; putting customers first; and empowering middle managers. The President's commitment and enthusiasm to streamline and downsize the federal government has spread to many local governments. A number of big-city mayors—in Chicago, New York, Philadelphia, Phoenix, Los Angeles, Cleveland, Baltimore and Indianapolis—have begun emulating the national movement in their own cities, particularly in program downsizing and contracting out services.[54]

PUBLIC RISK MANAGEMENT: COPING WITH THE LIABILITY INSURANCE CRISIS

Risk management has been identified as one of the fastest growing fields in local government.[55] Over the past decade or so, increased attention has been paid to how state and local governments can effectively manage risks.

By the early 1980s public risk management was gaining acceptance as an important governmental function. Numerous large cities and counties began hiring, or appointing from within, full-time risk managers who could oversee this very important function of government. Today, risk managers look at public safety, insurance and claims management, workers' compensation, employee training, employee benefits, litigation management, and emergency preparedness. In any operation where there is a risk of human or financial loss, risk managers are involved.[56] Risk management can be divided into five primary functions: exposure identification, risk evaluation, risk control, risk funding, and risk administration.[57]

What caused this new concern for risk management? Cities were facing a "liability crisis" unmatched in contemporary history, one that seriously threatened to impair the ability of local governments to provide residents with necessary and desired services. The two major factors precipitating this crisis were the unpredictability of commercial insurance as a means of protection and the changing nature of the tort system.

In the late 1970s and early 1980s, high interest rates helped create an extremely profitable picture for many commercial insurance companies. Insurance companies collected premiums covering their risks and then invested much of this money at high interest rates.[58] Some companies wrote policies on bad risks to increase their premiums, which in turn were reinvested at high rates of interest.

In the early 1980s both government and the private sector were reaping the benefits of one of the softest and most competitive insurance markets in history. Public agencies were buying extensive coverage, probably more than necessary, for incredibly low premiums. Insurers courted governments by offering multimillion dollar limits of coverage at bargain-basement prices.[59]

In the mid-1980s, however, the pendulum swung, interest rates plummeted, loans on bad risks came due, and the insurance market suffered extraordinary losses. Estimates put the losses for 1985 at $5.5 billion.[60] Some liability insurance coverage for public agencies disappeared almost overnight. State and local governments found themselves victimized by the insurance industry's reaction to the sudden and sharp drop in profitability. Insurance companies, scrambling to recoup their losses, abandoned municipalities and sought to insure what they perceived as the more "predictable risks" found in the private sector.[61]

Small and large jurisdictions from coast to coast saw their policies canceled at midterm. When it came time to renew their policies, many of these communities found their carrier was not interested. Most found that those willing to renew or write their coverage were increasing premiums and offering drastically reduced coverage. Several political jurisdictions without insurance initiated self-insurance programs, while others turned to rapidly growing risk-pooling organizations that were emerging.[62] Other jurisdictions had to cancel such activities as fun-runs and the sale of alcoholic beverages at community festivals due to potential liability problems.

It should be pointed out that the insurance industry did not view the crisis in the same light as did local governments. The insurance industry claimed that the crisis was generated by a litigious society suing state and local governments at an increasing rate. In their eyes the industry was experiencing a tort crisis, not an insurance crisis.[63]

In the summer of 1986, the Public Risk Management Association (PRIMA) surveyed its member cities, counties, states, school districts, and special districts to assess the extent of the damage. Municipalities reported an average increase in premiums of 86 percent, with some respondents reporting increases as high as 350 percent. These increases were accompanied by higher deductibles, lower limits of coverage, and exclusions. In many cases what was excluded made the coverage virtually worthless.[64]

The liability insurance crisis of the mid-1980s made many urban officials nervous. They became painfully aware of how quickly economic conditions could change and how precarious their liability insurance was. Once the crisis subsided and the market for liability insurance opened up again, many local governments began examining their risk management policies. In many instances risk managers were hired and new departments created. In other cases self-insurance became a major option for local governments and school districts. Most important of all was the full realization that municipal liability was a major financial consideration in local government and would continue to be so for the foreseeable future. Local government officials quickly realized the rising importance of professional risk management as a way to ensure that a city, county, or school district faced minimal liability exposure at the same time adequate resources were made available to insure against risk.

CONCLUSIONS

State and local finance is an integral part of the political process. Cities are limited in the taxes they are allowed to levy. The budget sets local political as well as economic priorities. Revenue policy and expenditure policy reflect the values of society as perceived and understood by the political branches of government. From time to time one or another emphasis may shift in response to changes in demands made upon the decision-making agencies.

Cities are faced with many problems that are, at the core, financial in nature. There are severe revenue limitations placed upon cities by states. National economic policy, with its effects upon inflation, unemployment, recession, and interest rates, has a strong impact on both local revenues and expenditures. Further, localities are often forced to spend money on required services as a result of state and federal mandates. The impact of national economic cycles and state and local mandates is felt in both growing and stagnating cities alike. In times of recession, the nation's most fiscally troubled cities have had problems in finding the funds necessary for infrastructure repair and the provision of needed social services. The result of such constrained fiscal circumstances has been an upswing in municipal borrowing, particularly in nonguaranteed urban debt.

Given these difficult conditions, it is conceivable that cities will not be able to assume the responsibilities assigned to them under the various New Federalism proposals, nor assume most of the costs of federal program cuts. There is little reason to believe that states and localities are financially capable of undertaking vast new investment programs in areas such as road construction, bridge repair, and public transit. Confronted by fiscal austerity, local governments have even had to postpone scheduled infrastructure improvements.

In the face of economic conditions that increase service costs while constricting local revenues, cities are often forced to raise taxes. Yet this can backfire by encouraging businesses to look elsewhere for more favorable tax situations. Cities and their surrounding suburbs are often embarked on intense competitive struggles both to retain existing businesses as well as to attract new ones. The struggle among the states is even more intense. Automobile manufacturers, airline hubs, and new athletic stadiums are among the most sought-after projects to assist economic development activities.[65] Many businesses, for instance, find it just as convenient to locate in New Jersey or Connecticut as in New York City. To the extent that such development patterns emerge, the city loses potential revenue.

One alternative to raising taxes is for cities to begin a program of cutback management. Several techniques are available to city officials in helping them to reduce costs. However, few of the choices are pleasant to make or easy to implement since they involve reducing spending in important service areas and shrinking the municipal work force. Each of these choices has political and administrative ramifications for the political actors in the city. Cutback management policies often redistribute power within the urban political system.[66]

As we have seen, cities continually seem to be experiencing tough fiscal times. A reshaped intergovernmental system has given states and cities new service responsibilities. Taxpayer revolts have further limited local revenues. Both growing and declining municipalities alike have had great difficulty in providing the full range of services expected by citizens. What, then, is the future of cities as the United States prepares to enter the twenty-first century? The answer to this question is the subject of our concluding chapter.

NOTES

1. Elaine B. Sharp, *Urban Politics and Administration: From Service Delivery to Economic Development* (New York: Longman, 1990), pp. 153–54.
2. John B. Smith and John S. Klemanski, *The Urban Politics Dictionary* (Santa Barbara, CA: ABC CLIO, 1990), p. I-5 ("Income Sources, Urban").
3. Sharp, *Urban Politics and Administration*, p. 162. Michigan in the early 1990s voted to limit the use of the property tax as a basis for school financing. Similar discussions are underway in Wisconsin, Idaho, Vermont, and South Carolina. See Scott Mackey, "The Property Tax Predicament," *State Legislatures* (August 1994), pp. 23–26.
4. Summer Benson, "A History of the General Property Tax," in *The American Property Tax: Its History, Administration, and Economic Impact*, ed. George C. S. Benson (Claremont, CA: Institute for Studies in Federalism, The Lincoln School of Finance, Claremont Men's College, 1965), pp. 33–44 and 52–59.
5. In a survey conducted by the ACIR, the property tax ranked just behind the federal income tax as the least fair tax paid by the public. See *Changing Public Attitudes on Governments and Taxes* (Washington, DC: Advisory Commission on Intergovernmental Relations, 1993), p. 3.
6. *State and Local Taxes: Significant Features* (Washington, DC: Advisory Commission of Intergovernmental Relations, 1986), p. 7.
7. For a discussion of the property tax, see J. Richard Aronson and John L. Hilley, *Financing State and Local Governments*, 4th ed. (Washington, DC: Brookings Institution, 1986), chapter 7. Also see Ronald C. Fisher, *State and Local Public Finance* (Glenview, IL: Scott, Foresman, 1988), chapters 7 and 8; and David R. Morgan, *Urban America*, 3rd ed. (Pacific Grove, CA: Brooks/Cole, 1989), pp. 262–71. For a discussion of recent changes in property taxes, see Scott Mackey, "The Property Tax Predicament," *State Legislatures* (August 1994), pp. 23–26. Also see Richard Netzer, "Property Taxes: Their Past, Present and Future Place in Government Finance," in *Urban Finance Under Siege*, ed. Thomas R. Swartz and Frank J. Bonello (Armonk, NY: M. E. Sharpe, Inc., 1993), pp. 51–78.
8. Sharp, *Urban Politics and Administration*, p. 153.
9. For a discussion of sales taxes, see Aronson and Hilley, *Financing State and Local Governments*, chapter 5; and Fisher, *State and Local Public Finance*, chapter 9.

10. Ronald K. Snell, "Our Outmoded Tax Systems," *State Legislatures* (August 1994), pp. 17–18. Also see Irene Rubin, *The Politics of Public Budgeting*, 2nd ed. (Chatham, NJ: Chatham House, 1993), chapter 2. Also see James J. Gosling, *Budgeting Politics in American Governments* (White Plains, NY: Longman Publishing, 1992), chapter 6.

11. Income taxes are discussed in Fisher, *State and Local Government Public Finance*, chapter 10.

12. Don Cozzetto, Mary Kweit, and Robert Kweit, *Public Budgeting: Politics, Institutions and Processes* (White Plains, NY: Longman Publishers, 1995), pp. 157–159.

13. For an analysis of user fees as a viable revenue raising source, see Morgan, *Managing Urban America*, pp. 267–69. Also see Aronson and Hilley, *Financing State and Local Government*, pp. 155–59; and Fisher, *State and Local Government Public Finance*, chapter 16. Also see C. Kurt Zorn, "User Charges and Fees," in *Local Government Finance*, ed. John Peterson and Dennis Strachota (Chicago: Government Finance Officers Association, 1991), chapter 8; and Paul B. Downing, "The Revenue Potential of User Charges in Municipal Finance," *Public Finance Quarterly* 20 (October 1992), pp. 512–27.

14. E. S. Savas, *Privatization: The Key to Better Government* (Chatham, NJ: Chatham House, 1987), pp. 248–50.

15. See ACIR, *Changing Public Attitudes on Government and Taxes*, p. 52.

16. Steven D. Gold and Brenda M. Erikson, "State Aid to Local Governments in the 1980s," *State and Local Government Review* 21 (Winter 1989): 11–22. Also see chapters 12 and 13 for further documentation as to the cutbacks in intergovernmental funding.

17. The various types of municipal bonds are described in Cozzetto, Kweit, and Kweit, *Public Budgeting*, pp. 167–69. Also see Mikesell, *Fiscal Administration* (Belmont, CA: 1991), chapter 13.

18. See Fisher, *State and Local Public Finance*, chapter 12; and Aronson and Hilley, *Financing State and Local Government*, chapter 9.

19. Sharp, *Urban Politics and Administration*, pp. 177 and 198–99.

20. "Trouble in Paradise," *U.S. News and World Report* (December 19, 1994), pp. 52–54; Frank Shafroth, "Muni Bond Market Evens Out as Orange County Situation Unfolds," *Nation's Cities Weekly* (December 19, 1994), p. 13; James Sterngold, "Orange County: Reluctant Fiscal Test Case," *The New York Times*, June 1, 1995; Leslie Wayne, "Banging a Tin Cup With a Silver Spoon: Orange County's Tough Approach Tests Municipal Finance System," *The New York Times*, June 4, 1995; and Mitchell Benson, "Rest of State Pays 'Orange County Tax,'" *San Jose Mercury News*, June 29, 1995.

21. Two interesting studies of the key actors in urban finance are Esther R. Fuchs, *Mayors and Money: Fiscal Policy in New York and Chicago* (Chicago: University of Chicago Press, 1992); and Charles Brecher and Raymond Horton, *Power Failure: New York City Politics and Policy Since 1960* (New York: Oxford University Press, 1993).

22. Robert W. Bailey, *The Crisis Regime: The MAC, the EFCB, and the Political Impact of the New York City Fiscal Crisis* (Albany, NY: State University of New York Press, 1984), p. 151. Also see Jack Newfield and Paul DuBrul, *The Abuse of Power: The Permanent Government and the Fall of New York* (New York: Penguin, 1977), pp. 18 –20 and 36.

23. Comprehensive analyses of the New York City fiscal crisis can be found in Martin Shefter, *Political Crisis, Fiscal Crisis: The Collapse and Revival of New York City* (New York: Basic Books, 1985); William K. Tabb, *The Long Default: New York City and the Urban Fiscal Crisis* (New York: Monthly Review Press, 1982); Charles Brecher and Raymond D. Horton, eds., *Setting Municipal Priorities: American Cities and the New York Experience* (New York: New York University Press, 1984); and Brecher and Horton, *Power Failure*, 1993.

24. See Shefter, *Political Crisis/Fiscal Crisis*, chapter 6.

25. Newfield and DuBrul, *The Abuse of Power*, pp. 17–21 and 36–49.

26. Rendell has proved to be very popular with the press. He came across as an urban hero. See Jacob Weisberg, "Philadelphia Story," *New York* (May 2, 1994), pp. 30–32; Neal Peirce, "The City of Philadelphia Tries Reinvented Government," *County News* (June 7, 1993), p. 14; Denise Baker, "Philadelphia Rebuilds Fiscal House with Savings," *Nation's Cities Weekly* (April 20, 1992), pp. 1 and 4; and Ben Yagoda, "Mayor on a Roll: Ed Rendell," *The New York Times Magazine* (May 22, 1994), pp. 26, 28, 29.

27. See Fisher, *State and Local Public Finance*, chapter 14; and Morgan, *Managing Urban America*, pp. 271–72.

28. Fisher, *State and Local Public Finance*, pp. 288–93.

29. ACIR, *Significant Features of Fiscal Federalism* (Washington, DC: Advisory Commission on Intergovernmental Relations, 1994), vol. 2, pp. 45 and 47.

30. For an overview of citizen feelings about taxes, see ACIR, *Changing Public Attitudes on Governments and Taxes*.

31. Rubin, *The Politics of Public Budgeting*. This is the most comprehensive analysis of public budgeting. Also see Cozzetto, Kweit, and Kweit, *Public Budgeting*, chapter 4.

32. Charles Lindblom, "The Science of Muddling Through," *Public Administration Review* 19 (Spring 1959): 79–88; and Aaron Wildavsky, "A Budget for All Seasons? Why the Traditional Budget Lasts," *Public Administration Review* (November/December 1978): pp. 501–502 and 508.

33. See Irene S. Rubin, ed., *New Directions in Budget Theory* (Albany, NY: State University of New York Press, 1988), pp. 3–5; Morgan, *Managing Urban America*, pp. 272–82; Susan A. MacManus, "Budget Battles: Strategies of Local Government Officers During Recession," *Journal of Urban Affairs* 15 (1993): 293–307; and Michael A. Pagano, "Balancing Cities' Books in 1992: An Assessment of City Fiscal Conditions," *Public Budgeting and Finance* (Spring 1993), pp. 19–30.

34. J. Richard Aronson and Eli Schwartz, *Management Policies in Local Government Finance* (Washington, DC: International City Management Association, 1987), p. 400. Also see Aronson and Hilley, *Financing State and Local Governments*, pp. 203–07.

35. Aronson and Schwartz, *Management Policies in Local Government Finance*, pp. 406–08. Also see Michael Pagano, *Tax Reform and City Capital Spending* (Washington, DC: National League of Cities, 1986), chapter 1. John P. Forrester, "Municipal Capital Budgeting: An Examination," *Public Budgeting and Finance* 13 (Summer 1993): 85–103. Also see Robert L. Bland and Samuel Nunn, "The Impact of Capital Spending on Municipal Operating Budgets," *Public Budgeting and Finance* 12 (Summer 1992): 32–47.

36. Aronson and Schwartz, *Management Policies in Local Government Finance*, pp. 400–01.

37. Terry Schwadron, ed., *California and the American Tax Revolt: Proposition 13 Five Years Later* (Berkeley, CA: University of California Press, 1984), pp. 104–12. Also see Peter J. May and Arnold J. Meltsner, "Limited Actions, Distressing Consequences: A Selected View of the California Experience," *Public Administration Review* 41 (January 1981), 172–79; and C. Kurt Zorn, "User Charges and Fees," in *Local Government Finance*, ed. Peterson and Strachota, chapter 8.

38. Lillianne Chase, "Funny-money Classrooms," *Golden State Report* (September 1986), p. 34. Also see David R. Elkins and Elaine B. Sharp, "Living with the Tax Revolt: Adaptions to Fiscal Limitations," *Public Administration Quarterly* 15 (Fall 1991): 272–86.

39. *Allegheny Pittsburgh Coal Co. v. County Commission of Webster County, West Virginia*, U.S. 87-1303 (1989). Also see Lee Ruck, "Supreme Court Requires Fairness in Assessments," *County News* (a publication of the National Association of Counties, Washington, DC), April 10, 1989.

40. See Marcia Whicker Taylor, "State Mandated Local Expenditures: Are They Panacea or Plague?" *National Civic Review* 69 (September 1980): 435–51.

41. ACIR, *Mandates: Cases in State and Local Relations* (Washington, DC: Advisory Commission on Intergovernmental Relations, September 1990); Joseph F. Zimmerman, "State Mandate Relief: A Quick Look," *Intergovernmental Perspective* (Spring 1994), pp. 28–30. Also see *Legislative Mandates: State Experiences Offer Insights for Federal Action* (Washington, DC: General Accounting Office, September 27, 1988).

42. Jeffrey D. Straussman, "Courts and Public Purse Strings: Have Portraits of Budgeting Missed Something?" *Public Administration Review* 46 (July/August 1986): 345–51.

43. Sharp, *Urban Politics and Administration*, p. 158.

44. Ibid.

45. Georginia Fiordalisi, "Municipal 'Junk Bonds' Piling Up," *City and State*, April 10, 1989, pp. 9–10.

46. Ibid., p. 9.

47. Sharp, *Urban Politics and Administration*, pp. 176–77 and 201–08. Also see Dennis Zimmerman, *The Private Use of Tax Exempt Bonds: Controlling Public Subsidy of Private Activity* (Washington, DC: The Urban Institute Press, 1991), chapters 2 and 4.

48. Jill Conley, "Blockbuster Wins Own Quasi-Government in Florida," *County News*, September 26, 1994, p. 10.

49. See Charles H. Levine, "More on Cutback Management: Hard Questions for Hard Times," *Public Administration Review* 39 (March/April 1979): 1; and Charles H. Levine, "Organizational Decline and Cutback Management," *Public Administration Review* 38 (July/August 1978): 316–25.

50. See Straussman, "Courts and Public Purse Strings," p. 345.

51. Levine, "More on Cutback Management," p. 180.

52. Levine, "Organizational Decline," p. 320; and Levine, "More on Cutback Management," pp. 181–82.

53. See Levine, Rubin, and Wolohojian, *The Politics of Retrenchment*, for a comparative analysis of how Oakland, Baltimore, Cincinnati, and Prince Georges County, Maryland, dealt with issues of retrenchment.

54. The reinventing government movement was spawned by the publication of David Osborne and Ted Gaebler, *Reinventing Government: How the Entrepreneurial Spirit is Transforming the Public Sector from Schoolhouse to*

Statehouse, City Hall to the Pentagon (Reading, MA: Addison-Wesley, 1992). Also see Al Gore, *From Red Tape to Results: Creating a Government that Works Better and Costs Less* (Washington, DC: U.S. Government Printing Office, 1993), pp. 35–40. For a first-year analysis, see Donald F. Kettl, *Reinventing Government? Appraising the National Performance Review* (Washington, DC: The Brookings Institution, 1994).

55. Lauren Cragg and H. Felix Kloman, "Risk Management: A Developed Discipline," in *Risk Management Today*, ed. Natalie Wasserman and Dean G. Phelus (Washington, DC: International City Management Association, 1985).

56. Nester Roos, "Risk Management: Selected Characteristics For Individual Cities and Counties," *Urban Data Service Reports* 14 (Washington, DC: International City Management Association, February 1982). Also see R. Bradley Johnson and Bernard H. Ross, "Risk Management in the Public Sector," *Municipal Yearbook* (Washington, DC: International City Management Association, 1989), pp. 1–11.

57. Cragg and Kloman, "Risk Management: A Developed Discipline," p. 7.

58. Jay Muzychenko, "Local Governments at Risk: The Crisis in Liability Insurance," *Municipal Yearbook* (Washington, DC: International City Management Association, 1987), pp. 3–7.

59. Roos, "Risk Management."

60. Muzychenko, "Local Governments at Risk," p. 3.

61. Eric Meyer, "The Morning After: Emerging from the Hard Market," *Public Management* 68 (November 1986): 6–8.

62. See Meyer, "The Morning After," pp. 6–8; Roos, "Risk Management"; and Kathleen Sylvester, "Do-It-Yourself Insurance," *Governing* (October 1987): 56–63.

63. Susan A. MacManus, "Litigation: A Real Budget Buster for Many U.S. Municipalities," *Government Finance Review* 10 (February 1994), pp. 27–31.

64. See Jay Muzychenko, "PRIMA Survey Reflects Insurance Trends," *Public Risk* (January/February, 1987): 8.

65. Charles Mahtesian, "Romancing the Smokestack," *Governing* (November 1994): 36–40. Also see "Hold Up in the Windy City," *U.S. News and World Report* (July 17, 1989): 40–41. Also see Andrew O'Rourke, "Counties Should Stop Free Rides When Corporations Skip Town," *County News* (March 16, 1992): 2.

66. Terry Nichols Clark and Lorna Crowley Ferguson, *City Money: Political Processes, Fiscal Strain and Retrenchment* (New York: Columbia University Press, 1983); and Robert W. Burchell and David Listokin, *Cities Under Stress: The Fiscal Crises of Urban America* (Piscataway, NJ: Center for Urban Policy Research, Rutgers University, 1981).

15

The Future of
Urban America

What is the future of urban America? In this chapter we point to three important factors that will continue to shape cities and suburbs as they enter the twenty-first century. First, we observe that economic development policy will continue to take primacy in the urban policy arena. Second, we explore the prospects for minority power. Finally, we conclude by discussing the future of national urban policy. As we shall see, American urban policy is at a crossroads. There is no consensus as to just what direction federal policy should take in attempting to ameliorate the problems faced by cities and suburbs.

CONTINUING EMPHASIS ON ECONOMIC DEVELOPMENT

Urban politics in the 1990s has become increasingly identified as the politics of local economic growth and development. While some urban observers believe that the preoccupation of local government with economic development will pass as the costs of growth become apparent, we believe that there will be no lessening in the near future in the intercity competition for business. In the wake of the tax revolt and the downscaling of federal aid, local governments will continue to pursue policies designed to attract and retain business. Only more affluent and better-off cities and suburbs will be able to resist the temptations of new development and, instead, seek to impose growth-control measures aimed at preserving the local quality of life.

As cities compete for economic development, business—particularly big business—will continue to occupy "the driver's seat" as it seeks tax advantages, infrastructure improvements, and other favorable considerations from local policy makers. Economists and other urban specialists frequently object that such awards are too freely dispensed. Numerous studies show that tax concessions are rarely as important a factor in business-siting decisions as is commonly believed. A firm must locate in reasonable proximity to suppliers, a trained labor force, and the market for its goods; tax considerations take secondary importance to these concerns.

Yet the evidence on this point is ambiguous. City officials cannot know for sure just when a tax concession will or will not prove to be an important influence in a business's decision. Local tax policy may prove to be an important influence on a corporation's choice of locales within a metropolitan area inasmuch as access to suppliers, a qualified labor force, and markets is relatively the same throughout much of the metropolis.[1]

But even if tax concessions and other subsidies lack a great influence on a firm's siting decision, just the perception that they are important gives a business power. Local officials believe that they must act aggressively in order to be "players" in a highly competitive, economic development game. They believe that they will lose business unless they are able to anticipate and match the package of development subsidies offered by neighboring and more distant jurisdictions.

Businesses that receive tax abatements and other concessions are the clear winners in this economic development game. But who are the losers in an urban arena increasingly preoccupied with economic development? Who pays for the concessions that are given businesses?

Local economic development officials and members of the local growth coalition contend that no one pays—that new businesses contribute to the city tax base and help to pay for other services. At times, this proves to be the case.

But at other times, the new revenues generated by a business do not cover the costs of the services that the city provides—especially if the full costs of tax abatements, infrastructure improvements, and other municipal service concessions demanded over time are factored into the equation. In such cases, the burden of supporting a business falls on a city's neighborhoods and small businesses. They will suffer as municipal services are redirected and their taxes are increased to support the new business. Added to this are the costs that development imposes on a community in terms of increased congestion, crime, and displacement. The local school system suffers when developmental policy cuts the rates of taxation on industrial property or creates a tax increment financing district or other structure that dedicates new tax revenues to the improvement of facilities in the industrial district.

Some urbanists observe that for cities to stay competitive, they will need to engage in even "more future-oriented public policies regarding infrastructure development."[2] As urban sociologist John Kasarda continues, the "successful cities of the future will develop computer-age infrastructures that will provide them with comparative advantages for processing and transmitting information."[3] Kasarda suggests that municipal officials "wire" cities to provide the infrastructure needed by business in an information age. Cities can even have municipal "supercomputer facilities" that can be leased to information-processing businesses on a cost-sharing basis. City officials must also address the quality-of-life concerns needed to make their cities more attractive to high-technology firms and their higher-income and better-educated work forces.

The danger, of course, is that cities will exacerbate **uneven development** by pursuing policies that meet the demands of corporations and their technologically competent work forces at the cost of ignoring the housing and service needs of their less fortunate residents.[4] For example, in New York City, offices, upscale retail, hotels, and restaurants have driven out all but luxury housing south of 96th Street. The city has acted to preserve older manufacturing areas as possible sites for future commercial expansion, denying their use as possible sites for affordable housing. The new convention center and other large-scale economic development projects have had the effect of driving up the price of housing in surrounding neighborhoods. In such a tight housing market, private developers build for the well-off. In the absence of strong municipal action, the housing needs of the poor, displaced manufacturing workers, and newly arrived immigrants are ignored.[5]

Why is it that city growth projects often face little effective opposition? In Chapter 3, we observed the considerable power advantages enjoyed by progrowth forces. Economic development projects enjoy yet another important advantage in terms of the relative visibility of the costs and benefits entailed by growth. The threat by a big business to leave a community can be quite dramatic. City decision makers do not want to be blamed for the closing of a major business or the loss of the local baseball or football team. The sponsors of a growth project have a substantial material stake in making sure that the project gains city approval. By contrast, the costs of paying subsidies are spread over the long term and are far less visible. The costs of financing a project are also more diffuse as they are borne by a much larger population. Only when a growth project imposes an immediate threat to a specific community does intense opposition usually mobilize.

In more and more cities, active citizen groups—homeowner associations, environmentalist organizations, small business owners resistant to new taxes, and inner-city racial minority and neighborhood groups—act as a partial counterweight challenging the power of corporate elites. At times, coalitions of such forces have led local governments to enact policies of balanced growth that seek to ameliorate the problems associated with unconstrained economic development. Yet, in many metropolitan areas, quasi-independent authorities and special districts have been created to insulate public-private growth partnerships from direct accountability to the public.

In the Sunbelt, the rise of citizen activism has already brought new challenges to the region's historic pattern of downtown-business-elite dominance. A new assertiveness by homeowners, environmentalists, and the region's rising number of minority citizens has tempered the power of the old civic elite and the managers of the newer international corporate elite. This new citizen activism has helped to add a new degree of balance to local political systems in the Sunbelt.[6] Yet the power of the civic and corporate elites still proves substantial.

Numerous public policy strategies could conceivably lessen local economic dependence. Federal revenue sharing, metropolitan tax base sharing, plant closing laws, strict land use regulation, and targeted economic development programs are all strategies that would leave cities in a less precarious economic position.[7] But there is little will in the United States to enact such solutions on a widespread basis. Free-market economists question the wisdom of plant closing laws and strong land use controls. Suburbanites generally object to tax base sharing with more impoverished jurisdictions. Federal policy has moved in the exact opposite direction—of exacerbating, not ameliorating, local economic dependence—by terminating revenue sharing and greatly reducing housing and community development programs. More than ever in recent decades, cities and suburbs will have to pursue economic development as they are left to fend for themselves.

In such an environment, there are no clear borders between economic development and other urban issues. Economic development concerns are seen to intrude on virtually all urban arenas. Such was the case when, in 1995, the Federal Department of Housing and Urban Development (HUD) announced that it was taking from the Chicago Housing Authority (CHA) the responsibility for managing the city's extensive public housing stock. HUD announced that, as part of its plan, it would demolish some of the larger CHA high rises after having first moved tenants into vacant units in other public housing buildings. HUD Secretary Henry Cisneros also announced that more habitable, low-rise buildings would be constructed in place of the units that were to be torn down. But residents of a number of the targeted housing projects were suspicious. HUD's initial demolition plans called for demolishing some of the bigger buildings in Henry Horner Homes and Cabrini-Green—two north side projects that bordered increasingly valuable land in the city. Henry Horner Homes was within blocks of the new United Center—the home of the Chicago Bulls and the 1996 Democratic convention—and other "West Loop" developments just outside of downtown. The city would want to "improve" this area for visitors. Similarly, Cabrini-Green was within walking distance of Chicago's "Magnificent Mile"—some of the most expensive property in the country—and the city's growing night-life areas. Would the federal takeover correct the mismanagement of the CHA and improve the conditions in public housing? Or would it also facilitate plans to displace large numbers of predominantly poor, black people in an effort to abet the city's economic development? Questions of housing policy and economic development were inexorably intertwined.

THE FUTURE OF MINORITY EMPOWERMENT

The more strident confrontations between minority groups and city hall of the 1960s and 1970s have yielded to a minority politics that emphasizes electoral power, coalition building with sympathetic elements in the white community, and the importance of community groups in service delivery. Commenting on the transformed style of Hispanic politics, Roberto Villarreal, Norma Hernandez, and Howard Neighbor observe that the radicalism of the 1970s has been replaced by "the policies of accommodation and recognition."[8]

Black and Hispanic citizens gained new opportunities for power as they made up increasingly large percentages of the population of central cities and inner-ring suburbs. But the growing minority percentages do not guarantee the genuine empowerment or political incorporation of these groups.[9] For Mexican-Americans, for instance, the gain of power "seems to be more an achievement of the conservative middle class than of the masses."[10] The Hispanic community also continues to be severely underrepresented in both elected office and top administrative policy-making positions. For instance, Chicanos in 1986 comprised 70 percent of El Paso's population but held only a third of the high-level positions in the municipal bureaucracy.[11] It took pressure from both citizen groups and the federal district court to force the Los Angeles County Board of Supervisors in 1990 to adopt a redistricting plan that would at long last give Hispanics a majority in one district. Minority vigilance is especially important during times of legislative redistricting to ensure that legislatures and courts draw district lines that maximize, rather than dilute, minority voting power.[12]

Since the 1940s, the Supreme Court has been a friend of African-American and Latino groups as they have attempted to win voting rights. But a number of more recent Supreme Court decisions may indicate that there is a limit to the extent that the Court will go in affirming plans that attempt to maximize minority voting representation. In **Shaw v. Reno** (1993), the Supreme Court struck down a race-conscious redistricting plan that strung together pockets of African-American concentration across North Carolina in an effort to create a black-majority congressional district.[13] Although the Court did not strike down all race-conscious redistricting plans (other race-conscious efforts to create minority-majority districts have been upheld by the federal courts), *Shaw v. Reno* clearly suggests that there is a limit as to how irregularly a district can be shaped or gerrymandered in an effort to maximize minority representation. White citizens can be expected to challenge as a denial of their voting rights any plan that entails the drawing of oddly shaped districts in an attempt to increase the representation of racial minorities.

In 1994, a staunchly divided Supreme Court gave yet another indication that it would not simply endorse just any plan designed to decrease existing barriers to minority voting rights. The municipal government in Bleckley, Georgia, was run by a single-commissioner arrangement. African-Americans, who made up one-fifth of the county's population, were effectively shut out from the county government by the single-commissioner plan. They claimed that the single-commissioner plan was used by this southern community in an attempt to deny them an elected voice in county government. But in **Holder v. Hall**, the Supreme Court majority was not willing to assume that there was a racial motivation behind the plan. The Court spurned the request to order Bleckley to replace its single-commissioner system with a five-member system elected by district that would likely result in the presence of an African-American on the reconstituted commission.[14]

Does an African-American or Latino electoral victory in city elections bring with it the full fruits of victory? Racial minorities have attempted to use their newfound access to city hall—especially in majority-minority communities—to use city resources in an effort to bring new job opportunities to minority communities. But can cities show a preference in dispensing city contracts to minority-owned firms and firms that agree to racial hiring targets? Here, too, Supreme Court decisions have had an important impact on the prospects for minority empowerment.

In 1989 the Supreme Court handed down three decisions imposing new restrictions on the use of minority set-aside and affirmative action programs. Of the three, the Court's decision in **Croson v. City of Richmond** had the greatest significance for minority incorporation.[15]

In *Croson*, the Court struck down a program under which the city of Richmond required that at least 30 percent of the total dollar amount of municipal contracts be awarded to minority firms. When blacks gained control of city hall a decade earlier, the minority set-aside program was one of the first measures the city council enacted. Before passage of the ordinance, black firms had received less than 1 percent of the city's business despite the fact that blacks accounted for over half the city's population. According to the law's supporters, the program was needed both to correct a clear case of discrimination and to build up businesses in, and bring jobs to, the black community. But white-owned businesses countered that the law amounted to reverse discrimination in that a white-owned firm submitting the lowest bid could not receive a contract unless it first agreed to award 30 percent of the work to minority contractors.

In striking down the statute in question, the Supreme Court effectively announced that such programs were to be subjected to "strict scrutiny," a stipulation that will likely be very difficult for many cities to meet. A city cannot just allege a history of past discrimination and thereby justify new, ameliorative minority preferences. Instead, the city must present evidence that demonstrates that the city had engaged in unconstitutional discrimination in the service area under question. Statistical analysis pointing to the disparity between the number of minority businesses in a market area and the percentage of a city's contracts they received could be used as evidence to help establish the existence of a pattern of discrimination. But before the court would approve the adoption of a minority set-aside program, the city must also show the court why more temporary and race-neutral programs cannot be relied upon to correct the discrimination.[16]

The *Croson* ruling impedes, but does not spell the end of, municipal affirmative action and contract compliance programs. Cities that can document a history of local discrimination can continue to justify the award of preferences as a remedy. But such programs would have to be narrowly drawn to survive court scrutiny. Also, programs that give minority group members special training or that set hiring and contracting targets and goals without imposing quotas are more likely to withstand court challenge.

The immediate effects of *Croson*, however, were substantial. In the wake of the Court's ruling, lower courts struck down similar programs in San Francisco, Atlanta, Philadelphia, Birmingham (Alabama), Jacksonville, Multnomah County (Oregon), and the states of Florida, Michigan, Minnesota, and Wisconsin. Local governments around the country began to repeal or severely limit their minority set-aside programs. San Jose, Ft. Lauderdale, South Bend (Indiana), Minneapolis, Durham (North Carolina), Salem County (Oregon), and the New Orleans school board were among the great many jurisdictions that suspended or terminated their set-aside programs in the wake of the *Croson* decision. The Port Authority of New York and New Jersey, too, voluntarily suspended its use of minority set-asides out of fear of possible lawsuits.[17]

Still, not all jurisdictions dropped their affirmative contracting efforts in the wake of the *Croson* ruling. Instead, many local governments began to amass the history of deliberate incidents of discrimination in local industries that could be used to defend minority preference programs before court challenge. New York City, Los Angeles, Atlanta, Milwaukee, Oakland, San Francisco, San Antonio, San Jose, and Tallahassee, as well as Hillsborough, Dade, and Palm Beach Counties in Florida, were among the many communities that initiated **disparity studies** in an attempt to establish the existence of discrimination against minority businesses in a market area. The city of Atlanta's disparity study was an 1,100-page report! In the post-*Croson* era, federal court rulings have upheld local minority business set-aside provisions that are narrowly drawn, enacted for a fixed period of time, and where both historical evidence and marketplace analysis have documented the pervasiveness of discrimination.[18]

As we have seen throughout this book, the Supreme Court has not been willing to support aggressive, equalizing action in such areas as affirmative action, minority business set-aside programs, inclusionary zoning, metropolitan school integration, and school finance reform. What accounts for the Supreme Court's timidity (for lack of a better word) in these areas? In part, the Nixon, Reagan, and Bush administrations made their influence felt in their large number of appointees to the federal bench, including the Supreme Court. A series of Republican presidential victories led to a more circumspect court when it comes to matters of race and integration.

Yet, a full explanation requires that we look at more than just the impact of presidential judicial appointments. Courts are not simply the reflections of the presidents who made the appointments, and, for many conservatives, the Supreme Court and the federal judiciary are still too liberal when it comes to claims of civil rights.

In fact, it is not a simple matter to predict exactly how the Court will vote in the future when a number of civil rights and voting rights issues are argued again in a different context. The Court is faced with the difficult task of drawing fine lines of legal distinction. For instance, the Court has to decide when and under what conditions minority preferences in hiring or contracting should be granted as well as just what form those preferences can take. A justice who votes against preferences for minorities in a case today may find that the different facts of a case will justify a vote in favor of preferences tomorrow. Justices have also been known to alter their views and mature in office over time. Further, the Court's ideological make-up may change as a result of retirements and new appointments. As of early 1995, President Clinton's appointments were already having the effect of moderating the balance on the Court.

The more conservative orientation of the federal bench as a result of its Nixon, Reagan, and Bush appointees has led activists to look to the state courts for progressive urban action. A federal system offers multiple access points for those seeking change. The New Jersey Supreme Court's action in striking down certain forms of exclusionary zoning serves as a notable case in point. But few state judiciaries have the activist orientation of the New Jersey Supreme Court. In other states, court action will tend to be influenced more by the doctrine of judicial restraint; their courts will be less inclined to reverse policy decisions made by elected officials absent a clear violation of a state's constitution or its duly established statutes.

Still, a relatively activist posture by state courts can be expected on questions of school finance reform, as many states have provisions in their constitutions regarding the quality of education. In the early 1990s, state supreme courts in Montana, Kentucky, Texas, New Jersey, and a number of other states all acted to reduce the fiscal disparities between poor and wealthy school districts.[19]

THE FUTURE OF NATIONAL URBAN POLICY

Just what should be the federal government's response to urban problems? After a half century of federal action, there is no consensus when it comes to answering this question. Some observers believe that a more aggressive and explicit national urban policy is necessary if the United States is ever to begin to undertake effective action to alleviate urban ills. Yet other observers take the exact opposite point of view. They argue that national policy action has been ineffective, wasteful, and oftentimes counterproductive. They argue that instead of national action, program and policy choices should be left to the more capable hands of states, cities, and local communities.

We conclude this book by presenting three radically different possible future scenarios for national urban policy. We seek to identify if there is any possibility of sustaining federal urban policy in an age when the public and the Congress have become increasingly hostile to more conventional urban aid efforts.

A NATIONAL URBAN POLICY

As we observed in Chapter 13, Jimmy Carter was the only President ever to attempt to formulate a national urban policy. Other than that one brief and futile attempt, the United States has never had a policy that has made conditions of cities the focus of national action.

The call for a national urban policy was articulated in the late 1960s by then-presidential adviser (more recently Senator from New York) Daniel Patrick Moynihan.[20] Moynihan and others noted the many gaps, inconsistencies, and coordination problems inherent in a fragmentary, program-by-program approach to urban problems. Rather than being aided by a national policy that sought to preserve the health of cities, cities were often victimized (as we noted in Chapter 2) by a "hidden urban policy"—the deleterious consequences of governmental actions in other policy areas.

Given the continuing decline of conditions in the inner city and older suburbs, the call for a national urban policy has been repeated in recent years by a number of academics and urban activists. Paul Kantor has proposed expanding the federal role in urban development as the most promising way of liberating cities from their economic dependence. While Kantor does not propose that federal policy protect all communities from decline, he does argue that the federal government should regulate the social costs of urban development and compensate "loser" communities. Kantor proposes, for instance, that enterprise zones be designed to assist distressed areas—not growing and distressed communities alike, as is the common practice in many states. He also proposes to lessen the intercity competition for business by reducing federal grants-in-aid to cities that give tax abatements and other subsidies to business. Kantor envisions reversing the direction of the New Federalism, with the national government taking greater responsibility for social welfare programs instead of decentralizing authority to states and cities that neglect social needs in their haste to promote business growth.[21]

A special issue of the *Journal of Urban Affairs* has similarly called for the enactment of a national urban policy. According to the editors, only strong governmental intervention can remedy the problems caused by the demographic shifts, economic dislocations, and changed intergovernmental aid patterns that buffeted cities in the United States in the 1970s, 1980s, and early 1990s. Fragmented governmental policy interventions will not be adequate to the task that lies ahead: "The need for a national urban policy is stressed."[22]

Each chapter of the special issue presented policy recommendations for a different policy area. But all pointed to the need for more comprehensive and coordinated national urban policy:

> The premise of each chapter, however, is that because contemporary urban problems are interdependent and systemic, policy interventions directed toward their resolution must be holistic and broad in scope. Policy interventions must be multifaceted and coordinated across sectors, agencies, and jurisdictions.[23]

The call was for broad-scale, national action to deal with problems posed by urban decline. As the authors of one article in the volume concluded: "Only a total rethinking of the nation's priorities and a reinvestment in social and human capital can transform urban life."[24]

In the aftermath of the Rodney King riots, the Urban Institute, a research organization of national prominence, too, joined in the call for a national urban policy. The institute observed that the conditions in the cities are in many ways worse than they were in the 1960s but that much is known about how to bring about improvements:

> One clear lesson is that the country does not need another generation of separate urban policy. It needs a coordinated reform of domestic policy that considers the distinctive problems of the cities. The integrated approach must be built firmly on a foundation of human investment, job availability, and mobility strategies that allow residents to get ahead as a result of their own efforts. The costs will be high, but well within the nation's capacity if the will to take on the job can be mustered and sustained.[25]

The advocates of a national urban policy are right in one critical regard. Nothing short of a broad rethinking and comprehensive, holistic, coordinated action can be expected to reverse the process of urban decline.

The only problem, as we discussed in Chapter 13, is that a national urban policy is no longer possible. Antitax fever, national budgetary limitations, and the swelling representation of suburban and Sunbelt constituencies in Congress have all acted to make it increasingly difficult, if not impossible, to enact such broad-scale, systemic policy interventions focused on urban decline. The constituency for national urban policy does not seem to be there. Federal policy makers and the public alike are convinced that big-spending federal programs do not work. They are equally unwilling to support new big-spending efforts that funnel money through the states. The age of national urban policy is not about to begin; it has already passed.[26]

What would it take to create a constituency for new broad-scale, urban-oriented policy interventions? One possibility, sad to say, might be the occurrence of a wave of urban riots in response to federal aid cuts and in response to the deteriorating fabric of life in impoverished central cities. As Frances Fox Piven and Richard Cloward report, federal domestic aid programs greatly expanded in the late 1960s—in response to the wave of violence that cut across urban centers. When political actors were scared, they threw off more conservative fiscal concerns and responded with programs intended to ameliorate the situation and lessen the threat of disorder. But, in later years, when political quiescence was restored, federal aid programs were cut. The moral is that "a placid poor get nothing, but a turbulent poor sometimes get something."[27] A new wave of urban violence, today, similarly might lead to a new sense of national urgency in fighting urban problems. But, then again, it might not. The Los Angeles riots led to no great outpouring of federal aid. The political context of the 1990s is quite different from that of the 1960s.

ELIMINATING THE FEDERAL ROLE IN URBAN POLICY

The frustrations with federal government programs and the inability of massive federal spending to solve urban problems have led to a call for eliminating, or at least sharply reducing, the role played by the federal government in urban affairs. These calls for reform were given heightened prominence in the wake of the Republican takeover of Congress in the 1994 elections. Clearly, according to budgetary "hawks," domestic programs would have to undergo severe restructuring, sacrifice, and downscaling as part of the effort needed to eliminate the federal budget deficit. Deteriorating urban conditions showed just how little has been accomplished by conventional domestic and urban aid programs. The more extreme advocates of redefining the federal government's role called for the dismantling of HUD and the Departments of Commerce and Education, as well as sharp cutbacks in the programs of the Departments of Labor, Transportation, and Health and Human Services.

The policy course of radically redefining the federal role is based on a recognition of the inadequacies inherent in the intergovernmental aid system as it has evolved over time. There are just too many urban aid programs, costing too much money, and accomplishing too little. From this point of view, urban aid programs cannot be developed effectively in Washington; nor can they be effectively and efficiently implemented. National laws are often necessarily imprecise and ambiguous; ambiguity is a consensus-building strategy that allows competing parties to come together. Federal agencies then develop detailed program rules and regulations, earning the animosity of state and local officials who claim that program goals are being distorted. Regulations regarding citizen participation and nondiscrimination, among other purposes, are routinely added (sometimes by Congress) to large numbers of federal programs across the board. Subnational officials also complain about "regulatory creep" and the constraints on flexibility that are imposed as the price of accepting federal aid. Over the years, the federal grant-in-aid system has become increasingly complex and cumbersome.[28]

In many areas, project grants have become very narrow and specialized, further denying recipient governments program flexibility. Many of these grants distribute relatively small sums of money but incur great accompanying overhead costs in terms of application processes, the drafting of administrative guidelines, and other paperwork, evaluation, and auditing requirements. Figures provided by the General Accounting Office indicate that in the early 1990s more than half the federal grant programs, 330 in all, were as small as $15 million! Nearly 200 grant programs were as small as $5 million each![29] Small grants are not cost effective. Can such small programs be justified if the costs of administration eat up so much of the funds in these small programs?

Not all federal programs, of course, can be regarded as inefficient and failures. Less radical critics of government argue that programs such as Head Start, WIC (a program that provides nutritional supplements to at-risk pregnant women and young children), and Community Health Centers have a demonstrated record of success and should be preserved. But in other program areas, the federal government should get out of the urban policy business and leave policy decisions to the states while maintaining responsibility for ensuring that civil rights laws and other constitutional obligations are met.

Advocates of the federal government's withdrawal from urban policy argue that the states are more capable of effective action than ever before. Over the years, the states have modernized and professionalized their governments and reapportioned their legislatures. They have demonstrated an increased sensitivity to the concerns of racial minorities within their borders. As a consequence, the need for a direct federal-city relationship (a need which was so obvious in the early 1960s) has abated.

The withdrawal of the federal government from active urban policy represents a radical change. But only such an extensive change will erase the worst excesses of the current costly and ineffective system and allow the states and localities new freedom to determine which programs work best for their constituents. With federal program responsibilities reduced, federal taxes can also be cut. This will give state and local governments the chance to decide service and taxing levels for themselves. Subnational governments will be responsive to the wishes of their residents.

Critics of this path of action, however, warn of the dangers inherent in such radical program devolution. They argue that the national government has a responsibility to pick up the costs of national problems. The states and localities did not cause the problems in such areas as immigration and a changed national economy. Is it fair to displace the costs of meeting national problems on jurisdictions that may not have the financial wherewithal to provide needed services?

Similarly, critics of devolution fear that states and localities will seek to maintain their economic competitiveness by cutting taxes, even if this means cutting important services to the poor. Further, environmental safeguards may be relaxed in the interstate and interlocal search for competitiveness. Only the federal government can afford to engage in equity programs and environmental protection without fearing that new taxes and regulations will shift business to a neighboring locale. Critics of state governments also fear that in the wake of any abandonment of federal programs, the states will just pass the responsibilities along to the cities. Fiscally hard-pressed cities will not have the cash to meet citizens' service needs. Especially during economic hard times, distressed communities may lack the ability to meet the expanding demand for services; once again, the urban poor will suffer.

Defenders of central cities further observe the influence enjoyed by growing suburban populations in the state houses. State legislatures can be depended on to enact programs that are popular, but these will not always be programs that address the needs of hard-pressed cities (with their declining share of state populations), racial minorities, and the urban poor.

Picking Up the Pieces?
Urban Policy for an Anti-urban Policy Age

Is there a middle ground between costly national urban policy and the withdrawal of federal action that leaves communities to the vicissitude of market forces and the good will of state governments? If the federal government is to play an active role in countering urban problems, its policy must be responsive to the political forces that shape the urban policy process. It must recognize that the national decision-making system has become increasingly hostile to the development of strong urban policies. It will have to develop an urban policy that is acceptable in an anti-urban policy age.

As sociologist William Julius Wilson once concluded in a discussion of social policy, "the real challenge is to develop programs that not only meaningfully address the problems of the underclass but that draw broad support."[30] The same challenge confronts urban policy. How can we design programs that meaningfully address the problems of distressed communities but that also draw broad political support?

Quite simply, distressed communities can be helped through the enactment of more popular ameliorative programs that are less obviously "urban" in nature. What follows is a set of ten keys for developing more pragmatic strategies, urban policy pieces, and "nonurban programs"[31] that will provide real assistance to troubled urban communities and their residents. The list provides tactical advice for developing programs to assist cities and urban populations in a decision-making environment that is not conducive to urban policy:

1. **Pursue universal and "race-neutral" programs that spread program benefits.** Social programs that spread benefits are in position to garner a large supportive constituency.[32] William Julius Wilson has similarly argued for broad, **race-neutral programs** that provide assistance to white, middle-class citizens, not just to people of color and the poor. Targeted programs are less capable of attracting a stable base of support. As recent criticisms of affirmative action underscore, programs that appear to be targeted on the basis of race are especially vulnerable in terms of their political viability. However, the public will support more universal job training and economic revitalization programs that include benefits for working- and middle-class citizens, even when those programs provide disproportionate benefits to the inner-city poor.[33] Urban constituencies will gain from reforms in education and national health care, reforms that promise benefits to middle-class constituencies as well as to the poor.

   Yet, strategies based on universalism suffer from numerous disadvantages. Spreading program benefits dilutes the assistance given to people and constituencies in need. The high cost of universal programs also eats up funds that might otherwise be available for more effective and targeted programs.

   Perhaps more significantly, in an age of tight budgets the high cost of universal benefit programs diminishes a proposed program's political viability. Spreading benefits is no longer a guarantee of political success. The Reagan administration terminated or greatly cut General Revenue Sharing, job training, and Community Development Block Grants, despite the large number of constituencies aided by each program. Reagan simply argued that the nation could no longer afford such broad, wasteful programs. Similarly, Bill Clinton sought the passage of a broad national health plan that promised to improve health coverage for millions of Americans. But the huge cost of the program, coupled with the regulatory aspects of the plan designed to control costs, ultimately led to its defeat. Fiscal constraints limit just how often universal approaches can be used.

2. **Target when possible; target within universalism.** There is no real need to choose between a strictly targeted or strictly universal approach to urban policy. A mixed approach can utilize both universal and targeted policies where appropriate.[34] Theda Skocpol provides sound practical advice with her strategy

of **targeting within universalism,** where eligibility is spread broadly but extra benefits and special services are given to certain poor people.[35]

For spatial-based programs, targeting within universalism can entail a two-step approach: The first step makes a large number of communities eligible to participate in a program; but in the second step, administrative mechanisms are used to whittle down the number of applications or otherwise target the bulk of program benefits to constituencies with greater need. Approximately 90 percent of the U.S. population lived in areas defined as distressed and eligible for Economic Development Administration (EDA) assistance; yet, the EDA was able to award the bulk of the program's monies to more distressed areas.

But in an age of budget-cutting politics, a targeting-within-universalism strategy suffers severe limits. A program that seeks to distribute even a portion of its benefits to communities with no obvious need immediately is subjected to close scrutiny by budget-cutters looking for wasteful programs to eliminate.

3. **Emphasize a program's middle-class constituency.** The political viability of a program is enhanced if it contains benefits for the middle class as well as for the poor. School reform promises benefits to the middle class as well as to the poor. Reforms in education promise to deal with the many problems that middle-class parents have in getting public schools to be responsive to the needs of their children.

Similarly, citizen participation and community empowerment strategies can be sold as giving middle-class citizens, not just the poor, greater control over bureaucratized and irresponsive service systems. Perhaps New York City Mayor John Lindsay's fatal mistake in the 1960s school decentralization experiments was that the city's initial program focused only on empowering poor and minority neighborhoods. The program did not attempt to build a broad coalition of supporters by establishing community school boards in white ethnic and middle-class parts of the city as well as in Ocean Hill–Brownsville.[36]

But in an age of budget-cutting politics, even a middle-class constituency no longer guarantees a program sufficient political protection. In the mid-1990s, Republican budget hawks in Congress focused on making major cuts in Medicare and student tuition aid programs, arguing that taxpayers could no longer afford to subsidize benefits to better-off recipients. Though under attack, these programs were still in better shape politically as compared to programs that had no middle-class constituency to rally to their defense.

4. **Emphasize programs that tie benefits to participation in the work place.**[37] Americans are more willing to support work as

opposed to welfare. Programs that emphasize work-force participation and the transition from welfare to work are consistent with
the high value that Americans in general place on work. A public
opposed to welfare may still tolerate expanded assistance given
to the "deserving poor," the working poor.

In his first year in office, Clinton succeeded in greatly expanding
the Earned Income Tax Credit (EITC), a program of assistance
provided the working poor, with virtually no public debate. Clinton
knew that the expansion of EITC enjoyed two great political advantages. First, the assistance is given to "deserving" people who
work but who still have great need. Second, as a credit administered through the tax system, most Americans cannot really
fathom how it works. Even if aware of the EITC, they are likely to
be confused and see it only as a complicated tax code provision,
not as welfare or assistance to the poor.

Even in an era of tight budgets, the public can be expected to
support job training programs—if they are seen as effective and
not as wasteful—and child care programs—if they aid the entry of
mothers into the job market. The public can also be expected to
subsidize mini-vans and other transportation programs that
enable inner-city residents to reach suburban job sites.

5. **Focus on education.** The American public, while suspicious of a
great many social welfare programs, nonetheless continues to
view education sympathetically. Consequently, as Jeffrey Raffel
and his colleagues observe, "Focusing on the needs of children
would be more politically positive than focusing on urban needs."[38]
"Education" enjoys three distinct advantages over explicitly "urban"
programs. First, children, especially young children, constitute a
sympathetic constituency. Second, education is accepted as a good
investment. Increased spending for education can be portrayed as
an alternative, even a cost-efficient alternative, to social spending.
If schools do their jobs and children learn, there will be less in the
way of costly social problems and crime for society to deal with
later. The nation can either pay now for education or pay later in
response to increased social problems. Third, the benefits of increased spending for education can be spread to increase political
support. Even if a major portion of new school spending is targeted for children or districts in need, a portion of new spending
can be allocated to improve educational opportunities for working-class and middle-class children as well.

Spending for education can also draw the support of a city's
business community as it prepares a technologically competent
work force essential for the city's economic competitiveness. Education and human resource development are essential to local
economic development. The authors of one survey of the economic development literature have concluded that investment in

education and job training is critical to maintaining a locale's economic competiveness: "In particular, we believe the evidence is clear that in the long run education and human resource policies are vastly more important to urban economic development than more narrowly and traditionally conceived development policies such as tax concessions, industrial bonds, or enterprise zones."[39]

6. **Build on programs with a demonstrated record of success.** The American public will continue to oppose social spending that is generally regarded as unnecessary and ineffective. However, the public will support programs targeted for the poor when there is demonstrated proof that the programs work, that they are not simply a waste of money. Head Start and the supplemental food program for women, infants, and children (WIC) are two programs that not only survived the Reagan budget onslaught but actually were expanded over time. Reagan attempted to cut these programs. But members of Congress and the various policy communities acted to save them, convinced of the programs' effectiveness as a result of their demonstrated records of success.[40]

Similarly at the state and local level, policy advocates can use demonstrated examples of program success to argue for program expansion. For instance, the Harold Washington Single-Room Occupancy (SRO) Hotel in Chicago's Uptown neighborhood prevents homelessness by providing safe, assisted housing, with appropriate counseling and recreational activities, to persons at risk. The Harold Washington SRO does not look like a typical single-room occupancy hotel. It respects the privacy and dignity of its residents. In contrast to more seedy SROs, the Harold Washington SRO is not seen to pose a threat to the surrounding neighborhood, and, while expensive, it works. It provides a demonstrated successful alternative to mass shelterization and programs that simply warehouse the homeless. Urban advocates can use the Harold Washington SRO model as an example in their efforts to seek funding for programs for the homeless.

7. **Play to powerful symbols and sympathetic constituencies.** Certain causes and constituencies evoke greater public sympathy than others. Media attention acts to dramatize certain problems, while others are ignored. The plight of the homeless, persons with AIDS, and battered women have received substantial, even if not full, public airing in recent years; programs aimed at helping the homeless, persons with AIDS, and battered women are more likely to receive public support than programs aimed at urban problems in general. The plight of families and veterans on the street, even if not typical of the majority of homeless individuals, can be used to mobilize support for homelessness prevention.

8. **Emphasize the needs of the elderly.** The elderly constitute another sympathetic constituency whom the public is willing to

help. Communities are willing to build subsidized housing for the elderly even when they resist new construction for the nonelderly poor. Construction of new housing, even if limited to projects for the elderly, will help to alleviate the housing shortage in tight housing markets. Expanded funding for law enforcement can also expect to draw the support of the elderly.

9. **Pursue public/private partnerships for local economic development.** As we have already observed, local economic development has become so popular that it has dominated urban policy in recent years. Urban advocates need to ride this wave. They should seek appropriate measures designed to assist entrepreneurship and job creation and remove barriers to urban economic performance. The public will support job creation over welfare. They will also support programs to assist private-sector job training over government "make-work" programs that provide no real training or job skills demanded by the private sector. Critics of public-private partnerships note the dangers of creating a dual city if assistance is dispensed to firms solely according to terms demanded by the business community. To avoid this, tax concessions and other subsidies given to business can be predicated on the number of jobs or training slots created for the poor. Public and community participation and strict accountability measures, too, will ensure that growth is structured for public as well as for private benefit.

10. **Utilize programs that work bottom-up through nonprofit and community organizations, not government.** A top-down, federal urban policy is no longer possible. Instead, the government must seek to nurture and sustain the creative, problem-solving energies of the tens of thousands of nonprofit and community organizations that exist in urban America. As urban affairs journalist Neal Peirce has observed, hope for the urban future lies with community development corporations, mutual housing associations, land trusts, reinvestment corporations, and the myriad of other disparate civic, neighborhood, and corporate and citizen volunteer organizations found on the urban scene.[41]

An approach that works through community, religious and other nonprofit organizations can enjoy great public legitimacy and tap greater public support than one that relies on government action alone. Nonprofit and community organizations know a neighborhood's needs; they have expertise as a result of their extensive experience in working with local problems over the years. Volunteer and client participation also extends the problem-solving reach of the government by supplementing limited federal resources. A decentralized approach to problem solving also promotes flexibility. Finally, as community and voluntary organizations also promote citizen empowerment, they represent a healthy alternative to continued dependency on government.

The problems with this approach are obvious. What voluntary and nonprofit organizations do they do very well. But they are limited in terms of their resources and what they can accomplish. Voluntary and nonprofit organizations can choose whom they will aid; government, in contrast, is more universal in its service provision.

Critics of these pragmatic steps will argue that either they are too much (as they do not attempt to revolutionarily redefine and limit the federal government's role in urban affairs) or that they are too little (as they fall far short of constituting a comprehensive national urban policy or even a set of policies that will effectively ameliorate a wide range of urban ills). The critics are right on both counts. The ten keys listed above comprise a pragmatic middle way between the federal government's abandonment of the cities and a greater (and, in the present-day political context, maybe impossible) federal assumption of urban program responsibility.

The pragmatic steps listed above do not add up to the full-fledged national assault required to combat deep-rooted urban ills. But politics is the art of the possible. Barring a cataclysmic event and a fundamental change in political attitudes, the achievement of strong national urban policies is not politically achievable in the United States as it enters the twenty-first century. Budgetary constraints and a lack of political determination will continue to constrain the development of a more comprehensive and effective national urban policy.

The famous community organizer Saul Alinsky once observed that a true radical was not an idealist but a pragmatic tactician whose attack on the political and social system started from where the world is, not from where one would like it to be.[42] In the United States, advocates of a national urban policy are idealists who describe the world as they would like it to be. The advocates of more limited, discrete urban programs, in contrast, recognize the limitations imposed by power realities. They are the more pragmatic tacticians who start from where the world is.

NOTES

1. Harold Wolman, "Local Economic Development Policy: What Explains the Divergence between Policy Analysis and Political Behavior?" *Journal of Urban Affairs* 10, no. 1 (1988): 19–28. According to Robert Guskind, "Games Cities Play," *National Journal*, March 18, 1989, pp. 634–40, cities have incurred "staggering" costs as a result of the "pricey deals" they have given in the inter-city competition for business.

2. John D. Kasarda, "Urban Change and Minority Opportunities," in the *New Urban Reality*, ed. Paul E. Peterson (Washington, DC: The Brookings Institution, 1985), p. 64.

3. Ibid.
4. Dennis R. Judd and Michael Parkinson, "Urban Revitalization in the United States and the United Kingdom: The Politics of Uneven Development," in *Regenerating the Cities: The UK Crisis and the US Experience*, ed. Michael Parkinson, Bernard Foley, and Dennis R. Judd (Glenview, IL: Scott, Foresman, 1989), pp. 1–8.
5. Norman I. Fainstein and Susan S. Fainstein, "The Politics of Planning New York as a World City," in *Regenerating the Cities: The UK Crisis and the US Experience*, pp. 143–62. Also see "Dishing Out Freebies in the Big Apple," *National Journal*, March 18, 1989, p. 638; and Josh Barbanel, "Koch Faces a Sore Point: The Poor," *The New York Times*, July 6, 1989. A more thorough and complex picture of the changing power relationships in a transformed New York City is provided by H. V. Savitch, *Post-Industrial Cities: Planning in New York, Paris and London* (Princeton, NJ: Princeton University Press, 1988), pp. 30–97.
6. Carl Abbott, *The New Urban America: Growth and Politics in Sunbelt Cities*, rev. ed. (Chapel Hill, NC: University of North Carolina Press, 1987), p. 252. For an extended discussion of the changed nature of power structures in the Sunbelt, see Abbott, pp. 252–55; and Philip J. Trounstine and Terry Christenson, *Movers and Shakers: The Study of Community Power* (New York: St. Martin's, 1982).
7. David L. Imbroscio, "Overcoming the Economic Dependence of Urban America," *Journal of Urban Affairs* 15 (1993): 173–90.
8. Roberto E. Villarreal, "The Politics of Mexican-American Empowerment," in *Latino Empowerment: Progress, Problems, and Prospects*, ed. Roberto E. Villarreal, Norma G. Hernandez, and Howard D. Neighbor (Westport, CT: Greenwood Press, 1988), p. 6.
9. Rufus P. Browning, Dale Rogers Marshall, and David H. Tabb, *Protest Is Not Enough: The Struggle of Blacks and Hispanics for Equality in Urban Politics* (Berkeley, CA: Univ. of California Press, 1984).
10. Roberto E. Villarreal and Howard D. Neighbor, "Conclusion: An Overview of Mexican-American Political Empowerment," in *Latino Empowerment: Progress, Problems, and Prospects*, p. 128.
11. Eugene I. Finke, "Mexican Americans in the Bureaucracy of Local Government," in *Latino Empowerment: Progress, Problems, and Prospects*, pp. 55–62.
12. For a case study of Latino activism in redistricting, see James A. Regalado, "Latino Representation in Los Angeles," in *Latino Empowerment: Progress, Problems, and Prospects*, pp. 94–104.
13. *Shaw v. Reno*, 113 S.Ct. 2816 (1993). In 1995, a sharply divided Supreme Court further ruled, in *Miller v. Johnson*, that race cannot be the "predominant factor" in drawing district lines.
14. *Holder v. Hall*, 114 S.Ct. 2581 (1994).
15. *City of Richmond v. J. A. Croson Co.*, 109 S.Ct. 706 (1989).
16. Mitchell F. Rice, "State and Local Government Set-Aside Programs, Disparity Studies, and Minority Business in the Post-*Croson* Era," *Journal of Urban Affairs* 15 (1993): 533.
17. Ibid., p. 534; and Robert Pear, "Courts Are Undoing Efforts to Aid Minority Contractors," *The New York Times*, July 16, 1990.
18. Rice, "State and Local Government Set-Aside Programs…," pp. 536–50.

19. Joseph F. Sullivan, "New Jersey Ruling to Lift School Aid for Poor District," *The New York Times*, June 6, 1990. The 1990 decision in New Jersey was *Abbot v. Burke*.

20. Daniel Patrick Moynihan, "Toward a National Urban Policy," *The Public Interest* 17 (Fall 1969).

21. Paul Kantor, *The Dependent City Revisited* (Boulder, CO: Westview Press, 1995), pp. 238–46, especially pp. 238–40 and 245–46.

22. David L. Ames, Nevin C. Brown, Mary Helen Callahan, Scott B. Cummings, Sue Marx Smock, and Jerome M. Ziegler, eds., "Rethinking American Urban Policy," *Journal of Urban Affairs* 14 (1992): 197.

23. Ibid., p. 213.

24. Edward J. Blakely and David L. Ames, "Changing Places: American Urban Planning Policy for the 1990s," *Journal of Urban Affairs* 14 (1992): 423.

25. "Confronting the Nation's Urban Crisis," *The Urban Institute Policy and Research Report* (Summer 1992): 1. Also see George Peterson et al., "Confronting the Nation's Urban Crisis: From Watts (1965) to South Central Los Angeles (1992)" (Paper available from the Urban Institute, Washington, DC, 1992).

26. Paul Kantor unconvincingly argues that a national urban policy is possible—that the nation's business community will support a national urban policy, as it is good for business, and that suburbanites, too, will be supportive of a policy that protects them—not just central-city residents—against the vagaries of economic shifts. See *The Dependent City Revisited*, pp. 240–43. Unfortunately, suburbanites and businesses may know their self-interest better than does Kantor. A national urban policy imposes costs—not just shared benefits—on these groups. Businesses will likely continue to reject proposals that limit their subsidies, tax advantages, and geographical mobility. Suburbanites will resist both cooperative efforts with central cities and costly federal programs supported by their taxes.

27. Frances Fox Piven and Richard A. Cloward, *Regulating the Poor: The Functions of Public Welfare*, 2nd ed. (New York: Vintage, 1993), p. 338.

28. For a review of the changing shape of the intergovernmental system and the difficulty that it poses for the development of effective national urban policies, see Bernard H. Ross, Cornelius M. Kerwin, and A. Lee Fritschler, *How Washington Works* (Englewood, NJ: Thomas Horton and Daughters, Inc., 1996).

29. U.S. General Accounting Office, *Federal Aid Programs Available to State and Local Governments* (Washington, DC: GAO, May 1991), pp. 14–15.

30. William Julius Wilson, "Public Policy Research and *The Truly Disadvantaged*," in *The Urban Underclass*, ed. Christopher Jencks and Paul E. Peterson (Washington, DC: Brookings Institution, 1991), p. 478.

31. Marshall Kaplan and Franklin James, eds., *The Future of National Urban Policy* (Durham, NC: Duke Univ. Press, 1990).

32. Theda Skocpol, "Targeting Within Universalism: Politically Viable Policies to Combat Poverty in the United States," in *The Urban Underclass*, ed. Christopher Jencks and Paul E. Peterson.

33. William Julius Wilson, *The Truly Disadvantaged* (Chicago: Univ. of Chicago Press, 1987); and Wilson, "Public Policy Research and *The Truly Disadvantaged*."

34. Robert Greenstein, "Universal and Targeted Programs to Relieving Poverty," in *The Urban Underclass*, ed. Christopher Jencks and Paul E. Peterson.

35. Skocpol, "Targeting Within Universalism: Politically Viable Policies to Combat Poverty in the United States," p. 414.
36. Douglas Yates, *The Ungovernable City* (Cambridge, MA: MIT Press, 1977).
37. Greenstein, "Universal and Targeted Programs to Relieving Poverty."
38. Jeffrey A. Raffel et al., "Policy Dilemmas in Urban Education: Addressing the Needs of Poor, At-Risk Children," *Journal of Urban Affairs* 14 (1992): 281.
39. Hal Wolman, Royce Hanson, Edward Hill, Marie Howland, and Larry Ledebur, "National Urban Economic Development Policy," *Journal of Urban Affairs* 14 (1992): 235.
40. Greenstein, "Universal and Targeted Programs to Relieving Poverty."
41. Neal Peirce, "An Urban Agenda for the President," *Journal of Urban Affairs* 15 (1993): 457–67.
42. Saul D. Alinsky, *Rules for Radicals: A Pragmatic Primer for Realistic Radicals* (New York: Vintage Books, 1971).

Appendix

Continued

513

ABBREVIATIONS—Continued

NACO	National Association of Counties
NAFTA	North American Free Trade Agreement
NASBO	National Association of State Budget Officers
NCL	National Civic League
NCSL	National Conference of State Legislatures
NGA	National Governors' Association
NIMBY	Not In My Backyard
NLC	National League of Cities
NOACA	Northeast Ohio Areawide Coordinating Agency
NRA	National Rifle Association
OMB	Office of Management and Budget
PAYGO	Pay-As-You-Go
PFF	Picket Fence Federalism
PIGs	Public Interest Groups
PRIMA	Public Risk Management Association
RLA	Rebuild Los Angeles
RPCs	Regional Planning Councils
SBA	Small Business Administration
SCAG	Southern California Association of Area Governments
SEMCOG	Southeast Michigan Council of Governments
SES	Socioeconomic Status
SON/SOC	Save Our Neighborhoods/Save Our City (Chicago)
SPDDs	State Planning and Development Districts
SRO	Single-Room Occupancy (Hotel)
TANS	Tax Anticipation Notes
TELACU	The East Los Angeles Community Union
TMO	The Metropolitan Organization (Houston)
TWO	The Woodlawn Organization (Chicago)
UDAG	Urban Development Action Grants
UNO	United Neighborhood Organization (Los Angeles)
URPG	Urban and Regional Policy Group
VA	Veterans Administration
VRA	Voting Rights Act of 1965
WIC	The Special Supplemental Nutrition Program for Women, Infants, and Children

Name Index

Subject Index

URBAN POLITICS: POWER IN METROPOLITAN AMERICA
Fifth Edition
Edited by John Beasley
Production supervision by Kim Vander Steen
Cover design by Jeanne Calabrese Design, Berwyn, Illinois
Composition by Point West, Inc., Carol Stream, Illinois
Paper, Finch Opaque
Printed and bound by Quebecor Printing, Kingsport, Tennessee